The
Human Species

Frederick S. Hulse

University of Arizona

SECOND EDITION

The Humanspecies

An Introduction to Physical Anthropology

Random House New York

ISBN 0–394–31010–1
Library of Congress Catalog Card Number: 78–99449

Manufactured in the United States of America

Illustrations by Vantage Art, Inc.

Cover photograph by Michel Desjardins—*Realites*.

Second Edition

9876543

To
All Our Ancestors

Foreword to the Second Edition

DURING THE SEVEN YEARS that have gone by since the publication of the first edition of *The Human Species*, new discoveries that cast light upon the biology of mankind have continued to be made. Consequently some hypotheses have been supported and others weakened. New ideas have been suggested, and some old ones disposed of. An increasing interest in the story of human evolution has developed. New techniques for the analysis of data have been developed and proved useful. But the most significant change, I believe, has been a growing awareness of the ecological crisis that the past activities of the human race have caused. At long last, millions of citizens are coming to realize that this crisis may become a catastrophe. If this is to be avoided, it is more than ever vital for us to understand the biological bases of human nature. It is my hope that the revised edition of this book will contribute to such an understanding.

Frederick S. Hulse

Tucson, Arizona
January 1971

Foreword to the First Edition

IT HAS BEEN FUN to write this book. It is probably most improper academically to admit this, but it happens to be true. It has been my good fortune to teach a beginning course in anthropology each year that I have taught at all, and I have learned a good deal from this experience. Being introduced to a scientific study of our own species need not be a dull and ponderous business. In fact, it should not be. People are naturally interested in one another, in why humans look and act as they do, and in how they came to be as they are. Physical anthropology attempts to explain the biological background and the biological aspects of mankind. The presentation of basic knowledge and elementary concepts in this field is therefore a standard method of introduction to the field of anthropology as a whole: it is not the only method, but it is a good one, full of wonder and excitement.

This book has grown out of my classroom experience. It contains the sorts of things which I have told my students, and which I have found, by experience, they appreciate. My first thanks must go to them, for they have taught me much.

All of those whose research has led to our increase of knowledge about man's biology, past and present, also deserve acknowledgment. Above all I and all my colleagues owe a debt of gratitude to Charles Darwin and Gregor Mendel, one neglected and the other vilified during his lifetime. I, in particular, must thank all of the scholars whose research formed the basis for what is in this book, for I have simply assembled and tried to integrate the results of their work. Some of my colleagues have been kind enough to read parts or all of the manuscript, and from their criticisms it has profited a great deal. They deserve my special thanks.

Most of the figures, including the maps, were designed by Leonie Hulse and Robert Foss. To them, and to their teacher in the techniques of scientific illustration, Mr. Donald Sayner, I wish to express my thanks. The photographs were contributed by many people—colleagues, students and friends. I am grateful to them all.

Finally I should like to thank all those thousands of men, women and children who have submitted to the examinations, tests and experiments of physical anthropologists, physicians, dentists, and psychologists. Had it not been for their good nature, neither this book nor any other on such a topic could have been written.

Frederick S. Hulse

Tucson, Arizona
June 1963

Contents

The
Human Species

CHAPTER 1

What Is Man?

THE UNIQUENESS OF MAN

Tens of thousands of years ago, during the Ice Ages, a little boy died at Teshik Tash in Central Asia. His body was not just left where it lay nor tossed behind a bush. Instead, a shallow grave was scraped out in a nearby cave and lined with a number of wild goat horns. Then the boy's body was placed in the grave, the limbs arranged in a special position and covered with earth and stones. Perhaps the people sang or wept or recited charms while they were disposing of his body. We cannot know. But it is clear that they felt the need to do something special, to go to some extra trouble because the boy had died. Their tools were poor, their existence hard. We would probably find them ugly, for they were Neanderthal men. But when one of their own died, they could not neglect their duty. The boy was not just another animal to them: he was a man.

What is a man? For more than 2,000 generations men have been asking this question. The fact that they have asked it and have used their imagination and their reason to try to answer it is indication enough that there is something special about man. No other creatures appear to worry about who they are or why they exist. Like us, they are born, they grow, they mate, they die. Many of them, like us, appear to be alert, inquisitive, and able to

1

learn. But, unlike us, they show no sign of wondering what their origin or destiny may be. We, on the other hand, have been perhaps a little vain in the assumptions we have made about ourselves and which we unconsciously build into the phrasing of our questions about the nature of man.

This is unfortunate because, since the question "What is man?" bothers us, the accuracy of the answer is important. We have sought answers which will comfort us, which will not disturb either our desires or our aspirations, which will preserve our sense of self-esteem, and which will permit us to be hopeful about our future— if not in this world, then in another. We have not hesitated to create, in our imaginations, other worlds in which we suppose that we are really at home, thinking that we must be strangers in this one. We have assumed that we, and we alone, are somehow important in the universe and that it was created for us. We have believed that we alone of all living creatures here on earth have souls, and at other times and places we have believed that we do not. Christians have claimed and Buddhists have abhorred immortality.

In the intellectual tradition of the Western world at least, a certain dualism has permeated our thinking: mind and matter, good and evil, body and soul have been contrasted to each other. For a long time we could think of the physical world about us as operating in accordance with ascertainable regularities. It was harder to think of living creatures, like inanimate objects, operating in the same way. Indeed, until we had surrounded ourselves with mechanical devices of our own invention which we operated to suit our fancy, we could not even think of plants or animals as essentially intricate machines. But by the time of Descartes, three centuries ago, man had created enough machinery to be able to entertain this notion. Although most people still believe that life is somehow different, we commonly recognize that the actual processes of living are in concord with certain physical and chemical regularities or, as they are sometimes called, laws.

Nevertheless, we humans have continued to endow ourselves with certain mystic and inexplicable qualities. We say our minds are entities distinct from the matter of which our brains are composed. Some of us say we have souls as well as bodies and that souls are separable from bodies. We alone are supposed to be able to distinguish good from evil, and our souls are responsible for making the proper choices between them. Or so we have been in the habit of reassuring ourselves.

Is the introduction of the mystic and the inexplicable really necessary? Perhaps we can never answer this question. Certainly we cannot answer it on the basis of data available at present. Yet, if we are to understand the phenomenon of man at all, we must seek as natural an explanation as we can find. The method of scientific inquiry should certainly be applied to the study of man in order to remove as much mystery as possible.

A QUESTION OF SCIENCE

What is the method of scientific inquiry, and what are its aims? The methods and aims must be consistent with one another or the whole endeavor is futile. As in other kinds of inquiries, the aim is fuller understanding through explanation. We want to know the causes of the events which we perceive. Unlike religious and philosophical explanations, however, a scientific explanation does not pretend to be all-embracing, universal, and eternal. Unlike a religious explanation, it does not demand unquestioning faith. Rather, in each and every detail, scientific explanation remains permanently open to question, to reassessment, reevaluation, or reversal in the light of later discoveries of data or better research methods. Unlike a religious explanation, a force outside of nature is never called upon to explain the otherwise inexplicable. On the contrary, things which seem inexplicable are to be examined further, in the future, as new methods permit us to acquire more data. Without adequate data, we may indulge in speculation but may dare not claim any degree of certainty.

As distinct from philosophy, a scientific explanation is highly skeptical of speculations based upon reason and logic alone. This does not mean that scientists do not philosophize, for they do. We all like neat and elegant solutions, but their elegance alone does not make them credible. The principle of parsimony, that is, avoiding the introduction of unnecessary factors or complexities, should be rigorously adhered to. Other things being equal, a simple explanation is preferable to a complex one. Yet we must keep an open mind. Things may be more complicated than they seem. We have sometimes discovered that what had seemed unnecessary was only hidden. There is a story of a man whose tribe had never heard of alcohol, but who observed the behavior of some Europeans in his country. Some drank whisky and soda, some drank brandy and soda, some even drank gin and soda. Whichever drink they mixed with the soda, they got tipsy. The man concluded, with complete logic, that drinking soda makes people tipsy. This was the simplest explanation.

A scientific explanation, like a philosophic one, must be rational and logical, but it must be more than that. It must account for evidence as well as logic, and it must seek evidence constantly by whatever means. Of course, the best evidence of all is derived from controlled experiment in which the various factors of the situation have been intentionally introduced by the experimenter so that he knows precisely and measurably how much of each factor is present. Measurement is the soul of experiment; for only measurement by some preexisting standard gives precision, and only with precision can an experiment be successfully repeated. A scientist, then, will seek by all means to devise techniques for measuring any phenomenon under investigation. Without measurement, experiment is impossible.

Indeed, under many circumstances experiment is impossible, and in these cases attempts at scientific explanation must depend upon very careful observation of such situations as exist in the world as it is. Under these conditions, too, measurements must be made for the purpose of accurate comparisons, for outside the laboratory comparison must substitute as best it may for controlled experiment. Here, as much as in the laboratory, care and precision in observation is required, perhaps more than ever since nothing can be taken for granted. Here, in the world of nature, the full complexities of existing situations are revealed to us if we will but look for them, and we must constantly reapply the method of scientific inquiry to this world. One of the major problems in observing the natural world has been inventing appropriate means of measuring what can be perceived, and another has been discovering the appropriate items to be measured. As we will later see, the scientific study of man has run into major difficulties on both counts, and all the problems are not yet solved.

Scientific inquiry attempts by its methods to reach an approximation of accuracy in describing the interrelations and operations of those items under investigation. Knowledge and comprehension are built upon the accumulation of data, not revealed suddenly. Although new and improved interpretations may often come suddenly, causing drastic alterations of our conclusions, they must always be demonstrated in an independently verifiable manner before we accept them. Without imagination any advances in scientific knowledge would be out of the question. But the imagination which is applied to the solution of a problem should be trained and under control. Speculation is perfectly legitimate if it is recognized as such. Often, of course, our own speculations are so appealing and so plausible that we may mistake them for valid inferences from the data. This is a hazard to which all human beings are subject and which scientists must guard against.

We can regard a statement which is difficult or impossible to disprove as a speculation. The available data which bear on a problem may be inadequate; two or more explanations may seem equally plausible on the basis of what we know. Thus, the goat horns may have been placed in the Teshik Tash grave to protect the dead boy's soul against evil spirits or to protect those who buried him against his evil spirit. Indeed, there may have been some other motive behind this action. We don't know, and we have no means of finding out. Or the data may be conflicting. Some characteristics of *Tarsius*, a small primate which lives in the East Indies, strongly resemble those of a monkey but other characteristics strongly resemble those of a lemur. To which is he a closer cousin? We don't know, but as we collect more data and learn to analyze it better, we may find out.

Speculations which can be tested are called hypotheses. The native who concluded that soda is intoxicating could have sampled some and so disproved his hypothesis. As a scientist, he would then have had to pursue his inquiries further until he discovered not only that whisky, rum, and gin contain many substances in common, but that one and only one of these has the property of intoxicating people.

An inference is a conclusion which is supported by a large body of data and which is not positively discredited by other data. We are quite safe in making the inference that the consumption of alcohol in sufficient quantity causes intoxication. Laboratory tests demonstrate this. We are quite safe in making the inference that *Tarsius* is more closely related to monkeys and lemurs than to horses and tigers, despite the fact that it is impossible to test this conclusion in the laboratory. The number of likenesses which these three sorts of animals share with one another but not with horses and tigers is convincing. No alternate explanation fits the data. It is a very probable but less certain inference that the people who buried the boy at Teshik Tash had some ideas about life and death. Among living people, the ritual disposal of the dead is connected with such ideas, so we cannot imagine why else his people took the trouble to bury him. All inferences are not equally strong. A scientific investigator is content to accept what appears to be well demonstrated and equally content to alter his opinion whenever new data are convincing. He should not have an empty mind, but he should have an open one.

Data themselves may sometimes prove a bit tricky. Those things which are perceptible to the senses have to be regarded as data, but the sense organs of any creature, including a human scientific investigator, record only a limited range of cues. Some of us, for instance, are color blind and, consequently, unaware of messages which the rest of us receive. None of us can record the very high pitched squeaks emitted by bats by the echoes of which they guide their flight in the dark. Nor are we able to discriminate between olfactory sensations as dogs can. Fortunately, mechanical equipment can be and has been constructed which enables us to learn of many things about which we would otherwise be unaware. Microscopes, Geiger counters, litmus paper, telephones, and many other pieces of apparatus transform impulses of all sorts into messages within the range of human perception. There is no doubt that much potential data escapes our attention. It is also clear that we can easily misinterpret the significance of such data as our sense organs do receive. Despite all this, we are forced to depend upon the cues which our senses record for our basic information concerning the outside world. These are, in fact, the data upon which, methodically or carelessly, we base our inferences. They must be treated with respect, if not blind faith. A scientific investigator will base his conclusions upon what appears to be the most reasonable interpretation of the data available to him.

For this reason work in a laboratory has certain advantages over work in the field, and the results of experiments conducted under controlled conditions carry more conviction than any other observations. Much of the apparatus which records data precisely cannot be carried about. A cyclotron, for example, is rather bulky, and so are the pieces of equipment needed for testing many of the physiological reactions of a living creature. Very precise observations and measurements are likely to be required in any form of scientific work, whether experimental or not. The standards used should be comprehensible to other scientific workers, so that knowledge may be pooled.

Experiments, when possible, should be conducted under conditions which are described well enough so that they may be repeated. Independent verification of the results of experiments and of field observations, too, often serves as a useful check on accuracy. Anyone can make an error in observation, but it is somewhat less likely that several well-trained persons will all make the same error than that they will make different ones. We are constantly devising more precise techniques for recording data which may well lead to new interpretations. Scientific investigators, therefore, should not become enamored of any existing theories, even their own. They should desert disproven ideas as readily as rats do a sinking ship, and they should be willing to examine new theories unsentimentally and dispassionately.

ANTHROPOLOGY

Perhaps it is this dispassionate attitude of mind when faced with problems which interest us deeply that most of us humans find difficult, if not impossible, to attain. Yet it is necessary. The scientific attitude is a ruthless one. We cannot "like to think" that something is or is not so. We can easily be—perhaps we usually are—uncertain about an answer, but we cannot accept one answer because it is more comforting or less flattering than another. Pertinent evidence must be considered, whether convenient or not, and spurious reasoning must be rejected even if it would lead to a conclusion we would enjoy. Of course, such considerations have made any attempt at the scientific study of man far more difficult than the scientific study of anything else. No human beings can reasonably be expected to surrender their privacy, without good reason, in order to become the object of scientific investigation. And people rarely accept the advancement of knowledge for its own sake as a good reason.

Nevertheless, we have been able by various means to accumulate a body of data concerning man which surpasses that available for any other topic. Man's curiosity is as great as his vanity or his sensitivity, so we have continued to investigate ourselves. The real problem has been reviewing the information available in a dispassionate manner. Man has been called a little lower than the angels and a mechanical misfit; the most dangerous creature alive and a ridiculous weakling. All of these labels can be viewed with sympathy, but all are based on value judgments. The task of the anthropologist is to study men and mankind objectively, from the viewpoint of natural science.

The study of man involves much more than an attempt to find out as much as possible about the structure and operation of his body. We are highly social and highly imaginative creatures. As the science of anthropology has grown, different scholars have become interested in different aspects of the field. Some have concerned themselves especially with problems concerning language, and the subdiscipline of linguistics has arisen. Others have specialized in studies of social structure, of culture history, of the diverse economic, religious, or political systems which are found among different peoples. Cultural anthropology, embracing all such studies, has become the focal point about which all other anthropological specialties are arranged. Still other scholars attempt to add time-depth to the study of man by engaging in archaeological investigations. It should be noted that each field of interest which has been mentioned impinges upon some other discipline. This is characteristic of anthropology. Historians, sociologists, psychologists, and economists are among the many scholars whose interests overlap those of anthropologists. It is the emphasis upon culture as a unifying theme which makes anthropology one discipline rather than many.

Physical anthropology is properly included within the field of anthropology as a whole, rather than being simply an allied subject, because it, too, is concerned primarily with human culture. Historically, medical men, geneticists, paleontologists, and anatomists have made great contributions to knowledge in physical anthropology, just as scholars in the behavioral sciences have contributed to other aspects of the field in general. But physical anthropology is more than the study of human biology, or of human evolution, or of human genetics. It is impossible to chop mankind, or the study of mankind, into separate fragments. The fact that man is a social being is inseparable from the fact that he is a biological organism. Culture has added a new dimension to human life, but it has not abolished the dimensions which already existed. As we shall see, culture originated and developed out of the pre-cultural activities of our remote ancestors and has served as an integral part of the environment of man ever since. The study of the biological aspects of human life can never neglect this fact. But this study will assist us in understanding that fact. The case of the burial of the boy at Teshik Tash illustrates both points. Burial is culturally determined behavior: only human beings feel the need to dispose of their dead in some specified manner. It is therefore evident that man's mental faculties and emotional responses had developed to a cultural level tens of thousands of years ago. This tells us far more about what sort of a creature he had become, by then, than we can learn by studying the buried bones themselves. We not only know how big his brain was but can begin to guess how his brain operated, a guess which has great biological significance. Biology is not the study of the anatomy of dead creatures but of the activity of living ones. What are some of the most important things which can be said about our species from a biological point of view?

THE SPECIES, MAN

In the first place, we are by far the most numerous of the giant forms of life: human bodies undoubtedly contain more living material than the bodies of any other single species. Our total bulk,

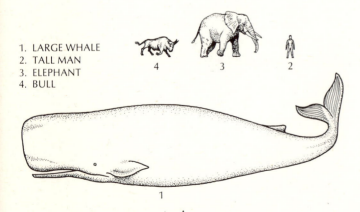

1. LARGE WHALE
2. TALL MAN
3. ELEPHANT
4. BULL

4 3 2

1

A
(Scale: All lengths reduced 300 times)

FIGURE 1-1A. We Are Neither the Largest . . .

that is, all the human beings living in the world added together, can be estimated at about 150 million tons. Of course, in comparison to whales or elephants we do not appear to be giants, but very few creatures attain dimensions such as theirs. A walk through the countryside or a visit to the zoo will reveal that most animals and plants are smaller than we are. A look through a microscope will show even more minute forms of life. These are almost innumerable; indeed, the numbers of individuals in any single species of microorganisms may exceed us by millions of times, yet their total bulk would be far less than that of a single man. Among the few animals which are larger than man the number in any one species is far less in almost all cases; among the plants which are larger the percentage of living tissue is relatively small. Figures 1–1 A and B illustrate the size of man in contrast to a few larger and a few smaller creatures.

Secondly, man is a widely scattered species geographically. Our only close competitors are those creatures which we have carried with us, such as rats, lice, and a variety of parasitic microorganisms. We have devised techniques which enable us to contend successfully with almost all environmental conditions and to extract a living from areas having the most varied sorts of resources. There can be no question that we are the most successful form of life which has appeared upon the planet up to now. This is all very flattering, but we had better not let our success make us vain. Our present dominant position provides no guarantee for the future. Indeed, some scholars have compared the human species to a rapidly metastasizing cancer because of the speed with which we are consuming the resources of our host, the earth. Since the first edition of this book was published in 1963, some 20 million tons of human protoplasm have been added to the burden the earth must carry. Figure 1–2 indicates the growth of the human population.

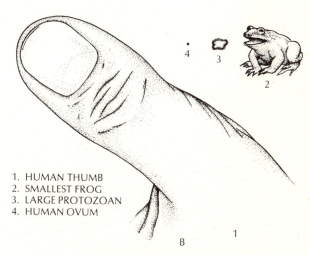

**FIGURE 1-1B. . . . Nor the Smallest
of Living Creatures**

1. HUMAN THUMB
2. SMALLEST FROG
3. LARGE PROTOZOAN
4. HUMAN OVUM

B

(Scale: All lengths enlarged 1¼ times)

The position of human beings as the most successful life forms up to now must be explained in terms of the characteristics of the creature concerned. What biological characteristics in anatomy, physiology, and overt behavior do we possess which may help us to understand our accomplishments? Let us begin with as simple a description as we can, thinking of anatomical detail in functional terms and comparing our bodies and our activities to those of other living creatures in those instances where such a comparison is illuminating.

Obviously, being so large, we are multicellular; indeed, there are billions of cells in a human brain alone. We are not rooted, or sessile; on the contrary, we are capable of very rapid movement. Containing no chlorophyll, we cannot synthesize our food and so must devour living things for our sustenance and expel rather than take in carbon dioxide in our metabolic processes. These are the characteristics of animals rather than plants, and we can without doubt be classified as animals. In basic pattern, people are among those animals which are constructed like segmented tubes and which are bilaterally symmetrical: that is to say, we have easily distinguishable fore and hind ends, and bellies and backs, while organs and appendages tend to be arranged in pairs associated with the different segments. By far the greater number of biologically successful animal varieties share all of these characteristics with us, from angleworms and ants to fish and birds.

We have, furthermore, a closed circulatory system provided with a single heart which carries all necessary materials in solution to and from all the cells of the body. Our digestive system, unlike that of a jellyfish, for instance, provides for one-way traffic: in at the head end and out at the other. The digestive system lies along the belly, or ventral side, of the body, whereas the central nervous system is closer to the back, or dorsal side. Specialized receptor sense organs are, for the most part, concentrated at the head end, and—perhaps in association with this fact—a great elaboration of the central nervous system is also located at the head end. We have an internal skeleton composed of over 200 separate bones in articulation with each other, rather than an external shell such as those of insects and lobsters.

Our species is bisexual, consisting of males and females, so that we do not reproduce by simple budding-off of new individuals as some creatures do. Neither can we practice self-fertilization nor change our sex from time to time, like a number of other creatures. Indeed, internal fertilization is required to continue the species, and in this we differ from some fish and frogs. The organs and ducts used in this process are in close association with the urinary system, an anatomical oddity which can only be explained by our evolutionary history. The mother's body retains the fertilized eggs, there giving them nourishment and protection until the time of birth, instead of providing them with a toughened shell and laying them in a nest to be hatched later, like turtles and birds. Indeed, even after birth, the mother continues to nourish her offspring with milk which her breasts secrete. This is a remarkably efficient reproductive system which both permits and encourages a low birth rate.

Our digestive system is highly efficient, too. Our mouths have jaws, of which the lower moves up and down, and both jaws have teeth. The teeth are of various sorts so that food may be sliced, pierced, and ground up before it is swallowed; the first set of teeth is entirely replaced by more firmly rooted ones during the growth period. A variety of glands produce digestive fluids, and symbiotic microorganisms which exist in the gut further aid the process of digestion. We are practically omnivorous as a species, although every tribe of humans practices food tabus of one sort or another. Americans refuse to eat dogs or caterpillars, while some other peoples will not consume fish, or pigs, or maize.

Human beings are terrestrial in habitat and have four appendages, each consisting of several articulated segments and terminating in five digits. They are unique in the type of differentiation between the hind and forelimbs and in the method of attachment of the hind limbs, which are capable of supporting the entire body in a vertical position. The forelimbs are far more flexible than the hind limbs. At the end of each forelimb is a hand with an opposable thumb, as well as four fingers. This makes grasping and manipulating all kinds of objects very easy. Paired lungs permit oxygen to be absorbed from and carbon dioxide returned to the atmosphere. The lungs, however, must be moist at all times. The body's ability to regulate its temperature and keep itself warm enough for rapid metabolism also makes life outside the water easier. Unlike most but not all warm-blooded creatures, man lacks the insulation of fur or feathers. We have, however, the most efficient sweating mechanism of any creature.

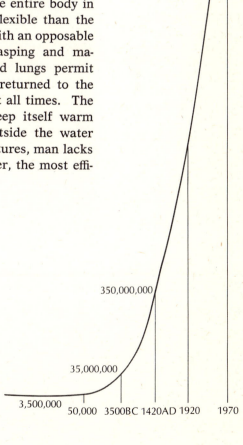

FIGURE 1-2. The Human Population Explosion. This Graph Shows How Much More Rapidly Our Population Has Been Increasing Recently than It Did in Earlier Times.

FIGURE 1-3. Packed in Like Sardines. A Subway Train during Rush Hours Shows the Discomfort of Crowding, at Present Alleged To Be Inevitable. (Photo: Minoru Aoki from Monkmeyer)

The brain is both relatively and absolutely large, although not uniquely so, and continues to grow after birth to a most unusual extent. Of the specialized senses, man appears to depend upon vision to the greatest extent, and he can do this because of the excellence of his eyes. Unlike most creatures, except apes and monkeys, he can distinguish various wavelengths of light and also judge distances very accurately by focusing both eyes upon an object. Hearing is also well developed in man, and his fingertips are especially rich in nerve endings and so are very sensitive to such things as texture, moisture, and temperature. Our sense of smell, on the contrary, is clearly less well developed than that of other creatures which resemble us.

The frontal and temporal lobes of man's brain are especially well developed, and it has been surmised that this may be associated with the high degree to which his behavior is organized under conscious control. In simple learning ability, we do not appear to excel such laboratory animals as rats, but the complexities of human mental behavior remain obvious. We grow slowly and live long, we are constantly exposed to one another in society, and the type as well as extent of our learning and memory are both related to these facts. With our eyes and our fingers we can gratify and thus perhaps sharpen the inquisitiveness which we share with many other creatures. Our manipulative ability is supreme. Humans alone of all animals can communicate by means of language, which has profoundly influenced our imaginations. Our childhood is so long, our life so easy, and our excess energy so great that play activity has assumed a very great importance in guiding behavior.

These traits are well exemplified by human mating behavior. Humans are among the relatively few mammals without a mating season, so that adult males are more or less constantly attracted to females, and sexual activity continues throughout the entire year. Furthermore, females of other species are likely to be sexually receptive only during those brief periods when they are most likely to be fertilized; and males are attracted to them only at these times. Courtship among other species, as a rule, is brief; mating procedure is stereotyped; and there is little evidence of female satisfaction. In our species this is by no means the case. Females are just as receptive, and males as eager, at times when fertilization is impossible as at times when it is likely. Courtship is likely to be accompanied by far more playful activity than among most other animals. The act of mating is often elaborated in diverse ways and accompanied by mutual caresses; and females are as capable of satisfaction as males. This has also had a profound effect on our mode of life.

Each species is, of course, unique in its relationship to its environment and, consequently, in its adaptation. But the special ways in which the human species is unique include the extent to which we dominate and control our surroundings. We have power, and the mythologies of many peoples, including our own, glory in this fact. Not only are our muscles perfectly adequate, but our mentalities have enabled us to exploit an increasing variety of energy sources. Thus we have not been content to live as other animals do, depending as they do upon the productiveness of nature as we find it. To cultivate crops, we cut down forests and irrigate deserts. To make tools, we extract metals from the earth. To supplement our own strength, we burn fossil fuels. We are highly efficient in these exploitative activities and during the past two centuries have become much more so. This has created conditions highly favorable to population increase, and the expectable result is that our species has become very numerous. It cannot be denied that the story of man has been a biological success story.

But the surface of the planet is not infinite, nor are its resources. Crowded conditions are now all too common, and scenes such as that shown in Figure 1–3 are found more and more frequently. Any area, large or small, has a limited carrying capacity, and the living creatures within it, including ourselves, are mutually dependent upon one another. Consequently, no population can continue to increase in numbers forever. Our increased and still increasing exploitative ability has hidden this fact during the past few generations, but it still remains a fact. The human species is living on its capital, despoiling its environment, and producing a world-wide ecological crisis. This is undoubtedly the major problem which we face today, and its solution will demand more forethought, cleverness, and sophistication than have been used in solving our past problems. The situation in which we find ourselves demonstrates the relevance of anthropology to modern life. Difficult though it may be, a dispassionate assessment of our characteristics and potentialities is among the primary necessities facing the present generation of the human species. Such an assessment must be based upon, although not restricted to, a much more precise knowledge than we have yet gained of the biology of mankind.

We have, however, learned enough to make anyone realize the degree to which we share characteristics of structure and behavior with other living creatures. We are members of the community of life. To investigate more deeply whether the phenomenon of man can be explained in natural terms should be worthwhile. The purpose of this book is to make such an investigation.

Sources and Suggested Readings

AYALA, F. J.
　　1968　Biology as an Autonomous Science. *American Scientist*, **56**, 207–221.

BATES, M.
　　1950　*The Nature of Natural History*. Scribner, New York.

CARSON, R.
　　1962　*Silent Spring*. Houghton Mifflin, Boston.

CONANT, J. B.
　　1951　*Science and Common Sense*. Yale University Press, New Haven.

EHRLICH, P. R.
　　1968　*The Population Bomb*. Ballantine, New York.

HUXLEY, T. H.
  1863   *Man's Place in Nature.* London.

KLUCKHOHN, C.
  1949   *Mirror for Man: The Relation of Anthropology to Modern Life.* Whittlesey House, New York.

SIMPSON, G. G.
  1964   *This View of Life.* Harcourt, Brace & World, New York.
  1969   *Biology and Man.* Harcourt, Brace & World, New York.

CHAPTER 2

The Qualities of Life

THE PROPERTIES OF LIFE

Superficially, it might appear that we have little in common with an oak tree or microbe. We do not look at all like either of them, nor do they resemble each other. Yet oak trees, microbes, and men are all alive, and long before the invention of scientific apparatus our ancestors had no difficulty in recognizing living entities as distinct from inanimate objects. In fact, as we increase our understanding of the world of nature, we find it more difficult than they did to draw a sharp line between life and nonlife. No one simple criterion can be given with which to make this distinction, yet there are certain statements which can be made about the qualities which all living things share, and which, in combination, are unique to them alone.

Life must be thought of as a process. Perhaps it is best described, or even explained, in terms of what it does rather than in terms of what it is. The properties of life are active, and the action is more important, in terms of living, than the raw materials of which living things are composed. The inherent properties of these raw materials are necessary to the activities which we identify as life, but it is the set of activities which we recognize: without activity life cannot be said to be going on. This much can be said about a flame, but whereas in that very elementary chemical reaction energy is dissipated at once, in the process which we call life the contrary is true. Life functions as an energy trap, accumulating and reassembling matter in such a way as to delay, if not inhibit, the rule of entropy which appears to govern the inanimate world.

As Homer Smith wrote in his perceptive book *Kamongo*, "Life is an eddy in the second law of thermodynamics." This may be a symbolic rather than a scientific way to state the truth, but it reveals the most significant quality of life and forms the essential base upon which the structure of all living things is constantly being erected. Perhaps it is this extraordinary quality which has led so many theorists to conclude that there must be some vital force, different in nature from all other sorts of energy, with which life is endowed. Yet as the processes of life are examined more deeply, no manifestation of any force unique to living organisms has been discovered. So this would appear to be an unnecessary hypothesis: it violates the principle of parsimony. The chemical elements found in living creatures are those of the inanimate world too, and the energy exhibited in living processes appears to be the same energy which is found in the inanimate world as well. It is the activity of life which is its distinctive feature.

Life exists in discrete individual entities, each one forming a closed, self-perpetuating system. The processes which take place within each of these systems are basically identical in nature, though minor modifications distinguish various types of organisms. It is therefore possible to describe the qualities, the properties, and the necessities of life in general, although we should never forget that each life is a unique affair. This individuality is indeed one of the important properties of life, for the reactions of each living thing to its surroundings and the interactions of living things are among their major forms of activity.

Biologists call the ability of a living thing to respond to the external world *irritability*. As biologists use the term, irritability describes responsiveness to stimuli and sensitivity to environmental changes. This is the only way that life can be continued and the integrity of the organism maintained. The external world, of course, is completely indifferent to the needs of any organism. It contains not only substances which a living thing might use but also those which might be dangerous, thus making the proper reaction to external conditions vital. Each individual organism must continuously avoid or overcome hazards and exploit opportunities from the moment it comes into existence. Although irritability does not imply awareness, the awareness which some creatures have developed obviously depends upon the underlying and more basic property of irritability which all living organisms share.

THE CHEMISTRY OF LIFE

Since life is a dynamic process and not a passive state of being, it requires raw materials for its substance and energy sources for its action. The chemical elements and compounds of which living things are composed and the sources of the energy which they constantly expend are found in the environment. They are constantly being absorbed into the stream of life, and excreted—often in altered form—into the environment. Furthermore, some are assimilated into living substance, so that organisms may both increase in size and change in structure.

Nutrition, metabolism, and growth are, therefore, among the basic properties of life, existing in such an intimate relationship with one another that a description of any one of these properties alone is not only difficult but misleading. One important aspect of metabolism, however, deserves special mention. This is respiration, whereby oxygen is obtained and carbon dioxide lost. Living things, in most cases, obtain their energy through oxidation, and the materials oxidized are typically derived from sugars, so that carbon dioxide and water are by-products of this vital process. After their production, the organism concerned may or may not use them fully, depending upon its requirements at the time. In the case of green plants, for instance, so much carbon dioxide is used in the creation of carbohydrates by photosynthesis that it is taken in from, and oxygen lost to, the environment—a reversal of the ordinary respiratory process. In the case of animals living on the land, a good supply of water is likely to be welcomed because liquid water is life's natural habitat.

The chemical processes which maintain life require an extraordinarily complex pattern of organization. Typically, though not universally, the cell is the basic, individual unit of organization which leads, to some degree, a life of its own. It is the cell rather than any of its constituent parts which behaves in such a manner that we can say it is alive. In many cases, a vast multitude of cells are so organized in relation to one another as to form a single creature, such as a pine tree or a man. These constituent cells are not independent units, but they are nonetheless the basic units of life, even when so dependent upon each other. There are also a great number of single-celled organisms, each carrying on a life of its own.

The cell's basic pattern of organization includes a membrane, which is a definite boundary between the living substance and the outside world; a nucleus, which appears to contain the chief organizing properties; and more or less cytoplasm, which itself contains many subsidiary but vital structures, such as the mitachondria, vacuoles, droplets of oil, and various filaments. Activity within a cell is constant as chemical reactions take place. Some of this activity is visible through a microscope, but most of it is at a submicroscopic level. Cells differ in size and shape, but single-celled organisms are rarely large enough to be seen without the aid of a microscope. Most of the constituent cells of a multicellular organism are much smaller than are independent single-celled organisms, yet it is within these minute units that life resides.

A cell is composed of a living substance known as protoplasm. This substance is somewhat like a jelly, somewhat like a colloid, and consists for the most part of water and a great variety of protein molecules, together with the raw materials from which protein is built up. Protein molecules are far larger and far more intricate in their arrangement than the molecules of the inanimate world. Even the simplest protein molecules such as insulin are composed of thousands of atoms, and some are several hundred times as large as molecules of insulin. Each protein has the precise structure which fits the function it performs in the life of the cell. Protein molecules are themselves built up of chemically linked molecules of the various amino acids, or of amino acids and nucleic acids which transfuse from the nucleus, where they have been formed.

The nucleic acids are unquestionably the most important chemical structures within the cell, since their activity appears to determine to a great extent everything else which takes place within a living cell. There are two kinds of nucleic acids, deoxyribonucleic and ribonucleic. The former, which is almost always termed DNA, is found in the chromosomal material of a cell. The latter, termed RNA, is found in the cytoplasm. Deoxyribonucleic acid, or DNA, is not a protein, being composed of certain sugar and phosphate groups which alternate in long spiral chains. In addition, each sugar molecule is attached to one of four organic bases. Apparently, these four substances alternate in a precise pattern, and normally two threads of chromosomal material are joined by these bases, each forming a mirror image of the other. The sequence in which the patterns exist on these threads determines the chemical events within the cell and, consequently, within the entire organism. Watson and Crick received the Nobel Prize in 1962 for their demonstration (1953) of the structure of DNA molecules and their arrangement on the chromosomes. (See Figure 2–1.) Ribonucleic acid, or RNA, is synthesized within the nucleus, doubtless with DNA as a template, and it carries the information encoded upon the chromosomes to the other parts of the living cell (Taylor, 1962). In this way the nucleus controls the events which take place in the cytoplasm, so that the organizational integrity of the cell is maintained, and the proper chemical reactions occur in the appropriate sequence.

THE NECESSITIES OF LIFE

The elements of which living substance is composed are, for the most part, abundant. Oxygen is the major constituent, with carbon, hydrogen, nitrogen, calcium, and phosphorous found in lesser but still important quantities. Many other elements are used in smaller

FIGURE 2-1. The Structure of Deoxyribonucleic Acid (DNA)

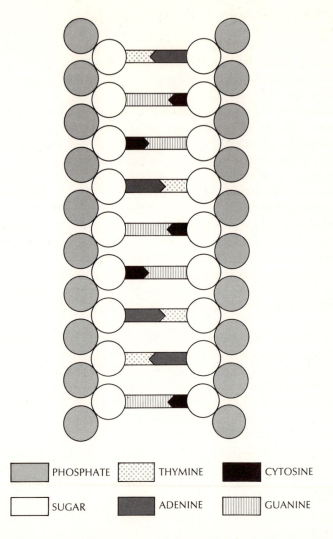

	PHOSPHATE		THYMINE		CYTOSINE
	SUGAR		ADENINE		GUANINE

amounts, and some of these, though minimal in quantity, are absolutely vital to the operation of an organism. Even more important is the correct balance between the proportions of various elements and types of compounds. For instance, if the balance shifts very far in either an acid or an alkaline direction, the organism will die. Furthermore, if the processes of life are to be carried on, much of the oxygen and hydrogen must be combined to form water, which must be in a fluid rather than a solid or gaseous state. Experiment has shown that after being frozen many organisms can later be restored to active life. But life is suspended during the period of their freezing. Should any organism be heated so that the water within its cells becomes steam, the explosive effect of the transformation is enough in itself to destroy the organism's structure beyond repair.

Life therefore exists only within a very restricted temperature range, a range found rather infrequently in the universe at large. The planet Earth happens to receive the appropriate amount of radiant energy from the sun in the form of light and heat to make possible the chemical reactions necessary for life to continue. It also happens to rotate upon its own axis in such a way that all parts of its surface are alternately exposed to and shaded from the sun's rays, and it does so at a speed which prevents surface temperatures from reaching extremes. The magnetic field of our planet, furthermore, helps to protect us from the constant bombardment of radiations from space which are harmful to life. The Earth happens to have a mass adequate enough to retain an atmospheric blanket of gaseous materials which adds to this protection and stabilizes temperatures still further. This invisible gaseous blanket, moreover, helps provide enough atmospheric pressure, at sea level, to ensure that water will not boil at temperatures favorable to metabolic processes. The recent visits of astronauts to the moon, which confirmed the prediction that lunar environment is totally hostile to life, have shown us how vitally important this combination of conditions has been for life. The lush bounty of the earth is contrasted to the utter sterility of the moon in Figure 2–2. It is only because of the simultaneous existence of all these conditions that the living organisms which we know have been able to survive, or, indeed, have been able to come into being in the first place. These are a few aspects of the set of physical conditions which have sometimes been called "the fitness of the environment" in recognition of the fact that the environment of life must fit the necessities of life.

As we suggested before, the necessities of life include plenty of liquid water and free oxygen. To be sure, there are certain anaerobic bacteria which exist without supplies of oxygen, but all other living creatures require it constantly to carry on metabolism. To perform any of life's activities, a liquid medium is also required, and for this all organisms use water. Indeed, so much of the content of any living thing is water that its specific gravity is very close to unity. Weight is not much of a problem for any organism which lives in the water, no matter how large or small it is. For those creatures such as man which live on the dry land, dehydration is a constant hazard, since all of our living substance must be bathed constantly. Our systems cannot absorb oxygen until it has been dissolved in the thin film of water which lines all the surfaces within our lungs. Our food must be dissolved before it can pass from the gut into the bloodstream. All land-dwelling organisms contain a bit of the ocean from which their ancestors at one time emerged.

Given an ample supply of liquid water and free oxygen, carbon is the element which appears to have the chemical properties most useful for life. It is able to enter into a vast number of complex chemical compounds which typically include veritable chains of carbon atoms. The molecules formed by these combinations have the versatility of reaction which is typical of and required for life. Molecules of protein and nucleic acid are, in a sense, based upon such carbon chains, and such molecules not only make up the sub-

stance of life but in many cases are the catalysts needed for the rapid sequence of chemical reactions necessary to life. The breaking down of previously existing compounds and their rearrangement is a major activity within a living cell, and enzymes, or biocatalysts, speed up this process (Butler, 1959). By their work, which leaves their own structure unimpaired, these biocatalysts produce more living substance. In some cases this substance duplicates their own,

FIGURE 2-2. The Earth Is Lush; the Moon Is Stark (Photo: Left, Carl Frank, Photo Researchers, Inc; Right, NASA)

so that living substance is not only maintained but increased, and new living individuals come into existence.

The creation of new living individuals is perhaps the most dramatic property of life. It is certainly the property which has enabled life to spread, to diversify, and to exploit the resources of the planet with increasing vigor and efficiency. It is just as basic and universal a characteristic as irritability, metabolic processes, growth, and individuality and is most closely correlated to the latter two. What a monstrous prospect the unhindered growth of an original and solitary organism would be! Of course such a process would have been self-defeating, since it would have exhausted all available raw materials long ago even had it been a structural possibility. The property of reproduction is a kind of insurance which has reconciled growth and individuality, for basically the process depends upon the ability of an individual cell to divide itself into two individuals, each containing the potentialities of the parent cell. There is of course much more to the process of reproduction than the simple splitting of a cell, and we still do not know what stimulates a cell to behave in this fashion. But the continuance of life clearly depends upon this property.

THE SIZES OF LIFE

Although we have, of necessity, outlined briefly the similarities among all forms of life, it is just as necessary to stress the differences among them. Living individuals exist in many sizes and shapes, exploit many diverse circumstances, face a variety of hazards, and seize upon all sorts of opportunities. All organisms face similar problems, but they solve them by vastly different methods. The lives of an amoeba, a rosebush, and a human being depend in each case upon the basic properties of protoplasm, yet each organism lives in a very different way from the other two. In dealing with the similarities, the properties and problems of the single cell are important, but many organisms, including ourselves, are multicellular. This has both advantages and disadvantages.

We, for instance, are giants, although by no means the largest giants. (See Figure 1–1.) Most of the living things we see are smaller than we are, yet the number of individual, independent, free-living creatures which are too small to be seen by the naked eye is enormously greater than the number of those within our range of vision. Such organisms, minute to us, need not contend with the force of gravity: the weight of each one is too slight. Indeed, even the smaller living things within our range of vision may be so buoyed up by atmospheric pressure that they are blown freely through the air and fall to the ground from any height without structural damage. Under a high-powered microscope, the cell membrane of an amoeba may be seen to vibrate under the impact of the moving molecules of water in which it lives. It must be strong enough to resist this never-ending bombardment, but its weight would be no problem even in the air. There, however, it would dry out at once, since its surface is so large compared to its volume. Very tiny creatures which live in the air rather than the water need some form of casing to avoid this fate. At the same time, because of their relatively huge surface area, they are able to absorb all the oxygen they require without trouble, as do the individual cells within our own bodies.

The forces of adhesion and cohesion in liquids present real problems, giving certain advantages to organisms the size of small insects or smaller. Some organisms skate along the surface of the water with ease, since they are not heavy enough to break its surface tension. Should they break through the surface, they would, of course, be sucked into the water. Should a creature of this size attempt to drink from any volume of water as large as itself, it would be at the peril of its life. It might well be sucked within the water by the force of adhesion and drowned (Pauli, 1949). The problem of heat loss is also a major one for tiny creatures, again because of their high ratio of surface area to volume.

The chemical reactions of life proceed most efficiently at certain temperatures, and although these reactions produce heat, this heat tends to be lost by radiation if the ambient temperature is lower. The smaller the organism, the more rapidly this occurs. On the other hand, if a single cell were large enough, too much heat would be generated in its deep interior for the cell to be able to operate efficiently.

THE PROBLEMS OF BEING MULTICELLED

It is ordinarily unprofitable for an independently living, single-celled organism to grow large enough to be seen by the naked eye. The creatures which we do see are generally many-celled and must face problems of a different sort from their microscopic cousins. These problems concern not only weight and heat but organization. A division of labor among the different cells is necessary, and the position of the cells in relation to each other must be such that all the basic functions of life can be carried on. The entire multicellular organism has to be coordinated so that it acts as a unit, replacing the freely living cell as the independently operating, self-contained individual.

The means employed to solve all of these problems simultaneously are highly varied. Animals, as distinct from plants, have the added problem of movement, for moving a large creature is a very different proposition from moving a single cell. Plants simply avoid the problem by not moving, and some adult animals such as oysters and sea anemones become sessile too. But since animals, unlike most plants, cannot synthesize their own basic foods, most of them seek food actively, moving from place to place to do so.

Humans are animals, and our problems and solutions depend upon this fact. We depend for our nourishment upon the ability of plants to synthesize food, we move, and, consequently, we compete in an active rather than a passive manner with other creatures. We share these characteristics with other many-celled animals. Among active, predatory creatures size is a prime advantage. They can feed upon a great range of other creatures and cannot be fed upon by so many.

Size alone does not afford protection, but other things being equal, it has proved advantageous to many different sorts of animals. Certain corollaries to size turn out to be useful as well. Large animals take longer than smaller ones to attain their full adult size, tending, as a result, to live longer. They have time to profit from experience if they are equipped to do so, and the lessons often prove useful to them. They are usually less prolific than small animals, so that each individual may receive more parental attention when young and inexperienced. The very fact that size imposes requirements of a more complex functional organization among their constituent cells permits the sharpening of many of the basic qualities of life. From simple irritability, for instance, specific reactions to varied stimuli are differentiated, and these in coordination may result in awareness.

All multicellular animals, or metazoans, require systems of internal transportation so that nutrient substances in solution may reach each living cell in the body and waste products may be carried away and discharged into the environment. They all require systems for at least the partial digestion of the food and a way for the food to enter the transportation system. They all require special systems for reproducing new individuals of their own kind, for each individual metazoan is bound to die. Single-celled organisms may reproduce by simple cell division, thus in a sense avoiding death. But all many-celled creatures meet this fate eventually. Only a few of their reproductive cells may survive. All active metazoans require systems of internal communication and coordination, so that each cell or group of cells may behave in a manner useful to the creature as a whole, no matter what the consequences to the cell itself. They require muscular systems to enable them to move, integuments as added protection for their existence as discrete individuals, and, very commonly, some supporting or skeletal tissues as well. Definite organs for the storage of food supplies, for the perception of different types of stimuli, and for the fuller integration of behavior are not always found, but these do perform such useful functions that they are very widespread among different types of active metazoans.

Certain body shapes are also more convenient for multicellular animals which move about. Streamlining is necessary for rapid movement within the water. Air is so much less dense a medium that extended plane surfaces are even more at a premium for flying animals. All except sessile creatures exhibit some form of symmetry, and bilateral symmetry is characteristic of those creatures whose life requires high speed. Bilaterally symmetrical animals have definite head and tail ends and ventral and dorsal surfaces, as well as right and left sides. This shape enhances directional mobility, so that the animal may pursue food actively and escape from becoming the food of another creature. Typically, although not universally, the mouth for receiving food is located at the head end, whereas waste products are eliminated toward the rear. This arrangement has an obvious convenience: the creature can seize food without delay and leave the excreta behind. Special sensory receptors such as eyes are also usually located at the head end, as there is more survival value in being able to see where one is going than where one has been. Organs and appendages, when these exist, are usually arranged in pairs along the two sides of a bilaterally symmetrical animal.

Animals which are shaped in this way need to and usually do behave in a more completely integrated way than animals organized on a different basic plan. As a rule, much of the nervous tissue is concentrated in a central cord extending through the long axis of the body, and often large masses of such tissue are concentrated at the head end. Nerves from sensory receptors are in contact within the central cords with nerves which direct special activities, such as muscular movements. Nerves from different sorts of receptors may be in direct or indirect contact as well. This is especially true in the masses of nervous tissue near the head end of the creature. In this way different sorts of messages from the outside world can be apprehended in an integrated manner, and more appropriate responses become possible. Animals with such complex nervous systems are frequently able to behave as though they were aware of what was going on around them, and those which have been tested show at least some ability to learn from experience, even though much of their activity is stereotyped (Dethier and Stellar, 1961).

THE VARIETIES OF LIFE

Variety in the forms of life is one of life's most easily recognizable characteristics, and, upon investigation, it can be seen that this variety is far from chaotic. Thus living creatures may be classified as well as named. The distinction between plants and animals was made long ago, as well as a number of groupings within each of these large categories. All early systems of classification contained many errors. There are, for example, some perfectly successful organisms which may combine plant and animal-like characteristics. Despite their name, sea anemones are not plants; despite their habitat, whales are not fish. Bats are not birds, and Tasmanian wolves are not actually wolves at all. Any classifications depending upon superficial accommodations to habitat are bound to be faulty.

About two centuries ago, Linnaeus (1758) devised the system which forms the basis for taxonomy even today. By that time European students of natural history were familiar with creatures from most parts of the world. They knew enough about the anatomy and habits of a great many creatures, so that systematic comparison was possible on a large scale. Similarities and differences between internal as well as external anatomy and between larval and adult forms could be studied. Thus Linnaeus was in a position to erect a systematic framework for his classification, based upon the idea of underlying or original affinities in structure, rather than analogous function. In systematizing what was known about the various forms of life in his day, he was not thinking in terms of biological relationships or mutual ancestry of different kinds of animals or plants. His taxonomy was simply a brilliant attempt to reduce to order the apparently chaotic variety of life. It contained, however, the essential seed from which natural history was during the next century to grow, for the similarities which he recognized were those of structure, of what Le Gros Clark (1955) has called the Total Morphological Pattern, rather than of behavior or function. Rather than classifying fish with shrimp because they both swim, or birds with wasps because they both fly, Linnaeus was able to observe that the essential form of the fish is like that of the bird, the essential form of the shrimp is closer to that of the wasp, despite their different modes of life. In his time, the idea of actual genetic relationship between different kinds of organisms had not been accepted. It was assumed as a matter of course that each species had been separately created. The different kinds of living things were placed in hierarchical order, with man at the top and the other creatures arranged each in its proper place below him.

Despite this basic misconception, Linnaeus provided the groundwork for the development of evolutionary thought in using the principle of basic affinities, or homologies, to assign each type of creature its proper place. He gave each creature both a generic and a specific name: thus *Homo sapiens* or *Equus caballus* and *Equus zebra*. Within each genus or general category of animal there might be more than one species, or specific type. Note that it is customary to italicize a taxonomic name for genus and species; the name of the genus is capitalized, but the name of the species is not. Furthermore, several genera are included within a larger grouping called an order, several orders within a class, and several classes within a phylum. It is clear that, though Linnaeus placed *Homo sapiens* at the top of the ladder, he recognized similarities among man, apes, and monkeys. Linnaeus included man in the same order with them and naturally called this order Primate, or first. He was thinking in terms of a great chain of being, not of evolution; yet the scheme of classification which Linnaeus drew up could not help but have evolutionary implications. The system of giving dual names is enough in itself to suggest that real biological relationships unite the different species of a genus.

We have learned so much since the eighteenth century about the history, the variety, and the characteristics of living things that a considerable expansion of the Linnaean system has become necessary. Modern taxonomists often consider intermediate taxonomic levels necessary such as the family, the sub-order, the tribe, the infra-class, and others. The function of all such terms is to express degrees of similarity and difference, and the aim of the taxonomist is to devise a system which will record the separate existence of natural groupings and represent, if possible, the degree of kinship among different varieties of living things. To accomplish this we need far more than a simple addition of similarities. Even after discounting superficial likenesses, we find that some points of similarity are far more important than others; that basic similarities may be disguised in many ways; that the fossil evidence of extinct forms of life may contradict conclusions which seem reasonable when we are studying only living forms; and perhaps, especially, that the total morphological pattern is much more significant than any number of discrete items. During the last century, the study of embryology yielded much information about phylogenetic or ancestral kinship, and it was often said that embryology recapitulates phylogeny: that each one of us climbs his own family tree as it were. As it turns out, this is not scientifically accurate, but it is poetically revealing. During the present century the study of physiology, biochemistry, and, more recently, behavior and genetics have assisted in solving problems of classification.

In the modern concept, the species is no longer thought of as a type. In every species there is variation, and it is a mistake to suppose that a creature which is not "average" is an inferior representative of his species. None of us is average. A species is a population of individuals united by common ancestry to such a degree that the similarity among its members is obvious. In bisexually reproducing organisms, such as ourselves, it is a population whose members, if left to their own devices, and if the opportunity arises, will mate and produce fertile offspring. Mating between members of different species which belong to the same genus may produce fertile offspring, but such matings are not too likely to occur under natural conditions. Normally, then, the mating habits of creatures maintain the unity of a species. This topic will be further discussed in Chapter 3.

A VARIETY OF BODY PLANS

In seeking to discover the proper place of the human species, as of any other species within the world of life, we cannot afford to neglect any clues, whether from gross or microscopic anatomy, the fossil record, the development from fertilized egg to adult, the metabolic processes, or even the ecological relationships. A brief review of the characteristics of a variety of metazoans is therefore in order, for there is a great range of variation among them, some being far more complex than others. A few of the lower invertebrates are illustrated in Figure 2–3.

The simplest of the metazoans, for example, the sponges, show only a minor degree of differentiation in their tissues. Some of their cells are specialized for sexual purposes, some build the limy skeleton of the creature, and some assist in digestion. Three layers of tissue are found in sponges, of which the central one consists mostly of inanimate jelly. No living parts are deeply buried: metabolism, including respiration, is facilitated by this structural pattern. But there really is not much that a sponge can do. It fastens itself to a single spot, awaits what food may come drifting by, and, if it is lucky, grows. Lacking nervous tissue, it scarcely behaves like an

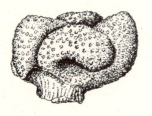  

PORIFORA: SPONGE   COELENTERATE: JELLYFISH   COELENTERATE: SEA ANEMONE

animal at all, and compared to many vigorously active single-celled animals, its life seems to us incredibly dull.

Jellyfish and sea anemones may not appear at first sight to resemble us more closely, but they do. Animals at their level of organization possess nervous tissue, muscular tissue, some cells which produce digestive enzymes, and others which produce poison to assist the animal in capturing its food. They have mouths and digestive cavities and are organized on a radially symmetrical plan about these organs: that is, they are shaped like discs or circles. Animals such as these are capable of coordinated action, and sensory cells enable them to perceive enough of their environment so that their reactions, although simple and stereotyped, may be regarded as purposeful. Although some, such as coral polyps, are sessile and build such large limy skeletons that they look like rocks, others, like jellyfish, have no hard parts at all. Their reproductive practices tend to be exotic. Often alternate generations will be firmly attached polyps which reproduce by budding and drifting jellyfish which reproduce sexually. Although their abilities are meager and the extent of their awareness dubious, creatures such as this begin to show the possibilities inherent in metazoan life.

Other important steps in the direction of the degree and type of organization which is characteristic of the human species are found among a number of creatures classified as flatworms. Their body plan shows bilateral instead of radial symmetry. Like us, they have three distinct layers of tissue: ectoderm, mesoderm, and endoderm. Their nervous system runs from the head to the tail end, but their digestive and excretory systems are more diffuse than ours, and some have mouths on the belly surface instead of the head. The flatworm's head does, however, contain a concentration of nervous tissue and eyes of a sort. Flatworms may reproduce by splitting in two or by laying fertilized eggs. Each individual produces both eggs and sperm. Although flatworms require an ample supply of moisture, they are not restricted to life in the water. Many of them, such

FIGURE 2-3. Some Lower Invertebrates

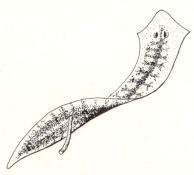

PLANARIA: FLATWORM

ASCARIS: ROUNDWORM

ANNELID: EARTHWORM

as liver flukes and tapeworms, have become parasitic upon larger creatures, but those which forage for their living independently behave much more vigorously and with a higher degree of coordination than jellyfish or sponges.

Roundworms exhibit further advances in the human direction with a digestive system in the form of a tube which runs from a mouth at the head end to an anus at the rear, and they possess a circulatory system as well. This circulatory system not only distributes food throughout the body, but oxygen as well, and like us they carry oxygen by means of hemoglobin. The roundworm's digestive tube is enclosed within a body cavity, or coelum, also like ours. Few varieties of roundworms consist of animals each of which produce both eggs and sperm; among most species the sexes are separate. Segmented bodies, found among some flatworms, are characteristic of the annelids such as earthworms and leeches which comprise still another phylum. This is a further basic improvement in body plan, for it is characteristic of most of the animals which have attained more complex forms of organization and behavior. Some annelids, but not all, have hemoglobin in their blood. Others make use of a rather different substance called chlorocruorin, which colors their blood green (Florkin and Morgulis, 1949). The distinction between males and females at this level of organization remains very different from ours, however. Each earthworm is both, so that when they copulate, each produces sperm to fertilize the eggs of the other. The *Bonellia*, one of their sea-dwelling cousins, has quite different habits. Should it succeed while still young in locating an unmated female, it enters her body where it lives as a parasite and produces sperm. If its search is unsuccessful, it grows up to become a female itself and settles down to await a wandering youth.

Beyond the level of organization represented by the creatures already mentioned, there is a great deal of diversity in basic body plans, of which some offer greater opportunities than others. Some of them are shown in Figure 2–4. The mollusks, for instance, typically live within shells which they secrete. These add to their weight as well as giving them protection against predators. Among

FIGURE 2-4. Some Higher Invertebrates

MOLLUSK: OCTOPUS

MOLLUSK: SNAIL

ARTHROPOD: LOBSTER

those mollusks which dwell on land, shells also serve to retain moisture, but the extra weight involved is a real burden. They move as slowly as snails: they are snails. The octopus and squid are mollusks which have emerged from their shells and are active, well-coordinated, and well-equipped with a variety of sense organs, but utterly unable to support their own weight except when buoyed up by water.

The arthropods have been more successful in adapting to diverse habitats. Among them the crustaceans, such as lobsters and most crabs, have remained water dwellers. Others, such as centipedes, spiders and insects have adjusted to life on the land. Their shells are much lighter than those of mollusks but fit their bodies snugly, making growth very difficult. A common solution among insects is to spend a large part of one's life as a caterpillar or larva and cease growing after metamorphosis. Some adults do not even eat after emerging from the cocoon but simply procreate and die. Even so, the problem of respiration remains, for the insect body plan provides neither lungs nor gills. A multitude of tiny passageways lead from openings in the shell to all parts of the body, so that oxygen can reach all their cells. The larger a creature is, the more such tubes are needed and the greater their diameters must be if gas is to diffuse through them efficiently. Yet this porous construction tends to weaken the structure of the shell which acts not only as a protective device but as a skeleton for support and muscle attachment. Insects may therefore grow long or wide, but not very thick lest they suffocate.

Many insects have developed remarkable abilities for such small creatures. Their sense organs are acute in many ways, their manipulative ability is often exceptionally skilled, and some species have had a highly developed social organization for millions of years. At the same time, their basic body plan imposes limitations which encourage stereotyped rather than flexible behavior. Insofar as we

ARTHROPOD: BUTTERFLY

ECHINODERM: STARFISH

CHORDATE: AMPHIOXUS

have been able to test them, their learning ability appears very limited. Most insects which have been tested can be conditioned in one way or another: bees can learn to associate food with certain colors, and ants often learn to find their way through mazes. Yet the most complex activities of insects, such as constructing cocoons or behaving properly within the colony, would seem to be inherent or instinctive and subject to only minor variations as a result of individual experience. In any case, most insects have such short lives that they could not profit from any lessons they might learn. Insects are certainly a successful class and, as such, their development parallels in a number of ways the line of evolution which has led to our own species, a parallel which is a rather sinister caricature.

Echinoderms such as sea urchins and starfish may seem simple creatures in contrast to insects. As adults, they are radially symmetrical. Lacking brains and having poorly developed special sense organs, their abilities are at best mediocre. Some are sessile, and none are in a hurry. Fossil evidence demonstrates continued vacillation in their evolution, yet embryological evidence carries the conviction to the greater number of zoologists that they are closer kin to us than the arthropods are. In the early stages of growth and development, the individual vertebrate resembles the individual echinoderm in many ways and differs from the embryos of the other sorts of animals so far mentioned. Furthermore, some, although not all echinoderms possess a substance known as creatine in their muscles (Moody, 1962). Chemical compounds called phosphagens are involved in the expenditure of energy during muscular contraction. Most invertebrates have phosphagen containing arginine, whereas all vertebrates have creatine instead. In this aspect of biochemistry, as in embryology, the echinoderms seem to bridge the gap between vertebrates and other animals. Finally, serological precipitin tests, which measure the degree of similarity of the serum proteins in the blood, indicate that the echinoderms and the vertebrates are allied in this respect as well (Wilhelmi, 1942).

THE VERTEBRATE BODY PLAN

We have a few other unpretentious relatives living in the sea, all classified with the vertebrates into the chordate phylum. These are the acorn worm, the tunicates, and the amphioxus. The embryos of all these creatures, like those of fish, birds, and people, contain a number of unique structural peculiarities. We all possess an elastic stiffening rod called the notochord toward the back and lying next to a hollow central nerve. We all possess a series of paired gill slits in the neck region which serves for respiration among sea dwellers. Among vertebrates, the notochord is replaced by the backbone early in growth, and among land-dwelling vertebrates, the gills are replaced by lungs. But the basic body plan of all vertebrates reveals their kinship to these simple creatures: it is simply an improved version, representing a more efficient level of organization.

Perhaps the best demonstration of the efficiency of the vertebrate body plan is the existence of an internal articulated skeleton. Different vertebrates have at times grown external shells as well, as have turtles, yet even they retain internal skeletons. Such a system permits continued growth: neither we, nor turtles, nor fish have to shed our supporting skeletons and expose ourselves from time to time to a predacious world as crabs must do. Nor do we need to wrap ourselves up in cocoons like caterpillars in order to reach our adult forms. Our bones grow within us, serving as muscular attachments and reservoirs of calcium, as well as giving us strength for mobility at all times. Furthermore, since the backbone consists of a long series of hollow rings, it provides not only ample flexibility but also protection for the central nerve cord within it. Best of all, the directing brain of the vertebrate is protected by the bones of the skull which encase it. The vertebrate skeleton gives support, permits freedom of the body, and supplies protection where it is most needed—to the all-important central nervous system which controls and directs behavior.

This feature alone was enough to demonstrate to Linnaeus and his contemporaries that any reasonable scheme of taxonomy must place the human species not only in the primate order but also among the vertebrates. His scheme of classification suggests the ancestral relationships which we now realize exist among all the forms of life. By itself, however, it cannot prove any such relationship. It simply shows how many variations can be played upon a theme, not how they came to be played, or when, or where. The forms of life vary in space and time, and the fact that different animals live in different places became obvious as European travelers saw more of the world. Some creatures are tropical, others are found only in temperate or arctic regions. The inhabitants of deserts differ from the inhabitants of grasslands or jungles. Different continents possess distinctive types of animals, and those found upon islands often have peculiarities of their own as well.

ISOLATION AND DIVERSIFICATION

Europeans were astonished at the exotic fauna described and sometimes brought back by returning voyagers. In America, for instance, mammals were found which kept their young in pouches on their bellies. These were the opossums. A great variety of pouched mammals were later found in Australia, too. Some, like the kan-

garoo, were utterly different in shape from anything known heretofore. Others, however, like the Tasmanian wolf, looked almost like
familiar creatures. The Americas lacked many animals which were
common in the Old World, such as leopards, camels, elephants, cattle, and pigs, but were inhabited instead by jaguars, llamas, bison,
and peccaries. Monkeys were found in the American tropics, but
they all had an extra set of premolar teeth, a different arrangement
of the nostrils and, in some cases, grasping or prehensile tails. Indeed, many animals in the American jungles were found to have
prehensile tails. As knowledge about the distribution of animals increased, it became clear that all species are limited in their range
and that most of them inhabit only a comparatively small region.
On the other hand, different species of the same genus may live in
many different areas, while different genera of the same order are
likely to be found spread over the greater part of the world. Some,
such as the pouched marsupials, may live only in a few isolated
areas. Some, such as the nonhuman primates, may be found only
in the warmer parts of continents. But in general the rule seems to
be that the higher the level of classification, the more widespread
the distribution.

Isolation appears to result in diversification within any group
of animals, whether a class, an order, or a genus. Darwin (1839)
noted during his trip around the world on the *Beagle* that many
kinds of finches, but very few other birds, lived on the Galapagos
Islands in the Pacific. In most places finches are seed eaters and
have beaks suitable for such a diet. In the Galapagos some finches
ate insects, some ate buds or fruit, and some substituted for absent
woodpeckers. The beaks of these finches were modified in accordance with their source of food, as is shown in Figure 2–5. A few
species were restricted to one or two nearby islands. None were
spread throughout the entire archipelago, and what one species did
on one island, another would do on a second. Darwin wondered
how to account for this, for it seemed odd the finches would differ
from one another in such ways as he noted, had each species been
separately created. Since his time, of course, many observers have
noted similar degrees of variation between related species which are
isolated from each other: snails in different valleys of Polynesian
islands and birds of paradise in Melanesia are standard examples.
As Darwin thought about this problem and about the other diverse
examples of adaptation which he noted during this voyage, he found
himself formulating the hypothesis that evolution rather than separate creation must be the answer.

Entire continents, as well as valleys and islands, are isolated
from each other, and sometimes high mountains, deserts, and climatic differences serve as barriers within large land masses. As a

result biologists now recognize various life zones. Each one appears to have its own typical flora and fauna, although there is some degree of overlapping between adjacent zones. Even when a certain sort of animal or plant has an extremely widespread distribution as is the case with the human species, minor differences are easily noted between the inhabitants of the different zones. The earliest attempts at racial classification, which date from the time of Linnaeus, take account of this fact. Linnaeus himself recognized European, African, Oriental, and American varieties of man, and since his time the geographical basis of systems of classification within the human stock has been commonly recognized.

FIGURE 2-5. Variety among Darwin's Finches. These Closely Related Birds on the Galapagos Islands Have Adapted to Different Ecological Niches by Evolving Different Kinds of Beaks. (Photos: Dr. I. Eibl-Eibesfeldt)

Some barriers have been much more effective than others in keeping living creatures apart. For instance, the Atlantic Ocean seems to have separated the Americas from the Old World to a greater extent than the Pacific, because Alaska and Siberia are so very close and have often formed a single land mass in the geological past. Wallace's line, a series of very deep troughs running through the East Indies, appears to have kept almost all Asiatic land-dwelling animals from reaching Australia and New Guinea for some 60 million years. This has protected marsupial or pouched mammals from competition with the eutherian varieties which nourish their unborn young through a placenta. Small kangaroos and other marsupials scramble about in the trees of New Guinea, but there are no monkeys. One area which we may clearly rule out as a possible site for the origin of the human stock is Australasia. Another is South America, despite the presence of some primates in the tree tops of that continent. We have already noted the way in which they differ from the primates of the Old World, and we resemble the latter. Furthermore, for millions of years South America, like Australia, was isolated by water from all the rest of the world and served as a haven for animals unknown elsewhere. The faunal regions of the world are mapped in Figure 2-6.

MUTUAL DEPENDENCE

Although much of any animal's behavior is directed toward its own survival, with no regard for the consequences to other creatures, one of the qualities of life is the mutual dependence of different creatures. This mutual dependence takes many forms, from predation and scavenging to symbiosis and even active cooperation between individuals. Mutual aid is not at all uncommon, but we have no reason to assume that it is generously given or gratefully received or even that the creatures concerned are in any sense aware of its existence. It is extremely hazardous to draw lessons in ethics from the relationships which exist between different organisms and from which some of them or the world of life in general may profit.

FIGURE 2-6. The Major Faunal Regions of the World

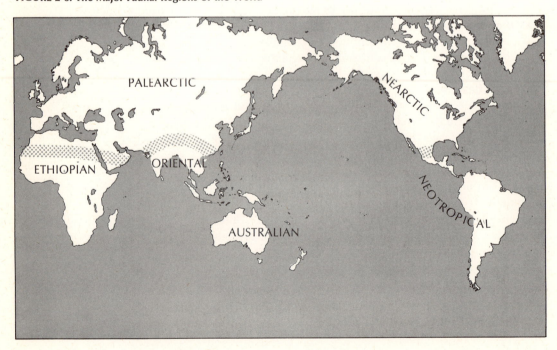

FIGURE 2-7. Sea Anemone and Fish. Although Most Fish Are Killed by the Poison of the Sea Anemone, a Few Species Live in Harmony. (Photo: A. W. Ambler from National Audubon Society)

Human beings cannot justify either cruel or kind actions on the grounds that they represent some hypothetical law of nature. The balance of nature is neither cruel nor kind. It simply exists. In general animals exploit the fact that plants create food and return oxygen to the atmosphere. Plants exploit the fact that animals produce nitrogenous wastes and return carbon dioxide to the atmosphere. Larger animals kill and eat smaller ones, while micro-organisms feed upon all sorts of larger creatures and are themselves the victims of virus infections. Many bacteria inhabiting the digestive tracts of bigger creatures assist them in digesting their food by enzymic activity.

A great many varieties of organisms live in groups of their own sort, for there is often protection in numbers. Sometimes organized societies with a division of functions may exist among animals. Ants and bees have the most complex and rigid societies of this sort, but many other creatures are also highly social. Social organization gives even more protection than simply flocking together in a group. Such societies may coexist with other types of organisms, too. Some fish, as shown in Figure 2–7, take refuge among the toxic tentacles of sea anemones. Small owls use prairie dog burrows; ant hills frequently contain a variety of other insects which produce secretions that ants lick up (Wells, Huxley, and Wells, 1931). Sometimes ants feed their own larvae to their guests. There are usually plenty of surplus larvae available, and ants need all the stimulation they can find for their ceaseless tasks. Not infrequently, mothers, or even fathers, protect and nourish their offspring even to their own detriment, discomfort, or death. Not infrequently, as in the case of fish such as guppies, mothers gobble up their young if they can catch them. And female spiders, after being fertilized, normally kill and suck dry the carcasses of their recent mates.

Nevertheless, reproductive processes among metazoans, usually, and among single-celled creatures, often, require cooperation between two individuals. Actual fertilization necessitates cooperation to the supreme point of extinction through the merging of two cells, so that their nuclear material is combined. This process has frequently been observed among single-celled organisms. The same thing happens when a sperm enters an egg, although in a different way. The act of mating between male and female metazoans, however, is a type of behavior on quite a different level from the conjugation of a sperm with an egg which may result from mating. Since most metazoans are bisexual, mating between males and females is essential for reproduction. The type of cooperation required for this procedure is varied, but it is always complicated and must be precise if it is to be successful. The impulses directing the activities of creatures during mating are very strong and sometimes even savage. Apparently they inhibit most of the other activities of the creatures concerned for the time. Insects have been observed which continued to copulate even after their heads were removed. Even when bodily contact is unnecessary, as it often is among animals which live in the water, males release their sperm only when stimulated by the emission of a female's eggs in their vicinity, often displaying hostile reactions to other males at the same time.

Some extra benefit must accrue to a population of organisms from the complicated forms of behavior involved in bisexual reproduction. If not, it would be difficult to understand how this method of creating a new generation has become so very widespread not only among animals but also among plants. It would be even more difficult to understand why single-celled organisms so frequently conjugate and merge their individualities when simple cell division can lead to their multiplication, as it ordinarily does. One might have supposed that the budding-off of some part of a metazoan would have been the standard form of reproduction, but although this does occur, it is far from typical. The advantages of bisexual reproduction, as well as the rules which appear to exist in the transmission of life, are so important in determining the various forms in which life appears that they deserve a separate chapter.

Sources and Suggested Readings

BUCHSBAUM, R.
1938   *Animals Without Backbones.*   University of Chicago Press, Chicago.

BUTLER, J. A. V.
1959   *Inside the Living Cell.*   George Allen & Unwin, London.

CLARK, W. C. LE GROS
1955   *The Fossil Evidence for Human Evolution.*   University of Chicago Press, Chicago.

DARLINGTON, P. J.
1957   *Zoogeography: The Geographical Distribution of Animals.*   Wiley, New York.

DARWIN, C.
1939   *The Voyage of the Beagle.*   The Natural History Library Edition, 1962.   Doubleday, Garden City.

DETHIER, V. and E. STELLAR
1961   *Animal Behavior.*   Prentice-Hall, Englewood Cliffs.

FLORKIN, E. and S. MORGULIS
1949   *Biochemical Evolution.*   Academic Press, New York.

HENDERSON, L. J.
1913   *The Fitness of the Environment.*   Macmillan, New York.

LINNAEUS, C.
1758   *Systema Naturae,* 10th edition.   Laurenti Salvii, Stockholm.

MOODY, P. A.
1962   *Introduction to Evolution,* 2nd edition.   Harper and Bros., New York.

NEURATH, H. and K. BAILEY
1954   *The Proteins.*   Academic Press, New York.

PAULI, W. F.
1949   *The World of Life.*   Houghton Mifflin, Cambridge.

SIMPSON, G. G.
    1949   *The Meaning of Evolution.* Yale University Press, New Haven.
    1961   *Principles of Animal Taxonomy.* Columbia University Press, New York.

SMITH, H. W.
    1956   *Kamongo, or the Lungfish and the Padre.* Viking, New York.

TAYLOR, J. H.
    1962   Chromosome Reproduction and the Problem of Coding and Transmitting the Genetic Heritage. *Science in Progress,* **12**th series. Yale University Press, New Haven.

THOMPSON, D'ARCY W.
    1942   *On Growth and Form.* Cambridge University Press, Cambridge.

WATSON, J. D. and F. H. C. CRICK
    1953   The Structure of DNA. *Cold Spring Harbor Symposia in Quantitative Biology,* **18,** 123–131.

WELLS, H. G., J. S. HUXLEY, and G. P. WELLS
    1931   *The Science of Life.* Cassel and Co., Ltd., London.

WOOLDRIDGE, D. E.
    1966   *The Machinery of Life.* McGraw-Hill, New York.

CHAPTER 3

The
Transmission
of
Life

REPRODUCTION: BY CELL AND BISEXUAL

Some geneticists have said that life is a device for manufacturing DNA. In fact, we could legitimately view people, like other animals and plants, as elaborate systems which function in such a way that this very complex chemical compound may have a constant supply of the raw materials it needs in order to reduplicate itself. We know that life depends upon the continued elaboration of DNA within living cells, for this material is absolutely vital in transmitting life from one generation to the next. Some cells, for example, the red cells, or erythrocytes, of our bloodstreams, may live for a time although they lack DNA. But such cells have a short life span, usually four months or less, and leave no offspring. Quite a few varieties of organisms, such as bacteria, not only survive but divide rapidly without nuclei. But these organisms possess nucleic materials scattered throughout their cytoplasm which duplicates itself so that equal and presumably identical parts of it are present in each daughter cell after division.

    Cell division such as that practiced by bacteria and other micro-organisms is, in a sense, the most elementary way of reproducing and transmitting life. However, it is not a simple process except when compared to the method followed by organisms which practice bisexual reproduction. A living cell does not simply split in two. This would mean death. And not all parts of a cell are capable of duplicating themselves in every detail. On the contrary, this is a property primarily, if not exclusively, of DNA. As we noted in Chapter Two, DNA appears to direct and coordinate events which occur within a cell. This appears to be true of cell division, too. Only after the DNA within a cell has duplicated itself is such a cell capable of dividing properly. After such division, the DNA directs the synthesis and assembly of the other constituent materials which compose the new cell as a whole.

In most of the cells of most organisms, large or small, by far the greater part of the DNA is assembled in threadlike bodies known as chromosomes. It is not at all unlikely that a few molecules of DNA are contained in the centrioles, for these bodies, which assume great importance at the time of cell division, share the power of self-duplication with chromosomes. Normally, each cell contains one centriole, a small body which lies just outside of the nuclear membranes. In preparation for cell division, the centriole divides. The new centrioles move to opposite ends of the cell, while each chromosome duplicates itself into a pair of identical twins. These twins then part company from one another, and one member of each twin pair is drawn to either end of the cell. A nuclear membrane forms to contain each set of chromosomes, and finally the cell becomes two (Stern, 1960). Thus each daughter cell contains not only the same number of chromosomes but, in a real sense, the identical chromosomes which their mother cell had possessed before the process began. In this way, each daughter cell has the same capabilities which the mother cell had. Mitosis, as this type of cell division is called, is illustrated in Figure 3–1.

Molecules of the substance called DNA are varied in their construction and, consequently, in the chemical reactions which they provoke. It is known that in some species the arrangement of such molecules with respect to one another—that is, their relative locations on a chromosome—is significant with respect to their functions. We do not know whether this is true with respect to the human species. We know that even slight alterations in the molecular structure of a fragment of DNA may produce profound differences in the effect upon the activities taking place within a cell and, consequently, upon an entire multicellular organism. Finally, each molecule of DNA is only capable of reduplicating itself. It cannot form some other sort of DNA. Because of this combination of facts, the sequence of events leading up to and including cell division must occur in a precise pattern to be effective. Yet cell division is constantly taking place. During the time which it has taken to read the last few sentences, many thousands of such cell divisions have taken place within the reader's body and many thousands more among the microorganisms which his body shelters.

Cell division is the way single-celled creatures produce new individual units of life. It is also the way multicellular organisms grow in size. Life is transmitted in both cases, but in the multicellular organism the activities of the individual cell are circumscribed to serve the functions it may be expected to perform for the life of the body as a whole. It is remarkable that in both cases the entire complement of chromosomal material is evenly divided. In a free-living, single-celled individual, cell division is adequate for all the needs of independent existence. In the cells of our various tissues, it is adequate for the needs and functions of those tissues. We have the same chromosomes in the cells composing our eyes, our muscles, our livers, our skins, and our gonads, or sex cells, just as trees have the same chromosomes in their roots, their leaves, and their flowers. Clearly, the way in which the DNA directs the activities of a cell depends not only on its chemical structure and its location on a chromosome, but upon other factors as well, such as the position of the cell in the body and the chemical influences which reach the cell from other parts of the body. The cell's environment and the DNA transmitted to it by its parent cell jointly determine what sort of cell it is going to be. Only a tiny proportion of the cells of most metazoans function in such a way that they may contribute life to another generation of creatures.

Many animals are capable of astonishing powers of regeneration. Each half of an earthworm which has been cut in two may grow

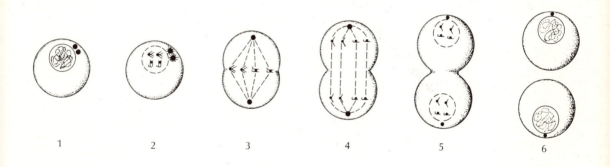

1   2   3   4   5   6

FIGURE 3-1. Mitosis. Stage 1: The Centriole Has Duplicated. Stage 2: The Nuclear Membrane Is Dissolving as the Chromosomes, Already Duplicated, Become Distinguishable. Stage 3: The Centrioles Are at Opposite Ends of the Cell, the Spindle Fibres Are Appearing, and the Chromosomes Assembling along a Central Line. Stage 4: The Chromosomes Are Moving along the Spindle to the Centrioles at the Two Ends of the Cell. Stage 5: New Nuclear Membranes Are Forming about Each Set of Chromosomes as the Cell Constricts in the Middle. Stage 6: The Nuclear Membranes Are Complete, the Chromosomes Are Vanishing, and the Cells Are Separated.

into a complete earthworm, but this is not the earthworm's normal method of reproduction. Yet many varieties of smaller and simpler metazoans do reproduce in this manner as a matter of course. Other metazoans may reproduce by budding, that is, a protuberance on some part of the parent's body eventually detaches itself as a new individual. Some sorts of jellyfish, as well as other creatures, alternate with each generation between budding and bisexual reproduction. A number of other marine creatures produce eggs which usually develop into mature individuals without the necessity of fertilization. It is clearly possible for life to go on for generations, even in the case of metazoans, without the merging of two cells which is the essence of bisexual reproduction. Yet by far the most frequent method of reproduction among multicellular organisms, whether animals or plants, involves such mergers and requires the development of special male or female reproductive cells. Sometimes among plants and usually among animals the entire organism may be characterized as male or female, thus adding still more to the complexity of life.

Long before anything approaching a scientific attitude had grown up among our ancestors, the astonishing results of sexual behavior had become apparent to them. We have no idea when or where our ancestors discovered that copulation may result in reproduction. It was certainly a great many thousands of years ago, although there are still tribes who prefer to imagine that all conceptions are supernaturally mediated or that females just naturally give birth to babies without any, or at most incidental assistance from males. In the Trobriand Islands, for example, the natives castrate all their domestic boars, yet their sows continue to reproduce. They point to this as proof that males have nothing to do with reproduction, conveniently overlooking the fact that there are plenty of wild boars on the islands from whose attentions they make no effort to protect their sows.

Yet most agricultural communities have long attempted to practice some kind of breeding to improve their stocks of animals and plants. Some plants, such as maize and dates, have had human care and assistance for so long that they are completely dependent upon it and do not reproduce if left to their own devices. Selective breeding is an ancient practice so far as cultivated plants and domestic animals are concerned, for people noticed that descendants were more likely to resemble their ancestors than they were to resemble unrelated creatures. Not only did sheep give birth to lambs rather than to dogs or donkeys, but in time, careful breeding of certain sheep produced sheep which had more and better wool for spinning. Different varieties and strains of both plants and animals were developed by agricultural breeders who used sufficient care. At the same time no coherent theory was developed to account for these results, and all sorts of misconceptions about breeding were prevalent. Two thousand years ago the Roman philosopher and poet Lucretius suggested in *De Rerum Natura* ideas about inheritance which are startlingly similar to those held by scientists today, but he did not perform experiments to demonstrate their validity (Sarton, 1959).

THE MENDELIAN LAWS OF HEREDITY

Indeed, until a century ago, no one performed experiments designed in such a fashion as to demonstrate the mode of inheritance characteristic of bisexually reproducing organisms. By that time it had been discovered that males produce sperm which fuse with female eggs, but it was the general opinion that the contributions of the two sexes to the hereditary characteristics of their offspring blended together and diluted each other in such a way that they became inseparable. Even such scientists as Darwin (1868) thought that changes which environment imposed upon the body could in some way affect the reproductive cells, so that acquired characteristics might be inherited. No one could explain how this might happen in any way that made sense, but the facts that one species evolved into another as time went on and that organisms appeared to be tailored to fit their living conditions led many scientists to suppose it must be so.

In a monastery in Moravia, meanwhile, Gregor Mendel was carefully sorting out and counting peas. He was a patient, careful man, and he raised the legumes in the monastery garden under strictly controlled conditions. From his study of previous experiments in breeding, he realized that it would be necessary to select clearly defined, alternate characters in some organism whose fertilization he could control and to analyze the inheritance of a single set of characters at a time, for several generations. This was the secret of his success. Mendel observed that there are a number of ways in which peas differ: in some the seeds are round, in others they are wrinkled; in some they are green, in others, yellow. The flowers in some peas are axial in position, in others, terminal. These are specific characteristics which do not merge into one another and are not subject to a continuous range of variation as human stature is. Mendel therefore picked purebred strains which differed from each other in one character only and cross-fertilized them. When the new plants grew, he observed them and counted what he found.

Mendel knew nothing of what goes on within a living cell. He did not need to in order to infer the mode of inheritance of the contrasting, discrete characters which he had wisely selected for study. For what he discovered when he took the trouble to count was that in the generation produced by cross-fertilization, all the peas were round, none were wrinkled. All were yellow, none were green. All the flowers were axial, none terminal in their position. It did not matter whether he had pollinated green by yellow or yellow by green; every one of the peas was yellow. Mendel might have deduced that the color green had been totally lost. But Mendel was a patient man. He was not satisfied to study a single generation. And he was curious. He wanted to know what had happened to the green. So he continued his experiment. He fertilized the seeds of each plant of this generation with its own pollen; this is called self-fertilization. He was careful to prevent any possible contamination from other plants. When another generation of peas grew, he observed them, and once more counted what he found. Thus he discovered what had happened: 6,022 peas were yellow, and 2,001 were green. In the same way, wrinkled peas had vanished in the first generation, but in the second there were 1,850 wrinkled peas and 5,474 round ones. In a third experiment terminal flowers, which were completely absent in the first hybrid generation, reappeared in the second to the number of 207, although 651 were axial. Mendel studied several other characters, and in each case obtained the same sort of result.

Mendel's curiosity was not yet satisfied. He bred still another generation of peas, again by self-fertilization alone. The wrinkled peas, green peas, and those with terminal flowers produced only their own type. But one-sixth of the offspring of round peas which had been self-fertilized were wrinkled, and one-sixth of the offspring of yellow peas were green. There was only one possible explanation to all this: the hereditary factor which produced green seeds had not been lost; it was only masked in all the members of the first generation and in three-quarters of the members of the second generation, too. This factor could only be effective in producing a green pea if it was received from both parents at fertilization. In the preparation of reproductive cells, the factor producing green must be segregated from that producing yellow. Because half of the cells which had united to form them were green producing and half yellow producing, in the first hybrid generation, half of these cells would carry the factor for yellow and half, the factor for green, although all the peas were yellow in color. With self-fertilization the chances of any one green-producing factor uniting with another are one-half of one-half, or one in four. One in four of the succeeding generation turned out, in fact, to be green. The results of self-fertilization in the third generation of the experiment confirmed this set of inferences and was not consistent with any other conclusion. Mendel proved that hereditary potentialities are clearly inherited as discrete units, which may be hidden in the presence of contrasting ones but are not lost and which may reappear untarnished in later generations. If any individual has received contrasting factors from his parents, these factors will be segregated from each other in the preparation of his reproductive cells, which are known as gametes.

THE LAW OF SEGREGATION

Mendel's first discovery is known as the Law of Segregation. Its mechanism is demonstrated in Figure 3–2. The importance of this rule to our understanding of heredity is overwhelming. In studying the heredity of human beings, it took a long time after Mendel, who lived a century ago, before suitable contrasting characters were discovered. Although we are unable to control human breeding as Mendel controlled the fertilization of his peas, we have learned

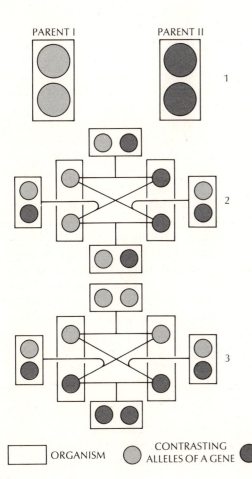

FIGURE 3-2. The Mechanics of Mendel's First Law: Segregation. 1. The Parental Generation. Each Parent Has Two Identical Genes. 2. The Genes of the Parents Join To Produce the First Filial Generation. Each Child Receives One of His Two Genes from Each Parent. The Two Genes of Each Child Are Different. 3. The Genes of Two Members of the First Filial Generation Join To Produce the Second Filial Generation. Note the Random Distribution of the Genes, which Are Seen To Have Remained Segregated throughout Their Transmission from Generation to Generation.

PARENT I   PARENT II

ORGANISM   CONTRASTING ALLELES OF A GENE

enough by analyzing family lines to be quite sure that the manner in which we inherit potentialities from our parents and transmit them to our children is precisely the same as Mendel discovered for peas. The discrete and segregating unit of inheritance, whether in a pea or in a man, is called a *gene* and the study of inheritance is termed *genetics*. We now know, as Mendel did not, that genes are located on chromosomes and are composed of DNA. Mendel's lack of this knowledge did not prevent his discovery of the functions of the genes in transmitting potentialities from one generation to the next.

In each of the characteristics which he studied, Mendel found that one of its two contrasting forms appeared in all members of the first hybrid generation and in three-fourths of the next. He called the form which was apparent, even among hybrids, *dominant*, and the form which was masked *recessive*. In a great many other cases which have been studied, one of two contrasting forms is dominant, but in a great many others neither dominance nor recessiveness exists. Sometimes dominance is not complete. Sometimes there are three or more alternative forms, of which only one will be totally recessive. Of course, no individual may have more than two in his own system: one from each parent. Such contrasting forms of a gene are called *alleles*.

An interesting case of this sort in the human population is that of the blood groups discovered at the beginning of the present century. Three alleles called I^A, I^B, and I^O exist in this system; I^O is recessive to both I^A and I^B, but neither of these is dominant over the other. Consequently, human blood may be of group O, group A, group B, or group AB. Persons of blood groups A or B may or may not possess the allele I^O. We have no way of testing directly but can often infer the answer from a study of the blood groups of their relatives. One of the easiest and yet most instructive questions in human genetics is to ask, "What are the blood group alleles and the testable blood groups of the parents of four brothers who have been tested and found to be O, A, B, and AB?" The reader should be able to solve this problem on the basis of what he has just read.

Any organism obviously possesses numerous potentialities which it has inherited. Peas may be both green and wrinkled. People may have blood group A and blue eyes. The tiny fruit fly used so often in genetic experimentation, may have a black body and garnet eyes. Can we expect that different characters which are associated in one generation will continue to be combined in the same way in later generations?

THE LAW OF INDEPENDENT ASSORTMENT

Mendel continued his experiments in order to find out how different pairs of potentialities are transmitted simultaneously. He crossed round yellow peas with wrinkled green ones. In the first hybrid generation, all the peas, without exception, were round and yellow. This was to be expected, since he had already learned that the alleles producing both these characters are dominant. Mendel self-fertilized this generation of peas, and then examined the characters present in the next generation. Both wrinkled peas and green peas reappeared, of course. In fact, he counted 315 round yellow peas, 101 wrinkled yellow, 108 round green, and 32 wrinkled green: the mathematical ratio was approximately 9:3:3:1. One-sixteenth of the peas combined both recessive characters, six-sixteenths combined a dominant with a recessive, and nine-sixteenths showed both dominant characters. It was clear that the potentiality for being green is not connected with the potentiality for being wrinkled. The two characters had been inherited quite independently of one another. By chance, and by chance alone, one-fourth of the alleles for green had combined with one-fourth of the alleles for wrinkled. One-fourth of one-fourth is one-sixteenth, so that one-sixteenth of the second generation showed both recessive characters. This second discovery by Mendel is known as the Law of Independent Assortment. The mechanism of Mendel's Second Law is shown in Figure 3–3.

The element of chance and probability in the mechanism of inheritance is very important. One cannot predict which male and female gametes will fuse to form a new individual. It is possible only to predict the relative frequency with which various alternative possibilities will occur and therefore the proportions of various combinations. We cannot expect to find the predicted proportions in any small group, but we can in a large group. You may win the first ten times in any game of chance, but if it *is* a game of chance your winning streak won't last forever. Human families are never large enough for us to expect the 3:1 or the 9:3:3:1 ratios to be found in any single group of brothers and sisters. The study of any large group, however, will demonstrate just the situation which Mendel found in counting peas.

It is embarrassing to have to record the fact that Mendel's work attracted no attention when it was published in 1866. A generation later, after other scientists had studied the physiology of cells and of reproduction extensively, it was brought to the attention of biologists, and many other experimenters confirmed it. By this time enough was known about cell division and especially the kind of cell division needed for the final preparation of gametes, or reproductive cells, for Mendel's work to be fully appreciated. Chromosomes had been observed under the microscope, and it was apparent that they were constant in number for any species from one generation to the next. Yet each parent contributed chromosomes in the fusion of gametes. Why didn't the number of chromosomes double with each generation? The German physiologist Weismann (1892) correctly predicted that a special type of cell devision must be required when gametes are formed, in which the number of chromosomes must be reduced by half. This is indeed the case. There are two kinds of cell division: that of ordinary cells, already described, is called *mitosis;* the other type of cell division, which produces gametes, is called *meiosis.*

MEIOSIS

In almost all of the body's cells, whether those of a person, a fruit fly, or a corn plant, the chromosomes are in pairs. Man has twenty-

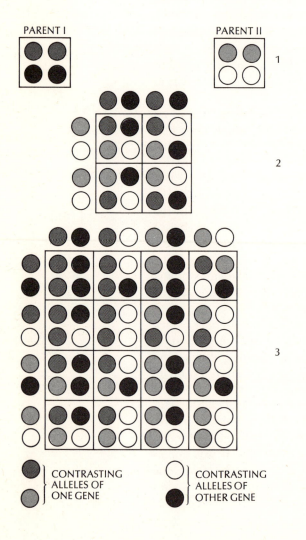

FIGURE 3-3. The Mechanics of Mendel's Second Law: Random Assortment. 1. The Parental Generation. Each Parent Has Two Identical Alleles for Each of Two Separate Genes. 2. The Genes of the Parents (Outside the Square) Join To Produce the First Filial Generation. All Children Have Both Alleles of Each Gene. Consequently, All Produce Four Types of Gametes, or Sex-Cells. 3. The Genes of Two Members of the First Filial Generation (Outside the Square) Join To Produce the Second Filial Generation. Each of the Four Types of Gametes from One Member May Join Any of the Four Types of Another Member. Consequently, All of the Sixteen Combinations Shown Are Equally Possible.

PARENT I PARENT II

CONTRASTING ALLELES OF ONE GENE

CONTRASTING ALLELES OF OTHER GENE

three pairs; different species of fruit fly, four or five pairs; a corn plant, ten pairs. Before mitosis takes place, both members of each pair duplicate themselves and become twins, so that all daughter cells receive a full complement of paired chromosomes. As Mendel's experiments demonstrated, one member of each pair of chromosomes is contributed by the mother and the other by the father. Bisexual reproduction gives each of us twenty-three chromosomes from each of our parents, and each chromosome contains many genetic potentialities.

For meiosis, two successive cell divisions are required. (See Figure 3–4). The first step is a coming together of the already duplicated pairs of chromosomes, which twist about one another in such firm embrace that they usually exchange portions of themselves with their partners. Following this intricate procedure, the chromosomes separate, and the primary cell division ensues. It should be noted that the chromosomes assort quite independently of each other in this separation. There is no fixed pattern of maternally and paternally derived chromosomes moving as a unit. Each resulting cell contains some of each. Since we humans have twenty-three pairs of chromosomes, 8,324,608 different combinations are equally likely to occur.

After the primary cell division, a second cell division takes place almost at once. The chromosome pairs have not reduplicated themselves, as they would have preceding mitosis. Consequently,

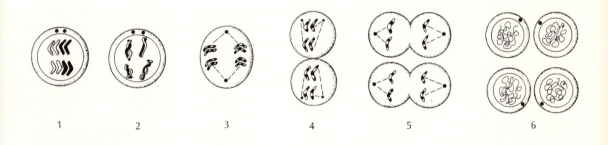

1   2   3   4   5   6

FIGURE 3-4. Meiosis. Stage 1: Duplicated Chromosomes, Black from Father and White from Mother, Pair. Stage 2: Chromosomes Twist about Each Other, Exchanging Genetic Material. Stage 3: The First Meiotic Division Begins. Stage 4: The First Division Completed, the Second Is about To Start. Stage 5: The Second Meiotic Division Reduces the Chromosome Number in Each Cell by One-half. Stage 6: Meiosis Is Complete.

the separation between the two members of a pair reduces by half the number of chromosomes in each of the resulting gametes. They are no longer in pairs but are single and ready to pair with similar chromosomes in a gamete from another individual upon fertilization. Furthermore, as a result of random assortment the maternally and paternally derived chromosomes have been thoroughly shuffled, as a deck of cards would be at the beginning of an honest game.

LINKAGE AND CROSSING OVER

It was fortunate for the development of our understanding of genetics that Mendel chose items controlled by genes which are located on different chromosomes in his study of the simultaneous inheritance of two separate characteristics. Had the genes which lead to seed color and surface texture been located on the same chromosome, he could not have discovered the Law of Independent Assortment. Genes on the same chromosome are said to be linked, for indeed they are fastened together like the links of a chain. They tend to be inherited as a unit and in the reduction division of meiosis, it is these units which are randomly assorted rather than the individual genes themselves. In most creatures which reproduce bisexually the fact of sex itself is genetically controlled, as one might expect. The chromosome which contains the sex-determining factor also includes other genes. These are said to be sex-linked because they are inherited together with one's sex. In our species, the genes which determine the presence, partial absence, or absence of color vision are sex-linked.

Also in our species, as in many others, females possess a chromosome pair of which the partners appear to be identical, whereas among males the partners are observably unequal, one chromosome

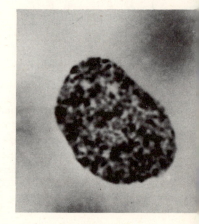

FIGURE 3-5. Barr Bodies, which Indicate the Number of x Chromosomes in a Cell (Photos: Dr. Arthur Robinson)

being much shorter than the other. The long chromosomes are known as x chromosomes, the short ones as y chromosomes. Among men, at the time when the number of chromosomes is reduced by half during meiosis, one-half of the cells which will become spermatozoa contain the y chromosome, the shorter member of the pair, and one-half contain the longer x chromosome. Among women both members of the pair are equal in length, so that all cells destined to become eggs contain a long sex-determining chromosome. Half of man's spermatozoa are capable, therefore, of producing sons and the other half of producing daughters, should they succeed in fertilizing an egg. Therefore the sex ratio approximates equality. Evidence suggests that a higher proportion of male-determining spermatozoa succeed in the race to the egg, and we know that males are more likely to die, even before birth, than females. We still don't know why either of these things happen but, in any case, they counterbalance each other.

About a decade ago it was found that cells from a female may be expected to contain, within the nucleus, a particle known as a Barr body (Barr, 1959), named for its discoverer. At times, there may be two or three such particles because meiosis, a very complex mechanical process, sometimes goes astray and leads to ova which contain two or even three x chromosomes, rather than the one which is standard. The number of Barr bodies, it seems, is always one less than the number of x chromosomes in the nucleus of a cell. Figure 3–5 shows nuclei with different numbers of Barr bodies. Of course, mechanical mistakes may occur in the production of sperm too. Some males have two or three instead of just a single y chromosome. Such abnormalities in the number of sex chromosomes may lead to deviations from the standard sexual characteristics of mammals.

Random assortment leads to an astonishing variety in the chromosomal composition of eggs and sperm. The exchange of genetic

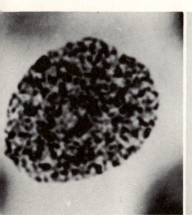 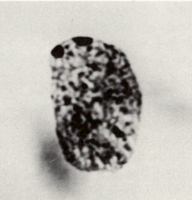 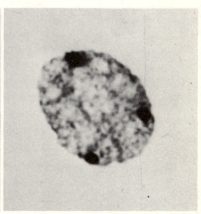

material between paired chromosomes which takes place before the assortment leads to an even greater degree of variety in the genetic composition of eggs and sperm produced among bisexually reproducing organisms. The inevitable result is that when twin chromosomes do part company, they are no longer completely maternal or paternal in derivation. This process is known as crossing over, and it has been possible to calculate the relative position of some genes on chromosomes by counting the frequency with which linked genes become unlinked. The farther apart on a chromosome any two genes are located, the more likely they are to cross over. We have good reason to believe that there are many hundreds of genes on most chromosomes and in some cases perhaps several thousand. We can understand then how meiosis produces new combinations of genes with every generation and promotes variety by the drastic redistribution of genetic material.

THE SPECIES

In the previous chapter, the species was mentioned as the basic taxonomic unit. It had been easy for people to observe the existence of species even before anything was known about the mode of inheritance of characteristics. Since the discoveries of Mendel and his successors, it has become obvious that we ought to define the species, in bisexually reproducing organisms, in genetic terms. One might have supposed that this would be simple, but, in fact, it is not. Mayr (1956) tells us, "A species is a single large Mendelian population pervaded in all directions by gene flow," and clearly this is true and worth remembering, but it is not quite enough. This statement implies that the species has sharp boundaries beyond which genes will not flow; yet we know that sometimes some boundaries are crossed, as when mares are bred by donkeys and give birth to mules. Note that the mule is sterile; this fact illustrates the means whereby species boundaries are maintained. The genetic system of *Equus caballus* differs just enough from that of *Equus asinus* to lead to this result. There are cases in which closely related species have genetic systems which are more compatible. But among most animals, and very obviously among mammals, new species do not appear to arise by hybridizing existing species. Under natural conditions, mammals of one species rarely become sexually interested in mammals of another species. Their mating habits contribute very strongly to the retention of species boundaries, although it is almost certain that other isolating mechanisms led to the building of the boundaries at sometime in the past.

The reason that gene flow does pervade the species population in all directions is that genes are transmitted in combination, as an integrated genetic system without too many internal contradictions. As geneticists phrase the situation, the genes are co-adapted to each other. It is only because of this that a zygote is able to develop into an integrated creature with all its parts and functions mutually suitable to each other. The genetic system of each species differs, to some degree, from that of every other species with the result that hybrids between species are likely to receive partially or wholly disintegrated genetic systems from their parents. The expectable result is the loss of some ability or abilities, which leads to lessened ability to live, to grow, or to reproduce.

Thus, even though instances can be cited in which the boundary of a species is not sharp at one point or another, in most cases it is sharp enough to inhibit frequent fertile hybridization. The species, as we find it in nature, is a unit for genetic reasons. As long as gene flow continues to pervade it in all directions, it will remain a single species, even though conditions change and evolution takes place. If a species occupies a large enough geographical range, some of its subpopulations may become isolated from the others. Then, in time, a new species may evolve, because there is always variation within a species, constantly generated by the recombination of genes which results from mating.

HEREDITY AND ENVIRONMENT

If all the individuals within a species were carbon copies of one another, the complicated process whereby eggs and sperm are produced would scarcely seem worth the trouble. But in fact, no two of us look alike; no two members of any population which engages in bisexual reproduction have precisely the same genetic endowment except twins derived from a single fertilized egg. The sperm and egg cells which united to form any one of us differed inevitably in other respects than sex. For instance, about half of all the people in the world today possess the blood type known as MN. They received the allele L^M from one parent, the allele L^N from the other; they are said to be heterozygous for this gene. Neither L^M nor L^N is dominant, so we are able to infer the *genotype*, or genetic endowment, from the *phenotype*, which is the actual, observable character. Persons having blood type M are homozygous, as are those of blood type N, since they obviously received the same allele from each parent. This is but one example of a gene which exists in two contrasting forms in the human population. There are hundreds if not thousands of other ways in which people differ from one another genetically, and the same is true of all bisexual animals and plants.

Of course the genes themselves transmit nothing but potentialities to the organism of which they are a part. Every gene appears to behave as an enzyme, so that what actually develops as a creature grows depends upon the reactions between the genes and their environment. The environment, as well as the genetic potentiality, is important in determining the phenotype, but it does not affect the genotype, which remains available, unchanged, for transmission to the next generation.

One aspect of the environment of any one gene consists of all the other genes. The reactions between two contrasting alleles are an example of this, as the phenomenon of dominance shows. In the presence of a dominant allele, the potentialities inherent in the recessive one do not come to fruition. If dominance is incomplete, which is often the case, neither allele produces the effect it would have if it had been alone. Often, two genes at different positions in the nucleus affect one another's results. For instance, among human beings, hair color appears to be under the joint control of several genes. The gene which is concerned with redness of hair is not linked to any which are concerned with lightness or darkness of hair. If a person inherits the alleles which give the potentiality for red and black hair, the red will be hidden in his phenotype. If he inherits alleles which give the potentiality for red and for light brown hair, the observable result will be auburn and if he inherits alleles which give the potentiality for red and for very blond hair, the result will be really red hair.

As we know, hair often darkens with age and may in later life turn gray, or perhaps white, or may even vanish more or less completely from our heads. Still other genes are concerned with the biochemical changes which take place in our bodies as we grow up and grow old. These changes modify the effects of the genes which control hair pigment, just as they modify the effects of many other genes which we possess. The whole internal environment of the body is one of the major modifiers of the effects which any gene might be expected to produce if left alone. It never is left alone. Although each gene is an independent unit, genes act in concert. It is clear that the development of many inherited features of the body is the result of the mutual actions of many genes. The simple Mendelian techniques of genetic analysis are inadequate in dealing with such quantitative traits. We are fortunate that some effects of some genes have been clear-cut and simple enough, as are those controlling the color of peas, so that genetic analysis was able to get started. These have given us the key to how the system works. It is highly probable that every gene has many effects upon the organism of which it is a part. As a rule, genes are named after the effect which was first observed, but there is no reason to believe that such genes do not produce other results as well. A large number of such cases are well known, and many are suspected though not proved.

The external environment in which a creature takes form, grows, and lives as an adult affects its phenotype in many ways. The first aspect of this environment, among creatures which retain the developing embryo within the body of its mother, is the uterine environment. Armadillos, for instance, give birth to monozygotic quadruplets, which must be genetically identical, since they originate from a single fertilized egg. Williams and Storrs (1968) found that no two members of such quadruplet sets are identical. On the contrary, they differ greatly from one another both anatomically and biochemically. The authors attribute these differences to cytoplasmic differences within the egg, but the relative position of the fetuses in the uterus may also be effective.

The conditions surrounding an unborn infant, whether a human or a shark, are very different from the conditions which he will meet in later life. In general we can assume that a worthwhile degree of protection is afforded to the young creature, but there are still hazards. Unborn sharks have a habit of eating their brothers and sisters, which puts a premium on the possession of alleles which promote rapid development. The survivors receive good training for their postnatal life in the open seas. Unborn human babies may have blood factors which are incompatible with the blood factors in their mother's circulation. The reaction between Rh negative mothers and Rh positive fetuses is the most notable but not the only case of this sort. This reaction can destroy the red cells in a baby's bloodstream, a condition known as erythroblastosis foetalis. Other less drastic maternal influences also affect the phenotype of the offspring. Certain infections such as measles and even the age of the mother are among the environmental conditions which influence the development of a baby before birth.

Plasticity in body form never reaches the extremes among animals which it does among many plants, yet closely related animals may develop in markedly different ways if they grow up under different living conditions. Certain breeds of rabbits have black-tipped paws if they are reared in cold weather but will lack this distinctive feature when reared in a hotter climate. Litters of rats have been separated at birth, some being kept under very hot temperatures during their growth period, while their brothers and sisters were permitted to grow up in a cooler climate. The former grew considerably longer tails than the latter. Harrison, Morton, and Weiner (1959) surmise that the longer tails functioned to dissipate extra heat, which is a reasonable conclusion. Many animals, including man, reach greater size and mature earlier when well fed and free of disease than when undernourished and subject to many illnesses. We seem to be less plastic in body size than many fish or mice and certainly more so than flying birds for which extra weight would be a disaster rather than a mere encumbrance.

A creature's environment includes the presence of other members of his species. Among highly social creatures such as ants and bees, all members of a colony are sisters, except for a few brothers reserved for stud purposes only. Yet by special feeding and differential care, some develop remarkably different features to suit their social function: some are fighters, some workers, others living storage jars, and a few are queens. Any type of creature which is cared for and fed by a parent as birds and mammals are is bound to be affected during the period of dependency by the efficiency of its mother and perhaps its father. Likewise each member of a litter will be affected by the presence of competing brothers and sisters, especially at feeding time. Some are likely to grow more rapidly than others, and it has not been demonstrated that this is regularly due to differences in genetic endowment. Competition for food is likely to be keen if there are many individuals sharing the same food preferences, even after the period of parental feeding, and this may also result in differences of size which cannot be attributed to genes. Our own species, as time has gone on, has created social systems which involve, in many cases, the coexistence of the wealthy and the poverty-stricken. The children of some families are better nourished and cared for than the children of others. Consequently, it is not uncommon for members of the upper classes to be taller, heavier, and healthier than the lower classes. It was noted in England that, as a result of 1940–1945 wartime rationing, such differences were minimized, and improved living conditions have been found in association with greater size in many parts of the world at various times.

We have succeeded, by improving technology, in altering the human environment to such a degree that a rather fatuous doctrine has been promulgated maintaining that genes are irrelevant because environment alone accounts for all the differences among men. Human plasticity, both in body form and in personality structure, is certainly great. It is indeed one of our important genetic characteristics. But plasticity is not infinite. The cultural environment within which all people live modifies the expression of genetic potentialities in many ways. We have learned to exploit natural forces to our advantage to a far greater extent than any other creature does. Yet we remain subject to these forces. We can and do put up our hair on curlers, but the new hair grows out straight, if that is the potential of our genes. We dye it, and new hair grows out brown, or black, as the case may be, if that is what we inherited. We eat well and grow fat or even tall, yet our offspring, if undernourished, will not. We have modified our environment most remarkably so that it is the cultural rather than the natural environment which reacts with our genetic endowment.

But the effect of the environment upon the phenotype has no direct result upon the genotype, in man or in any other organism.

MUTATION

Sometimes, however, the environment affects the genotype itself. Since August 7, 1945, we have been hearing a lot about mutations, and many people have worried about them. A mutation appears to be an alteration in the structure of a gene. Atoms are gained or lost, the DNA molecule is rearranged in a new pattern, and the nature of its activity is changed as a result. We have long known that radioactivity is one of the causes of mutation, so that it is only reasonable to be concerned over any increase in the amount of radioactivity in our environment. But other environmental circumstances may cause mutations as well, while by far the greater number of such genetic alterations are as yet unexplained. We only know that at times a gene does undergo this type of change. Estimates of the rate of mutation vary, but geneticists agree that under normal conditions such events have been comparatively rare. So far as we know, most genes have less than one chance in 100,000 to mutate in any one generation under ordinary circumstances.

After a gene has undergone mutation it not only functions in a new and different way in the physiological processes of the cell but duplicates its new form, so that the potentialities which it transmits to the next generation will be new ones. At least one and perhaps many of our early ancestors possessed DNA which had mutated in such a way that their great toes grew in line with their other toes. These individuals found that they could not use their great toes like thumbs to be opposed to the other toes. This made grasping with their feet somewhat difficult. For life in the trees, this new condition would be quite unfortunate. Queen Victoria's DNA had mutated in such a way that she transmitted a sex-linked gene which leads to a lack of ability to coagulate blood. This condition, known as hemophilia, spread among several European royal families because of the marriages which she arranged for her daughters. One cannot predict whether a mutation will be disastrous or only appear to be so at the time, but it is most unlikely that a mutation will be immediately useful to the creature concerned. Mutations occur at random, not because it would be convenient to have one. Any chance alteration in the composition and properties of a highly complex operating system is not likely to improve its manner of operation, and most mutations are disadvantageous for this reason. There is a delicate balance between an organism and its environment, which a mutation can easily upset. One could as well expect that altering the position of the foot brake or the gas pedal at random would improve the operation of an automobile.

PLEIOTROPY, HETEROGONY, AND NEOTENY

A population with a genetic constitution such that a single mutation will produce a considerable effect upon the phenotype is also in a favorable situation. A single favorable mutation is rare enough; half a dozen in succession are even less likely. Economy in the number of mutations required for evolutionary change is therefore very useful. Pleiotropy, heterogony, and neoteny are three means of exploiting economy in the number of mutations in the service of evolutionary change.

Genes which affect several traits are called pleiotropic. Probably many genes, if not most, have pleiotropic effects, of which some are more important than others to the continued life of a population. According to Keeler (1942), hair color in rats is determined by a gene which also affects the animal's disposition. If aggressiveness is useful in the rat's ecological niche, he may, of necessity, be of a color which would make him conspicuous to predators against certain backgrounds. This would restrict his habitat. Many examples of pleiotropy are known, and we may confidently expect more to be discovered. They are bound to have had a considerable effect upon the evolution of many descent lines.

Heterogony is differential or allometric growth of separate parts of the body. Among humans, the legs increase in length much more than the arms during postnatal growth; the head circumference increases less than either of these. Among horses, the snout lengthens, and the molar teeth grow disproportionately; among many felines, the canine teeth do. It is a notable fact that many species of animals, otherwise quite similar in form, differ in shape because of the emphasis during growth upon some particular segment of the body. We can see this even within a species: tall men are likely to have especially long legs, and most of the tallest have proportionately the most elongated shins. Selection for a given size may produce a change in the shape of a creature, or selection for shape may produce a difference in size (Thompson, 1942). What appears superficially to be a major evolutionary change may, in fact, have required but a single mutation.

Neoteny is the retention of a youthful or even infantile characteristic into adult life. Sometimes, perhaps often, this is accomplished by a genetic change which postpones the acquisition of some trait or traits which in the ancestral stock had been concomitant with sexual maturity. Thus the axolotl, a Mexican salamander, continues to have gills and to be able to breathe under water even after it is fully grown. In the arid regions where it lives, venturing out of the water has no survival value. Indeed, it may well be that the whole subphylum of vertebrates owes its origin to the retention of larval characteristics such as motility which its relatives lost upon becoming adult. Thus a great variety of environments became available for active exploration (Young, 1950). Humans retain traits which are characteristic of baby apes rather than of adult apes, such as flat faces, small jaws, and other characteristics described in Chapter Seven. There seem to be many circumstances in which it is quite functional to postpone or even eliminate entirely the final stage of development.

We see that there are various ways of adapting to the environment. But it is worth remembering that however the adaptation is made, it is not static, nor is it something granted a creature to make its life more easy, pleasant, or worthy. Adaptation is due rather to the fortunate coincidence of the proper set of circumstances and the proper set of genes. Most animals die without issue, and most species become extinct rather than evolving into different species. Selection prunes the branches and twigs of the tree of life with impersonal ruthlessness. All living creatures are the descendants of only a minute proportion of those who inhabited the world 10 million years ago. Moreover, as Waddington (1957) has pointed out, the selection which leads to the attainment of adaptation operates upon the organism as a whole rather than upon the genetic constitution directly. A useful genotype can be transmitted only by an individual possessing phenotypic traits which have kept it alive during its entire growth period. Selection operates very largely upon the young, so that devices of any nature which keep the young alive are at a premium. Finally, we must never forget that we all have ancestors as well as necessities. The lines of evolutionary change which are possible for any population depend upon its genetic system. Basic structural similarities continue to exist within entire phyla of animals, no matter how distorted they may be.

THE ADVANTAGES OF POLYMORPHISM

If only by chance, a small percentage of random mutations would turn out to be useful for one purpose or another; some would do no particular harm, and some might enable a creature to live in a different if not better way. In many cases mutant alleles are recessive to the normal form of a gene and thus unable to affect the operation of the organism except when homozygous. Together with rearrangements of the linkage chain, mutations are the raw material for evolutionary change, and all species which have been examined possess different alleles of many genes which could only have come into existence as mutations. The differences between green and yellow peas and between persons of blood types M and N are due to past mutations. A population which possesses genetic diversity of this kind is said to be polymorphic, and this condition has certain advantages in itself.

The phenomenon called heterosis, or hybrid vigor, is one such advantage. Mendel noted such vigor among his peas. When he hybridized long-stemmed and short-stemmed peas, their offspring grew taller than either parent. Hybrid corn is now planted extensively in this country because of its superior yield: an increase of at least 50 percent over parental stocks raised under the same conditions. The fitness of an organism appears in many cases to be improved if it is heterozygous, but the physiological explanation of such increased fitness is often most obscure.

No one has yet been able to find out why there are more persons whose blood type is MN than would be expected from the frequencies of the two alleles L^M and L^N. On the other hand, some alleles which are most unfortunate for the creature which possesses them when they are homozygous may be very useful indeed when heterozygous. This has been found to be the case for many genetic factors among fruit flies and at least one among human beings—the sickle-cell trait, which is discussed in detail in Chapters Ten and Eleven. There is evidence that greater stature among the children of people who have married outside their ancestral villages is

due, at least partly, to increased heterozygosity (Damon, 1965; Ferak *et al.*, 1968; Hulse, 1969). Closely consanguinous matings, in contrast, lead to a higher frequency of homozygous individuals in the next generation. This does not force, as some have supposed, any reduction in phenotypic variability in a population. Bonné (1966) found a high degree of variation in many characteristics among the Samaritans, who have been closely inbred for no one knows how long.

Such variation, however caused, often turns out to be useful for its own sake among creatures living in social groups, if the characters which vary are perceptible to their sense organs. Thus we find that among African antelopes there is an amazing degree of variation in the appearance of the horns, both between species and within a species (Simpson, 1953), as is shown in Figure 3–6. This enables these creatures to recognize each other at a glance. Because of the fact that different members of the group are likely to vary in their social reactions, it can be vital for a young animal to learn to distinguish which is which in the group; thus he learns how to behave in his dealings with each separate member of the group. If Uncle John has a nasty temper, whereas Uncle Jim is easygoing, it is worthwhile to be able to tell one from the other at a reasonable distance, either by sight, smell, or sound. Therefore, since polymorphism promotes variation on an individual basis, it is not surprising to find so much of it among social animals.

FIGURE 3-6. African Antelopes Have Horns of Many Shapes (Photos: From Left to Right, Zoological Society of London; Zoological Society of London; A. W. Ambler from National Audubon Society; and Gabor Czaky from National Audubon Society)

As we noted before, polymorphism provides genetic systems with a kind of insurance. The future is unpredictable. We only know that conditions will change. Most organisms are completely unaware of any future, even if they have some consciousness of the present or memory of the past. Their phenotypes must be adapted to present circumstances if they are to survive as individuals. Their genotypes must be adapted to future circumstances as well if they are to continue surviving as populations. Internal diversity within a population may be thought of as hedging a bet. New abilities may turn out to be useful in the future, even if they were not in the past, and genetic variety may be exploited in this way. Some people have curly hair but others have straight hair; some can taste chemicals of which others are unaware. Some fruit flies have rudimentary wings while others have large ones; some are resistant to DDT while others are not. These differences are due to the concurrent existence of different alleles in the genetic systems of the species. At this moment in history, neither straight nor curly hair appears to have survival value. Thirty years ago, a genetic resistance to DDT had no survival value for a fruit fly. But it does now. New hazards and new opportunities arise in time for all the various species of life. Genetic variety is necessary to exploit future possibilities. A total lack of deviant or unusual forms can lead only into a blind alley and sooner or later to extinction.

Bisexual reproduction leads to a repeated shuffling and reshuffling of genetic material. The constant recombination of different alleles, which is due to the egg's fertilization by a sperm, multiplies the amount of diversity which is possible within a species. All populations which depend upon sex for reproduction conduct a continuous experiment in new adjustments to the environment. An animal which has simply budded off from one parent is bound to be identical to that parent genetically, save in the rare case of a mutation. If by good luck such a mutation occurs at a suitable time, there is no way for the new advantage gained to be spread throughout the species. On the other hand, an animal which has two parents cannot possibly be identical to either genetically. Mutant alleles which originated thousands of generations ago may be received from either parent. Its brothers and sisters will only rarely have the identical genetic equipment. Each individual in a bisexually reproducing population is just a little different from all the others. In most cases the difference will be unimportant; in even more cases it will seem unimportant. Sometimes it will be an unfortunate difference. Insurance is often expensive, and certain individuals are frequently sacrificed for the benefit of the population. But insurance pays: those species which take the trouble to practice bisexual reproduction are those which are the most successful of all the varieties of life.

Sources and Suggested Readings

BARR, M. L.
  1959   Sex Chromatin and Phenotype in Man. *Science,* **130:** 679–685.

BONNÉ, B.
  1966   Are There Hebrews Left? *American Journal of Physical Anthropology,* **24,** 135–146.

DAMON, A.
  1965   Stature Increase Among Italian-Americans: Environmental, Genetic, or Both? *American Journal of Physical Anthropology,* **23,** 401–408.

DARWIN, C.
  1868   *Variation of Animals and Plants Under Domestication.* Orange Judd and Co., New York.

DOBZHANSKY, T.
  1951   *Genetics and the Origin of Species,* 3rd edition. Columbia University Press, New York.

FERAK, V., Z. LICHARDOVA, and V. BORJINOVA
  1968   Endogamy, Exogamy and Stature. *Eugenics Quarterly,* **15,** 273–276.

HARRISON, G. A., R. J. MORTON, and J. S. WEINER
  1959   The Growth in Weight and Tail Length of Inbred and Hybrid Mice Reared in Two Different Temperatures. *Philosophical Transactions of the Royal Society,* London.

HULSE, F. S.
  1968   Migration and Cultural Selection in Human Genetics. *The Anthropologist,* Special Volume, 1–21.

KEELER, C. E.
  1942   The Association of the Black (non-agouti) Gene with Behavior in the Norway Rat. *Journal of Heredity,* **33,** 371–384.

MAYR, E.
  1956   Geographical Character Gradients and Climatic Adaptation. *Evolution,* **10,** 105–108.

MENDEL, G.
  1866   Experiments in Plant Hybridization. *Proceedings of the Natural History Society of Brünn.* English Translation, Harvard University Press, Cambridge, 1948.

METTLER, L. E. and T. G. GREGG
  1969   *Population Genetics and Evolution.* Prentice-Hall, Englewood Cliffs.

SARTON, G.
  1959   *A History of Science,* Vol. **II.** Harvard University Press, Cambridge.

SIMPSON, G. G.
  1953   *The Major Features of Evolution.* Columbia University Press, New York.

STERN, C.
  1960   *Principles of Human Genetics,* revised edition. Freeman, San Francisco.

THOMPSON, D'ARCY W.
  1942   *On Growth and Form,* 2nd edition. Cambridge University Press, Cambridge.

WADDINGTON, G. H.
  1957   *The Strategy of the Genes.* George Allen & Unwin, London.

WEISMANN, A.
  1892   *Essays upon Heredity.* Oxford University Press, Oxford.

WILLIAMS, R. J. and E. E. STORRS
  1968   A Study of Monozygous Quadruplet Armadillos in Relation to Mammalian Inheritance. *Proceedings of the National Academy of Sciences,* **60.**

YOUNG, J. Z.
  1950   *The Life of Vertebrates.* Clarendon Press, Oxford.

CHAPTER 4

Ecology and Evolution

THE BALANCE OF NATURE

A kindly and thoughtful sea captain once introduced a colony of rabbits to an uninhabited atoll in the South Pacific. He had earlier been shipwrecked on such an island and, remembering his own hunger, wanted to help any possible future castaways by providing a ready source of food for them. The rabbits ate well and multiplied, as rabbits will, but the island lacked any predators. Without any natural check on population increase, they had devoured all the local vegetation within a few generations. After the last rabbit had eaten the last plant, it died of starvation, leaving the atoll more desolate than ever.

In Africa, malaria-transmitting mosquitoes were luckier. As Livingstone (1958) has pointed out, the spread of farming practices in the tropical rain forest on that continent has created conditions most favorable to an increase in the number of mosquitoes. The primeval jungle is rarely mosquito infested, but the clearings made by farmers, and often abandoned after a few years, contain many small stagnant pools in which these insects breed. Farming also leads to population increase and greater population density, since people gather together in villages, providing the mosquitoes with an easily available food supply and, at the same time, facilitating the transfer of the malaria plasmodium from one person to the

69

next. Almost everyone is infected, and those who for any reason are more resistant to the disease have the best chance to survive and reproduce. The resulting effect upon the genetic structure of the human populations is recounted in detail in a later chapter.

In the Great Lakes, especially Lakes Huron, Michigan, and Superior, the native fish, although not yet extinct, may soon be, for they too have suffered from sudden changes brought about by the introduction of new elements into their environment. In order to permit shipping to by-pass Niagara Falls, the Welland Canal was dug and later deepened. Lampreys as well as ships used the canal and began to prey upon the fish in the upper lakes with most disastrous results. In an attempt to protect crops against insects—which enjoy eating them as much as we do—enormous quantities of insecticides, especially DDT, began to be used in the drainage basin of the Great Lakes. DDT is among the most persistent of chemicals, and much of it is washed into the streams which feed the lakes, so that fish as well as "pests" were affected by the poison. Given enough time, many populations acquire the ability to adjust to new hazards, but many of course do not, and what the end result will be for the Great Lakes' fish no one knows. Figure 4–1 indicates the huge death toll exacted by man-made pollution.

These are contrasting examples of the dynamic nature of the relationships between different kinds of living things in a community. These relationships form one of the most important aspects of the environment to which creatures must adapt. Since life itself is a process and since each organism is born, grows, and dies, the relationships between organisms are constantly changing. Even if the purely physical aspects of the environment remain constant, as they may over considerable periods of time, the biotic aspects, those due to the activities of animals and plants, cannot be the same even from day to day. In any community of living creatures we can imagine a state of equilibrium in which just enough of each variety would exist so that the adjustment of the creatures to one another would continue without change from generation to generation. The ecologist, whose interest is in analyzing the relationships between living forms and their environment, may often find such a steady state of affairs a convenient model for his studies. Indeed, if we lack the perspective of time, a static balance of nature may appear to be the ideal state of affairs. The degree to which most creatures appear to be adapted to their ways of life at any given moment may easily lead one to conclude that each variety was designed to fit its proper place and to fulfill its proper function in the living community.

In each living community the various sorts of organisms seem to fit together in a system which is self-sufficient except for the energy constantly being received from the sun. Plants use this en-

FIGURE 4-1. Dead Fish Floating in a Polluted River. As Man-made Pollution
Increases, We Destroy Our Own Resources. (Photo: Hays from Monkmeyer)

ergy to manufacture food. Animals eat some of this food. Most of it returns to the soil to be decomposed by bacteria. Some of the herbivorous animals are preyed upon by carnivores, some by internal or external parasites. Bacteria may decompose those animals which are not devoured by predators or scavengers may eat them. In any case, the raw material of life returns to the general store, available for the next generation of organisms. Life could not continue without this decomposition. Each form of life contributes in its own manner to the maintenance of the community. Without predation, herbivorous creatures might sweep the land clear of vegetation, as did the rabbits on the atoll; without cellulose-digesting bacteria, many herbivores could not break down the cellulose in their food. Many seedlings depend on the shade of larger plants to establish themselves, and many flowering plants could not reproduce without bees to spread the pollen. Likewise, without the nectar from the flowers, the bees would starve. Most well-established biological communities provide many ways of making a living which biologists call ecological niches. In a balanced community we find that these ecological niches are likely to be occupied.

This is the static picture. There may be fluctuations this way or that, but they are supposed to cancel one another within a given cycle of years. Extra rainfall may promote extra plant growth, which will support more herbivorous animals, which will in turn feed more carnivores. But as rainfall returns to normal, the numbers of creatures at each higher link of the food chain will be correspondingly reduced. Or overcrowding may lead to contagion and a high death rate or low birth rate. But the balance of nature is precarious and, if disequilibrium goes beyond a certain point, it may collapse entirely to be drastically rearranged in a new fashion. Sometimes the rainfall does not return to normal: climate changes during geological time. Lakes slowly fill with silt, becoming marshes and then meadows. The biological community of the lake is extinguished, and a new ecological system suitable for dry land replaces it. Even quite minor changes in the habits of one of the species inhabiting a community may start a chain of events which affects the entire system. Darwin (1881) provides us with a classic example. As one minor result of the industrial revolution, the number of spinsters living in English villages increased during the nineteenth century. It was a popular custom among them to have cats as pets, so the number of cats increased, too. Cats kill small animals such as dormice and moles which, in turn, consume many earthworms and bumblebees. More cats = fewer predators upon earthworms and bumblebees = more earthworms and bumblebees. More earthworms enriched the soil by their mode of life, while more bumblebees made pollination of clover easier, so that more clover grew in the fields near the villages where many spinsters lived.

Although Darwin did not know about it, he would have been gratified to learn of another result of the industrial revolution in England. Vast quantities of soft coal smoke from millions of chimneys settled in the wooded areas about industrial cities, killing the lichen which used to cover tree trunks and blackening the bark. Moths of many species have long had the habit of resting upon the bark of trees during the day. Since birds prey upon moths, it is clearly to the moth's advantage to attract as little attention as possible while resting. One variety, the peppered moth, derived its name from the appearance of its wings, which render it almost invisible when resting upon lichen. In Darwin's day a few of these moths had black wings: now almost all of them do. Kettlewell's experiments (1957) show what caused this change. In areas where the trees are still covered with lichen, birds found and ate three times as many black moths as those with peppered wings. In woods where the tree trunks were black, the results were exactly the reverse. Let the reader examine Figure 4–2 and test the keenness of his vision. The change in ecological circumstances has given added survival value to those moths with black wings

FIGURE 4-2. How Many Moths Do You See on Each Tree? (Photos: Dr. H. B. D. Kettlewell)

which, consequently, reproduce at a much more rapid rate than they did one hundred years ago. The climate has not changed, nor the topography, nor the habits of either moths or birds; only the color of the tree trunks has been altered. But the result is a shift in the allele frequencies of the moths. This is evolution, and its mechanism is natural selection.

We should emphasize several points of such evolution:

1. It involves change as time goes on. The useful adaptation of today may be disastrous next year.
2. The cause of the change is external to the creatures involved. Neither birds, moths, nor trees produced the industrial revolution, yet it affected a vital detail in their mutual relationship.
3. The evolution was due to this shift in the habitual behavior of living creatures in relation to one another. If moths did not rest on trees or if birds did not eat moths, there would have been no evolution.
4. The change which occurred exploited an existing detail of moth anatomy. If no moths had possessed the allele for black wings to begin with, it could not have been selected. Perhaps the moths would have become extinct; perhaps they would have altered their habits. We cannot know.
5. Selective pressures affect whole populations. The individuals concerned are incidental. Those adaptations are useful which promote the continuance, through generations, of the species.
6. The same changes were observed in many wooded areas which were subject to blackening by smoke. Under similar circumstances, similar populations can be expected to react in similar ways.
7. Rather large populations were involved in this example. In a very short sequence luck plays a greater part than in a long one, as anyone who has gambled knows. Natural selection, consequently, can be expected to be more effective in large and less effective in small populations.

SELECTIVE ENVIRONMENTAL PRESSURES

There can be many sorts of selective pressure, for any species of organism has to solve varied problems. The above example concerns predation, but the food supply is an even more important factor. Some species of animals are much less likely to be devoured than others, but they all have to eat. Competition is often keen for available food of the proper sort. There is an advantage in eating things which other animals neglect: the case of Darwin's finches, cited in Chapter Two, is probably an example of evolution due to the willingness of some of these birds to try a new diet when faced with a shortage of seeds. The potential population increase of any species is, of course, in geometric proportion, whereas the amount of food available cannot be expected to increase at all under normal circumstances. In the natural world the expectation that any fertilized egg picked at random will hatch, grow, mate, and produce offspring is rather meager. Almost all die young, and among those which die will be those incapable of finding, eating, or digesting enough food.

Those incapable of withstanding infections will also die young. Parasites of all sorts as well as microorganisms depend upon larger animals for their food supply, and infestation by such creatures is the inevitable lot of larger beasts. Only those which can tolerate coexistence with lice, tapeworms, bacteria, and similar forms of life will be able to contribute their genes to the next generation. At the same time, it is to the advantage of parasites that their hosts should continue to feed them as long as possible. Relations of mutual advantage often evolve, as in the case of cellulose-digesting bacteria already mentioned. But in any case, disease has been a potent selective factor among innumerable populations, and resistance to disease confers a great advantage to any creature. Biochemical defenses, such as the production of antibodies, are among the most frequent but far from the only means of resistance which have been selected in many species, including our own.

Finding a mate is another problem among bisexually reproducing organisms which have avoided or overcome the hazards of youth. Except among highly social animals, such as termites or human beings, a celibate adult is a detriment to the species since it devours resources without contributing to future generations. No species will continue to possess any genetic peculiarities of creatures which have not mated. Among plants the process of fertilization is impersonal and may even require the services of a third party, as when a bee carries pollen from one flower to another. Animals must not only find but recognize mates, and it is not unlikely that sexual dimorphism, that is, an obvious difference between the two sexes of a species, has evolved in response to this problem. We humans perceive the world by means of our eyes, and so are likely to think of sexual dimorphism in terms of size, shape, or color. But many creatures, such as moths among others, depend upon the sense of smell, and males attracted by the perfume of the females may fly long distances to find them. Creatures may develop displays of unusual behavior to facilitate the process of mating: posturing, dancing, singing, and giving presents are examples.

All of the problems listed above involve the relationships of different organisms in the community to one another. Adaptations in

form and behavior which have evolved in response to the selective
pressure of such relationships are those most likely to prove useless
on sudden notice, for as we have seen, the equilibrium of a biological community is often precarious. Adaptations to the physical
aspects of the environment are just as vital, but there is less chance
of a sudden change in climate, soil chemistry, or topography. As
time goes on, the physical environment is altered, and the presence
of life itself has produced some of the alterations. The quality of
the soil is largely dependent upon the activity of plants and of
burrowing animals. Clams, corals, and other creatures constantly
extract the calcium dissolved in seawater. The proportions of oxygen and carbon dioxide in the atmosphere are certainly due to the
respiration and photosynthesis of living things. But the physical
environment changes slowly and is apt to follow trends which
continue in a single direction for a long time.

Whether slow or fast, however, environmental change is always
one of the perils with which any species of organism must contend.
Those which have been most successful are those which have overcome this danger by one means or another. Some species have maintained themselves with little or no change for tens of millions of
years: the horseshoe crab, for instance, is a relic of the Paleozoic
period. This is most exceptional. Success through continued evolution is far more typical. The members of succeeding generations
become less and less like the ancestral forms. A population composed of creatures whose basic efficiency in contending with a
variety of stresses is well developed enjoys a real advantage in the
struggle for existence. A polymorphic population, that is, one in
which contrasting alleles exist at a number of loci, has provided for
the future. Witness the peppered moths of England.

THE HISTORICAL EVIDENCE FOR EVOLUTION

Linnaeus did not know that the forms of life vary in time as
well as in space, but between his time and Darwin's enough data
had been uncovered to convince all students of natural history that
this was so. Some fossils were known in Linnaeus' day, but no
one knew their meaning. As time went on, excavations for all sorts
of purposes uncovered more and more bones. By the end of the
eighteenth century the inescapable inference was that the creatures
which had once inhabited the earth differed from those which live
here now. The earlier finds were few and scattered, and each layer
contained bones very different from those found in layers above
or below it. It seemed as though the world had passed through a
series of cataclysms, each one of which wiped out all living creatures. Then, it was supposed, a completely new set of inhabitants

came into existence, somewhat like the previous creatures, but each time including animals a little bit more like those alive today. Figure 4–3 shows the sequence of eras and epochs as revealed by these strata. Only in the most recent strata, or layers deposited since the latest catastrophe, were found the bones of human beings. The bones of earlier animals had fossilized, absorbing minerals until they had become like rock, but the bones of men had not been buried long enough for this to have occurred—or so it seemed.

But as more and more digging was done, and as more and more fossils were uncovered and studied, this interpretation was seen to be at fault. Instead of a sequence of catastrophes, the evidence of the earth demonstrated that changes in the forms of life had been, for the most part, gradual. What had seemed, on the basis of

ERA	EPOCH	CREATURES ANCESTRAL TO MAN
CENOZOIC	SEE FIGURE 6-1: THE LAST 100,000,000 YEARS	
MESOZOIC	CRETACEOUS	INSECTIVORES
	JURASSIC	
	TRIASSIC	THERIODONTS
PALEOZOIC	PERMIAN	THERAPSIDS
	CARBONIFEROUS	EARLY REPTILES
	DEVONIAN	AMPHIBIANS
	SILURIAN	FISH
	ORDOVICIAN	EARLY VERTEBRATES
	CAMBRIAN	POSSIBLE CHORDATE ANCESTORS
PROTEROZOIC		
ARCHEOZOIC		

(Scale: 1 inch = 230,000,000 years)

FIGURE 4-3. Chart of Geological Time I: The Last Billion Years

scanty data, to be a series of unconnected types of life became instead a chain of living varieties. Many links which had been missing from the chain continued to be found. Gaps between different sort of creatures became narrower until they were, to all intents and purposes, closed. Order was found to exist in the history of life as well as in the classification of living creatures, and, best of all, the evidence derived from the study of living forms could be reconciled with the evidence derived from the study of extinct ones.

THE LIVING PAST

Paleontology is the name given to the study of ancient life, and the students of human life have much to learn from this branch of science, for it provides the evidence of our ancestry. It has by now become clear, from analysis of the evidence, that the surface of the earth has undergone constant but gradual changes of many sorts during the past few billion years. Land is constantly being pushed upward by subterranean forces and, just as constantly, is being worn away by the erosion of wind and flowing water.

Material washed down from mountain heights is deposited at some lower level where it builds up in layers, or strata, of earth. As time goes on, the sediments deposited become rock such as shale or sandstone. At the same time, the limy skeletons of marine creatures, large and small, are constantly falling to the bottom of the sea to build deposits of chalk or limestone, which at a later date may rise above the surface of the water. The first material to reach any spot will naturally lie at the bottom of the deposit which is built up, so that normally the later strata will be the highest, the earlier strata the lowest, in any sequence which erosion may expose. Sometimes the pressures within the crust of the earth may bend and twist these layers out of place and even fold earlier layers over on top of later ones, but in general the rule is that more recent strata lie above more ancient ones.

When living creatures die, their bodies are likely to be devoured by scavengers or decayed by bacteria. In most cases calcium is leached away and distributed throughout the soil. A few creatures meet a different fate. If buried quickly enough and deeply enough, their bones and other hard parts may fossilize instead. Perhaps millions of years later, they will even be discovered and so bring knowledge and joy to a paleontologist. About as good a way as any to become a fossil is to be swept away in a flash flood and deposited within a mud bank or a sand bar as it forms. But sinking into the ooze at the bottom of a swamp or being engulfed in quicksand may be just as effective.

Because of the nature of the soil and the weather, dwellers on a prairie are more likely to leave fossil remains then dwellers in a forest, especially a tropical rain forest; for such jungles are apt to be deficient in minerals as well as swarming with hungry creatures of all sizes. With good fortune a bone may lie buried so securely that the molecules of which it is composed are replaced one by one by molecules of other minerals without any change in the form of the bone. In this way, although the bone's substance changes, its shape does not. Millions of such fossils have been discovered, and billions of undiscovered ones must lie within the earth. Yet all of them are but a minute fraction of all the hard parts of the creatures which have lived in the past.

Since teeth are the hardest of organic substances, they are more likely to be preserved than any other part of the anatomy. Many extinct creatures are known to us only from their teeth, but fortunately one can infer a great deal about an animal from this sort of evidence alone. Jaws and skulls also last well: the somewhat globular shape of the latter assists in its preservation by distributing pressure, and it may be filled rapidly with soil through its various openings. The pelvis, on the contrary, is so shaped that it is very likely to be broken into small fragments. Many unlikely things, besides bones or shells, have also been preserved: scales of fish, impressions made by feathers or horny knobs on the hide, footprints, and even worm burrows. Microscopic details of the internal construction of hard parts often remain perfectly clear, making it possible in many cases to tell whether bones were broken before or after death. From the condition of their teeth, we may infer quite confidently that some dinosaurs, like people today, had caries. Recently, Soriano (1969), by comparing an oddly shaped outgrowth of bone on the femur of "Pithecanthropus" to similar lesions on patients whose ailments had been diagnosed, demonstrated that this early ancestor of ours very probably suffered from an excess of fluorine in his diet. The study of paleopathology may provide us with many new clues concerning the nature and extent of selective pressures in the past.

Although the reconstruction of an entire animal from some small bony fragment is out of the question, an experienced paleontologist is often able to infer a great deal from very little. Our knowledge of the anatomy of presently living creatures can always be called upon to help fill in missing parts and so can our understanding of how various parts of the body function together. Of course, mistakes have been made, but remarkably accurate forecasts have not been at all uncommon. For example, paleontologists had recovered many fossils of the Coelacanthini, an order of fish thought to have been extinct for 60 million years, and they had reconstructed its external appearance, complete with soft parts and scales. Since the reconstructions of this fish resembled no living fish at all closely, they had to be considered as tentative although highly plausible speculations. Then some twenty years ago, a living representative of the order was caught by a fisherman in the Indian Ocean (Smith, 1956). The external appearance of this fish, named *Latimeria*, was amazingly similar to the reconstructions, demonstrating the degree to which a skillful and experienced man can extrapolate beyond direct evidence and still be correct. At the same time, we must understand that reconstructions are exercises of the imagination and are therefore subject to any preconceptions in the mind of the reconstructor. Pictures of our own prehistoric ancestors, often used to illustrate books concerning them, can be dangerously misleading, for we know absolutely nothing about their pigmentation, the extent of their body hair, or the thickness of their lips.

For a long time it remained impossible to estimate the length of time represented by any set of strata. Some strata were obviously older than others, but the thickness of any layer of rock was not a very good basis for the guesses which were made about the number of years which must have elapsed between the beginning and the ending of its deposition. The rate of decay of radioactive elements is now beginning to provide us with a clock which we have every reason to hope is accurate. Using this technique, we can estimate that the period represented by fossil-bearing strata has endured for more than a billion years. Rather more than half of this time had elapsed before strata were deposited which contain the earliest fossils of vertebrates: fish covered with bony plates but lacking jaws. Ancestral arthropods, mollusks, and echinoderms are found from still earlier periods but like the vertebrates were confined to the seas for many millions of years. Apparently, plants emerged from the water long before any animals did. We should remember that plants provide the oxygen for animals to breathe and food for them to eat.

By the end of the Devonian period, perhaps 300 million years ago, amphibians began to leave footprints in the mud flats along shores in some parts of the world. During this time ferns and the ancestors of conifers and flowering plants were widespread on dry land, and insects had come ashore as well. Within 50 million years both insects and amphibians had become numerous, widespread, and diverse, and reptiles had appeared. A glacial period of undetermined length succeeded the warmer weather which had prevailed before, and by the time it ended some of the reptiles had evolved a remarkable number of mammalian characteristics. The following era, the Mesozoic, is often called the Age of Reptiles. It lasted for well over 100 million years, nearly twice as long as all succeeding time. Mammals were in existence, and birds appeared as well, but they had to compete with flying reptiles for millions of years. One of the most beautiful fossils ever found is that of the very early bird, Archaeopteryx, shown in Figure 4–4. Some reptiles returned to the sea, but the most famous were the dinosaurs, many of which, like kangaroos and men, moved about on their hind legs. Others, including the largest land-dwelling animals which have ever lived, needed all four legs to support their bulk, and many doubtless lived in swamps, where the water helped to support them. It has often been remarked that mankind is fortunate in not having come into existence until long after these enormous animals had all died, but our prehuman ancestors did coexist with them successfully for millions of years.

Eventually, for reasons as yet undetermined, the dinosaurs and most of the other reptiles became extinct, and the Cenozoic era, or the Age of Mammals, began some 60 million years ago. But

FIGURE 4-4. Archaeopteryx, a Fossil Bird. This Extinct Species Retained Many Reptilian Features, Such as Teeth, which Modern Birds Have Lost. (Photo: Courtesy of the American Museum of Natural History)

for a long time these creatures were not very much like their descendants with which we are familiar. Each succeeding epoch within the Cenozoic produced animals a little more like those we know today and a few, such as the opossum, appear to have changed very little in all this time. But neither lambs nor lions, humans nor horses appeared upon the scene until relatively late. A study of the fossils shows us which of the earlier mammals were ancestral to these living species, but many changes in anatomy and adaptation have taken place, and many early sorts of mammals became extinct without leaving offspring, as had the dinosaurs before them. Life has continued to vary in its manifestations in time, just as we find it does in space, and we must expect this process to continue. As time has gone on, new forms have constantly come into existence, changed, diversified, and sometimes prospered and then, much more often than not, become extinct. Creatures have discovered and exploited new ways to make a living and have attained new levels of efficiency. But the balance of nature is dynamic rather than static, and the adaptation which is highly functional at one time may become obsolete without warning: something different will be required to meet a new set of circumstances.

BEHAVIOR AND EVOLUTION

When we become cold, for instance, tiny muscles in the skin tighten, and it develops a bumpy appearance commonly called goose flesh. Animals with plenty of hair succeed in raising all the individual hairs when they do this and so create an added insulation to protect their bodies against cold. We lack the hair, but continue quite automatically to attempt the same response. In our case the response has become self-defeating, because it simply increases the surface area from which we will loose heat: we become colder than ever by doing what made our ancestors warm. The necessary connection between anatomy and behavior is shown by this example. Structure is bound to restrict the sorts of behavior which are functional or even possible, while the actual behavior of any animal species cannot help but affect the way in which selection operates upon the species. It is appropriate behavior, after all, rather than anatomical detail as such, which leads to success or failure in the struggle for survival. Fortunately for us, the hair-raising reaction has not been too crucial for the survival of the human stock. Our ancestors presumably lived in warm places until they acquired other means of retaining body heat.

When new problems, hazards, or opportunities arise in the life of any species, several solutions may work equally well. Different populations within a species may utilize different solutions. The various ways in which bisexuality exists is an example of this fact: apparently the essential thing is that two sexes should exist. Whether sex is determined by age, by nutrition, or by genetic constitution is less important. However, the way in which sex is expressed greatly affects the behavior of the members of the species toward one another, and this behavior will, in turn, help to guide the future evolution of the group. If sex among vertebrates, as among *Bonellia*, were determined by age, can we imagine that the evolution of the vertebrates would have been the same? If only one female vertebrate in many thousands had been capable of reproduction, as is the case with ants, would this not have required the sort of social life characteristic of ants? The fact is that sex among vertebrates depends upon genes. It is therefore subject to the statistical rules concerning the transmission of genes, earlier discovered by Mendel, with the result that the two sexes are much more likely than not to be produced in more or less equal numbers. This in turn makes stable matings between one male and one female and hostility between members of the same sex both possible and functional.

Several varieties of vertebrates have succeeded in flying. In all cases wings were evolved from their forelimbs. The precise details of anatomy involved in the wing construction of a bird differ from those of a bat. Both, however, render the use of the forelimb as a grasping organ difficult and its use as a manipulative organ impossible. The necessities of flight are rigorous, and creatures which have attained this ability simply have had to sacrifice the possibility of attaining many other abilities. To make a living, all animals must become experts in one way or another: some become superexperts in a restricted way of life, making it difficult for their descendants to shift to another way. What is difficult is not necessarily impossible. Penguins, for instance, do not fly in the air; they use their wings in swimming under water. Their technique in doing so is unlike that of any fish: they remain birds and exemplify the way in which anatomy and behavior are related.

Paleontologists long ago noted that as they studied the fossil remains of any variety of creature from lower to higher strata, its typical characteristics tended to become more and more emphasized or even exaggerated. Reversions to earlier or ancestral forms appeared to be lacking. This led them to formulate the Law of Irreversibility of Evolution, which some took as absolute dogma. This was unfortunate, for it led to misinterpretation of data, as the belief in a dogma is likely to do. As a matter of fact, in any given item of anatomy or behavior, the reversal of a trend is perfectly possible: the genes responsible may mutate at any time in such a way as to enable selection in any direction. Animals may become bigger and then smaller; teeth may become longer and then shorter; hair may be gained and then lost. It is unlikely, on the other hand, that a whole sequence of reversals will occur and even more unlikely that the whole environment of a species will revert to its previous condition at the same time. Any population of creatures must adapt to the entire set of circumstances in which it finds itself, and some of these circumstances are likely to be due to the activities of its own ancestors. It is the sequence of events which has produced the present environment which is irreversible rather than any mystical trend or evolutionary law.

We humans, for example, have altered the balance of nature to a great extent during the course of our history. Should we, as a population, undergo a series of mutations which returned to us the bodies and the behaviors of our ancestors of 500,000 years ago, the world in which our species would be living would be quite different from that in which those ancestors survived. Doubtless, their characteristics were useful to them then. There is no reason to suppose that such characteristics would have the same survival value now. And so it is for other creatures too. The world changes as time goes on. Even without the activity of man, the balance of nature shifts. Ecological niches which once seemed secure vanish with the interplay of the activities of all the forms of life, of climatic shifts, and geological change.

Because of this, the course of evolution tends to be opportunistic. Populations must adapt, in one way or another, to the situations in which they find themselves, or become extinct. More often than not, the adaptations which solve immediate problems lead to overspecialization. Most species have eventually found themselves boxed in, as it were, and have died out, leaving no descendants. Evolution, furthermore, may be quite rapid—in paleontological terms—or very slow indeed, depending upon the degree of selective pressure exerted upon a species by ecological changes. Thus evolution does not proceed at a constant rate. It may produce parallel results in different taxa: the eye of the octopus is remarkably similar to the eye of the vertebrate. Parallel evolution is especially likely among creatures which share the same basic structure, however. The manner in which vertebrates fly, mentioned just previously, illustrates this, and other cases will be mentioned in later chapters. It would seem that creatures who are cousins living far apart but who are faced with similar problems or opportunities are likely to behave in more or less the same way. The more similar their structures are to begin with, the better the chance that similar structural changes will be selected for, under these circumstances. At times, evolution has even resulted in convergence, so that quite distant cousins acquire a degree of resemblance to one another which their ancestors lacked (Simpson, 1953).

VERTEBRATE STRUCTURE

The evolutionary variations in the structure of vertebrates exemplify all of the principles just mentioned. They all share the
same basic structure, but selective pressures of all sorts have led
the vertebrates to evolve, during the last half billion years, into
forms as diverse as sharks, frogs, dinosaurs, eagles, lions and people.
Adaptations to various ways of life have been accomplished, as
Darwin (1859) so well demonstrated, by the slow accumulation and
selection of minute variations which, over the generations, altered
the anatomy, physiology, and psychology of populations in many
diverse ways. But the basic structure of the vertebrates has
remained: that is, the possession of a backbone composed of
a series of rings within which runs the spinal cord. The digestive system within the abdominal cavity is ventral to this structure. The vertebrate body is bilaterally symmetrical, with a mouth
containing teeth at the head end. Just behind the mouth lie the
gill slits; these vanish, of course, among land-dwelling vertebrates
as they develop. At the same end of the body, above the mouth, is
the skull, which encloses the brain. Special sense organs such as
eyes, ears, and nostrils are also located in the head. Taste buds are
located upon the tongue; some fish have similar chemoreceptors elsewhere as well. The internal, articulated skeleton and the muscles,
many of which run from one bone to another, facilitate movement.
The vertebrates have a closed circulatory system with a heart which
pumps the blood, first to the gills or lungs, and then throughout the
body. The blood carries oxygen, nutrients, and hormonal secretions
from the endocrine glands to all the tissues. Furthermore, all vertebrates possess both livers for food storage and urinary systems for
maintaining the proper osmotic pressure in the blood and eliminating nitrogenous wastes. This urinary system is always closely associated with the sexual organs. The entire body is protected by the
skin, typically, although not always, flexible.

So far this is the most efficient pattern for overcoming varied
difficulties and exploiting diverse circumstances which has evolved.
As time has passed, most vertebrates have evolved further basic
improvements, but, except for the loss of teeth in some lines of descent, nothing in the basic pattern has been lost. Vertebrates are
active, energetic creatures. Their body plan permits both rapid
and delicate movements. The use of hemoglobin in the bloodstream permits large amounts of oxygen to be transported to all
bodily tissues, and the beating of the heart provides speedy circulation. The nervous system is highly organized and well integrated, so that vertebrates are capable of learning and of modifying
their behavior to a higher degree than any other group of animals.
Their body plan permits growth to an unprecedented degree, so

that some, like whales and dinosaurs, have reached truly enormous proportions.

The relationships between the various groups of vertebrates are shown in Figure 4–5. Of the eight classes of vertebrates only one lacks jaws, and it is appropriately named Agnatha. Today the only

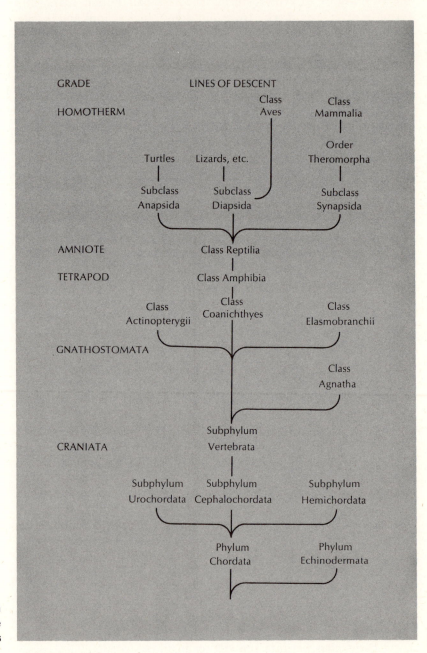

FIGURE 4-5. Approximation of the Family Tree of the Vertebrates

animals left in this group are lampreys and hagfish, but some of the earliest vertebrates known, the Ostracoderms of the Silurian period, belonged to this class too. The lamprey's mouth is circular, containing a tongue and lips with many rasping teeth. This arrangement permits lampreys to suck blood from fish to which they fasten themselves. They lack true stomachs, retain the notochord throughout life, and have imperfectly developed cartilaginous vertebrae.

Lampreys barely qualify as members of the vertebrate group, but the earliest Agnatha apparently possessed more bony tissue. So far as we know from the fossil record, they lived in fresh water, which probably explains why the vertebrate body fluids are less saline than seawater. By the Devonian period, however, water-dwelling vertebrates had not only entered the ocean but had evolved movable jaws which permitted active and voracious predation. This was the first basic improvement in the vertebrate pattern, the key to a freer type of life.

All the other classes of what we usually call fish have well-developed movable jaws, equipped with sharp pointed teeth with which to seize their food and hold it fast should it try to escape. Unlike the mandibles of arthropods which, as modified legs, grasp from both sides, the vertebrate mandible whether in fish or man is a modified gill arch and, consequently, moves up and down. The muscles which move the jaw are fastened to the cranium, which also serves as the bony case protecting the brain. This dual function of the cranium has proved to be a most useful economy, one of many in the vertebrate pattern. Another typical economy in the vertebrate pattern is the dual function of the ear as an organ of equilibrium and of hearing. The latter sensation is apparently secondary, but all vertebrates with jaws possess three semicircular canals placed at right angles to each other on each side of the skull near the jaw articulation. Movement in any direction is registered by tiny hairs within these canals. The existence of biting jaws, furthermore, enabled vertebrates to dispense with inconveniently heavy external armor. Most vertebrates find that attack is the best defense.

It is worth noting that vertebrates which bite also possess stomachs, enlarged pouches in the gut which receive and help digest large pieces of food. The intestine, which lies beyond the stomach, completes the digestion. The backbone and spinal cord of fish always extend well beyond the anus into the tail, which acts as a rudder and stabilizer in swimming. A pair of fins near the gills and another pair near the anus also serve as stabilizing organs in two classes of fish: the Elasmobranchs, which include sharks, and the Actinopterygians, or bony fish, most of which are active swimmers. In the class Coanichthyes, however, these fins are much more like limbs and may even be used to push the body forward along the bottom.

Since they live in the water, fish are not much bothered by the problem of weight. Most Actinopterygians, however, possess an air bladder which functions as a hydrostatic organ. They can thus increase or decrease their specific gravity and rise or sink as may be convenient. The air bladder is often connected with the esophagus, and a fish may rise to the surface and gulp air into it. Such a bladder also serves as a respiratory organ, and a few fish, exploiting this fact, may spend a great deal of time out of the water. Lungfish, an order of the class Coanichthyes, are so named because among them this bladder has become a true though simple lung upon which they depend for their supply of oxygen, and their nostrils serve as air passages as well as smelling organs. Such fish can survive long periods of drought when the streams they inhabit dry up. Burying itself in the mud with only a small hole from its mouth to the surface, such a fish can breathe and avoid drying out while all the other fish in the stream perish. When rains replenish the water supply, it becomes active once more, crawling about on the stream bottom and feeding on small invertebrates and decaying vegetation. Fossil evidence indicates the existence of fish, very similar to the modern lungfish, in the Devonian period; today they are scarce, living only in parts of South America, Africa, and Australia.

The water in which fish live also provides the necessary fluid element for transmitting sperm to eggs to fertilize them. Consequently, in the greater number of species of fishes, mating need not involve any bodily contact between male and female. All the body wastes from kidney and intestine alike are discharged through the cloaca and so are eggs and sperm. When eggs and sperm are ripe, the presence of the male commonly stimulates the female to discharge eggs, and this event in turn stimulates the male to shed sperm. One or both of the pair may engage in a variety of courting or nest-preparing activities at this time. Some of these practices are quite exotic, as in the case of sea horses. In this family, females lay their eggs in a pouch on the belly of the male, where they are fertilized and then remain until they are fully developed and able to swim out. The utility of protecting the egg until it has developed is obvious: eggs are quite unable to protect themselves and are excellent food. Consequently, the practice of internal fertilization has become established among many different kinds of fish. In these species the males' pelvic fins are modified as "claspers," which may

LAMPREY

CODFISH

FROG

LIZARD

be erected and inserted into the female cloaca for the transmission of sperm. Some are viviparous: the fertilized eggs are retained within the mother's body until the young fish are fully formed. As might be expected, the number of eggs formed in such species is very much reduced, which is a considerable economy. We have no evidence, however, that viviparous fish increase in numbers either more or less rapidly under natural circumstances than do others. For life in the water, diverse systems of reproduction seem to work equally well.

THE ORGANIZATION OF BEHAVIOR

The extent to which the behavior of vertebrates is organized within the central nervous system has been the real key to their success. Even the lamprey has a better developed brain than any invertebrate (Young, 1950). The human brain and nervous system are simply elaborations of the brain and nervous system of the fish. In the course of vertebrate evolution, a process known as encephalization has taken place: the brain, and especially the cerebral cortex, have come into more complete control of behavior. But the basic organization of the spinal cord has not changed very much. The central nervous system is a hollow tube composed of millions of separate fibers along which pass waves of excitation and which are in contact by means of synapses. A special feature is the fact that messages to and from the left side of the body are under the control of the right side of the central nervous system and vice versa. From between each pair of vertebrae emerge nerves which reach what are, in the fish, nearby parts of the body. The distortion in form which we and other land-dwelling vertebrates have undergone has not altered this aspect of the nervous system at all. The connections of the cranial nerves with the brain retain the same basically segmented pattern. Figure 4–6 indicates some of the rearrangements which have taken place in the vertebrate brain during evolution.

FIGURE 4-6. The Brains of Six Representative Vertebrates. The Brain Is Viewed from One Side and, in Size, Each Is Drawn to the Same Scale.
1. Olfactory Lobe.
2. Cerebrum. 3. Cerebellum.

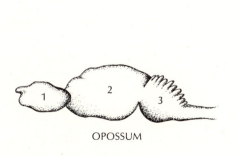

OPOSSUM

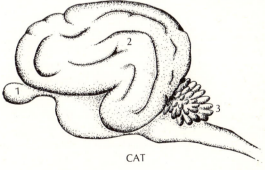

CAT

The functions of the spinal cord are to integrate reflex behavior and to conduct nervous impulses to and from the brain itself. The second function, already vital among fish, increases in importance among reptiles and even more so among mammals. The brain itself is subdivided into several sections. The medulla is the hindmost part and is concerned with such aspects of internal behavior as breathing, heartbeat, and the like. The cerebellum, lying next, is concerned with balance and coordination of movement. The midbrain, in fish and in amphibia, is the primary visual center; simple visual and auditory functions are localized here among mammals. The forebrain is the chief center for sensory integration. One section of it, the cerebrum, is divided into two hemispheres by a deep fissure extending from the front to the rear. These hemispheres have expanded enormously in the course of evolution from fish to mammals so that they cover most of the other parts of the brain. The deeper regions in the cerebrum, such as the hypothalamus, are concerned with hunger, thirst, water balance, and emotional states. The foremost section of the cerebrum, the olfactory bulb, is concerned with the sense of smell. The cerebral cortex, or neopallium, has come to be the most important part of the cerebrum among creatures with highly developed mental abilities. Its surface area has increased by folding into deep convolutions in such animals and especially in man.

Vertebrates, then, have central nervous systems which operate with a high degree of efficiency, as well as bodies which are well designed for an active life and sensory organs from which they can gain all sorts of information about their surroundings. It is not surprising that they were among the first of the animals to venture ashore.

Apparently their earlier visits were inadvertent. The climate during the late Devonian became increasingly arid, and many streams and lakes were only intermittently filled with water. It is in such streams today that the lungfish dwells. He hides away during dry seasons, but an alternative mode of behavior would be to slither from pond to pond, actively seeking water. A standard speculation is that this is precisely what the first land-dwelling vertebrates, the amphibians, did. By venturing out of the water, these creatures succeeded in entering a habitat which gave rich opportunities of many sorts. Water at normal pressure contains less than 1 percent, by volume, of dissolved oxygen, whereas the atmosphere of the earth contains about 21 percent. The increased metabolic rate made possible under these circumstances is shown by the differences between fish and air-breathing vertebrates in the ratio of carbon dioxide production to body weight. Among fish, the ratio is from .10 to .20 percent, among lizards 3.00 percent, among men 6.50 percent, and among birds 27.00 percent (Pauli, 1949). Of course, a creature able to breathe out of water could feed upon his more unfortunate neighbors, the fish which were left in the bottoms of streams as they dried out. Most people have no great regard for scavenging as a means of making a living, but it is often a profitable ecological niche to occupy, none the less. In all probability, there was little to eat on the land itself when the first vertebrates came out of the water, and it is only reasonable to suppose that there were many failures as well as the successful invasion of this strange new habitat.

LIFE ON LAND

We find life on land so natural that it is easy to forget the mechanical and physiological problems which it involves. It took millions of years for the early amphibians to solve them, and no members of this class have solved the problem of reproducing on land. Locomotion is the most conspicuous but certainly not the most difficult of these problems. Fish have pectoral and pelvic fins, and many fish use these as limbs. The limbs of land vertebrates are attached to the pectoral and pelvic girdles, so that the homology to the arrangement among fish is clear. No vertebrates have more limbs than these: four is the standard number, so land vertebrates are known as tetrapods. Furthermore, the construction of the limbs is homologous: they are jointed, and the segments are the same in the forelimb as in the hind limb. The first segment of a tetrapod limb contains one long bone, the next contains two; beyond this are a larger number of bones, in two rows, which may be derived from segments containing three and four, and finally five. The final segments are commonly separated from one another, at least to some degree, becoming distinct digits tipped with a horny substance. The manner in which evolution has altered the limbs in diverse ways illustrates how flexible the tetrapod body plan is. Its basic unity is evidence of common origin from a single ancestral stock.

Without the support of the water, an animal has to contend with the problem of weight. Early amphibians and some living ones rest on their bellies, using their limbs somewhat like paddles. Bones, ligaments, and muscles must be strengthened to raise the body, to move rapidly, or to jump. Lacking the protection of water, an animal is likely to dry out, and the skin must be modified to resist this hazard. Some amphibians keep their skins moist and breathe through them. Their habitat is restricted to damp areas. Creatures like toads which live on really dry land need tougher skins, for the internal environment must be kept wet if life is to continue. Gills no longer have any utility. The lungs, which were already useful, are now vital and must take over the main job of respiration. Amphibians use movements of the mouth and throat to gulp in the air through the nostrils, forcing it to and from the lungs. These last must remain moist to assist in the transfusion of gases between the atmosphere and the bloodstream, but they must not be filled with water. Nostrils, which most fish use for smelling, provide a passage for air even when the mouth is closed. The circulation, designed to carry oxygen from the gills to all parts of the body, needs some re-arrangement if oxygen is obtained from the lungs instead.

Temperature changes very slowly in the water. A fish can easily swim away from areas which are too hot or too cold in the open seas. On land, however, the temperature goes up after sunrise and falls after sunset. In many parts of the world, furthermore, it is much colder in winter than in summer. These fluctuations pose a real problem, for metabolic processes are always carried on more rapidly and effectively at certain temperatures than at others. The atmosphere permits the rays of the sun to be transmitted far more easily than does the water. Some of these rays may damage the tissues of the body, but the sense of vision of a land-dwelling crea-ture does not have to contend with distortions caused by the water's turbulence, and during the day the amount of light is likely to be greater than in the water. The production of a variety of sounds by an air-breathing creature is easy. Fish grunt, gurgle, and click their

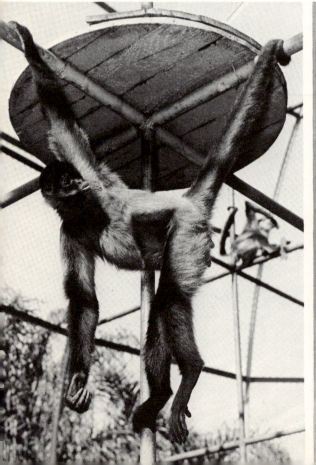

teeth, but possess no real vocal apparatus. Tetrapods, on the contrary, have exploited the possibility of making all sorts of noises, making use of the passages which carry air to and from their lungs. They hear sounds by means of an extraordinary shift in the function of the gills for which they would otherwise have no use in the air. Embryologically, the eardrum is derived from tissues which become a gill slit in fish, while the *stapes*, the bone which transmits the vibrations of the eardrum to the inner ear, is homologous to the hyomandibular bone of the fish, by which its jaw is articulated to the skull.

This is just one example of the way in which the fishlike form of the earlier vertebrates evolved by a distortion in shape and change in function of certain parts of the body. In the line of evolution leading from fish through Amphibia and Reptilia to the class Mammalia, there has been a general reduction in the number of separate bones, especially in the skull. The tail, which functions as a rudder and contributes to locomotion in water, is unable to serve either purpose on the land. In many creatures, including frogs, bears, and humans, the vertebral column comes to an end at or directly beyond the pelvis. Other creatures have found new uses for the tail (as Figure 4–7 shows): squirrels to keep warm, rats to keep cool, kangaroos for balance, birds for guidance in flight, some monkeys for

FIGURE 4-7. A Few of the Varied Uses of the Tail (Photos: From Left to Right, San Diego Zoo Photo; Dr. Harvey I. Fisher from National Audubon Society; and A. W. Ambler from National Audubon Society)

grasping, and horses for fly swatting. As a leftover organ, the tail is available for any number of uses. In the embryonic stage all vertebrates including man have tails. Members of the class Amphibia retain these in the larval or tadpole stage, but frogs and toads resorb them into the body tissue. Other amphibians such as salamanders retain tails permanently, but these tails do not resemble those of fish. Most adult tetrapods differ in shape from fish near the head end, too. The body and head are sharply separated by a neck which permits the head to be moved sideways or up and down, a maneuver which fish find quite unnecessary.

Amphibians as a class have never entirely escaped from the water, for their method of reproduction makes this quite impossible. All of them lay eggs in the water, and upon fertilization these develop into larvae with functional gills and limbless, fishy shapes. Only later do legs sprout and lungs develop, enabling the creature to crawl out onto dry land. Various devices have evolved to evade, but none to overcome, this difficulty. The ecological plateau or adaptive zone which these creatures occupy is still worth exploiting after some 300 million years. The greater efficiency of truly land-dwelling tetrapods, such as reptiles, birds, and mammals, has led these latter classes into habitats which apparently do not interfere with those which frogs, toads, and salamanders occupy. The amphibian way of life both restricts these creatures and keeps them out of harm's way.

Sources and Suggested Readings

BATES, M.
   1963   *Animal Worlds.* Random House, New York.

DARWIN, C.
   1859   *The Origin of Species.* Murray, London.
   1881   *The Formation of Vegetable Mould Through the Action of Worms, with Observations on Their Habits.* Murray, London.

GRANT, V.
   1963   *The Origin of Adaptations.* Columbia University Press, New York.

HUTCHINSON, C. E.
   1957   Homage to Santa Rosalia, or Why Are There So Many Kinds of Animals? *American Naturalist,* **93,** 117–126.

KETTLEWELL, H. B. D.
1957   The Contribution of Industrial Melanism in the Lepi-
       doptera to Our Knowledge of Evolution. *British Asso-
       ciation for the Advancement of Science,* **52,** 245–252.

LIVINGSTONE, F.
1958   Anthropological Implications of Sickle Cell Gene Dis-
       tribution in West Africa. *American Anthropologist,*
       60, 533–562.

MAYR, E.
1963   *Animal Species and Evolution.*   Harvard University
       Press, Cambridge.

METTLER, L. E. and T. C. GREGG
1969   *Population Genetics and Evolution.*   Prentice-Hall,
       Englewood Cliffs.

PAULI, W. F.
1949   *The World of Life.*   Houghton Mifflin, Boston.

ROMER, A. S.
1968   *The Procession of Life.*   World Publishing, Cleveland.

SIMPSON, G. G.
1953   *The Major Features of Evolution.*   Columbia Univer-
       sity Press, New York.

SMITH, J. L. B.
1956   *The Search Beneath the Sea.*   Holt, New York.

SORIANO, M.
1970   The Fluoric Origin of the Bone Lesion in the Pithecan-
       thropus Erectus Femur. *American Journal of Physical
       Anthropology,* **32,** 49–58.

WALLACE, B. and A. B. SRB
1961   *Adaptation.*   Prentice-Hall, Englewood Cliffs.

YOUNG, J. Z.
1950   *The Life of Vertebrates.*   Clarendon Press, Oxford.

CHAPTER 5

The Evolution of the Mammals

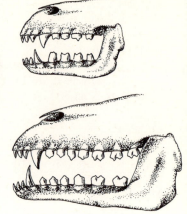

THE AMNIOTE EGG

Evolution has been described as a device for generating a high degree of improbability. Certainly some of its results are rather bizarre. At the same time, the existence of long-term directional trends in evolution are well established (Simpson, 1944). As we look back at any sequence of events, they may well appear to have been inevitable or at least highly probable. Yet this does not warrant predictions concerning the future. Mutations occur at random, and, unless they happen to improve the efficiency of a species, evolutionary progress must wait. Yet given enough time, advance does take place.

During the Carboniferous period, vertebrates solved the problem of reproducing on land, and the Amniote grade or level of organization came into existence. The solution of this problem opened up entirely new areas of the world and ways of livelihood to tetrapods, involving such an increase in overall efficiency that many of them have succeeded in taking to the air, several have returned to the water and competed successfully with fish, and one, after a long and educational sojourn in the trees, has become human.

The amphibian egg, like most fish eggs, is jellylike and unprotected. It demands a liquid and, specifically, a watery environment for respiration and development into an active creature. Such eggs can be fertilized after the female sheds them, yet many fish practice internal fertilization, and some retain the egg until it has developed into an active, though small, creature. For reproduction on dry land, internal fertilization is necessary. To avoid drying out in the air, eggs must be encased in a shell or tough membrane which permits respiration but prevents loss of water. Such a membrane is necessarily also impermeable to sperm. Consequently, fertilization must take place before it develops, that is, within the body of the mother. As a result, mating among amniotes necessitates copulation. A form of social cooperation which takes place only in some sorts of fish must take place in all sorts of reptiles, birds, and mammals. The implications of this fact for the evolution of new forms of behavior as well as new details of anatomy and physiology are numerous. Males and females must be attracted to one another under the proper conditions at the right times and places. This by no means ensures the later evolution of continued association between male and female, but it is a necessary step in that direction. Glands to provide fluid for the transport of sperm are necessary for the male, and a special chamber to retain eggs until they are ready to be laid is necessary for the female.

The amnion and the allantois, however, are the structures most vital to the egg as it develops into a fully formed creature, ready for activity in the outside world. These are saclike membranes derived from the embryo itself during its development. Figure 5–1 represents the amniote egg in schematic form. The amnion completely encloses the growing embryo and is filled with liquid, so that it provides the watery environment supplied by nature to the eggs of amphibians. The allantois develops later and serves a dual function. In the first place it collects the urine which the kidneys produce as they begin to function. The nitrogenous wastes of fish and amphibians are usually converted into urea, which is highly soluble in water. In high concentration urea is toxic, and the continued collection of this substance in the allantois would endanger the life of the growing embryo. Egg-laying amniotes convert urea into uric acid which is much less soluble and may safely be stored within the egg. Once established during embryonic life, the practice of ex-

FIGURE 5-1. The Scheme of the Amniote Egg

creting uric acid is continued, by reptiles and birds, after they have hatched. Secondly, the allantois operates as a breathing organ, for it has many blood vessels which carry oxygen from and carbon dioxide to the surface which encloses the entire egg. By means of this intricate yet economical set of arrangements, the embryo within the egg has all the advantages but none of the disadvantages of an egg floating in a pond or ocean. By bringing a miniature replica of their ancestor's environment onto dry land, the early amniotes were able to avoid returning to the water to breed.

FURTHER PROBLEMS OF LIFE ON LAND

Having solved the vital problem of reproduction, early amniotes were faced with others. The class of reptiles, first of the amniotes to evolve and ancestral both to birds and mammals, solved enough of them to become highly successful. Reptiles breathe by a backward movement of the ribs, so that the lungs expand and suck in air. They expel the air by reversing this process. Many reptiles have limbs strong enough to raise themselves so that they can run easily. Indeed, many of the ancient reptiles ran about on their hind legs, using the forelimbs to seize food, while others took to the air. The separation in function of the forelimbs and hind limbs which is observed in many tetrapods is nothing new. Since the forelimbs are closer to the mouth, it is not strange that in many varieties of tetrapods they are used in feeding as well as in locomotion. Since the eyes are located in the head, it is not strange that this part of the body may frequently be raised so that the creature may look around. The hind limbs, consequently, are apt to receive the greater part of the weight of the body and are especially useful in thrusting the creature forward as well. A strengthened pelvis and hind limb and a more flexible forelimb are quite characteristic of the greater number of amniotes and even of some amphibians.

The reptile's central nervous system is an improved version of the amphibian's. The cerebral hemispheres are enlarged, and there is evidently some transfer of the highest integrative functions into this area. But reptile behavior is, for the most part, stereotyped and relatively simple. The degree to which it is modified by learning from experience is certainly greater than among fish, since the diversity of experiences on land is considerable. Yet the size of the brain in most of the living as well as of the extinct giant reptiles is astonishingly small, especially in proportion to their bulk. It was clearly adequate for survival, since many of these genera continued to exist for tens of millions of years. But one suspects that the competition with other living forms depended very little upon mental ability in those days. Large and small, the reptiles during most of the Mesozoic had only one another as serious competitors. They were anatomically and physiologically more efficient than other existing creatures. Consequently, their evolution followed the most diverse lines, as did that of Darwin's finches millions of years later, but to an even greater degree. Several distinct phyletic lines returned to the sea, where they were highly successful for prolonged periods. Indeed, some turtles continue to pursue this form of life even up to the present. Others took to the air and flew: their forelimbs evolved into wings. The greater number remained terrestrial in habitat, but among these both herbivorous and carnivorous varieties existed.

For a very long time tropical and subtropical climates prevailed throughout most of the world. Under these conditions, the reptiles flourished, as they are apt to do in similar environments today. Like fish and amphibians, they possess no internal mechanism for maintaining a constant body temperature. In the water this is a matter of no great importance, and in the more humid tropics it does not inhibit activity unduly, for fluctuations in the temperature of the atmosphere are minor. In arid or temperate areas, on the other hand, the air may become warm or cold quite rapidly, and reptiles suffer a real disadvantage in contrast to mammals and birds today for this reason. They are likely to remain torpid and subject to predation until they have absorbed warmth from their surroundings. Nor can they withstand great heat. The importance of being able to avoid torpidity is illustrated by the adaptation of *Dimetrodon*, a reptile of the Permian period (Simpson, 1953). This creature possessed a set of long spines articulated dorsally to its vertebrae, enabling them to be raised and lowered. The spines contained large blood vessels and were connected by a membrane through which the blood must have flowed. By raising the spines, the creature was able to expose the surface of the membrane to the rays of the rising sun early in the morning. The blood flowing through it would be warmed and, in its further circulation, would raise the temperature of the animal's body. Thus he could become active earlier than his neighbors and, perhaps, breakfast upon them while they were still half asleep.

Such an adaptation would scarcely be efficient enough to fit the ecological circumstances of the present. The presence of even more active mammals and the scarcity of less active reptiles render this technique for increasing body temperature obsolete. In the same manner, perhaps, the flying reptiles of the Mesozoic, the pterodactyls, which did very well for a long time, may have been put out of business by the birds. Birds, like mammals, have gained control over their own internal temperatures. It seems likely that what a pterodactyl could do, a bird can do even better. But since we ourselves are mammals, it is with the course of mammalian evolution that we are especially interested.

THE MAMMALS

The pattern of mammalian organization is so obviously efficient that once established, its success was assured. But the fact that this pattern originated would seem remarkable if we failed to consider the problems involved in the mutual adaptations of living creatures. We recall that the balance of nature resembles the balance of a tight-rope walker: the one impossibility is continued success in standing still. Even during the humid warmth of the Mesozoic there was advantage to be gained by a heightened degree of activity. To be able to maintain an even temperature internally despite changes in the amount of heat received from the environment adds to the efficiency of physiological processes. The evolution of the two quite separate classes of homotherms, the birds and the mammals from different subclasses of the reptilian stocks by the middle of the Mesozoic, is evidence of the utility of temperature control among land-dwelling vertebrates. Indeed, according to Simpson (1959) the grade of organization which is termed mammalian evolved more than once, although this is disputed by many (Reed, 1960).

The fossil evidence indicates that adaptive radiation into a number of quite distinctive lines of descent occurred early in the evolution of the reptiles. It is not uncommon for this to take place soon after any phyletic line has evolved a really basic improvement in its mode of life. In this case it was the amniote egg. Among the various groups which diverged from the common stem were the turtles and the now extinct Parapsida, which both returned to the water with much success; the Diapsida, the ancestral stock of lizards, snakes, crocodiles, dinosaurs, and birds; and the Synapsida. Mammals evolved from this last subclass. Even as early as the Permian period, which was long before the appearance of dinosaurs, there were a number of reptilian genera which possessed such mammalian traits as deep mandibles, projecting canine teeth, enlarged brain cases and temporal fossae for the reception of jaw muscles. From the increased size and altered shape of the pelvic and pectoral girdles and from the disposition of the articular surfaces on the limb bones, we must infer that these creatures did not normally rest on their bellies like lizards, but raised their bodies from the ground like dogs, cats, or horses. None of them show any trace of bipedalism, but in many the thumbs and big toes contained only two bones each, whereas the other digits all had three. The reader should examine his own digits to see if he has the same arrangement.

During the Triassic period, perhaps 160 million years ago, still further evolution away from the standard reptilian and toward the standard mammalian condition had taken place in this phyletic line. Among the various creatures known collectively as Theriodonts the teeth were differentiated into incisors, canines which were single-cusped, and grinders, each of which contained several cusps. The tooth-carrying bone of the lower jaw was much enlarged, and the method of articulation of the jaws enabled these creatures to chew as well as simply seize their food before swallowing it. Mammals today have highly developed salivary glands, but these, of course, have left no fossil remains. Chewing and pouring saliva upon one's food speeds up the digestive process and enables an animal to make use of the energy thus obtained within a short time. Overloading the stomach can result in torpidity: several hours which might be spent in exploring, playing, or hunting are wasted. The condition of a snake after each meal or of a human after Thanksgiving dinner both illustrate this point.

Before the end of the Triassic some genera of Theriodonts possessed a secondary palate which kept the nostrils separated from the mouth. This enabled them to chew and breathe at the same time, which is a convenience. Some of them were as much as nine feet long, and all seem to have had rather massive builds, with thick tails, short necks, and sturdy legs. The braincases remained reptilian in type and, by mammalian standards, really small. We do not know whether the learning ability of these creatures was better developed than that of their contemporaries.

The fact that no fossils of a similar nature have been found in Jurassic and later strata suggests that they were no more intelligent than their competitors. The larger forms all became extinct without issue, and dinosaurs usurped their ecological niches. During a period of 90 million years the mammals do not seem to have offered any effective competition to the great diversity of reptiles which inhabited the earth. The reasons for this are obscure. Mammals of a sort were certainly in existence, as their fossil remains have been found scattered throughout both Jurassic and Cretaceous strata. Paleontologists identify mammals as a class by their possession of a single bone in the lower jaw. Their ancestors, the Therapsids, had several such bones although all but the dentary became smaller as time went on. Figure 5–2 pictures the evolution of the mammalian mandible. A few of the Mesozoic mammals, which had teeth like rodents, became reasonably large, but all of the others were of much smaller dimensions. We infer from their teeth that they were insectivorous. We know many forms only from their teeth or jaws, and we know almost nothing of their postcranial anatomy. The braincases were higher than those of reptiles: the cerebrum must have begun to expand. It would seem logical that they

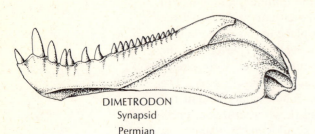

DIMETRODON
Synapsid
Permian

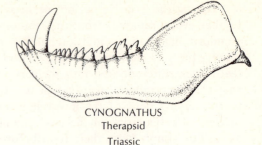

CYNOGNATHUS
Therapsid
Triassic

**FIGURE 5-2. The Evolution of
the Mammalian Mandible**

DOG
Carnivore
Present

had better integrated central nervous systems as well as more efficient digestive systems than their contemporaries, so their long-continued obscurity seems odd. Quite possibly they suffered from physiological disadvantages which have left no fossil evidence but which were great enough to counterbalance the advantages of quicker wits and better digestions.

Such a speculation is suggested by the fact that what characterizes living mammals is a whole new set of physiological mechanisms which function to maintain homeostasis. They are able to keep the internal environment in a steady state, both biochemically and mechanically, in the face of rapid external changes, which reptiles cannot do (Young, 1957). Each mammal possesses biochemical individuality to a degree unknown among other creatures. For instance, tissue transplants, which are readily accomplished between salamanders, simply do not take in the case of rats or rabbits. This is well illustrated by the difficulties which have attended the transplanting of human hearts and other organs in recent years. Each mammal functions under an even higher degree of central nervous control than any reptile. Its responses to complex stimuli are therefore more likely to be effective. These two aspects of improved efficiency are interrelated, for the proper operation of the brain depends upon lack of fluctuations in the composition as well as in the supply of blood. The result is that mammals are able to live more freely than any other vertebrates, just as vertebrates can live more freely than invertebrates. To attain the intricate biochemical balance which makes this possible may well have been a difficult and long-drawn-out process.

In any case and again for obscure reasons, all of the large and most of the small reptiles became extinct at the end of the Mesozoic era. We know that extensive topographical and climatic changes took place at this time, but how these could have led to the death of aquatic as well as terrestrial genera, families, and orders is difficult to understand. From the Paleocene to the present, a time span of perhaps 70 million years, the class of mammals has been as prominent as it had previously been obscure. As the reptiles before them, the mammals underwent a process of adaptive radiation into a great many different ways of life. Forms evolved which were suitable only for life in the water; others developed the ability to fly; but most remained terrestrial. Some specialized in eating vegetation, others in eating flesh. But the mammals were also able to do previously impossible things, such as remaining active during months of very cold weather.

Not only did new tenants occupy existing ecological niches, but also many new ones were created through the interaction of different species. All these changes were due to the biological capabilities of the creatures concerned rather than any shifts in the physical aspects of the environment. As any capacities for new and more complex forms of activity evolved in some particular species, the balance of nature in its ecological community shifted, providing a stimulus for the further evolution of other species. Since mammals came to depend a great deal upon the proper functioning of the central nervous system, it is not strange that orthoselection for further improvements in that system became widespread.

MAMMALIAN ADAPTATIONS

Mammals as a class have a great many shared characteristics, aside from the most efficiently organized central nervous systems in existence. We have already mentioned their highly developed biochemical individuality, as well as their excellent digestive system. Some degree of ability to control the internal temperature and maintain it at the point most useful for the current activities of the animal is universal among mammals. The teeth are differentiated to serve various functions: incisors, canines, premolars, and molars are standard. There are two sets of teeth, deciduous and permanent. The mammalian lower jaw is composed of a single bone, the mandible. Two of the bones which form part of the lower jaw in reptiles are found in mammals in the middle ear as part of the hearing apparatus.

The bones of mammalian limbs articulate in such a manner as to lift the body clear of the ground. With the exception of a few species in two orders, seven cervical vertebrae are always found. These lack ribs, as do the lumbar vertebrae. Bones have several centers of ossification as a rule, which fuse only at the end of their growth periods. Thus the bones can be strong even while still growing, which is most advantageous. The fossil hunter has plenty of clues to help him decide whether or not his discoveries are mammal bones.

In studying the characteristics of living mammals we find more similarities among them, many of which are unique to the class (Young, 1957). Especially important, perhaps, is the mammalian skin, a very remarkable tissue of great importance. It is elastic, tough, and capable of constant self-repair. Among the major distinctions of the skin of mammals are the proliferation of excretory glands and the growth of hair (Montagna, 1962). Fish and amphibians tend to have many slime-producing glands distributed over their bodies, but the living reptiles do not. Mammals, however, excrete an astonishing variety of materials from glands in their skins. Milk is, of course, one of these materials, about which more will be said later. Sweat, which is another, is particularly important in the human species. Sebaceous glands ordinarily empty into hair follicles, and their oily secretion covers the surface of newly emerging hairs. Apocrine glands, which are also likely to be found in association with hair, produce a variety of scents which have come to function as social signals among many mammals. Eccrine glands secrete water and sodium; in most species they are confined to friction surfaces, but our species has exploited them as a means of keeping cool, and they are widely distributed over the entire body.

Hair serves many functions and has been modified in some rather bizarre ways. Normally, a mammal's body is rather well covered with a hairy coat which insulates him against rapid changes in temperature and protects the skin from scratches and bruises. In a number of genera, however, such as armadillos and pangolins, much of the hair has been modified into overlapping scales; in the rhinoceros the horn is, in fact, composed of modified hair, and hedgehogs and porcupines are among the mammals most of whose hair is stiff and spiny. The vast majority of land mammals possess stiff vibrissae on either side of the snout which are highly sensitive to touch. Hair also serves an ornamental function in many cases, growing in tufts or being pigmented in various hues. It is almost never found on contact surfaces such as palms, soles, or the tips of digits and may be lost from other areas as well. Whales and porpoises have hair only during fetal life.

In most species of mammals the organs of perception, including the nerve endings just under the surface of the skin, operate at a high degree of efficiency and discrimination, enabling mammals to be aware of a great variety of cues. To be sure, adaptation to very different habitats has led to emphasis on different sensory perceptors and even to the loss of some. Since attempting to breathe underwater would result in drowning, for instance, whales and porpoises have lost the sense of smell completely. Bats can fly as skillfully if blinded as with their eyes open and operating, for they depend upon the locating of echoes and have marvelously acute hearing. Since the cerebrum has taken over the function of integrating all sensory cues, mammals can make proper and, indeed, subtle responses. The speed of nerve conduction is rapid, so that mammals can make the most complex responses very quickly. The well-developed hormonal system serves to divert bodily activity speedily into new channels when necessary, making an integrated response easier. A four-chambered heart pumps blood first to the lungs and only afterward throughout the rest of the body. This is enormously helpful as a mechanical aid to adequate biochemical reactions, since oxygen-rich blood is not mixed with venous blood. Large supplies of oxygen are, therefore, constantly available to the brain. Deep breathing is required if this system is to operate well and is made possible by the presence of a diaphragm which separates the thoracic from the abdominal cavity. When the muscles of the diaphragm contract, the lungs expand and take in large quantities of air. Aeration of the lungs is also improved by their complex structure and extensive surface area. The large amounts of oxygen needed to maintain a high body temperature are thus available.

But although this high body temperature is generally advantageous, it happens to be deleterious to spermatogenesis. Yet sperm must be produced in sufficient quantity if any species is to continue existing. The descent of the testes into the scrotum, a sac outside of the body where it is cooler, solves the problem for most adult male mammals. This has been a remarkable evolutionary achievement, since among the other vertebrates the testes lie near the kidneys and discharge sperm into the kidney duct, which leads to the cloaca. Mammals have developed a new set of kidneys which discharge into a bladder, while the testes have taken over exclusive use of the old kidney ducts. These join the urinary system just below the bladder, so that semen and urine are still discharged among mammals by a common duct, but this duct transverses an extensible penis rather than joining the cloaca. Indeed, the cloaca is lacking in all mammals except for Monotremes and Marsupials.

The female body has undergone a still more remarkable set of adaptive alterations, one of which has given the class its name. This is the possession of milk-producing glands. Among the Monotremes these glands are diffuse and lack nipples. Among Marsupials the nipples are located in the pouch where the young undergo most of their development and inject milk by periodic reflex action. Among Eutherian mammals, however, the nipples must be actively suckled by the young. They are placed in one or more pairs on the ventral side of the body, sometimes concentrated in either the pelvic or pectoral region, but often in a long series reaching from one of these regions to the other.

As a device for protecting the newborn, the provision of nourishment in the form of milk is superb. The baby animal is not forced out into a hostile or, at best, indifferent world at the moment of hatching to make its own living. It remains in its mother's care. Milk itself is so nutritious that the baby does not require such continuous feeding as young birds which also depend upon parental care. It contains antibodies developed by the mother which are useful in protecting the young against disease. At the same time, distention of the milk glands renders the mother as dependent upon her nurselings as they are upon her. The emotional bond which develops between mammalian mother and child is well known, and the existence of this bond has been crucial in the development of mammalian societies. Milk glands are indeed the most vital as well as the most striking, unique, and universal traits of the mammals. The class is well named.

The reproductive tracts of the female mammals have also undergone changes in accordance with their new functions. The Monotremes lay eggs with yolks, as reptiles do, but both Marsupials and Eutherians retain the fertilized egg within the uterus, a newly

FIGURE 5-3A. Some Mammalian Advances in Efficiency, I

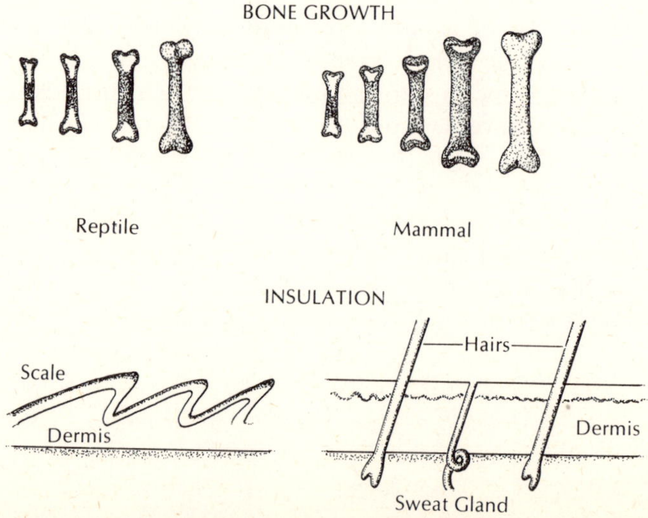

BONE GROWTH

Reptile   Mammal

INSULATION

Scale

Dermis

Hairs

Dermis

Sweat Gland

evolved organ. Among Marsupials the young are born in semiembryonic condition and transferred to the pouch for further development. The Eutherian embryo, however, develops a placenta which attaches to the uterine wall. Through the very thin membranes of this structure oxygen and nutrients pass from the mother's bloodstream into that of the fetus, while waste materials transfuse in the opposite direction. As among fish and amphibians urea rather than uric acid may safely be excreted by mammals. Within the uterus the baby can develop and grow, sometimes for many months. Although quite a few other vertebrates are viviparous, none of them possess such an efficient method of protecting and nourishing the young. One consequence of this is that mammals do not need nearly so high a birth rate in order to maintain or even increase their numbers. Humans exploit this more than most other mammals, although elephants and perhaps whales produce relatively few offspring during a lifetime as well.

Nor does the mammalian ovary need to produce a great quantity of eggs. Mammalian fertilization occurs deeply enough within the body so that the placenta will have a uterine wall to which it may attach itself. The vagina, a separate tube which leads outward from the uterus, provides a passageway for sperm coming in and babies going out. These organs are paired in Marsupials, but Eutherians have a single vagina with its own opening to the surface of the body, although they may have two uteri, or a partly divided one. During mating the extended penis is inserted into this tube rather than into the cloaca, which improves the chances for sperm to encounter and fertilize an egg, of which very few and often only one are available at any given time. Figures 5–3A and B picture some of the mammalian advances in efficiency.

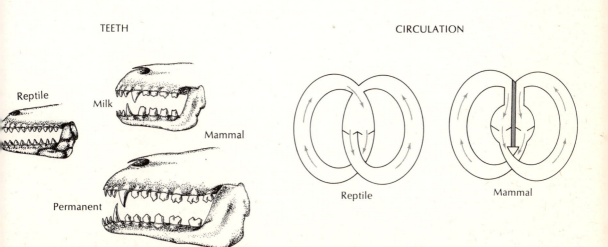

TEETH

Reptile

Milk

Mammal

Permanent

CIRCULATION

Reptile

Mammal

MAMMALIAN BEHAVIOR

The efficiency of mammalian reproductive physiology and behavior avoids a great deal of waste. Furthermore, just as the emotional bond between mother and child provides the primary base for mammalian society, so the sexual bond between male and female provides a secondary one. Among many species the sexual relationship is transient, but among others it becomes much more lasting. This is especially true in cases which involve a triangular relationship between father, mother, and offspring. Just as among the equally warm-blooded birds, the association of two adults with growing infants has had survival value in many ecological circumstances. In a number of species a male will continue his companionship with the female who has mated with him for a long time, despite the fact that they copulate only during a few days in a year. The mere presence of an adult male, even a lazy or indifferent one, often discourages potential rivals or predators.

Consequently, young mammals of many species are apt to grow up in the company of their parents, and more often than not, of their brothers and sisters. These are commonly their litter mates, but sometimes such siblings are older or younger, since the growth period of mammals is prolonged. Mammals have a greater capability than other creatures to learn by experience. Much of this experience is provided by their social relationships: one of the most important aspects of mammalian behavior is revealed by the fact that mammals play.

Play activity, in which young creatures test out their various abilities in response to one another, without danger of serious consequences ensuing, functions to train them for the real hazards of adult life. They find out what they can do and how to do it during a time of life when they are still kept out of harm's way. As we humans know, playing is not only educational, but also fun. It may lead and, indeed, often has led to imaginative inventions, to the creation of something new. Whether we dare extrapolate from our human experience and attribute to other animals the emotions

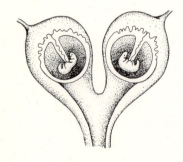

MAMMALIAN REPRODUCTION AND CHILD CARE

which we feel in similar situations is dubious. We are, however, so profoundly mammalian in all observable structures and testable reactions that anthropomorphic explanations of mammalian behavior are less rash than similar explanations of the activity of snakes, snails, or spiders would be. People frequently establish empathetic relationships with other mammals, but somewhat less with birds, and apparently never with fish or frogs. A great deal, although far from all, of human behavior can be and has been quite accurately described in terms of biology. It seems as reasonable to explain our own addiction to play as part of our mammalian heritage as it is to explain our four limbs, warm blood, and body chemistry. In other mammals, as in man, socialization mediated by playfulness has survival value.

Among a great many species of living mammals, social organization goes far beyond simple pair-bonds between male and female. In such species troops, bands, or packs exist, each containing adults of both sexes as well as youngsters and each retaining their identity year after year. One of the major lessons learned in youthful play, in these cases, is that hierarchy exists within the group: some animals are dominant over others. Ethologists, those who study the naturalistic behavior of animals, find that dominance plays a major role in the social relations of many kinds of creatures. Conflict within a group is kept at a minimum when each individual is aware of his status, and the social stability which results from this awareness has a certain degree of survival value for the group as a group and, consequently, for its individual members. It is important to note that males, in by far the greater number of species, show greater interest in their position in the hierarchy than do females. But it is also important to note and rather surprising to most humans to learn that dominant males more often assert their priority in reference to food than in reference to females.

Really serious battles between rivals appear to be rare in well-established bands or packs, although there may be brief flare-ups of violence. Signals indicating submission, given by the loser, seem to inhibit the winner of a combat from inflicting further damage (Lorenz, 1966). Such signals are but one of the many forms of social communication which ethologists have found to exist among

REPTILIAN REPRODUCTION AND LACK OF CHILD CARE

FIGURE 5-3B. Some Mammalian Advances in Efficiency, II

mammals as well as some other creatures. Because of the fact that human beings communicate largely by the use of spoken language, we tend to think of the sense of hearing as the primary signal receptor. This is not necessarily true: we ourselves communicate by facial expression, gesture, and bodily posture as well as by talking. A dog with its tail between its legs gives a message perfectly comprehensible to other dogs. A hard fixed stare or a silent snarl are understandable even across species lines. Many mammalian species have elaborated these and other silent signals into complex rituals which have proved highly adaptive. Because most mammals have a far keener sense of smell than we, many of their signals are olfactory, and the development of glands which secrete a variety of odoriferous substances is widely exploited in a large number of species. A female in heat, for instance, produces aromas which attract and excite males of the same species. Furthermore, we know how canines mark out their territories by spraying urine in appropriate places. Farley Mowat (1963), during a field study of the behavior of wolves in northern Canada, found that these animals respected the boundary lines about his dwelling when he marked them in the same manner. He found that he had to drink several quarts of tea each day in order to accomplish this.

The establishment of territories with boundaries which are protected serves to space out the members or the bands of members of a species. Since such spacing, in turn, serves to inhibit or at least reduce the overexploitation of resources, territorialism is often quite advantageous to a species. It is not surprising that we find territorial behavior in many species of mammals. But the degree to which it is developed varies, not only from species to species, but in accordance with circumstances. In many cases, for instance, only a small core area may be jealously defended by a band, which exploits a much larger range in common with other bands of the same species. In other cases seasonal migrations from one region to another may take place. The concept of territorialism turns out to be a rather vague one, and it cannot be regarded as the unifying theme which explains mammalian social behavior, including the behavior of human beings.

Another way in which human behavior resembles that of other mammals—or, if you will, the behavior of other mammals resembles ours—in the necessity for periodic sleep. Here our behavior parallels that of birds without being identical. It is almost certain that the high degree of nervous activity characteristic of both warm-blooded classes is responsible for this phenomenon. In any case, there is a sharp distinction between waking and sleeping states among mammals. Many other vertebrates or even invertebrates alternate, as circumstances require, between hibernation, estivation, or complete torpor on the one hand and a state of activity, sometimes alert activity, on the other. Perhaps, however, it would be more of an error to say that a clam or a lamprey is ever awake, even though active, than to say the reverse. When most of a creature's activities are automatic and not subject to cerebral direction, it is impossible to tell. On the other hand, when a creature not only learns readily but also exhibits a great deal of behavior which is directed from the cerebrum, it is reasonable to say that the creature is aware to the extent of being awake. So it is with mammals. Like us, they can continue to function in a haphazard fashion even after extensive damage to the cerebrum, but the well-organized activity whereby they make their livings in the wild requires integration in this section of the brain.

DIVERSIFICATION OF THE MAMMALIAN STOCK

The diversification of the mammalian stock (see Figure 5–4) began so long ago that some lines of descent do not possess all of the characteristics which we think of as typical of the class. As we noted, the Monotremes lay eggs. In many ways their skeletons resemble those of reptiles. They have hair but their temperature is lower and less constant than that of other mammals. No fossil remains of this group have yet been discovered from times earlier than the Pleistocene, but they differ so much from all other mammals that it is commonly supposed that their line of ancestry diverged early in the Mesozoic. They are therefore considered to belong to a subclass of their own, the Prototheria. Today they occupy highly specialized ecological niches in Australia and New Guinea to which they are closely adapted. Doubtless, the protection from competition with Eutherian mammals afforded by Wallace's line has helped to preserve the Monotremes from extinction.

Most Marsupials live behind the protection of this same barrier. Although the members of this order are considered to be of the same subclass, the Theria, as other mammals, they are so distinctive that they are placed in the infraclass Metatheria (Simpson, 1945). In anatomy and behavior the Metatheria retain far fewer reptilian characteristics than the Prototheria, but obviously more than the Eutheria. The fossil record shows that such Metatherian types as opossums were quite widespread during the Cretaceous, but that later they became restricted to the more isolated parts of the world. Opossums continue to exist in America with skeletons almost identical to those of their ancestors of 75 million years ago. In Australia and New Guinea, however, the absence of Eutherian mammals left many ecological niches vacant, and the Marsupials diversified to fill them. Forms as different as the kangaroo and the koala are in-

FIGURE 5-4. Approximation of a Family Tree of the Mammals

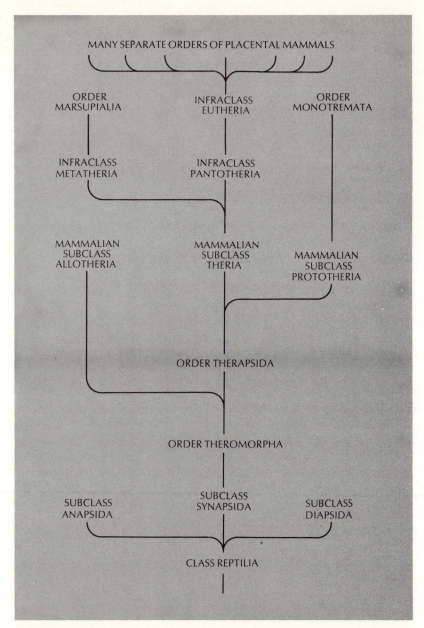

cluded within one superfamily of Marsupials, while another includes creatures which look and act almost like moles as well as others which look and act almost like wolves. The Marsupial pattern is not as efficiently organized as the Eutherian: this is exemplified by the lack of a well-developed method of nourishing the embryo within the uterus.

The Eutherians, on the other hand, have often been called placental mammals because their embryos are provided with a placenta. Babies are often born in a helpless condition—puppies are blind, rats hairless, humans weak and uncoordinated—but none are so utterly undeveloped as baby kangaroos; and many, such as calves and whales, are quite competent either at birth or within a few minutes after birth. The species' way of life is the deciding factor, but it is important for a mammal to be born with a cerebrum which is capable of considerable development during infancy at least. The ability of mammals to learn from experience is one of their major competitive advantages. Any device which will promote improvements in this ability has selective value, unless it interferes a great deal with other aspects of life.

We have mentioned the enlargement of the cerebral hemispheres as a characteristic of the Eutheria. Significantly, one of the major trends in mammalian evolution has been a still further increase in the size of this part of the brain. More recent species show increased development of the nonolfactory areas of the cerebral cortex and the frontal lobes and other changes related to complex behavior, in contrast to ancestral species. Primates and of course the human species in particular have carried this general trend further than have other mammals, but even such a stupid beast as the rhinoceros has a larger cerebrum and probably greater mental ability than his Eocene ancestors possessed. The brains of horses, dogs, elephants, and many other sorts of mammals have increased greatly during the Cenozoic. If all of one's neighbors are behaving more intelligently, it is often worthwhile to do the same thing.

The earliest Eutherians of which we have fossil evidence were small, probably insectivorous creatures with forty-four teeth: three incisors, one canine, four bicuspids, and three molars on either side in each jaw. Their legs were short and their feet plantigrade, each having five digits. They had long snouts and well-developed olfactory lobes. It is more than likely that most of them were nocturnal and many of them semiarboreal. This was during the Cretaceous period, but by the Paleocene the adaptive radiation of the Eutheria had started, as well as trends toward reduction in the number of teeth and digits, lengthening of the limbs, and increase in size in many separate lines of descent. To be sure, some mammals, especially those of the Insectivore order, retain all or most of these old-fashioned characteristics. Reduction in the number of teeth has become very widespread, however, or even extreme. We primates have more teeth than most mammals, and our teeth have not become specialized for some particular diet as have those of horses, whales, or hyenas.

Reduction in the number of digits has also been common. Many mammals run about on their toes rather than their feet, sometimes even on the tips of their toes. For such purposes one or two toes are adequate or even preferable, unless the weight of the creature is so great as to require exceptionally thick legs like the elephant's. Lengthening of the limbs has proved highly functional for various purposes including added speed and climbing. The increase in body size, which has occurred separately in numerous descent lines, may be explained in many ways.

In order to maintain a constant high temperature, mammals must eat food containing enough calories to provide for their warmth, their energetic activity, and the replacement of bodily tissues. If a body doubles its lineal dimensions, its surface area will increase by four times but its volume by eight. Heat is lost by radiation from the surface of any object, including an animal's body. Increase in bulk, consequently, minimizes heat loss and eases the nutritional problems of a mammal which lives where the air temperature is quite a few degrees lower than that of its body, as is most ordinarily the case. Growth of hair, reduction in the number of sweat glands, shortening of appendages, and other changes in proportion also help to conserve body heat. Yet the smallest mammals, such as shrews, must eat their own weight every day just to remain active.

Mammals of any one variety which inhabit colder regions are as a rule larger than those of the same variety in warmer regions. This rule, which is often known as Bergman's Rule, has been found to apply to many species and genera which have a wide climatic range. Allen's Rule refers to the extension of appendages to maintain the proper heat balance. Figure 5–5, showing the varied sizes of foxes' ears, illustrates this rule. There is strong evidence that Allen's Rule and weaker evidence that Bergman's Rule had as much effect upon the evolution of the human species as upon the evolution of many others. Climate is but one of many aspects of the environment to which any creature must adapt. Elephants and shrews inhabit the same jungles and musk oxen and lemmings the same tundras.

Body size is also a function of the animal's method of making a living. Often it reflects very precisely the activities in which the species engage. The giraffe, for instance, has no competitors in

FIGURE 5-5. Foxes' Ears—A Climatic Adaptation. The Arctic Fox, to the Left, Has the Shortest Ears; the Desert Fox, to the Right, the Longest Ears. These Appendages Radiate Heat. (Photo: By Permission of Chanticleer Press, Inc.)

browsing the leaves from high branches. In the single genus *Felis* are found species as small as domestic cats and as large as lions, each preying upon animals of appropriate dimensions. If sexual combats between males are customary as a prelude to mating, as among stags and seals, extra size may often tip the scales so that the larger of two competitors transmits his genes. In all these examples the ecological relationships between the different animals in a community are important, no matter whether it is hot or cold, wet or dry. In many cases, of course, small size is advantageous. A flying creature such as a bat gets along better if he does not weigh too much. Arboreal creatures such as squirrels and monkeys can exploit the lesser branches of trees only if they are not heavy.

Larger animals are more likely than smaller ones to grow slowly and have a longer life span. They also have brains which are absolutely bigger although relatively smaller than their undersized relatives. Among creatures which depend as much upon learning as mammals do, it is worthwhile to live long enough so that one's experience really matters. Partly due to allometric growth, large animals are also more likely to have chewing apparatus adequate to deal with food which could not be consumed by a smaller creature. For such reasons, too, a trend to increase in size as the generations go on is perfectly logical among mammals. Of course, the largest of all, the whales, live in the water where weight, as such, is a matter of complete indifference.

We have noted that hair is a characteristic common to all mammals and unique to the class. Its primary function has doubtless been to insulate the body, but modification of hair has been a widespread trend in mammalian evolution. In some cases almost all of it is lost very early in life, as among whales. In others it is very sparsely distributed, as among hippopotamuses and elephants. It may be significant that in such cases the skin is generally very dark.

Hair may also be modified into spines, as it is among porcupines. Or certain parts of the body may be hairier than others. There may be sexual dimorphism in the pattern of hair growth: lions and male baboons, among other species, have manes; human males grow beards and sometimes chest hair. Patterns of hair color are very common: stripes, spots, and blotches occur in a great number of species, functioning as camouflage or for display. As among a number of Arctic species, hair color may change with the season. The opportunism of evolutionary change is well illustrated by the varied uses to which hair has been put.

Such opportunism is also demonstrated by the highly diverse modes of life to which mammals had adapted as long ago as the Eocene. Already by that time forms readily identifiable as the ancestors of nearly all the present orders were flourishing. The extent of adaptive radiation in our class is illustrated by Figure 5–6. Fos-

FIGURE 5-6. Adaptive Radiation among the Mammals. The Vastly Different Shapes of the Mammals in These Photographs Show How Natural Selection Has Caused Them To Evolve To Fit Many Different Ways of Life. (Photos: Above, The Bettmann Archive, Inc.; Below, Zoological Society of London; Upper Right, Courtesy of Marineland of the Pacific; and Lower Right, Mark Boulton from National Audubon Society)

sils of the orders Cetacea and Sirenia show that both whales and sea cows had returned to a purely aquatic existence, adapting, however, in profoundly different ways. The earliest Sirenians show striking similarities to the ancestors of elephants, but the Cetaceans have been very distinct from all other forms of mammals for as far back as the fossil record takes us.

Fossils of the orders Chiroptera and Dermopteria show that both bats and the so-called flying lemur had taken to the air. The latter simply glides by means of stretching out a membrane between the forelimb and hind limb, as a flying squirrel does. Bats, however, support their membranous wings by stretching out enormously elongated fingers. Their existence demonstrates the division of labor in ecological communities. Most birds fly by day, guided by their excellent vision. Many of them catch insects on the wing by the speed and precision of their flight. Bats, on the other hand, emerge to patrol the air as the birds retire at nightfall. They are guided by means of built-in sonar equipment. Emitting a series of noises so high-pitched that we cannot hear them, they catch the echoes and know precisely where obstructions or insects are to be found. Competition between birds and bats is minimized and each functions to stabilize the balance of nature.

The rest of the Eutherians continued to run around on all four legs for a long time but found many ways to make a living even before the Eocene began. From the fossil evidence, we can readily infer that they all depended a great deal upon the sense of smell in their interpretation of the nature of the world around them, but differences in anatomical detail became well established by the Eocene. The order of Lagomorphs (which includes rabbits) and the order of Rodents (which includes squirrels, rats, beavers, porcupines, guinea pigs and others) both evolved large incisors which enable them to gnaw through hard substances. As time has passed rodents have become more and more numerous and diversified. This order is among the few which have never evolved very large forms, even though some of them live in cold areas. Most of them mature rapidly and give birth to large litters quite frequently. Because many rodents live in colonies, contagions are readily spread among them, and large-scale fluctuations in population are common. Most of them are exclusively and all of them are largely vegetarian in diet, consuming bark and roots as readily as leaves.

In contrast to these successful orders, the Edentates, which have always been restricted to America, have poorly developed teeth or no teeth at all. This order includes such improbable creatures as the sloth, the anteater, and the armadillo, all of which are closely adapted to very narrow ecological niches.

The Proboscidea is another order which dates back to the Eocene. Today elephants alone represent this group, but in earlier times there were many five-toed herbivorous mammals of closely related orders. Some of them, in fact, became almost as large as elephants, but most of them died out as other herbivores began to flourish. In many regions the order of Perissodactyls succeeded them as the chief large herbivores. This order, which now includes only the three families of horses, tapirs, and rhinoceroses, produced some three-toed genera of elephantine proportions in quite early times. A great area of the world was forested in those days, and apparently the herbivorous mammals were browsers rather than grazers. A very common speculation to account for their extinction is that their teeth and feet proved to be inadequate (Lull, 1945). The problem of grinding up enough forage to supply the caloric and dietary needs of a mammal weighing several tons is formidable. The ancestors of horses themselves remained small, three-toed forest dwellers for a long time, but, by the Miocene, grasslands began to spread at the expense of forests. Modern horses are descended from those creatures which ventured out into these prairies, to which they adapted by developing more deeply rooted teeth for grazing, by losing all but one toe on each foot, and by becoming much larger.

The even-toed herbivores, classified as the order of Artiodactyls, also existed as early as the Eocene. The earliest fossils are of creatures rather like pigs, which of course do not restrict their diet to vegetation, but ancestral camels are almost as early. Like the rodents, this order has continued to flourish and diversify since early times, and most of the living herbivorous mammals such as deer, cattle, goats, and many others belong to it. Many of them have adapted to grazing instead of, or as well as, to browsing by the evolution of special digestive arrangements. We all have microorganisms in our digestive tract, some of which may assist in digestion. The ruminants have exploited this fact, having what amounts to an extra stomach in which these tiny guests produce enzymes which break up cellulose and produce organic acids. This symbiotic arrangement has proved most profitable for the ruminants and no doubt for the microorganisms as well.

The fact that the earliest Eutherians preyed upon insects and other very small creatures might lead one to expect that predation upon large mammals would have begun as soon as they had evolved. This indeed occurred. Fossils of the order of Carnivores are found even in Paleocene strata, and some were as large as bears. Like their prey, they had small brains by modern mammalian standards, and most of them became extinct very long ago. Modern carnivores are probably all descended from rather doglike creatures, of which the earliest fossils date from the Eocene. Before that period had ended, the catlike sabertooths had also differentiated from within the order. Their very much enlarged upper canines were useful in attacking thickskinned herbivores. When, as eventually happened, the sabertooth's prey became extinct, he vanished to be replaced by other cats with smaller canines but bigger brains. In fact, the history of the ecological relationships between mammalian carnivores and herbivores is a constant repetition of speed and shrewdness replacing size and strength. Some of the species in the order of Carnivores found other ways of making a living besides preying upon their mammalian cousins. Hyenas are scavengers. Bears have become largely and pandas entirely noncarnivorous. Seals returned to the ocean where they were well established by the Miocene but have remained predacious.

The order of Insectivores was clearly the ancestral stock from which the other Eutherians diverged, yet it has continued to exist. Its ecological zone may seem a lowly one, but apparently it is secure. There are always plenty of bugs, grubs, and other forms of small life available as food, and some families of insectivores have persisted since before the Eocene. Shrews, moles, and hedgehogs are among the commoner varieties alive today. Almost indistinguishable from the fossils of Paleocene insectivores are those of the Paleocene primates. Even at present taxonomists disagree on the question of classifying the tree shrew *Tupaia*. Some claim that this alert little beast is the primate most similar to insectivores, while others affirm that it is the insectivore most similar to primates. This disagreement demonstrates how closely allied our own order is to the insectivores and how many of the basic mammalian characteristics we and our closest cousins retain. Other orders took to the air or the ocean, to predation or grazing or browsing or eating ants to the exclusion of other means of livelihood. Many of them did well for a long time, often millions of years. Many of them still do well. But our ancestors, in the comparative safety of the trees, began to observe the world around them with growing inquisitiveness.

Sources and Suggested Readings

BROOM, R.
   1932   *The Mammal-like Reptiles of South Africa and the Origin of the Mammals.* Witherby, London.

COLBERT, E. H.
   1958   Morphology and Behavior, in *Behavior and Evolution*, edited by A. Roe and G. G. Simpson. Yale University Press, New Haven.

GREGORY, W. K.
1929   *Our Face from Fish to Man.* Putnam, New York.

LORENZ, K.
1966   *On Aggression.* Harcourt, Brace & World, New York.

LULL, R. S.
1945   *Organic Evolution,* revised edition. Macmillan, New York.

MONTAGNA, W.
1962   *The Structure and Function of Skin,* 2nd edition. Academic Press, New York.

MOODY, P. A.
1962   *Introduction to Evolution,* 2nd edition. Harper and Bros., New York.

MOWAT, F.
1963   *Never Cry Wolf.* Atlantic Monthly Press, Boston.

REED, C. A.
1960   Polyphyletic or Monophyletic Ancestry of Mammals, or: What Is a Class? *Evolution,* **14,** 314–322.

ROMER, A. S.
1955   *The Vertebrate Body,* 2nd edition. Saunders, Philadelphia.
1968   *The Procession of Life.* World Publishing, Cleveland.

SIMPSON, G. G.
1944   *Tempo and Mode in Evolution.* Columbia University Press, New York.
1945   The Principles of Classification and a Classification of the Mammals. *Bulletin of the American Museum of Natural History,* **85.**
1953   *The Major Features of Evolution.* Columbia University Press, New York.
1959   Mesozoic Mammals and the Polyphyletic Origins of Mammals. *Evolution,* **13,** 405–414.

YOUNG, J. Z.
1950   *The Life of Vertebrates.* Clarendon Press, Oxford.
1957   *The Life of Mammals.* Clarendon Press, Oxford.

CHAPTER 6

The Primate Pattern

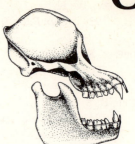

ADAPTING TO ARBOREAL LIFE

If you really want to live in the trees, there are certain requirements which you must meet, but it will also give you some interesting opportunities. We human beings meet so many of the requirements that our kinship with tree-dwelling animals is obvious. Our early ancestors, during the long period shown in Figure 6–1, took full advantage of the opportunities of arboreal life. Anatomically, physiologically, and in social behavior we carry with us the marks of a continuous process of selection which persisted through at least several million generations of arboreal existence. Adaptations for efficient operation in this ecological zone are responsible for many of man's abilities and disabilities. This set of adaptations may be considered the primate pattern. Of course, many other animals live in trees too, and primates share certain characteristics with them. But it was the good fortune of our ancestors to make the sorts of adaptations which later proved to have been most adequate as a basis for evolutionary developments in the direction of generalized rather than specialized ability.

Nesting in a tree, as many birds do, is not the same thing as living in the trees. Climbing into a tree, as raccoons, cats, and other essentially terrestrial mammals do, is not the same thing either. Some creatures such as sloths and koalas actually do live in

122

the trees all the time, but they have not seized upon the opportunities offered by this form of life. Evolution does not necessarily mean "progress." The ways in which a species solves the problems it faces depend in part upon its existing characteristics, in part upon environment, and in part upon chance. The primates certainly profited from the experiences of arboreal existence more than their arboreal neighbors, and some primates profited more than others. Birds, for instance, face the overriding necessity of adapting for flight: their forelimbs cannot be efficient grasping organs. Some birds do not fly, but none of these nest in trees. Mammals which spend all their time in the trees need efficient flexible grasping organs such as those of sloths, koalas, and primates. Furthermore, they are light in build, as are all creatures which go out on the branches of trees. They have to be if the branches are to support their weight.

The grasping organs required for climbing about in trees are varied. Long sharp claws, like those of a leopard, will do very well. Sucker-disc pads on fingers and toes are excellent if a creature weighs only a few ounces or less. Lizards and tarsiers find these pads most useful. Long, flexible digits, of which at least

ERA	EPOCH	FOSSIL
CENOZOIC	PLEISTOCENE	HOMO
	PLIOCENE	AUSTRALOPITHECUS OREOPITHECUS RAMAPITHECUS
	MIOCENE	RAMAPITHECUS DRYOPITHECUS "PROCONSUL"
	OLIGOCENE	AEGYPTOPITHECUS
	EOCENE	AMPHIPITHECUS TETONIUS
	PALEOCENE	TARSIOIDS AND LEMUROIDS
MESOZOIC	CRETACEOUS	INSECTIVORES AND MARSUPIALS

(Scale: 1 inch = 28,000,000 years)

FIGURE 6-1. Chart of Geological Time II: The Last Hundred Million Years

one may be separated from the others so that it will reach around the branch, are best of all. If the digits' surfaces are roughened as, for example, by fingerprints and slightly moistened by perspiration, then the grasp is firmer than ever. With true fingers such as these, claws are unnecessary. Claws may even get in the way: sloths and koalas, both of which have claws, rarely hurry from place to place. On the other hand, primates are much more active, and one of the few almost unique things about them is the possession of flattened nails rather than claws. The tree shrew, which is on the borderline between the Primate and the Insectivore orders, lacks flattened nails, and some primates have claws on one or more digits and nails on the rest. But in general, fingernails and toenails are typical of the primates as an order. The differences between claws and fingernails, as distinguished by Le Gros Clark (1936), are shown in Figure 6–2.

Small size and light weight are also typical of primates. All of the early Eutherian mammals were small, but as we pointed out in Chapter Five, there has been a trend to increase in size in many orders since the extinction of the giant reptile species. The necessities of arboreal life have held this trend in check among the primates: those species which have descended from the trees, such as baboons, gorillas, and men, are much heavier than most of their arboreal cousins. Some adult orang-utans weigh over 200 pounds, but they are cautious climbers. Skeletal examinations show that more than one-third of them suffer limb fractures during their youth (Schultz, 1939). Chimpanzees, which grow to be nearly as heavy, spend most of their adult lives on the ground, despite their acrobatic ability. It is interesting that the life spans of primates seem to be longer than those of other mammals of equal size. We need more information on this subject, but available evidence indicates that some of the smaller primates live for as long as twenty years, while baboons and the larger apes live as long as horses; and our life span rivals or even surpasses that of the elephant.

An animal which lives in a tree rather than simply visiting it must find his food there as well as a place to perch, hide, or lie in wait. If the animal lacks sharp claws, its ability as a predator may be reduced. Some primates, especially very small ones, are insect eaters, and most species are perfectly willing to eat meat should the opportunity arise. Their digestive systems are quite capable of

FIGURE 6-2. Claws and Fingernails. Note that the Claw Has a Deep Layer of Horny Substance which the Nail Lacks and that the Claw Has a Much More Curved Surface than the Nail.

CLAW OF TYPICAL MAMMAL

Lateral Cross Section   View from End

NAIL OF TYPICAL PRIMATE

Lateral Cross Section   View from End

dealing with a high protein diet. When making their own living, however, most primates rarely find such opportunities, and their diet is overwhelmingly vegetarian. (It is interesting to note that our species and the few other anthropoid species which have been tested lack the ability to synthesize ascorbic acid, or vitamin C. Almost all other animals are able to do this, but it appears (Stone, 1965) that we lack the gene which controls the final step required to manufacture this vital substance.) In other environments they would suffer from scurvy and die. Creatures living where there is a constant supply of fresh vegetation do not suffer from this condition, for they can obtain the small amounts of ascorbic acid which they need from their food. Fruits, nuts, and leaves offer no resistance: they can be plucked by hand. Whether vegetarian or not, primates grasp their food by hand, not with their jaws. Hands with flexible digits are all-purpose tools. As we all know, however, fingers lose much of their flexibility when they are chilled. Nor are many fruits, nuts, leaves, or insects to be found during a cold winter. A few primates other than man, such as the Japanese macaque, live where they encounter snow, but only a few. The primates' ecological zone is largely restricted to the warmer parts of the world.

The earliest tetrapods not only had five digits but also broad shoulders. The clavicle, or collarbone, serves as a strut to keep the forelimbs firmly separated, each on its own side of the body. Many land-dwelling mammals have little use for such a strut; it is more efficient for them to have the forelimbs beneath the body. For arboreal life, the more conservative arrangement is better, and primates, like frogs and iguanas, retain a well-developed, functional clavicle. The ability to rotate the forearm so that the hand can be turned in or out, up or down, is another characteristic most useful for arboreal life. A creature must reach the branches of a tree, no matter where they are, before it can grasp them. Primates are among the few mammals so constructed that they can do this easily. In moving about among the branches, the long axis of the body may be horizontal, diagonal, or even perpendicular with unpredictable frequency. In actual climbing it cannot be horizontal. Among primates, consequently, semierect or even completely erect posture is quite frequent, and bipedalism is not at all uncommon. This in itself is nothing new. Many dinosaurs were bipedal, as are birds; kangaroos often are, and many other mammals will stand on their hind legs with adequate motivation (Snyder, 1967). The greater number of primate species, however, are able to stretch their legs out to an extent not usually found in other animals, since being in a vertical position is so frequently necessary for them.

It is always convenient to be able to see where one is going, but most mammals depend upon their sense of smell as a directional guide to a great extent. Aromas, which are abundant just above the surface of the ground, can convey as much information at midnight as at noon. But vision requires light, and the ability to distinguish different colors requires a lot of light. Many terrestrial mammals are active at night rather than during the day and find their way about quite readily.

Life in the trees is a different proposition. Accurate judgment of the precise distance and position of various branches may be a matter of life or death to a creature moving about, and split-second timing may be vital if one is in a hurry or if one's target is swaying. Primates depend far more upon their eyes than upon their noses, and the greater number of them confine their activities to the daylight hours, or to dawn and dusk. Most of them have rather large eyes. Even the tree shrew has larger eyes than other shrews, while the tarsier's eyes are enormous. One species of tree shrew and all other primates have a ring of bone completely circling the exterior side of the eyeball. This is the postorbital bar. Furthermore, the reduction of dependence upon the olfactory sense permits an equal reduction of the size of the snout. This, in turn, permits the eyes to be set closer together so that they tend to face forward instead of laterally, as do those of a fish or a horse.

The improved optical equipment of the primates would be of little benefit if it were not accompanied by an enlarged visual cortex, that section of the neopallium concerned with the sense of sight. This area of the surface of the brain has expanded among all primates, and the areas devoted to the sense of smell have diminished in size. The visual centers of all vertebrates are located in the occipital lobe at the rear, the olfactory centers in front. The shape of the primate brain reflects this fact, and so does the shape of the skull which encloses the brain. The spinal cord emerges from underneath the brain, and the foramen magnum is located below the skull, rather than at the rear. The entire skull is to some degree bent down in front as a result of this. This is a great convenience for animals apt to assume a vertical posture. The shift in the position of the foramen magnum is greater among monkeys than among lemurs and reaches its extreme only among human beings.

The hairless, clawless fingers and toes of primates are useful not only for grasping but also for feeling, for they are highly sensitive to touch. The areas of the cerebrum concerned with these sensations are enlarged, just as are those concerned with vision. So-called association areas on the surface of the brain, where messages from the eyes and from the fingertips can be coordinated and integrated, are expanded as well. In circumstances which cause a rat to sniff and feel with its moist muzzle, a primate is likely to respond by staring intently, feeling with its fingertips, and perhaps picking up an object for even more careful inspection. The shortening of the snout which is typical of primates appears to be connected with this sort of behavior, as well as with hand-feeding; primates are so constructed that they can learn more about their surroundings by a combined use of the hand and the eyes than by any other means. Some scholars have maintained that this standard primate technique of investigation is primarily responsible for the eventual development of the human mentality (Jones, 1916). At any rate, it would seem that the sorts of sensory information which nonhuman primates can appreciate resemble those which are available to us, rather than those available to a dog or a rat.

Bats, bears, and primates share a genital peculiarity. In all these groups the male has a pendulous penis. Elephants, sea cows, and most primates share another: the female has only two breasts and they are located near the forelimbs. Babies must be carried as well as fed, and, even though they cling tightly, an encircling arm is good insurance against falling out of a tree. In most species of primates babies are physically dependent for a relatively long time and emotionally dependent for even longer. No primates produce litters, although a few species habitually have twins. One baby at a time keeps the mother well occupied but also permits more individual attention. Until very recently, it was thought that most, if not all, primates resemble us in lacking a breeding season. Further study is beginning to show that this is not so. Mating habits apparently vary in response to circumstances as well as in accordance with species, so that observations made in zoos or laboratories cannot be taken to represent the way primates act when free. Even at times when sexual interest is not aroused, however, primates are likely to pay a good deal of attention to one another. Mutual grooming is frequent among most species. It has been suggested (Marett, 1936) that salt, a biochemical necessity rarely found in tropical jungles, is exchanged in this way among the different members of the group. At any rate, mutual grooming certainly adds to the degree of social cohesion and thus has survival value.

During the phase of adaptive radiation early in the evolution of the primates, a good many varieties found ecological niches from which they did not budge. Most of these varieties became extinct long ago due to changes in circumstances which made their ways of life no longer profitable. Some are still extant in various tropical parts of the Old World. These creatures are commonly lumped together under the label of Prosimians because their evolution has never reached the grade represented by monkeys (see Figure 6–3).

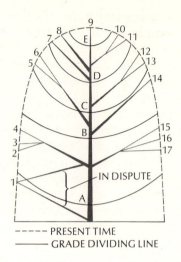

FIGURE 6-3. Approximation of the Family Tree of Primates. A. Prosimian. B. Haplorrhine. C. Monkey. D. Ape. E. Man. 1. Tree Shrew. 2. Aye-Aye. 3. Indris. 4. Lemur. 5. Hapalidae. 6. Cebidae. 7. Gibbon. 8. Orang-Utan. 9. Homo Sapiens. 10. Gorilla. 11. Chimpanzee. 12. Cercopithicinae. 13. Semnopithicinae. 14. Tarsier. 15. Loris. 16. Potto. 17. Galago.

PROSIMIANS

Since this grade or suborder of primates is quite diverse, taxonomists disagree about just how to classify them. Each major grouping of the Prosimii has remained conservative in its own way, but each also has its own peculiar specializations. Tree shrews, for instance, are scarcely primates at all. These little animals of Southeast Asia have reduced olfactory lobes in their brains, despite their long narrow snouts and moist muzzles with tactile bristles on either side. Their eyes and the visual centers of their brains are enlarged, but only one species has a postorbital bar defining the orbit. Their digits resemble those of primates save for the fact that they lack flattened nails, but their limbs are relatively short. Whether classified as primates as by Simpson (1945) or as insectivores as by Osman Hill (1953), they form a link between these two orders.

Lorisiformes, Lemuriformes, and Tarsiiformes are universally accepted as primates. The first of these groups contains two families, the Lorisdae and the Galagidae. The slow loris and the slender loris live in tropical Asia, while the potto and the angwantibo live in the rain forests of West Africa. These nocturnal creatures are the least sociable of all primates. Although exclusively arboreal, they are very deliberate climbers with an exceedingly tight grip (Grand, 1967). Their index fingers are short and can be opposed with the thumb to the other digits. The corresponding toe, also short, bears a sharp claw instead of a toenail. They have large eyes which lie close together, since the narrow snout projects below rather than between them. They are primarily insect eaters. The carotid artery supplying blood for the brain follows a direct route, as with monkeys, apes, and men, rather than an indirect one, as in lemurs and many other mammals, but there is no evidence that this more efficient arrangement has improved their mental abilities. An infant potto is shown in Figure 6-4.

Galagos or bush babies form the other Lorisiform family. These little creatures are distributed throughout the forests of Africa, where they occupy the same ecological niche held by tarsiers in the East Indies. Ordinarily, they move by leaping, sometimes for astonishing distances, plucking their prey out of the air with their hands. They can do this because their feet have been considerably lengthened in the tarsal region—a good example of the way in which selection produces parallel adaptations when related animals

FIGURE 6-4. A Baby Potto (Photo: Photo Department, Oregon Regional Primate Research Center)

are faced with similar situations. Although the loris and the potto both have very short tails, the galago has a long bushy one. So far as we know, all Lorisiformes have one or two breeding seasons each year (Hill, 1953), and none are capable of any facial expression more complicated than a snarl. Like Lemuriformes and most mammals, they have moist muzzles, and their upper lips are cleft, with stiff tactile hairs on both sides of the snout.

The Lemuriformes are much more varied in appearance and activity than the Lorisiformes but much more restricted in habitat. Although they lived in Europe and North America during the Eocene, all the living species are confined to Madagascar. This large island has been isolated for so long that only a few carnivores ever established themselves there, and there are no monkeys to compete with the Lemuriformes at all. Some species are no larger than mice, but others grow to the size of a big dog. A recently extinct form, *Megaladapis*, was as big as a donkey. Some are strictly nocturnal; others are active only during the day; while still others may wake or sleep at any time. None, however, appear capable of distinguishing colors, and few have eyes as large as those of the Lorisiformes. Some are strictly arboreal, but one species lives on the ground in rocky areas, much as the baboon does in Africa. A few are solitary creatures, but most live in social groups of up to twenty or more individuals. Although they generally move about on all fours, they are not averse to running on their hind legs, thus freeing their hands for other purposes, such as grabbing and scratching. Some species, especially the smaller ones, are almost entirely insectivorous. The Indris family seems to be exclusively vegetarian, depending especially on leaves and buds; still other families are omnivorous. It would seem that Lemuriformes, like Lorisiformes, have one or two breeding seasons a year, although males bored by captivity may become sexually excited at any time. Like people and platyrrhine monkeys, Lemuriformes have legs which are longer than their arms.

Of the three families of living Lemuriformes, the Daubentoniidae, or aye-aye, is the most aberrant. It was thought to be a squirrel when first discovered because its most obvious specialization is a rodentlike emphasis on the central incisors, but unlike rodents, it has enlarged lower rather than upper incisors. These teeth are adapted for gnawing through the bark of trees, for the chief items of the aye-aye's diet are wood-boring grubs. The creatures lack canines and lower premolars, so there is a wide space, or diastema, between the enormous incisors in front and the small molars to the rear. Only their great toe has a flattened nail; the other digits have claws. The third and fourth fingers are exceptionally long and the third is attenuated as well. The alleged use of this finger is to skewer such grubs as the aye-aye reaches by gnawing (Hill, 1953).

The other two families of Lemuriformes, the Lemuridae and the Indriidae, have less exotic ways of life, but their dental arrangements are odd enough. Their lower incisors and lower canines protrude almost horizontally, and the canine itself is flattened into the shape of an incisor. These teeth form a dental comb which the animals use most assiduously to comb their fur. All the species in the family Lemuridae have three premolars, of which the first in the lower jaw is enlarged to substitute for the canine. Living species of Indriidae have only two premolars. They have also lost a lower incisor and their upper incisors are somewhat enlarged. Some species in this family have rather globular skulls and reduced snouts, and the species *Indris indris* has a very short tail. Another species of Indris, the sifaka, is shown in Figure 6–5. None of the Lemuriformes have very large brains, nor do any of them display the signs of intellectual activity characteristic of most monkeys. This may be related to their method of using their hands.

In studying the evolution of the use of the hand, Bishop (1962) notes that Lemuriformes reach for food or a branch with the digits extended and parallel, so that the fingertips will touch it first. Lorisiformes, in contrast, spread their fingers widely, and touch what they are reaching for with their palms before encircling it with their fingers. Neither group appears to have separate control over individual digits. Their grasping ability is great, but their manipulative ability is meager.

Nor, except when bored by captivity, do they show any interest in playing with inanimate objects: rather, their attention is directed to other members of their troop. In an interesting field study of lemur behavior the same author (Jolly, 1966) notes the high degree of social interaction among these creatures and their ability to adjust their behavior suitably in dealing with those of different status or temperament. She concludes that their "social intelligence is comparable to that of monkeys, although their under-

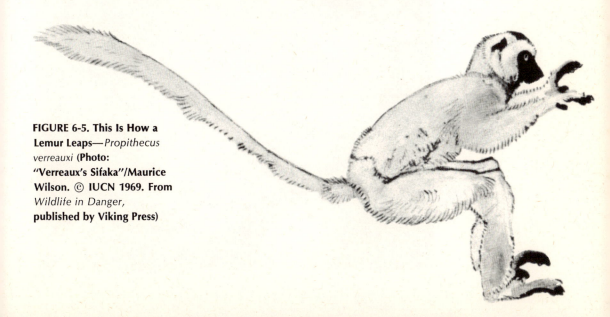

FIGURE 6-5. This Is How a
Lemur Leaps—*Propithecus
verreauxi* (Photo:
"Verreaux's Sifaka"/Maurice
Wilson. © IUCN 1969. From
Wildlife in Danger,
published by Viking Press)

standing of objects lags far behind." The troops which she studied defended their home territories and reacted to contact with their neighbors quite aggressively, and the males appeared to be far more status-conscious than the females. Family resemblances in appearance within each troop suggest a minimum of mating between different troops. A lemur of a different species lived with one of the troops: its presence was tolerated, but no female permitted any sexual advances.

The tarsier's eyes are bigger than its stomach, as you might guess from viewing Figure 6–6. Indeed, their combined volume is greater than its brain's, even though the brain of this three-ounce creature is by no means small in proportion to its body size (see Figure 6–7). The tarsal bones of the foot are about as long as the humerus of the upper arm, a characteristic which has given the tarsier its name. Although these proportions may seem exaggerated to us, they are functional in this animal's ecological niche. Like the galago, the tarsier makes its living by jumping for and catching insects; and there is always an ample supply on hand in the East Indies where it lives, especially at dawn and dusk when the light is dim. The tarsier's enormous eyes make its vision especially keen

FIGURE 6-6. An Adult Tarsier. Note the Length of His Tarsal Bones, from which He Gets His Name. (Photo: Photo Department, Oregon Regional Primate Research Center)

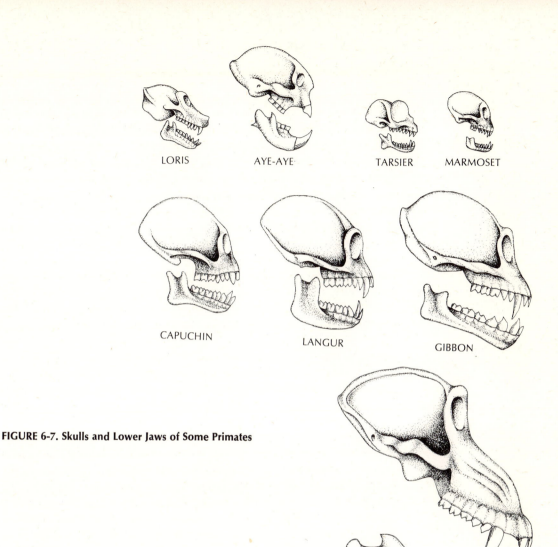

FIGURE 6-7. Skulls and Lower Jaws of Some Primates

LORIS   AYE-AYE   TARSIER   MARMOSET

CAPUCHIN   LANGUR   GIBBON

MANDRILL

at such times, but they are unsuitable for daytime activity. Like the other Prosimii, the tarsier lacks color vision. Unlike other Prosimii, the tarsier's eyes are set in complete bony sockets, and they lie so close together that the nose is reduced to a little up-turned nubbin below them. Their eye-moving muscles are vestigial, so they do not move the eyeballs in their sockets, even to focus on an object. In compensation, they can swivel their heads about in either direction until they look directly behind them. They look so much like little furry people that this gives them a somewhat uncanny appearance. Their arms are much shorter than their legs; their rumps are very well developed; their faces are rather flat

LEMUR

TARSIER

CEBOID

CATARRHINE

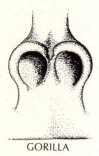

GORILLA

FIGURE 6-8. Some Primate Noses

with a protruding nose; and their heads are rather globular in shape. Some scholars (Jones, 1916) have thought of tarsiers as our closest cousins, but they were jumping to conclusions as far, but not as accurately, as the tarsier jumps for a moth.

A closer look shows that their resemblance to us is as superficial as their resemblance to galagos. Like other prosimians, they have claws on some of their toes, and their ears are large, somewhat pointed, and very flexible. Tarsiers lack extensive convolutions on the surface of the brain, are highly specialized for a narrow range of activities, and lap or lick in drinking. The female's uterus is divided like that of the female lemur or loris. Yet they produce only one baby at a time, have placentas resembling those of humans, and have a menstrual cycle just as female monkeys, apes, and humans do. Unlike other prosimians, they have true noses, not moist muzzles, and their upper lips are free and mobile, not cleft. The tarsier's olfactory lobe is much reduced, and its behavior suggests much greater dependence upon eyes and fingertips than upon the nose. Tarsiers are intermediate between the other Prosimii and the Anthropoidea in much the same way that tree shrews are intermediate between Primates and Insectivora. They are one of the many links which are not missing in the evolutionary chain. The controversies which tarsiers cause among taxonomists demonstrate that evolutionary forces do not produce convenient pigeonholes in which to insert the varied forms of life. Simpson (1945) is quite correct in describing tarsiers as prosimian, for they lack many of the characteristics which unite monkeys, apes and men. Osman Hill (1953) is also quite correct in describing them as haplorhine, for their noses and lips resemble ours rather than those of the other prosimians, as Figure 6–8 shows. Whether grouped by themselves, with the Anthropoidea, or with the Prosimii, they are the only living representatives of the Tarsiiformes.

During the Eocene, however, there were many genera of such creatures both in Europe and in North America. The fossilized tarsal bones which have been found force us to infer that some of these little animals had already adopted the bouncing mode of movement which is typical of tarsiers today. The oldest known primate endocranial cast is that of a Tarsioid, *Tetonius*, who lived in Wyoming about 55 million years ago. The olfactory lobes are less reduced in size than in any living primate, yet the temporal and occipital lobes of the brain are relatively enlarged. From this we can infer that vision had already become of primary importance in our order; and that the association areas, in which messages from the various sense organs are integrated, had begun to expand. It is a highly plausible speculation, therefore, that the mental abilities which set primates apart from other mammals date back to the Eocene (Radinsky, 1967).

ANTHROPOIDS

None of the prosimians have exploited the possibilities of arboreal life as fully as the anthropoids have. This group of primates, which includes monkeys, apes, and men, may properly be considered as both a suborder and a grade. The term grade is frequently used to indicate a level of organization, without necessarily implying a single origin for the entire stock concerned. It seems appropriate in this case, for the available evidence leads to a strong inference that the evolution of monkeys took place twice. Just as tarsiers and galagos evolved parallel adaptations for a specialized way of life, the ancestors of the anthropoids evolved parallel adaptations of a more generally advantageous nature both in the Old and in the New World. Environmental circumstances in the tropical areas of both these land masses were and are quite similar, so the selective pressure upon their prosimian inhabitants led, in both cases, to amazingly similar basic improvements in bodily organization and operation. The monkeys on both sides of the Atlantic resemble one another in their general mode of life and in their methods of dealing with environmental stresses and opportunities. The differences in structural detail which distinguish the monkeys of America from the Old World anthropoids do not interfere with these basic improvements and can best be explained as signs of the separate origin of the two lines of descent.

During the Cenozoic, the weather slowly grew colder throughout the temperate and arctic regions of the world. The migration route between America and Asia via the region where the Bering Strait now exists ceased to be available for creatures adapted to a continuously warm, well-wooded habitat. Fossil evidence does not permit us to infer that anthropoids had evolved before these colder conditions had come into existence. We are therefore forced to conclude that only parallel evolution is able to explain the existence of monkeys in both the Old World and the New.

Anthropoids are characterized by: the possession of nails rather than claws on all digits; stereoscopic vision and the ability to distinguish colors; well-developed manipulative ability; cerebral expansion to the rear, covering the cerebellum completely; increased convolution of the cerebral cortex or neopallium; facial muscles which permit a variety of expressions; tongues unsuitable for lapping; and a high degree of dependence upon social learning as a substitute for innate reflexes. All of these characteristics may be regarded as refinements of traits found among some or most prosimians. When found in combination, however, they produce a type of animal which is capable of a much greater range of activities than any prosimian and which, as the name anthropoid implies, is manlike.

The integration in the brain between the tactile sensations from the fingertips and the visual sensations from the eyes permits more precise discriminations, and the behavior of monkeys indicates that they do make such discriminations. We can picture the appearance of what is felt but not seen and imagine the texture of what is seen but not touched. The similarities between the neural anatomy of apes and monkeys and the neural antomy of men suggest that the former may also have these abilities. Stereoscopic and color vision permit more refined discrimination, too; creatures possessing either of these basic improvements can respond to cues of which other creatures are unaware. Animals like man and other anthropoids possessing both are capable of an enormously extended range of adequate responses. These abilities are so important to the adaptation of ape, monkey, and man to their environment that it is necessary to describe briefly the anthropoid visual equipment.

The eyeball is nearly spherical with an interior lined by the retina as by a film. As an outgrowth of the brain, the retina is composed largely of nervous tissue, the cells of which are sensitive to light. Among anthropoids that part of the retina directly in line with the lens of the eye contains cone-shaped cells packed closely together. This area is the macula, or yellow spot. The concentration of cones and the absence of blood vessels or any other structures which might interfere provide very acute, sharply defined vision but require plenty of light. The rest of the retina contains both cone-shaped and rodlike cells, as well as nerve fibers and blood vessels. It is more easily stimulated, even by dim light, than the macula, but gives less precise images. Rods are equally sensitive to all wavelengths of light within the visual range, but cones have the added property of discriminating between different wavelengths and thus provide us with color vision. It is not strange that nocturnally active animals are apt to lack cone cells, for being able to see in very dim light is far more useful for them than the ability to tell red from green. Significantly, many animals which are active during daylight are also color blind. Of all the mammals the anthropoids have developed color vision to the highest degree.

The anthropoid's stereoscopic vision depends upon anatomical refinements of another nature. The nervous tracts connecting the retina to the visual areas of the cerebral cortex are composed of thousands of separate fibers. Nerves from the left side of the brain lead to organs on the right side of the body, while those from the right side of the brain reach the left side of the body. Impulses from the left ear reach the right side of the brain, the movements of the right eyelid are controlled from the left side of the brain, and so on. Among most vertebrates all the nervous fibers from the retina of either eye follow the same pattern, crossing over at a point known as the optic chiasma. Among some vertebrates, such as the cat, which has eyes that are not widely separated, some of the fibers from the retina of the left eye do not cross over but reach the left side of the brain, and vice versa. Among anthropoids all of the fibers from the left side of each eye reach the left side of the brain, while those from the right side of the same eye reach the right side of the brain, as is shown in Figure 6–9.

Visual images from each eye are recorded on each side of the cerebral cortex where they can be integrated with those from the other eye. Although an anthropoid's eyes look directly forward, each eye sees any object from a slightly different angle than does the other. It is easy to test this statement. Simply close one eye and hold a finger up a foot or so in front of your face, so that it hides some more distant object. Then close the other eye and open the one which was closed. Your finger will appear to have moved, although you know that you have held it still. We gain perspective and can judge distance by means of stereoscopic vision, and so do apes and monkeys. If our life depends upon perceiving that the branch we are jumping for is eleven feet away rather than ten feet away, this ability is very useful. The life of a monkey may depend upon such precise observation several hundred times a day.

MONKEYS

The continued life of any species of monkey depends upon what its members learn from one another. This fact, of which earlier scholars were unaware, has become clear as a result of many experiments and is confirmed by careful observation of these animals in the field. Learning from experience and modifying one's activities in consequence is typical of mammals, and the association between mammalian mothers and their offspring sets the stage for the development of social learning. Anthropoids have simply ex-

FIGURE 6-9. The Anthropoid Eye Contrasted with Eyes of Most Other Mammals. 1. Eyeballs. 2. Optic Chiasma. 3. Visual Centers of the Cerebrum. Note the Complete Crossing Over of Nerve Tracts from Eye to Brain in Most Mammals and the Incomplete Crossing Over in Anthropoids.

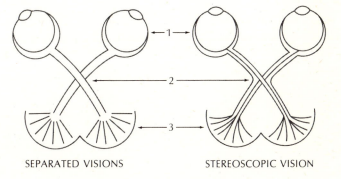

SEPARATED VISIONS   STEREOSCOPIC VISION

ploited the possibilities inherent in such associations to a greater degree than any other mammals. Almost none of them are solitary by preference, and they pay a great deal of attention to one another. Many activities which are of a reflex nature among most or all other mammals are under some degree of cortical control among anthropoids; when speaking of human beings, we would say under conscious control. Recent experiments show that even the techniques of mating behavior are learned rather than instinctive among monkeys. Harlow (1960) reports that he raised young monkeys in isolation from their elders, so that they never observed copulation. When they reached sexual maturity, they did not mate even though they showed all the signs of sexual tensions and even though males and females intermingled freely and engaged in mutual grooming. Indeed, females introduced to more sophisticated males defended their virtue most ferociously. It has also been observed that unless captive female apes have had the chance to observe the mother-child relationship, they do not know what to do with their newborn babies (Hooton, 1946).

Such behavior would, of course, result in the immediate extinction of any species unless its members lived in social groups where they had the opportunity to learn by means of personal observation or verbal instruction. People transmit information by means of language. The other anthropoids must depend upon direct perceptions. They must learn, among other things, how to get along with the other members of their society. Forms of social organization among the anthropoids are quite varied and only during the past decade have they been extensively studied and analyzed. Consequently, we are only now beginning to know very much about them, and it has been found that we know less than we thought we knew a few years ago. For instance, we used to think that monkeys and apes lacked breeding seasons and that continued sexual ac-

FIGURE 6-10A. The Brains of Primates, I. The Brain Is Viewed from One Side and Its Size Is Relative to the Length of the Creature from Crown to Rump.

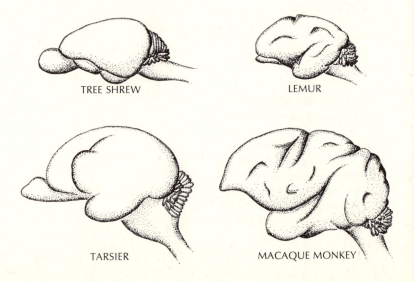

TREE SHREW

LEMUR

TARSIER

MACAQUE MONKEY

tivities served as an important bond in holding their societies together. Now it appears that most species of monkeys mate far more frequently at some seasons than at others and may show no interest in sex during the greater part of the year. Yet the gang sticks together. Its members are habituated to one another and rarely permit an outsider to join them.

Up to the present, available evidence indicates that one thing all young monkeys learn is that they will be able to boss some of their fellows but will have to be submissive to others. Sometimes a troop will be dominated by a single male, sometimes by a clique. Sometimes a young male whose mother ranks high will gain self-confidence because of this, and so he will be able to dominate his fellows from an early age (Imanishi, 1960; Sade, 1965). In any case, for creatures which depend upon learning, knowing how to behave in society implies a great deal of self-control and probably of self-awareness. The expansion of the cerebral cortex found among anthropoids appears to facilitate their social behavior, for they must be constantly alert to cues provided by interactions between the members of their group. Moreover, unlike lemurs, the monkey's ability to discriminate seems to extend to inanimate objects. Thus they can almost always solve mechanical problems far better than lemurs do, with the result that the psychologists who give lemurs such problems consider them much more stupid (Jolly, 1966).

Although it varies from species to species in size and proportion to body weight, the anthropoid cerebrum is much enlarged in comparison to that of any prosimian and is more globular in form (Osman Hill, 1955). The lateral views of primate brains in Figures 6–10A and B should be compared to those of some other vertebrates in Figure 4–6. Occipital, temporal, and frontal lobes have all expanded. As a rule the presence of convolutions further increases the surface area or cortex. Apparently, this cerebral

FIGURE 6-10B. The Brains of Primates, II. The Brain Is Viewed from One Side and Its Size Is Relative to the Length of the Creature from Crown to Rump.

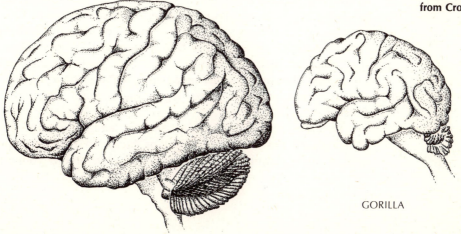

GORILLA

HOMO SAPIENS

cortex is especially concerned with those activities which are under conscious control among humans. The behavior of nonhuman anthropoids resembles ours enough to support the idea that the cortex serves a similar function among them. Psychological experiments of all sorts have been performed using these animals as subjects, and it is a general conclusion that their mental abilities transcend the requirements of their lives in the wild. This is quite possibly a misinterpretation. Psychologists may have neglected to consider the demands made upon their mentalities by the complexities of their social life. For instance, aggressive behavior is not required by anthropoids in obtaining food: bananas do not have to be pursued and subdued before they can be eaten. Just the right amount of aggressive behavior is required in social life, however. In some monkeys severing parts of the frontal lobe has led to a complete loss of aggressiveness and apparent indifference to the demands of society. It is doubtful if such creatures would survive long in the wild. We could certainly not expect that males with such inert dispositions would produce offspring or that similarly affected females would care effectively for any babies they bore.

The shape of the skull reflects to some extent the shape of the brain which it encloses, but the skull must also serve for the attachment of the muscles of the jaw and the neck. Since the foramen magnum is underneath the skull but close to the rear, neck muscles must be large and strong in order to hold the head in place and move it from side to side. The jaw muscles, as a rule, enclose most of the braincase and are disposed in a nearly vertical direction just behind the orbits. The bony plate behind the orbit which is characteristic of anthropoids protects the eyeballs from pressure which jaw muscles might exert. The face may be nearly flat or very projecting, but the muscles which permit facial expression are always well developed and in frequent use. The degree of lip mobility common to infant mammals and useful for nursing is retained in later life by anthropoids. This may be an example of neoteny, already described in Chapter Four. None of the anthropoids lap like dogs or cats in drinking, although they may lick their own hair when it is wet. In quite a few other ways the anthropoids retain youthful or even infantile characteristics, even after they have become sexually mature. One theory of human evolution holds that this process has made us what we are today and that the apes and monkeys have begun the process which we have finished.

Observations of anthropoid behavior lend support to the idea that neoteny has been an important factor in their evolution as well as ours. Inquisitiveness is a strong drive among young mammals, but it declines in importance among most of them as they get older. It tends to remain strong among anthropoids. Psychologists have found that rewarding this drive will often work as well with monkeys as rewarding hunger works with other creatures. A psychologist, finishing up his work for the day, found that one of his monkeys continued to peer at him through the window of her cage (Butler, 1954). He closed it; she opened it. He closed it again; she opened it again. He decided to see how soon she would become bored and kept closing the window when the monkey opened it. Several hours later, the psychologist's hunger drive overcame his inquisitive drive, and he admitted defeat by going home. The monkey had continued to open the window just as soon as he closed it during all that time. Her only reward was being able to see what was going on. Or was she testing the psychologist?

NEW WORLD MONKEYS

Although anthropoids throughout the world share many characteristics, those of the American tropics are distinctive in some ways. Their blood reacts much more faintly to antihuman serum than does that of any Old World monkey (Goodman, 1967). They are often called platyrrhines because many of them have nostrils which diverge instead of running parallel, as those of Old World monkeys, apes, and men do. Taxonomically, they constitute the superfamily Ceboidea. Members of this superfamily have three premolars on each side of the jaw, above and below, whereas the other anthropoids have two. None of the Ceboidea have protruding browridges or other extensive bony crests on their skulls; none have cheek pouches, and none have bared, calloused rumps. Many Old World apes and monkeys possess one or more of these traits. On the other hand, all New World monkeys have tails, usually long, and in some species prehensile. The thumb is not fully opposable to the fingers, although the great toe is easily opposed to the other toes. Spider monkeys have no thumbs, but the grasping ability of the tail makes up for this. These monkeys and a few others in South America have hairless areas on their tails with dermatoglyphics such as our fingers possess. Platyrrhines are typically (though not always) quite linear in build, and none are as large as baboons. They are all strictly arboreal, and, except for the owl monkey, none are nocturnal.

The superfamily Ceboidea contains two families: the marmosets, or Hapalidae, and the Cebidae. Marmosets are small and largely insectivorous. They differ from the Cebidae and indeed from the other primates in general in having only two molars instead of three on each side of the upper and lower jaws. Ordinarily they produce twins, and ordinarily they are found living as mated pairs. Their faces are sparsely haired at best, but most of them resemble lions and human beings in growing manes. Some marmosets have mustaches or beards and frequently long, silky, and often brightly colored body hair. Their tails are long but never prehensile. Marmosets' nails are much more clawlike than is common among other anthropoids (Thorndike, 1968). The earliest fossil ceboid yet discovered, dating from the Oligocene, was probably a marmoset, although larger than any of those alive today.

The Cebidae are more variable than Hapalidae but fit much better into the popular idea of what a monkey ought to be. Perhaps this is because one genus of this family, *Cebus*, often called the capuchin, is so often seen in zoos, while another, *Ateles*, the spider monkey (shown in Figure 4–7), has the most active prehensile tail of any animal. The spider monkey is a most attenuated creature and the only platyrrhine to employ brachiation to any extent in moving about. Most monkeys run along on top of a branch, using all four limbs, and leap from one branch to another. A brachiating creature hangs below a branch, moving hand over hand, and swings from one branch to another; at times, he may fling himself through the air for a considerable distance. Spider monkeys not only do this, but at times will hang by means of the tail alone, leaving all four hands available for other activities. In behavior both capuchins and spider monkeys are alert, restless, and apparently as capable of problem solution as any of the Old World monkeys.

FIGURE 6-11. A Group of Squirrel Monkeys (Photo: Joel Ito, Photo Department, Oregon Regional Primate Research Center)

Like most of the Cebidae, they live in bands or troops, each of which seems to have a definite range through which it wanders. Sometimes these troops have scores of members, as in the case of the squirrel monkey in Figure 6–11. The few field studies which have been made of Cebidae (Carpenter 1934, 1935, 1965; Mason,

1968; Moynihan, 1964) suggest that adult females outnumber adult males in such bands and that babies are likely to be born at any time of the year. Aggressive behavior within the group has rarely been observed, but hostility toward members of other groups is commonly expressed by screaming. They have a great range of vocalizations. We have found few fossil remains attributable to this family, none dated earlier than Miocene. Paleontologists who have studied the Eocene Prosimii of North America are not agreed that any type yet discovered is a probable ancestor, although *Omomys*, an extinct genus, is often mentioned as a likely candidate.

CATARRHINES

Fossil remains of anthropoids are much more abundant from Asia, Africa, and Europe, but the problem of which prosimian was their actual ancestor is still unsolved. Fragments of teeth and mandibles from as far apart as Spain and Burma may indicate that anthropoids were in existence before the end of the Eocene. During the Oligocene and Miocene, a variety of apes and monkeys lived in many parts of the Old World, and by the Pliocene some genera which still flourish had evolved. The fact that *Amphipithecus*, the Burman form, had three premolars may be taken to indicate either that the earliest anthropoids retained some aspects of the ancestral pattern of dentition or that this form was a prosimian. All Oligocene and later Old World anthropoids have two premolars, resembling the prosimian Indris in this respect as in a few others.

From Egypt, for example, come the jaws and teeth of *Propliopithecus* and the facial bones of *Oligopithecus* (Simons, 1959) which have completely closed orbits. *Parapithecus*, an Egyptian contemporary of which two species are known, one larger than the other, seems to be a monkey, whereas *Aegyptopithecus* is much more apelike (Simons, 1967). *Propliopithecus* is often thought of as the ancestor of gibbons, but it seems to have had a tail. The mandible of this animal was short and less protruding than that of any gibbon living today. None of these creatures had lower canines which were very projecting. All of them were smaller than their presumed modern descendants. The fossil record of the Miocene is much fuller than that of the Oligocene and provides data from which we can infer that the Catarrhines had already diversified. Such fossils as those of *Limnopithecus* in Africa and *Pliopithecus* in Europe have clear affinities to the gibbon line of descent. The humerus of each form has a straight slender shaft indicating gracile body built. The face and teeth of the latter show no essential differences from those of later gibbons. *Mesopithecus*, on the other hand, had bilophodont or monkeylike molar teeth with four sharply defined crests, unlike those of apes and men (Clark, 1959). Three distinct species of *Dryopithecus* lived in Kenya during the Miocene. Until recently they were given the generic name of "Proconsul," but it is now recognized that they are not a distinct genus at all (Simons and Pilbeam, 1965). One species of "Proconsul" was probably as least as big as most human beings. The characteristics of this "genus" are described in more detail in Chapter Eight, as are those of the later genera *Oreopithecus* and *Ramapithecus*, because of their particular significance to the problem of human ancestry.

We share with the apes and monkeys of the Old World so many and such diverse characteristics that there can be no question of our kinship to them rather than to the platyrrhines. Not only is our dental formula the same—two incisors, one canine, two premolars and three molars on each side of each jaw—but we have nasal passages which are parallel rather than diverging. We are all Catarrhines. Menstrual bleeding and a menstrual cycle of four to five weeks are common to female Catarrhines during the childbearing period of life. The biochemical properties of human blood resemble those of the other Catarrhines much more closely than they do those of the Ceboidea or Prosimii (Goodman, 1967). Typically, the thumb diverges from the fingers much more among Old World than among New World anthropoids. Many species use it in grasping, although some do not, and a few have quite useless or vestigial thumbs on their hands. Only among Old World anthropoids do we find any ground-dwelling or any giant forms, any varieties with protuberant noses such as we and the proboscis monkey display, any genera with cheek pouches or ischial callosities, or any with vestigial tails.

OLD WORLD MONKEYS

Taxonomists usually classify the Catarrhines into two superfamilies, the Cercopithecoidea and the Hominoidea. Monkeys comprise the first superfamily, while the second includes both apes and men. There are two natural groupings among the monkeys and two among the apes. Each of these may be regarded as a subfamily, but the human stock is ordinarily called a family. The major difference between the two subfamilies of monkeys relates to their feeding habits. Monkeys of the subfamily Cercopithicinae have a varied diet and store food in cheek pouches which open next to their lower molars. Monkeys of the subfamily Semnopithicinae subsist for the most part on leaves and shoots and have an extra lobe or pouch of the stomach. Their cheek pouches are either very small or altogether absent. Most, but not at all, of the leaf-eaters remain in the trees more of the time than the more omnivorous monkeys, some of which are almost as terrestrial as we are.

Of those characteristics common to both groups, the ischial callosity, a hairless, calloused patch on the rump, is the most obvious. Among the adult males of some species, such as mandrills, the ischial callosities are brightly colored, while among many species the rump is habitually presented as a symbol of submission to any passing monkey of higher status. Among females the skin surrounding the genitals becomes engorged with blood and swells out during the period when they are most fertile. Males are bigger than females, most especially among the larger monkeys and among those species which are primarily ground-dwelling, like the baboons. Other signs of sexual dimorphism are quite common, such as large canine teeth, especially long or brightly colored hair, manes, and beards, among other items. Arms and legs are usually about equal in length, and it is habitual for catarrhine monkeys to walk by placing the soles and palms flat on the ground, as is shown in Figure 6–12. Except in a few species, all four thumbs are well developed and used with facility in grasping.

There may be less than a dozen or more than one hundred animals in a social group. Local circumstances rather than species of monkey determine the number. Washburn and Devore (1961) have observed that most play among baboons is interpersonal rather than with objects, and observers of other species of monkeys note the same thing. Most communication results from visual cues among those species (such as baboons, macaques, and patas monkeys) which spend much of their time on the ground in the open. Among the more arboreal species a great variety of calls function to maintain group cohesion. Jungle-dwelling monkeys are notoriously noisy (Schultz, 1961).

After weaning, a young monkey must find his own food. Food is never shared. The mother may retain a protective attitude toward her offspring, which is likely to rush to her for protection, but she does not feed it (Washburn and Devore, 1961). The band has a range, but evidence of a protected home territory is dubious at best. Catarrhine monkeys use their hands for exploratory and manipulative purposes but rarely for carrying objects, except among captive specimens whose behavior is much altered in many other ways, too. The violent sexual jealousy which has been observed in zoos (Zuckerman, 1932), for instance, is rarely encountered among free-ranging monkeys. By the time all of the permanent teeth have erupted, a quarter of a monkey's life span has elapsed, in contrast to one-sixth in the case of a lemur. Only the mutual protection afforded by membership in a band makes such slow maturation possible. At the same time, it is probable that delayed maturity facilitates band cohesion, since it provides

ample time for the young to learn their manners. Social play is a very important means of learning. Young monkeys are highly inquisitive and constantly active, and among animals with traits like these play has a very positive function.

It has been orthodox among anthropologists to assume that only the human species possesses culture, but the more we learn about the naturalistic social behavior of monkeys, the more we have to wonder about how meaningful this statement is. Culture,

as anthropologists use the term, means behavior which is learned rather than instinctive, shared by the members of a social group, and transmitted from one generation to the next. Clearly, monkeys learn most of their behavioral patterns. They certainly live in social groups of which the members share many such patterns, and in which some have higher status than others. How much of their learned behavior is transmitted by tradition over the years? As was mentioned previously, dominance may be passed on from mother to son, at least in some species. Japanese ethologists, whose observations on monkey behavior have been both extensive and intensive, have noted the innovation of new forms of behavior in some bands of monkeys, such as the washing of sweet potatoes (Kawamura, 1959) which led to differences in the customary habits of different bands. Altman (1967) found that rhesus monkeys, when urbanized, alter their social relations and many of their other habits; Maples (1969) noted a rapid adoption of new customs by baboons in areas where farms are being established. Perhaps the difference between cultural and noncultural behavior is not as great as we, in our anthropocentric pride, used to suppose.

Catarrhine monkeys resemble us so very closely physiologically that we use them extensively and profitably in medical experimentation. They are subject to the same contagions and infections that afflict mankind. Arthritis and dental decay are not at all uncommon among older individuals, and I have found growths diagnosed as cancerous in several specimens. It does not seem unlikely that disease rather than accident or predation is a major cause of death among monkeys or at least so weakens many of them that they fall easy prey to other troubles (Bramblett, 1968). Monkeys may show concern for their ailing companions, but there is nothing they can do to help the sick. Except when protected by captivity, the life span rarely exceeds the reproductive period, which is true of apes as well.

The extent of genetic polymorphism, which contributes so much to the differences in individual appearance among people, certainly extends throughout the entire catarrhine group (Schultz, 1947). In facial appearance, body proportions, and other characteristics, most if not all species are so variable that until recently many taxonomists listed far more species than really exist. Individuals of the same species differ in such genetic characteristics as blood type and the constituents of the urine, just as we do. Apes and monkeys, like people, are highly individualized creatures. Apparently, this degree of variability is adaptive for the sort of life they lead, just as it is with us.

APES

There are four clearly distinct varieties of apes living today, but we have discovered fossil remains of many others. One variety, the gibbon, is small, but the other three are giant forms. These are the orang-utan, the chimpanzee, and the gorilla. Their geographical distribution is much more restricted than that of the Old World monkeys. Gibbons, of which there are several species and two genera, live in the East Indies and Southeast Asia. Orang-utans are confined to the islands of Borneo and Sumatra, although at one time their range extended to China and India. Chimpanzees inhabit the tropical rain forest of Africa. Gorillas are divided into two groups, one of which dwells in the lowland jungles near the Atlantic Coast of Africa and the other in the mountains which separate the Nile from the Congo and in the nearby lowlands.

Like us, the apes lack any trace of an external tail, but like monkeys, the sexual skin of adult females undergoes periodic swelling. Like us, but unlike monkeys or indeed other mammals in general, they excrete uric acid as well as urea. Like monkeys, their faces and jaws protrude more and more as they mature, and their canine teeth come to project, while their brains grow less than ours do. Ischial callosities are typical of gibbons but are found in only a minority of the larger apes. Apes brachiate in moving through the trees and are accustomed, therefore, to a vertical position. Their legs, however, are much shorter than their arms, and cannot be fully extended either at the hip or the knee. Nevertheless, juvenile members of all species frequently use bipedal posture and gait. Adults of the giant species will stand and walk upright upon occasion, but are more apt to lean over and rest on their knuckles or fists, not the palms of their hands. Kortlandt (1962) attributes the quadrupedal gait of chimpanzees to their jungle habitat. He states that it is easier to move rapidly through the underbrush on all fours than when standing erect. Some individuals raised in human families continue to stand and walk erect until they have seen other apes which do not. Gibbons' fingertips reach the ground even when they are standing up, and they habitually run with the arms waving above them in order to keep their balance.

GIBBONS

Thus equipped, gibbons are the most skillful and daring of brachiators, able to move at high speed through the treetops. Figure 6–13 suggests their acrobatic skill. Gibbons weigh only about twelve pounds and lack the muscular development of the larger apes, but like the spider monkey, they are elongated in build and find little use for the thumbs on their hands in swinging from branch to branch. These thumbs are separated from the palm of the hand almost to the wrist thus permitting the gibbon to reach around a rather large branch. Since musculature is not greatly developed, gibbons lack the bony crests on the skull which we find among other apes (see Figure 6–14), and their faces are not especially prognathous.

Male gibbons are only slightly larger than females, but they do have larger canine teeth. Male and female gibbons are usually found in pairs, together with offspring, rather than in larger groups.

FIGURE 6-13. The Supreme Arboreal Acrobat. A Gibbon Sails through the Air with the Greatest of Ease—But, Unlike that Daring Young Man on the Flying Trapeze, He Has Four Hands, which Is Good Insurance.
(Photo: A. W. Ambler from National Audubon Society)

These small families are reported (Carpenter, 1940) to display at least vocal hostility to all neighboring gibbons, and we do not know just how youngsters find their mates. Ellefson (1968) confirms the importance of territorial behavior among these graceful creatures. In proportion to body weight the gibbon brain is nearly as large as that of a human being, but there are a number of even smaller primates with relatively larger brains. There is no evidence to suggest that the intellectual ability of an average gibbon surpasses that of such monkeys as the macaque or the capuchin. Very little psychological experimentation has been done with gibbons, despite the fact that many of them are in captivity. They tend to be exuberant, demanding of affection, and temperamental, which does not make them ideal subjects for laboratory tests.

ORANG-UTANS

Although they approximate human size, orang-utans (see Figure 6–15) are as dependent upon the trees as are gibbons. They cannot, of course, venture out onto small branches when fully grown, and they are very careful climbers. They are the least hairy of the apes, but their hair is very long and reddish in color, and they often grow beards and mustaches. With somewhat high and globular skulls, the orang-utan's browridge is the least developed of any of the apes and they often lack sagittal crests. Like other great apes, orang-utans have quite protrusive faces and very large teeth, with a mandible somewhat like a horseshoe in shape. This is reinforced in front by a growth of bone known as the simian shelf. A diastema for the reception of the very projecting upper canine separates the lower canine from the first premolar. This premolar is sectorial: that is, one of its two cusps projects far more than the other, so that it shears against the upper canine when the animal bites.

Throat pouches which may be inflated with air are characteristic of all great apes but reach extreme proportions in adult male orang-utans. The legs of these apes are exceedingly mobile at the hip, for they lack the ligament which binds the femur to the pelvis in all other primates. Their wrists and ankles are very flexible, their finger and toe bones slightly curved, and all four thumbs rather reduced. All of these limb specializations are excellent for arboreal life, but disastrous for living on the ground. Since the weight of an adult orang-utan precludes the use of small trees as a habitat, the extensive clearing of jungles for farming has been a real tragedy for this amiable species, and there may be less than 5,000 of them alive today.

Field studies of orang-utan behavior are just beginning. It is already known, however (Harrison, 1962), that they construct nests in which to sleep; that adult males spend much time by themselves; that mothers remain solicitous of their children for many years; and that they do not live in troops or bands. We know nothing of

FIGURE 6-14: Skulls and Lower Jaws of the Great Apes

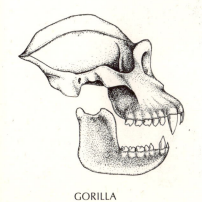
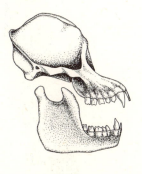
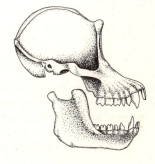

GORILLA

ORANG-UTAN

CHIMPANZEE

(Lateral views, about 1/6 natural size)

FIGURE 6-15. The Orang-utan from Borneo—Now Almost Extinct (Photo: "Orang-utan"/Barry Driscoll. © IUCN 1969. From *Wildlife in Danger*, published by Viking Press)

their breeding habits, but births take place throughout the year. Adult males grow to at least twice the size of females. Such sexual dimorphism among the terrestrial baboons has been explained as an adaptation to give the troop protection, but, clearly, this is not so in the case of orang-utans. Most observers have characterized orang-utans as lethargic or even pessimistic in disposition, but like the gibbon, very few of them have been subjected to psychological tests. They appear to be equal in problem-solving ability to chimpanzees but more deliberate in their methods.

CHIMPANZEES

Chimpanzees, approximately equal in size to orang-utans, are quite different in build, as Figure 6–16 shows. They are the most demonstrative of the apes, vociferous, eager, and active. They delight in rough play and practical jokes. These are the creatures most commonly used by psychologists in their attempts to probe the simian mentality, and they tend to be highly motivated in most cases, although some are bright, and others are stupid. Students of chimpanzee behavior have noted their capacity to make simple tools, to employ symbols, and to foresee future desires. On the other hand, they seem to lack motivation to speak, although their vocal apparatus is adequate to produce a great variety of calls. These are evoked by different emotional states (Hayes, 1951) but serve as signals to other members of the group, as do similar calls among many other animals. It is clear that they are automatic, not learned, so that they resemble coughs or sneezes rather than words. Lack of linguistic ability is partly compensated by a great range of facial expression, so that chimpanzees do succeed in communicating with one another almost as well as any of us might do with someone whose language we didn't know. Consequently, they are quite capable of coordinating their efforts to gain a desired result. In one test (Crawford, 1937) a weight too heavy to be moved by a single animal had to be lifted before the reward was obtained. Faced with this problem, two chimpanzees joined their efforts, pulled in unison, and were successful.

Chimpanzees often use any loose object as a tool in order to get something beyond the reach of their arms (Köhler, 1925). They often pile boxes one on top of the other in order to climb to the top of a cage, although their piles are so casually constructed as to have no stability. Fastening two bamboo poles together by inserting one within the other, so that a single, longer pole is available, is a feat which many but not all chimpanzees accomplish without any hints from the psychologist.

Cowles (1937) was even able to teach chimpanzees thrift. The experiment which demonstrated this involved two steps. First the

FIGURE 6-16.
A Chimpanzee
—Fortunately Not Almost
Extinct (San Diego
Zoo Photo)

experimenter rewarded the chimpanzee for accomplishing some task with a coin or token, not food. The chimpanzee had to insert this coin in a slot machine in order to obtain food. Learning to accept and use a symbol of this sort did not strain his mental abilities unduly. Then the price was increased. The chimpanzee had to insert several coins instead of one. We can sympathize with the animals' usual first reaction. Each would have a tantrum, lying on his back, kicking and screaming. Upon recovering, however, the chimpanzee would go back to work and accumulate the required number of coins, even though he might have to save them for several days. When they were tempted by rewards which cost less than others, some chimpanzees even saved up for a more highly desired prize.

Most chimpanzees have a very short attention span, but their memory seems to be well developed, and their observation is acute. Learning by imitation is rapid, and in manipulation, despite his short thumb, the chimpanzee shows great dexterity. Perhaps this is the wrong word, for it implies skill in using the right hand. Chimpanzees do develop more skill with one hand than the other, but about half of them learn to use the left hand more skillfully (Yerkes and Yerkes, 1929). Furthermore, if their first efforts at problem-solving fail, many of them will stop trying and sit quietly for a while. Then their next attempt will be successful. It is as though they had been considering and rejecting alternative lines of attack until they reached a proper solution.

The chimpanzee's brain, like the orang-utan's, rarely exceeds 400 cubic centimeters, less than one-third of the human average. It is rich in convolutions, however, and the frontal lobe is extensive. At birth the brain is almost half the adult size, although body bulk increases by twenty times or more. By the age of six a chimpanzee's brain has stopped growing, and the sutures of the skull begin to fuse. His massive jaw muscles require firm attachment, and he still solves more problems by brawn than brain, at least until the psychologist gets to work on him.

When living free in their native habitat, chimpanzees are found in bands of changing composition and varying size. Females and their young form the only stable groups, for the adult males come and go as suits their fancy. Goodall (1963, 1967, 1968) in her long extended studies of chimpanzees in Tanzania has increased our knowledge of the biosocial characteristics of these creatures tremendously. Although wary of strangers and of novel objects, chimpanzees have a strong drive for companionship and a real curiosity, which counteracts shyness sooner or later. Females and children cower when a dominant adult male puts on an aggressive display, yet neighboring bands have been observed to intermingle in a most friendly fashion. There is no evidence of territorial exclusiveness; indeed, when visitors drop in they may be welcomed with joyous hoots, embraces, and excited dancing. There is no evidence at all of a breeding season, but males become sexually aroused only when a female is in estrus (that is, during the few days each month when an egg has matured and is ready for fertilization), which is made obvious by the swelling of her sexual skin and by her soliciting male attention.

During the day chimpanzees spend much of their time eating, digesting, or searching for food either on the ground or in trees. Fruit appears to be a staple, but leaves, shoots and flowers are also consumed in large quantities. When the opportunity arises, however, a chimpanzee will kill and eat any small animal which it can catch, such as a monkey. On such occasions it may share some of the meat: at any rate, any other chimpanzees who are nearby will beg for a morsel. At least at the Gombe Reserve where Goodall worked, termites are considered a delicacy, too, and are captured by chimpanzees in a very shrewd manner. Twigs and stiff blades of grass are trimmed into proper shape by a chimpanzee, which he will then insert into one of the entrances of the termite nest. The insects attack them with their jaws; the tools are then withdrawn, and the termites are licked off by the chimpanzee. This is, indeed, tool manufacture—a sophisticated form of behavior which must, at minimum, be considered protocultural. At night they climb into trees and make individual nests of branches and leaves in which to sleep. Until a youngster has learned how to do this—and early attempts are usually most unskillful—he sleeps with his mother; he often continues to do this even later, for the emotional bond between them is very strong. Life, on the whole, appears to be very easy for these animals, so that they are able to spend a lot of time at play or grooming one another.

Adult males are bigger than adult females, although not by a great deal, and are normally more aggressive and bossy. Mothers do not seem to become subordinate to their sons, however, even after the latter are fully grown. The fact that regional differences in biological characteristics are at most subspecific in territory extending from Senegal to Tanganyika suggests extensive interbreeding. Chimpanzees have longer, lower skull vaults than orang-utans, bigger browridges, and much bigger ears. Their hair is thicker, shorter, and darker, their build less bulky, their legs longer and stronger, their fingers and toes less curved.

GORILLAS

The gorilla is the largest living primate. Adult males rarely weigh less than 400 pounds and may weigh twice as much, and they often stand six feet high, with a span of as much as nine feet. Females are considerably smaller, as are female orang-utans. To support such weight, the feet become broad during growth, the rather short legs grow thick, and iliac wings of the pelvis flare. The gorilla has short fingers and toes, but his great toe remains divergent and prehensile. Bony crests of astonishing size develop as added attachment for the very powerful neck and jaw muscles, and massive browridges and cheekbones enhance the rather determined look of the gorilla's face. The nasal wings are very prominent, and the nostrils large. As in all apes but no men, the lips are not everted. The gorilla's skin is black and, except for palms, knuckles, soles, and face, is covered with hair which tends to be abundant. The hair, too, is black during youth and remains so among adult females. A sure sign of full adulthood among male gorillas, however, is the depigmentation of the hair from below the shoulders to the rump, so that they are commonly called "silverbacks." A thick pad of connective tissue surmonts the top of the male's head; females have a much smaller one, just as their bony crests are smaller, too. The brain ordinarily has a volume of some 550 cubic centimeters, but as among men, there is a considerable range in size. These creatures appear to be formidable, and they are.

Fortunately for those who deal with them, gorillas are rarely ferocious. Even when young, they do not often behave in the uninhibited fashion so typical of chimpanzees but exhibit both self-assurance and the ability to refrain from using their full strength when dealing with weaklings like us. However, a gorilla is rarely subordinate even when friendly. A young gorilla of my acquaintance became used to riding on my back when he weighed only twenty pounds. A few years later, having gained over one hundred pounds, he continued to insist upon doing this whenever I entered his cage. It is difficult to resist the importunities of a gorilla, so eventually it became necessary to stop visiting him. There is no reason to suppose that their mental abilities are inferior to those of chimpanzees, but gorillas tend to react to test situations much more calmly and may indeed refuse to react at all, to the annoyance of their testers. This points up the difficulty which we have in assessing the IQ, not only of members of other species, but of human beings whose cultural background differs from our own. Motivations are inevitably associated with the way of life to which an individual has become accustomed. And gorillas seem to have led an easygoing life for the past several million years in areas where their food supply has been ample and where predation upon them, until well-armed men appeared, has been discouraged by their size and their habit of living in groups.

George Schaller (1963) spent nearly a year studying the activities of free-ranging mountain gorillas who became used to his presence and learned to tolerate it. Only rarely did any of them try to intimidate him by a chest-beating display or by shaking the branch upon which he sat quietly to observe their behavior. Their band organization is less fluid than that of chimpanzees: usually one or more silverback males live with a considerably greater number of adult females, juveniles, and babies. A mother and her infant are shown in Figure 6–17. Some adult males wander about by themselves, sometimes visiting with a band for a few days and then moving on. From time to time two bands may intermingle, but without showing the enthusiasm which marks such an event among chimpanzees. Most of the day is spent in eating or napping; adult males easily consume thirty-five pounds or more of vegetation every day, picking out only those parts of a plant which appear most succulent. No meat-eating has been observed. The children play actively, but adults do not; as the day passes the band wanders, usually in the wake of the most dominant male, from place to place in the forest. By late afternoon they may have gone from a few hundred yards to several miles. Then the females and juveniles prepare nests in the trees to sleep in, but the much heavier adult males make theirs on or very close to the ground. Births take place during all months of the year, but apparently the sex drive is low: in ten months Schaller observed only two copulations.

FIGURE 6-17. Infant
Gorilla and Mother (Photo:
Paul Steinemann from
Camera Press, London)

Like chimpanzees and orang-utans, both the menstrual cycle and the gestation period are of approximately the same length as among humans.

Primates may not have exploited every conceivable ecological niche in the arboreal zone available to mammals with grasping fingers and excellent eyesight, but they have certainly turned their hands to a great diversity of ways of life in the trees and even on the ground. Selection has operated upon them in such a way as to lead, in many cases, to adaptations of a generally useful nature.

The primate pattern which has resulted from the totality of these adaptations has involved behavior as well as structure which closely resembles our own. As evolution proceeded during the last 50 million years, some varieties remained perched on branches at relatively low levels of overall efficiency, but others found better means of using the opportunities afforded by arboreal life. As a group, the Prosimii specialized in such diverse ways that they must be classified into a large number of families. Monkeys differ from one another much less, although there are many genera in this grade. The high degree of visual acuteness and manipulative skill which monkeys attained permitted some, like the baboon, to return to the ground many million years ago while still habitually pronograde. Abilities which are the result of selection for tree living proved more than adequate for this new environment.

There are even fewer varieties of apes than of monkeys. In their case selection has produced bodies adapted to frequent assumption of erect posture and other basic improvements, especially in the organization and cortical control of behavior. Each improvement in the degree of mental ability makes anatomical specialization less necessary, except for those parts of the anatomy which contribute to mental ability itself. Thus each stage of primate evolution provided the necessary preadaptations for the next, until finally, from the primate pattern the hominid pattern of existence emerged.

Sources and Suggested Readings

ALTMAN, S. A., ed.
  1967   *Social Communication Among Primates.* University of Chicago Press, Chicago.

BISHOP, A.
  1962   Control of the Hand in Lower Primates. The Relatives of Man. *Annals of the New York Academy of Sciences,* **102,** 316–337.

BRAMBLETT, C.
  1967   Pathology in the Darajani Baboons. *American Journal of Physical Anthropology,* **26,** 331–340.

BUTLER, R. A.
  1954   Curiosity in Monkeys. *Scientific American,* **190,** 70–75.

CARPENTER, C. R.
  1934   A Field Study of the Behavior and Social Relations of Howling Monkeys (Alouatta palliata). *Comparative Psychology Monographs,* **10,** no. 2.

1935 Behavior of Red Spider Monkeys in Panama. *Journal of Mammalogy,* **16,** no. 3.

1940 A Field Study in Siam of the Behavior and Social Relations of the Gibbon (Hylobates lar). *Comparative Psychology Monographs,* **16,** no. 5, no. 84.

1965 The Howlers of Barro Colorado Island, in *Primate Behavior: Field Studies of Monkeys and Apes,* edited by I. De Vore, pp. 250–291. Holt, Rinehart and Winston, New York.

CLARK, W. E. LE GROS

1936 The Problem of the Claw in Primates. *Proceedings of the Zoological Society,* **I.**

1959 *The Antecedents of Man.* Edinburgh University Press, Edinburgh.

COWLES, J. T.

1937 Food-Tokens as Incentives for Learning by Chimpanzees. *Comparative Psychology Monographs,* **14,** no. 5, no. 71.

CRAWFORD, M. P.

1937 The Cooperative Solving of Problems by Young Chimpanzees. *Comparative Psychology Monographs,* **14,** no. 2, no. 68.

DE VORE, I., ed.

1965 *Primate Behavior: Field Studies of Monkeys and Apes.* Holt, Rinehart and Winston, New York.

ELLEFSON, J. O.

1968 Territorial Behavior in the Common White-Handed Gibbon, Hylobates lar Linn, in *Primates: Studies in Adaptation and Variability,* edited by P. C. Jay, pp. 180–199. Holt, Rinehart and Winston, New York.

GOODALL, J. VAN L.

1963 Feeding Behavior of Wild Chimpanzees, in *The Primates, Symposia of the Zoological Society of London,* edited by J. Napier and N. A. Barnicot, no. 10, pp. 39–48. Zoological Society, London.

1967 *My Friends the Wild Chimpanzees.* National Geographic Society, Washington, D.C.

1968 A Preliminary Report on Expressive Movements and Communication in the Gombe Stream Chimpanzees, in *Primates: Studies in Adaptation and Variability,* edited by P. C. Jay, pp. 313–374. Holt, Rinehart and Winston, New York.

GOODMAN, M.
1967   Deciphering Primate Phylogeny from Macromolecular Specificities, in Symposium on Primate Locomotion, pp. 255–273. *American Journal of Physical Anthropology*, **26**, no. 2.

GRAND, T. I.
1967   The Functional Anatomy of the Ankle and Foot of the Slow Loris (Nycticebus coucang), in Symposium on Primate Locomotion, pp. 207–218. *American Journal of Physical Anthropology*, **26**, no. 2.

HARLOW, H.
1966   Development of Patterns of Affection in Macaques. *Yearbook of Physical Anthropology*, **14**, 1–7.

HARRISON, B.
1962   *Orangutan.* Collings, London.

HAYES, C.
1957   *The Ape in Our House.* Harper and Bros., New York.

HILL, W. C. O.
1953–1968   *Primates: Comparative Anatomy and Taxonomy*, Vols. **I, II, III, IV, V, VI, VII,** and **VIII.** Edinburgh University Press, Edinburgh.

HOOTON, E. A.
1946   *Man's Poor Relations.* Doubleday, Garden City.

IMANISHI, K.
1960   Social Organization of Subhuman Primates in Their Natural Habitat. *Current Anthropology*, **1**, 393–407.

JAY, P. C., ed.
1968   *Primates: Studies in Adaptation and Variability.* Holt, Rinehart and Winston, New York.

JOLLY, A.
1966   *Lemur Behavior: A Madagascar Field Study.* University of Chicago Press, Chicago.

JONES, F. WOOD
1916   *Arboreal Man.* Arnold, London.

KAWAMURA, S.
1959 The Process of Sub-Culture Propagation Among Japanese Macaques. *Primates,* **2,** 43–60.

KÖHLER, W.
1925 *The Mentality of Apes.* Harcourt, Brace, New York.

KORTLANDT, A.
1962 Chimpanzees in the Wild. *Scientific American,* **206,** no. 5.

MAPLES, W. R.
1969 Adaptive Behavior in Baboons. *American Journal of Physical Anthropology,* new series, **31,** 107–110.

MARETT, J. R. DE LA H.
1936 *Race, Sex and Environment: A Study of Mineral Deficiencies in Human Evolution.* Hutchinson's, London.

MASON, W. A.
1968 Use of Space by Callicebus Groups, in *Primates: Studies in Adaptation and Variability,* edited by P. C. Jay, pp. 200–216. Holt, Rinehart and Winston, New York.

MORRIS, D., ed.
1967 *Primate Ethology.* Weidenfeld and Nicholson, London.

MOYNIHAN, M.
1964 Some Behavior Patterns of Platyrrhine Monkeys. I The Night Monkey (Aotus trivirgatus). *Smithsonian Miscellaneous Collection,* **146,** 1–84.

NISSEN, H. W.
1931 A Field Study of the Chimpanzee. *Comparative Psychology Monographs,* **8,** no. 17.

RADINSKY, L. B.
1967 The Oldest Primate Endocast. *American Journal of Physical Anthropology,* **27,** 385–388.

REYNOLDS, V.
1967 *The Apes.* Dutton, New York.

SADE, D. S.
1965   Some Aspects of Parent-Offspring and Sibling Relations in a Group of Rhesus Monkeys, with a Discussion of Grooming. *American Journal of Physical Anthropology,* **23,** 1–17.

SCHALLER, G. B.
1963   *The Mountain Gorilla: Ecology and Behavior.* University of Chicago Press, Chicago.

SCHULTZ, A. H.
1939   Notes on Diseases and Healed Fractures of Wild Apes and Their Bearing on the Antiquity of Pathological Conditions in Man. *Bulletin of the History of Medicine,* **7,** 571–582.
1947   Variability in Man and Other Primates. *American Journal of Physical Anthropology,* new series, **5,** 1–14.
1961   Some Factors Influencing the Social Life of Primates in General and of Early Man in Particular. *Social Life of Early Man.* Viking Fund Publications in Anthropology, no. 31, New York.

SIMONS, E. L.
1959   An Anthropoid Frontal Bone from the Fayum Oligocene of Egypt: The Oldest Skull Fragment of a Higher Primate. *American Museum Novitates,* no. 1976.
1967   The Significance of Primate Palaeontology for Anthropological Studies. *American Journal of Physical Anthropology,* new series, **27,** 307–332.

SIMONS, E. L. and D. R. PILBEAM
1965   Preliminary Revision of the Dryopithecinae (Pongidae, Anthropoidea). *Folia Primatologica,* **3,** 81–152.

SIMPSON, G. G.
1945   The Principles of Classification and a Classification of the Mammals. *Bulletin of the Museum of Natural History,* **85,** New York.

SNYDER, R. C.
1967   Adaptive Values of Bipedalism, in Symposium on Primate Locomotion, pp. 131–134. *American Journal of Physical Anthropology,* **26,** no. 2.

STONE, I.
> 1965 Studies of a Mammalian Enzyme System for Producing Evolutionary Evidence on Man. *American Journal of Physical Anthropology*, **23**, 83–86.

THORNDIKE, E. E.
> 1968 A Microscopic Study of the Marmoset Claw and Nail. *American Journal of Physical Anthropology*, **28**, 247–262.

WASHBURN, S. L. and I. DE VORE
> 1961 Social Behavior of Baboons and Early Man. *Social Life of Early Man*. Viking Fund Publications in Anthropology, no. 31, New York.

YERKES, R. M.
> 1925 *Almost Human.* Century, New York.

YERKES, R. M. and A. W.
> 1929 *The Great Apes.* Yale University Press, New Haven.

ZUCKERMAN, S.
> 1932 *The Social Life of Monkeys and Apes.* Harcourt, Brace, New York.

CHAPTER 7

The Hominid Pattern

THE ISOLATION OF MAN

Men today are more distinct from their closest cousins than all but a few other mammalian species are from theirs. This is recognized in taxonomy by the assignment of specific, generic, and familial status to our stock. Almost all taxonomists consider that the apes should be placed in the same superfamily, the Hominoidea, although Van Valen (1969), on the basis of our unique abilities, excludes the apes from this superfamily. Goodman (1962) on the other hand, on the basis of our very close biochemical similarities to the gorilla and chimpanzee, separates these African apes from the Pongidae and includes them in our own family. *Homo sapiens* is the only species of man living today, and later chapters will show that our genus has been unified to the same degree for as far back as fossil evidence is yet available. We retain a rather large number of characteristics which are often called primitive or generalized. The use of these terms carries implications which may be misleading: the first has rather insulting overtones, and the second is really quite vague. Primitive simply means that there are some ways in which we have changed less from the ancestral pattern than have the creatures to which we are compared; generalized means that we continue to be able to do a good number of things very well. These statements are both true and both very significant. Human evolution has emphasized the further development and reinforcement of the most essential central tendencies of the class Mammalia. It has avoided too great a dependence on developing any one simple skill at the expense of all others. In many ways we are the most mammalian of all mammals.

At the same time, as Sir Julian Huxley (1941) has insisted, "Man stands alone." His choice of words, as always, is very apt, for the primary fact about man is that he stands erect, usually with no conscious effort and has thus isolated himself from all other mammals. Fossil evidence leads to the inference that this distinction was first in time as well as in significance and that our other distinctions evolved subsequently. We are not the only bipedal animals, as has been mentioned earlier. Birds also walk on their hind limbs, their forelimbs having evolved into wings for flight. Kangaroos and some other mammals frequently hop and often rest, supported by their hind legs. But only man stretches his legs out straight, stands vertically at ease with his head directly above his feet, and strides ahead with his trunk erect. The entire body has had to be rearranged to accomplish this, so that its various parts are mutually adapted and kept in balance. Even after some millions of years of this unique stance and method of progression, each human baby has to learn the trick anew. A detailed examination of the structural arrangements which are involved in erect posture is in order.

FIGURE 7-1. Adaptations of the Primate Foot. From Left to Right, We See the Foot of a Howler Monkey, which is Highly Arboreal; of a Macaque, which Spends Much Time on the Ground; of a Gorilla, which Rarely Climbs and Often Stands Erect; and of a Human Being, Who Habitually Stands and Strides Erect.

HUMAN POSTURE

In shape the human foot is the most uniquely specialized section of our anatomy, as Figure 7–1 shows, because it has to support the entire weight of the body, yet it was evolved from a grasping organ. Its earlier mobility has had to be sacrificed for stability. The tarsal bones are strong and wedge-shaped and articulate closely, forming together with the robust metatarsals an arch which can

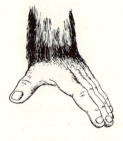
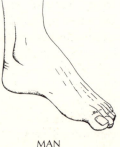

HOWLER MONKEY   MACAQUE   GORILLA   MAN

absorb the shock each time a step is taken. The great toe, instead of being short and opposable to the other digits, is long, strong, and in line with the rest. These, on the contrary, have become very short and have little utility in grasping. The talus and calcaneus at the heel are much enlarged and fit tightly together. The latter extends to the rear as a lever which is used in lifting the heel from the ground by the contraction of the soleus and gastrocnemius muscles. Among most people who habitually walk barefoot the heel is much narrower than the ball of the foot. It is very instructive to place one's hand, palm down, beside the foot: one can observe at once the changes in proportion which have taken place during human evolution. The gorilla's foot, which must also sustain a heavy weight, bears a faint resemblance to man's, but this resemblance develops during his lifetime, whereas we are born with feet which are prepared for their future task. Nor does the gorilla's calcaneus project enough to give much leverage.

Lowering the center of gravity is important for the proper balance of a creature which stands on its hind legs, as we can see when watching a gibbon waving his arms as he walks on the ground to keep from toppling over. His center of gravity is just below the rib cage; that of an adult human is close to the lower part of the sacrum. It is not surprising that the legs comprise about half of the total stature in a human adult. In an adult ape or a newborn human baby they comprise little more than one-third. Human legs increase in length and girth during childhood much more rapidly than the trunk does, an example of allometric growth. The articular surfaces and areas of muscular attachment permit the leg to straighten out completely at the knee without discomfort. The gastrocnemius, or calf muscle, swells to pleasing proportions. The plantaris muscle, important in most mammals, is vestigial in man, whereas the soleus, so useful in striding, is much enlarged. The tibia, or shin bone, is more robust than in any other primate and makes up at least one-fifth of the total stature. The femur, or thighbone, is even longer and sturdier. In man, as distinct from apes, the femora are at a slight angle to each other rather than parallel, so that the knees are close together when upright posture is assumed. Figure 7–2 illustrates the differences between the hind limbs of man and ape. The neck and head of the femur, which articulate that bone to the pelvis at the acetabulum, extend obliquely upward—rather than at a right angle from the shaft as among apes—to facilitate the transmission of weight from the pelvic arch onto the legs. Furthermore, the head of the femur is larger, so that the greater trochanter is farther from the pelvis. Thus the muscles which abduct the thigh have greater le-

FIGURE 7-2. The Lower Limb of Man and Gorilla. The Bones of the Pelvis and Leg Indicate the Difference in Bodily Proportions between a Man and a Gorilla of the Same Stature.

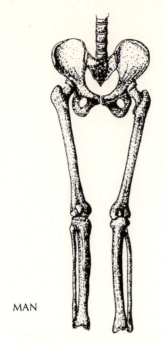

MAN

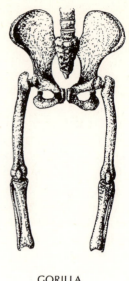

GORILLA

verage in man.   All of these modifications from the standard primate pattern are useful in helping us to stand and walk erect.

The trunk of the human body is pulled up and back to be balanced directly above the legs by a strong sacrospinalis muscle which runs from the sacrum and the backward flare of the iliac crest of the pelvis to the thorax behind the vertebral column.   A counter-acting muscle in front of the vertebral column, the psoas minor, is always small and often absent in our species; in pronograde mammals it is far larger and enables them to arch their backs, which we find unnecessary.   The gluteus maximus, too small to de-serve that designation in other anthropoids, is indeed very massive in human beings.   This muscle runs from the posterior part of the ilium and behind the sacrum to the linea aspera, a ridge running down the back of the femur, with some tendonous connections even to the tibia.   In association with our erect posture, which re-quires full extension of the femur, the gluteus maximus is located to the rear of the greater trochanter, so that it can pull the femur back into a vertical position below the pelvis.   The buttocks, con-sequently, show considerable backward protrusion among humans, a feature quite lacking in apes.   The gracilis muscle reaching from the pubis to the tibia becomes much smaller than among other pri-mates.   Indeed, as Washburn (1951) has pointed out, these two muscles deserve their names only in relation to human anatomy. The rectus femoris, which we use in kicking, and the three vastus muscles are all of exceptionally large size in man.

The pelvic region itself has become distorted from its ancestral shape with a remarkable degree of success.   For moving or standing in a pronograde position, that is, on all fours, a somewhat tube-shaped pelvis is quite adequate in most tetrapods. The ilium is situated so far forward that a large opening is left between the sacrum and the pubis; childbirth is rarely a problem among animals with such a pelvis. At the same time, it is mechanically impossible to transmit the entire weight of a heavy, vertically held body to the legs by means of a pelvis with such a shape. The human pelvis has been tilted over, shortened, broadened, and constricted in order to fulfill this function. The ilium flares to the rear with its posterior section bent downward; the sacrum, at which the pelvis and backbone join, becomes larger and more solidly wedged into place. The human sacrum normally consists of five fused vertebrae, as is the case among the large apes. Monkeys have only three. In man, as in apes, an external tail is absent, but we are likely to have a greater number of small coccygeal vertebrae below the sacrum than they. Attached to these small bones are several muscles which support the viscera—a real necessity in vertical posture. The ischium is shortened, so that the sacrum is brought closer to the acetabulum; and the ischial spine, to which coccygeal muscles are attached, is accentuated. The ischial tuberosity (upon which we sit) is also brought closer to the acetabulum and somewhat to its rear: this eases the job of the hamstring muscles in extending the femur for erect posture. These various rearrangements of bone and muscle solve the problem of standing and walking in a vertical posture very neatly but, in doing so, create a new problem by constricting the birth canal. As a rule, human females have broader pelves with wider openings than human males: this is one of the best ways to tell the sex of a human skeleton (see Figure 7–3). If human babies

FIGURE 7-3. Sectional View of the Human Pelvis, Showing Sexual Differences

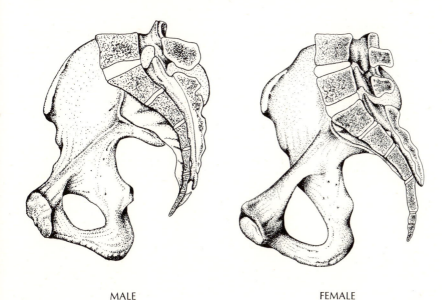

MALE   FEMALE

were born when still tiny or with smaller heads, there would be no difficulty in reconciling the contradictory functions of the pelvis. But a large brain is necessary for a human being, and babies are born with heads which can just barely slip through the opening provided. The fact that we have succeeded in overcoming the difficulties involved in standing and walking as we do demonstrates what great advantages our ancestors must have gained by this new posture.

The vertebral column and the trunk have undergone less obvious but equally important modifications because of our perpendicular stance. In the pronograde position the backbone forms a single arch from which the various internal organs are hung, although the neck may be moved about and sometimes recurved if the animal needs to raise its head. Such an arrangement would be far too weak structurally for a creature which stands vertically, although it serves for one which hangs vertically from time to time. The twisting of the pelvis would throw the body completely out of balance were it not pulled back by a reverse curve in the lumbar region directly above the sacrum: this is what saves us from falling flat on our faces. Below the sacrum, also, the few tiny bones which are the remnant of the ancestral tail are equally curved forward. Above the lumbar region with its five vertebrae the original arch remains throughout the thoracic, or rib-bearing, section which has twelve, but our necks curve backward so that we can look forward, not just down at our feet, without conscious strain. Figure 7–4 shows how this series of complex curves, each counterbalancing the next, enables us to maintain our center of gravity. But other details help. The shoulders are pulled back by the trapezius muscle, the rib cage is flattened, and the suspensory ligaments which hold our internal organs in place attach from the diaphragm as well as dorsally. Among human females the extra projection of the buttocks to the rear is counterbalanced by the forward swell of the mammary glands, which are better developed than among other

FIGURE 7-4. Posture and Structure. These Diagrams Show, in Basic Outline, the Structural Differences in the Skeletons of These Three Creatures. A Backbone which Is a Simple Arch Functions Best for the Pronograde Creature. For Arboreal Life It is Convenient for the Head To Be Lifted Up and Shifted Back. An Upright Posture Requires a Lumbar Curve To Pull the Trunk Back and Up Over the Legs.

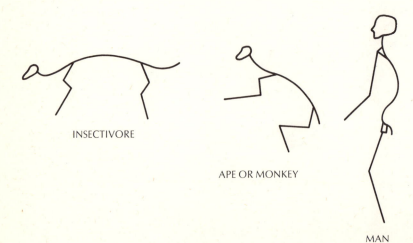

INSECTIVORE

APE OR MONKEY

MAN

primates. Only rarely are female apes endowed with even slightly projecting bosoms.

The upper arms remain long but the forearms are shortened. It has been pointed out that apes are far more likely to pull their bodies up to a branch from which they are hanging, whereas we are much more likely to lift objects up from below. Apes move the upper arm in their usual activity, we the lower arm in ours, and in each creature the leverage is appropriate to the activity. Furthermore, our arms are less heavily muscled in proportion to our body weight than those of other primates. Figure 7–5 indicates the distinctive traits of the human hand. The palm of the hand is shortened and broadened, and the fingers are shortened and straightened, compared to those of apes. The last segment of the thumb is slightly enlarged, and the thumb itself is so articulated that it moves with great freedom. Thus it becomes readily opposable to the tips of the fingers, and we are able to grasp objects precisely and delicately (Napier, 1961). The facility which we enjoy in the use of the thumb is anatomically a minor, but functionally a major distinction. Since our forelimbs have been totally freed from the jobs of clinging to branches or being used as forefeet, their alternate job of manipulation is all that remains to keep them busy. The old proverb says that Satan finds work for idle hands to do; but human hands have certainly been far from idle since their emancipation as our ancestors began to stand and walk erect. Their skill in manipulation is as extraordinary as it is essential.

It is a delicate problem to balance the human head in its appropriate position upon the occipital condyles of the skull, which articulate with the topmost vertebrae. Among pronograde animals the foramen magnum is located at or close to the back of the skull, and large neck muscles run from above it over the shoulders, since whenever they carry anything, they use their mouths to do so. The semierect posture typical of apes and monkeys is associated with

FIGURE 7-5. Adaptations of
the Primate Hand. The
Baboon Walks on the Palms
of His Hands Yet Also Picks
Up Small Objects and Seizes
Large Ones Easily. The
Gibbon, Climbing and
Swinging, Can Reach around
Quite Large Branches
Because of the Position of
His Thumb. Homo Sapiens
Uses His Hands for
Precise Manipulation.

BABOON　　　　　　GIBBON　　　　　HOMO SAPIENS

a shift of this foramen to a position beneath the skull but far back to the rear. Neck musculature remains very strong since the head needs to be lifted in order for the animal to look forward. Among humans there has been a still further shift, accompanied by a backward curve of the cervical vertebrae, so that the foramen magnum is not only underneath but far forward and tilted back slightly. Since the balance is almost perfect, human neck muscles need not be so large, nor need they be attached to such a large area of the occiput as among other mammals in order for the head to be held up.

Had our faces remained as projecting as apes', we would not have attained this balance. But as our braincase has expanded, our jaws have retreated. The chin may project below as the nose may protrude above the human mouth, but the face as a whole is rather flat. Both teeth and jaw muscles are much reduced in size, and the mandible does not need to be large to accommodate them. Very little of the skull is required as an area of muscular attachment.

An infant ape has little facial protrusion and small neck and jaw muscles. But his mode of life soon demands that he develop much larger ones. In his case it is functional that the brain should cease growing and the skull sutures close to provide a solid basis of muscular attachment. Precisely the contrary is true of a human child. His muscles remain weak, but continued brain growth throughout childhood requires that the skull sutures remain open.

THE HUMAN BRAIN

We tend to be proudest of our brains. We have every reason to be. No other animal possesses nearly so efficient an instrument for integrating awareness, behavior, and emotion. Our brains are not the biggest to be found in the animal world. Only rarely does a human being have a brain with a volume of 2,000 cubic centimeters, which is less than the size of an elephant's. Whales have even larger brains. Nor are human brains the biggest in proportion to body size. The human brain as a rule weighs about 2 percent as much as the body which it controls. Some small monkeys better us in this respect. As a general rule large mammals have a lower ratio of brain size to body size than their smaller cousins. But there is no creature of dimensions approaching ours which has a brain nearly as large. Chimpanzees and orang-utans rarely have cranial capacities of more than 400 cubic centimeters, or gorillas of more than 550. The brains of normal human adults have an extreme range of from 900 to 2,200 cubic centimeters with the average at about 1,450.

Nor is there any creature at all with a brain having such an expanded frontal lobe. The surface of this lobe comprises 47 percent of the cerebral cortex among humans, in contrast to about 33 percent in any of the large apes and 23 percent in the lemur. No other creature has such an extensively or deeply convoluted surface or cortex as we have. Apes and porpoises have complex patterns of convolutions, but theirs are less complex than ours. Our brains are clearly primate brains, but they carry to extremes the evolutionary tendencies which are only partially developed among other primates. It will be recalled that in previous chapters the vertebrate and the primate brain were briefly described, and the transfer of emphasis from olfactory to visual cues among primates was explained. The extension of the association areas in the brains of monkeys and apes was also mentioned.

All of these developments have culminated in the human species. Naturally, so active an organ as the human brain needs constant nourishment and oxygenation: the amount of blood which is pumped through it every minute nearly equals its own weight (Harrison and Montagna, 1969). Lack of freshly aerated blood for so short a time as seven seconds leads to unconsciousness. The carotid and vertebral arteries all unite to form a circle at the base of the brain, which serves to ensure that all parts of the brain are equally well supplied with blood. The cerebral cortex, often called the gray matter, is particularly well nourished; it is within this surface area of the forebrain that the final integration of nervous activity takes place. Convolutions increase the area of the cortex out of all proportion to the increase in volume of the cerebrum: it may have an extent of 200 square inches or more, which is at least 50 percent greater than the surface area of a sphere of equal size. Furthermore, it contains more than 7 billion separate neurons, or nerve cells.

Each of the cerebral hemipheres, among the anthropoids, is divided into four more or less distinct lobes. The central sulcus separates the frontal lobe from the parietal, and the lunate, or simian, sulcus separates the latter from the occipital lobe. The temporal lobe lies below the sylvian sulcus. It will be recalled that the visual cortex is upon the occipital lobe. The auditory cortex is on the temporal lobe, close to the sylvian sulcus, while the tactile cortex runs along the edge of the central sulcus upon the parietal lobe. Association areas, very much expanded in man, lie between these three sensory centers (see Figure 7–6). For the most part, the functions of the two cerebral hemispheres are identical. But, remarkably enough, the major section of the cortex which concerns human language is on the left hemisphere only, in the temporal and parietal association area (Penfield and Roberts, 1959). The motor areas of the cortex, which control conscious movements, lie along the central sulcus upon the frontal lobe. This lobe, which has expanded a very great deal in the course of human evolution, is presumed to function as an inhibitor. Thus we are able to extend

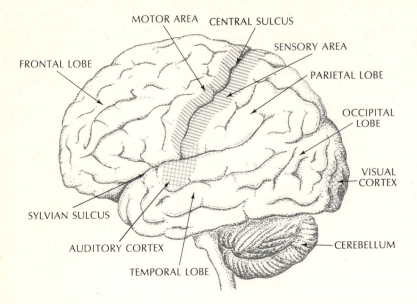

FIGURE 7-6. The Human Brain, Showing Its Functional Areas

MOTOR AREA CENTRAL SULCUS
SENSORY AREA
FRONTAL LOBE
PARIETAL LOBE
OCCIPITAL LOBE
VISUAL CORTEX
SYLVIAN SULCUS
AUDITORY CORTEX
CEREBELLUM
TEMPORAL LOBE

our attention span, maintain our drive toward a goal by screening out stimuli which might divert us and, as a result, behave like human beings. For the human brain, as an anatomical item, is not nearly so unique as the forms of behavior which result from its activity.

Not only unique but of the utmost significance is that form of behavior known as articulate and meaningful speech. This exclusively human accomplishment involves social interaction to the highest degree: speech would be functionless unless understood. The area in the cortex of the temporal and parietal lobes of the cerebrum associated with the comprehension of spoken words is somewhat enlarged in human beings, but it is doubtful if the study of fossil skulls can tell us whether their possessors had a language.

To produce sounds in speech, the vocal cords, larynx, and tongue must be precisely coordinated. The retreat of the jaws and the advance of the foramen magnum in our species have caused a rearrangement of these organs: the larynx, or Adam's apple, being very obvious in the throat, for instance. The modifications in the mouth which have probably facilitated—not caused—articulate speech include the broadening of the mandible and the pushing forward of the chin, which give more freedom of movement to the tongue, and the evolution of the genial tubercles inside the mandible near its symphysis, from which the genioglossus muscle of the tongue originates. Our tongues are attached further forward than those of other primates, and only humans have genial tubercles and double paired vocal cords in the larynx.

In the other anthropoids, many of which emit vocal signals which serve to communicate information concerning their emotional states, the esophagus and trachea run diagonally back at an oblique angle from the mouth. As a necessary consequence of erect posture, both of these tubes drop at a right angle just behind the human mouth; the larynx is directly beneath the rearmost part of the tongue. Vocalizations are produced, when air is expelled through the vocal cords, by muscular contractions which cause the cords to separate and come together. The different sounds of human speech, however, are produced by movements of the soft palate, tongue, and lips, which modify the vibrations of the escaping air in varied ways. Vowels, for instance, are produced when the soft palate is raised. The lips assume different shapes for different vowels. Obstructing the even flow of air momentarily in one way or another produces a consonant. The differences in anatomical detail between man and ape are, as in the case of the thumb, rather minor but apparently enough to make articulate speech easy and "natural" for us but not for them. These differences are shown in Figure 7–7.

Yet the variety of different noises which other primates make is diverse enough to provide the basis for intellectual communication, if these noises were rearranged and combined in sequence. This, however, does not occur. Apes, monkeys, and lemurs use their vocalizations to communicate transient emotional states in a social context, and that is all. They may signal "I feel friendly," or "I'm scared," or perhaps even "Watch out!" but they do not say, "That leopard has spots," or "Let's visit that grove of fig trees tomorrow," or "The moon is made of green cheese." The lack of this kind of communication is not simply due to the anatomical differences in

FIGURE 7-7. Hominoid Vocal Apparatus

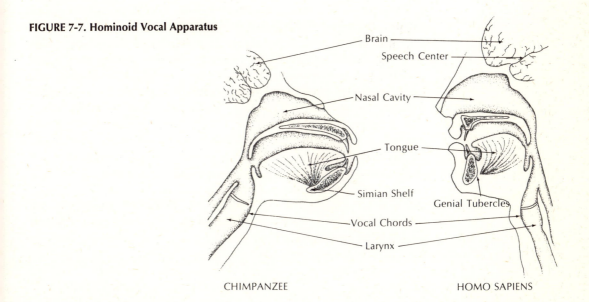

CHIMPANZEE   HOMO SAPIENS

the vocal apparatus. It is much more concerned with differences in the brain. As Professor E. A. Hooton used to say in class: "The reason that an ape doesn't speak is because he doesn't have anything to say."

Nor do apes sing. It is amazing and somewhat distressing to note that, although much has been written by students of evolution concerning the origin of human language, the origin of human song has been neglected. Of course we are not the only vertebrates who sing: many birds do. But among the primates our species is unique in its interest in producing, as well as listening to, melodious sequences of sounds. Since apes and monkeys often vary the pitch of sounds which they emit, we can infer that they are anatomically equipped to sing. But the impulse to use the voice in this way, just like the impulse to use the voice in enunciating words and sentences, appears to be confined to man. Both of these uses of the voice are species-specific biological characteristics of *Homo sapiens*.

Were there no ears to hear, neither would be functional. Human language serves to convey information, and the sounds which compose it must be emitted at frequencies audible to the human ear. Our ears make us aware of tones as low in frequency as twenty cycles per second and as high (until we age) as 25,000 cycles. As was mentioned in Chapter Five, bats can hear sounds with a frequency more than twice as great. Chimpanzees resemble us in hearing ability, but some monkeys can hear notes of higher pitch (Harrison and Montagna, 1969). The human ear is not one of our unique distinctions. We require, and possess, a high degree of auditory discrimination: without it, we could not distinguish one word from another. But we do not know that we excel the other primates in this ability. If we do, the auditory cortex, so well developed in our species, is largely if not entirely responsible. Externally, our ears are quite varied in size and shape, although never so large as those of chimpanzees and rarely as small as those of orang-utans. Our ears are rarely moveable—in this respect we differ from most primates, although apes do not do a much better job than we. A minor tubercle on the inner edge of the rim of the helix seems to be all that remains of the pointed tip which characterizes the standard mammalian ear. This ear tip has been quite appropriately named Darwin's point, since it is a relic of our evolutionary past. The fleshy lobe which forms the lowest part of the external ear is rudimentary at best in other anthropoids and in man may be large or small, free swinging or attached in front. What the function of the earlobe may be is not known, although Morris (1968) has suggested that it is an erogenous zone.

OTHER DISTINGUISHING CHARACTERISTICS OF MAN

The facial characteristics of *Homo sapiens* are probably best explained as adaptations to the kind of life which erect posture has made possible. They are by no means necessary consequences of such posture, as a study of our fossil relatives shows. Probably the great reduction in size of the canine teeth, which do not project to any perceptible degree, is connected both with the use of the hands and the retreat of the jaw. Canine roots remain large. The projecting canine teeth of other primates are often used for display in conflict situations. Since our hands are free, we are more likely to threaten each other with a clenched fist or by grasping a weapon. It is worth noting that in apes and monkeys the permanent canines erupt late, after the individual has nearly matured. Should one of these creatures appear aggressive before he grew strong enough to defend himself, he would suffer, or worse. In the human species these teeth erupt much earlier in the sequence, by the beginning of puberty. A human adult need not feel threatened when he observes the canines of a youngster, so early eruption is safe. Up to the present we have not found enough fossils of twelve-year-old humans to tell when the shift in tooth eruption sequence took place.

Quite possibly the turning out of the membranous section of the lip is a secondary effect of the reduction of facial protrusion. Whatever its origin, this is certainly another of our unique, species-specific characteristics. Chimpanzees have exceedingly mobile lips, but, when at rest, no eversion at all is shown, and so it is with the other primates and, indeed, with mammals in general. Among humans the degree of lip eversion, commonly called lip thickness, varies a great deal both within and between the races, but even the thinnest-lipped human beings among us differ from the apes. It would be interesting to know how long ago our ancestors began to acquire everted lips, but of course fossil evidence can tell us nothing. The eminence of the human nasal tip might seem to be the result of the jaws' retreat from beneath the nose, yet none of us have such magnificent protuberances as the proboscis monkey, whose jaws have not retreated. The alae, or wings of the nose, are also prominent in man but cannot match those of the gorilla. As in the case of lips, these fleshy parts of the nose leave no fossil traces to satisfy our curiosity about origins.

The nasal bones in our species are not so long and narrow as among apes but tend to project more or less; this probably *is* related to the retreat of the jaws and adjacent parts of the facial skeleton. Even though nasal bones are fragile and often lost from the fossil remains of our ancestors, we do have some evidence concerning the evolution of this part of the human face. In our species today the maxillae flare slightly or sharply on either side of the nasal aperture and below it as well, creating what is termed the nasal sill, a distinctive trait of recent mankind. The transition between the floor of the nasal passages and the exterior surface of the maxilla is more gradual in apes and monkeys and also in early hominid fossils. Finally, in our species the entrance to the nostrils points downward: that of the other living primates is directed forward, except in the case of the proboscis monkey just mentioned. All in all, the human nose is a rather distinctive and obvious organ.

As time went on, our ancestors came to depend more and more upon tools and, consequently, less and less upon teeth to accomplish a variety of tasks. Having less heavy work to do, the human mandible has become smaller, and a chin at its foremost lower border is adequate to buttress it. The incisor teeth, like the canines, are reduced and are placed vertically. The upper incisors, in most cases, are slightly in front of the lowers, so that we lack the edge to edge-bite which was typical of our ancestors. The masseter and temporal muscles which move the jaw, having less work to do, are not so large as those of the apes and need less extensive attachment to the skull. The temporal muscles of other primates often reach the very top of the braincase where a sagittal crest may develop. We lack this adornment. The reader, by feeling the sides of his skull while making chewing movements, can perceive readily that his temporal muscles do not rise very high. Inasmuch as the browridges, which function in part as buttresses against the stress exerted by powerful jaw muscles in action, no longer need to fulfill this function, they too have become much reduced in the course of human evolution. Thus the human face has become much altered in appearance since our ancestors first stood up and freed their hands from the task of supporting any part of the body's weight.

Whether other details in which human bodily appearance differs from that of other primates are derived from the same cause is dubious. For instance, the pattern of hair distribution in the human species is completely bizarre. We are by no means the least hairy of the mammals or even of the terrestrial mammals. Elephants and rhinoceroses are among the creatures which are even more glabrous. We are, however, the least hairy of the primates. Human hair is nothing but a fine down over most of the body. Of this we have plenty. Our hair follicles are as numerous as those of other primates: we appear hairless because most of them do not produce long, coarse hair. Nor are we the only mammals or primates possessing manes, although sometimes ours may grow to great length. The beards and mustaches found among some other primates are never as long as those which some men grow. Nor do any of our closer relatives have curly or wooly hair. But the concentration of hair in the pubic and axillary regions in both sexes, its scantiness elsewhere in females, the extent of sexual dimorphism in the amount of hair on chest, arms, and legs, and the sudden appearance of facial and body hair at adolescence form a truly distinctive combination not found among other animals.

We are also completely lacking in tactile hairs, and human hair does not function as insulation, nor to shed rain, nor to protect the skin against scratches. Even the hairiest man does not have a thick enough coat of hair for efficient protection against these hazards. For this reason Darwin (1871) suggested that its distribution might be accounted for in terms of sexual selection. His view has not been generally accepted, but Harrison and Montagna (1969) accept the idea that these scattered tufts of hair are ornamental. It is worth noting that whereas in other primates sexual dimorphism is commonly expressed by means of body size, canine size, and sometimes by pigmentation, among humans the sexes differ more in bodily shape and hair distribution (see Figure 7–8). Men are, on the average, taller than women, but stature is so variable in our species that this is not a reliable criterion of sex, while differences in weight are even less distinctive. Sexual differences in canine size are minimal, and hair color is not related to sex in our species. Now that the skin is not hidden beneath a coat of hair, skin color has come to be a minor aspect of sexual dimorphism, however. Almost all studies indicate that adult males unexposed to sunlight have slightly darker skins than females of the same population (Hulse, 1967).

Other land mammals which lack a furry coat always have skins

FIGURE 7-8. Sexual Dimorphism in Man and Ape

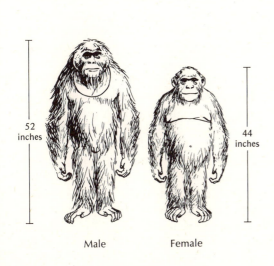

52 inches

44 inches

Male Female

ORANG-UTAN

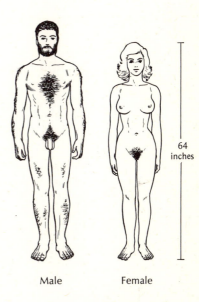

64 inches

Male Female

HOMO SAPIENS

which are much thicker and tougher than ours. As a substitute means of protection, such a hide is adequate, at least for a large animal in the tropics, where heat loss is minimal. In most cases, the skin of such hairless beasts is full of melanin and, consequently, much darker than the skin of a majority of mankind. The skin on the grasping surfaces of the hands and fingers and the walking surfaces of the feet and toes is not only thickened but ridged. It is sometimes called friction skin, because the ridging helps to prevent slipping.

But we resemble other primates in these characteristics. Our fingerprints are rather more complex than theirs, but this is not an outstanding difference. Another characteristic of human skin is that it tends to be rather even in color on most parts of the body unless exposed to strong sunlight. The palms and soles of dark-skinned persons are usually lighter and the nipples and genitals of lightskinned persons darker than the rest of the body, but patterns made up of contrasting colors are otherwise lacking. In response to sunlight, however, some persons freckle, and most human beings tan. It is the combination of these traits rather than any one of them which is distinctive of our species.

It must be remembered that the visible part of the skin is simply the dead, horny layer at the top of the epidermis, which is constantly being shed and replaced from below. Below the epidermis is the dermis, a much thicker, very flexible layer, richly supplied with blood. Indeed, it is by means of the flow of blood to the skin that we are able to adjust our body temperature, for this flow transfers heat from the interior of the body to the surface, so that it may be radiated into the air. The tiny blood vessels of the skin are well equipped with interconnections and valves, so that more or less blood may be pumped close to the surface. Thus we are able to blush—a form of social communication which has great significance —as well as, of course, to become paler than usual. Both of these conditions may be activated by hormones in the bloodstream in correlation with emotional states, but physical exertion or external temperature may be causative factors as well.

The glands of the skin have been mentioned in Chapter Five. We find, however, that our species has developed the ability to throw off excess heat by sweating to a truly outstanding degree. The eccrine glands of a human body number between 2 and 5 million, all of them present at birth. They are especially numerous on the head, but no part of the skin is without them: scarcely a square inch has less than a thousand. The water which they secrete evaporates into the atmosphere, a process which, as we all know, has a cooling effect. This is why humid heat feels so much more oppressive than dry heat. Inasmuch as the other primates, although living for the most part in warm regions, do not perspire with nearly as much efficiency as we, it is natural to wonder how, when and why we attained this unique ability. Ashley Montagu (1964) has speculated, in my opinion very plausibly, that the real need for sweating arose among our ancestors when they began to hunt large game animals on the open plains; these were creatures which had to be followed at some speed for many hours. Natural selection, under these circumstances, would obviously favor those hunters who could do this without collapsing from heat exhaustion, and throwing off heat by heavy sweating is the best means of doing this, if there is water available to replenish the body fluids lost in this manner. At the same time, lack of a thick hairy coat facilitates the necessary evaporation of sweat. The ability to perspire and nakedness of the skin, then, do seem to fit together in a most functional way.

Man has been called a mechanical misfit (Estabrook, 1941) but this is strictly untrue. It is immaterial that we are not all trapeze artists like gibbons, or tremendously strong like elephants, or possessed of teeth and jaw muscles like lions, or able to run as fast as gazelles, or leap as far as kangaroos, or swim like porpoises. These are all dead-end overspecializations, and the mammals which win top honors in any one field of athletic ability do poorly at the decathlon. We climb far better than most mammals, are bigger, stronger, and more fleet of foot; we can swim, jump, kick, dance, and throw. At biting and sniffing out scents we are definitely inferior to the average, but in all-around physical abilities we are not.

There can be no doubt that superior cleverness has been the main factor in our species' success, but our early ancestors needed sound, well-coordinated bodies as well, and they possessed them. In the ability to throw fast, far, and accurately we are—as doubtless they became—the undisputed champions. Chimpanzees can often be trained to throw quite accurately but are not known to do so when left to their own devices. Archaeological data permit us to infer, however, that our ancestors had begun to throw either stones or spears in hunting long before our present species evolved (Leakey, 1961). There can be little doubt that for a long time the ability to throw was of the greatest importance to man in seeking his livelihood. The assumption of erect posture has resulted in certain unusual strains on the human body, but man has solved the problems involved very successfully.

ECOLOGICAL INFLUENCES ON BIPEDALISM

It is only reasonable to consider the ecological circumstances which might have been influential in leading a Miocene or Pliocene primate to adopt terrestrial bipedalism in preference to any other method of exploiting his habitat. In those days large primates ranged from

China to France and throughout much of Africa. Some of the countryside was forested, but much was open prairie; transitional zones, partly wooded, must have been numerous. Fossil remains of baboons dating from the Pliocene tell us that large monkeys had already attempted quadrupedal terrestrialism with success. Fossil remains of the early apes, usually called Dryopithecines, suggest that they had not become as adapted for brachiation as the living apes are.

Large primates must find much of their food on or near the ground; this would have been as true then as it is now. Those which lived on the edge of a wooded area would have had the incentive as well as the opportunity to venture from one wooded area to another across intervening open regions. Creatures in the process of becoming adapted for brachiation would have been those most likely to move bipedally—as chimpanzees often do when in the open (Kortlandt, 1962)—in contrast to the continued pronograde habit of such monkeys as baboons. Hewes (1961) has suggested that our erect posture may have originated because it freed the arms to carry such things as tools or food. Goodall (1967) notes that chimpanzees find this convenient. The previously existing habit of erect posture in climbing would make it easier for an animal to exploit the advantages of carrying objects or being able to look around. A primate partially but not fully adapted for brachiation is in fact preadapted for erect walking on the land (Avis, 1962).

Such a late Miocene or early Pliocene ape would have found many advantages in his new habitat. Since almost all anthropoids live in bands of which the members are bound together by habit if not by emotional ties, we may reasonably infer that their and our Miocene ancestors lived in this way too. The safety from predators which baboons today find by living in groups would have been effective then for creatures as big as or bigger than baboons. Fossil skulls of African Dryopithecines indicate rather small cranial capacity by modern standards, but we can be confident that they were at least as shrewd, alert, and well-coordinated as any of their potential predators or competitors. Lacking the quills of a porcupine, the thick hide of a rhinoceros, or the fertility of a rabbit, they could not have afforded to be stupid. The heritage of arboreal life should have prepared them to respond effectively to all sorts of hazards and opportunities.

With hands and arms free from the necessity of supporting the body, the manipulative skills typical of all anthropoids would have had the chance to develop much more freely. With digestive systems capable of utilizing a great variety of foodstuffs, the dietary problem should not have been difficult. Baboons not only scavenge but will sometimes even kill a small helpless creature (Washburn and Devore, 1961), as do chimpanzees. Any large swiftly moving primate can become a much more accomplished predator, as our ancestors eventually did. We do not yet know how long ago they came to depend upon predation as a major source of nourishment, but we know that they added meat to their diet a long time ago.

The development of adequate hunting techniques was probably crucial in the evolution of humanity. Primates other than ourselves simply collect food and eat it. When caged, dominant apes may share food after becoming satiated (Nowlis, 1941), and chimpanzees sometimes part with pieces of monkey meat (Goodall, 1967); but otherwise, they do not share. A band functions to protect its members against outsiders, to satisfy their sexual needs, to teach them their proper places in society, and to give them a sense of security. It does not provide them with food. In this rather important aspect of life, an ape or monkey is on its own after being weaned. The situation is quite different among a number of hunting animals. The very young are in no position to catch their own prey, and the mother brings food to the den for them, as the vixen in Figure 7–9 is doing for her pups. In many cases a group, such as a wolf pack, hunts together and shares the kill. Social cooperation in providing food for the group has survival value but involves activities which depend upon some degree of self-control by each of the animals in-

FIGURE 7-9. Vixen Bringing Food to Her Cubs (Photo: Leonard Lee Rue III from National Audubon Society)

volved. At some time in the past our ancestors learned to master themselves well enough to hunt and to share their food.

It is not unreasonable to speculate that the division of labor between the sexes arose in association with this degree of self-mastery. As pointed out earlier in this chapter, man's erect posture has involved pelvic rearrangements which make childbirth less easy. Human babies are helpless for a long time, during which they require their mother's care. Women can easily collect vegetation, scavenge, or catch small animals, as baboon females do. But a nursing mother cannot engage in long or distant hunting expeditions. Among all hunting tribes which have been studied, the men hunt and bring food back to the women and children: a very practical arrangement. This system allows the infant to mature very slowly. Apes mature less rapidly than monkeys, but our children carry this primate tendency to an extreme. Although our brains grow most rapidly during the first few years of life, they do not stop growing completely until puberty or even later (Watson and Lowry, 1962). We do not, as a rule, become sexually mature until almost one quarter of the life span has elapsed. As Ashley Montagu points out in *Adolescent Sterility* (1946), the fertility of pubescent girls is rather low. Prolonging the period of youth has unquestionably promoted the acquisition of the cultural achievements which make our lives so different from those of other animals.

Animals which depend almost entirely upon vegetation for their food must spend much of their time eating. Most apes and monkeys have a diet that contains much roughage, lots of vitamins, little protein, and few calories per unit volume. Such food is readily accessible and easy to collect, but foraging leaves them comparatively little free time. In contrast, hunting animals such as lions need not spend so much time in eating: flesh is highly nutritious, full of calories, and contains little roughage.

There is no evidence that lions spend their free time in improving their minds. Primates, in contrast, are very inquisitive creatures. Young primates in particular are exploratory and playful. A large primate which had left the trees, taken to walking on its hind legs, found means of including ample meat in its diet, and enjoyed the luxury of a somewhat prolonged youth could not be expected to behave like a lion. The heritage of temperamental characteristics derived from the primate form of society would not vanish overnight. Such a creature might be expected to use his brain, his hands, and his free time for all sorts of activities beyond the capacity of any previously existing form of life. This, of course, is precisely what our ancestors did. Perhaps we will never collect the proper sort of evidence to indicate when food was first carried home or words first exchanged. But all these events did take place, and, as they did so, human culture and human personality emerged.

Some scholars think that the delay in sexual maturation was especially significant in the evolution of the capacity for culture. Chance and Mead (1953) suppose that those young males whose sexual drives overcame them before their physical prowess was adequate for them to challenge mature males successfully would have been driven off or killed. In either case their genetic potential would be lost. Only those able to restrain themselves would father the next generation.

We know that the frontal lobes, so much expanded in man, are concerned with inhibitions, worrying, and good judgment. Social responsibility—so the supposition goes—develops hand in hand with the evolution of greater mental abilities. It is certainly true that human sexual activity is under a very high degree of cortical control. Not only must techniques be learned, as among monkeys, but the drive itself may be repressed. The human personality is such that inhibitions concerning sex are readily instilled. Among non-human primates, on the other hand, such inhibitions and repressions have not been observed. Overeager young males may in some cases be denied access to females, and surplus males may be expelled from a band. Lone adult males and bachelor gangs are found in many primate species.

But it would appear that under natural conditions, living in their own habitat, a male ape or monkey rarely feels the impulse to mate except when a nearby female is in estrus. At this time the female is quite uninhibited in signaling her desire to be mated. Copulations may take place many times in a day while this period lasts, and chances are very good indeed that she will be impregnated. Thereafter, she will not come into estrus again until after she has given birth or suffered a miscarriage. In some species, but not all, nursing also inhibits estrus. Whether breeding seasons exist or not, therefore, sexual activities are recurrent rather than constant.

The human species not only lacks a breeding season, but among us the estral cycle is of no importance so far as sexual behavior is concerned. The temperature of an adult female may rise slightly at the time a mature egg is released, but so far as we know, her interest in sex does not increase at this time, and her appearance does not change in such a way as to stimulate greater male interest. Most adult human males, inhibited or not, are as likely to be interested in females on any one day of the cycle as on any other. The mating patterns of different peoples vary, but all agree in paying no attention to the fact that females can be fertilized only during a brief period each month, just as they all agree in the expectation that men and women enjoy sexual intercourse as much in one month as in the next. Tabus against touching or even having any sort of contact with menstruating women are very common. Tabus concerning a multitude of sexual activities are not only very common but very different in different human societies. All of them indicate the degree to which we have brought our sexual impulses under cortical control, but none of them are connected with the estral cycle of which, indeed, no one was aware until the present century.

That we have retained the habit of breeding the year round, even in parts of the world where seasonal concentration of births has survival value for other species, is certainly a symbol of our effectiveness in dealing with all sorts of environmental hazards. But it is more than that: this habit is associated with the habit of food-sharing which also distinguishes human beings from other primates, for food-sharing is related to the sexual division of labor mentioned earlier. Food-sharing and the social groups which share food are not seasonal events in our species but are lasting institutions. The stability of these social groups is promoted by the constant availability of sex partners within each of them, just as hostility between neighboring groups is often reduced by exchanging sex partners between them. Human boys and girls are trained very early in life to be aware of the different sexually determined roles which they are to play as adults, so that males are aware of their masculinity and females of their femininity at all times. The habit of cooperation between the individuals who form a band or community is reenforced by the constant exchange of goods and services in a reciprocal manner among them, and this includes sex as well as food.

Under the circumstances of human life sexual expression has become far more than simply the available means of propagating the species. Like other forms of cooperative endeavor, it serves as a means of binding society together. With a mentality so organized that we are aware of the future as well as of the past and the present, with a very high degree of cortical control over our immediate urges, and with a continued interest in play activities and exploratory behavior derived from our primate ancestry, we humans have an awareness of pleasure which stimulates us to seek it consciously. It is perfectly possible that other creatures are also conscious, at least to some degree, of future pleasures: the fact that chimpanzees can be taught thrift, as was mentioned in the previous chapter, is very suggestive of this. But in our species this faculty has become of enormous importance, so that human behavior is not at all simple, whether with respect to food, social relations, or sexual activities. Culture, which has developed and elaborated as our species has evolved, has modified and rechanneled all aspects of our behavior. It takes a good deal of time for a child to learn how to adjust properly.

In what may be called the prothominid stage of our ancestors' evolution, when they were already walking erect and sharing food,

the necessity for learning became even greater than it is among baboons or chimpanzees. Learning to cooperate in hunting, to be
willing to share food, and eventually to make tools must have been
important. It probably was difficult for creatures with small brains.
Selection should have favored individuals with larger brains, yet
brain size at birth could not easily have been increased. Extra brain
growth during childhood would be the only solution. Certainly a
longer childhood and possibly one free of intense sexual interests
would be of help. We have no way of knowing whether the bands
in which our ancestors lived at this time were small or large,
whether few or many adult females were sexually receptive at any
given time. The Freudian idea of jealousy between father and son,
although certainly applicable to many later human societies, is not
necessary to explain the great lengthening of the period of childhood
which so distinguishes the present human species. Slow development and the retention of many infantile characteristics would have
been useful in any case.

We have already mentioned neoteny, or the retention of youthful characteristics even after sexual maturity has taken place, as an
evolutionary mechanism for producing change with an economy of
mutations. Chapter Six lists several instances of neoteny among
primates. The assumption of constant rather than sporadic erect
posture in the human line of descent has led to additional advantages for the prolongation or lifelong retention of some traits of
infancy. Our body proportions never change in such a way as to
make standing upright uncomfortable or difficult. But there are
other ways in which neoteny seems to be expressed among us.
Among human females the labia majora continue to be well developed and the vaginal opening to be directed forward as in juvenile
but not in adult chimpanzees. A human adult's pattern of hair distribution resembles that of a chimpanzee shortly before birth. The
brain continues to grow for a longer time than among apes, and the
face never develops the projecting snout which adult apes have.
We retain the ability to learn, which is associated with youthful
inquisitiveness. Our ecological zone makes more demands upon the
brain than upon the jaws, and, up to the present, this shift has been
biologically successful for the species.

The final result has been a unique degree of power by the human species over the earth and its inhabitants. We are not only the
dominant form of life on Earth, but we have now gained the ability
to abolish life from our planet. We are not only inquisitive, but in-
ventive. We not only learn from each other but engage in teaching
each other. We have become aware of the future and plan for it.
The ability to use language facilitates cooperative endeavors which
add to the extent of our accomplishments. Consequently, the presence of our species in any part of the world is bound to cause ex-

tensive modifications in environmental conditions. As time has gone on and as we have learned more, our power has increased, so that drastic ecological rearrangements become commonplace. All forms of life cause inadvertent changes in their habitat, of course. Oppenheimer and Lang (1969) remarked on the increased branching of certain trees, the leaves and growing twigs of which are fed upon by monkeys. Removing the ends of branches stimulates a greater number of new branches to sprout. But this effect is far from disastrous. Elephants in Kenya are alleged to be destroying the vegetation upon which they subsist more rapidly than it can grow again. This is disastrous, but the habitat of elephants is restricted.

Our habitat, however, is the entire globe, rather than some small area. The efficiency with which we exploit resources has become so great that we have already made enormous changes in the environment of other creatures, not just our own. An immediate result of greater exploitative efficiency is an increase in population. Since the dawn of recorded history, less than 300 generations ago, the human population has increased perhaps a hundredfold. More recently, after the invention of power machinery depending upon the energy of fossil fuels such as coal, there has been a much more rapid increase in the crowding of the planet. Not only that, it has led to concentrations of population in urban areas to an unprecedented extent. There may be as many human beings in Tokyo today as there were in the entire world a thousand generations ago. This is alleged to be convenient for the operation of factories and businesses, but it is not necessarily convenient for the human beings involved, who are subject to crowding, pollution, and other new hazards to which they are not biologically adapted, such as the traffic jam shown in Figure 7–10.

Another aspect of culture which is pertinent to the study of ecology is the development to ethical and esthetic standards and judgments. Child-rearing practices in all societies include the inculcation of values, so that the young may know not only how to behave but why they ought to behave. The rough-and-tumble encounters which teach a youthful baboon or chimpanzee his manners are not eliminated from the human experience, but they are supplemented by positive instruction. We constantly judge things, people, and events in terms of good and bad, beautiful and ugly. In all cultures the feelings which people have about such matters provide the ideological bases for the sort of social structure which they will accept and the justification for actions which they will undertake. Cultures differ in their judgments to be sure, but, all the same, judgments are made. Mutual sympathy, human kindness, and a sense of duty actually do exist and have influenced the manner in which resources have been exploited. Ecologically, these imponder-

FIGURE 7-10. A Traffic Jam. Modern Crowding Leads Not Only to Frustration But Also to Pollution. (Photo: Robert Doisneau from Rapho Guillumette Pictures)

ables have had varied results. Land has been overcultivated and ruined by farmers intent on feeding their families. Forest clearings have provided excellent breeding grounds for mosquitoes which spread malaria. The inertia of tradition has prevented the adoption of conservation practices. Sympathy for human suffering has led to the introduction of lifesaving drugs, widening the gap between the birth rate and the death rate, and thus accelerating the speed of the population explosion (Ehrlich, 1968). Religious tabus in some areas, a sense of obligation to the family line in others, simple love of babies, or pride in virility have inhibited the application of birth control methods. In contrast to these dismal results of kindness and virtue, it must be said that it is possible to appeal for action against pollution, against overcrowding, and against destructive practices, on moral and esthetic grounds. People may well respond to such appeals more readily than to an appeal couched in terms of immediate self-interest, which is likely to sound unconvincing.

The development of self-consciousness has also, surprisingly enough, had ecological consequences. Each of us observes himself, his own condition and circumstances in contrast to those of others. Ambition becomes possible as, of course, does vanity. Human beings are not content to live like other animals. We have been hearing a great deal, lately, about the "Revolution of Expectations," but this is really nothing new. To desire and to strive for greater comfort, greater prosperity, greater beauty, or greater distinction is expectable in all cultures. Therefore, it is standard practice for human beings to exploit their environment for more than food alone. Bodily ornamentation has been practiced for at least more than a thousand generations. Bodily covering, at least to protect against frigid weather, seems to have been in use much earlier, and this required the use of animal skins. Fire was used at least half a million years ago by some of our ancestors, and this requires fuel: until recently, wood was used more often than not. All the larger apes make nests in which to sleep; with the advent of human technology, more complicated shelters began to be constructed, which require the use of still more materials obtained from the environment. As the standard of living rises, an ever greater drain is made upon irreplaceable resources. Fossil fuels began to come into common use a few generations ago. Of these there is only a limited supply, and the rate of consumption rises constantly. In the meantime, the atmosphere is becoming polluted with smog. Indeed, in the opinion of some scientists, the amount of carbon dioxide in the air has already begun to change the climate of the whole world. This might have a great variety of interesting consequences.

A few thousand years ago, the cultivation of crops began. Improvements in the efficiency of agriculture have accumulated ever since, and each improvement has had, as a by-product, some effect upon the balance of nature. Many feet of valuable topsoil have been flushed down the drain of the Mississippi River into the Gulf of Mexico. Enormous fields have been planted with a single crop, providing wonderful opportunities for population explosions of species other than man which find them good to eat. We call our competitors pests, or varmints, and apply enormous amounts of poisons (often in a most reckless fashion) for the protection of "our" crops. A universal consequence of food production is the increase of population within the area concerned. People become more crowded together, facilitating the transmission of infectious disease. Human wastes become a hazard to health, and gastrointestinal disorders become common. Only recently have public sanitation measures become at all adequate to deal with this self-imposed problem. Furthermore, of course, since sanitation has improved, fewer children die and crowding becomes more accentuated, for the surface of our planet is no larger now than it was millions of years ago when our ancestral stock first separated from that of the apes. Their biological characteristics were only minutely different from those of the ancestors of apes in those days, so there has been much debate among paleontologists, anthropologists, and other scientists interested in human origins about the fossil remains of the Hominoidea. Which are the bones of our ancestors?

Sources and Suggested Readings

AVIS, V.
  1962 Brachiation, the Crucial Issue for Man's Ancestry. *Southwestern Journal of Anthropology,* **18,** 119–148.

CHANCE, R. A. and A. P. MEAD
  1953 Social Behavior and Primate Evolution. *Symposia of the Society for Experimental Biology,* **7,** 395–439. Academic Press, New York.

DARWIN, C.
  1871 *The Descent of Man and Selection in Relation to Sex.* Murray, London.

EHRLICH, P. R.
  1968 *The Population Bomb.* Ballantine, New York.

ESTABROOK, G. A.
  1941 *Man the Mechanical Misfit.* Macmillan, New York.

GOODALL, J. VAN L.
  1967 *My Friends the Wild Chimpanzees.* National Geographic Society, Washington, D.C.

GOODMAN, M.
  1962 Evolution of Immunological Species Specificity of Human Serum Proteins. *Human Biology,* **34,** 104–151.

HARRISON, R. J. and W. MONTAGNA
  1969 *Man.* Appleton-Century-Crofts, New York.

HEWES, G.
  1961 Food Transport and the Origin of Hominid Bipedalism. *American Anthropologist,* **63,** 687–710.

HULSE, F. S.
  1967 Selection for Skin Color Among the Japanese. *American Journal of Physical Anthropology,* new series, **27,** 143–156.

HUXLEY, J. S.
  1941 *Man Stands Alone.* Harper and Bros., New York.

KORTLANDT, A.
  1962 Chimpanzees in the Wild. *Scientific American,* **206,** no. 5.

LEAKEY, L. S. B.
  1961 *The Progress and Evolution of Man in Africa.* Oxford University Press, New York.

MONTAGNA, W.
  1962 *The Structure and Function of Skin,* 2nd edition. Academic Press, New York.

MONTAGU, M. F. A.
  1946 *Adolescent Sterility.* Thomas, Springfield, Ill.
  1964 *The Human Revolution.* World Press, Cleveland.

MORRIS, D.
  1967 *The Naked Ape.* McGraw-Hill, New York.

NAPIER, J. R.
  1961 Prehensibility and Opposability in the Hands of Primates. *Symposia of the Zoological Society of London,* **5,** 115–132.

NISSEN, H. W. and A. H. REISEN
  1964 The Eruption of the Permanent Dentition of Chimpanzees. *American Journal of Physical Anthropology,* new series, **22,** 285–294.

NOWLIS, V.
  1941 The Relation of the Degree of Hunger to Competitive Interaction in Chimpanzee. *Journal of Comparative Psychology,* **32,** 1.

OPPENHEIMER, J. R. and G. E. LANG
  1969 Cebus Monkey: Effect on Branching of Gastavia Tree. *Science,* **165,** 187–188.

PENFIELD, W. and L. ROBERTS
  1959 *Speech and Brain Mechanisms.* Princeton University Press, Princeton.

SCHULTZ, A.
  1935 Eruption and Decay of Teeth in Primates. *American Journal of Physical Anthropology,* **19,** 489–587.

WASHBURN, S. L.
   1951   The Analysis of Primate Evolution with Particular
          Reference to the Origin of Man. *Cold Spring Harbor
          Symposia on Quantitative Biology,* **15,** 67–76.

WASHBURN, S. L. and I. DE VORE
   1961   Social Behavior of Baboons and Early Man, in *Social
          Life of Early Man.* Viking Fund Publication in Anthro-
          pology, no. 31, New York.

WATSON, E. H. and G. H. LOWRY
   1962   *Growth and Development of Children.* Year Book, Chi-
          cago.

VAN VALEN, L.
   1969   A Classification of the Primates. *American Journal of
          Physical Anthropology,* new series, **30,** 295–296.

CHAPTER 8

Human Origins

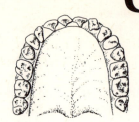

THE SEARCH FOR ORIGINS

Darwin remarked near the end of *The Origin of Species* (1858) that "much light will be cast upon the origin and history of man." He had effectively demonstrated that natural selection guides evolution, but at that time no fossil evidence of the evolution of our species from an earlier one had been brought to light. A few ancient human bones of somewhat odd appearance had been dug up, but both their antiquity and their significance remained to be proved. Before Darwin's death, excavations in rock shelters and in caves in Europe had produced more such remains. Those which could be dated well back into the Pleistocene age seemed to have an aspect unlike that of any living race of man. Very low foreheads, huge browridges arched over deep eye sockets, and retreating chins were typical. Since the first of these human fossils to be scientifically described came from the German valley called Neanderthal, they were called Neanderthal men. To the scientists who studied them, they seemed far more apelike than we, so they were assigned to a species of their own, *Homo neanderthalensis*. Professor E. A. Hooton (1946) has aptly called the Neanderthal man Darwin's first witness, and, indeed, the testimony of those bones proved very convincing.

But there was still a wide gap between man and ape. The Neanderthal fossils did not differ enough from the bones of living men so that they could be excluded from our genus. It was not until 1890,

several years after Darwin's death, that Dubois, a Dutch army surgeon searching in Java for evidence which might cast light upon the
origin of man, excavated at Trinil a fossilized skullcap to which he
gave the name "Pithecanthropus erectus," or the erect ape-man. It
was not until still another twenty-five years had passed that Pilgrim
(1915) suggested, rather timidly, that a maxillary fragment which
he had dug up earlier in the Siwalik Hills in northwestern India
might not really be that of a *Dryopithecus*. It was not until 1925
that Dart published a description of the skull from Taung in South
Africa to which he gave the name *Australopithecus africanus*. Since
that time more and more fossil evidence has been discovered and
analyzed, but these three pieces of ancient bone are of the greatest
importance, for they appear to represent three stages in the evolutionary history of man. Simons (1961, 1967) has clarified the proper

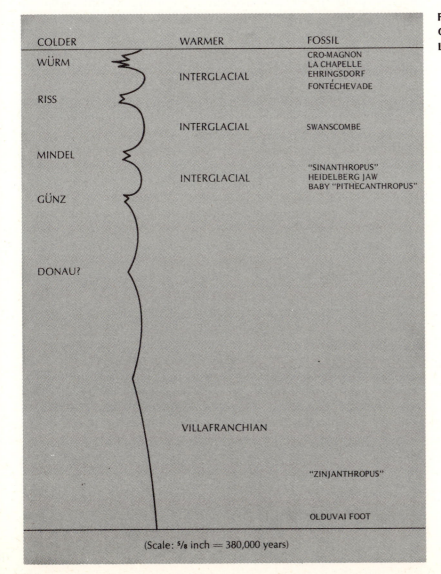

FIGURE 8-1. Chart of
Geological Time III: The
Last Two Million Years

COLDER	WARMER	FOSSIL
WÜRM	INTERGLACIAL	CRO-MAGNON / LA CHAPELLE / EHRINGSDORF / FONTÉCHEVADE
RISS	INTERGLACIAL	SWANSCOMBE
MINDEL	INTERGLACIAL	"SINANTHROPUS" / HEIDELBERG JAW / BABY "PITHECANTHROPUS"
GÜNZ		
DONAU?		
	VILLAFRANCHIAN	
		"ZINJANTHROPUS"
		OLDUVAI FOOT

(Scale: ⅝ inch = 380,000 years)

taxonomic position of the genera represented by the hominid fossils, so that we now have a pretty good idea of where each one stands in our family tree. Figure 8–1 represents the time span during which man evolved.

As long ago as 1856, before *The Origin of Species* had been published, Lartet described a mandible of Miocene age from France, which he named *Dryopithecus fontani* and which, as he pointed out, resembled the lower jaw of a living ape. Since that time teeth, jaw fragments, and a few limb bones of very similar creatures have been found in Miocene and Pliocene strata from Spain and several other parts of Europe, western Asia, eastern Africa, India, and even China. Despite the fact that taxonomists recognized their similarities and therefore included them in a subfamily, Dryopithecinae, each discoverer felt impelled to give a new generic name to his discovery. At least twenty-six such names clutter up the literature, misleading and confusing readers and disgusting beginning students, who are required to memorize them. As we will see, the proper analysis of human fossil remains has been impeded by the unjustified granting of generic and specific titles to fossils which are not, in fact, morphologically different from each other. A number of these names are found so frequently in the literature that I will have to use them from time to time for the sake of convenience. (Such names, when used, will appear in quotation marks.) Some specimens and some groups of specimens need personal or family names, like Helen Smith or the Jones family. But such names are *not* to be considered as taxonomic.

One of the most distinctive features of the Dryopithecinae is the cusp pattern of the mandibular molars, already mentioned in Chapter Six. This pattern resembles that of living apes and men and is distinct from that of the catarrhine monkeys, as Figure 8–2 shows. What has been called the Dryopithecine pattern is not bilophodont in its cusp arrangement. Instead, the cusps—often five instead of four in number—are individually distinct, and there is no narrowing of the crown between the forward cusps and those to the rear. The crown itself approaches a square in shape rather than being clearly oblong like that of a monkey molar. So far as we know, a molar with this pattern is neither more nor less efficient for mashing up fibrous vegetation than is a molar of the bilophodont pattern. It has therefore been widely accepted as a diagnostic trait enabling paleontologists to distinguish between the ancestors of monkeys, on the one hand, and the ancestors of apes and men, on the other. Another dental characteristic that serves to distinguish apes from men is the shape of the first lower premolar. Among apes, ancient and modern, this premolar is sectorial; that is, one cusp rises much

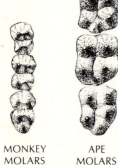

MONKEY
MOLARS

APE
MOLARS

FIGURE 8-2. Molar Crown Patterns of Primates. The Difference between the Bilophodont Molars of Old World Monkeys, Shown on the Left, and the "Dryopithecus Pattern" of the Molars of Apes and Man, Shown on the Right, Is Obvious.

higher than the other to shear against the projecting canine of the upper jaw. A sectorial premolar implies that the opposing canine did in fact project, even though the fossil hunter may not have found evidence of it. We need to keep these dental details in mind when examining the various candidates for human ancestry.

"PROCONSUL"

How much dental fossils can tell us about the mode of life of the animals concerned is another matter. Fortunately, fossil evidence of the East African Dryopithecines is much more complete than from other parts of the world. Until recently, these primates were given the generic name "Proconsul," but it is now recognized that they should be included in the genus *Dryopithecus*. They came in three sizes, the largest being as big as a gorilla (Clark, 1959), and lived from early Miocene times until, in all probability, the Pliocene. From the smallest species, which was not much larger than a baboon, we have a reasonably complete skull, including most of the mandible. The braincase is small relative to the size of the face, as compared to the proportions found in living apes; but it lacks sharp crests for muscular attachments, and the browridges are not marked. The mandible and palate are narrow in front and broad in back, and there is no simian shelf. The incisors and premolars are small. Cusps are arranged on the lower molars in the same basic pattern as that of later apes and men: the grooves which separate them are in the shape of the letter Y. The limb bones are more like those of monkeys or even men than of any living ape. The humerus, for instance, is relatively long and slender, and so are the thumb bones. The femur has a straight shaft, is less robust than in any of the large modern apes, and would seem to articulate to the pelvis in a manner more like that of man than of any living ape. The tarsal bones resemble a monkey's, except for their greater size.

A creature with such a skeleton must have been of lighter build than the large apes of today and was certainly less specialized for brachiation. In the time of "Proconsul," as today, the highlands of East Africa, where he lived, were open parkland, so that a primate able to get about on the ground as well as in the trees would have been in a fortunate position to exploit all of his habitat.

From examining a partial endocranial cast, zoologists have inferred that "Proconsul's" brain had an anatomical pattern rather less developed in a human direction than is found among modern great apes. The cerebellum and the convolutional patterns of the cerebrum must have been similar to those of monkeys. From this we can draw the less certain inference that his mentality was also less like ours. However, few other mammals of his ecological community had yet evolved brains as efficient as those of their present descendants. It is not unreasonable to suppose that he had a good competitive position, that he was, in fact, the most intelligent creature of his time and place.

Nothing contradicts the supposition that he could range freely from one forested area to the next or that he could have moved about bipedally at least as freely as any modern ape. The common ancestor of man and the African apes ought to have been very much like one or another of the species of "Proconsul." There is little reason to suppose that our line of descent had separated from that of the apes before the Miocene began, and, until recently, many scientists supposed that this separation did not take place until much later. Indeed, Sarich (1968), on the basis of his analyses of differences in the precise biochemical composition of serum albumin in various primate species, proposes that we shared a common ancestor with the chimpanzee and gorilla no longer than 3 or 4 million years ago. He bases this conclusion on the hypothesis that evolutionary change at the locus controlling this substance continues at a uniform rate rather than being subject to natural selection—an idea that most students of evolution view with profound skepticism.

Nor does this conclusion agree with the growing body of fossil evidence. In fact, Leakey (1967) now believes that several teeth, jaw fragments, and limb bones which he had earlier attributed to "Sivapithecus" and "Proconsul" are truly hominid as distinct from pongid and also that they are early rather than late Miocene in date. If he is correct, we know less about "Proconsul" than we had earlier supposed; furthermore, it would appear that our ancestors separated from those of the apes at least 25 million years ago. However, the more recent methods of dating fossil-bearing strata, about which more will be said, do not support such an early date for these finds, and Leakey's earlier opinion concerning which creature the fossils represent may be as accurate as his more recent decision. What does seem quite certain is that by the end of the Miocene there were a number of large primates in existence and that during the Pliocene, if not before, more than one taxon among them had evolved adaptations which force us to consider them among the candidates for human ancestry.

OREOPITHECUS

Perhaps the most puzzling of these forms is *Oreopithecus bambolii*, an early Pliocene primate whose remains have been found in several European countries. The most complete fossils of this variety have been extracted, badly crushed, from coal mines in Tuscany where the remains of more than fifty individuals have been recovered. Coal is derived from trees that were once alive in swampy areas. Few primates live in swampy areas, but *Oreopithecus* obviously must have visited them, although, unless he was as fully arboreal as the gibbon, he could scarcely have survived in such a place. Hürzler (1958) finds that the hand bones are those of a brachiator, and Straus (1963) finds that the arms are longer than the legs, as among living apes. The great toe was opposable, the talus quite monkeylike, but the calcaneus has an odd mixture of traits—some of which are like those of human beings. The breadth of the ilium and the development of its anterior inferior iliac spine are also such as to suggest erect posture and bipedal gait. These animals apparently stood about four feet in height, if indeed they did stand up, and might have weighed as much as eighty pounds.

The skull of *Oreopithecus*, as reconstructed, has a number of interesting features. The cranial capacity is most uncertain but was surely much greater than that of "Proconsul" and may have been equal to that of a chimpanzee. This implies a larger brain than would have been anticipated for an ape who lived 12 million years ago. There is no sagittal crest, but the browridges are very large. The face is shorter and less prognathous than in living adult apes; the nasal bones project; and the position of the malars, or cheekbones, is quite hominid rather than pongid. The mandible lacks a simian shelf. The canines are by no means large, and, in relation to this, no diastema exists between the lower canine and the first premolar. Nor is this premolar sectorial: indeed, it looks remarkably human in shape. This is one of the main arguments advanced by Hürzler in support of his contention that *Oreopithecus* is really a hominid rather than an ape or monkey. The molar teeth, however, do not have the *Dryopithecus* pattern, which has been standard for apes and men alike. Simons (1960) noted that *Oreopithecus'* teeth resemble those of the very much earlier *Apidium*, an Oligocene primate from Egypt. Inasmuch as the Dryopithecine pattern had already developed long before the time of *Oreopithecus*, we are forced to conclude that the latter was not a close relative of ours. This conclusion is reenforced by the existence, at the same time as well as earlier, of another creature with far more significant similarities to the human stock.

RAMAPITHECUS

As early as 1934, Lewis described a partial maxilla from the Siwaliks, obviously similar to that which had earlier aroused Pilgrim's cautious doubts and to which he gave the generic name *Ramapithecus*. This piece of bone is small, but it is very important because it comes from a part of the mouth in which apes and men differ greatly in a number of functionally significant ways. Since our incisors and canines are much smaller than those of apes, our palates are narrow in front, and our dental arch curves inward. The socket containing the canine root, in man, is not only smaller than that of an ape but is vertical, whereas the ape's extends in a curve from above the premolar sockets. The first premolar of an ape is somewhat enlarged compared to that of a man, too; furthermore, the internal or lingual face of the ape molar slopes, but that of a man is almost vertical. *Ramapithecus* resembles men much more than apes in all of these details, although he lived in the late Miocene and early Pliocene. Simons (1963, 1967) has reexamined the fossils attributed to this genus and to the Dryopithecinae extensively and intensively. He has been able to reclassify quite a number of the specimens earlier attributed to other genera, and he continues to find mandibles hidden away in museum basements, which are worthy of closer study than they have heretofore received. As a result of Simons' work, it is now apparent that *Ramapithecus*, of which there may or may not be more than one species, had a mouth far more like ours than did any of his contemporaries. One of Simons' more interesting conclusions is that the fossils termed "Kenyapithecus wickeri" by Leakey are, in fact, attributable to *Ramapithecus*.

How far may we safely extrapolate from these data? We lack crania and limb bones, it must be remembered, so that our knowledge of the body size of *Ramapithecus* is most uncertain. It has been estimated that he was a small animal, but this is quite impossible to prove. It has been stated that a creature with so human a dentition must have used his hands for feeding more than apes do, but in fact apes use their hands a great deal in feeding. Now that studies of primate social behavior have shown us that canine display is used as a signaling device, we cannot think of a primate's dental equipment only in terms of feeding, in any case. It is quite possible that *Ramapithecus* was bipedal; *Oreopithecus* may have been too; but lack of projecting canines is inadequate evidence to demonstrate bipedalism. On the other hand, the fact that *Ramapithecus* lived in Africa, India, and apparently China (Simons, 1967) is strong evidence that this genus was not confined to forested areas. This does suggest bipedalism. We await with much interest the discovery of the bones which will solve this problem, for this creature is by far the best candidate for the position of the earliest hominid yet discovered. No matter how *Ramapithecus* walked, his dental arrangements place him in the family Hominidae.

LATER PLIOCENE HOMINIDS

Until very recently fossil evidence of human ancestry during the Middle and Upper Pliocene remained hidden in the ground. But finally, paleontologists have begun to extract it—so far, only in eastern Africa—but who knows what the future has in store? For almost a generation L. S. B. Leakey of the Corydon Museum at Nairobi worked alone in this area, and his discoveries did not receive the attention they deserved. But after his publication of a photograph (see Figure 8-3) of the skull which he had named "Zinjanthropus," found in the Olduvai Gorge in 1959, more and more scientists have joined his search for evidence of early hominids in East Africa. The results have been excellent. It would be most unwise to claim that this part of the world is the cradle of mankind, but certainly it is among the regions inhabited by primates which were directly ancestral to the human species. *Ramapithecus*, as we have just seen, lived there as well as in Asia in the early Pliocene. Work by French and United States expeditions, the latter directed by F. Clark Howell of the University of Chicago, in the Omo Valley of southernmost Ethiopia has shown that hominids lived there more than 4 million years ago: their teeth and mandibles have been found and dated. The lower end of a hominid humerus, including

FIGURE 8-3. Two Australopithecine Skulls. "Zinjanthropus," to the Left, and "Plesianthropus" to the Right, Were Both Members of the Genus Australopithecus. The Photographs Are of Casts Made by the Wenner-Gren Foundation, and Are Shown Side by Side To Indicate the Extent of Individual Variety in This Genus. "Zinj" Lived in East Africa Nearly Two Million Years Ago and is among the More Robust Groups. "Mrs. Ples" lived in South Africa, Date Uncertain, and Represents the More Gracile Sort of *Australopithecus.* **(Photo: Arizona State Museum)**

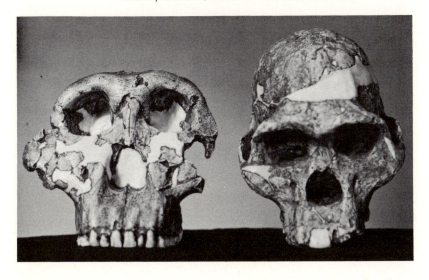

the elbow joint, was recovered by Patterson of Harvard University at Kanapoi, not very far from the Omo Valley. This specimen can be dated to more than 2.5 million years ago, by which time the Pliocene was merging into the Villafranchian. The name Villafranchian is given to the earliest part of the Pleistocene and is characterized by the appearance of numerous new genera of mammals which are still living today. The fossil remains of other animals living in these areas at that time indicate open country, not forest, although there were enough trees along the riverbanks to support bands of monkeys. It would, therefore, be most astonishing were we to discover evidence, at some time in the future, that these early hominids were not bipedal in gait. In fact, it is probably safe to assign them to the genus *Australopithecus*, of which the first specimen was reported by Dart in 1925.

THE AUSTRALOPITHECINES

When Dart had the audacity to point out the hominid characteristics of the juvenile skull from Taung, his conclusions were not well received. It was current opinion that man had evolved in Asia, and this notion was supported by the fact that "Pithecanthropus" had been found in Java. It was pointed out, accurately, that chimpanzee infants look somewhat more human than do chimpanzee adults. The date assigned to the Taung fossil was said to be far too late, in any case, for his taxon to have been ancestral to ours. But although this child's face was as projecting as that of a baby chimpanzee, his canines were much too small, his dental arch strikingly human in shape, and his braincase already larger than that of most adult chimpanzees. Furthermore, the date assigned was wrong: there is little doubt, now, that this individual lived during Villafranchian times (Oakley, 1966) perhaps as much as 2 million years ago. Finally, after more than a decade of loneliness, fossil remains of relatives of the boy from Taung began to be discovered in other South African limestone deposits—from Sterkfontein in 1936 (see Fig. 8–3) and Kromdraai in 1938. More and more are being recovered every year. More than eighty individuals of the group known as Australopithecines have left at least a tooth for scientists to study. South Africa was not their only home; East Africa, Java, and China were also within their geographical range. It now seems clear, too, that this group had evolved before the end of the Pliocene and did not vanish from the earth until the Middle Pleistocene, perhaps less than half a million years ago. Fortunately, fossil hunters have discovered the remains of males and females, of adults as well as children. Even more fortunately, several pelves, many limb bones,

one almost complete foot, fingers, toes, heel and wrist bones, vertebrae, a good number of nearly complete skulls, a collarbone, part of
a shoulder blade, quantities of spare teeth, and even ribs are
available for study.

Consequently, we have been able to find out more concerning
the anatomy of the Australopithecines than about any earlier and
most subsequent fossil anthropoids. It is no longer possible to
consider them just another sort of extinct ape. Controversies over
interpretation of the data are continuous, but very few of those who
have studied the evidence now deny that among the *Australopithecinae* are our direct ancestors. Whether the African or, more
especially, the South African specimens were as individuals ancestral to you and me is irrelevant. The first specimen to be found
had obviously died at too early an age to have been anyone's ancestor. But creatures like him, whether they lived in Africa, Asia,
or Europe, had the characteristics which made human evolution
possible. They represent an adaptive stage through which the
hominid phyletic line passed in the transition from animal status
to human standing.

For these creatures did stand, although perhaps with less ease
than we. The position of the foramen magnum, the shape of the
femur, and, above all, the construction of the pelvis, as indicated in
Figure 8–4, leave no room for doubt about this. The shape of the
ilium is almost identical with that of a modern human being:
the gluteus maximus and sacrospinalis muscles must have been
adapted for holding the body erect. Although the ischium is not so
completely human in shape, it is unlike an ape's. The articular surfaces of the femora as well as their shape are suitable for straight-
ening the leg at the knee. The inclination of the occipital condyles
and position of the foramen magnum are consistent with erect posture but indicate that the head was thrust forward more than in
the present species of man. The mastoid process just behind the
ear, which is very little developed in any of the apes, is found on
the skulls of Australopithecines just as it is on the skulls of *Homo
sapiens*.

These features alone are enough to satisfy taxonomists that
these creatures were members of our own family, the Hominidae,
rather than the very closely related family to which apes belong, the

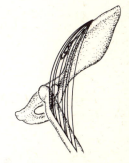

CHIMPANZEE

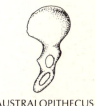

AUSTRALOPITHECUS

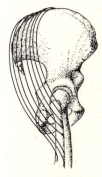

HOMO SAPIENS

**FIGURE 8-4. The Pelvis and Posture. The Pelves of the Three Varieties Are All Viewed
from the Side and Are in the Position which the Creature Would Assume When Standing
at Ease. Note that the Ape's Leg Is Bent, But that of the Man Is Not. The Striped Area
Represents the Gluteus Maximus Muscle, which Holds the Femur Directly Below the Body
of a Man, But Functions Normally as an Abductor among Apes and Monkeys. The
Reader Should Be Able, When Looking at the Pelvis of Australopithecus, To Realize What
Sort of Gluteus Maximus Would Have Been Suitable for This Creature.**

Pongidae. But the discovery of an almost complete foot skeleton at Olduvai Gorge is the final proof of erect posture and bipedal gait among the Australopithecines. At this site in northern Tanzania the Leakeys have, by their persistent efforts, uncovered hominid remains dating from about 2 million years to less than half a million years ago, and in the lowest level of all were found these foot bones. As Figure 8–5 shows, they are far more like those of a man than of an ape; there is nothing to suggest that the great toe diverges. It is a small foot, however, and this is only one of the evidences that *Australopithecus* was a small animal. The pelves, too, are small, and Lovejoy and Heiple, who have made the most recent estimate of the femoral length (1970), conclude that the femur was only 276 millimeters long in at least one individual from Sterkfontein and 310 millimeters in a Swartkrans specimen, which may belong to a larger species. Had their proportions been similar to those of *Homo sapiens*, neither would have had a stature of more than four feet. But modern proportions may not have evolved until after modern posture; we dare not extrapolate too far.

One of the disagreements in the interpretation of Australopithecine data concerns the number of taxa involved and their relationships to one another. It has been maintained that the larger individuals are males and the smaller, females. It has been maintained that the larger individuals are later in time and represent a stage intermediate between *Australopithecus africanus* and our own genus, *Homo*. It has been maintained that the larger individuals are members of a separate species, *Australopithecus robustus*, which eventually died out, whereas *Australopithecus africanus* evolved into *Homo erectus*, perhaps through an intermediate stage, "Homo habilis." Unfortunately, except at Olduvai Gorge, the sites from which the fossils come lack clear stratigraphic sequences, and in most cases their relative dates are unknown. Careful studies have demonstrated a succession of wet and dry periods in the South African fossil-bearing sites (Brain, 1959), and such climatic alterations took place in East Africa, too; but there is still disagreement as to whether these periods are contemporaneous with the advances

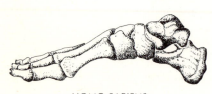

HOMO SAPIENS

OLDUVAI BED I,
LOWEST HOMINID

GORILLA

FIGURE 8-5. Hominid and Pongid Foot Bones. Note the Arch of the Foot in Homo Sapiens and the Diverging Great Toe in Gorilla. Compare Them to the Fossil Bones from Bed I of Olduvai Gorge. Then Decide for Yourself How This Ancient Primate Used His Feet.

and retreats of the glaciers which characterized the Pleistocene in North America and Europe. In time, no doubt, the continually improving techniques of the geochronologists, such as potassium-argon dating, will settle some of the disagreements.

The potassium-argon technique of dating was developed recently and, like a number of other means of attaining precision in dating prehistoric events, depends upon the regular rate of decay of radioactive isotopes as time goes on (Evernden and Curtis, 1965). A certain proportion of potassium is found to be radioactive, and atoms of argon are among the products of its decay. One-half of the radioactive potassium changes to argon in 1,300 million years. This argon is trapped if the material containing potassium happens to be buried. When a deposit is excavated, the amount of argon can be measured and compared to the amount of potassium: the proportion of one to the other indicates the date when the deposit was formed. Contamination from various sources is always possible. The technique of dating by this method is new, and sometimes conflicting dates have been ascertained. Consequently, there is a margin of error, and many authorities are not at all convinced of the accuracy of the date assigned to a deposit. This was particularly apparent when the date of the fossil called "Zinjanthropus" by Leakey was announced as 1,750,000 years ago. This was far earlier than anyone had previously imagined the Australopithecines had flourished, but repeated tests have confirmed this dating. Similar incredulity has been expressed at the results of other objective dating methods, particularly when they give unexpected results. But a scientist should never be so wedded to his theories that he refuses to accept data which disagree with them, and, in fact, the use of chemistry and physics in the study of human evolution has already made the course of human evolution more clear.

In this case the use of chemistry and physics has shown us that the period available for the transition from clever dexterous primate of uncertain posture to modern man is, after all, long enough for natural selection to have been effective. After initial astonishment almost all anthropologists accepted the expansion of the Pleistocene and the demonstration of very early toolmaking with equanimity. For not only did the dating of the occupation level at which "Zinjanthropus" was found tell us how long ago he lived but also that the manufacture of chipped stone tools has at least equal antiquity. Years before the finding of this Australopithecine fossil, large numbers of roughly fashioned stone choppers, of a type accepted as the earliest African pebble tools, had been collected in the neighborhood and other parts of the continent and had been given the name Oldowan. Clearly, some intelligent being had made them, but this was the first time that such tools had been discovered in clear association with hominid bones.

Objects of bone, horn, and teeth found with Australopithecine fossils have been claimed to be manufactured tools, especially by Dart (1957). Certainly some would have been useful weapons. But the evidence of intentional modification is dubious at best. Pebble tools, crudely but effectively chipped to obtain cutting edges, have been found at Sterkfontein, but their association with Australopithecines is most uncertain. The Olduvai discoveries, however, appear to be decisive. The presence of intentionally chipped pebble tools on the same level as the "Zinjanthropus" skull is convincing evidence. They cannot assure us that the creature whose skull was found among them was the maker, but, if he was not, a contemporary creature must have been. From his time to the present the association between man and tools has been intimate, and there can be little doubt that natural selection has operated to give survival value to the mental and manual ability required for the manufacture and skillful use of tools.

The first stone tools served for cutting something, and this is what really distinguishes them from the tools made by other animals. Sea otters use stones to crack the shells of mollusks; one of Darwin's finches uses cactus needles to pierce grubs and bugs. Chimpanzees, as we have noted previously, prepare twigs with which to catch termites and, in captivity, have been known to join two short poles in order to make a longer one. Many creatures, including the large apes, prepare nests; and beavers build dams skillfully. But the need for a cutting tool does not seem to have been felt by any creature except man and his ancestors. It would seem that he had begun to do quite new sorts of things in exploiting his environment.

Such activities clearly require a combination of forethought and necessity. Only if ecological circumstances put a real premium on the constant use of tools can we expect them to be manufactured. If a creature can collect food readily by hand, or if any stick is as good as any other for digging some desired object out of the ground, the capacity for tool manufacture will have no selective advantage. But if a creature is to attack an animal or to butcher a large one in order to carry it away more easily, a previously prepared stabbing or cutting tool will come in handy. Some natural objects have sharp edges and one might carry these about in the search for food. But conscious preparation of a tool produces something which has not existed before. It implies imagination as well as prudence.

We have already seen that the canine teeth of *Ramapithecus* were reduced in size. Those of the Australopithecines were no larger than yours and mine and did not project at all. Their incisors were small and, in some cases, badly crowded. But their molar teeth were large and, in some cases, huge. Robinson (1954) believes that there were two major varieties of Australopithecines, which had adapted in different ways to their environment, and he bases his conclusions largely on differences in the dentition. He includes in the species *Australopithecus robustus* those specimens with the largest molars, such as "Zinjanthropus"; these specimens also tend to have the smallest incisors and canines, and often the enamel on the molars is chipped as though by grit in the diet. The face was broad and not especially prognathous; the skull vault was low and carried a sagittal crest for jaw muscle attachment. These are interpreted as adaptations for a vegetarian diet which requires much chewing, yet the data suggest that "Zinjanthropus" was not exclusively vegetarian.

Australopithecus africanus had larger canines but smaller molars, a higher skull vault with a rounded forehead, and no sagittal crest. Apparently, he was the smaller animal of the two. In both forms the palate, although very large, was rounded as in modern man rather than expanding in front like that of an ape. Neither variety had diastemas to accommodate projecting canines. The cranial capacity in both averaged between 500 and 600 cubic centimeters. This is as much as that of a typical gorilla and a good deal more than that of a chimpanzee but less than half the capacity of a modern human skull.

Although the most complete remains of Australopithecines come from Africa, certain lower jaw fragments of hominid conformation indicate that Australopithecines lived in Java also. Fragments of two mandibles, each containing teeth and both very thick, were excavated from the so-called Djetis beds near Solo on the island of Java about thirty years ago. These strata are either of Lower Pleistocene or early Middle Pleistocene time, probably half a million years ago or more. A third fragment of the same sort was found in 1952. The canine sockets are small, the premolars bicuspid, but the molars enormous. Careful comparison with the teeth and jaws of *Australopithecus robustus* demonstrates the essential similarity between them (Robinson, 1955). No valid taxonomic reason can be found for assigning a separate generic name to the Javanese specimens. We can say the same about "Zinjanthropus." All of these forms should be thought of as representatives of the genus *Australopithecus*, and they may all be members of the same species. (See Figure 8–6.)

It is of interest to note that the fossil remains of "Pithecanthropus" had been found earlier in the same Djetis beds. At Swartkrans in South Africa Robinson found remains of both *Australopithecus robustus* and *Homo erectus* at the same level which is usually attributed to the earliest Middle Pleistocene. Oldowan pebble tools are also present. Furthermore, at Olduvai Gorge, not only Bed I but also Bed II (which is much later in date) has yielded fossil remains of *Australopithecus robustus* as well as of another hominid which

Tobias (1965) calls "Homo habilis" but which many other scholars call *Australopithecus africanus* (Robinson, 1965). All of these finds support the inference that there were two separate but contemporary taxa of our family, the Hominidae, in different parts of the world during early Pleistocene times. Stone tools have never yet been found where *Australopithecus robustus* alone was discovered, and this suggests that only the other taxon (by whatever name) manufactured them.

In support of the theory that *Australopithecus africanus* evolved into *Australopithecus robustus* who in turn evolved into *Homo erectus*, it has been urged that two species of the same genus are unable to coexist. Their adaptations, it is said, are bound to be so similar that the more efficient will drive the less efficient out of business if both of them try to exploit the same region at the same time. This appears very logical, but it may be that their adaptations are not quite so similar as one would expect. If, indeed, one species made stone tools with cutting edges, whereas the other did not, their ways of life could not have been the same. It is quite possible, although by no means certain, that *Australopithecus robustus*, like chimpanzees today, rarely ate animal food and depended upon vegetation for his nourishment almost exclusively. It is highly likely that *Australopithecus africanus* was much more carnivorous. The broken bones of a variety of small animals and, in some cases, larger ones have been found in close association with his fossil remains. Furthermore, Oldowan tools, crude though they may be, are adequate to dismember as well as to kill all sorts of game. At some time in the past our ancestors began to depend upon hunting for a large proportion of their diet. There is no question that they did this by using weapons which they had manufactured for the purpose. As we will see, they acquired great skill in this practice by the Middle Pleistocene at the latest. This alone would have transformed their ecological relationships; they would not have been competitors with their more vegetarian cousins.

FIGURE 8-6. Hominoid Palates (All the Same Scale). A. The Palate of Modern Man is Short, Relatively Broad, and Shaped Like the Letter "U." All the Teeth Are Small. B. The Palate of the Chimpanzee Is Long, Relatively Narrow, and Shaped Like a Horseshoe. The Canines and Incisors Are Large, But Third Molars May Be small. C. The Palate of the *Australopithecus* Was Long But Shaped Like the Letter "U." The Canines and Incisors Were Small, but the Molar Teeth Were Large. Meganthropus, However, Had Even Larger Molars than the African Forms of *Australopithecus*.

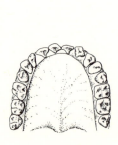

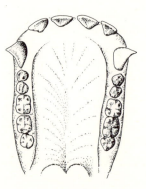

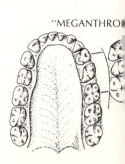

HOMO SAPIENS

CHIMPANZEE

AUTRALOPITHECUS ROBUSTUS

"MEGANTHRO

A

B

C

In any case, this much seems sure. Despite his small brain, *Australopithecus* became capable, nearly 2 million years ago, of creating a desired object for future use. Technology had come into existence. A new and previously nonexistent ecological zone had been opened up for exploitation. Selective pressures upon populations of toolmakers began to shift. From the hominid pattern of existence, already clearly different from that of other primates, the genus *Homo* was able to evolve.

THE GLACIAL AGES

Just as our ancestors adapted to erect posture before the end of the Pliocene, so they adapted to the use of tools during the Pleistocene. This was the period of recurrent glaciations in Europe and North America, and some attention must be paid to this unusual set of phenomena in order to clarify the concurrent sequence of events in human prehistory. Until recently most authorities estimated the total length of the Pleistocene at rather more than half a million years. The date assigned to "Zinjanthropus" suggests that the period must have lasted a great deal longer. Since extensive icecaps still exist in such places as Greenland and Antarctica, we cannot say with any assurance that the Pleistocene is over, although paleontologists call the present period the Holocene. The great North American icecap extended into Wisconsin as recently as 11,000 years ago. Most preceding geological periods, in contrast, have been considerably warmer in the zones which are now temperate or cold. The final and most important phases of human evolution took place during a most unusual series of climatic changes. These changes may have exerted a considerable influence upon the way in which early human populations evolved.

During the transitional period between the Pliocene and the Pleistocene, termed the Villafranchian, the climate gradually became cooler, and evidence is accumulating that extensive glaciers grew and then melted away several times. We have long had even better evidence of five major advances of the glaciers later in the Pleistocene, each with at least two peaks separated by less frigid periods called interstadials. These glaciations, known in Europe as Donau, Günz, Mindel, Riss, and Würm, were named after certain valleys in which they left moraines. North America and Europe appear to have been the areas most affected by glaciation. The tropics remained tropical, and glaciers do not seem to have been extensive in eastern Asia. During the times when much of Europe lay under icecap and the rest had a Siberian climate, such desert regions as the Sahara became less arid than they are today. Because so much water was frozen into glaciers, the sea level dropped several hundred feet. Many of the campsites of early man are now doubtless far off shore and deep beneath the sea, and such islands as Great Britain, Java, and Borneo were sometimes connected with their adjacent continents because of the fall in the sea level.

The glaciers did not advance and retreat at regular intervals. Perhaps 400,000 years separated the Donau and Günz glaciations (Evernden and Curtis, 1965). Less than 100,000 years of warm weather separated the Günz glaciation from the Mindel; the Riss and Würm glaciations were separated by a longer period. But the Mindel-Riss Interglacial, during which the earliest varieties of the genus *Homo* were flourishing, lasted for at least twice as long. It is often called the Great Interglacial because of its length. During this time the weather in such areas as Europe was considerably warmer than it has been since the Würm glacier melted away, and tropical animals such as the hippopotamus lived in France. Glacial advances and retreats rearranged the scenery quite drastically again and again. Deep valleys were gouged out of the mountains and moraines left at the edge of the glacier, for advancing glaciers scour the land deeply. River valleys eroded and then filled up again and again. Thousands of human tools dating from the first three-quarters or more of the Pleistocene have been found in the river gravels of England, France, and Germany, but living sites undisturbed by the results of glacial activity must be sought elsewhere. We cannot expect that any campsite of our early ancestors escaped if it lay in the path of a glacial advance.

Nevertheless, the fact that different sorts of animals flourished during different periods within the Pleistocene enables us, in many cases, to place the remains of man and his tools in the proper chronological sequence. We usually assume that materials found in close association were deposited together at the same time. In many parts of Europe, as glaciers advanced, river terraces were formed, which were cut into as the ice melted and water flowed more rapidly. The river cut deeper with each glaciation, so that the highest terraces, farthest from the riverbank, are the oldest and contain the earliest remains of animals and man. Periods of increased rainfall, in river valleys far from glaciers, lead to the same terracing process which is illustrated by Figure 8–7. There are hazards in this method of dating, since materials may be redeposited and found out of their proper context, but means have been devised for taking these hazards into account. Some of these will be discussed in connection with cases in which they have proved useful in checking on previously assumed dates of human remains.

Since the study of prehistoric man began in Europe, much of our knowledge about him has been derived from the study of tools and occasional human bones found in river terraces there. But until

FIGURE 8-7. The Formation of River Terraces. 1. A River Flowing Slowly Deposits Gravel which Fills Its Valley. 2. Flowing Faster, the Same River Erodes the Terrace It Had Deposited and Digs Its Valley Even Deeper. 3. At This Stage, Flowing Slowly Again, the River Deposits a Second, Lower Terrace of Gravel. 4. Once More Flowing Fast, the River Cuts Down through the Second Terrace. These Alterations of Cutting and Filling May Occur Again and Again. The Lowest Will Be the Latest.

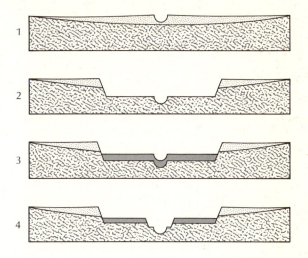

recently, undisturbed sites of really early date have not been found on that continent. However, during the 1960s at Vértesszöllös in Hungary and at Torralba and Ambrona in Spain, which have not been disturbed by glacial activities, such living sites were uncovered and carefully studied. Small animal bones as well as Oldowan stone tools have been found at Vértesszöllös, as well as a number of burned objects. Small bands of hunters probably left these objects there about 400,000 years ago. At the Spanish sites, which are adjacent to each other, there is evidence that elephants as well as many smaller animals, including horses, deer, and cattle, were driven into a bog, slaughtered, and then cut up into pieces small enough to be carried away. Large quantities of stone cleavers, hand axes, and other stone tools have also been found there, as well as pointed pieces of wood, no doubt the remnants of spears. The stone tools are of style called Acheulian, which came into use during the Great Interglacial period. Figure 8–8 shows Oldowan and Acheulian tools. Probably these sites were being used more than 250,000 years ago, but this is not yet certain.

HOMO ERECTUS

When Dubois discovered the fossil remains which he called "Pithecanthropus erectus," he assigned them to a genus separate from our own because the skullcap was so small and had such heavy brow-ridges that it appeared to be halfway between ape and man. A fragment of a lower jaw, found at the same site, confirmed his opinion. The species name, *erectus*, was given because a femur, fully suitable for erect bipedal walking, was found nearby. Now we know from Australopithecine data that an upright posture was attained by our ancestors much earlier, for the Trinil beds where Dubois worked are dated at not more than about half a million years ago. Now we realize, too, that a separate generic name for the population represented by his finds is unjustified. In fact, it has been seriously proposed by some qualified taxonomists that even the Australopithecines should be classified as members of the genus *Homo* (Mayr, 1950), but most do not agree. Since Dubois' discovery other human fossils with similar characteristics have been discovered in widely scattered places throughout the Old World. We now recognize that they all represent the same stage in human evolution, and the proper taxonomic name to be applied to all of them is *Homo erectus*.

During the 1930s Von Koenigswald (1939) excavated in Java and discovered five more individuals of the same stock which seem to have been in existence there even earlier than the time of Dubois' specimen; Von Koenigswald's find includes the skull of a small child. Later, in the 1960s, two more fragmentary skulls were found, one of which is illustrated in Figure 8–9. This specimen, under the title Pithecanthropus VI, has been excellently described by Jacob (1966).

Each of the adult "Pithecanthropus" skulls was thick and somewhat keel-shaped, low-vaulted, and broadest near the base. As in men today, the mastoid process, to which are attached the muscles which rotate the head from side to side, was well developed. Apes, in contrast, have poorly developed mastoid processes. The browridges were marked. The face, however, was shorter than among any of the Australopithecines, and the prognathism was concentrated in the region about the mouth. The nasal openings were short and broad. The roof of the mouth was high. The mandible lacked a chin, but it was not as deep as that of the Australopithecines. The molar teeth were not so large as those of *Australopithecus* but, like his, increased in size from front to rear. At least among males, however, the canines were larger, and the presence of a slight di-

FIGURE 8-8. Some Tools of Early Man. Note the Simplicity of the Oldowan Tools, in Contrast to the Neatly Finished Style of the Acheulian Tools.

ACHEULIAN TOOLS

OLDOWAN TOOLS

POINT

SCRAPER

OLDOWAN PEBBLE CHOPPERS

HAND AX

astema in two specimens indicates that the canines may have inter-
locked (Weidenreich, 1946).

"Pithecanthropus" babies developed rapidly. In the specimen
discovered the bones of the cranium were thin and sutures un-
closed, but the fontanelles, or soft spots, were small. Although the
forehead rose steeply and browridges had not yet developed, there
was already a postorbital constriction of the temples. The cranial
vault had reached the same height as in adult specimens, and its
capacity is estimated at about 700 cubic centimeters. Just as the
little *Australopithecus* boy from Taung had a brain as big as an adult
chimpanzee, this even younger "Pithecanthropus" had a brain at
least as big as an adult *Australopithecus*. This comparison represents a further step in the direction of our species. Yet orthoselection for larger brains had not yet produced a population in which
the youngsters could remain infantile for a prolonged period.

Like the earlier Australopithecines and all other sorts of later

FIGURE 8-9. "Pithecanthropus VI," One of the More Recently Discovered Specimens
of the Species *Homo erectus*. This Frontal View of the Broken Skull Shows the Low,
Keeled Vault and the Thickness of the Cranial Bones So Frequently Found in
This Species. (Photo: Ngadimin)

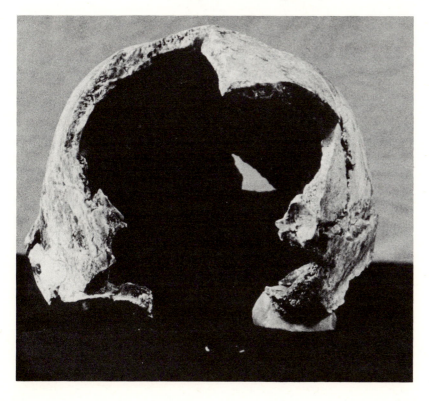

hominids, these creatures stood erect. The foramen magnum is located even farther forward than among Australopithecines, so that the head was better balanced on the neck. However, a large torus at the occiput, or rear, of the skull indicates the presence of very powerful neck muscles. The femora previously mentioned have been dated as of the same period as the skulls. It seems most likely, therefore, that they are of individuals of the same population. Their owners must have stood erect and had a stature of well over five feet. No pelves have been found, but it is clear that they had solved the problem of posture. Our ancestors had obviously become accustomed to this stance a very long time before their brains increased to modern size or their faces retreated beneath their foreheads. Estimates of the adult brain size of "Pithecanthropus" are derived from reconstructions of their crania, of which none are complete. But it is apparent that 800 to 950 cubic centimeters was normal for this population. Although an adult "Pithecanthropus" lacked a recognizable forehead, his frontal lobe was proportionately larger than any ape's but distinctly smaller than ours.

It is interesting that, as with most modern people, the left side of this lobe was slightly expanded in contrast to the right. Tilney (1928) concluded from this "the inception of unidexterity," in other words, that "Pithecanthropus" was right-handed. This is a perfectly plausible speculation, but we need more evidence before we can be sure. At some time in the history of our stock right-handedness did become the prevailing characteristic. Unidexterity would seem to be associated with the very high degree of manipulative skill which we possess, but we do not know why the right hand and not the left came to be preferred. There is convincing evidence that the trait is inherited, although training can modify the preference. All tribes and nations of the world today contain a very large majority, usually from 85 to 95 percent, of right-handed people, and all cultures frown upon left-handedness. This leads us to believe that the characteristic is of very considerable antiquity. Quite possibly, right-handedness does indeed date back to the Middle Pleistocene.

This is an interesting combination of characteristics. The short face, broad nose, and thick skull are typical of many early types of men, not apes. The cranial capacity is much greater than among apes and approaches that of *Homo sapiens*. But the canine teeth are more apelike, and no one has advanced a satisfactory hypothesis to explain this fact.

No one has found any tools in association with the "Pithecanthropus" fossils, but they have excavated crudely chipped pebbles from strata of equal antiquity in Java. One of the "Pithecanthropus" skulls shows many signs of having been caved in by the blows of some heavy implement. A number of the bones were broken and dislocated, but the fact that the fragments are in contact with each other indicates that the skull was broken before the skin and flesh of the scalp had decayed. Some of the Australopithecine skulls appear to have been crushed in a similar manner, so we must infer that interpersonal violence was one of the earliest uses to which our ancestors put their weapons. Evidence pointing to the same conclusion is found at practically all later periods of human prehistory as well. It is bad reasoning, however, to extrapolate from this evidence that every man's hand was turned against his brother. All the living primates are capable of extreme violence effectively directed, but at the same time they live in bands within which relationships are usually amicable. As a rule, hostilities appear to be directed toward outsiders. As our ancestors began to develop hunting techniques and the weapons appropriate for killing animals, their ability to damage one another would certainly have improved. Competition between different bands over hunting territory, well known in historic times, could have originated as hunting itself developed. We do not know. But the fact that our early ancestors were as nasty as we sometimes are should not be taken to mean that they could not also be as friendly as we sometimes are.

"SINANTHROPUS"

Discoveries made near Peking during the present century have given us much more knowledge of the early hominids in eastern Asia. The remains of nearly forty individuals, mostly in fragmentary condition, were excavated from deposits of Middle Pleistocene age in a cave at Choukoutien in northern China and have been most carefully studied, especially by Weidenreich (1936, 1937, 1943). On the basis of the characteristics of a single lower molar tooth, this variety was named "Sinanthropus pekinensis." Most taxonomists now agree that it was a mistake to assign generic or even specific status to this population. "Sinanthropus" certainly belonged to the same genus and species as "Pithecanthropus."

Both had large browridges, short faces, broad noses, chinless mandibles, midfacial prognathism, and occipital tori. The skull vaults of the Peking specimens are higher and a bit longer: consequently, the cranial capacity is greater. The largest is 1,300 cubic centimeters, which is not too far below the average for *Homo sapiens*. None has a diastema. Differences of similar type and magnitude separate various human races today, yet by every test we are all members of one species.

Discoverers have commonly given each new hominid fossil its own generic name, although this is most inappropriate taxonomically and certainly creates artificial difficulties for the student. Until about a generation ago very few really ancient human fossils had been discovered. Since they had been found in different parts of the world and in strata deposited during different times, the differences between these fossils were rather more obvious than their similarities. We now have much more material available. In a number of instances, extensive remains of several to many individuals—instead of a single tooth or jaw—represent a given population. The gaps separating one group or variety from another are being closed. Our sample is not only more extensive but more representative. The differences between various groups are worth studying for the light which they may cast upon the processes of human evolution, but so are the similarities. Consequently, almost all anthropologists today agree that the proliferation of genera and species which used to be common was an error.

Although the "Sinanthropus" teeth are large, they share many characteristics with those of later fossils and some living groups of men. The molars have large pulp cavities, and the wisdom tooth is the smallest of the series. The upper incisors are scooped out on the side toward the tongue, or shovel-shaped. But the lower incisors are remarkably large. Genial tubercles for the attachment of the genioglossus, one of the tongue muscles, exist in the mandible, which is thickened toward the front with an extra bony growth or torus. The malars project forward as among Mongoloids today, and one of the skulls possesses an Inca bone: the upper part of the occipital is separated from the remainder by a suture, a condition not uncommon in the Mongoloid stock. From calculations based upon the estimated length of the femur, we conclude that the average stature of adult males was slightly more than five feet. The femora are very robust and thick-walled. They are slightly bowed and flattened from front to back, a condition known as platymeria. X-ray photographs of the internal structure of the femoral head show less efficient arrangement of the spongy tissue to withstand stress than is the case among humans today.

We are able to make a number of significant inferences concerning the behavior of "Sinanthropus" from a study of the deposits which contained his fossil remains. The broken bones of many animals were found in the same strata as the broken bones of "Sinanthropus." The animals are of types which were adapted to rather cooler and damper weather than prevails in this part of China today. The flora indicate that he lived during the later part of the Mindel Glacial. Many animal bones appear to have been cut, and many to have been exposed to fire. This is also true of the greater number of "Sinanthropus" bones.

Tools chipped from quartz, which does not occur nearby, were found before any of the bones—indeed, it was their presence which led archaeologists to excavate the site. These tools are shaped in what is known as the Chopper-Chopping Tool tradition, which persisted in eastern Asia for hundreds of thousands of years. In workmanship they are distinctly superior to the pebble tools found with "Zinjanthropus." There can be no doubt that "Sinanthropus" was an able hunter and that he used fire. The manner in which the hominid skulls had been broken open suggests strongly that their brains had been extracted. Indeed, it seems most likely that he was a cannibal, just as many other humans in later times have been.

TECHNOLOGY AND SOCIALIZATION

Although fire may have been used even before the time of "Sinanthropus," we have no evidence of this. Exploiting fire for heating, cooking, and for producing chemical changes in a variety of materials long ago became one of the few universal traits of human culture. As a technological accomplishment, the conquest of fire ranks with toolmaking in importance, for it enabled man to extend his range to colder areas, to break down tough vegetable fibers by cooking, to split stones, to drive animals into his traps, and even to stay up late at night. As time passed, men found many other uses for fire, but even in early periods fire changed man's environment so that the direction of selection must have shifted.

All animals adapt to their habitats or die. We humans began a long time ago to alter our environment by using tools and fire and, having done so, had to adapt to the environment as we had modified it. Human life, according to Hobbes (1651), is nasty, brutish, and short, but these inventions, like later ones, made it a little less brutish and possibly less short. Although 40 percent of the individuals whose bones have been recovered from Choukoutien died before maturity, one skull is that of an elderly female.

Wild animals are most unlikely to live much beyond their period of reproductive activity, although some do. They are of no use to their species after they have ceased childbearing. But it will be recalled that among highly social animals, adults may play other useful roles. If such roles enhance the survival value of the group as a whole, selection may increase the lifespan. If the creatures which compose the group are late in maturing, somewhat neotenous, and dependent upon learning rather than upon inborn reflexes in their behavior, they are likely to profit from a long life. *Homo sapiens* is a species which fits this model, and the human body ordinarily wears out only after six or seven decades.

Elderly people are often of much assistance in caring for children: this frees young parents for other activities. They may continue to make tools, to repair them, and to perform household tasks of various sorts. In societies which lack writing their accumulated knowledge is enormously valuable to the community. They commonly serve as teachers, transmitting the lore of the past to future generations. In this way the ideas and values as well as the matter-of-fact techniques of the group are maintained. These functions have a great deal of utility in any human society, since they enable its members to live and reproduce much more easily and to keep a greater proportion of their offspring alive than they could otherwise.

Many if not most of the functions of the elderly involve talking. In Chapter Seven we noted that the ability to use and understand language is a unique and universal characteristic of our species. But we do not know when or how human speech began. The only sorts of evidence which we have are indirect. The continued use over prolonged periods of any particular style in tool-making suggests but cannot prove that language existed. Teaching a standardized procedure is much easier if words and example can be combined. The expansion of the proper areas of the brain, the existence of genial tubercles, and the rearrangement of the neck associated with erect posture are probably necessary anatomical preconditions. The presence of old folks in the community is also suggestive. The "Sinanthropus" assemblage is the earliest to meet all of these requirements. The evidence is too weak for us to infer that the members of this population spoke to one another, but it is a plausible speculation.

OTHER VERY EARLY HOMINIDS

Discoveries of human fossil remains in several other parts of the world permit us to infer that the genus *Homo* was widespread by the time of "Sinanthropus." As early as 1907 the Heidelberg jaw had been recovered from a depth of eighty-two feet in a sandpit near the village of Mauer in Germany. From associated faunal remains this mandible has been dated as Günz-Mindel Interglacial or possibly as belonging to a warm period during the Mindel Glacial. The man to whom this jaw belonged lived at least as early as "Sinanthropus" and "Pithecanthropus." No other skeletal remains were found nor were any tools. The remarkable thing about the Heidelberg find is that although the mandible itself is huge, the teeth are not. In size and conformation they are within the range of variation of our own species, so that there has never been any question of assigning a separate generic name to the Heidelberg man. The jaw has no chin, and the ascending ramus to which the jaw muscles attach is very broad. There are no genial tubercles. If this mandible is representative, we can only say that the earliest known Europeans of our genus were neither more nor less like us than the earliest known Chinese.

During the 1950s three incomplete mandibles and a parietal bone were discovered at Ternifine in Algeria (Boule and Vallois, 1957). They are similar in all essential details to the "Sinanthropus" remains, and the stratification indicates that they are of approximately equal antiquity. The parietal is thick, the chin absent, the molars large. Tools of quartzite and sandstone were found in close association with the bones. They were made in a very different style or tradition from those of eastern Asia, however. But although their style of tool-making was different from that practiced by "Sinanthropus," there is no reason to assign the Ternifine fossils to a separate genus or even species on the basis of evidence at hand.

An incomplete cranium found by Leakey (1961) in the Olduvai Gorge indicates that populations of the genus *Homo* inhabited East Africa during this same period. This skull, unfortunately lacking all facial parts, lay in a layer which had previously yielded many stone tools of the Chellean tradition. Tools of this kind were first discovered in France more than a century ago in river terraces which are older than those containing Acheulian tools. Chellean tools are made by chipping flakes from both sides of a stone, a technique which gives a better cutting edge than is found in Oldowan pebble tools, but they are cruder than the Acheulian forms. Because, as time went on, the style in which stone tools were made changed, tool style has often been used for estimating the date of an occupation level. But in this case we also have a potassium-argon date of 490,000 years. The vault of this skull is low, the bone itself very thick, the occipital torus for the neck muscle attachment large, and the browridges even more massive than those of other *Homo erectus* specimens. Cranial capacity has been estimated (Tobias, 1965) at about 1,000 cubic centimeters. Figure 8–10 contrasts the North Chinese with the East African specimen.

FIGURE 8-10. *Homo erectus* from Asia and Africa. Sinanthropus, to the Left, and the Olduvai Man, to the Right, Both Lived about Half a Million Years Ago. The Photographs Are of Casts: that of the Asian Sinanthropus Is a Reconstruction by the Pennsylvania University Museum, that of the African from Olduvai by the Wenner-Gren Foundation. (Photos: Left, Courtesy of the American Museum of Natural History; Right, Arizona State Museum)

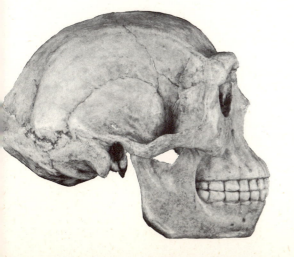

As was mentioned previously, an early Middle Pleistocene deposit at Swartkrans in South Africa contains not only Australopithecine remains, but also those of another hominid which were at first given the name of "Telanthropus." These remains consist of two mandibles with teeth as well as a few other bones. Oldowan tools accompany these fossils. Robinson (1961) believes that these remains should be classified as *Homo erectus*. The more nearly complete mandible is in depth somewhat like the one from Heidelberg. The teeth are certainly smaller than those of the Australopithecines, and some of the hand bones appear to be quite human, so his conclusion is the most likely one.

Tobias (1966), who has studied the very fragmentary remains of a hominid discovered near Lake Tiberias in Israel, classifies them as *Homo erectus*, although earlier it had been supposed that they might represent an Australopithecine population. It is to be expected, of course, that intermediate forms will appear as more fossils are found. *Australopithecus* evolved into *Homo erectus*, and the various stages of this evolution should be represented by specimens which are difficult to classify as certainly belonging to either: this is bound to be the nature of transitional forms.

At Lantian in northern China a *Homo erectus* mandible was discovered in 1963 and described by Woo (1964). The next year a skullcap and parts of a face were discovered not far away. Clearly, these bones belonged to individuals whose appearance was very similar to that of the people who lived at Choukoutien during the Middle Pleistocene. The newly found specimens may have lived at an even earlier date, and the cranial capacity seems to have been less. The jaw is said to be that of an elderly female who, interestingly enough, lacked third molars. This is a trait found most frequently today among American Indians.

Of equivalent antiquity but quite different appearance is an occipital bone from Vertesszölös in Hungary, a site mentioned earlier in this chapter. In 1965 this fossil, from the back of someone's cranium, was excavated and is described by Thoma (1966). Typically, the skull vault of *Homo erectus* is low, its broadest part being near the base. In *Homo sapiens*, on the contrary, the vault is higher, sometimes much higher, and the greatest breadth is at least halfway up to its top. The Vertesszölös find, despite its great age, indicates a rather high skull vault, which is frankly surprising. The most recently reported discoveries of hominids who lived a half million years ago or earlier come from Czechoslovakia (Fejfar, 1969). At Prezletice, near Prague, a site dating from the Günz-Mindel Interglacial has produced about fifty crudely chipped stone tools and one fragment of molar tooth which has been diagnosed as human. Whether this diagnosis is correct or not, the

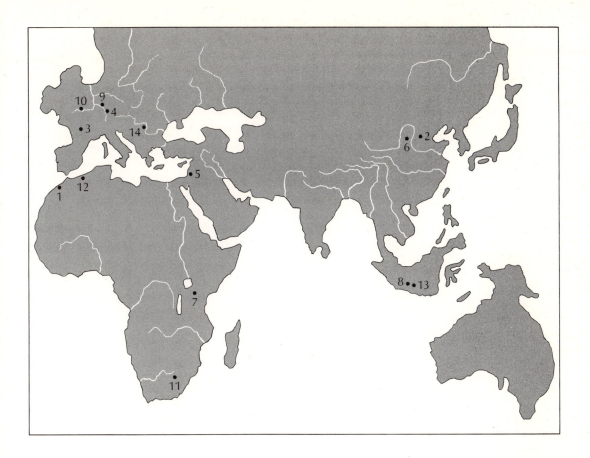

presence of tools indicates a toolmaker. Figure 8–11 shows sites where human fossils that are more than 100,000 years old have been found.

Thus it is apparent that populations of our own genus, resembling one another in many ways, had already extended their habitat throughout most if not all of the temperate and tropical parts of the Old World by the earliest part of the Middle Pleistocene. The use of tools which they manufactured was unquestionably a major factor in their success, and many anthropologists suppose that the process of toolmaking operated as the chief selective force in their evolution. Those whose mentality or temperament was not equal to the task, it is said, were unable to survive as long, reproduce as successfully, or provide for one another as well as those who were able to imagine, create, and employ tools with skill. There is much to be said for this point of view, although increased skill in social relations was certainly favored by natural selection, too. In any case, both aspects of life require the use of the cerebral cortex to a degree previously unknown. Populations of the genus *Homo* are distinguished by having brains much larger than those of any ape and at least somewhat larger than those we find in the genus *Australopithecus*.

FIGURE 8-11. Sites Where Human Fossil Remains More than 100,000 Years Old Have Been Discovered. 1. Casablanca. 2. Chou-kou-tien. 3. Fontechévade. 4. Heidelberg. 5. Israel. 6. Lantian. 7. Olduvai Gorge. 8. Sangiran. 9. Steinheim. 10. Swascombe. 11. Swartkrans. 12. Ternifine. 13. Trinil. 14. Vertesszolos.

The fossil record as it is now interpreted makes it clear that this increase in brain size did not take place until after tools had begun to be used, and it is highly probable that it did not take place until after tools had begun to be made. Recognizing this, the name "Homo faber" has been proposed for the pre-*sapiens* varieties of our genus, since the word *faber* means *maker*. As a descriptive term, this title has much to recommend it, but it does not qualify as a taxonomic label. In fact, we know a great deal more about the tool kits of these early men than we do about their anatomical characteristics, and some attempts have been made to guess at details of early human biology from a study of tools. It is said, for instance, that the tools found with the "Sinanthropus" remains were suitable for holding in the right hand rather than the left.

Styles in toolmaking persisted for incredibly long periods of time. From India through the Near East and into Europe the tradition from very early times was to chip flakes from both sides of a core, at first in a rather rough style known as Chellean or Abbevillian, but later with more care and precision in a style called Acheulian. In Africa the early pebble tools were slowly modified and replaced by hand axes and other implements flaked on both sides, so that they began to resemble the Chellean and later the Acheulian styles of Europe. Smaller flakes of stone were fashioned into knives and scrapers, and wooden shafts which must have been used as spears were also made. In eastern Asia the Chopper-Chopping Tool tradition persisted unaffected by such foreign influences. We know that toolmakers were present and can infer that there was less contact between eastern Asia and the rest of the world than between Europe and Africa. The fact that tools were not made in a haphazard manner but in accordance with standards and tradition implies that members of each generation learned style as well as utility from their elders. The fact that there are regional variations implies that there was cultural variety then as there is now.

Sources and Suggested Readings

BOULE, M. and H. VALLOIS
   1957   *Fossil Man.* Dryden Press, New York.

BRAIN, C. K.
   1959   Transvaal Apeman-Bearing Cave Deposits. *Transvaal Museum Memoir,* no. 11, Pretoria.

CLARK, W. E. LE GROS
   1959   *The Antecedents of Man.* Edinburgh University Press, Edinburgh.
   1967   *Man-Apes or Ape-Men?* Holt, Rinehart and Winston, New York.

DART, R. A.
   1925   Australopithecus africanus: The Ape-Man of South Africa. *Nature,* **115,** 195–199.
   1957   The Osteodontokeratic Culture of Australopithecus Prometheus. *Transvaal Museum Memoir,* no. 10, Pretoria.

DARWIN, C.
   1859   *The Origin of Species.* Murray, London.

DAY, M. H.
   1969   *Guide to Fossil Man.* Camelot Press, Ltd., London.

EVERNDEN, J. F. and G. H. CURTIS
   1965   Potassium-Argon Dating of Late Cenozoic Rocks in East Africa and Italy. *Current Anthropology,* **6,** 342–385.

FEJFAR, O.
   1969   Human Remains from the Early Pleistocene in Czechoslovakia. *Current Anthropology,* **10,** 170–173.

HOBBES, T.
   1651   *Leviathan.* Andrew Cook, London.

HOOTON, E. A.
   1946   *Up from the Ape,* revised edition. Macmillan, New York.

HOWELL, F. C.
   1960   European and Northwest African Middle Pleistocene Hominids. *Current Anthropology,* **1,** 195–232.

HOWELLS, W. W.
1967   *Mankind in the Making*, revised edition. Doubleday, Garden City.

HÜRZLER, J.
1958   Oreopithecus bambolii Gervais: A Preliminary Report. *Mitteilungen Naturforschenden Gesellschaft* in *Bern*, **69**, 1–48.

JACOB, T.
1966   The Sixth Skull Cap of Pithecanthropus Erectus. *American Journal of Physical Anthropology*, new series, **25**, 243–260.

KOENIGSWALD, G. H. R.
1939   Anthropological and Historical Studies Relating to the Earliest Evidence of Man. *Carnegie Institute Year Book,* no. 38.

LARTET, E.
1856   *Note sur un grand Singe fossile qui se rattache au groupe des Singes Supérieurs.* C. R. Academie des Sciences, **43**, 219–223.

LEAKEY, L. S. B.
1961   *The Progress and Evolution of Man in Africa.* Oxford University Press, New York.
1967   An Early Miocene Member of the Hominidae. *Nature*, **213**, 155–163.

LEWIS, G. E.
1934   Preliminary Notice of New Man-like Apes from India. *American Journal of Science*, **27**, 161–179.

LOVEJOY, C. O. and K. G. HEIPLE
1970   A Reconstruction of the Femur of Australopithecus africanus. *American Journal of Physical Anthropology*, **32**, 33–40.

MAYR, E.
1951   Taxonomic Categories in Fossil Hominids. The Origin and Evolution of Man. *Cold Spring Harbor Symposia on Quantitative Biology*, **15**, 109–118.

OAKLEY, K. P.

1966   *Frameworks for Dating Fossil Man*, 2nd edition. Aldine, Chicago.

PILGRIM, G. E.

1915   New Siwalik Primates and Their Bearing on Questions of Evolution of Man and the Anthropoidae. *Records of the Geological Survey of India*, **45**, 1–74.

ROBINSON, J. T.

1954   The Genera and Species of the Australopithecinae. *American Journal of Physical Anthropology*, new series, **12**, 181–200.

1955   Further Remarks on the Relationship between "Meganthropus" and Australopithecines. *American Journal of Physical Anthropology*, new series, **13**, 429–446.

1961   The Australopithecines and Their Bearing on the Origin of Man and of Stone Tool-Making. *South African Journal of Science*, **57**, 3–16.

1965   Homo "habilis" and the Australopithecines. *Nature*, **305**, 121–124.

SARICH, V.

1968   The Origin of the Hominids: An Immunological Approach. *Perspectives on Human Evolution*, **1**, 94–121.

SIMONS, E. L.

1961   The Phyletic Position of Ramapithecus. *Peabody Museum Postilla*, **57**, 1–9.

1963   Some Fallacies in the Study of Hominid Phylogeny. *Science*, **141**, 879–889.

1964   Apidium and Oreopithecus. *Nature*, **186**, 824–826.

1967   The Significance of Primate Palaeontology for Anthropological Studies. *American Journal of Physical Anthropology*, new series, **27**, 307–322.

STRAUS, W. L.

1963   The Classification of Oreopithecus, in *Classification and Human Evolution*. Wenner-Gren Foundation, New York.

THOMA, A.

1966   L'Occipital de l'Homme Mindelien de Vertesszölös. *L'Anthropologie*, **70**, 495–533.

TILNEY, F.

1928   *The Brain from Ape to Man*. Paul Hoerber, New York.

TOBIAS, P. V.
    1965   New Discoveries in Tanganyika: Their Bearing on Hominid Evolution. *Current Anthropology*, **6**, 391–411.

    1966   Fossil Hominid Remains from Ubeidya, Israel. *Nature*, **211**, 130–133.

    1967   *Olduvai Gorge 1951–1961*, Vol. 2. Cambridge University Press, Cambridge.

WASHBURN, S. L., ed.
    1963   *Classification and Human Evolution.* Wenner-Gren Foundation, New York.

WEIDENREICH, F.
    1936   Sinanthropus Pekinensis and Its Position in the Line of Human Evolution. *Peking Natural History Bulletin*, **X**, part 4.

    1937   The Relation of Sinanthropus Pekinensis to Pithecanthropus, Javanthropus and Rhodesian Man. *Journal of the Royal Anthropological Institute*, **LXIII.**

    1943   The Skull of Sinanthropus Pekinensis: A Comparative Study of a Primitive Hominid Skull. *Palaeontologia Sinica*, new series D, no. 10.

    1946   *Apes, Giants and Men.* University of Chicago Press, New York.

WOO, J. K.
    1964   Discovery of the Mandible of Sinanthropus Lantianensis in Shensi Province, China. *Current Anthropology*, **5**, 98–101.

CHAPTER 9

The Evolution of Homo Sapiens

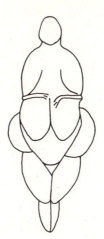

FOSSIL SPECIES

The species as a unit can be defined in genetic terms when we deal with living animals, as we have seen in Chapter Three. In most cases two contemporaneous species can be distinguished without too much trouble: they are separated by the incompatibility of their genetic systems. A workable definition of species from an evolutionary point of view has to be less precise. In dealing with species which no longer exist the paleontologist has only fossil remains to guide his judgment. He notes the differences which separate one fossil from another and compares these to the degree of difference between living species of the

FIGURE 9-1. Chart of Geological Time IV: The Last 100,000 Years

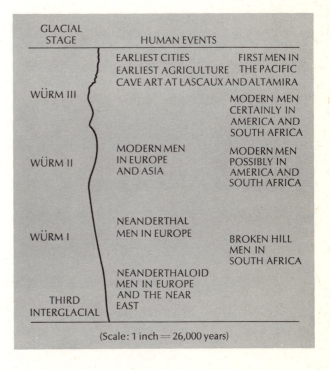

GLACIAL STAGE	HUMAN EVENTS	
	EARLIEST CITIES	FIRST MEN IN
	EARLIEST AGRICULTURE	THE PACIFIC
	CAVE ART AT LASCAUX AND ALTAMIRA	
WÜRM III		MODERN MEN CERTAINLY IN AMERICA AND SOUTH AFRICA
WÜRM II	MODERN MEN IN EUROPE AND ASIA	MODERN MEN POSSIBLY IN AMERICA AND SOUTH AFRICA
WÜRM I	NEANDERTHAL MEN IN EUROPE	BROKEN HILL MEN IN SOUTH AFRICA
THIRD INTERGLACIAL	NEANDERTHALOID MEN IN EUROPE AND THE NEAR EAST	

(Scale: 1 inch = 26,000 years)

227

same order or family. He also ascertains the amount of variation within such living species. If the difference between two fossil populations is as great as that between living species, the taxonomist is justified in considering that they were in fact separate species, even though one may have been ancestral to the other, which is often the case.

All too often, fossil evidence is so scanty that more than one interpretation is possible. Perfectly legitimate disagreements exist concerning the number of species of *Australopithecus*, for instance. Until quite recently, many anthropologists supposed that there were several species of "Pithecanthropus." Now, however, enough data have been recovered and analyzed to assure us that these varieties should all be included in the species *Homo erectus*. Almost all scientists who have studied the course of human evolution agree that this species was ancestral to our own. A few, indeed, do not consider the distinctions between people who lived 500,000 years ago and those who live today great enough to justify full specific rank for *Homo erectus*, whom they consider an early subspecies of *Homo sapiens*. There is general agreement, however, that such differences as do exist reflect the growing importance of culture as an aspect of the human environment, to which our ancestors became better and better adapted as time went on. Evolutionary

FIGURE 9-2. STEINHEIM AND SWANSCOMBE SKULLS. These Two Skulls, Neither Complete, Provide Us with the Only Information We Have about the Facial Appearance and Brain Size of Our Ancestors during the Latter Part of the Great Interglacial, about Two Hundred Thousand Years Ago. Note that the Steinheim Specimen Has Large Browridges, But that We Can Only Guess about the Browridges of the Swanscombe Specimen. (Photos: Left, Karl Dietrich Adam, Staalliches Museum für Naturkunde, Stuttgart, West Germany; Right, British Museum)

changes of this sort have been found in many creatures. When the members of a population begin to do something new and different, they may be rather clumsy. If their new activities are important, natural selection will increase the proportion of those who are skillful: this process—known as orthoselection—has been discussed in Chapter Four.

By the time of the Great Interglacial, between the Mindel and Riss glaciations, *Homo erectus* seems to have been a well-established and biologically successful species. His closest cousin, *Australopithecus*, if not already extinct, was dying out, so that *Homo erectus'* own position in the world of life was preeminent. By the skillful use of the tools which he made, he was able to kill large game animals and thus to occupy an adaptive zone unavailable to other primates. The astonishingly large number of stone tools which he discarded or mislaid informs us that his habitat extended from northern China to southern Africa and from northwestern Europe to southeastern Asia, which at that time included Java. Yet evolution continued. Once the genus *Homo* had begun to live this new sort of life, new possibilities for progress were opened. The problem of erect posture had been solved by *Australopithecus;* the problems involved in the creation of tools and the sharing of food began to be solved by *Homo erectus.* We have by no means finished solving them yet. But orthoselection for the ability to deal with them has been continuous and has led to the evolution of a species with much larger and, let us hope, better brains. It is impossible to draw a line at some date in the past between ancestral and descendent species. No *Homo erectus* mother ever gave birth to a *Homo sapiens* baby: the change from the genetic system of the earlier species to the genetic system of the later species had to be slow and imperceptible if the population was to survive.

As we recover the fossil remains of people who lived between 500,000 and 150,000 years ago, we can expect to find forms which will be difficult to pigeonhole into either *Homo erectus* or *Homo sapiens*, for these fossils are bound to represent the transition from one species to the other. But our direct knowledge of human anatomy for this entire period is dependent upon two broken skulls from Europe, shown in Figure 9–2, and a few jaw fragments from Morocco.

STEINHEIM

The Steinheim specimen—a skull—was found in river gravel near Stuttgart in southern Germany in 1933. These strata are said (Howell, 1960) to date from near the end of the Great Interglacial.

The skull is a young lady's and the left side of her face appears to have been crushed by a heavy blow. The browridges are very large, the mastoid processes small, and the skull bones very thick. However, she had a perfectly good forehead, and the contours of her skull are of essentially modern type, with its greatest breadth rather high. The front teeth are missing, but the molars are small. Her nose was broad, but her face lacked the prognathism of earlier fossils. Brain size as estimated from the cranial capacity was between 1,100 and 1,200 cubic centimeters. She was not a beauty queen by our standards, but she must have looked a great deal more like us than any of the earlier types yet known. In appearance her browridges and nose are reminiscent of the Neanderthal people who lived in Europe much later, so that it has been proposed that she is an early representative of that race. But the shape of the braincase and the lack of facial protrusion remind one of modern *Homo sapiens*. Indeed, Coon (1962) accepts Steinheim as a member of our species, but most anthropologists do not.

SWANSCOMBE

The Swanscombe specimen, from England, consists of the occipital and both parietal bones, but the forward part of the skull is missing. Since the sutures between the bones had not begun to fuse at all, we must infer that the individual to whom they belonged had died young, perhaps at about twenty years of age. The bones are very thick, but as with the Steinheim skull the conformation is modern with the foramen magnum well forward as among ourselves, and there are no indications of excessively developed neck muscles. The mastoid processes are small. The skull is said to be that of a female, and females usually have smaller mastoid processes than males. The Swanscombe cranial capacity has been estimated at more than 1,300 cubic centimeters, but in the absence of a frontal bone this estimate is tentative although perfectly reasonable. We simply do not know whether the face was more or less prognathous than Steinheim's nor whether the browridges were large or small. Had such fossils been dug up from a recent deposit, no one would have hesitated to assume a physiognomy like that of *Homo sapiens*, but in fact they came from a river terrace containing Acheulian tools and dated as late in the Great Interglacial period. The most reasonable speculation is that the young lady of Swanscombe lived more than 200,000 years ago, that is, about 10,000 generations after the time of "Sinanthropus."

Since it was surprising to find bones of such modern shape in such an ancient deposit, the fluorine test has been given to the Swanscombe fossils to determine whether they really are as old as their context would affirm. The fluorine present in ground water accumulates steadily in buried bones and teeth. The rate of accumulation depends upon how much fluorine is dissolved in the ground water; the amount differs vastly from one drainage basin to another. Therefore, the fluorine test cannot tell us how long in years bones have been buried. But we can discover whether various bones found in close association in a single deposit have all been together for the same length of time. The bones which have been buried longest will have taken up more fluorine; those added at a later date will contain proportionately less. Since bone is porous, the fluorine tends to be distributed rather evenly as it accumulates, and small samples from a fossil are adequate for testing.

In the stratum containing the Swanscombe fossils there were also many bones of animals typical of the Great Interglacial in England, such as extinct species of elephant and rhinoceros. The fluorine content of the animal bones varies from 1.7 percent to 2.8 percent. That of the Swanscombe occipital bone is 1.9 percent and of the parietal, 2.0 percent (Oakley and Montagu, 1949). We can only infer that the human remains are not intrusive but represent an individual who was alive at the same time as the other creatures. The human stock had obviously evolved at a rapid rate during the Great Interglacial.

The use of chemical and physical methods of dating is being constantly improved and extended. It has proved invaluable as a check upon the authenticity of bones alleged to be those of early mankind and his relatives. For a long time authorities thought that the Galley Hill skeleton, found only 500 yards from the Swanscombe remains, was of equal antiquity despite its completely modern appearance. The fluorine content of the different bones in this skeleton, however, amounts to only 0.2 percent to 0.4 percent, which is approximately the same as that in postglacial animal bones in the vicinity. We must conclude that the Galley Hill skeleton was intentionally buried in a grave and is not truly ancient at all.

THE PILTDOWN HOAX

The most spectacular case in which fluorine and other tests have been used is the notorious Piltdown hoax, perpetrated in England. Early in this century, when the Heidelberg jaw and the first "Pithecanthropus" skullcap were the only really ancient human fossils yet discovered, the Piltdown remains were brought to public attention. They consisted of several bones from a braincase, a lower canine tooth, and most of the left half of a mandible. They seemed to have come from gravels laid down early in the Pleistocene which also yielded bones of elephant, hippopotamus, and beaver. A few fragmentary bones of similar nature were later found not far away. The extraordinary thing about this collection of bones was that the cranial fragments were like those of *Homo sapiens*, whereas the jaw and canine were completely apish. Neither *Homo sapiens* nor an ape ought to have been living in England during the Lower Pleistocene. Yet the finds indicated that a creature combining the characteristics of both had done so. Since the cranium and jaw had been found in close proximity, it was supposed that they must have come from a single individual. At the time no one knew the sequence of events in the course of human evolution because so very few fossils had been discovered. Many scientists flatly refused to accept the Piltdown specimens as authentic, yet no one could explain them away.

During the succeeding thirty years, however, there were so many new finds that the outline of human origins became much more clear. The Piltdown remains, weird enough before, now appeared rather absurd. But there they were. Oakley (Oakley and Hoskins, 1950) subjected both skull and mandible to the fluorine test and found that they had accumulated only about one-fifth as much of this element as had the elephant bones in the deposit. They had clearly been misplaced and could not be of greater antiquity than the end of the Ice Age. Since the existence of such a creature as the Piltdown Man during a recent time was even more puzzling than it would have been during an earlier epoch, a much more thorough investigation was launched. The fluorine test methods were improved, and all the fragments were tested for the presence of nitrogen, carbon, water, and collagen. These materials should decrease in amount as time goes on, just as fluorine increases. All the tests led to the same conclusion (Weiner, 1955): the mandible and canine are fresh bone, whereas the skull fragments are indeed from the end of the Pleistocene. Their association was false. Further examination indicated beyond doubt that the teeth had been filed down and the jaw stained with chromate and iron to give it an ancient appearance. It is, in fact, the jaw of a young orang-utan. The elephant teeth are probably from Tunisia, those of the hippopotamus from Malta, and both had been stained to agree in color with the human skull. The hoax was an elaborate one, accomplished with great skill and careful planning. What its perpetrator neglected to take into account was the future. He had no means of knowing that physical and chemical tests, capable of detecting such fraud, would later be developed. He depended upon the fact that scientists, even when they disagree, assume honesty in the search for truth on the part of their colleagues.

MORE PLEISTOCENE FOSSILS

With the Piltdown hoax exposed, it is possible to return to the account of honest discoveries of fossil men. During the long period after the time of Swanscombe and Steinheim, the Riss glacier advanced and melted away. In Europe and parts of Africa people continued to make tools in the Acheulian tradition, but they improved them as time went on. Before the end of the Final Interglacial in Europe many smaller implements, such as hide scrapers and spearheads among others, had been invented, and the Mousterian tradition began to form.

FONTÉCHEVADE

Only a few human fossils, mostly skull fragments, have been found in association with Acheulian tools or in strata of equivalent age. Fragments of two skulls were found at Fontéchevade in France in 1947 (Boule and Vallois, 1957). The first is a small piece of the frontal bone, including the inner corner of the orbit and the area called glabella just above the root of the nose. The second is an almost complete skullcap which shows no trace of postorbital constriction. The curve of the frontal bone indicates a forehead of the modern type. It has been estimated that the cranial capacity was over 1,400 cubic centimeters. As in almost all of the earlier varieties of man, the greatest breadth is well toward the rear, but the parietal bones are shaped as in *Homo sapiens*. The fragment of the frontal bone lacks the large browridges present in all other specimens of equal antiquity and also in the Neanderthal variety which lived later. It is, in fact, the sort of browridge expected on a modern female. It has been claimed that this is a sign of immaturity, but the presence of a well-developed frontal sinus militates against this assertion, and the sutures are well fused also.

A few years ago I had the opportunity to examine and handle the Swanscombe and the Fontéchevade specimens within a few days of each other. I was struck by the greater thickness of the Swanscombe parietals, although the Fontéchevade braincase is, by modern standards, a robust one. The crania from La Chapelle-aux-Saints and from La Ferrassie, both classified as Neanderthal, were made available to me at the same time as the Fontéchevade specimen. These crania, when palpated, are found to have thinner parietals than Swanscombe, resembling Fontéchevade in this respect. But in conformation they are quite different, indicating a range of variation in the European population of the Final Interglacial period which would not have been anticipated.

The dating of the Fontéchevade specimens is authenticated, as Figure 9–3 indicates, by their presence beneath a stalagmite floor at

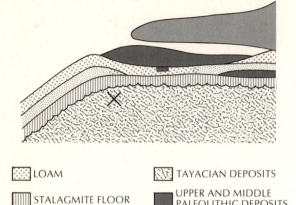

FIGURE 9-3. Cross-section of the Fontéchevade Cave. This Diagram Shows the Stratigraphic Position of the Two Skull Fragments. X Marks the Spot Where They Were Found.

LOAM

STALAGMITE FLOOR

SAND

TAYACIAN DEPOSITS

UPPER AND MIDDLE PALEOLITHIC DEPOSITS

BEDROCK

the mouth of a cave. Above this floor are strata containing Mousterian tools, and above these are strata containing Upper Paleolithic tools. Furthermore, the fluorine test shows that the bones are of the same age as the surrounding animal bones: rhinoceros, deer, and tortoise among others, a group typical of the Riss-Würm Interglacial. The only inference we can draw is that evolution had been continuing in the direction of *Homo sapiens*, as might be expected, since the time of Swanscombe and Steinheim, so that some individuals at least had lost the very large browridges which had previously been characteristic of our ancestors. The implication is that such massive facial architecture was losing its survival value, presumably because with larger brains, powerful jaws were no longer required. In fact, we will see that the Fontéchevade frontal bone is quite different from almost all others of its time and of times considerably later. Imposing browridges remained in style for thousands of generations.

NEANDERTHAL MAN: GEOGRAPHICAL RACE OR UNIVERSAL STAGE?

Only late during the Final Interglacial, as Figure 9–1 shows, does Darwin's first witness begin his testimony. This testimony is not what had been expected, but it makes the nature of evolution in general and of human evolution in particular much more comprehensible. The development of the Neanderthal variety of man demonstrates, among other things, the opportunism of evolution and certainly refutes the notion of orthogenesis. It may be interpreted as an example of climatic adaptation as well, for the Neanderthal populations were the first we know about to have lived in a really cold climate.

Ehringsdorf in Germany, Saccopastore in Italy, Montmaurin in France, and Ganovce in Czechoslovakia have provided fossil remains which show the characteristics of this variety while the European weather was still warm. More than one hundred specimens have been recovered from strata dating from later, during the first half of the Würm Glaciation in Europe. A number, of equivalent antiquity, come from several sites in the Near East, notably Mount Carmel and Shanidar. A few Neanderthaloid fossils, still from the same time period, have been found in North Africa, and one in Central Asia.

All of the skulls, whether early or late and whether or not of individuals who lived in cold places, share some common characteristics. This is true even of the bones of children. The bones tend to be somewhat thick, as in all types of early men. The browridges are perhaps especially distinctive: they are not only large and continuous, but curve up over each eye socket, to which they give a somewhat cavernous look. The Steinheim and Zambian specimens are somewhat like this, but the *Homo erectus* browridges form a single horizontal bar. The Neanderthal skull vault is long, low, and narrow, and quite flat on top; its greatest breadth is not high on the parietals. The nose is broad but with nasal bones suggesting a high bridge. The mandible has a broad ascending ramus and little or no chin. The palate is large, but there is little alveolar prognathism. Instead, the entire face is likely to project forward and to be very long. The cheekbones, on the contrary, rarely project forward as they so often do in *Homo sapiens* today.

Those specimens which date from the interglacial period, however, are frequently of lighter build than are those of the succeeding frigid era. Their foreheads are usually higher, but their cranial capacity is smaller, for the occiput is not protrusive. The wisdom teeth found in some of these early specimens are exceptionally small, even as among some of us nowadays. The characteristics in which the later Neanderthal people differ most from us are either absent or incipient rather than fully developed among the earlier representatives of this group.

It must be emphasized, too, that the European specimens show the most extreme differentiation from the mainstream of human evolution. These were the first to be discovered; they have been the most fully described; and there are more of them. It is easy to think of the most extreme cases, such as the La Chapelle-aux-Saints skeleton, as being representative, just as it is easy to think of all Scandinavians as being tall and blond. In both cases the error is the same. The Neanderthal variety of *Homo sapiens* had as much individual variation as any other sort of man. Fortunately, both old and young male and female specimens are available for study, and there are more of them than of any of the varieties of hominids who lived before their time.

Typically, the later Neanderthal people had occiputs of a peculiar shape, drawn out like a bun, rather low, which balanced the forward projection of the face. The mastoid processes are small. The cranial capacity was at least as great, on average, as that of Europeans today, but the frontal lobe is rather smaller. The orbits are very round and deep. The cheekbones slope back from either side of the nose, and the maxilla, or upper jaw, is not cut away beneath the cheekbones as yours and mine but appears rather puffed out. In osteological terms, the canine fossa is lacking. The palate is exceptionally broad, but the teeth, although ordinarily large, are by no means outside the range of variation found in modern man.

A few of the skeletons of the later Neanderthal variety are complete enough to give us a good picture of body build as well as facial appearance and cranial characteristics. The spinous processes of the cervical vertebrae are long and heavy, from which, as well as from the shape of the occiput, we must infer strong neck muscles. The ribs indicate a barrel-shaped chest; the lumbar vertebrae and sacrum suggest that the reverse curves found in modern man were less emphasized. The humerus is short, and in all known cases, the right humerus is more massive than the left (Boule and Vallois, 1957). The radius is also short and curved, leaving a large space for the muscles of the forearm. The finger bones are short. Femora and tibiae have massive shafts and articular surfaces; the former is usually curved more than is typical of modern man. The calcaneus and astralagus bones of the foot are shaped in such a way as to suggest that much of the body weight rested on the outside of the foot. Two footprints in an Italian cave indicate that the foot was broad and the arch low, but we have no other direct evidence of the external appearance of Neanderthal individuals.

If a Neanderthal man stood up straight, he should have had a stature of five feet and a few inches. But some authorities (Boule and Vallois, 1957) think that he slouched a bit at the knees, as one is likely to do when thrusting the head forward, whereas others (Straus and Cave, 1957) believe that the specimens which suggest slouching were those of arthritic rather than healthy individuals. The latter opinion is now generally accepted.

In any case he was a burly fellow. A compact body with short extremities is an excellent adaptation for cold weather, and the Neanderthal people were the first to remain in Europe during an intensely cold period. Puffy cheeks may have served to help warm the air which he breathed, and his eyes should have been well protected in their deep sockets. Very often Neanderthal man is represented as having been hairy, but Arctic peoples today rarely are; since he used tools, his fingers would have had to be so exposed that no amount of hair would have helped him much. Very often, too, he is represented as having thick lips, but this seems most inappropriate for an Arctic creature.

Fortunately, these people, like most, were a rather untidy lot, often mislaying their tools for archaeologists to pick up 50,000 years later. Consequently, we know quite a lot about their living habits as well as about their skeletal structure. Many of them dwelt in rock shelters or the mouths of caves, and after generations deposits of the trash and garbage which they dropped built up in layer above layer at such sites. Their tools included knives, points for spears of various sizes, scrapers for treating animal hides, and gouges among other things. They seem to have been the developers of the Mousterian style or tradition in toolmaking, which involves the use of flakes chipped off from larger cores of stone, usually flint. They made use of fire; this must have been absolutely vital for their continued life during the Würm Glaciation. The presence of great quantities of scrapers at their habitation sites forces us to infer that they used the hides of animals which they killed; the presence of gouges strongly suggests that they bored holes in the hides so that they might be fastened together, perhaps with leather thongs. The most reasonable conclusion is that they fashioned some sort of clothing from animal hides.

The bones of various Arctic-adapted animals such as the mammoth, the wooly rhinoceros, and the cave bear are found at their hearths: we can be sure that they succeeded in killing these large creatures as well as smaller ones for food. The type of wear which is characteristic of Neanderthal teeth indicates a great deal of chewing, such as is required by a diet which includes a large quantity of coarse fibrous vegetation. But it may indicate constant chewing on animal hides to keep them flexible, too. Doubtless, they were as omnivorous as other humans before or since. The bones of more than a dozen men, women, and children found at Krapina are not only broken up, but some show signs of burning, which has led some authorities to believe that they were the victims of cannibalism. This is plausible but certainly not proved. The Neanderthal people do not seem to have suffered from caries, but pyorrhea was not uncommon, and their teeth became badly worn even in early maturity, so that apical abcesses formed, and they lost teeth. The so-called Old Man of La Chapelle-aux-Saints—who was certainly both mature and arthritic but far from senile—had lost the greater number of his teeth before death. Nor was he the only specimen who had clearly lived for many years despite being partially incapacitated.

Stewart (1959) has described the condition of one of the individuals found in a cave at Shanidar in Iraq. The man's right arm was withered and had been successfully amputated, yet he survived this misfortune for many years. It is obvious that no matter how many cannibal feasts they engaged in, Neanderthal people did their best to assist other members of their own kin or community and were sometimes skilled enough to keep disabled people alive for a prolonged period.

They also buried the dead. Whether earlier members of our genus did so we do not know, but a fair proportion of the Neanderthal skeletons are from graves, laboriously excavated with inadequate tools and sometimes adorned with objects which could only have a supernatural significance. The little boy of Teshik Tash, mentioned in the first chapter, was of the Neanderthal race and one of a number whose bones had been ceremoniously treated. All peoples in recorded history have felt the necessity of doing something about the dead bodies of their companions: they are not just left lying around. Sometimes they are buried, sometimes burned; sometimes parts of them are ceremonially eaten. But the ritual disposal of the dead is one of the universal items of human culture, and it dates back clearly at least to the time of Neanderthal man. We can infer from this that these people must have had some ideas about death and that they lived in communities of older and younger individuals. If we add to these obvious inferences the evidence of care of the disabled and of the manufacture of a variety of cleverly made tools in traditional style, we must infer that they used language as we do for exchanging ideas and information, as well as for expressing emotional states.

Articulate speech, a possibility for the Pithecanthropoids, is a certainty for the Neanderthaloids. We do not know what they talked about nor what their ideas about death were, any more than we know what their skin color may have been. But we can be sure that they had skins, and the data concerning their behavior make us sure that they had ideas as well. Since man's mentality is his most outstanding biological characteristic, it is important for students of human evolution to seek for those clues concerning it which the archaeologist may obtain.

Culture is, in a sense, not only our creation but our creator. When our forefathers began to modify their environment by new inventions, such as a tool or cooked food, their offspring had to adapt to the new, not to the outmoded environment. When they began to share ideas, whether those ideas were sensible or silly, their offspring had to adapt to behavior in line with those ideas. Linton (1945) has defined culture as behavior which is learned, shared, and transmitted from generation to generation. It modifies or controls all aspects of conscious behavior by human beings. The evolution of the capacity for culture is, in fact, the evolution of the human stock. Arbitrary standards, symbols, and ethical judgments are among the essential characteristics of culture. These depend upon the type of mentality which has both imagination and the ability to restrain immediate impulses and which is also capable of speaking and understanding language. From the behavior of Neanderthal man, as indicated by materials found in association with his bones, we have no reason to suppose that he lacked these characteristics. From his time on, our species has had to adapt more and more to an ecological niche which we have created. *Homo erectus*, an exceedingly clever animal, consequently evolved into *Homo sapiens*, who had eaten the fruit of the tree of knowledge of good and evil.

The later Neanderthal populations were not restricted to Europe, although they evolved their most distinctive characteristics on that continent. The Würm Glaciation not only made the climate very cold but set barriers which these people must have found difficult if not impossible to cross. The extent to which these barriers isolated western Europe is shown by Figure 9–4. They created the ideal circumstances for the evolution of a separate variety (Howell, 1952). In the Near East the situation was different: communication with other human populations remained open. Some, but not all, of the Near Eastern fossil remains of the early part of this last glacial period have thoroughly Neanderthal features: the cripple of Shanidar is an example of this sort, except for his chin. So is a skull discovered at Amud in Galilee (Suzuki, 1965). The skull of a young lady accompanied by the lower jaw of a man which were found at the Tabun Cave in Israel are slightly less characteristic; they lived during the middle of the Würm Glaciation.

In the cave known as Skhul, nearby, but perhaps some thou-

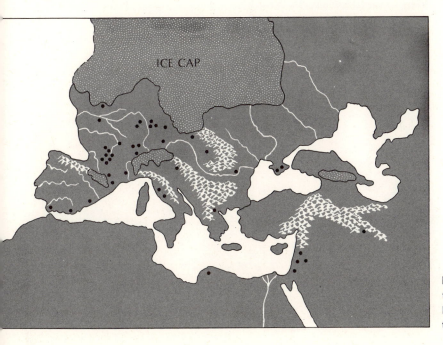

FIGURE 9-4. The Habitat of the Neanderthaloids. Each Dot Indicates a Neanderthaloid Fossil Site.

sands of years later, lived a group which was barely on the verge of being Neanderthal at all. Full face and profile views of one of the skulls from this cave are shown in Figure 9–5. All had big brow-ridges and some facial protrusion, but none had either the bun-shaped occiputs or the flattened skull vault which are so diagnostic of the full-fledged Neanderthal man. The canine fossae and the mastoid processes were developed as among modern man. The cranial capacity of the adult males was more than 1,500 cubic centimeters. These men were rather tall in stature but had short powerful forearms. The characteristics of this small population, quite possibly representing several generations of a family encamped at the spot, have been explained in several ways (Keith and McCown, 1939). Some consider them to be hybrids between the Neanderthal variety and the more recent type of mankind. Others consider them a stage in a presumed evolution from Neanderthal to ourselves. Perhaps, however, they simply represent the appearance of another of the populations of the time. Almost everyone had big browridges in those days, but we have no evidence that the Neanderthal populations had a world-wide distribution.

FIGURE 9-5. Two Views of the Skhul V Skull. These Are Photographs of a Cast Made by the Wenner-Gren Foundation of an Adult Male Skull from Mt. Carmel in Israel. (Photos: Arizona State Museum)

Another cave in Israel at Djebel Quafzeh near Nazareth has also produced interesting evidence about the Middle Paleolithic inhabitants of this region. People used this cave repeatedly, leaving great

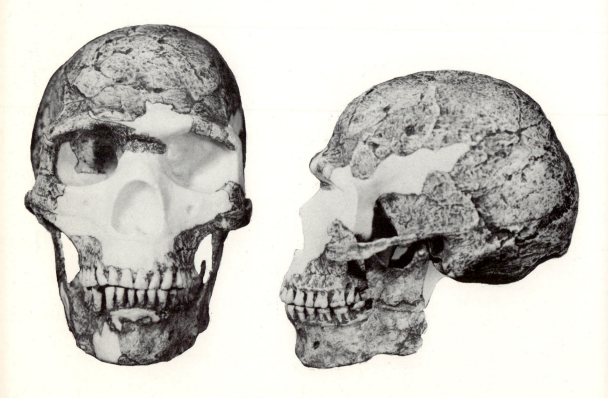

quantities of stone tools and burying their dead near the cave mouth. In one occupational level deposited during a time when Mousterian tools were being used, the skeletons of six adults and two infants have been found. The skulls of the adults are high vaulted and lack bun-shaped occiputs; the mastoid processes are well developed. The browridges, although large, are not Neanderthaloid in conformation, and canine fossae are present. There is very little facial prognathism, and the mandibles have quite obvious chins. These are not the skeletons of Neanderthal men.

RADIOCARBON DATING

Neanderthal man's habit of building fires has proved as useful to the archaeologist as his custom of burying the dead has been for physical anthropologists. The latter custom enhances the probability of the skeleton's preservation. The former makes it possible to obtain accurate dates for habitation sites by using the carbon-14 test. Only a few Neanderthal dwelling places have been uncovered since this test was developed, and most are so early as to be at the extreme limit of reliability, at least by present methods. Shanidar Cave, for instance, was inhabited by Neanderthaloids at various times between 65,000 and 46,000 years ago, and a fragmentary mandible from Libya, which may be Neanderthaloid, has been dated at 38,000 B.C. A Mousterian site at La Quina in France, at which a female skull was found, is dated at 33,000 B.C., later than any other Neanderthaloid (Oakley, 1966). But the carbon-14 means of dating the past has proved so useful for later times that it must be described.

Carbon 14 is a radioactive isotope of carbon. So far as we know, it is created at a constant rate by cosmic rays in the upper atmosphere. Its rate of decay is also constant: it has a half life of 5,720 years. This means that one-half of all the carbon 14 in existence at any moment will have ceased to exist after that number of years; one-half of the remainder after 11,440 years; one-half of what still remains after 17,160 years; and so on indefinitely. Ordinary carbon 12 is not radioactive and so does not vanish in this way at all. All living things contain a great deal of carbon, but no organism is able to distinguish the radioactive isotope. A living plant will therefore contain ordinary and radioactive carbon in the proportions which exist on the surface of the earth. At death, of course, carbon ceases to be taken up into the plant, and from that moment on, the proportion of carbon 14 to carbon 12 which it contains will decrease at a regular rate. When wood is burned, some charcoal is likely to be left as a residue, and this charcoal is composed very largely of carbon. If the hearth is buried, this carbon remains for a future archaeologist to extract. After 5,720 years, the proportion of carbon 14 to carbon 12 will be only one-half as great as it had been when the firewood died. After 11,440 years the proportion will be one-quarter. Laboratory tests for the degree of radioactivity in a sample of charcoal from an ancient hearth can, therefore, tell us how long ago the plants which were burned had been killed. There is, of course, a margin of error, but this is relatively small. There are possibilities of contamination from roots of plants growing upon the site later, or from some burrowing animal bringing in more recent carbon, or from other causes. But these contingencies can be taken care of, although in some cases sufficient precautions have not been taken.

Bone, of course, contains carbon just as wood does, but this is likely to be lost in the process of fossilization, so the charcoal from a hearth is the most dependable source of material for testing. The technique of carbon-14 dating has been enormously valuable to all who are interested in prehistoric events. It is very widely and most successfully used for obtaining dates from a few thousand to a few tens of thousands of years ago. After some 50,000 years have elapsed the proportion of carbon 14 to carbon 12 is only one five-hundredth as great as in living things. This amount is so small that it is extremely difficult to measure with any degree of accuracy. From all the prehistoric periods more recent than that time, however, we now have a means of dating any site upon which a fire had burned and left charcoal for analysis. As a result, we have learned a great deal about the sequence of prehistoric events.

OTHER EARLY FORMS OF HOMO SAPIENS

Paleoanthropologists who use the term Neanderthal Man when referring to all people who lived anywhere during the period which we have just been discussing do so because they believe that the European and Near Eastern fossils represent a universal stage in human evolution. Others, of whom I am one, have concluded that the data available support the thesis that Neanderthal Man was a local race living on the periphery of human habitation, under adverse climatic conditions. Most scientists agree, however, that he was a member of our own species, *Homo sapiens*, although earlier taxonomists used the term "Homo neanderthalensis." Whether this variety of man was a geographical race or a chronological stage, he did not differ enough from living populations to be given formal taxonomic status. The fossil evidence shows a genetic continuum rather than a gap between the Neanderthal populations and other varieties of *Homo sapiens*.

As we have seen, some of the Near Eastern populations, although they were contemporaries of the later and more extreme

Neanderthal people of Europe, resembled modern men in many ways. The little boy who was buried at Teshik Tash falls into the same category. In China several fossils of Neanderthal contemporaries have been found. The Ma-pa skull (Woo and Peng, 1959) has a low vault and orbits rounded in the Neanderthal fashion, a broad nose, and, of course, heavy browridges. These browridges, however, are shaped more like those of the Solo specimens than like typical Neanderthal specimens; and the forehead is less retreating than in either of these varieties. The other finds are too fragmentary to tell us much.

The Solo population, which lived in Java sometime during the Würm Glaciation, is known to us from eleven crania and two tibiae. No faces or jaws were found, and the skulls had been cracked open at the base: it is suspected that they were victims of foul play and perhaps of a cannibal feast. Cracking open the skull in this manner is not uncommon among cannibals in recent times. Neither the browridges nor the occipital tori resemble those typical of Neanderthal Man. According to Weidenreich (1951), they are like the similar parts of the skulls of "Pithecanthropus." Inasmuch as they lived in the same area, this similarity should not astonish us. The cranial capacity has been estimated to range from 1,200 to 1,300 cubic centimeters, which is far less than among the Neanderthal people. The size of the brain varies greatly in modern man, and apparently this was the case in early times as well. There is no evidence that, beyond a certain threshold, human intelligence is dependent upon the volume of the brain.

From North Africa we have scanty evidence of early forms of *Homo sapiens*, most of it so fragmentary that it is subject to diverse interpretations (Briggs, 1968). Two pieces of mandible dug up near Casablanca in Morocco may date from the time of the Riss Glaciation in Europe. They are said to resemble the earlier Ternifine specimens mentioned in the last chapter. A badly broken up skull from Rabat, not far away, and perhaps, but not certainly, of more recent date, has a number of the same characteristics, but the canine fossa is meagerly developed, which suggests Neanderthaloid affinities. Two skulls from Jebel Irhoud, farther south, clearly date from the period of the Würm Glaciation and are accompanied by Mousterian tools. Their appearance is even more like that of Neanderthal Man (Ennouchi, 1962), although their noses were broader and flatter and their browridges less pronounced. A number of other fossils from northwestern Africa add to the impression that the course of human evolution in this part of the world was only slightly influenced by gene flow from Europe. The Strait of Gibraltar, although narrow, is deep. It remained open when the sea level fell during glacial periods, and there is no evidence that man had ventured onto the water until many thousands of years later.

South of the Sahara, fossil evidences of contemporaries of Neanderthal Man are more numerous. In East Africa Leakey has found quite a few specimens which probably date from the same period. From Kanjera come fragments of four skulls and a few other bones, together with Acheulian tools. These skulls are quite large, and two of them lack browridges. The single piece of maxilla available has a canine fossa. Human fossils from other sites in this area are fragmentary, but none of them resemble Neanderthal Man.

From still farther south in Africa come specimens which are more complete and, probably, not quite so ancient. Two skulls which resemble one another closely are those found at Broken Hill in Zambia and at Saldanha in the Cape province of South Africa. The browridges are the largest of any fossil man yet discovered; the forehead and skull vault are very low; and the occipital torus is extensive. The cranial capacity is between 1,200 and 1,300 cubic centimeters. Yet the position of the foramen magnum is the same as in *Homo sapiens*, and the mastoid processes are well developed. A profile view of the Broken Hill specimen is shown in Figure 9–6. Clearly, the head was balanced as among members of our species. The face was quite prognathous, the nose very broad, and the palate enormous, but the teeth are very much like our own. This is true even to the extent that in the first skull to be found, the one from Zambia, ten of the fifteen teeth were carious, and alveolar abscesses had formed at the roots of several. The Broken Hill specimen, which is a complete cranium, lacks a canine fossa, but a separate maxilla found with it possesses one (Wells, 1957). At the Cave of Hearths in South Africa Dart found a fragment of mandible which is presumed to date from the same period as the Saldanha skull; the fragment is clearly that of a human child who was rather chinless. The Florisbad skull from this region, although incomplete, shows

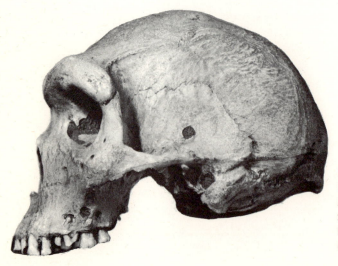

FIGURE 9-6. Homo Sapiens from Broken Hill in Zambia. This Photograph of a Cast Made by the Wenner-Gren Foundation Shows a Probable Contemporary of the People Who Lived at Skhul.
(Photo: Arizona State Museum)

much of the face and the skull vault. Its large browridges are not at all of the same shape as those of Neanderthal specimens. The cranial vault is low; alveolar prognathism is marked; the canine fossa is obvious; and the nasal root is very depressed and broad. Carbon-14 dates of materials in the deposits containing this fossil indicate an age of 37,000 years or more, but these materials may have been contaminated (Oakley, 1957) by more ancient carbon. Although the term Neanderthaloid has been applied to all of these remains (Singer, 1958), none of them look very much like the Neanderthal people of Europe and the Near East. Geographical variety, presumably adaptive in origin, seems to have existed within the human species then as it does now.

THE PEOPLE OF THE UPPER PALEOLITHIC

By the time the peak of the Würm Glaciation had passed, new methods of toolmaking had replaced the Mousterian techniques in Europe, and a new variety of people had replaced the Neanderthal race. The new tradition of toolmaking consisted of striking long blades with parallel sides from a prepared core of flint or obsidian. Some tools of this sort were found in the Tabun Cave in Israel. These came from a much earlier time, and it is quite possible that tribes which migrated from the Near East brought the blade-making tradition to Europe. We do not know. It is clear, however, that the Neanderthal peoples vanished. Those who lived in Europe may have frozen or starved during the worst of the glacial weather, but those who had lived in other areas, such as in the Near East itself, vanished also. Brace (1962) maintains that they evolved into the modern variety of man in both areas. It is more generally supposed that such an evolution is more likely to have taken place in the Near East than in Europe. In any case, they were succeeded by peoples whose anatomical characteristics are like those of modern man.

Earlier taxonomists hotly debated whether we should be considered as a separate species from the Neanderthal variety. The fact that groups having intermediate characteristics lived in the Near East, where genetic contact was possible, and the fact that the earliest Neanderthaloids had less extreme specializations than the later ones in Europe, both support the idea that they should be considered as a race of *Homo sapiens* rather than as a species. The four skulls in Figure 9–7 show the similarities and differences between Neanderthal and later types of man.

The stone tool industries earlier than the Mousterian are known commonly and collectively as Lower Paleolithic; the Mousterian itself and others of the same age as Middle Paleolithic; and those which succeeded it as Upper Paleolithic. Figure 9–8 illustrates Mous-

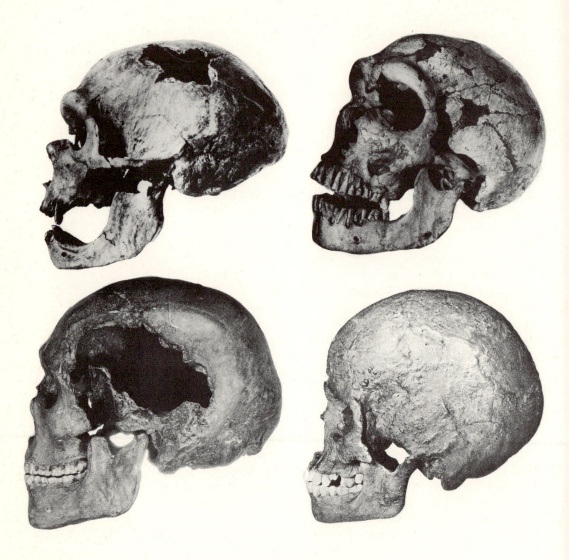

FIGURE 9-7. The Skulls of Four Ice-Age Frenchmen: Upper Left, LaChapelle;
Upper Right, LaFerrassie; Lower Left, Combe Capelle; Lower Right, Grimaldi
(Photos: Upper Left, Collection Musée de l'Homme; Upper Right, Collection
Musee de l'Homme; Lower Left, Courtesy of the American Museum of Natural
History; and Lower Right, Courtesy of the American Museum of Natural History)

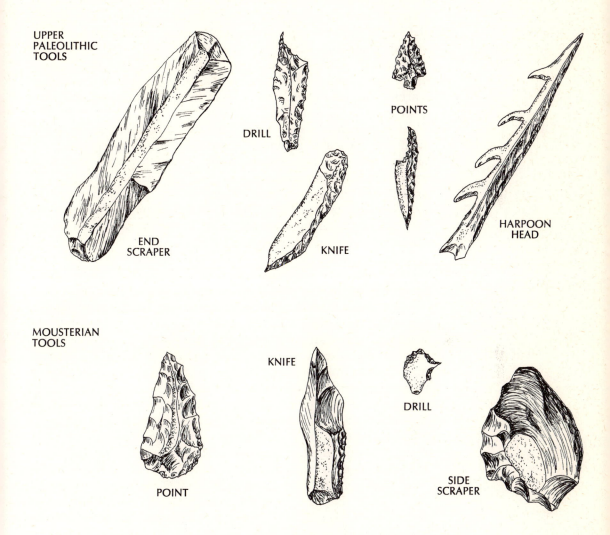

UPPER
PALEOLITHIC
TOOLS

DRILL

END
SCRAPER

KNIFE

POINTS

HARPOON
HEAD

MOUSTERIAN
TOOLS

KNIFE

DRILL

POINT

SIDE
SCRAPER

FIGURE 9-8. Tools of Later Paleolithic Men. As Time Went On, Our Ancestors
Made Better and More Specialized Tools, as These Mousterian
and Upper Paleolithic Implements Show.

terian and Upper Paleolithic tool types. In Europe the earliest Upper Paleolithic industry is called Chatelperronian; the latest is called Magdalenian. There is no debate about including all men of the Upper Paleolithic and still later times in the species *Homo sapiens*. We have derived most of our information about the people of the Upper Paleolithic from excavations in Europe, but we know enough about this period in other parts of the world to be quite sure of this. There has been more digging in Europe than in other areas, and as archaeologists examine sites in Asia and Africa, we are learning that the picture derived from Europe is not necessarily representative of the situation elsewhere.

But we can safely say that during the period lasting from 40,000 to 10,000 years ago, members of our species continued to live as hunters and collectors in small bands. Their technology began to improve at a much more rapid rate than before, and it is not at all unlikely that the human population increased. It certainly spread to previously uninhabited regions. Man lived under a greater variety of environmental conditions than he had previously, and adaptations to these varied conditions have evolved. But the protection of better technology and the requirement for adaptation to culture assumed additional importance as time went on. We find racial but no species differences among the men of the Upper Paleolithic.

The skeletal remains of Neanderthal man and his contemporaries so far discovered represent scarcely more than one hundred individuals. Excavations in European sites of the Upper Paleolithic have produced more than twice as many. We have, therefore, a much greater amount of material for study, a bigger and probably a more representative sample upon which to base judgments. Furthermore, the skeletal remains are so much like those of people living today that we can feel more confident about reconstructing missing parts than we are when dealing with fragmentary fossils which, though clearly hominid, are very different from similar structures in modern man. Finally and best of all, the men of the Upper Paleolithic were artists. They carved and painted the forms of many of the creatures of their times and a much smaller number of representations of one another. Their art, like all other art, followed conventions and standards. They did not take photographs. But they have left the evidence to prove that, as we would have expected, their external appearance was as similar to ours as their bony structure.

Earlier prehistorians and anthropologists were as fond of creating Upper Paleolithic races as they were of creating Lower Paleolithic genera. In both cases, they outraged the principles of taxonomy. Just as the not really so old man of La-Chapelle-aux-Saints was taken to be the ideal type of Neanderthal, so the Cro-Magnon man was taken to be the ideal type of early *Homo sapiens* in Europe.

Reconstruction of the exterior appearance of this gentleman usually gave him a most noble and clean-shaven appearance, firm and proud, yet not fierce or arrogant. In contrast, his European predecessor was made to look disheveled, vacant-eyed, slack-lipped and hairy-faced: a most unpleasant fellow. Such reconstructions are, of course, nothing but the projection of race prejudice into the past. The skeletons found at the Cro-Magnon rock shelter are but a few of the many of Upper Paleolithic date, and the idea of basing a race upon these finds alone is absurd. Other so-called races, such as those based upon finds at Combe-Capelle, Grimaldi, Chancelade, and Predmost, are equally invalid. Morant (1930) showed that the variability of the cranial remains from the European Upper Paleolithic was no greater than could be expected in any interbreeding population. Some men were taller than others; some had broader faces or longer noses. But there is no real evidence that a number of different races existed, either side by side or one after another.

Compared to Europeans of more recent times, those of the Upper Paleolithic had longer skulls, greater head circumference, and broader faces. The average cranial capacity, like that of Neanderthal man, was at least as great as ours. Most of them were dolichocephalic: that is, the skull was less than 75 percent as broad as it was long. In this they resembled earlier hominids, but in more recent times the proportion of people with rounder heads has increased very much. Most of them were leptorrhine: that is, the breadth of the nasal openings was less than 48 percent of its height or length. Here they resemble a large majority of recent Europeans but differ from all the earlier varieties of our genus, among whom broad noses were typical. Most of them had short broad faces. In this they resemble such living races as the native Australians, but neither the Neanderthal race nor a majority of living Europeans. Only a few of the Upper Paleolithic skulls show alveolar prognathism, and none show the facial prognathism typical of earlier varieties. In this they resemble later Europeans and many Asians more than other living peoples. The forehead was typically both high and broad and as frequently vertical as among Europeans today; but adult males frequently had bigger browridges and more depressed nasal roots than are typical now, except among such people as the natives of Australia. The chin was usually very prominent and so were the gonial angles at the rear of the mandible.

Due to burial, many almost complete skeletons have been preserved, so that we know a great deal about the body build of Europeans during the Upper Paleolithic. In stature the adult males were at least as tall as modern Europeans, but women seem to have been rather short. Limb proportions are as variable as in modern peoples and in general approximate those found among later Europeans. A few finds, such as that of a boy and a mature woman buried together at the Grotte des Enfants near Monaco, have exceptionally long limbs and a slightly Negroid facial appearance (Boule and Vallois, 1957). In general the bones indicate a robust build but not of the really burly type so common among the Neanderthal people. One can easily imagine that the Europeans of the Upper Paleolithic looked more like athletes in good condition than most of us do. In order to survive, they probably needed to be rather tough specimens, for their technology, although a distinct improvement over any earlier type, would seem most inadequate to us.

We can infer that before the end of the Paleolithic they had added fish to their diet from the presence of bone fish hooks and harpoon points in the strata containing their remains. The spear-thrower, an implement usually made of antler, was another useful invention of the period. This is a stick with a hook at one end into which the butt end of the spear is fitted. Its length added to that of one's arm permits a man to put more power into throwing the spear. Drills, needles, chisels, and a variety of small points suitable for light missiles were also standard parts of the Upper Paleolithic tool kit. Semisubterranean pit houses, in which mammoth ribs were used as beams, have been found in areas where no caves were available as dwellings.

Indeed, dwellings were sometimes placed within cave mouths. Post holes at the Grotte du Renne indicate the size and shape of a hut constructed by its Chatelperronian occupants (Movius, 1969). This is one of the sites which best reveals the nature of the transition from Mousterian to Upper Paleolithic ways of life, which took place here at least 34,000 years ago. Even the topmost Mousterian occupation level contains no evidence of artistic endeavor, or of any structures.

"Whereas the demonstrable Neanderthalers lived in the cave in the midst of the filth and rotten carcasses of their game, beginning with Level X things began to change in a fundamental manner. To the bad luck of the palaeontologist, who will no longer find the mattress of bones on which the Mousterians had dwelled, the cave was now levelled off by man. Right up to the time of Level III one finds signs of Palaeolithic household work—the bulk of the rubbish and debris was now gathered up and thrown outside in small heaps" (Movius, 1969, p. 122).

Toolmaking traditions, on the contrary, were not altered so rapidly or drastically, for the last two Mousterian levels contain a good number of tools worked in Upper Paleolithic style, and tools made in the Mousterian tradition are scattered throughout the Chatelperronian levels. A few teeth from the earliest Chatelperronian level are like those of Neanderthal rather than Upper Paleolithic men. But such transitional sites are rare in Europe.

Upper Paleolithic men (or women?) wore necklaces of shell or teeth and, on some occasions, masks. They made cords and baskets. Hides were used as clothing and perhaps to cover cave entrances. Since the bones of many game animals have been found at the cliff bases in a number of places, we infer that the collective drive was one method of hunting. We know from paintings which date from that period that by the end of the Upper Paleolithic they used the bow and arrow in hunting and in war.

Many paintings and engravings have been found on the walls of caverns, often far from their entrances. The representations of animals are most lively and often superbly executed. Upper Paleolithic men did not draw the human form as frequently. When they did, however, it is the form of a modern man with a hairless body which we see or, more often, the form of a woman. Facial features are sketchy, or indistinguishable, or covered by a mask which represents an animal or bird. Ivory or stone carvings of nude females are very common. One of these, the so-called "Venus of Lespugue," is shown in Figure 9–9. In all instances, they emphasized secondary sexual characteristics, sometimes to an astonishing degree. Breasts are enormous and pendulous, hips expansive, thighs tapered. The women look about eight months pregnant; possibly they are just very fat. Head hair is sometimes but not always represented; it may be straight or very curly. We have our earliest evidence of such human characteristics as curly hair and swelling breasts from these artistic creations.

Feet are never represented, hands very rarely. As in drawing, facial features are sketchy at best. Usually they are absent: obviously these sculptures do not represent females as they really were, for it is quite certain that they had feet and faces. Indeed, a few footprints on the clay floors of caves indicate that the exterior appearance of the foot was exactly what one would anticipate from a study of the foot bones; nor do hand prints on some cave walls present any surprises. These are the hands and feet of people like ourselves.

Skeletal material from the Near East and North Africa resembles that from Europe very closely, and archaeological data from all these areas indicates a good deal of intercommunication throughout all this part of the world. The Würm glacier was still extensive, the sea level still low, and distances not too great from Italy to Britain or from Iran to the Balkans. Available evidence does not permit us to infer a number of different breeding populations separated from one another within this part of the world. With the extinction of Neanderthal man, a single variety seems to have inhabited all the area around the Mediterranean Sea and as far north as climate permitted hunters to venture. Nor do there seem to have been changes

STATUETTE
OF FEMALE
AT LESPUGUE

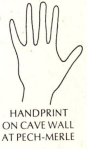

HANDPRINT
ON CAVE WALL
AT PECH-MERLE

HUMAN MALE
AT LASCAUX

FIGURE 9-9. Evidence of Human Appearance during the Upper Paleolithic

in anatomical form during the 1,500 generations of the Upper Paleolithic period in this whole area. The men of the late Magdalenian do not differ from those of the early Chatelperronian in any regular way, although styles in art and toolmaking had undergone a number of changes.

The climate fluctuated but remained generally cold in Europe and chilly and wet around the Mediterranean. Neither the bones nor the art tell us about the pigmentation of the people who lived in this area during the latter half of the Würm Glaciation. From the ecological circumstances known to have existed, however, it is perfectly reasonable to speculate about the origin of depigmentation in our species and the reason for its concentration in this part of the world.

A fair skin together with light eyes and hair are found among a greater proportion of the populations derived from northwestern Europe than among any other populations today. Such a combination is not found in any other living species of primate. It must, therefore, have become established at some time during human evolution. Sporadic instances of depigmentation are found among most human populations, but selection in favor of this characteristic would seem to have operated only in Europe and the areas around the Mediterranean and to have operated most strongly in the northern and northwestern parts of this region. The genetics and physiology of pigmentation are discussed in later chapters. Here it suffices to say that several genes are involved, that darkness increases with age to some extent, and that the ultraviolet rays from the sun create vitamin D in the human skin as well as burning and tanning it. Consequently, a fair skin may be adaptive in cloudy but dangerous in sunny regions. Various fish oils are also rich in vitamin D, which functions to prevent rickets among growing children, but there is no archaeological evidence of the consumption of sea food in this part of the world until rather late in the Upper Paleolithic.

Even today fair skins are not at all uncommon in North Africa and the Near East. Light eyes are less common and blond hair least of all, although they may appear among children. These traits have often been explained by assuming migrations from northern Europe into these regions, but such explanations are most inadequate. It is often among tribes in refuge areas least affected by migrations that the greatest amount of blondness has been found. If a light skin is indeed adaptive in areas where the cloud cover prevents much exposure of the skin to sunlight, it is worth remembering that most of this area, during the Upper Paleolithic period, had a climate as cloudy as that of northern Europe today. It is, therefore, quite likely that blondness became established in this part of the world some thousands of generations ago. As climatic zones shifted to the

north with the melting away of the Würm icecap, a fair skin would
have lost its adaptive value in the Mediterranean area. Among the
tribes which moved north and remained under cloud cover, on the
contrary, selection for depigmentation should have continued. The
most probable speculation is that blondness was as common among
the Upper Paleolithic peoples of the European-Mediterranean area
as it is today in Europe itself.

In other parts of the world during this same time period, people
lived under different ecological circumstances, yet the archaeological data indicate that everywhere the earlier varieties of man had
given way to or evolved into *Homo sapiens* as we know him today.
With improved tools and perhaps also because of expanding population, regions which before had few inhabitants or none at all now
became populated. Just as better technology enabled the Neanderthal race to live in the frigid conditions of Europe when the Würm
glacier expanded, so now that the glacier was retreating, a still more
extensive tool kit enabled mankind to contend with all sorts of climatic conditions.

FOSSIL EVIDENCE OF RACES

IN AFRICA

By the end of the Pleistocene the Sahara had become broad
enough, hot enough, and dry enough to serve as an effective barrier
to extensive population movements of tribes with the Paleolithic
technology. Skeletons of this period which have been found near
the Mediterranean coast resemble those of the Europeans who lived
at the same time. The site known as Afalou Bou Rhummel contained the remains of nearly fifty individuals who may have lived
10,000 years ago. Their chief distinctions were broader noses and
skulls and heavier browridges than their European contemporaries.
They appear to have been a particularly muscular group, even for
the Upper Paleolithic, but there is nothing about their bones which
suggests Negroid affiliations (Arambourg, Boule, Vallois and Ver-
neau, 1934).

On the other hand, a faceless skullcap from Singa in the Sudan,
which may be more than 20,000 years old, has a narrow forehead
which swells out above the browridges in the fashion commonly
found among the skulls of African Negroes today and, especially,
among Bushmen. The thickness of the skull and the size of the
browridges are more typical of early man in general than of modern
Negroes. Another skeleton, clearly a burial, in the Olduvai Gorge
in East Africa was found with Upper Paleolithic tools. It is that of
a tall man, and the skull is dolichocephalic with a long face. The

browridges are very small and the nose not very wide. Alveolar prognathism is not marked. Several skeletons found in Gamble's Cave in East Africa are quite similar; they probably date from the very end of the Upper Paleolithic which may, in this part of the world, have been less than 10,000 years ago. None of the East African finds are so obviously Negroid as the Asselar specimen, but they are not dissimilar to skeletons of some of the modern natives.

Asselar is in Mali near the southern edge of the Sahara desert, and the skeleton which was excavated there in 1927 is almost complete. It has been dated by the radiocarbon method at a bit earlier than 6,000 years ago and is the first unquestionable Negroid. It was found in a deposit laid down by a river which has been waterless for thousands of years. The bones are those of an adult male, at least 5 feet 7 inches in height, with long forearms and shins. The skull is large, long, and narrow, with small browridges and a slightly bulbous forehead. The nasal bones are concave and fused, the nose broad, the jaw really prognathous (Boule and Vallois, 1932). These characteristics are all typical of present-day African Negroids, so this population was unquestionably a distinct one, already living in tropical Africa by the end of the Pleistocene.

The Florisbad skull, already mentioned, as well as a few others of the Paleolithic period from South Africa have often been likened to those of native Australians of today. Indeed, a large number of Upper Paleolithic skulls from different parts of the world resemble those of many living Australians except for the generally larger size of the fossil skulls.

The technological means of exploiting the habitat which peoples of the Upper Paleolithic used were superseded many thousand years ago in most parts of the world. As improved means of livelihood were devised, selective pressures upon human populations changed. In a few areas, of which Australia has been one, there have been few technological improvements. The geographical isolation of Australia has, furthermore, kept gene flow into the continent at a minimum. It is quite possible that anatomical traits which were adaptive in most regions during the Upper Paleolithic remained useful in Australia long after they had lost their functional significance elsewhere.

In South Africa, however, people having quite different characteristics appeared before the end of the Paleolithic, despite the lack of any obvious improvements at the local tool kit. A skull found at Boskop in the Transvaal and illustrated in Figure 9–10 has given its name to this group. This is one of the largest prehistoric crania ever found. The browridges are very small, the forehead nearly vertical, but the vault rather flattened. Its greatest breadth is near the back, and the forehead is rather narrow. The mastoid process is small. More than half a dozen individuals are represented by skulls, mandibles, or other skeletal fragments which many authorities say resemble the Boskop find. Faces were short and not prognathous, the nose broad and not depressed at its root, the teeth remarkably small. In many respects these traits remind one of children rather than adults, yet the skulls are of mature individuals with large braincases; and estimates of stature derived from measurements of the limb bones indicate that these people were not short. Bushmen and Hottentots, both of whom have lived for a long time in South Africa, have features very much like those of their Boskopoid predecessors, but these living tribes are much shorter in stature.

The fossils available for study appear to indicate two separate varieties of *Homo sapiens* in South Africa, of which the one with neotenous characteristics is, in general, later in time. The range in appearance is certainly greater than in Upper Paleolithic Europe; yet there are not many fossils, and later finds may show that there was but a single although highly variable group. It is clear that the earliest skulls having neotenous traits are from South Africa, where the most neotenous living population is found today. Moreover, this population, like the racially very different native population of Australia, still follows a hunting and food-collecting way of life. South Africa has not, however, been nearly so effectively screened against outside penetration as Australia. For thousands of years, for instance, South Africans have used such machines as the bow, which was never known to the aborigines of the latter continent. Environments which seem similar may in fact be exploited by man in very different ways. The use of new implements and new techniques, even though it may not modify the landscape, often allows more intense utilization of natural resources. The result is that the human population is subject to new conditions, and this can lead to a shift in the selective pressures to which it is subject. Culture modifies the environment in many subtle ways, and the bodily characteristics of the Bushmen demonstrate that an archaic way of life does not require the anatomical details in which the native Australians resemble so many Upper Paleolithic men in other parts of the world, although it may favor their retention.

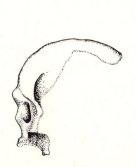

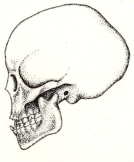

FIGURE 9-10. Three Paleolithic African Skulls

FLORISBAD   ASSELAR   BOSKOP

IN ASIA AND AUSTRALIA

There are a few human remains in Israel, Lebanon, and Iran dating from very late Pleistocene times, and they resemble those found in Europe. Perhaps they are a little less rugged in build and features, but the sample is too small for us to be sure that such minor differences are not due to chance. From India and the peninsula of Southeast Asia we have no human fossil remains of this or, indeed, of any early period. The presence of tools informs us that toolmakers were about, but we know nothing of their physical characteristics. Until the icecap melted, however, Borneo, Sumatra, and Java were all parts of southeastern Asia rather than separate islands. A skull found at Niah Cave in North Borneo has been given a carbon-14 date of 40,000 years, which would place it about halfway through the Würm Glaciation. There seems to be little doubt that this skull is of the type so common in those days—*Homo sapiens* with many of the characteristics typical of modern native Australians.

Probably at the very end of the Pleistocene but perhaps even later, Java had among its inhabitants the two individuals whose skulls were found at Wadjak in 1890. Figure 9–11 is an outline drawing of one of these skulls. They also possessed the combination of heavy browridges, receding foreheads, deep nasal roots, alveolar prognathism, and strong jaws combined with a dolichocephalic skull having a large cranial capacity with which the reader is now familiar. The palates are large and so are the teeth. It is quite obvious that, like the Niah Cave specimen, these two skulls demonstrate the presence of populations very much like those of Australia in what was then the farthest southeast tip of Asia. Several skulls from Australia itself, most notably the one excavated from Keilor, are evidence that *Homo sapiens* reached that continent during the lowering of the sea level which resulted from the expansion of icecaps in the northern hemisphere. Up to the present no earlier fossil remains of any species of hominid have been

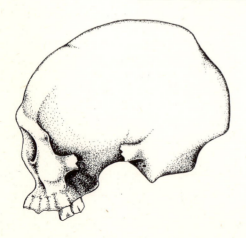

FIGURE 9-11. A Very Late Paleolithic Skull from Wadjak in Java

found east of Wallace's line. It will be recalled that this multiple barrier of deepwater channels through the Indonesian islands kept the marsupial fauna of New Guinea and Australia protected from competition by eutherian mammals for 60 million years or more. It is doubtful that any early man or proto-man swam across it. However, the crossing would be easy even with the most elementary type of shipping. A raft or even a log might suffice.

To transport a family or several families, however, takes enterprise as well as opportunity. Until the time when our forefathers' attention had been turned to the possibility of exploiting marine resources, we may doubt that they engaged in even the shortest voyages just for a lark. Archaeological data assure us that during the Upper Paleolithic in Europe men engaged in fishing. The people at Hotu caught seals in the Caspian Sea more than 9,000 years ago (Coon, 1957). It is a reasonable speculation that people in what is now Indonesia made use of rafts if not of dugout canoes at least as early as this. Technology had reached the point at which such craft could have been made quite readily. Crossing Wallace's line became possible and was obviously accomplished frequently enough to populate the areas to the east. Thereafter, the total occupation of New Guinea, Australia, and Tasmania was inevitable and easy, for they formed a single land mass as recently as 15,000 years ago or less. Birdsell (1957) has calculated that by population expansion alone all of Australia should have been occupied in about 125 generations after it was first entered, and only a few bands need have contributed to the total population. With no competition from any creature more intelligent than the kangaroo, the first human arrivals had only the unfamiliar terrain and climate to contend with. Under such favorable circumstances population ought to have doubled at least with each generation until the land reached its full carrying capacity. Calculations by numerous authorities for many areas show that a population with Upper Paleolithic technology requires some ten square miles, on average, to support each individual. The area of Australia is 2,974,581 square miles. Let the reader calculate two to the one-hundred-twenty-fifth power (2^{125}), and he will see that this figure—one person for each ten square miles—is far exceeded, even if we assume a single couple as the progenitors of all later native Australians.

Human bones of Paleolithic date are being discovered with increasing frequency in China and, more recently, even in Japan. Those from a later Upper Paleolithic horizon at Chou-kou-tien, which were found thirty years ago, have been the most completely described and are probably as representative as any. The remains of seven individuals ranging in age from a rather old man to a tiny baby were uncovered at this site. The skull of the old man (shown in Figure 9–12), having heavy browridges, a depressed nasal root, and

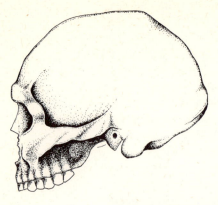

FIGURE 9-12. An Adult Male Skull of Upper Paleolithic Date from Chou-kou-tien in Northern China

a slight degree of alveolar prognathism, reminds one of many other Upper Paleolithic skulls. But his cheekbones jut forward in modern Mongoloid style, the shape of his nose is similar to that of a modern Chinese, and he has shovel-shaped incisors. The female skulls show the same characteristics, although some details of one have been labeled Eskimo-like and of the other Melanesian-like. All these individuals had short broad faces, and their cranial capacities were about average for specimens of *Homo sapiens*. In stature none of these individuals was short (Weidenreich, 1939). The existence of some but not all of the traits commonly found among the present inhabitants of eastern Asia is notable. Hooton (1946) states that the skull of the old man could be duplicated in any series of Ainu skulls, which would not be surprising, but the number of Mongoloid traits in these, as in the other remains of early man in eastern Asia, is even greater. To some anthropologists, these Paleolithic skulls resemble those of certain American Indians even more.

IN AMERICA

Just as Australia was empty of hominid inhabitants until technology was adequate for crossing the water barrier of Wallace's line, so were the Americas until men developed equipment enabling them to penetrate the Arctic. Only between Alaska and Siberia does America come at all close to the Old World: Bering Strait, which separates them, became dry land every time a glaciation lowered the sea level enough and broadened during periods which were warmer than at present. The fact that the Neanderthal race continued to inhabit Europe during the Würm Glaciation indicates that they had devised some techniques for Arctic life. There is no fossil evidence to suggest that this race ever reached America or, for that matter, eastern Asia. It was left for the men of the Upper Paleolithic, whose tools were even better, to accomplish this feat. They fished; they built pit houses; they were equipped with blade tools; they may even have invented tailored clothing.

Coon, C. P.
1957   *The Seven Caves.* Knopf, New York.
1962   *The Origin of Races.* Knopf, New York.

Day, M.
1965   *Guide to Fossil Man.* World Publishing, Cleveland.

Ennouchi, E.
1962   Un Neanderthalien: L'Homme de Jebel Irhoud (Maroc). *L'Anthropologie*, **66**, 279–299.

Hooton, E. A.
1946   *Up from the Ape.* Macmillan, New York.

Howell, F. C.
1952   Pleistocene Glacial Ecology and the Evolution of "Classic" Neanderthal Man. *Southwestern Journal of Anthropology*, **8**, 377–410.
1960   European and Northwest African Middle Pleistocene Hominids. *Current Anthropology*, **1**, 195–232.

Howells, W. W.
1967   *Mankind in the Making*, 2nd edition. Doubleday, New York.

Keith, A. and T. D. McCown
1939   *The Stone Age of Mount Carmel*, **II**. Clarendon Press, Oxford.

Koeningswald, G. H. R. Von, ed.
1958   *Hundert Jahre Neanderthaler.* Kemink en Zoon, Utrecht.

Linton, R.
1945   *The Cultural Background of Personality.* Appleton-Century-Crofts, New York.

Morant, G. M.
1930   Studies of Palaeolithic Man LV. *Annals of Eugenics*, **4**, 109–214.

Movius, H. L., Jr.
1969   The Chatelperronian in French Archaeology: The Evidence of Arcy-sur-Cur. *Antiquity*, **43**, 111–123.

OAKLEY, K. P.
  1957   The Dating of the Broken Hill, Florisbad and Saldanha
          Skulls. *Proceedings of the Third Pan-African Congress
          of Prehistory*, 56–57.
  1966   *Frameworks for Dating Fossil Man*, 2nd edition. Al-
          dine, Chicago.

OAKLEY, K. P. and M. F. ASHLEY MONTAGU
  1949   The Galley Hill Skeleton. *Bulletin of the British Mu-
          seum of Natural History*, no. 1.

OAKLEY, K. P. and C. R. HOSKINS
  1950   New Evidence on the Antiquity of the Piltdown Man.
          Nature, **165.**

SINGER, R.
  1958   The Rhodesian, Florisbad and Saldanha Skulls, in
          Hundert Jahre Neanderthaler, pp. 52–62. Kemink en
          Zoon, Utrecht.

STEWART, T. D.
  1959   The Restored Shanidar I Skull. *Smithsonian Report
          for 1958*, 473–480. Smithsonian Institution, Washing-
          ton, D.C.

STRAUS, W. L. and A. J. E. CAVE
  1957   Pathology and Posture of Neanderthal Man. *Quarterly
          Review of Biology*, **32,** 348–363.
SUZUKI, H.
  1965   Personal Communication.

WEIDENREICH, F.
  1939   On the Earliest Representatives of Modern Mankind
          Recovered on the Soil of East Asia. *Peking Natural
          History Bulletin*, **13,** 3.
  1951   Morphology of Solo Man. *Anthropological Papers of
          the Museum of Natural History*, **43,** part 3, 205–290.

WEINER, J. S.
  1955   *The Piltdown Forgery*. Oxford University Press, New
          York.

WELLS, L. H.
  1957   A Note on the Broken Maxillary Fragment from Broken
          Hill Cave. *Journal of the Royal Anthropological Insti-
          tute*, **77,** 11–12.

Woo, L. K. and Peng

    1959   Fossil Human Skull of Early Palaeanthropic Stage
          Found at Mapa, Shaoquian, Kwantung Province.
          Vertebrate Paleasiatica, **3,** 176–182.

CHAPTER 10

Human Genetics

THE ANTHROPOLOGIST'S INTEREST

Neither we nor our ancestors have been exempt from the rules, of genetics. In Chapter Three the discovery and significance of genetic mechanisms were discussed. In the chapters dealing with the characteristics of our ancestors and their relatives, the operation of these mechanisms was assumed. The evolution of the various forms of life, including human life, has been completely dependent upon the reactions between these operations and the environments of the populations involved. Had either been different in any way, the results of their interaction would have been different also. There is no conflict between heredity and environment: their joint action produces the characteristics of all living things including ourselves. This is worth remembering, since there have been so many attempts to create a dichotomy between them. In experiments we must keep one of the two factors constant if we are to measure a change in the other.

This is relatively easy to do in dealing with fruit flies or maize. Laboratory situations can be created in which all the organisms have an equal opportunity for food, light, heat, and other conditions or in which all are subjected to precisely measured stresses. In a laboratory the experimenter in charge can control the situation. He can pollinate his plants in accordance with a predetermined plan. He can expose males and females to one another in whatever fashion he desires and mate them as he wishes. His techniques may be faulty, of course, and his experiment may fail. But he can do it again, and again, and again. Other scholars can check on the validity of his findings by experiments of their own. Independent verification of this sort is a most important aspect of controlled experimentation in genetics as in other branches of science. When repetition under identical circumstances produces the same result as an earlier experiment, we have increased confidence in the validity of the result.

Such laboratory experiments are impossible in studying human genetics. The sanctions and tabus which surround mating behavior in our species effectively inhibit the required procedures. Even if this were not so, no one is likely to be interested in starting an experiment which may not be concluded until long after he has died. We can breed many generations of fruit flies in a single year. We have large numbers of them available, and each mother is likely to produce many offspring. Human beings are not good experimental animals for genetic studies; probably only elephants or whales would be less practical.

If experimental breeding of creatures with known characteristics under controlled conditions were the only means of obtaining any knowledge of human genetics, we would be in a state of complete ignorance. Fortunately, this is not the case. Our ancestors were quite correct in assuming that sexual intercourse is a prerequisite to the production of human as well as other offspring long before they had found out why this is so. By observing the results of human mating more carefully, though not in a laboratory, we have added enormously to our knowledge. Laboratory tests may be and are conducted to determine the precise biological nature of many human traits. Genealogical knowledge can be obtained by questioning and the study of documents. Information gained from laboratory experiments in animal breeding is useful in explaining the mode of inheritance and the distribution of hereditary characteristics in our species. As a result of a combined attack upon problems of human heredity, we have learned a great deal about it, despite the difficulties involved. Certainly more data are available about the genetics of man than of any other mammal.

At the same time, the greater part of the data concern rare pathological traits which are of more interest to the physician than to the student of human evolution. Many of the clues which have led to discoveries in the field are derived from clinical practice. A mother will note some malformation or oddity in her baby's appearance and bring it to the attention of the family doctor; or a medical man trained to note symptoms which escape the layman will observe that several members of a family are afflicted with some unusual health problem; or a blood transfusion which by all previous tests should have been routinely successful will induce convulsions in a patient. In attempting to diagnose the cause of the trouble, the doctor will note the pattern of a hereditary trait. By means such as this, dozens of ways in which genes may cause a malfunction in the physiology of the body have been found. Reading case histories in medical genetics can be a rather morbid pastime. Fortunately for the human species, most of the inborn errors of metabolism are very rare. Not many of us, for instance, suffer from Wilson's disease, the result of an inability to synthesize the proper quantity of a blood protein called ceruloplasmin. This protein contains copper, and if it is not formed, the copper atoms ingested as normal parts of food are deposited in the liver and the brain, among other organs, where they produce degeneration of the tissues. Few are afflicted by phenylketonuria, wherein the lack of an enzyme required for normal biochemical transformations within the body leads to the excretion of a large amount of phenylpyruvic acid and to severe mental deficiency. Each of these afflictions is the result of a recessive allele.

What is fortunate for the species is in some ways unfortunate for the advance of scientific knowledge. The rare and the spectacular attract attention, while more common characteristics, even if unfortunate, are more likely to be taken for granted. During the past twenty or thirty years, more attention has been paid to the study of genetically based traits exhibited by a large proportion of humans, whether deleterious or not. But our knowledge is still most inadequate. It is still impossible to design chromosome maps for our species, for instance. Attempts to demonstrate linkage between different genes have not all failed, but very few are certain. The extent to which and the ways in which the highly varied environments of different populations may affect the mode of expression of a gene have been difficult to estimate. Yet discounting environmental effects to no more and no less than the correct degree is required in any genetic analysis. Phenotypic traits which appear to be identical may, in fact, be end results of the action of genes at different loci. Although the amount of data concerning human genetics is voluminous, satisfactory analyses of such data are all too often lacking. Research in human genetics is, however, a very active field of study, and our understanding of its complexities is rapidly increasing.

As we mentioned earlier, twenty-three pairs is the standard and proper number of chromosomes in *Homo sapiens*. Some other primates have closely similar numbers: chimpanzees, for instance, have twenty-four pairs. There is, however, a considerable range in chromosome number within the order. The haploid number in most of the species so far examined lies between seventeen and thirty-six. The quantity of chromosomal material, however, seems to vary much less than these figures would suggest; as a rule, the chromosomes are small when there are many of them (Chu and Bender, 1963). We need not expect that the number of genes in the human species is of a different order of magnitude from that of any other primate. Indeed, Stern (1960) sees no reason to believe that our species differs very much, in the number of genic loci, even from such a creature as the fruit fly, which is said to have between 5,000 and 15,000. Spuhler (1948), on the other hand, estimated as many as 40,000 genes for man. All methods of estimation are highly indirect: we really do not know the answer to this question.

The accepted theory, at present, is that genes manage the development of the organism, whether a man or a yeast, by means of controlling the production of enzymes. It has been demonstrated that the arrangement of DNA at each locus determines the structure of the enzyme produced, so that the relationship is, at this level, relatively simple and direct: one gene equals one enzyme. In some cases this is certainly true; but the pathway between genic action and phenotypic trait is usually so complex and so affected by environmental influences within the cell as well as from outside that we are not really certain that genes always act in this manner. In any case we must remember that what we inherit are potentialities, not phenotypic traits.

From the degree of similarity which our species has to other primates, it would seem only reasonable to conclude that we share a large majority of genes with them, perhaps 90 percent or more. The extent to which we share genes with other mammals must be less, and with all vertebrates, still less. But the basic operations of life must require the services of a very considerable proportion of the information carried by molecules of DNA. Years of research will be required before statements concerning the percentage of genes in which we are identical with other creatures can be made with confidence. It was only a few years ago that methods of cell preparation were perfected enough so that Tjio and Levan (Stern, 1960) were able to demonstrate beyond doubt that twenty-three pairs of chromosomes, as shown in Figure 10–1, is standard for man.

In somatic cells, which do not produce eggs or sperm, the chromosome number often varies from this norm, sometimes to a surprising degree. Apparently, this does not interfere with the normal functioning of the body. However, when an abnormal number of chromosomes is present in a gamete (or reproductive cell) the situation is different. In such cases, when sperm and egg unite, and their chromosomes pair up, each with its proper partner, one chromosome is left over. Such a situation may be lethal and prevent the development of the embryo. It may, on the other hand, lead to extensive pathological abnormalities (Lerner, 1968). An

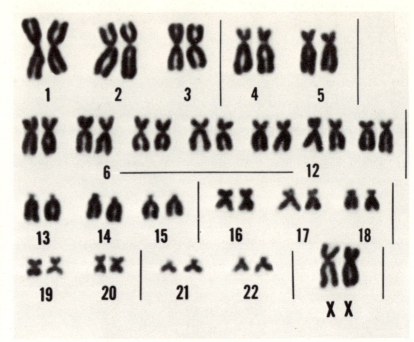

FIGURE 10-1. Human Chromosomes. Note that the Only Differences between Female (Left) and Male (Right) Sets of Chromosomes Is that the Female Has Two x Chromosomes of Equal Size, Whereas the Male Has One x Chromosome and a Much Shorter y Chromosome. (Photos: Dr. J. H. Tjio)

individual with an extra chromosome 21, for instance, suffers from Down's syndrome, also known as Mongolism. A male with an extra y chromosome is often tall, dull, and subject to impulsive action.

One member of each pair of chromosomes has been received from each parent. Due to the random assortment of chromosomes during meiosis, some of our grandparents are likely to have contributed more to our supply of chromosomes than other grandparents. On the average, of course, a grandparent could be expected to contribute one-quarter, and a great-grandparent one-eighth of a person's chromosome complement. If we go back three more generations, we find sixty-four ancestors. Since each of us possesses only forty-six chromosomes, it is clear that some of these individuals will have been left out. Because of the crossing over of genetic material during meiosis, it is not unlikely that some of the eighteen extra ancestors may have made some genetic contribution to any one of us. But this is far from certain. Random assortment and crossing over, it must be repeated, assure genetic diversity. None of us can possibly be identical with any of our ancestors.

Although each parent contributes an equal number of chromosomes, the human egg is enormously larger than the human sperm. An egg weighs about one twenty-millionth of an ounce and has a diameter of one-seventh of a millimeter. It would be a

1	2	3	4	5	6	X
7	8	9	10	11	12	
13	14	15	16	17	18	
19	20	21	22			Y

barely visible speck against a background of a different color. This may seem small, yet it is really one of the biggest of all human cells. A sperm, in contrast, has a length which is only about one-third of the egg's diameter, and most of this consists of a long and exceedingly thin tail. It would take thousands of sperm to occupy the volume of a single egg (see Figure 10–2). Yet the chro-

FIGURE 10-2. Human Ovum and Sperm
(Photo: Dr. Landrum B. Shettles)

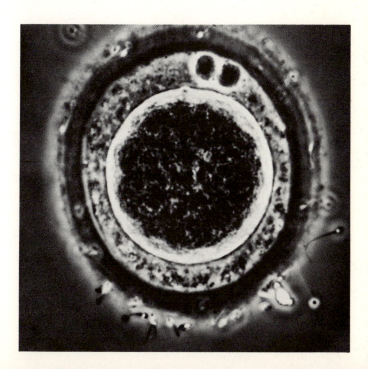

mosomal material contained in the egg is no more than that contained in the sperm. Most of the egg's volume consists of the protoplasm which is waiting to be organized by fertilization into a new human individual. The hereditary contribution of each parent is equal: this is the essence of bisexual reproduction. The one exception to this rule, of course, is that a male receives a y chromosome from his father, whereas a female receives an x chromosome from each parent.

You will recall that the chromosomes are essentially long threads of DNA molecules and that it is possible to recognize genes as the units of inheritance. So far as we know, each gene is capable of influencing more than one observable trait, and the development of any such trait is likely to be controlled by the interactions of several genes. The two hereditary misfortunes mentioned previously are examples of the former principle. Differences in skin pigmentation are among the more obvious examples of the latter. The observable color of the skin depends upon a number of factors, including the presence of more or fewer capillaries close to the surface, the manufacture of melanin, the distribution of melanin, and so on, each of which is quite independent of the others. It is usually the final step in a series of reactions which produces a perceivable phenotypic trait. The gene which we name from such a character is likely to be that concerned with this final step, as, for instance, when we speak of the gene for blue eyes or for early baldness.

Since the discovery of a genetic trait as an entity depends upon the existence of at least two contrasting forms, we have no way of knowing how many genes in the human species occur in only one form. The ways in which every man differs from any member of another species are probably controlled by genes of this sort. During the Miocene, when our ancestors and those of the apes were in a single gene pool, some of these genes must have occurred in several allelic forms. But selection for different ecological niches eliminated all of one allele from our stock and all of the contrasting allele from the pongid stock as Figure 10–3 makes clear. Since we are a highly polymorphic species, there are hundreds of loci on our chromosomes which may be occupied by contrasting alleles. Human genetics is especially concerned with the ways in which our species is polymorphic. The anthropological as contrasted to the medical interest in human genetics focuses upon the evolutionary and racial aspects of polymorphism. We want to find out how it is that one allele has a high frequency in population A but another is more common in population B. We are interested in the varying adaptive values of different genetic systems under contrasting environmental conditions.

The interest of anthropologists in adaptation overlaps the interest of medical men in hereditary malfunctions and abnormalities. Some genetic characteristics would seem to be unfortunate under any imaginable set of circumstances. Hemophilia, or the lack of ability of the blood to clot upon exposure to the air, is one such example. Others are unfortunate only for certain species, including our own. Color blindness of any sort, and there are several, illustrates this point. Animals which move about only at night have no use for color vision; indeed, this would be a defect for them, since it would interfere with their need to see in the dark. But we find good use for color vision. Still other traits are more or less unfortunate depending upon the habitat and culture of the population concerned. A tribe with a way of life which includes running around naked in a desert will not long include a large number of members with very fair skins. They will either wrap themselves up in flowing robes, as Arabs do, or go to live somewhere else, or come out only at night, or die. Diabetes mellitus, a metabolic disorder involving the utilization of sugar, is less dangerous to those whose way of life precludes the accumulation of much sugar. Most of our early ancestors may have been almost unaware of suffering from it. Neel (1962) advances the hypothesis that this ailment is an untoward aspect of a genotype which, in the days of hunting and gathering, led to exceptional efficiency in food utilization. Inherited biochemical predispositions to or immunity from one disease or another are irrelevant to the question of survival if the disease itself is not present.

Selection continually eliminates individuals whose phenotypes are not adapted to their habitats. If the poor adaptation is the result of genic activity, the deleterious allele is eliminated from the breeding population. Such an allele may be dominant or recessive. Should it be dominant, the number of alleles leading to

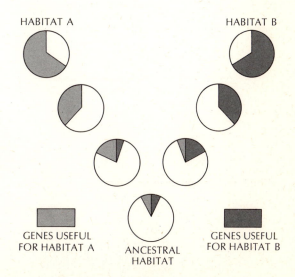

FIGURE 10-3. Genetic Differentiation. A Single Original Polymorphic Gene Pool, or Breeding Population, May Give Rise to Two Separate Populations which, in Adapting to Different Habitats, Become More and More Distinct as Time Goes on.

HABITAT A

HABITAT B

GENES USEFUL
FOR HABITAT A

ANCESTRAL
HABITAT

GENES USEFUL
FOR HABITAT B

malfunction in the breeding population concerned will be reduced by one or two. Should it be recessive, it will be reduced by two, since recessives by definition do not affect the phenotype except when homozygous. Since selection acts upon the phenotype, it can be effective against recessive alleles only when an individual is homozygous for the trait concerned. Thus a store of hidden recessives will be retained within a population for many generations. The less frequent the trait, the more rarely will it appear and become subject to removal by selection. Dominant alleles are removed much more readily. Of course, in many cases heterozygosity leads to a milder and homozygosity to a more severe affliction, or the ailment may not appear until the reproductive period has passed, or medical skill may postpone death for a long time. However this may be, the tendency over the generations is for the numbers of deleterious genes to be reduced. It is not surprising that they are rare. In all probability, their frequency in a population is due almost entirely to recurring mutations which are known to take place.

This is the simplest model of the action of selection upon genes. In fact, as we shall see, there are many situations which this model does not fit. It depends upon the assumption that a given allele will produce only a fortunate or only an unfortunate characteristic in the phenotype. This is not necessarily true. In most, but not all, of the cases of genetically based ailments which come to a physician's attention, the model as stated is adequate. In most of the cases of genetic polymorphism which interest anthropologists, the model is inadequate. There are a great number of genetic differences between the members of any human breeding population. In only a few of these cases is the possession of one allele rather than another at a given locus advantageous in any obvious way. In a great many cases we are yet to discover what the selective ad-

FIGURE 10-4. Genetic Selection Versus Genetic Drift

SELECTION

vantage of a genetically determined trait may be. For quite a long time, this was taken to demonstrate that natural selection had ceased to be relevant under the conditions of human life today—a very comforting illusion to many people. But, more recently, other views have become popular. At present one supposition vigorously urged by many scientists is that adaptation must be the sole cause of variation and that we will eventually uncover a selective advantage for every known characteristic. Another popular view is that many, if not almost all, of the ways in which human populations differ are the result of genetic drift, or chance variation. Examples which support both of these viewpoints are readily found, and statistical models which fit each of them are readily created. But none of these interpretations explains all of the data now available. Both selection and drift appear to be effective, now as in the past, in guiding the course of evolution (see Figure 10–4). In either case the anthropologist is always interested in genetic differences between human populations.

PROBABILITY

We have already noted that although it may be possible to predict the ratio in which contrasting characteristics will be observed among the offspring of matings between individuals who themselves have such contrasting characteristics, it is not possible to predict which individual will have which of the possible alternates. For example, if a father's blood is of type M, we know that he can produce only sperm containing the allele L^M. If a mother's blood is of type MN, half of her eggs will contain the allele L^M and the other half the allele L^N. Neither of these alleles is dominant. If such a pair produce enough children, half of them must

DRIFT

have blood type M, and the other half must have blood type MN, since these will be the alleles received from their parents. But there is no possible way of knowing which child will have which trait. Each individual child has an equal chance of receiving one or the other of these two contrasting sets of alleles. Predictions concerning the genetic characteristics of individuals or the comparative frequency of contrasting genetic characteristics in whole populations must therefore be made in terms of probability. The chances are 50/50, or 70/30, or 99/1, that a given event will take place. They may, of course, be 100 to 0; for example, no human matings ever produce fish or frogs, and no mating between individuals both of whom are homozygous for a given trait produces any offspring who are not homozygous for the same trait also, except when a mutation occurs. The laws of chance govern the distribution of genes so that genetic predictions are statements concerning probability.

In dealing with probabilities we can always expect a certain amount of deviation from any precise ratio. Let the reader flip a coin 30 times, and he will find that it is not bound to fall heads up exactly 15 times. In fact, chances are 1 in 4 that it will be heads up as many as 18 times out of the 30. Chances are only 1 in 15 that it will be heads up 20 times, however, and 1 in 100 that it will be heads up 22 times. *The greater the deviation, the less frequently it may be expected.* If unexpected results continue to occur, we suspect a cause other than pure chance.

The greater the deviation, the more suspicious we become and rightly so. In a short series, of course, anything may happen, but if we are dealing with a large number of observations, deviations from expected results are worth examining. If the deviation is great enough, it sticks out like a sore thumb, and common sense tells us that it must mean something. No knowledge of statistics is required for us to become curious about the significance of an odd event. We will wish to find out what it signifies. In dealing with a statistical series of observations it is customary to speak of a deviation as being significant at the 10 percent, the 5 percent, or the 1 percent level of probability. By this we mean that chances are 1 in 10, or 1 in 20, or 1 in 100 that luck alone is responsible for the oddity which we have observed. A deviation above the 10 percent level of probability is scarcely worth bothering about. It does not need to be explained. A deviation at the 5 percent level makes many people inquisitive as to its cause. A deviation at the 1 percent level means that the probability is only 1 in 100 that chance, or luck, is responsible. With odds like this, we require investigation.

There are tests which measure the extent to which the observed ratios of contrasting items, such as presumed genetic traits, fit theoretical expectations. For instance, we expect that as a result of a large number of matings between men of blood type M and women of blood type MN, one-half of the offspring will have blood type MN and the other half blood type M. In fact, in giving tests to a group of people we may find that 107 are of the former, but only 93 of the latter type. The chi-square test, often written χ^2, can tell us whether this amount of deviation should make us doubt our assumption.

In this test we first calculate the difference between the observed and the ideal, or expected, numbers in each class of the sample. Here the expected numbers would be 100 MN and 100 M, and the observed numbers are 107 and 93: the difference in each case is seven. Next, we square the difference: $7 \times 7 = 49$. Third, we divide the square by the expected number in each class: $49 \div 100 = .49$. Finally, we add these two figures: $.49 + .49 = .98$. The sum, in this case .98, is termed χ^2. Statisticians have calculated the probability that a deviation of such magnitude is due to chance. Tables containing the probabilities of many χ^2 values have been published, and a much abridged one is included in Table 1.

TABLE 1. SOME VALUES OF CHI-SQUARE.*

Degrees of Freedom	Probability						
	.50	.30	.20	.10	.05	.01	.001
1	.45	1.07	1.64	2.71	3.84	6.64	10.83
2	1.39	2.41	3.22	4.60	5.99	9.21	13.82
3	2.37	3.67	4.64	6.25	7.82	11.34	16.27
4	3.36	4.89	5.99	7.78	9.49	13.58	18.46
5	4.35	6.06	7.29	9.24	11.07	15.09	20.52

* Acknowledgment is made to Professor E. S. Pearson and the Biometrika Trustees for permission to reprint the material contained in this table, which is abridged from the table published on pages 130–131 of *Biometrika Tables for Statisticians*, Vol. 1, by E. S. Pearson and H. O. Hartley.

It will be seen that the first column in Table 1 is titled "Degrees of Freedom." This term must be explained. If a group has only two classes—in our example, M and MN—and we know the number in the entire group—200—and we know also the number in one class—100—then we also know the number in the other class because $200 - 100 = 100$. Only one class is "free" to vary. Our example, therefore, has one degree of freedom, and it may be seen that the χ^2 value of .98 has a probability of occurring in one case out of every three by chance alone. It is by no means significant. The deviation from expectation is too small to worry about. Our confidence in the assumption that matings between MN and M parents will produce offspring of whom half are MN and half are M need not be shaken.

A group is often divided into three or more classes instead of two, but the chi-square test can be used in such cases also. Since neither the allele L^M nor the allele L^N is dominant, we can expect that matings between many males and females, all of whom are of blood type MN, will produce offspring of whom one-quarter will have blood type M, one-quarter blood type N, and one-half blood type MN. This agrees with Mendel's first law. After testing a group of 300 such people, we find that in fact 81 have blood type M, 152 blood type MN, and 67 blood type N. The expected numbers would have been 75, 150, and 75. Table 2 shows how to compute the chi-square values in a case of this sort.

TABLE 2. COMPUTATION OF CHI-SQUARE VALUES.

	M	MN	N	*Total*
Observed	81	152	67	150
Expected	75	150	75	150
Difference	6	2	8	
Squared Difference	36	4	64	
Chi-square	$\frac{36}{75} = .48\ +$	$\frac{4}{150} = .03\ +$	$\frac{64}{75} = .85\ =$	1.36

Since there are three classes in this group, there are two degrees of freedom. A glance at the table of probabilities shows that the χ^2 value of 1.39 equals a 50 percent probability. As in the case above, such a deviation is so trivial as to be meaningless. It does not contradict Mendel.

Anthropologists often wish to compare the genetic characteristics of different groups of men, to find out if they are distinctive. A few years ago I noted certain differences in gross body size between two groups of Swiss, all of whom came from the same small area. One group was composed of men both of whose parents had been born in the same small village. The other was composed of men whose parents came from separate villages; these men were considerably taller than the others. In order to test whether there were genetic differences between them which might help account for the differences in stature, I compared the relative frequencies of a few traits such as eye color. We can assume that, if there are no differences in the frequency of the alleles for eye color, the proportions of various eye colors will be the same in the two groups. Table 3 for eye color is presented with numbers rounded off for greater ease in calculation.

Since there are four classes, one for each type of eye color in this example, and two groups of men, there are three degrees of freedom. The table of probabilities shows that for such a case a chi-square of .69 is equivalent to an 80 percent probability that the

TABLE 3. EYE COLORS AMONG THE SWISS.

	Blue	Light	Mixed	Brown	Total
Total Observed	160	223	152	164	699
Group One Observed	86	120	79	82	367
Group One Expected	84	117.1	79.8	86.1	367
Group Two Observed	74	103	73	82	332
Group Two Expected	76	105.9	72.2	77.9	332
Differences, Each	2	2.9	.8	4.1	
Chi-square	.05 + .05 + .07 + .08 + .01 + .01 + .20 + .22 = .69				

observed differences are due to chance alone. Therefore, we cannot claim that the eye colors of these two groups differ to a significant extent.

The chi-square test for significance is a very flexible tool. We must remember that it can only demonstrate that two groups or classes are really different from one another. It does not tell us why. It cannot prove that they are identical, only that they are indistinguishable. Differences which are by no means significant in comparing small groups may become highly significant if they continue on the same scale in large groups. Consequently, subjecting observational data to a chi-square test is only a preliminary step. If the results indicate that the differences between two sets of observations are too great to be explained by chance, the anthropologist will feel it worthwhile to seek for a cause. The chi-square test has shown that the assumption of no difference was so improbable that we can safely consider it to have been wrong.

POPULATION GENETICS

Any scientific study should start with some model or set of assumptions which can be tested. The first two examples of chi-square were based on the assumption that Mendel's first law is correct, and the observations agreed with this assumption. The third example was based on the assumption that the two groups being compared do not differ in the relative frequency of the various alleles which lead to different eye colors. This assumption could not be disproved either. In this last case we are dealing with the distribution of alleles in a population, not simply with the mode of inheritance of a trait. This brings us into the field of population genetics.

Since anthropologists are interested in the differences and similarities among groups of people, population genetics is a vital aspect of their approach to genetic problems. The groups of people to be studied, in order to compare their characteristics to those of other groups, are those who are in the habit of mating with one another rather than with members of other groups. Such a group is known as a breeding population, or as a gene pool, or as a genetic isolate. Unless rigid barriers stand in the way, a gene pool is not completely isolated from other gene pools. The previous chapter should have made that clear. A Dane is very much more likely to mate with another Dane than with a Hottentot or a Chinese, if only because other Danes are nearby while Hottentots and Chinese live a long way off. But a Dane is not unlikely to mate with a German or a Swede.

One of the assumptions made in population genetics is that mating is at random within a breeding population. In dealing with the human species this statement should perhaps be rephrased. Within such a population, a person is as likely to marry any person of the opposite sex as any other person of the opposite sex. The chances that Betty will marry Tom, Dick, or Harry are approximately equal; the chances that Tom will marry Betty, Mary, or Susie are about the same. If Dick is much less likely to marry Dolores, or Michiko, or Tanya, these girls are not really in the same gene pool as he is. The boundaries of a gene pool do not have to be clearly defined, although they are often sharper than most of us realize. Some genes flow in, some genes flow out, but most of them continue to circulate within the pool for generation after generation. Most babies are born to parents who belong to the same isolate. Even when mating is not restricted to married couples, this statement remains true. We need not expect that the members of a breeding population are all alike. They are not. They are simply more likely to mate and marry with one another than with anyone else.

Therefore, the genetic endowment possessed by a breeding population many generations ago can be expected to have continued into the present. On the assumption that curly hair is genetically determined, if one-third of the population had curly hair then, one-third of the population should have curly hair now. We cannot assume that there has been any change in the frequency of the alleles for curly hair if genes have been neither introduced nor subtracted and if breeding has been at random. Unless we have information to the contrary, the only safe assumption is that genetic stability will be maintained over the generations. Indeed, a single generation of random mating suffices to establish equilibrium in the distribution of genotypes within a population with respect to any single gene. When two previously distinct breeding populations happen to be fused for any reason into one, such equilibrium will come about in the next generation and be maintained thereafter. This fact is expressed in mathematical terms by the Hardy-Weinberg Law.

Since this law is stated in terms of allele frequencies, it is necessary to transform the data, which of course concern the relative proportions of different observed phenotypes, into the percentages of the various alleles responsible for the phenotypes. This calculation may be extremely simple or rather more complicated, depending upon the mode of inheritance of the character involved. The inheritance of the characters known as M and N in one of the many blood type systems is simple, for it depends upon two alleles, and neither is dominant over the other. Among the Quinault Indians (Hulse and Firestone, 1961) 77 were type M, 101 type MN, and 23 type N. Each individual of type M possessed two L^M alleles, and each of type N possessed two L^N alleles. Each individual of type MN possessed one L^M allele and one L^N allele. The total number of L^M alleles is $77 + 77 + 101 = 255$. The total number of L^N alleles is $23 + 23 + 101 = 147$. Two hundred and one persons have, of course, 402 alleles at this locus. To obtain the allele frequency of L^M, divide 255 by 402. The answer is 63 percent. To obtain the allele frequency of L^N, divide 147 by 402. The answer is 37 percent. With this information we can find out whether the Quinault are in fact a breeding population in genetic equilibrium by applying the Hardy-Weinberg Law and testing the results by chi-square.

THE HARDY-WEINBERG LAW

The Hardy-Weinberg Law simply applies the algebraic formula known as the expansion of the binomial to the problems of population genetics. This formula is $p^2 + 2pq + q^2 = 1$, or totality, the whole population. In the case of the MN blood types of the Quinault, p stands for the relative frequency of the allele L^M, and q stands for the relative frequency of the allele L^N. The phenotype M can be produced only when one receives the allele L^M from each parent. This frequency will necessarily be $L^M \times L^M$, or p^2. The phenotype N can be produced only under opposite conditions; its frequency must be q^2. The phenotype MN can be produced only when the allele L^M is received from one parent and the allele L^N from the other. The fertilization of L^N eggs by L^M sperm will be in the frequency pq; the fertilization of L^M eggs by L^N sperm will be equally common, so that we obtain the frequency $2pq$ for all MN phenotypes. Consequently, to apply the formula, we multiply .63 by .63: this equals .397; we multiply .37 by .37, which equals .137; we multiply .37 by .63: this equals .233. We double this last number and obtain .466. The total is, of course, 1.000, representing 201 individuals. The diagram in Table 4 may help to simplify this calculation.

p^2, or .397 of 201, is 80 people who are expected to have blood type M. q^2, or .137 of 201, is 28 people who are expected to have blood type N. $2pq$, or .466 of 201, is 93 people who are expected

TABLE 4. CALCULATION OF MN GENOTYPE FREQUENCIES AMONG THE QUINAULT INDIANS.

	$.63L^M$	$.37L^N$
$.63L^M$	$.397L^ML^M$	$.233 L^ML^N$
$.37L^N$	$.233 L^ML^N$	$.137 L^NL^N$

to have blood type MN. The observed numbers were 77, 23, and 101, respectively. The reader should now apply the chi-square test, recalling that two degrees of freedom are appropriate in this case. He should then be able to state whether this tribe of Indians is in a state of genetic equilibrium, so far as the MN blood types are concerned.

The Hardy-Weinberg formula is applicable no matter what the proportions or relative frequencies of various alleles at a locus. Among most American Indian tribes, the allele L^N has a low frequency; among native Australians, it is high; but this does not matter in the least. An algebraic formula such as this can accommodate whatever values exist. That is its virtue and its utility. We should note, too, that its function is to tell us whether the group which has been observed is a breeding population in genetic equilibrium or whether there has been some genetic disturbance worth investigating. We should note, finally, that it cannot be used unless we are able to calculate the gene frequencies of the population being studied.

We learn about the mode of inheritance of a given trait by studying families, not by studying populations. Some traits have been assumed to be of genetic origin simply because their frequency differs from one population to another, but this is a rash assumption. Sons of physicians are much more apt to become physicians than are the sons of other men, but there is no gene for being a physician. There are many traits which we are confident are genetically based but of which the mode of inheritance remains unknown.

A common reason for our ignorance is that several to many genes are involved in developing most observable traits. The simplicity of the mode of inheritance of blood types is one reason why they have been studied so much. Several alleles at a single locus are concerned in most and perhaps all of the blood type systems.

CALCULATING ALLELE FREQUENCIES

All calculations of allele frequencies are based upon the fact that under conditions of random mating, the percentage of homozygotes will be the square of the percentage of the allele concerned. A recessive trait will appear in the phenotype only when the individual is homozygous for that trait. It is, therefore, possible to calculate the frequency of a recessive allele very readily; it will be the square root of the phenotypic frequency. Pure albinism is an example. The biochemistry of an albino does not transform the substances of which melanin is formed into this pigment. This condition is normally due to a single recessive allele. Among European populations which have been investigated, about one person in 20,000 is an albino. The square root of 20,000 is 142, so the allele frequency is .007.

The Duffy blood type system may serve as another example. In most populations there are only two alleles at this locus, designated Fy^a and Fy^b, of which the latter is recessive. Blood which reacts negatively to the Duffy serum is of type Fy^b. Among the Quinault Indians, 10 individuals of 84 tested had this type of blood. The phenotypic frequency of this recessive condition is .12, so the allele frequency is $\sqrt{.12}$, or .35. If only two alleles are present, the allele frequency of the dominant is, of course, the difference between that of the recessive and the total. For nonalbinism in Europe this frequency is $1.000 - .007$, or .993; for the Duffy allele Fy^a among the Quinault, the frequency is $1.00 - .35$, or .65.

ABO BLOOD GROUPS

A little more work is required in calculating the frequencies of multiple alleles, such as are found in the ABO system of blood groups, but the principles remain the same. The mode of inheritance of this system was described in Chapter Three. The allele for blood group O is recessive, while those for A and B are codominant. There are two forms of type A, known as A^1 and A^2, but for the purposes of this example we can disregard this fact. The symbols most commonly used in calculating ABO allele frequencies are: p for the allele I^A, q for the allele I^B, and r for the allele I^O. The frequency of r is calculated as for any recessive: $r = \sqrt{O}$. The frequency of p and r combined is necessarily the square root of the sum of the two phenotypes: $p + r = \sqrt{O + A}$. Consequently, the frequency of p alone is expressed by the formula $\sqrt{O + A} - \sqrt{O}$. The frequency of q is found by the same method; the formula is $\sqrt{O + B} - \sqrt{O}$.

The Quinault Indians may serve to illustrate the application of these formulas. The phenotypic distribution as tested was 163 individuals of blood group O, 26 of blood group A, and 12 of blood group B. In percentages these figures are .81, .13, and .06, respectively. The square root of .81 is .90, which is the allele frequency of I^O. The square root of .94 is .97; by subtracting .90 from .97, we find that .07 is the allele frequency of I^A. The square root of .87 is .93; by subtracting .90 from .93, we find that .03 is the allele frequency of I^B. The theoretical frequency of the blood group AB is expressed, of course, as $2pq$, just as in the case of the MN phenotype. On grounds of chance alone, we might have expected $.07 \times .03 \times 2 = .0042$ in the Quinault series to have tested AB. In a group of 201 individuals, this would be a single case. In fact, no such person was found, but the deviation from expectation is very minor indeed.

We have naturally found deviations from expectation in the analyses of genetic data from many populations. The explanations are varied. Sometimes faulty techniques of observation were used: in other words, our information was wrong. But this does not explain all the deviations. Sometimes preferential mating exists, so that what appears on the surface to be a simple gene pool has a more complicated breeding structure than we realized. Sometimes selection is constantly eliminating individuals of a certain genotype. We know this to be the case with respect to the blood types, because there are incompatibilities in some cases between the blood of a mother and that of her unborn child. The most noted, although by no means the only example of incompatibility, is found in the Rh system.

THE RH FACTOR

A very large majority of our species has blood which contains an antigen known as Rh. This is an abbreviation for the name Rhesus, for the blood of Rhesus monkeys has an almost identical factor carried on the red cells. Individuals with this antigen are known as Rh positives; those who lack it are Rh negatives. These two types of blood are said to be incompatible because when Rh positive cells are injected into an Rh negative bloodstream, the latter will produce antibodies which otherwise would not have existed. Antibodies are normally formed in the blood as a protective device against foreign proteins, which they destroy. During pregnancy the bloodstreams of mother and child are in exceedingly close contact at the permeable membrane of the placenta. They should not actually mix, but the area of contact is so great that there is always a possibility for the Rh antigen of the fetus to penetrate into its mother's bloodstream. If the mother is Rh negative, the presence of the Rh antigen from the fetus will stimulate the production of antibodies in the mother's bloodstream; these may, in turn, penetrate back into the fetal bloodstream. Should they do so, they will naturally fulfill their function of destroying Rh positive cells. As a result, an Rh positive baby will suffer from erythroblastosis foetalis, which may easily result in death either before birth or shortly thereafter. Antibodies usually develop only after the Rh negative blood has been exposed to the positive antigen a number of times, so that a first pregnancy will be less hazardous than later ones.

The absence on red cells of the Rh antigen is inherited as a recessive characteristic. Consequently, the allele frequency is easy to calculate, and it has been found that different populations vary greatly in this trait. American Indians, native Australians, and some other people lack the Rh negative allele completely. Western Europe is the area of greatest frequency, and the Basques, a people who live at the western end of the Pyrenees mountains, on the borders of France and Spain, carry this tendency to the extreme. Among them the frequency of the Rh negative allele is approximately .50, whereas in other parts of western Europe it is rarely much more than .40. The farther away from the Basque country one goes, the smaller the proportion of Rh negative individuals one finds.

So far as anyone has yet discovered, neither the presence nor the absence of this allele confers any selective advantage. The misfortune takes place only when an Rh negative mother's blood destroys the blood of her unborn Rh positive baby. Such a baby is bound to be heterozygous: since the mother must have two negative alleles, all her offspring will have at least one. If the baby were not Rh positive, it would not suffer: consequently, it must have received its positive allele from the father. The father therefore must be positive, although he may be either homozygous or heterozygous.

Each time such a baby dies, it eliminates one positive and one negative allele from the local gene pool. As a result, in an isolate containing a precisely even balance between the frequency of positives and negatives, the genetic equilibrium will be maintained, but in all others it will shift constantly. The minority will become smaller and smaller as time goes on. If we subtract 20 from 60, the remainder is 40, while if we subtract 20 from 40, the remainder is 20. The early ratio of 3 to 2 has become a ratio of 2 to 1. The low frequency of Rh negative alleles in most populations is quite possibly due to this fact, but this would not explain the varying proportions of other alleles at this locus. The Rh system is very complex, and the division between positives and negatives is simply its most dramatic aspect.

A number of antigens, C, D and E, are known, and geneticists disagree about the proper genetic interpretation of this fact. Wiener (1954) is convinced that only one locus is concerned with many alleles, whereas Race and Sanger (1959) agree with Fisher (1947) that there are several which are very closely linked: one locus for each antigen, which may be present or absent. Almost all cases of incompatibility between mother and fetus involve the D antigen, but a few cases of C and of E incompatibility have been recorded. Any person may have blood containing none, one, two, or all three of these antigens, some of which occur in slightly variant form. Table 5 shows the correspondence between Wiener's terminology and that used by Race and Sanger for the more commonly occurring alleles or set of alleles.

TABLE 5. TERMINOLOGY OF THE RH SYSTEM.

Wiener	R^1	R^{1w}	R^2	R^0	$R^{0''}$	R^z	r	r′	r″
Race and Sanger	CDe	C^{w}De	cDE	cDe	cD^{u}e	CDE	cde	Cde	cdE

Many other alleles are known but are found so rarely in any population that they need not be listed here. On a worldwide basis, R^1, R^2, R^0, $R^{0''}$, and r occur with the greatest frequency.

Selection is sometimes a very intricate process. A good example of this fact is the relationship between Rh incompatibility and ABO incompatibility (Reepmaker *et al.*, 1962). Mothers of blood type O normally have antibodies against A and B. Such antibodies are capable of reacting against the blood of their unborn children, much as Rh antibodies do, and for this reason spontaneous abortions are not infrequent in some populations. However, if mother's blood and fetal blood are incompatible with respect to both systems, the fetal red cells which penetrate into the mother's circulatory system are usually destroyed by her anti-A or anti-B antibodies before they have stimulated the production of anti-Rh antibodies. In this way one incompatibility counteracts the other, reducing mortality among the unborn.

How different this picture of the selective process at work is from the simple view of lions chasing zebras! It should serve to remind us that population is the unit which must be "fit," rather than each individual in the population. Selection is likely to act in such a way that the population is in balance and prepared to meet a variety of circumstances, any one of which might be hazardous if all the members of the population resembled one another closely. Incompatibility selects against heterozygotes. Some other situations select in their favor. This results in a situation known as balanced polymorphism.

HETEROZYGOTE ADVANTAGE

An examination of the worldwide distribution of the MN and ABO blood groups strongly suggests some degree of heterozygote advantage in both cases. Except in Australia, New Guinea, and Micronesia, where the incidence of blood type N is very high, and among American Indians, who have a high incidence of blood type M, the two alleles controlling these contrasting blood types are found in ratios which approximate equality. Such ratios as 55 to 45 in favor of either of the two are common in populations containing close to 90 percent of the world's inhabitants. A perfectly even division would, of course, give rise to the greatest proportion of heterozygotes. This situation is rarely reached but usually approached. The suggestion of some heterozygote advantage is supported by the fact that family studies ordinarily show a slight excess of individuals with blood type MN.

Brues (1955) analyzed the distribution of ABO frequencies in 215 separate populations. The results are seen in Figure 10–5, and it will be noted that there is a great concentration within a very limited range of the whole set of possibilities. With three alleles the greatest amount of heterozygosity would be produced if each allele had a frequency of .33. No population has such a frequency, but nearly half of the populations have allele frequencies which assure the propagation of 40 percent or more of heterozygous individuals. It may be seen by an examination of the map in Figure 10–6 that the largest populations, especially those of Asia, are those in which heterozygosity is most frequent. We do not know what the nature of any heterozygote advantage with respect to these blood types may be.

We do know the utility of heterozygosis at the sickle-cell locus, however. The gene at this locus is concerned with the production

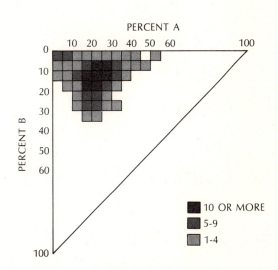

FIGURE 10-5. Allele Frequencies at the ABO Locus (Brues, 1954). 215 Populations from All Parts of the World Are Represented.

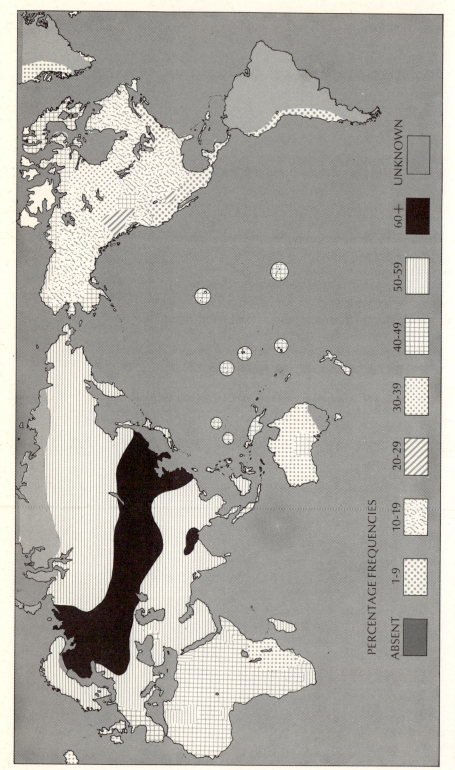

FIGURE 10-6. Heterozygosity at the ABO Locus throughout the World

of hemoglobin, which transports oxygen. Most of us have hemoglobin molecules containing several fractions of glutamic acid, because we possess the normal allele, Hb^A, of this gene. Those who are homozygous for the contrasting allele, Hb^s, have hemoglobin containing valine at one section of the molecule where glutamic acid belongs. As a result, their red blood cells, which contain hemoglobin, collapse into the shape of sickles rather than being round and fat (see Figure 10–7). Their capacity to transport oxygen is much reduced, and people with sickle cells suffer from anemia. As a rule they die young, often in early infancy. They almost never reproduce. Heterozygous individuals do not suffer from anemia, although some of their red blood cells are sickle-shaped. One would expect that selection against such an allele would be very strong. It should be as rare as the alleles leading to albinism or hemophilia. But it is not. Among some African tribes the allele frequency of Hb^s approaches 20 percent. Proponents of the idea that natural selection operates in modern mankind found this difficult to explain.

Then an odd fact was noted by health authorities. Where sickle cell anemia was prevalent, malaria, especially of the type caused by *Plasmodium falciparum*, was endemic. A series of investigations showed that persons who are heterozygous, possessing both alleles

FIGURE 10-7. Normal Red Blood Cells (Left) and Sickle Cells (Right) (Photos: Dr. A. C. Allison)

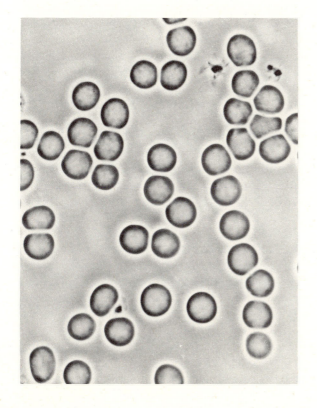
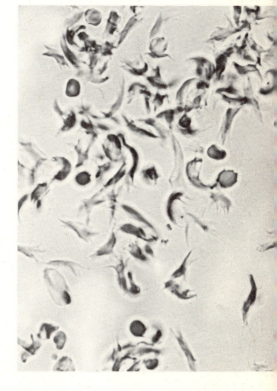

Hb^A and Hb^s, have a much greater resistance to this type of malaria and that heterozygous mothers suffer fewer spontaneous abortions than is the case with people who are homozygous for the normal allele. Various explanations have been offered for the heterozygote advantage in the struggle against malarial infection. Whichever explanations are correct, the important fact is that the advantage exists.

In many of these African populations the death from anemia of all or almost all persons having the genotype Hb^{s}Hb^s has been balanced by the death from malaria of a great many persons having the genotype Hb^{A}Hb^A. Anemia is disadvantageous under any circumstances; the loss of the allele Hb^s should be constant no matter what the environment. Only certain environments include malaria as a standard component; the loss of the allele Hb^A depends upon the proportion of the population which is infected. In any population in which the allele exists, as malaria becomes more prevalent, so does the sickle-cell allele until the point is reached at which deaths from malaria balance those from anemia.

At this point equilibrium is established, but since our species is in the habit of manipulating the environment by means of culture, the equilibrium may not last long. As Livingstone (1961) pointed out, the spread of farming practices in Africa creates conditions favorable to the breeding of mosquitoes, which carry the malarial plasmodium from one person to another. The primeval jungle is rarely mosquito infested, but the clearings made by farmers contain many small stagnant pools in which these insects breed. Farming also leads to population increase and greater population density, since people gather together into villages. Then the infected mosquitoes have all too easy a time in transferring the plasmodium from one person to the next. The migration of farming groups into new areas also spreads this genetic mechanism for combating malarial infection. But modern methods of sanitation decrease this trait's utility, for mosquitoes can be eliminated. Genetic adaptation to the hazard of malaria becomes irrelevant if malaria does not exist.

HOW CULTURE AFFECTS GENETICS

The profound effect of human culture upon human genetics is well indicated by the example of the sickle cell. There are other examples in later chapters, but a statement of some of the more obvious ways in which culture is capable of skewing the relative frequency of contrasting alleles should be made here. All human sexual behavior is subject to cortical control, and all human societies place restraints upon it, as was mentioned in Chapter Seven. Such restraints may be imposed for a variety of reasons. Many of these reasons have to do with social structure, especially with kinship, and they tend to interfere with the random mating postulated by the Hardy-Weinberg Law. A certain amount of skewing in the distribution of alleles may be expected because of this, even without the action of natural selection. Consequently, students of human genetics, when studying any population, must take into account the social regulations concerning mating habits within that population.

THE INCEST TABU

The most widespread of these cultural practices is the incest tabu, which in one form or another is found in all human societies. Intercourse between mother and son is invariably outlawed: this is one of the few cultural universals. Probably this is an exceedingly ancient tabu, and it may have evolved from prehuman social structure. We find that the incest tabu is commonly extended to forbid other sexual relations in almost all societies. Father-daughter and brother-sister matings are permitted in only a few cases, and still further prohibitions are very common, as well as quite varied. In general, however, mating with individuals who are thought of as close relatives is abhorred. The effect of the incest tabu has been to promote gene flow. If the local group is numerous enough, appropriate mates may be found within the neighborhood; otherwise, young males may have to look elsewhere for sexual gratification.

Available data, such as that provided by Washburn and Devore (1961), indicate that other primates mate within their group of origin. They observed only two successful cases of intergroup migration in months of field observation. It is quite clear that human breeding habits, due to the effects of culture, have become quite different. There is among us a far greater amount of pressure favoring the exchange of genes between different groups than exists among nonhuman primates. The lines of genetic communication within the human species have been kept open because of this universal habit, and the result must have been to minimize differences which would otherwise have developed between populations.

EXOGAMY AND ENDOGAMY

The practice of mating or of marriage outside of one's group of origin is known as exogamy. Mating and marriage within the group are called endogamy. It is very common for human societies to have rules concerning both. Some peoples consider first cousin marriage to be incestuous; others believe that a mother's brother's offspring or perhaps a father's sister's are not really close relatives at all. They may, in fact, be preferred as spouses; this is known as cross-cousin marriage. Still other societies forbid marriage between people of the same surname or between people who belong to the same clan, even though the genetic relationship may be remote. These are exogamous practices which carry further the pressure which favors gene flow.

In contrast, we find that in some societies the best possible mate is the father's brother's child. This has been traditional since biblical times in the Near East and is still very common there. Bonné (1969) in her study of the Jewish isolate from Habban, found that 56 percent of the marriages were between first cousins, of this sort, and that marriages between individuals of different surnames were most unusual. In other societies it has been regarded as very bad form to marry outside of one's village, even though first cousins are tabu as mates. In Switzerland, for instance, I found that in many villages during the nineteenth century 90 percent or more of the recorded marriages were between fellow villagers. These are examples of rather close endogamy, which tends to restrict gene flow.

Social stratification also affects the mating habits of at least 99 percent of the world's population, in one way or another. Most marriages are between people of more or less the same status in their societies; mating is by no means random between the rich and the poor. In many cultures, to be sure, rich men have been given and have taken the opportunity to beget children upon several or many women of the poorer classes as well as upon their legal wives. But rich women are less frequently encouraged to bear the children of poor fathers. Among other societies men who are ambitious to raise their social status have found it advantageous to father very few offspring or none at all. Caste barriers, which are much more rigid than those which separate socioeconomic classes, act as even stronger barriers to gene flow.

Differences in religious preference and in ethnic origin have become, during the past hundred generations at least, still further obstacles to random mating in many societies. This is, of course, especially noticeable in countries in which a variety of ecclesiastical organizations coexist or to which migrants from many other countries have come, such as the United States. Very few localities in this country can be thought of as comprising a single breeding population, although there are some communities of a religious nature which are in fact genetic isolates. Some barriers to random mating are illustrated in Figure 10–8.

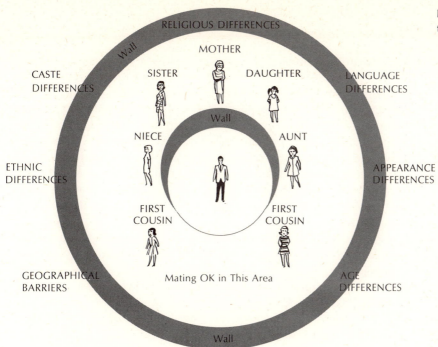

FIGURE 10-8. Some Barriers to Random Mating

RELIGIOUS DIFFERENCES

Wall

MOTHER

CASTE DIFFERENCES

SISTER

DAUGHTER

LANGUAGE DIFFERENCES

Wall

NIECE

AUNT

ETHNIC DIFFERENCES

APPEARANCE DIFFERENCES

FIRST COUSIN

FIRST COUSIN

GEOGRAPHICAL BARRIERS

Mating OK in This Area

AGE DIFFERENCES

Wall

MARRIAGE

Perhaps in spite of or, perhaps, because of the lack of a breeding season in the human species, the vast majority of children are conceived as a result of intercourse between a married couple. Marriage need not be religiously sanctioned or even legally recognized to be real in the eyes of the couple and their social peers; in any case it serves to reduce the random flow of genes within a group, as well as between groups. Nor need marriage be life-long; by far the greater number of societies recognize divorce. A student of human genetics attempting to account for the distribution of alleles in a population must pay attention to the local beliefs and practices of the people concerning the institutions and obligations of matrimony. But he had better not assume that these beliefs and practices resemble those of his homeland, because a great deal of cultural diversity exists.

Polygyny, for those who can afford more than one wife, is highly approved of in many societies, as is concubinage. Dorjahn (1958) found that in one tribe, at least, husbands with several wives fathered more children than did monogamous husbands. This result might have been expected, but Dorjahn also found that a co-wife did not bear as many offspring as a sole wife. Allele frequencies might be expected to shift from one generation to the next under these circumstances.

Polyandry, although rare, is also found. Sometimes a group of brothers will share a single wife, as in Tibet; the social father is the oldest brother. Sometimes younger brothers are permitted access to an older brother's wife or wives; the social father is the official husband. Arrangements of this sort can confuse geneticists who are accustomed to the European forms of marriage, leading them to suppose that promiscuity exists, when, in fact, genes are channeled in an orderly way from one generation to the next. Figure 10–9 shows some expectable results of different forms of marriages.

Human geneticists must also ascertain, if they can, the frequency of adoption and the rules concerning it in any society under study. Where kinship bonds are strong, as in Japan for instance, cousins are often adopted, especially if a wife has not provided the family with a son. Close questioning may be required to ascertain genetic rather than social relationships. Estimates of the degree of consanguinity, or of the mode of inheritance of a trait, or of the amount of differential fertility depend upon precise knowledge of biological parenthood.

DIFFERENTIAL FERTILITY

One of the most obvious facts of life is that some parents have many more children than others do, yet the Hardy-Weinberg Law assumes that all men and women contribute equally to the next generation. When we find, as we often have, that the allele frequencies at a certain locus remain unchanged for a long time in a population, we can only conclude that the parents of large sibships do not differ, at that locus, from the parents of small sibships. But we have no a priori assurance that this will be the case. Indeed, if it were always the case, evolution could not have occurred. It is always of interest, therefore, to look for genetic differences between large and small families. The characteristics which we note may or may not give a selective advantage to the individuals who possess them, but their frequency in the future must depend upon whether they are associated with sibships which continue to be numerous over the generations. Economic and other cultural practices may, and commonly have, overcome biological disadvantages. Table 6 shows the results of differential fertility.

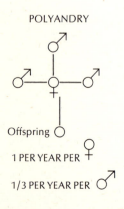

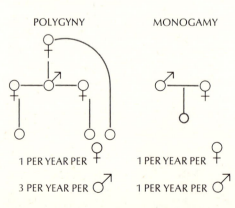

FIGURE 10-9. Three Forms of Marriage. Note the Differences, in Demographic Results, of These Three Forms of Marriage: Monogamy, Polygyny, and Polyandry.

TABLE 6. FOUR LINEAGES.

	2 Children	3 Children	4 Children	5 Children
1st Generation	100	100	100	100
2nd Generation	100	150	200	250
3rd Generation	100	225	400	625
4th Generation	100	338	800	1562
5th Generation	100	507	1600	3905

There can be little doubt that genetic factors contribute to differential fertility; twins are found much more frequently in some lines of descent than in others, for instance. But cultural factors appear to have been more important throughout all historic times, and the use of contraceptive techniques is undoubtedly the most important of these. Such techniques range from total avoidance of sexual intercourse to the modern use of the Pill. Both reduce the number of births in ways which are irrelevant to the survival value of the biological traits of their users. Consequently, human geneticists must be alert to cultural practices which affect the birth rate in a population which they are investigating.

PREFERENTIAL MATING

Inasmuch as sexual activity in our species is under cortical control, a considerable degree of choice in selecting sex partners is expectable. Even in *Drosophila* Dobzhansky (1967) has found a certain amount of choice: newcomers to a group seem to have more sex appeal than old-timers. We are far more selective in choosing our mates. The tabus which prevent certain matings have already been mentioned. But there are positive preferences as well. In many societies brides are supposed to be virgins, and in an enormous majority of cases men pick younger women as their wives. Attempts at self-beautification, known in all societies, indicate the extent to which physical attraction arouses the interest of the opposite sex.

Assortative mating is another well-known practice. More often than not, it is positive, as exemplified by the fact that tall men and women marry one another more frequently than would be expected by chance alone (Moody, 1967). As a positive factor, this serves to reenforce any rules which may exist against mating outside of one's caste or ethnic group. Even without such rules, people are likely to marry those whom they imagine to be similar to themselves. Many of the traits which lead a young man or woman to imagine this are by no means strongly influenced by genetic factors. But to the extent that the traits concerned *are* genetically determined, the inevitable result of long-continued positive assortative mating will be a reduction in the frequency of heterozygotes at the locus or loci related to such traits. Negative assortative mating, which has been found among people with red hair (Buettner-Janusch, 1966), will of course have the contrary result, but also, if it should be invariably practiced, would have other consequences which can be readily calculated by the reader.

Preferential mating of a nonassortative nature also takes place. Much more often than not, the reasons for this are social. Galton (1869) noted that in England an unusually high percentage of judges had married wealthy heiresses. At that time, a girl did not inherit unless she lacked brothers, which indicated a good deal less than average fertility in her family. To the extent that lessened fertility is influenced by genetics, the judges had therefore married less fertile wives. Henriques (1953) has documented a conscious preference, on the part of ambitious Negro males in Jamaica, for wives with some degree of European appearance, which symbolized higher social status. In Japan, too, girls with fair complexions have been held in high esteem. Although family considerations are primary in the selection of a spouse, this seems to have had an effect. I found (Hulse, 1967) that lighter skins are associated with higher social position in that country. All these findings lend support to Darwin's (1871) opinion concerning the importance of sexual selection in human evolution. The selection may be inadvert; but human geneticists need to ascertain the habits concerning preferential mating of the peoples whom they study as one of the potential variables which affect the distribution of genes.

GENETIC DRIFT

The maintenance of genetic stability over long periods of time is an expression of the laws of chance, or probability. Therefore, whether or not the proportions of contrasting alleles in a population will remain constant depends upon the size of the population, as well as upon selection. It will be recalled that a small sample is not necessarily a representative one; deviations from average values are very common in such cases. Since human mothers rarely have as many as ten children, a single sibship is most unlikely to exemplify the Hardy-Weinberg Law. A sample of one hundred families picked at random from a population, on the other hand, should do so, unless selection has been at work. The phenomenon known as genetic drift is produced only when a population itself is so small that chance becomes a significant factor in determining the frequency of contrasting alleles at one locus or another. Dr. Sewell Wright (1948 ff.) has worked out the mathematics of genetic drift extensively. Our interest is in its application to the problems of human population genetics.

Human social organization and technology have been so effective, for thousands of years at least, that very small populations indeed have managed to survive for many generations. It is among such tiny populations that genetic drift is most likely to operate. At the present time, most human breeding populations are so large that it would be surprising to find chance deviations from the norm as effective instruments of genetic change among them. But many inbred communities which are known to be derived from a very small number of ancestors exist even today. The people of Pitcairn's Island in the South Pacific have very few ancestors aside from the seven mutineers from the *Bounty* and their Tahitian consorts, for instance. Were these mutineers a random, representative sample, at *every* genetic locus, of the British population in the late eighteenth century? This would have been almost impossible.

What is called the founder effect is an aspect of genetic drift; that is, the alleles possessed by a small number of ancestors are all that are available to later generations descended from them, no matter how numerous the population may become. A recent study by Martin (1970) of the Hutterites, a religious group which has been endogamous for many generations, illustrates the way in which the founder effect has undoubtedly worked again and again during the course of human evolution. Ninety-one founders have left almost 10,000 living descendants, who now live in more than one hundred separate communities. The number of founders who have contributed any genes to any single existing community ranges from thirty-seven to fifty-seven, and of course the extent of the contribution of any one of the original ninety-one to each of these small groups varies much more. A remarkable degree of divergence in allele frequencies between the different communities is the expectable consequence of this. It is not at all unreasonable to suppose that many of the differences between the inhabitants of different parts of the world are due to the founder effect. We seem to find that peoples who live in remote places or who are believed to have originated from very small groups are the ones most likely to have unusual allele frequencies.

To be sure, if the genetic constitutions resulting from genetic drift prove inadaptive, either natural selection will operate to reverse the trend or the populations concerned will become extinct. But as culture has spread a protective screen between the human species and the natural environment, selection has been to some extent relaxed. Few of us who are alive today would have survived to reproductive age during the Paleolithic. The death rate of children has been reduced, and it is reduced by preserving individuals who would otherwise die: this is a relaxation of selection. But natural selection has not ceased to operate. Its direction changes in accordance with changed circumstances. So it does with any species which moves into a new habitat. Not everyone who is born reproduces, and some reproduce more extensively than others. Evolution continues, and the basic principles of genetics, effective in the evolution of other creatures, continue to be effective in the case of *Homo sapiens*.

Sources and Suggested Readings

BONNÉ, B.
>   1969   Polymorphic Systems in the Habbanite Isolate. *Abstracts of the XII International Congress of Genetics*, **I**, Tokyo.

BRUES, A. M.
>   1954   Selection and Polymorphism in the ABO Blood Groups. *American Journal of Physical Anthropology*, new series, **12**, 559–597.

BUETTNER-JANUSCH, J.
>   1966   *The Origins of Man.* Wiley, New York.

CHU, E. H. Y. and M. A. BENDER
>   1962   Cytogenetics and Evolution of Primates. *The Relatives of Man.* New York Academy of Science, New York.

DARWIN, C.
>   1871   *The Descent of Man and Selection in the Relation to Sex.* Murray, London.

DOBZHANSKY, T.
>   1962   *Mankind Evolving.* Yale University Press, New Haven.
>   1967   Genetic Diversity and the Diversity of Environments. *Proceedings of the 5th Berkeley Symposium on Mathematical Statistics and Probability*, **IV**, 295–304. University of California Press, Berkeley.

DORJAHN, V. R.
>   1958   Fertility, Polygyny and Their Interrelations in Temne Society. *American Anthropologist*, **60**, 838–860.

FISHER, R. A.
  1947 The Rhesus Factor: A Study in Scientific Method. *American Scientist*, **35**, 95–103.

GALTON, F.
  1869 *Hereditary Genius.* Macmillan, London.

HENRIQUES, F. N.
  1953 *Family and Color in Jamaica.* George Allen & Unwin, London.

HULSE, F. S.
  1967 Selection for Skin Color Among the Japanese. *American Journal of Physical Anthropology*, new series, **27**, 143–156.

HULSE, F. S. and M. M. FIRESTONE
  1963 Blood-Type Frequencies Among the Quinault Reservation Indians. *Proceedings of the Second International Conference of Human Genetics*, **2**, 845–847. Rome.

LERNER, I. M.
  1968 *Heredity, Evolution and Society.* Freeman, San Francisco.

LIVINGSTONE, F. B.
  1961 Balancing the Human Hemoglobin Polymorphisms. *Human Biology*, **33**, 205–214.

MARTIN, A. O.
  1970 The Founder Effect in a Human Isolate: Evolutionary Implications. *American Journal of Physical Anthropology*, new series, **32**, 351–367.

METTLER, L. E. and T. G. GREGG
  1969 *Population Genetics and Evolution.* Prentice-Hall, Englewood Cliffs.

MOODY, P. A.
  1967 *Genetics of Man.* Norton, New York.

NEEL, J. V.
  1962 Diabetes Mellitus: A "Thrifty" Genotype Rendered Detrimental by "Progress." *American Journal of Human Genetics*, **14,** 353–362.

PEARSON, E. S. and H. O. HARTLEY
  1953 *Biometrika Tables for Statisticians.* Cambridge University Press, Cambridge.

RACE, R. R. and R. SANGER
  1959 *Blood Groups in Man,* 3rd edition. Thomas, Springfield, Ill.

REEPMAKER, J., L. E. NIJENHUIS, and J. J. VAN LOGHEM
  1962 The Inhibiting Effect of ABO Incompatibility on RH Immunization in Pregnancy. *American Journal of Human Genetics,* **14,** 185–198.

SPUHLER, J. N.
  1948 On the Number of Genes in Man. *Science,* **108,** 279–280.

STERN, C.
  1960 *Principles of Human Genetics.* Freeman, San Francisco.

WASHBURN, S. L. and I. DE VORE
  1961 Social Behavior of Baboons and Early Man. *Social Life of Early Man.* Viking Fund Publications in Anthropology, **31,** New York.

WIENER, A. S.
  1954 *An Rh-Hr Syllabus.* Grune and Stratton, New York.

WRIGHT, S.
  1948 On the Roles of Directed and Random Changes in Gene Frequency in the Genetics of Populations. *Evolution,* **2,** 279–294.

CHAPTER 11

The Present Diversity of Man

The present diversity of man is partly but not entirely due to the continuing evolution which has led to varying gene frequencies in different breeding populations. The environment in which any individual grows up is bound to affect many of his phenotypic characteristics. Genic action, we must remember, will lead to different consequences under different circumstances. Most readily observable traits are plastic to a greater or lesser extent. If we eat a lot, we are quite likely to get fat, for instance, and no one can help observing this. A more careful analysis may show that a tendency toward obesity is genetically determined, but the genes by themselves cannot do the trick. Furthermore, the environment in which we live has been much modified by culture. What we eat and how much we eat depends very little upon the naturally occurring sources of food in the neighborhood. For most of us, it depends upon what the grocery store has available, what food preferences we have as individuals, how well our wives or mothers cook, and how much money we have to spend on food. These are all cultural factors.

It has always been the aim of physical anthropologists to ascertain the genetic component of human variation, but this has been no easy task. Such characteristics as obesity are obviously dependent upon environmental modification. Other traits, just as readily observable, such as body proportions and the shape of the face and the head, have been studied extensively and intensively with the hope that environment affected them less or perhaps even not at all. But all of them are due to growth and must, therefore, be considered as potentially subject to some modification during that process. None of them are inherited in simple form. Since it is clear that different populations vary with respect to pigmentation and hair type, these characteristics have been studied too. It has been easy to eliminate environmental effects in analyzing such traits, but not at all easy to determine their mode of inheritance in most cases.

BIOCHEMICAL POLYMORPHISMS

There are some characteristics, such as the various systems of blood types used as examples in the previous chapter, which depend upon single loci, which are not modified by any external conditions and which do not alter as one grows older. It is, therefore, possible to calculate allele frequencies for separate populations with respect to these characteristics, and it is of interest to note that these frequencies vary sometimes to an extreme degree. In some cases, we may reasonably consider a certain trait to be unfortunate, even though not clearly pathological; in others, we do not know what, if any, adaptive utility the trait has.

Yet regional variation exists in both sorts of characteristics. It is clear that the human species is genetically polytypic: allele frequencies at a large number of loci differ from one population to another. Each breeding population is polymorphic: at many loci two or more alleles are found in proportions which, presumably, are maintained by selection. Very few alleles are entirely restricted to the populations of any one region. Neighboring populations are more likely to resemble one another in allele frequencies than they are to resemble populations living at a distance, although historically known migrations have tended to make this less so than it used to be. The maps showing allele frequencies at various loci throughout the world are based upon the location of tribes and nations before the great overseas expansion of the Europeans.

Since this population began expanding about twenty generations ago with the discovery of America by Columbus, some changes in frequencies are known to have occurred. A number of tribes have become extinct, and many have been decimated. The spread of new diseases has probably shifted allele frequencies in some cases. Extensive intermixture has certainly altered the relative proportions of alleles in many others. We lack data for much of the world; the necessary field work is yet to be done. Where it is reasonable to

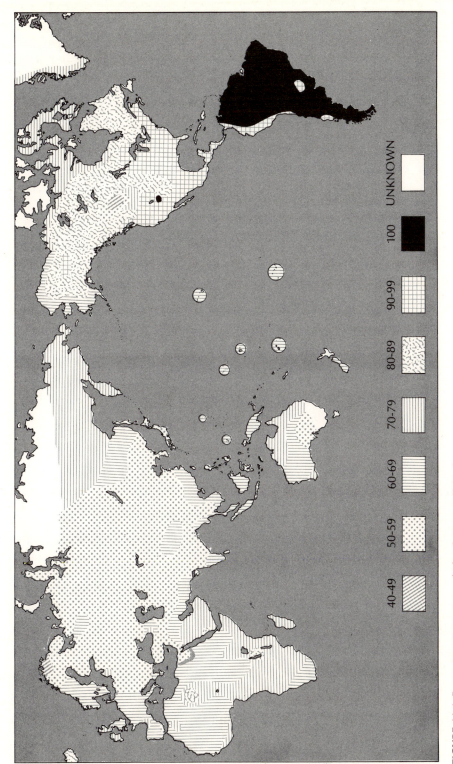

FIGURE 11-1. Percentage Frequency of Blood Group Allele I⁰

show clines on the basis of present evidence, they are drawn. In some cases our knowledge is very spotty. We can give frequencies of a certain allele here and there, leaving the reader free to guess at what might be expected at intermediate points. Such guesses will probably be wrong, but if they stimulate him to added inquisitiveness, so much the better. Perhaps he may become an anthropologist and, when well enough trained, go and find out for himself.

THE ABO BLOOD-GROUP SYSTEM

The first three maps (Figures 11–1, 11–2, and 11–3) are concerned with the ABO system of blood groups. Since this system was the first to be discovered, and since it is so important that blood transfusions be compatible, there is more information about this system than any other. Millions of people have been typed in all parts of the world, even remote and isolated communities of preliterate peoples. The importance of the ABO system to anthropology was first recognized during the Balkan campaign in World War I. In war soldiers are likely to lose blood and need transfusions. The soldiers whom the French and British assembled for this campaign came from many colonies in Africa and Asia, as well as from France, England, and the Balkans. Surgeons noted that the relative frequencies of groups O, A, B, and AB to which they had been accustomed in western Europe differed from the frequencies found among their patients from India and Africa. During and since the following decade, more and more investigators have collected data about the geographical distribution of the alleles at this locus and, more recently, about the adaptive value of the different alleles.

The recessive alle I^o has the highest frequency in almost all breeding populations, and it is very much more common than either I^A or I^B in a large majority of peoples. This led to the idea that blood group O was at one time universal among mankind, but we have discovered that antigens almost identical to A and B exist among nonhuman primates. Clearly polymorphism at this locus is exceedingly ancient, antedating the evolution of the family Hominidae by millions of years. Since mothers of blood group O are a little more likely to lose infants whose blood contains either the A or the B antigen than they are to lose infants of blood group O, there is constant selective pressure in favor of I^o. However, we have found that in many populations a positive correlation exists between blood group O and various ulcers, which may cause some selective pressure against I^o.

Vogel (1961) reported that the bubonic plague bacillus contains a substance termed H, which also exists in blood group O; he concluded that antibodies which destroy the virus should also attack the red cells of people having this type of blood. Recently, however, some experiments have tended to refute this claim. Nevertheless,

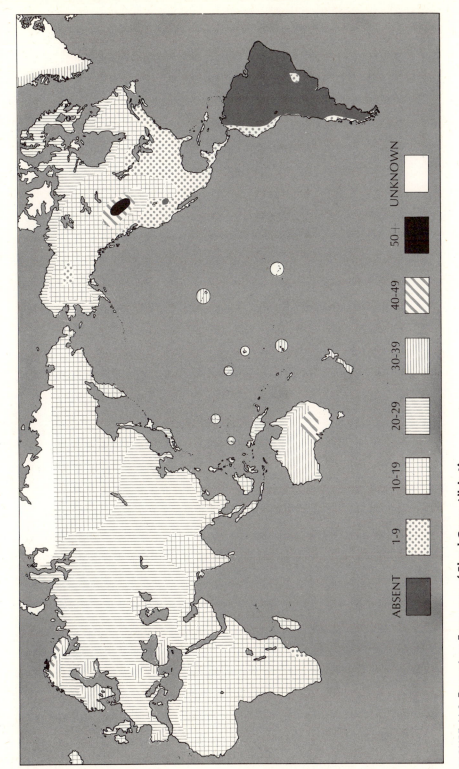

FIGURE 11-2. Percentage Frequency of Blood Group Allele I^A

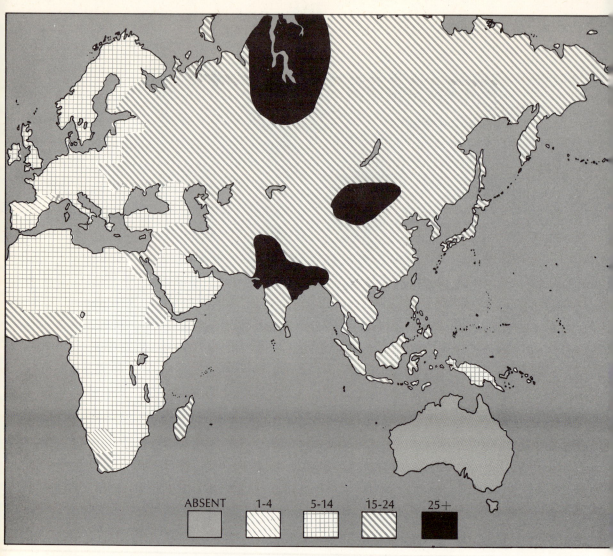

| ABSENT | 1-4 | 5-14 | 15-24 | 25+ |

FIGURE 11-3. Percentage Frequency of Blood Group Allele I^B

it is only fair to note that there is a low incidence of the allele I^o in the region stretching from Egypt, through India, to China, where plague has been most common. South America has the highest frequency of this allele. North America and Australia follow, while western Europe and parts of southern Africa come next. All these areas are somewhat remote from the world's population center.

The allele I^A ranks second in frequency on a worldwide basis. This allele has an absolute majority among the Scandinavian Lapps and the Blackfoot Indians of the northern Plains, while in western Europe, Polynesia, and southern Australia, it is very common. Only in some parts of India, China, and adjacent regions is this blood group less frequent than blood group B.

According to Vogel (1970), smallpox, at least in India, is significantly associated with groups A and AB, because the virus contains the A antigen. Consequently, antibodies useful against the disease may also attack the red cells of persons of groups A and AB.

Smallpox, like the bubonic plague, has been endemic to this part of the world. Livingstone (1960) reports associations between one or another of the blood groups and a variety of infectious diseases, and it is not at all unlikely that some of these associations have had significant selective results. Persons of blood group A are rather more likely to suffer from stomach cancer and diabetes than others are. The first misfortune, however, does not often attack anyone until after the reproductive period of life is coming to an end.

Blood group A appears in two forms, A^1 and A^2. The allele I^{A^2} is recessive to I^{A^1}, but codominant with I^B and dominant over I^0. This variant of A is much more restricted in the extent of its geographical distribution than the other alleles of the ABO system. It is almost completely lacking in eastern Asia and totally absent in the Pacific Islands and America. In East Africa, in southern Arabia, and at various spots along the seacoast of Europe, the relative proportion of A^2 to A^1 is higher than elsewhere. The explanation for this irregular distribution is unknown, although Kirk (1962) points out a significant relationship between the frequency of A^2 and the allele r of the Rh system. Higher caste genetic isolates in India commonly have higher frequencies of this allele than lower castes do. Indeed, in India, variation between castes at many loci is as great as variation between regions.

The allele I^B is more common in southern, central, and eastern Asia than in other parts of the world. It is absent throughout most of America and most of Australia and rare in western Europe, especially among the Basques and Lapps. Those areas in Europe where this allele is most common are also the areas which have been most frequently invaded by pastoral nomads from Asia, such as Huns, Mongols and many others, and Candela (1942) suggested that these invasions greatly increased its incidence. This is not at all unlikely, for invading soldiers often leave offspring behind. Any prejudice against individuals of Mongol appearance in later generations could not have operated against individuals who inherited the allele I^B but not facial features from such invaders, because no one was aware that blood types existed. We should also note that no associations between blood group B and any infectious disease or constitutional ailment have been clearly demonstrated as yet. If selection operates against persons of blood groups A and O, the frequency of the allele I^B ought to increase.

THE RH SYSTEM

A clear presentation of the geographical distribution of the alleles at the Rh locus is difficult because of their large number. Furthermore, there are many areas from which no reports of population surveys of this polymorphism have yet been received. The frequency of each of the four most common and widespread alleles as recognized by Wiener is presented in Figures 11–4, 11–5, 11–6, and 11–7. It will be noted that the allele R^1 is found in all parts of the world. A few scattered tribes in Africa may lack this allele, and it has a low incidence among most African peoples except those who live on the Mediterranean coast. The contrary situation exists in Melanesia, Indonesia, and Micronesia, where the frequency of the allele R^1 is very high. In Australia, Polynesia, and most of Asia this allele has a frequency of 50 percent or more, as it does among a good many tribes of American Indians. In Europe and the nearby parts of Asia and Africa, it is not quite so common.

The allele R^2 is also present in all regions and in almost every breeding population which has been tested. Except in some American, Polynesian, and East Asian groups, however, its frequency is less than 25 percent. The highest incidence of this allele is found among the Indians of British Columbia, but there are many nearby tribes and others in South America among whom it is very common. In Europe its frequency is slightly less common in the west, especially among the Basques, than in the east. The populations of Africa, India, and Melanesia have a low percentage of the allele R^2.

None of the other alleles at this locus have such a widespread distribution as R^1 and R^2. The recessive allele r is quite lacking in America and the Pacific Islands and very rare indeed in eastern Asia. It is, of course, found among a number of groups of mixed ancestry, since migrants from western Europe have settled in so many parts of the world, and sailors have had girl friends in many seaports. Only among the Basques does the allele r reach a frequency of 50 percent. Throughout western Europe it is nearly as common as the allele R^1. Throughout southwestern Asia and India the incidence of r is between 15 and 30 percent. The higher caste populations of India have a greater frequency of this allele than do the lower castes. In Africa, south of the Sahara, there is a great deal of intertribal variation. In the extreme south this allele is very rare indeed, but in many of the central African populations it is as common as in the Near East.

The alleles R^0 and $R^{0''}$ are typical of Africa. Among most of the Negro peoples of that continent, the incidence of R^0 is 50 percent or more, sometimes much more. The Sahara desert must have formed a real barrier to gene flow, since in North Africa this allele is only about one-third as frequent. In the Near East and southern Europe it is even less common, while in northern Europe, it is very rare indeed. The frequency of this allele in India, Southeast Asia, and Indonesia is quite variable: usually present, but rarely frequent. Native Australians have a slightly higher incidence of R^0, while the peoples of eastern Asia have a lower one. We do not know whether this allele was present among American Indians in early times. It

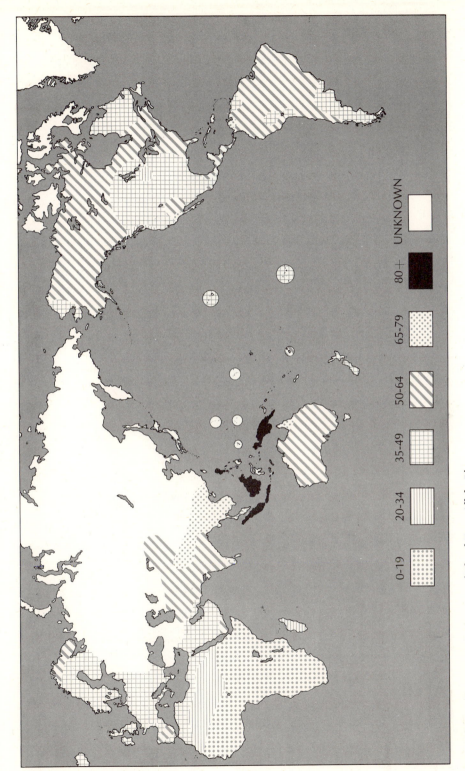

FIGURE 11-4. Percentage Frequency of Blood-Type Allele R¹

Legend:

0-19 · 20-34 ‖ 35-49 ⊞ 50-64 ⟋ 65-79 ⊡ 80+ ■ UNKNOWN ☐

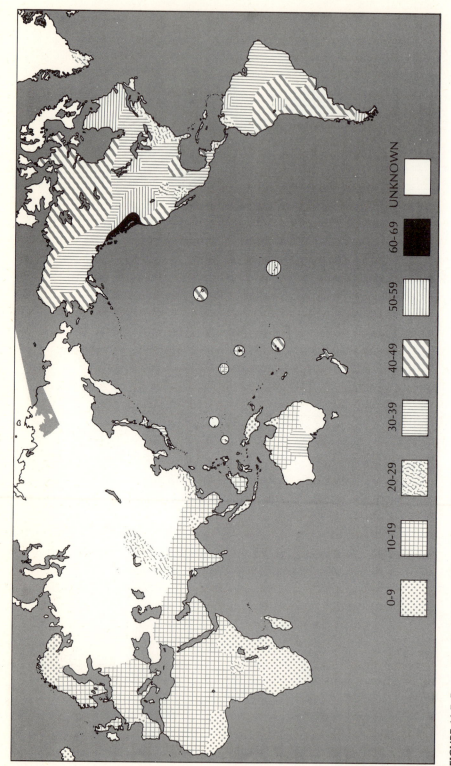

FIGURE 11-5. Percentage Frequency of Blood-Type Allele R²

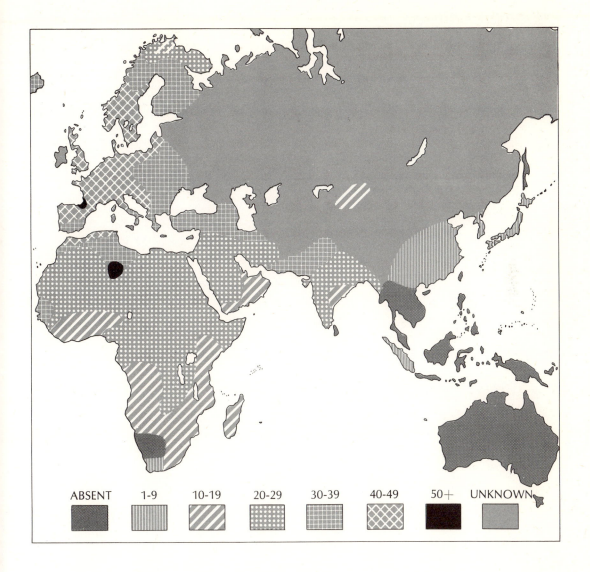

| ABSENT | 1-9 | 10-19 | 20-29 | 30-39 | 40-49 | 50+ | UNKNOWN |

may well have existed in a few tribes but certainly not in most. The allele R°″ appears to be a variant of R°. It is restricted almost entirely to Africa and the countries around the eastern end of the Mediterranean.

ABO and the Rh blood types deal with quite different properties of red blood cells. The alleles which determine a person's ABO group are at a different locus on a different chromosome from the locus controlling the Rh blood type. They have no more to do with each other than the color of one's hair has to do with its degree of curliness. This fact is easily forgotten but should always be remembered.

FIGURE 11-6. Percentage Frequency of Blood-Type Allele r (RH Negative)

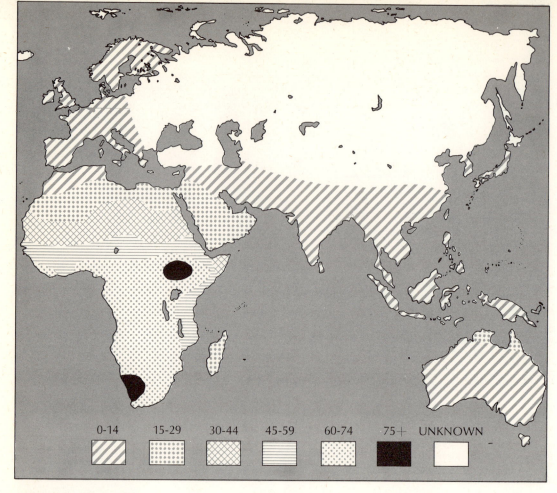

| 0-14 | 15-29 | 30-44 | 45-59 | 60-74 | 75+ | UNKNOWN |

FIGURE 11-7. Percentage Frequency of Blood-Type Allele R^0

THE MNSU SYSTEM

At still other loci not linked with either Rh or ABO, there are various genes of which the alleles determine still other biochemical properties of the red blood cell. The MNSU system is among them, and we have a lot of information about the relative frequency in different parts of the world of the different alleles of this system. Just as it is possible that several very closely linked genes, rather than a single gene, are involved in the Rh system, it is possible that the MNSU system is composed of several loci also tightly linked. Genetic analyses have not given a conclusive answer. Twenty years after the discovery of the M and N antigens, it was found that they were closely related to two other antigens which were given the names S and s. The antigen labeled U, also under the control of the same system, is a still more recent discovery.

In our present state of knowledge, we can only say that no one save a small minority of African Negroes lacks the antigen U. The antigen S is lacking among the natives of Australia, quite rare throughout the Pacific Islands and eastern Asia, and less frequent in southern than in central or northern Africa. In America the frequency is variable, whereas in Europe, the Near East, and India, it is more common than anywhere else. The M and N antigens are rather evenly balanced in most of the world, but there is a great deal of variation between populations with respect to the relative frequency of the alleles L^{MS}, L^{Ms}, and L^{Ns}. The incidence of L^{Ns} does not vary so much; it is never common and usually less than half as frequent as L^{Ns}. The proportions of L^{MS} and L^{Ms} are rarely so uneven. In Europe L^{MS} is almost as frequent as L^{Ms}, and this is true of some of the populations of the Near East and India as well. The maps in Figures 11–8, 11–9, 11–10, and 11–11 give the world distribution of these alleles.

OTHER BLOOD-TYPE SYSTEMS

Many other systems of blood types have been discovered, and for a few we have information indicating that allele frequencies vary considerably between different populations. At the Duffy locus there are probably at least three alleles. The one which produces the antigen discovered first, by Cutbush, Mollison, and Parkin (1950), is known as Fy^a. A different antigen is produced by the allele called Fy^b. Since many individuals, especially of African Negro origin, lack both antigens, a third allele must be postulated. As one may see by looking at Figure 11–12, the allele Fy^a is universal or nearly so among native Australians, Melanesians, Micronesians, and some of the peoples of eastern Asia. Among Polynesians and in India, it is less common. In America there is a great deal of intertribal variation. The allele Fy^b is more frequent in western Europe, except among the Basques. In Africa, south of the Sahara, the allele Fy^a is very rare indeed. As in the ABO, Rh, and MNSU systems, so in the Duffy system the darkskinned peoples of Africa differ profoundly from the darkskinned peoples of Melanesia and Australia.

We do not yet have enough data to map the worldwide frequencies of alleles in other blood-type systems, but we can make a few remarks about them. The contrasting alleles P and p control one of these types. Their frequency is rather even in Europe, leading, of course, to a high degree of heterozygosity. In central and southern Africa the allele P is much more frequent, whereas in India and eastern Asia, it is less so. Scanty data indicate that the populations of America and Australia resemble those of Europe in allele frequencies at this locus. At the Kell locus the positive allele, very rare in all populations, appears to be absent among the native peoples of America and some of those in eastern and southeastern Asia. The Kidd is another blood-type system. As in the other systems, the presence of the dominant allele results in the production of an antigen and is, therefore, called positive. The highest frequency of this allele is found in western Africa, where it reaches 70 percent.

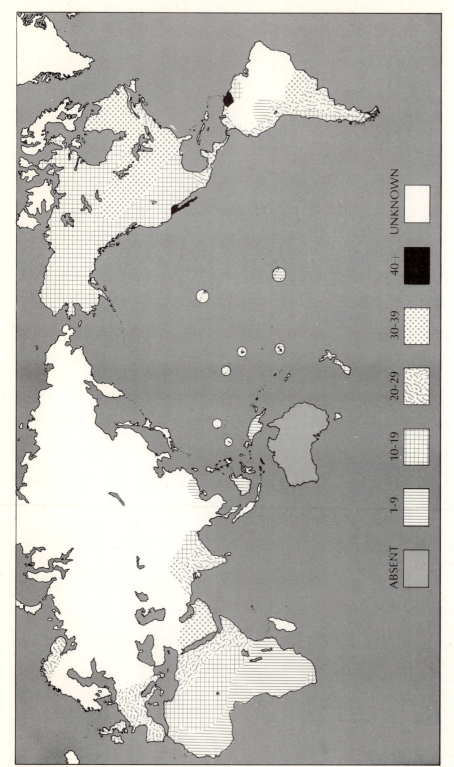

FIGURE 11-8. Percentage Frequency of Blood-Type Allele L^MS

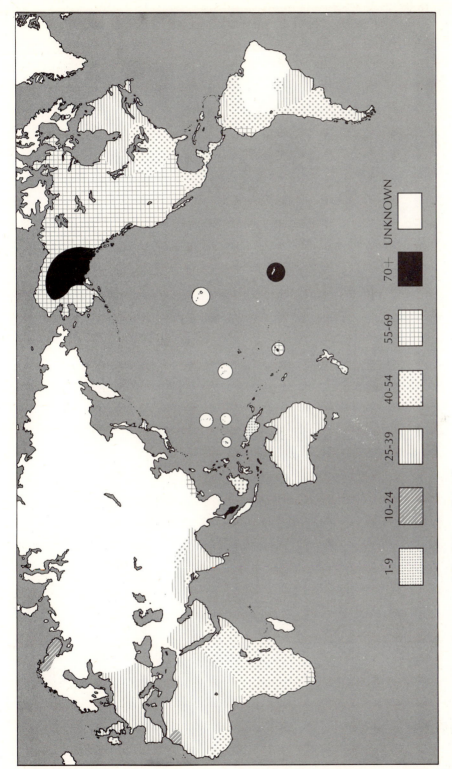

FIGURE 11-9. Percentage Frequency of Blood-Type Allele L^Ms

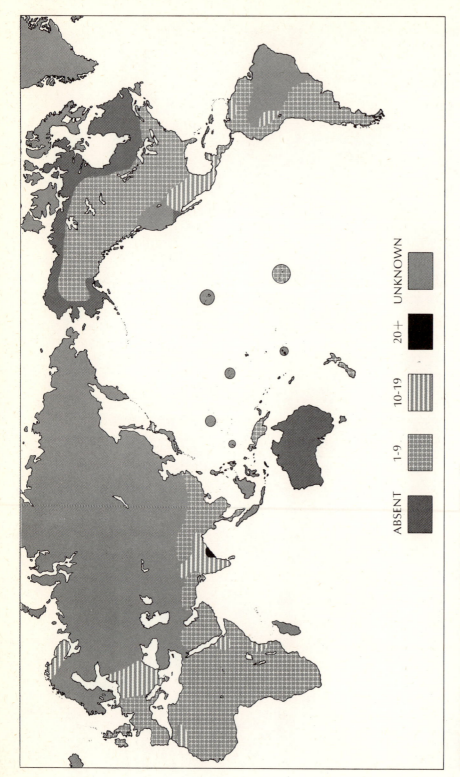

ABSENT   1-9   10-19   20+   UNKNOWN

FIGURE 11-10. Percentage Frequency of Blood-Type Allele L^{NS}

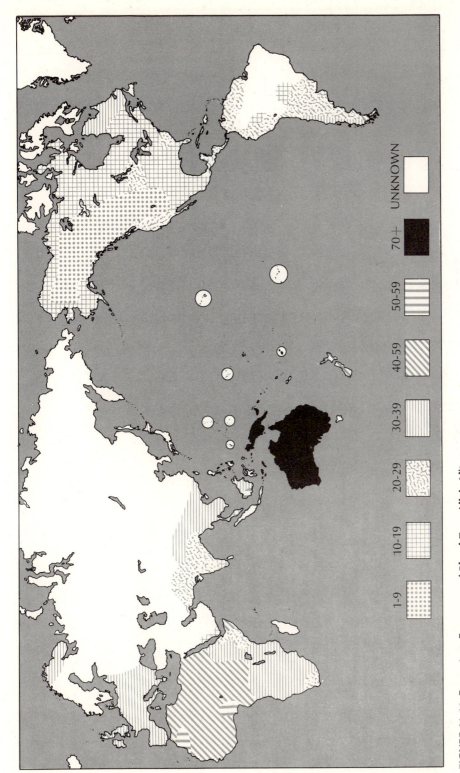

FIGURE 11-11. Percentage Frequency of Blood-Type Allele L^Ns

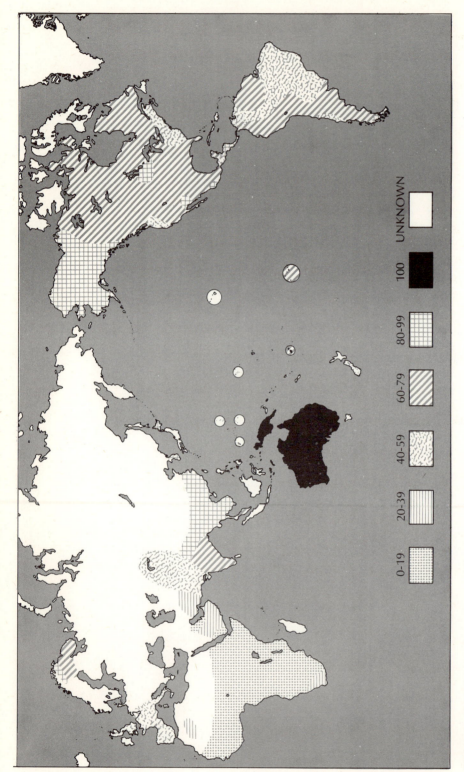

FIGURE 11-12. Percentage Frequency of Blood-Type Allele Duffy a

In Europe and North America Kidd positives are less common, and the lowest frequency is found in eastern Asia. In each of these blood-type systems polymorphism exists in almost all of the populations which have been tested. Some American Indian tribes are distinctive in having but one allele at the ABO locus, and probably all of them are uniform in lacking the Kell antigen.

They are distinctive, too, in the extent of polymorphism at the Diego blood-type locus. The Diego positive allele has a most irregular distribution among the natives of the Americas, is rare in East Asia and Indonesia, and has been found in only half a dozen individuals from other parts of the world. Layrisse and Wilbert (1961) attempted to explain its distribution among American Indians by the speculation that it was introduced by late migrants from Asia. More recent surveys have extended our knowledge of the frequency of the Diego positive allele to many populations not previously tested, so that Wilson and Franklin (1968) have been able to show a relationship between warm humid areas and high frequencies of the positive allele. It seems quite possible that insect-borne diseases have been among the selective factors at work, for in drier colder areas insects are not year-round pests as a rule. It is worth noting that the Diego factor is not found in the Old World wet tropics, except, rarely, in Indonesia, just as the abnormal hemoglobins are not found in the New World.

GENETIC DEFENSES AGAINST MALARIA

We know something about the geographical distribution and relative frequencies of contrasting alleles at a number of other loci, but in no case do we have such complete knowledge as we do of some of the blood-type systems. We have already mentioned the abnormal sickle-cell hemoglobin. The recessive allele Hb^s, although typical of Africa, is not restricted to that continent. It is also found at various spots where malaria is endemic—on both sides of the Mediterranean, in the Near East, and among some of the hill tribes in southern India. Nor are Hb^s and Hb^A the only alleles at this locus. Hemoglobin C, not uncommon in western Africa, is produced by another, Hb^c, and hemoglobin E, found in Southeast Asia and Indonesia, by a fourth allele, Hb^E. Individuals homozygous for either of these hemoglobins suffer from milder anemia than that which results from the genetic constitution Hb^sHb^s; but heterozygosity seems to give some protection against malaria.

The extent to which malaria has been a danger to the continued existence of many populations is shown by the fact that other genetic defenses against it have been found. At another locus are the alleles which we may call Th^1 and Th^2, since they are concerned with a red cell abnormality known as Thalassemia. Persons homozygous for Th^2 suffer from a highly lethal anemia, but the heterozygote Th^1Th^2 is protected against malaria. Studies by Ceppellini (1959) show sharp differences between the incidence of Th^2 in mosquito-infested coastal villages and mosquito-free mountain settlements on the island of Sardinia. There are four times as many heterozygous individuals in the lowlands as in the highlands. Thalassemia is found in populations throughout the basin of the Mediterranean, the Near East, India, China, Southeast Asia, Indonesia, and the lowlands of New Guinea, all of which have been afflicted with malaria for thousands of years.

Still another gene, apparently sex-linked, is concerned with protection against malaria. This gene controls the production of a red cell enzyme known as glucose-6-phosphate dehydrogenase. Either of two mutant alleles of this gene causes a deficiency in this enzyme, especially in older red cells. Enzyme-deficient cells contain very little glutathione, upon which malarial plasmodia depend for their growth. Some species of plasmodia are known to enter and live in the older red cells rather than the younger ones; they will be out of luck in the bloodstream of anyone having this enzyme deficiency. The person himself will probably not suffer, unless he is given certain drugs which cause his blood to hemolyze.

One of these drugs is derived from the fava bean, commonly grown in southern Europe and the Near East, and severe reactions to eating such beans or even smelling their flowers have long been known to exist among a small proportion of individuals living in those areas. This condition is known as favism. Another of these drugs is primaquine, a newly developed antimalarial compound. Favism, or primaquine sensitivity, is found in many African, Mediterranean, and Near Eastern populations, in some Southeast Asian populations, and even in New Guinea.

Livingstone (1967) has brought together and analyzed the available data on the various genetic defenses against malaria which have been so briefly mentioned previously. (See Figures 11–13, 11–14, and 11–15.) It is most interesting to note the complete absence of such defenses among the Indians of the American tropics, despite the presence of malaria. There is a very good chance that malarial plasmodia, together with the species of mosquitoes which transmit them, are relative newcomers to the New World. Perhaps, indeed, they were introduced at the same time that slaves were first imported from Africa. This is by no means certain, however. Not all malarial regions in the Old World are inhabited by human populations with such defenses, either. Mutations, useful or deleterious, arise by chance. Selection can lead to a shift in allele frequencies, but it can work only upon the material at hand.

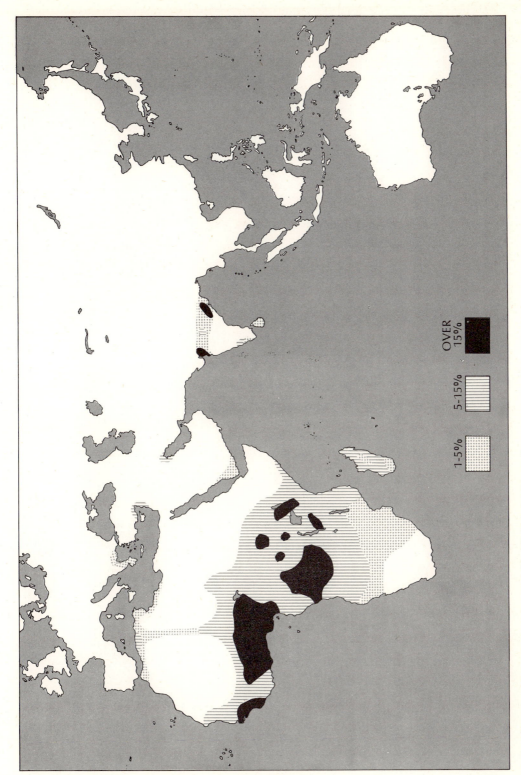

FIGURE 11-13. Percentage Frequency of the Allele for Sickle Cell

OVER 15%

5-15%

1-5%

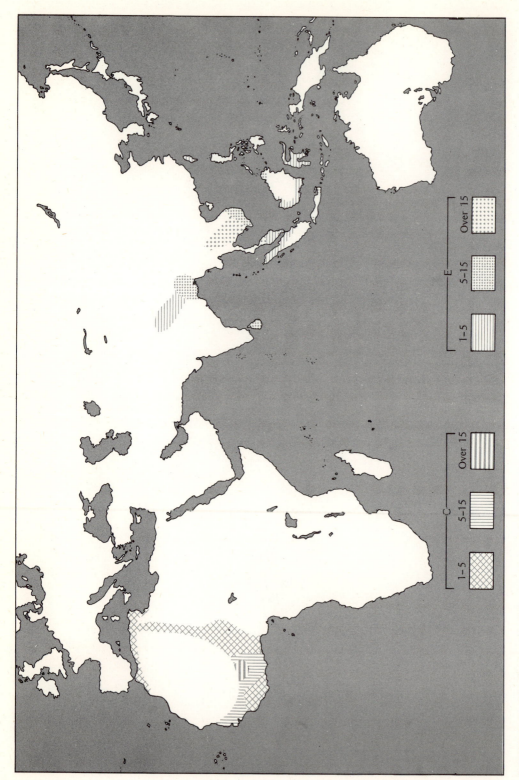

FIGURE 11-14. Distribution of Alleles for Hemoglobins C and E

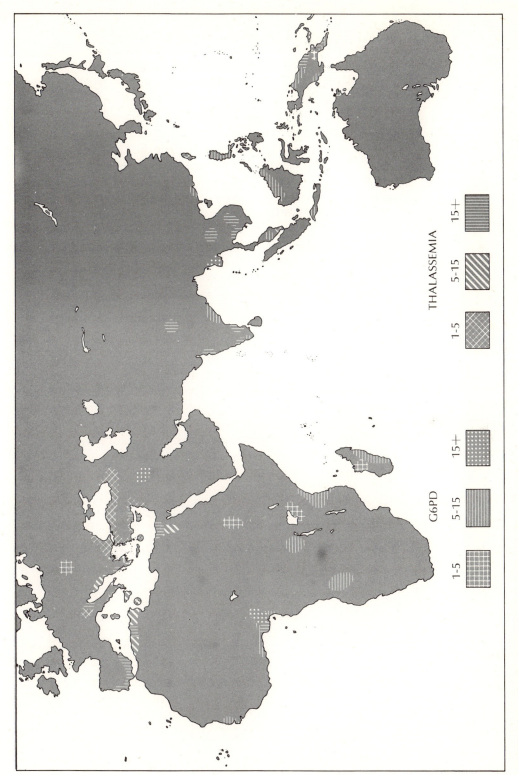

FIGURE 11-15. Distribution of Alleles for G6PD and Thalassemia

FURTHER BIOCHEMICAL CHARACTERISTICS

The ability to secrete ABH antigens in saliva is another trait dependent upon the presence or absence of a single allele, but it has a curious effect upon the activity of the Lewis blood-type systems also. The dominant allele Se, which leads to secretion of ABH antigens, is almost universal in America. It has a frequency of 50 percent in Europe but of only about 30 percent in Africa, south of the Sahara. The Lewis antigen is present in the saliva if the positive allele Le is present either homozygously or heterozygously without reference to the presence or absence of the allelle Se. It is present on the red blood cells of individuals of the genotype sese—that is, nonsecretors of ABH antigens. This complication has made it difficult to calculate the relative frequency among different populations of the Lewis blood alleles, but Lewis positives are probably most common among peoples of European ancestry. This example illustrates the complexities of genetic analysis due to the interaction of different genes.

There are many other characteristics of the blood which are rather close reflections of genic action because of the direct relation between genes and enzymes on the one hand and enzymes and blood chemistry on the other. The genic activity is just as direct upon some other aspects of metabolism, too. For instance, certain amino acids are excreted in the urine by those persons having one allele but not by persons with a contrasting allele. In the case of at least one of these, Beta aminoisobutyric acid, which is called BAIB for short, the proportion of affected individuals is much higher in European populations than in the very few others which have been studied (Harris, 1959).

ALBINISM

Total albinism appears to be caused by failure to synthesize melanin due to a deficiency of the enzyme tyrosinase. Probably a recessive allele at any one of several loci is capable of causing this deficiency. Albinism is less rare in some populations than others. It is never common but appears sporadically in widely separated places; in the San Blas tribe of Panama Indians the phenotypic frequency is .007, or 150 times as much as among Europeans. The frequency of albinism among the Hopi is also high, and the condition is known in Africa, Melanesia, and Japan. On grounds of natural selection alone, it might have been supposed that the frequency would be lower in sunny areas, such as that occupied by the Hopi, and that the Europeans' technological superiority and habit of working indoors might have led to a higher frequency among them. Since we do not find this to be the case, we remain ignorant of the reason for the existing frequencies of albinism and are likely to explain them by speaking of genetic drift.

PTC

Ability or lack of ability to taste a substance known as phenylthiocarbamide, called PTC for short, depends essentially upon a single gene. There are differences in the proportions of men and women of the same gene pool who can taste this substance; more women than men are tasters except among the Basques. Among tasters, some find the substance more bitter than others do; some perceive only on the tip, others only at the root of the tongue, and so on (Taylor, 1961). Ability to taste PTC seems to depend upon the level of di-idiotyrosine in the saliva (Fischer and Griffin, 1959). The discovery of this example of genetic polymorphism was quite accidental. A small amount of the chemical—a synthetic compound not found in nature—happened to be spilled in a laboratory, and one of the chemists mentioned the bitterness of the dust. Others were unaware of any taste at all. Still others, called in to settle the argument about whether PTC was tasteless or distasteful, also disagreed. A majority were certain that it was bitter, but the minority could not be convinced. Neither side was right or wrong. Their sensory equipment differed, so of course they arrived at different conclusions.

The matter was brought to the attention of geneticists, and family studies soon showed that ability to taste PTC is inherited as a dominant trait. The frequency of the positive allele is lowest in Australia—30 percent or less. It is low among some castes in India and some ethnic communities in the Near East. Alaskan Eskimos and most European populations, geographically remote from each other, are similar in frequencies at this locus—a small majority of the recessive allele. In Southeast Asia the frequency of the dominant allele is 60 percent or more; farther north the percentage becomes even higher. Among African Negroes the frequency of the positive allele is well over 70 percent, and among American Indians it reaches a frequency of 85 or 90 percent.

Just what good it does anyone to taste PTC nobody knows. Quite possibly this ability is related to other chemical perceptions which do confer some benefit, but these have not been discovered. There may be some relationship between tasting ability and goiter. The fact that chimpanzees, like human beings, are polymorphic at the taster locus (Fisher, Ford, and Huxley, 1939) indicates that both alleles have long been present in our ancestry. From this they argue that heterozygosity must confer some advantage. If so, this must be related to some aspect of life which we share with other anthropoids, as appears to be the case with respect to the balanced polymorphisms among some, at least, of the blood-type systems.

GENETICS AND ANATOMY

FINGERPRINTS

It is notorious that no two of us have identical fingerprints. With such a high degree of individuality it might easily be supposed that genetic analysis would be difficult. However, fingerprints can be classified into types, such as loops, whorls, and arches which render them more amenable to study. Similarities in pattern, as shown by family studies, demonstrate the genetic basis of fingerprints, but it is clear that several genes are involved. In Europe and Africa there is a high frequency of loops, whereas whorls are much less common. In the Near East and India loops become less and whorls more frequent. In Australia the incidence of loops is still lower and that of whorls much higher. There is great variation in eastern Asia and North America, but in general loops and whorls are more or less even in number. In South America as in Europe loops are more common than whorls. Only among the African Pygmies and Bushmen does the incidence of arches reach 10 percent or more.

COLOR BLINDNESS

The term color blindness covers a number of defects in the ability to distinguish different wavelengths of light. All of them are sex-linked, being determined by loci on the x chromosome as recessives. Consequently, the percentage of color-blind females in a population is the square root of the percentage of color-blind males. It has been maintained (Post, 1962) that there is an inverse correlation between the frequency of such defects and the amount of protection which technological advances give to individuals in a population. However, more recent studies with proper instrumentation for detecting and distinguishing between the various defects cast grave doubt upon this hypothesis (Adam et al., 1970). Anomalies in the perception of green appear to vary a great deal between different populations; red anomalies and total confusion of red with green (anopia) do not differ nearly so much in the groups which have been studied up to now. Figure 11–16 shows the frequencies of these defects in the only populations which have been adequately sampled. Earlier surveys, using less precise methods, suggested an almost complete absence of color blindness among American Indians and the peoples of the Pacific and a very low incidence indeed among African Negroes. We need a great deal more information on this subject.

GENETIC DETERMINATION OF HAIR

There are sexual differences in the incidence of tasting ability and color blindness: in the latter case, because the condition is due to a sex-linked gene; in the former, perhaps because of the influence of sex hormones. This seems to be true of another trait which is due to a single gene and not modified by the environment—the presence or absence of hair on the middle segment of the fingers. Unfortunately, no one has studied the frequency of this trait among most of the world's populations, nor are we at all sure how many alleles exist at the locus. Complete absence of such hair is recessive. In almost all samples which have been studied, however, females are much less likely to have such mid-digital hair than men are. This is almost certainly an aspect of the lesser hairiness of women in general. In the Near East a very large majority of adult males have hair on the middle segment of at least one and usually several fingers. The frequency of the trait is less in Russia and rises again in northwestern Europe. In East Africa only a small minority of individuals have mid-digital hair. In eastern Asia the minority is even smaller, and in America the trait is almost absent in some tribes and completely lacking in others.

These distributions agree with the extent to which body hair is found among the different peoples of the world. The presence or absence of hair on one part of the body or another is genetically de-

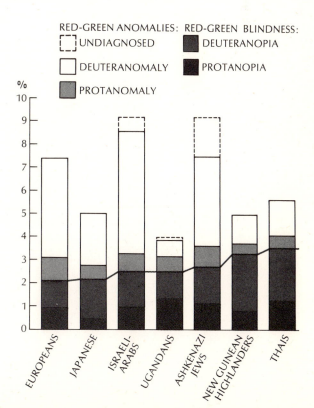

FIGURE 11-16. Frequency of Defects in Color-Vision among Selected Populations

termined, but we know next to nothing of the mode of inheritance. Most of our information leads us to believe that lack of hair is recessive to its presence and that greater is dominant over lesser hair quantity. Multiple alleles are probably involved in determining the quantity of hair. Populations native to different parts of the world differ from one another in the degree of bodily hirsuteness. But allele frequencies have been impossible to calculate on the basis of current data. That accomplishment remains for the future. It is certainly safe to assume that the frequency of hairy phenotypes in any population depends upon the frequency of the necessary alleles in the local gene pool.

Absence of body hair seems to be most marked among the peoples of eastern Asia—save for the Ainu—and America. Africa, south of the Sahara, is another area where the incidence of the alleles necessary for the growth of hair on the body is very low. In Australia, however, such alleles are very common. India, the Near East, and Europe are other areas where adult males are more than likely to have some body hair. Yet individual differences are very great both in quantity and pattern of hair growth.

The mode of inheritance of baldness is in dispute, but there is no doubt that the characteristic is inherited, and the allele or alleles involved have different frequencies in different populations. Snyder and Yingling (1935) consider it to be sex-controlled and dependent upon a single gene. The presence of a single allele for baldness will lead to the condition among males, but a female must be homozygous for this allele in order to become bald. The sex hormone is apparently effective, one way or the other, among people who are heterozygous.

Harris (1946) distinguishes between early baldness, which is certainly dominant in males, and baldness in later life. Baldness is most frequent in Europe, the Near East, and India. It is also very common in Australia and not uncommon in Africa and some parts of eastern Asia. Among American Indians, however, it is almost completely lacking. The geographical distribution of baldness resembles that of body hair, but this is not evidence of genetic linkage, which could only be demonstrated by studying pedigrees.

We know even less about the genetics of hair type than of hair quantity. The allele or alleles responsible for woolly hair are dominant over those for fine straight hair but probably not over coarse straight hair. In some cases wavy hair may be due to heterozygosity between the alleles for straight and curly hair. The degree of coarseness or fineness in any individual's hair is quite variable. But there are marked geographical differences in hair type between different populations.

Quite a few of these populations show less evidence of polymorphism in hair type than in blood type. Coarse straight hair is very typical in eastern Asia and America and woolly hair in Africa south of the Sahara and in parts of Melanesia. Curly or wavy hair is more frequently found in other parts of the world, but fine straight hair is common in Europe. Coon, Garn, and Birdsell (1950) speculate that woolly hair may have adaptive value in hot dry areas by providing insulation at the top of the head. The extent to which people of all tribes exploit the ornamental value of head hair by all sorts of modifications suggests that sexual selection may have played some part in the evolution of diverse types of hair. We really are very ignorant in this matter.

Hair color has already been mentioned in connection with skin color. Phenotypically, dark brown or almost inky black head hair is found among adults of both sexes in most parts of the world, but the genetics of hair color is far from simple. There must be multiple alleles of a single gene, several genes, or both. The very dark hair of Africans and American Indians is often due to such complete stuffing of the hair shafts with melanin granules that halving the quantity of pigment does not perceptibly lighten the color. Genetic polymorphism may exist without being expressed in the phenotype. It seems likely that this causes what is often called dominance of dark hair and that, in reality, the various genes or alleles have additive effect. Of course, if no melanin is synthesized in the body, as in the case of albinos, alleles calling for the deposit of this pigment in the hair call in vain.

Red hair studied with a spectrophotometer shows very slight reflectance in the green-blue regions of the spectrum. The red pigment is either incompletely synthesized or partially oxidized melanin. The mode of inheritance of red hair was discussed in Chapter Three. Hair color is dependent upon age as well as genes concerned with pigment. Hair which is light during childhood often darkens during adolescence or early maturity. In old age or even earlier, hair of any shade may become gray or even white. The genes concerned with these processes are certainly not those which determine hair color as such. In Europe and adjacent areas there is a high frequency of all alleles leading to depigmentation. The highest incidence of all is in the area about the Baltic Sea, as Figure 11–17 shows. Here and in neighboring countries, almost all children and half or more of the adult population are light-haired. In the Alps, the Caucasus, and in mountain ranges even further away live populations with a high incidence of light hair. Western Australia is a secondary center of light hair; here, too, children are more likely than adults to express this character. The center of highest frequency for the alleles producing red hair is along the Atlantic Coast of Europe. Since alleles for red and for blond are both very frequent in Scotland, a high proportion of people in that country have really red hair. But alleles for red hair exist as exotic rarities even

| NONE | 1-9 | 10-19 | 20-34 | 35-49 | 50-64 | 65-79 | 80+ |

Figure 11-17. Percentage Frequency of Light Hair in and near Europe

as far away as Melanesia. Beards are more likely to show red shades than head hair is.

Graying is caused by a decrease in the quantity of pigment granules. This phenomenon is known to occur in many species of mammals among individuals which live long enough. Since a large proportion of humans do live for a long time, their hair becomes gray or even white. However, very old people in some populations retain their hair pigment. This is especially true of the natives of America. A great number of Europeans become gray by the time they are forty or fifty years old. Some have white hair before they are thirty. The head hair is the first to lose pigment, next the facial hair, if any, while pubic hair does not as a rule become gray until very much later, if at all.

DIVERSITY IN PIGMENTATION OF EYES AND SKIN

Eye pigmentation, like that of hair, is genetically determined, and as with hair color, multiple alleles are involved. When we speak of eye color, we refer to the pigmentation of the iris, the membrane which regulates the amount of light admitted into the eye by its expansion and contraction. The deepest interior layer of the iris is always pigmented, except in the case of total albinos. What we perceive as the color of the iris is due to the way in which it reflects light. Blue-eyed persons have pigment only at this deepest layer; lack of pigment elsewhere is due to a recessive allele in almost all cases. When there are pigment cells in the middle layer of the iris, their number and arrangement cut off to some extent the reflection of light from the innermost layer, and we perceive such colors as gray, gray-green, hazel, or gray-brown. Pigment cells are usually arranged in concentric circles about the pupil or in rays which radiate from it like the spokes of a wheel. If most of the cells of this middle layer are pigmented, the iris will appear to be brown. The outermost layer may also be pigmented. If so, the eye will be even darker, sometimes almost black.

The pigment of the iris serves to protect the retina, upon which images are cast by the lens of the eye, from unnecessary light and to concentrate the entrance of light rays through the pupil alone. It is not surprising that most individuals in most mammalian species have brown eyes since this feature has positive adaptive value. Several hundred million members of our species, however, have irides which are depigmented to some extent. Just as hair which was light during childhood often darkens during growth, so does eye color, although not quite so frequently. Some instances of depigmentation have been noted among the elderly. Many dark-haired adults have light or even blue eyes. The proportion of men with light eyes in most populations possessing this character is greater than the proportion of women. Except for the recessiveness of the allele leading to pure blue eyes, the genetics of iris color have not been well worked out.

The highest frequencies of light eyes, as of blond hair and fair skin, are found in Europe near the Baltic Sea. Regions where the incidence of light eyes is very high are much more extensive, however, than regions where blond hair is common, as a comparison of Figures 11–17 and 11–18 makes clear. Among European countries, only in Bulgaria, Greece, Italy, Spain, and Portugal are such eye colors in a minority. The functional utility of reduced pigment in the iris is as great a mystery as that of reduced pigment in the hair. Inasmuch as these two characters are typical of populations with fair skin, one might speculate that they are among the pleiotropic effects of alleles for skin depigmentation. But although this is rea-

1-9 10-19 20-34 35-49 50-64 65-79 80+

FIGURE 11-18. Percentage Frequency of Light Eyes in and near Europe

sonable, there is no positive evidence which permits us to regard it as factual. We must know more about the mode of inheritance of pigmentation before the problem can be attacked with any hope of success.

Stern (1953) proposed that genes at five or six loci, each with two codominant alleles, were required to account for the difference in skin color between African Negroes and Europeans. His analysis was based upon the observations of several anthropologists who had done their work before reflectance spectrophotometers were available. By the use of the reflectance spectrophotometer, now readily available, it has been possible to record the degree of pigmentation much more objectively, and such studies have been made on more than a score of populations by now. Harrison and Owen (1964), on the basis of their work on first and second generation hybrids in Liverpool, concluded that four loci are rather more likely. Certainly several, but not too many, contrasting sets of alleles are likely to be involved in the total world-wide range of skin color. Multiple alleles and varying degrees of dominance may exist, for all anyone yet knows. We cannot draw a map showing allele frequencies for skin color, as we can for blood type A. We cannot even draw a map showing phenotypic frequencies, since geographic variation and variation within each gene pool are rather continuous. The frequency of occurrence of a discrete character can be recorded objectively. Only by setting up quite arbitrary and subjective subdivisions within a continuum can we record continuously varying characteristics in terms of frequencies. Sometimes this can be justified; there is always an arbitrary break-off point between those who pass and those who fail a driving test or a school examination. The percentage of people who are very dark or very fair within a population may tell us more than a statement about average, or normal, or typical skin color. But we dare not forget the arbitrary nature of such a technique.

Furthermore, skin color responds to environment quite readily, whereas eye color and blood type do not. Suntan lotion companies would go bankrupt if this were not so. Some of us burn and peel upon exposure to the sun and do not succeed in developing a tan. Some of us are so dark that no added tanning is visible. But most people have skins which are stimulated to deposit pigment by the sun's rays. This ability, like the unexposed color, is genetically determined. In recording skin color it is important to select an area of the body which is difficult to expose, such as the inner side of the upper arm. Skin color in many people darkens with age, and faulty metabolism can produce the same effect. We must, then, consider it to be a plastic character, which adds still more to the difficulties of genetic analysis. It is, nevertheless, a character in which the populations of the world differ from each other to a very marked degree. It is also a character of which the geographic distribution demonstrates both adaptive value and the results of history. In tropical Africa, most of India, Melanesia, and Australia almost all populations are darkskinned. The incidence of alleles for pigmentation must be very high. In Southeast Asia, Indonesia, Polynesia, and tropical America, the populations are not so darkskinned. All of these areas have been occupied by migrants from temperate or even arctic regions within the last 20,000 years or less. At the same time, darkskinned peoples penetrated into the southern temperate zones of Africa and Australia.

Recent studies of skin color with the reflectance spectrophotometer have demonstrated a number of interesting points. The percentage of light reflected is always greater toward the red end of the visible spectrum than toward the blue where wavelengths are shorter. This is most strongly marked in the case of people who appear fairskinned to the unaided eye. Furthermore, in the greenish section of the spectrum less light is reflected than in the blue-green section among those whose skin texture permits hemoglobin in the capillaries to be seen. Adult females in almost all populations so far examined are less deeply pigmented than adult males of the same group. In at least some cases, females become lighter during puberty, whereas males become darker (Hulse, 1970). Even without direct exposure to sunlight, the percentage of reflectance may vary with the seasons.

Any given degree of pigmentation has both advantages and disadvantages, so that the selective value of skin color must be related to other factors. It does not stand alone. A pale skin reflects the rays of the sun far more effectively than a dark one. Under heat stress, as when working in a desert, the body temperature of a Negro usually rises more than that of a European (Baker, 1958). At the same time, it is probable that melanin granules in the skin reflect ultraviolet rays. There is evidence that protection against this sort of radiation is also provided by the close-packed cells within the epidermis; the thicker this layer is, the more rays are reflected. Cells containing more or less melanin lie just below this layer as Figure 11–19 shows, and in most of us, exposure to the sun stimulates the deposit of melanin. In moderate amounts, ultraviolet rays produce vitamin D, which is beneficial. In large amounts, these rays destroy the skin tissues, which is detrimental. Extra heat may be dissipated by extra sweating. An expansion of the areas of the skin where perspiration glands are numerous facilitates extra sweating. Possibly a high ratio of skin area to

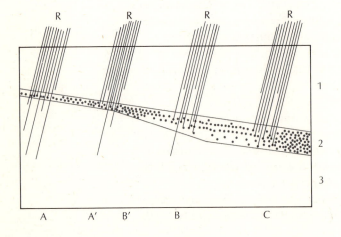

FIGURE 11-19. The Skin and Ultraviolet Light. 1. Epidermis. 2. Pigmented Layer. 3. Dermis. A. Naturally Fair Skin, Untanned. A'. Naturally Fair Skin, Tanned. B. Naturally Medium Skin, Untanned. B'. Naturally Medium Skin, Tanned. C. Naturally Dark Skin. R. Ultraviolet Rays.

Note that Both the Epidermis and the Pigmented Layer May Be Thick or Thin. Some Ultraviolet Rays Do Not Even Penetrate to the Pigmented Layer.

body volume may be useful, too, because sweating is less efficient in humid climates than in dry ones, since the sweat does not evaporate so readily. A skin which becomes tanned upon exposure to the sun increases the degree of protection against ultraviolet rays but also absorbs more heat. A skin which is already dark may tan to some extent, but the proportion of melanin added is too small to increase the absorption of heat very much.

Perhaps tanning ability is especially useful in habitats where the sunlight is likely to be bright, but the days are not hot all year around. Certainly populations which are darkskinned even before tanning are native to the tropical areas of the Old World, while those whose members are most frequently able to tan deeply are native to parts of Asia which are further north and to America.

THE EFFECT OF ENVIRONMENT ON BODILY PROPORTIONS

Inferring the genotype from a more or less plastic phenotype is still more difficult when we consider other aspects of bodily and facial appearance in which man's present diversity is obvious. The environment's capacity to alter the expression of those genes which establish the potentialities for growth is well known. The manner in which they do so and the extent of environmental modification are not nearly so well understood. Stature is one of the aspects in which human beings differ most obviously from one another, and it is one of the traits clearly affected by circumstances external to the individual genetic constitution. Improved diet and health conditions during childhood certainly make people grow taller. The case of the British school children mentioned in Chapter Three is one of many proofs of this. Yet the fact that monozygotic twins are much closer to each other in stature than dizygotic twins shows the strength of its hereditary component (Osborne and De George, 1959).

We do not know the genes involved in determining stature. It is a secondary sexual characteristic, doubtless affected by sex hormones. The range of stature in both sexes is so great, however, that many women are taller than many men. In all populations the female average is less than the male average stature, but the difference is less marked among shorter peoples than among taller ones. From birth to adulthood the total length of the body usually increases about three and one-half times. As we grow older, it becomes more difficult to stand at attention, and the elastic discs between our vertebrae become less resilient. Elderly people are not quite so tall as they were when younger.

Very few adult human beings are less than four or more than

seven feet tall. No breeding populations have average statures within eight inches of these figures. It is interesting that the very tall Watutsi, who comprise the aristocratic class rather than the entire population of their country, live in close proximity to Pygmies whose mean stature is more than a foot shorter. It is more usual for adjacent populations to be similar in stature, but the world-wide distribution of tall, medium, and short people is most irregular.

As a general rule, peoples living in warm, humid climates and those living in very cold ones are likely to be short, but there are many exceptions. Some desert dwellers and many groups native to temperate areas, especially grasslands, are likely to be above average in stature. During the past century and a half average stature has increased in all nations where nutrition and public health measures have improved. In a few regions this increase has amounted to six inches. In studying the skeletons of ancient Greeks, Angel (1946) found fluctuations in stature from one century to another which could be related to varying economic conditions. Stature is a dimensional characteristic; that is, it can be measured in inches or centimeters. Therefore, physical anthropologists have customarily recorded interpopulation differences in terms of averages rather than in terms of frequencies. In fact, for many decades most of the work of physical anthropologists consisted of measuring dimensions of various parts of the body and then calculating that expression of the average which is called the mean, together with a number of other statistical constants. They found long ago that in any unified group such as a breeding population, a great many individuals have dimensions which lie close to the mean, while only a few have dimensions which deviate to an extreme degree. In some cases the concentration of large numbers of individual measurements is greater than in others.

The extent to which a population is variable is expressed by the standard deviation. About two-thirds of the individuals in a group will have dimensions for any measurable trait within one standard deviation of the mean. Methods for calculating the mean, the standard deviation, and for comparing any two groups in order to find out how probable it is that they really differ from each other, are given in Chapter Thirteen. Here we need only say that in the dimensions and proportions of the body and of various parts of the body, different populations are as varied as they are in characteristics for which we can calculate allele frequencies.

Since all of the dimensional traits of the body depend upon growth, as blood types, for instance, do not, environmental influences have every opportunity to affect the phenotype which we measure. Ascertaining the genotype from the phenotype has proved impossible under these circumstances. For instance, people may be short in stature because of illness or poor nutrition during childhood, just as they may be short for genetic reasons. In some cases we know enough about a particular population to make a sound inference; in others we can make an informed guess; but in many cases we simply do not know.

There is little doubt that the various Pygmy populations in the tropical parts of the Old World are short for genetic reasons. The Watutsi, the Sioux Indians, and the Scotch Highlanders are tall because they have inherited the necessary alleles. As such, stature is probably not an adaptive trait, but there is good reason to suppose that it is a necessary expression of certain aspects of body build which have been adaptive (Newman, 1962).

Weight, which is even more responsive to one's environment than stature, is another such expression. Roberts (1953) has demonstrated a clear-cut relationship between average weight and prevailing climate. Populations in which the typical or normal weight of an adult male is greater than 130 pounds are found almost exclusively in temperate and cold regions. Such regions are found in mountainous areas within the tropical zone, of course, just as warm areas are sometimes found outside it. Tall people may be skinny and weigh little. Such a body build is commonly found among darkskinned tropical populations of great stature. Short people may be slight or stocky. Much more often than not, short people native to cold areas are stocky in build, whereas short people native to hot regions are slight. An Eskimo and a Melanesian in Figure 11–20, both about 5 feet 6 inches tall, illustrate this difference in body build very well. The Eskimo weighs thirty-three pounds more than the Melanesian. Bergman's and Allen's rules have some application to *Homo sapiens*.

Our cultural achievements have permitted or even encouraged a certain degree of evasion of these rules. Most of us like to eat, and this can easily make us gain weight, even if we live in the tropics. In many societies, prestige accrues to those who demonstrate their prosperity by becoming fat or by feeding their wives so that they become fat. Rich people can do this. Poor people, who must engage in physical labor, cannot. Populations living at the bare subsistence level are those most likely to abide by the rule that, to function most efficiently in the tropics, one should be of light build and not accumulate fat.

Our technology has also permitted very extensive migration, and today we find many populations which have not yet adapted genetically or adjusted phenotypically to their present habitats. Roberts (1953) found that Mongoloids, whose ancestors probably lived for a long time in a cold region, are less variable in weight in response to climate than are Europeans or Africans. Mongoloids tend to be somewhat solid in build, no matter where they

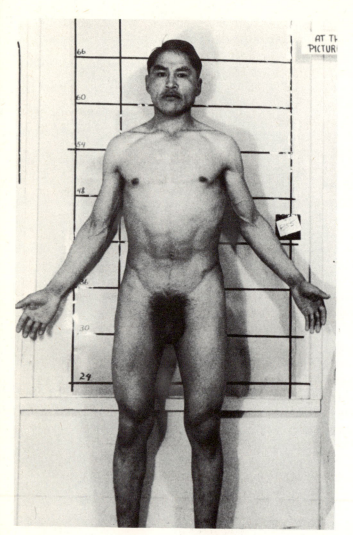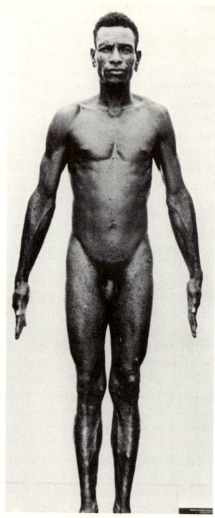

FIGURE 11-20. Arctic and Tropic Body Build. An Eskimo and a Melanesian of the Same Stature.

live. Those who live in the wet tropics are usually short but not really lean. Africans, except for the Pygmies, tend to be rather tall for dwellers in the tropics. Those who live in dry areas are usually very lean indeed.

Limb proportions as well as stature and weight are aspects of body form which have probably had adaptive value when technology was less adequate than it is today. Some desert-dwelling tribes, such as the Papago of Arizona, have bulky trunks but rather lean arms and legs. Since there is a concentration of sweat glands on the forearms, long extremities may permit enough heat loss to permit survival during the hot daylight hours when work must be done, while the trunk is bulky enough to retain heat during the night. Eskimos are much more likely to have short extremities

than they are to have squat figures. When hunting, their bodies
are clad in heavy furs, but their hands and fingers may have to be
exposed from time to time. In general, the native peoples of tropical Africa and of Melanesia have relatively long arms and legs,
while those of eastern Asia and the nearby islands have relatively
short ones. The forearms and lower legs are especially elongated
among African Negroes. In general, taller individuals have long
limbs in proportion to body size. But these are tendencies, not
rigid rules. The increase in stature during the past few generations
is not accompanied by any change in relative leg length in the
populations concerned (Tanner, 1964). This indicates that the
proportions of the body are less plastic than its gross size which is
clearly subject to considerable modification by environment.

Breadth measurements, such as those of the shoulders, chest,
and hips, reflect the influences of age and sex as well as ancestry.
It is well known that for functional reasons connected with childbirth, women as a rule have broader hips than men in proportion
to their stature and their shoulder breadth. Despite this fact, there
is a considerable overlap in relative hip breadth between the
sexes. Not all males have ideal masculine figures, nor do all females
have ideal feminine ones. The hips tend to expand during maturity but the breadth of the shoulders remains more nearly constant,
although elderly people may not be capable of keeping them spread
to their maximum width.

Sexual dimorphism in the shoulder-hip index is less marked
among African Negroes than among most other populations. This
may be associated with the linearity of build which is so frequently found in Africa. The breadth and depth of the chest are
frequently, but by no means always, greater among mountain-
dwelling than among lowland populations. It would seem reasonable to suppose that extra lung capacity would have added survival
value for those who live at high altitudes and for people who
spend a great deal of time climbing. At the same time, chest
dimensions may be increased by exercise, so that we cannot be at
all sure that selection has been required. Chest depth increases
during maturity, but as in the case of spreading hips, this is a
sign of aging rather than of improved function.

The dimensions and proportions of the head and face have been
recorded for populations in most parts of the globe. Anthropologists have found some major and a good many minor geographical
differences. Since skulls have better lasting qualities than most of
the other bones, enough of them from ancient times are available
to enable us to compare early and recent types of man, too. Earlier
chapters described some of the ways in which the characteristics
of the skull and, consequently, of the head and face have changed
during the course of human evolution. The degree to which living

peoples differ from one another in the average size and shape of the head and its various parts is considerable and, for the most part, unexplained. A very few characteristics have a fairly clear adaptive value. Plausible speculations have been made to account for some aspects of variation, but we remain quite ignorant of the reasons for the greater number of differences. Only a few of the ways in which population averages vary most from each other will be discussed in this chapter.

The size of the brain as reflected by the cranial capacity has obvious functional significance. Brains below a certain minimum size are inadequate to manage a human body successfully, but in no population does the mean cranial capacity come close to such a low figure. Brain size is correlated to body size. Consequently, men have, on the average, larger brains than women, and populations in which the average body size is large are likely to have large brains as well. Moreover, a sphere is the most economical form of container. A high vaulted or broad skull may be short and yet provide ample cranial capacity. Some of the big, burly, brachycephalic populations of Siberia, North America, and Polynesia have the largest average cranial capacities of any living peoples: 1,500 cubic centimeters or more for adult males. Japanese, northern Chinese, and central and northern Europeans have cranial capacities which average well over 1,400 cubic centimeters. The smaller peoples living in warmer areas of Europe, Asia, and America, and the African populations in general, have cranial capacities which average between 1,300 and 1,400 cubic centimeters. Some Pygmy groups and the natives of Australia have average cranial capacities of less than 1,300 cubic centimeters. The range in brain size in each of these groups is at least as great as the range in body size. Some Siberians have smaller brains than some Australians, and many Africans have much bigger ones than many Europeans.

Brachycephaly means broad-headedness, and a person is said to be brachycephalic if his head is 82 percent as wide as it is long. He is dolichocephalic or long headed if the proportion is 77 percent or less. The ratio between the length and breadth of the head is called the cephalic index. Most Paleolithic individuals were dolichocephalic, but a great majority of living human beings are not. Because alteration in the shape of the skull is among the most obvious aspects of recent human evolution, it is discussed in more detail in Chapter Fourteen.

The absolute size of the face and its shape, as shown by various indices, is as variable as the size and the shape of the braincase. Males normally have bigger faces than females just as they have bigger brains. This is simply an aspect of their greater size in general. Faces which are long and relatively narrow are more common in the mountainous area stretching from the Balkans through the Near and Middle East and along the Atlantic coast of Europe than they are in other parts of the world. Faces which are shorter and broader are quite typical of Africa and Australia, while oval faces are standard in the Mediterranean basin and much of India. The average breadth of the forehead is great in Europe, especially western Europe, but the reverse is true among the populations of the Pacific. In his study of the Norfolk and Pitcairn Islanders, who are the hybrid offspring of British and Polynesian ancestors, Shapiro (1936) presented evidence which suggests that narrowness of the forehead is due to a dominant allele. Great breadth of the jaw is most frequently found among Eskimos, and narrowness among South African Bushmen and European Basques. A few of the differences in facial shape are illustrated by Figure 11–21.

The most convincing case for adaptation in facial features is the correlation between climate and nasal index. To obtain the nasal index, one divides the breadth of the nasal wings by the total length of the nose. A narrow nose has a low index. The average nasal index of peoples such as the Eskimo who live in frigid areas is almost always low, whereas the average for populations in torrid areas is commonly rather high, as may be seen by an examination of Table 7. The correlation between absolute humidity and nasal index is .82. This is even higher than the correlation between dry-bulb temperature and nasal index, which is .63. Air should be both warm and moist by the time it reaches the lungs (Weiner, 1954). Broad nostrils are less efficient for warming or moistening the air one breathes than narrow nostrils. Wolpoff, in a very

FIGURE 11-21. Variety of Facial Conformation. A Japanese Farmer, a Spanish Student, and a West Indian Scientist, Dr. D. A. N. Hoyte, Represent Some of the Differences Found in the Shape of the Face in Modern Mankind. (Photos: Frederick S. Hulse)

neatly designed study (1968), has demonstrated that the breadth of the bony nasal aperture declines among Alaskan Eskimos, from south to north, and among Australian aborigines in New South Wales, from north to south. In both cases the narrowest noses are found where the climate is coldest and driest. Many people who live in arid lands have narrow noses. There are enough exceptions to the ecological explanation of nasal index to assure us that other factors are concerned as well as temperature and humidity, as Washburn (1963) has pointed out.

TABLE 7. THE MEAN NASAL INDICES OF POPULATIONS NATIVE TO VARIOUS CLIMATIC ZONES.

Region	Mean Nasal Index of Local Peoples	Mean Annual Temperature	Mean Annual Humidity
Africa			
Hot and Moist	76–105	72–83°	71–90%
Hot and Dry	65– 87	70–84°	33–52%
Asia			
Hot and Moist	69– 95	71–84°	63–81%
Hot and Dry	71– 82	72–82°	45–59%
Cold and Moist	59– 78	42–60°	67–88%
Cold and Dry	58– 76	48–59°	45–61%
Pacific Islands	75– 94	72–80°	77–86%
Australia	85–100	60–75°	40–60%
America			
Hot and Moist	76– 82	72–85°	73–83%
Hot and Dry	72– 78	65–80°	41–47%
Cold and Moist	56 80	22–54°	74–87%
Europe	56– 70	36–63°	50–82%

Many features which are readily observable are difficult to measure: for example, the height of the nasal bridge, the shape of the ear, the conformation of the lips and jaw, the presence and extent of folds of skin drooping over the eyelids. In each of these and in other traits as well, populations as well as individuals differ to an obvious extent. We know little or nothing of the mode of inheritance or the adaptive value, if any, of these traits. Some peculiarity of one or another may characterize a family line, as in the case of the drooping lower lip of the Hapsburgs, one of the European ex-royal families; or a small genetic isolate, such as the extra prominent noses of Pitcairn's Islanders or the villagers of Moghegno; or a vast congeries of related breeding populations, for example, the epicanthic eyefold so typical of the peoples of eastern

Asia. We can see that these features exist, and they are sometimes useful as diagnostic criteria, but explaining them is a different matter.

Even more difficult to deal with from the viewpoint of physical anthropology has been the obvious variety in body build among humans, which is readily seen but far from readily measured. Some aspects of the relation between body build and climate have already been mentioned. In all populations, however, some people are fatter, some more muscular, and some more attenuated than others. Sheldon (1941) devised a system of constitutional types, based upon three components, endomorphy, mesomorphy and ectomorphy, by which he proposed to classify the whole range of body builds. Sheldon uses the term endomorphy to stand for the viscera and fat of the body; the term mesomorphy to stand for the skeleton and muscles; and the term ectomorphy to stand for the skin and the nervous system. He used a seven point rating scale for each component to indicate the relative degree of development in each. The Eskimo in Figure 11–20 is rated 3–6–1; the Melanesian 1–6–3. Both are well above average in muscularity, as indicated by the rating of 6 for mesomorphy. The Eskimo is very solid without

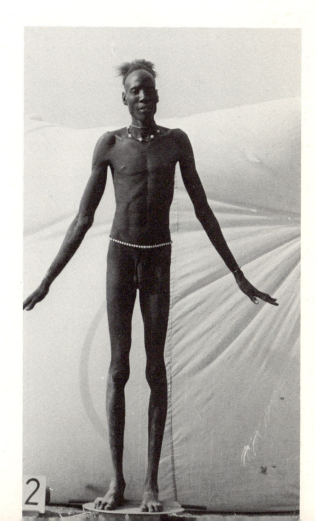

FIGURE 11-22. Nilotic Physique (Photo: D. F. Roberts and D. Bainbridge)

being at all fat, so that his endomorphy rating is 3; whereas the Melanesian, who has a minimum of subcutaneous fat, is rated 1. In contrast, for ectomorphy, the latter, who is the more linear in build of the two, has a rating of 3, but the former is rated 1. Men of identical constitutional types can be found in any large population, although some types occur more frequently in one part of the world, others more frequently elsewhere.

Indeed, since Sheldon developed his technique by working among American adult males, some anthropologists, attempting to apply them to members of other populations, have found it necessary to give ratings higher than 7 to certain individuals. Roberts and Bainbridge (1963) classify the Nilotic shown in Figure 11–22 at 1-2-8: he is certainly very attenuated. Heath *et al.* (1970) finds the men at Manus, in Melanesia, equally strong in mesomorphy. Even women, who in all populations are less muscular and have more subcutaneous fat than men of the same stock, may be remarkably lacking in ectomorphy at Manus, as is shown by Figure 11–23, the photograph of a young lady, whose somatotype rating is 5–4–1. She should be compared to the female of Northwest European ancestry, whose somatotype is 4–4–3.

Although the concept of constitutional type has been found to have clinical utility by many physicians, it has a number of grave weaknesses from a strictly scientific point of view. Claims have been made that it is a key to personality, but there is no evidence

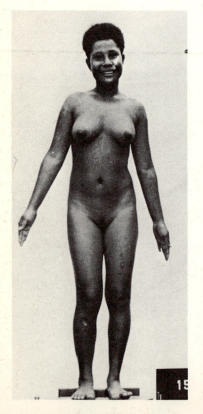
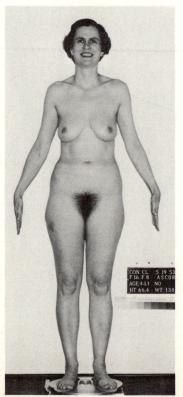

FIGURE 11-23. Adaptive Variety in Female Physique: A Melanesian and a North European

whatever to support such notions. Claims have been made that somatotype, being derived from one's genetic constitution, remains constant throughout life. It does not remain constant, and is as far removed from direct genic action as any other anatomical characteristic. It cannot be measured, as stature can, but depends upon the judgment of trained observers. In recent years, some progress has been made in the development of more objective techniques for judging constitutional type (Heath and Carter, 1966), but at present a somatotype rating is simply a convenient summary statement of overall anatomical appearance.

Sources and Suggested Readings

ADAM, A., E. MWESIGYE, and E. TABANI
  1970 Ugandan Colorblinds Revisited. *American Journal of Physical Anthropology*, new series, **32**, 59–64.

ANGEL, J. L.
  1946 Social Biology of Greek Culture Growth. *American Anthropologist*, **68**, 223–233.

BAKER, P. T.
  1958 Racial Differences in Heat Tolerance. *American Journal of Physical Anthropology*, new series, **16**, 287–306.

BAKER, P. T. and J. S. WEINER, eds.
  1966 *The Biology of Human Adaptability*. Clarendon Press, Oxford.

CANDELA, P. B.
  1942 The Introduction of Blood Group B into Europe. *Human Biology*, **14**, 413–443.

CEPPELLINI, R.
  1959 Blood Groups and Hematological Data as a Source of Ethnic Information. *Medical Biology and Etruscan Origins*. Little, Brown, Boston.

COON, C. S., S. M. GARN, and J. B. BIRDSELL
  1950 *Races*. Thomas, Springfield, Ill.

CUMMINS, H. and C. MIDLO
  1943 *Finger Prints, Palms and Soles*. Blakiston, Philadelphia.

CUTBUSH, M., P. L. MOLLISON, and D. M. PARK
1950   A New Human Blood Group. *Nature,* **165,** 188.

FISCHER, R. and F. GRIFFIN
1959   On Factors Involved in the Mechanism of "Taste Blindness." *Experimenta,* **15,** 447–451.

FISHER, R. A., E. B. FORD, and J. S. HUXLEY
1939   Taste-Testing the Anthropoid Apes. *Nature,* **144,** 750.

GARN, S. M.
1969   *Human Races,* revised edition. Thomas, Springfield, Ill.

HARRIS, H.
1946   Heredity and Premature Baldness in Men. *Annals of Eugenics,* **13,** 172–181.
1959   *Human Biochemical Genetics.* Cambridge University Press, Cambridge.

HARRISON, G. A. and J. J. T. OWEN
1964   Studies on the Inheritance of Human Skin-Color. *Annals of Human Genetics,* **28,** 27–38.

HEATH, B. H. and J. E. L. CARTER
1966   A Comparison of Somatotype Methods. *American Journal of Physical Anthropology,* new series, **24,** 87–99.

HEATH, B. H., M. MEAD and T. SCHWARTZ
1970   A Somatotype Study of a Melanesian Population. *Proceedings of VIII International Congress of Anthropological and Ethnological Sciences,* **1,** 9–11, Tokyo.

HULSE, F. S.
1970   Skin Color Among Yemenite Jews of the Isolate from Habban. *Proceedings of the VIII International Congress of Anthropological and Ethnological Sciences,* **1,** 226–228, Tokyo.

LAYRISSE, M. and J. WILBERT
1961   Absence of the Diego Antigen, a Genetic Characteristic of Early Immigrants to South America. *Science,* **134,** 1077–1078.

LIVINGSTONE, F. B.
1960   Natural Selection, Disease and Ongoing Human Evolution. *The Processes of Ongoing Human Evolution.* Wayne State University Press, Detroit.

1967   *Abnormal Hemoglobins in Human Populations.*   Aldine, Chicago.

KIRK, R. L.
1961   Blood-Group Interaction and the World Distribution of ABO Gene p^2 and the RH Gene r (cde). *American Journal of Human Genetics,* **13,** 224–232.

MOURANT, A. E.
1954   *The Distribution of the Human Blood Groups.* Blackwell Scientific Publications, Oxford.

MOURANT, A. E., A. C. KOPEC, and K. DOMANIEWSKA-SOBCZAK
1958   *The ABO Blood-Groups: Comprehensive Tables and Maps of World Distribution.* Blackwell Scientific Publications, Oxford.

NEWMAN, M. T.
1962   Evolutionary Changes in Body Size and Head Form in American Indians. *American Anthropologist,* **64,** 237–257.

OSBORNE, R. H. and F. V. DE GEORGE
1959   *Genetic Basis of Morphological Variation: An Evaluation and Application of the Twin Study Method.* Harvard University Press, Cambridge.

POST, R. H.
1962   Population Differences in Red and Green Color Vision Deficiency. *Eugenics Quarterly,* **9,** 131–146.

ROBERTS, D. F.
1953   Body Weight, Race and Climate. *American Journal of Physical Anthropology,* new series, **11,** 533–558.

ROBERTS, D. F. and D. R. BAINBRIDGE
1963   Nilotic Physique. *American Journal of Physical Anthropology,* new series, **21,** 341–370.

SHAPIRO, H. L.
1936   *Heritage of the Bounty.* Simon and Schuster, New York.

SHELDON, W. H. and W. B. TUCKER
    1941   *The Varieties of Human Physique.* Hafner, New York.

SNYDER, L. H. and H. C. YINGLING
    1935   Studies in Human Inheritance XII. The Application of the Gene-Frequency Method of Analysis to Sex-Influenced Factors, with Especial Reference to Baldness. *Human Biology,* **7,** 608–615.

STERN, C.
    1953   Model Estimates of the Frequency of White and Near White Segregants in the American Negro. *Acta Genetica et Statista Medica,* **4,** 287–298.

TANNER, J. M.
    1964   Human Growth and Constitution, in *Human Biology,* by G. A. Harrison, J. S. Weiner, J. M. Tanner, and N. A. Barnicot. Clarendon Press, Oxford.

TAYLOR, C. W.
    1961   A Note on Differential Taste Responses to PTC (Phenylthiocarbamide). *Human Biology,* **33,** 220–222.

VOGEL, F.
    1961   The Theory of Natural Selection in the ABO Blood Group System. *Abstracts of Proceedings of the Second International Congress of Human Genetics.* Excerpta Medica Publications, Amsterdam.
    1970   Anthropological Implications of the Relationship Between ABO Blood Groups and Infection. *Proceedings of VIII International Congress of Anthropological and Ethnological Sciences,* **1,** 365–370, Tokyo.

WASHBURN, S. L.
    1963   The Study of Race. *American Anthropologist,* **65,** 521–531.

WEINER, J. S.
    1954   Nose Shape and Climate. *American Journal of Physical Anthropology,* new series, **12,** 1–4.

WILSON, A. P. and I. R. FRANKLIN
    1968   The Distribution of the Diego Blood Group and Its Relationship to Climate. *Caribbean Journal of Science,* **8,** 1–13.

WOLPOFF, M. H.
    1968   Climatic Influence on the Skeletal Nasal Aperture. *American Journal of Physical Anthropology,* new series, **29,** 405–423.

CHAPTER 12

The Historical Distribution of Racial Varieties

Even before the latest of the continental icecaps had melted away, mankind had occupied not only the Old World but the New. The presence of manufactured artifacts as well as human fossil remains attest to the existence of our ancestors both in tropical and temperate climatic zones. From the fossil remains we have much information concerning the physique and appearance of Paleolithic men. For the earliest times, to be sure, our data are woefully meager, but fortunately we have a frame of reference from which to examine them, a frame provided by our knowledge of other species and of living groups.

It is quite clear, for instance, that any species of creature which occupies an extended range will be subject to various forces which will tend to divide it into different segments. The conditions of life are not the same in a tropical savannah as they are in temperate parkland; nor do boreal forests provide the same opportunities and hazards as do tropical jungles. Adaptation to purely local circumstances may well be necessary, so that the pressure of natural selection is likely to promote the retention of certain characteristics in one area but their alteration in another. Simple geographic distance acts as a check to completely random mating and consequently to gene flow. Among animals which live in any sort of social groupings, no matter how naturally and unconsciously these groupings may be organized, there are social as well as geographical barriers to intermating. Mutations occurring in one group do not automatically spread throughout an entire species, even though they be potentially useful.

We might well anticipate then that as a species spreads over a range extending from Peking to Ternifine and from Heidelberg to Java and Swartkrans, it might begin to differentiate. When it has occupied such isolated continents as America and Australia, the chance of diversification is even greater. Indeed, under such circumstances most animal species are known to divide, to come apart at the seams as it were, and evolve into a number of separate species.

An examination of living human groups shows that we have not been exempt from the normal processes of local evolutionary change. It would be difficult to mistake a Chinese for a Dane or a Hottentot for a Sioux. The skeletons of Upper Paleolithic men can tell us less than a study of the living, but even 15,000 years ago the extent of geographically based variety is clear. Genetic differences between populations inhabiting different parts of the globe had accumulated throughout the thousands of generations during which they shared only a minute portion of their ancestry. This process has continued since that time, so that some characteristics have become typical of the peoples of East Asia, while others have become just as typical of Europeans or South Africans. It is both interesting and significant that evolutionary diversification has not proceeded still further among humans and that, by all biological criteria, we remain members of a single species.

Since we are all members of a single species today, and since the human fossils from very early times are in many respects so different from any modern skeletal material, it has become a common opinion that racial diversity postdates the appearance of *Homo sapiens*. A very popular family tree among anthropologists is shown in Figure 12–1. The various fossils antedating those of the Upper Paleolithic are ordinarily shown as side branches which terminated through extinction without offspring rather than through evolution. Often they have been given specific or even generic status, at least by their discoverers. Only one central line is shown ascending triumphantly to the very peak of the tree, upon which twigs represent whichever racial stocks suit the fancy of the designer. It would appear from an examination of such a diagram that we have never succeeded in digging up our grandfathers' bones but only those of our great uncles, who were childless.

Not all students of human evolution have accepted this scheme in all details. Many scholars have maintained that Neanderthal man was ancestral to ourselves. Hooton (1946) could not bring himself to believe that hybridity had not taken place between our unfound ancestors and at least some Neanderthaloids. And a few authors, going to the opposite extreme, assumed a total separation between the so-called major racial stocks dating back to the Pliocene or earlier. The fossils of the past and the peoples of the present provide no evidence of any nature to support this extreme opinion.

At the same time there is an inherent improbability in the notion that only a small proportion of the earlier populations of men left any offspring at all. It would seem strange that the bones of our direct ancestors elude us, while we continue to find those of their close relatives. Perhaps the standard design of the ancestral tree, so useful in representing the descent of different species, has misled us. Such a design is invalid as a representation of subspecific diversification. The human fossils of the Pleistocene do not differ enough from one another at any single period of time to deserve such separate specific designations. Weidenreich (1947) proposed a design to represent the immediate phylogeny of *Homo sapiens*, not in the form of a branching tree but of a grid or trellis similar to that shown in Figure 12–2. Coon (1962) proposes a similar but not identical scheme. Hooton (1946) showed a vine of which the branches coalesce as well as separate to indicate what he believed to be the relationships between the living human races.

Both Weidenreich and Hooton realized that genetic continuity exists within a species and that any diagram which does not show this is bound to be misleading. Weidenreich pointed out that certain characteristics of "Sinanthropus" and of the later Chinese fossils foreshadow some of the characteristics of the living inhabitants of eastern Asia, and certain characteristics of Solo man foreshadow

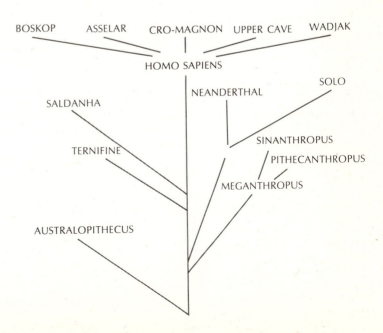

FIGURE 12-1. A Phylogenetic Tree. This Represents an Older Idea about the Evolution of Mankind, to which Many Anthropologists Still Adhere.

those of Wadjak and the present natives of Australia. On grounds of chance alone one would expect to find a greater concentration of genes derived from "Sinanthropus" in East Asia than in Europe or Africa. This does not mean, of course, that "Sinanthropus" when alive looked like a modern Chinese. An examination of the fossil remains of this early variety demonstrates that he did not. Mankind as a whole has evolved to a very considerable degree during the last 30,000 generations, and we have no evidence to suggest that any contemporary of "Sinanthropus" could be mistaken for any contemporary of ours.

Although the fossil evidence from this period is slim except for "Sinanthropus" and "Pithecanthropus," we find most taxonomists agreed that the human beings of that early time should be classified in a species other than our own. Until a generation ago "Sinan-

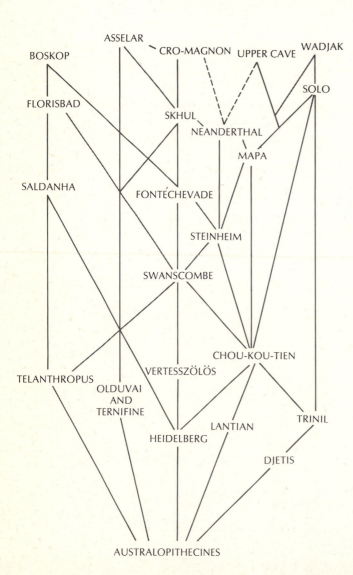

FIGURE 12-2. A Phylogenetic Trellis. This Represents a Modern Conception of the Evolution of Mankind as at All Times a Polytypic Species with Genes Flowing between Different Populations.

thropus" and "Pithecanthropus" were given separate generic status. Since we are fortunate enough to have several individuals from both of these groups, it is possible and therefore necessary to say that they do appear to represent separate populations. The available remains of their Atlantic coast contemporaries found at Heidelberg and Ternifine are so scanty as to demand great caution in our conclusions concerning them, yet the small teeth in the large Heidelberg jaw suggest, at least, a certain degree of difference between this form and the others. It seems more reasonable, therefore, to think in terms of population differences in different parts of the world during the Lower Paleolithic of the same order of magnitude which we find among populations living in different parts of the world today. The evidence which we have at present leads to the inference that then, as now, human populations living in various parts of the world could reasonably be classified into separate races but not into different species.

RACE FORMATION

What is implied by the term "race"? To some people it is just another nasty four-letter word, not to be uttered in decent company with the hope that it may thus be conjured out of existence. This abhorrence is easy to understand, for the word has been badly misused in many ways and has carried varied implications. But banning a word does not help solve the problems connected with its use. It has sometimes been alleged that the word does not correspond to any reality in the actual world and is therefore dangerously misleading. The word race has been said to imply eternal unchangeability, which puts it outside an evolutionary framework of thought. It is true, of course, that the use of the word race is rather older than Darwin's (1858) demonstration of how evolution is brought about. But Darwin does not appear to have felt it necessary to avoid the use of the word species, which in earlier days had implied eternal unchangeability as well as separate creation.

No matter what the origin and destiny of species may be, the word represents a valid taxonomic category. In the same way, recognizable subspecific categories are known to exist within many but not necessarily all species. According to Simpson (1961) the recognition of subspecific taxa is appropriate if this happens to be useful to the taxonomist, and it will be if there is some nonarbitrary element in the definition of the groupings concerned. A grouping may be considered as real and as existing in nature rather than in the taxonomist's mind if three-fourths of the individuals in adjacent subspecies are unequivocally determinable.

Subspecific categories, whether we call them races, stocks, breeds, varieties, subspecies, demes, breeding populations, isolates, or anything else are likely to lack the sharp boundaries which characterize species. In the absence of artificial hindrances, genetic communication between any one of them and its neighbors is open and is likely to take place when the opportunity is offered, in direct contrast to the lack of genetic communication between adjacent species. Breeding between members of separate species, although often technically possible, is likely to take place only when artificially encouraged, as for instance in the case of captive animals which have no other sexual partners available. Hybrids between valid species are therefore as rare in the natural world as hybrids between subspecific categories are common.

Despite this, it is sometimes easier to distinguish members of one breed of a species from members of another breed of the same species than it is to distinguish members of one breed within that species from members of another species. An Alsatian, for example, looks more like a wolf than it looks like a dachshund. Variety within a species can clearly proceed to a remarkable degree with no break in the chain of genetic continuity. So long as this chain is not broken, the subspecific taxa are always capable of merging with one another and vanishing: animal breeders must exercise constant care to maintain those genetic characteristics which they happen to favor. In the wild only geographic isolation can be depended upon to keep naturally existing subspecies distinct from one another. One would expect then in the history of any species that subspecific taxa should evolve from time to time within it, but that most of them would eventually disappear as such because of random mating, as the opportunity arose, between the members of the various natural groupings.

Dobzhansky (1958) states that "Races are sometimes referred to as incipient species. . . . it does not, however, follow that every race will at some future time be a species. . . . When the interbreeding of populations does not lower the fitness, the stimulus for the development of reproductive isolation is lacking." He is writing in this instance about genetic mechanisms enforcing, or at least promoting, reproductive isolation; he is not writing about external circumstances, such as geographical barriers, which may lead to such isolation for a certain period of time. Among living human populations, all the evidence at our disposal would indicate that interbreeding between populations whose ancestors had long been isolated from each other does not lower the fitness.

After their invasion of the Americas, Europeans interbred freely with the Indians, producing offspring who appear to be at least as fit as either parental stock. The account in Chapter Nine of man's coming to the Americas indicates that these two groups had shared no ancestry whatever for at least a thousand generations. Millions of Latin Americans today are of such mixed ancestry, and they are as fit and as fertile as any other population. Scientific studies of European-Hottentot hybrids in South Africa (Fischer, 1913) and of European-Polynesian hybrids in the South Pacific (Shapiro, 1929) demonstrate that fitness has been preserved, and perhaps even enhanced, by such mixtures.

Human races show no signs whatever of being incipient species. On the contrary, some of the populations which Coon, Garn, and Birdsell (1950) class as races have come into existence as a result of mixtures which took place within the last few score generations. In the genetic continuum of any species the genesis of a new race by means of hybridization may be anticipated whenever the circumstances are opportune. It will be recalled that one explanation of the characteristics of the Skhul population has been that they were the hybrid offspring of Neanderthaloids and men of more modern appearance.

It is also clear, however, that long-continued, free interchange of genes on a random basis must result in the complete merging of such previously distinctive populations as may have existed earlier. In the absence of historic documentation, whether in the form of written records or of skeletal remains, any attempt at describing the biological characteristics of such now submerged racial groupings is hazardous at best. It is often alleged, for instance, that separate races such as Nordics, Alpines, and Mediterraneans once existed in Europe. At present there are clines of frequency for such characteristics as blondness of hair and lightness of eyes, various series of blood types, brachycephaly, stature, and numerous other items on that continent. It must be noted at once, however, that clines divide frequencies of characters, not sorts of organisms: the clines which we find in Europe are not racial boundaries in any sense. Blondness is most frequent in the north, red hair along the Atlantic Coast, brachycephaly in the center and east, short stature in the south, and so on. If we draw clines for the frequency of as many as half a dozen characteristics on a map of Europe, a crazy-quilt pattern is seen and nothing more. It would be out of the question to reconstruct racial history on the basis of such data, and Huxley and Haddon (1936) exploded the notion of separate races within this region.

Fortunately, historic and prehistoric documentation does exist for this continent. The Paleolithic drew to a close as the icecap continued to melt away, forests grew, and a new fauna replaced the old. Men began using dogs to assist them in hunting and devised other new techniques to deal with their changing environment. An increased proportion of the skeletons from this later period are of smaller people and of people with shorter, broader heads in contrast to earlier Europeans. First in the Near East but later all through the basin of the Mediterranean, individuals of less rugged build appeared. The practice of agriculture began spreading, very slowly at first, throughout the whole continent. Population increased greatly, and archaeological remains attest to tribal migrations. By the dawn of European history population movements had taken place in all directions.

During the period of the Roman Empire, the continued movements of soldiers and traders did still more to promote gene flow, and the wandering of Germanic and Slavic tribes which succeeded it continued this process. Later during the Middle Ages such population movements declined in magnitude, but by that time the peoples had been mixed. Any classification of Europeans purporting to show subspecific or racial differences is really arbitrary rather than natural and would have to be abstracted from such a diagram as is shown in Figure 12–3, which is inspired by one in Simpson's *Principles of Animal Taxonomy* (1961). As we can see, any one of a number of groupings would appear to be equally valid. Different types may be rather more frequent in some areas than in others. Individuals of so-called Nordic type—tall, leptorrhine, dolichocephalic, and blond—are rare in Italy, Greece and Spain; whereas in Norway and Sweden as much as 10 percent of the popu-

FIGURE 12-3. Lines of Genetic Communication in Europe

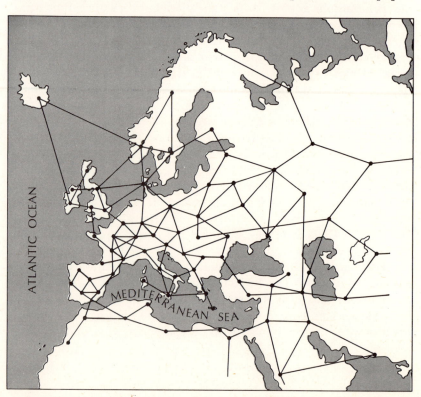

lation of some valleys may combine all of these features. Only a few minor populations, such as the Basques and the Lapps, appear to differ at all sharply in gene frequencies at several loci from their neighbors. Indeed, as Chapter Nine demonstrated, the range and variety among the European skeletal remains from the Upper Paleolithic indicate the lack of racial divisions among them.

PATTERNS OF GENE FLOW

Yet these Upper Paleolithic specimens from Europe and adjacent areas have many characteristics which ally them to the later inhabitants of the same regions rather than to all later mankind. In Africa south of the Sahara, in eastern Asia, and in the Americas the fossil men of the Upper Paleolithic show to an equivalent degree resemblances to later peoples living in their particular parts of the world. In still earlier periods rather scanty data suggest that different regions were inhabited by populations having different anatomical characteristics. By the Upper Paleolithic the data are ample enough to assure us that this was so. Most but not all of these ancient specimens are more rugged in build than is the bulk of the world's population today. Since modern Europeans are, on average, distinctly less neotenous than are most non-Europeans, this fact tends to obscure the extent of divergence among early populations which would otherwise be apparent. Evolution within the various populations has certainly been proceeding since, just as it had been before, and differing circumstances have led to selective pressures in different directions.

In Paleolithic times communication between widely separated parts of the world was certainly difficult and probably slow. Hunters and collectors may range over a considerable territory, but for sound, practical reasons are reluctant to move beyond the range they are accustomed to. There is ample evidence of some migration, but to extrapolate from this and jump to the conclusion that our Paleolithic ancestors were milling around all over the world is quite unjustified. We should be profoundly skeptical of the hypothesis of widespread migrations as an explanation of assumed similarities between populations in different parts of the world, unless supporting data from archaeology and linguistic distribution accompany it.

Thus, the notion that the Bushmen and Hottentots of South Africa derive some of their characteristics from a migration of Mongoloids from eastern Asia during prehistoric times need not be taken seriously. The notion that Polynesians must be descended from American Indians because of the high frequency of R^2 among both groups is equally unsupported. The notion that all dark-skinned peoples of the Old World tropics, whether now living in Fiji, Ceylon, or Africa, are representatives of a single Negro race, derived from a single area from which they all migrated at some time in the past is almost certainly mistaken. None of these notions agrees with our present knowledge of genetics or of archaeology.

It seems more reasonable to assume that gene flow due to mating between adjacent groups has been the more ordinary means for spreading hereditary characteristics. Such gene flow takes place in all widespread species, its extent being related to the social organization of the groups concerned. Present data suggest, for instance, that it is more common among chimpanzees than among baboons. Human mating patterns, especially the rules concerning incest and exogamy mentioned in Chapter Ten, serve to promote a considerable amount of gene flow in our species. We know that gene flow is continuous today, and we have no reason to suppose that it was not continuous in prehistoric times. We know that far more often than not changes in allele frequencies, as we move from one part of the world to another, are gradual rather than abrupt. The maps in Chapter Eleven, which represent the distribution of blood-group frequencies throughout the world, illustrate this fact. Given enough time, any mutation which is not eliminated by natural selection can be expected to spread throughout the world. Of course, a long time may be required if the average distance between the birthplace of those who mate is slight, as among the Juang, an aboriginal tribe in India studied by Ajit (1961). Since the human population was scanty in Lower Paleolithic times, the average distance between settlements must have been much greater, so that gene flow would have been more rapid. Nevertheless, it is 6,000 miles from Heidelberg to Chou-kou-tien, which is a long way to walk. It is not strange that the mandibles found at these localities differ from each other, even though both of them date from more or less the same time.

Distances within Europe are minimal compared to distances between France and China or either of these with South Africa. We could reasonably expect that such natural geographical barriers as oceans, glaciated mountain ranges, or deserts would channel such gene flow as existed along specific routes. If this did happen, the proper diagram to represent the relationships between peoples in the world before Columbus discovered America would resemble that in Figure 12–4, which is also inspired by one in Simpson's *Principles of Animal Taxonomy* (1961).

This contrasts sharply to the European-Mediterranean situation, since it shows a natural rather than an arbitrary set of divisions into subgroups within the species. At other times during human history existing lines of communication would certainly alter: old ones might vanish, and new ones appear. But at all times some barriers would be bound to exist to channel gene flow. Thus the conditions which might be expected to promote the evolution and fluctuation of perfectly valid subspecific taxa have existed since our ancestors came to occupy an extended range.

A number of things should be noted in the clustering of populations apparent on this chart. In the first place, not all are of equal dimensions. Racial groups need not be equal in population or even of the same order of magnitude because population size is totally irrelevant to the degree of genetic distinctness. Small groups are not necessarily branches of big ones. In the second place, some are intermediate between other clusters. Racial groups may be intermediate in gene frequencies between other such groups, and this need not be the result of hybridity. It may be a response to intermediate conditions. In the third place, some clusters are in communication with only one other, some with two, and some with even more than that. This chart does not represent a neatly ordered filing system. It simply attempts to represent lines of genetic communication.

FIGURE 12-4. Lines of Genetic Communication in the World

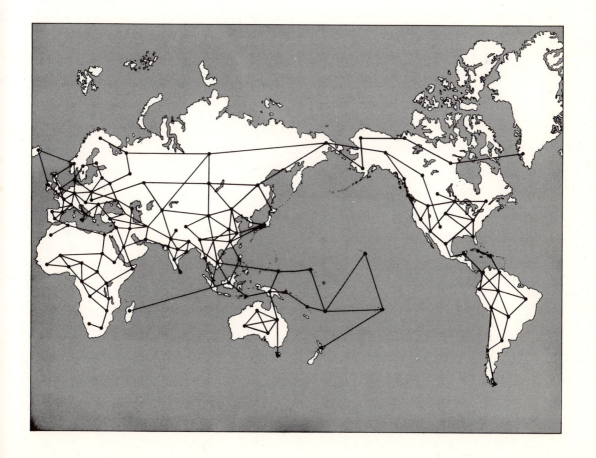

HOW MANY RACES?

Most of the attempts to reconstruct racial history postulate an original threefold division of our species into Mongoloid, Negroid, and Caucasoid stock, each of which later divided into subraces. Minority opinions maintain that the original division was twofold, fourfold, or even sixfold. Some anthropologists have stressed the role of hybridization between "major stocks" as well as divisions within each of them. As the previous chapters have demonstrated, however, we cannot expect taxonomic neatness at the subspecific level, and there is really little evidence to support the notion that at one time there were just two, or three, or four distinct races of *Homo sapiens*.

The evidence of human genetics does not support Hooton's statement (1946) that the differences between the subgroups which he listed are obviously more recent and smaller than those which separate the major stocks. The evidence of morphological characteristics of which the mode of inheritance is unclear or unknown does not support this hypothesis of a very few, original stocks. The geographical distribution of living peoples is difficult to explain on the basis of the idea that each of these stocks had an original homeland. And recent studies (Baker and Weiner, 1966) showing the role of adaptation in racial as well as in species evolution render the notion of two or three primary races unnecessary.

Some of the genetically distinct populations which exist today are far more numerous than others. In contrast to a few thousand Andamanese, for instance, there are several hundred million individuals of European ancestry. Some show a much greater degree of polymorphism than others; the same examples will serve to illustrate this point. Some are known to be of very recent origin by hybridization, like the American Colored. Others, like the African Khoisans, have existed for many thousands of years at least. Some actually do appear to be branches or subdivisions of others, as American Indians are a subdivision of Mongoloids. Others, just as clearly, cannot be pigeonholed so neatly: for example, the Ainu. However, each one of the groups just named can be described in terms of allele frequencies which are distinctive from those of other groups and also in terms of phenotypic traits which are characteristic and readily observable. They are among the groups which can legitimately be termed races.

It would be impossible to make a complete list of all existing races. We do not know enough about the genetic distinctions of many peoples in the world. It is both possible and worthwhile, however, to present in brief outline the more significant things we know about the characteristics of the populations native to different parts of the world.

THE AMERICAN INDIANS

Before the Europeans arrived nearly five centuries ago the New World was inhabited by peoples whose genetic connections with any non-American groups had been at a minimum for hundreds of generations, except in the northern and northwestern parts of North America. Even in these regions, where contact with Asia remained relatively easy, climatic conditions discouraged large-scale population movements, and gene flow seems to have been reduced to no more than a trickle. Nevertheless, most anthropologists agree that the Americas were originally populated by bands of Upper Paleolithic hunting peoples who wandered from Siberia into Alaska. There is no evidence that anyone lived in either North or South America until after the invention of clothing, hunting gear, and habitations suitable for survival in the Arctic. We do not know how many separate tribes may have reached America from Asia during the last 30,000 years, but we can be sure that all but an infinitesimal part of the Indian ancestry is derived from tribes which followed this route and which were subject to the selective pressures of an Arctic climate for a more or less prolonged period. Compared to the diversity in bodily form and genetic constitution found among the peoples on the eastern side of the Atlantic, the American Indians show a surprising degree of uniformity. Figures 12–5 and 12–6 show American Indians.

The earliest immigrants found themselves in the fortunate position of having 16 million square miles of virgin territory in which to hunt with no competition. We can imagine no better situation for rapid population increase, at least until the void had been filled. By comparison, later migrants would have had more restricted opportunities unless their technology was much superior. Linguistic distribution suggests that the last group to arrive from Asia had penetrated no further south than Arizona before the Europeans arrived. Linguistic and other ethnological distributions also suggest that in earlier times there had been a great deal of wandering back and forth by many tribes.

Whether the ancestors of many local populations among the American Indians had lived long enough within the same geographical region to become climatically adapted by means of selection is somewhat dubious. Archaeological data show that later populations in the southeastern part of the United States have distinctly taller stature than earlier populations, whereas in California the later populations were shorter (Newman, 1962). These trends are best explained as the results of selection. But for most areas we lack evidence of such evolutionary changes. Body size among American Indians is quite variable, but we do not know to what extent this variation is merely phenotypic.

FIGURE 12-5. South American Indians—Two Amazonians (Photos: Napoleon A. Chagnon)

Indians living in areas with cold winters and hot summers are much more likely to be tall and heavy than those who live where it is either rarely or always very hot (Newman, 1953, 1960). The degree of skin pigmentation and of nasal breadth varies, too, but there is less correlation between these characteristics and climatic conditions.

The variations which exist in such traits as head shape, lip thickness, blood-type frequencies, and fingerprints do not appear to be associated with climate. In fact, narrow heads are most frequently found in remote places like Greenland and lower California or in earlier horizons of archaeological sites. Simpler fingerprint patterns and high frequency of the Diego blood type are more frequently found among tribes which live south of the Mexican border than north of it. Wavy hair is found more often among tribes living in tropical jungles than among others. The frequency of blood group allele I^A reaches a world maximum in the Blackfeet and is quite high among Athapaskan-speaking tribes and Eskimos, but among other tribes it is rare or absent. Among most tribes the incidence of the allele I⁰ is very high indeed, whereas the allele I^B is absent. The frequency of blood type N is higher among the Blackfeet and some southwestern tribes than elsewhere. The blood type allele R^2 is exceptionally high in frequency along the Northwest Coast. There are many albinos among the Hopi and the San Blas Indians of Panama. In brief, American Indians show a certain degree of polymorphism, both individually and tribally, genetically and phenotypically.

There remains, however, a large number of ways in which the entire population is distinctive from all other populations except those of eastern Asia and a number of ways in which it is genetically unique. No American Indian tribe which has been tested has a frequency as much as 50 percent of blood type N. The alleles for such varied traits as red-green color blindness, absence of the palmaris longus muscle, and presence of hair on the middle segment of the fingers are also very low.

The Diego blood factor is present only among American Indians and a few peoples of eastern Asia. Their eyes and hair are commonly very dark, even black, and their hair is likely to be coarse and straight. As a rule, body and facial hair is scanty in both sexes. American Indian females are quite likely to have an epicanthic

FIGURE 12-6. North American Indians—Two Athapascans (Photo: Arizona State Museum)

eyefold and unlikely to have large breasts. In both sexes body build tends to be stocky whether the individual is tall or short; very few Indians have the elongated, gracile appearance found so often among Nilotics and some of their neighbors.

The skin color of these people never reaches the degree of pigmentation characteristic of many tropical peoples in the Old World, nor is it florid, as among so many northwestern Europeans. The ability to tan seems exceptionally well developed. The alleles for the blood types A^2, B, D^u, r, and Kell positive seem to be lacking, although some Peruvian Indians may have had a low frequency of I^B. The blood type allele R^0 was probably lacking and certainly very rare, but evidence is inconclusive here. Admittedly scanty evidence suggests a very high incidence of ability to taste PTC. Shovel-shaped incisors are very common, teeth tend to be large, and quite often third molars are absent.

American Indians are almost never bald, even in extreme old age, and they rarely have gray hair. Malars usually project both laterally and forward, and a slight degree of alveolar prognathism is common. There is a higher frequency than among Europeans of counterclockwise lambdoidal hair whorl, of the Inca bone, of small wormian bones in the lambdoidal suture, and of arches rather than whorls in the fingerprints. The alleles for the various abnormal hemoglobins like sickle cell are completely lacking, even among those tribes which live in malaria-infested regions.

Indeed, the meager extent to which any sort of tropical adaptation can be found among the Amazonian Indians affords us some idea of the length of time required for selection to alter the genetic constitution. On the other hand, adaptation for life in such mountain highlands as those of Peru seems to be well developed. Possibly this is a result of the prolonged period of selection for cold weather adaptations which the ancestors of the Indians underwent in Siberia and Alaska.

ARCTIC PEOPLES: ESKIMOS AND SIBERIANS

The Eskimo and the various peoples of Siberia—from Chuckchee through Tungus to Samoyed—have been geographically closer to the vast populations of eastern Asia than the American Indians. But the climate of their homelands, which has been too harsh to attract extensive immigration from the south, has probably been a continuing selective agent until the most modern times. Such characteristics as broad jaws, low, narrow noses, forward-jutting and fat-padded malars, small browridges, epicanthic eyefolds, and lack of facial hair are found among most individuals in all of these groups. Stocky build and rather short legs are also common, as are dark eyes and hair.

Except near the Atlantic most of the inhabitants of the Arctic are brachycephalic. Their skin is usually fair but not ruddy (see Figure 11–20), with the same ability to tan deeply which has already been noted for American Indians. These are all phenotypic characteristics of which the mode of inheritance is, in general, poorly known.

We know almost nothing about allele frequencies in these populations. It is clear, however, that blood type B, absent among the Greenland Eskimos, is found with increasingly high frequency further west, as is blood type A. Among the Siberians the incidence of blood type B is very high indeed. Arctic conditions are apparently irrelevant in selection at the ABO locus. The Diego blood type seems to be absent, as does r, and N has a low frequency. Inability to taste PTC is much more common and excretion of BAIB in the urine is much less common among Eskimos than among American Indians or the peoples of eastern Asia. Although the Arctic peoples are geographically intermediate between these two related groups, they are not intermediate in many of their biological characteristics.

THE PEOPLES OF EASTERN ASIA

The term Mongoloid is commonly used to designate one of the hypothetical major racial stocks because populations in this group are supposed to resemble Mongols. Certainly most of the peoples of eastern Asia, including the Arctic tribes, do share many phenotypic traits. Most people in this part of the world have dark eyes with an internal eyefold, very dark, coarse, straight hair, and little body or facial hair except at the temples. A counterclockwise hair whorl is more common than among any other peoples. Their skin color is apt to be a pale ivory shade when unexposed, but as among lighter-skinned American Indians, it tans readily. Quite often, especially when young, they have a bluish patch of skin at the base of the spine. Both sexes are likely to have smoothly molded facial features. Neither their browridges nor chins are prominent, but the malars are broad. There is a high percentage of individuals with shovel-shaped incisors.

Mongoloids usually have short legs and well-developed chests and shoulders. Gray hair and baldness are less common among them than among Europeans but more frequent than among American Indians. The natives of this part of the world now number at least 900 million, so they cannot be expected to form a single breeding population. However, there are fewer regional differences than in Europe, which suggests a greater degree of genetic unity. Archaeological and historic evidence demonstrate that this group of peoples has been expanding to the south, slowly but steadily, for at least several thousand years.

CHINESE

Tall stature is not uncommon in Mongolia, Tibet, and northern China, and a large majority of people are brachycephalic. The average cranial capacity is high. In these regions, too, the allele frequency of I^B is nearly 30 percent. Unfortunately, we know almost nothing about the genetic characteristics of these populations.

The Chinese, as a whole, form a set of interconnected gene pools, and neither national nor caste barriers divide them to the extent that such barriers divide the peoples of Europe or India. However, during the southward expansion of the Chinese they mixed with a variety of other peoples and have occupied areas with climates quite different from that of the north. Pestilence and famine have subjected them to drastic selection by weeding out all but the most resistant. And whereas wheat and millet are staples in the north, rice is the major item of diet in the south. All of these factors may have produced shifts in gene frequencies; they certainly affect bodily development during growth. It would be rash to extrapolate to China as a whole the results of the numerous studies of Cantonese emigrants since they come from southern China. Furthermore, most emigrants have come from a small proportion of villages which may not be representative of even southern China. Studies of such migrants have shown that, like American Indians, they possess the allele for the Diego blood type, that the incidence of Duffy positive is very high, that they lack the blood types A^2 and Kell negative, and that many of them excrete BAIB. They differ from American Indians in having a higher incidence of the blood type alleles L^N, R^1, and I^{A_1}, and in possessing the blood type alleles R^0, r, and I^B, the last of these with an incidence of 20 percent. They have the lowest recorded incidence of the Kidd positive and P positive blood types. The percentage able to taste PTC is intermediate between Eskimo and American Indian proportions.

SOUTHEAST ASIANS

During their southward expansion the Chinese absorbed many local peoples, but others like the Thai moved still further south. The peninsula of Southeast Asia contains a large number of breeding populations which are genetically and phenotypically very diverse as a result of this historic process. In Burma, for instance, a group known as the Mon has lived the longest. Burmese and later Shans came in from the north. Even more recently, both Chinese and Tamil immigrants came to Burma, the latter from southern India. The Chinese are the tallest, burliest, least pigmented, most brachycephalic, and most apt to have epicanthic eyefolds. The Shan resemble the Chinese closely, but the Burmese are intermediate between them and the Mon, who are almost as dark as the Tamils (Oschinsky, 1957). All of these except the Shan live in the hot, damp lowlands. The Burmese have been there long enough to have interbred with the Mon, but selection may have begun to modify their Mongoloid traits also.

We find a similar profusion of earlier, later, and still later peoples in the other countries of Southeast Asia. In most cases the shortest, slightest, darkest tribes have been in the tropics for the longest period. Some of them have wavy hair; few of them have epicanthic eyefolds. Hemoglobin E is very common, reaching a frequency of 35 percent in Cambodia, a malaria-infested country. The incidence of blood type alleles L^M, R^o, and I^B is higher than in southern China among most of these peoples. In these respects, these Southeast Asians resemble a number of the tribal peoples of India. Our knowledge of this area is sketchy at best, but it is clear that cultural barriers have kept many local gene pools partly separate from one another.

KOREANS

Like Southeast Asia, Korea is a peninsula, but one much closer to north China where there is a high frequency of Mongoloid traits. Korean allele frequencies at the ABO, MN, and Duffy loci resemble those of the Cantonese. The frequency of somewhat ruddy complexions is higher in Korea than in China, and the Korean facial outline is apt to be angular rather than softly rounded. Picking a Korean from a crowd of Chinese or vice versa, however, would be an impossible task on the basis of bodily structure alone, just as picking an Irishman from a crowd of Englishmen would be.

THE AINU

In sharp contrast to the similarities between neighboring populations which exist elsewhere in eastern Asia, the Ainu are obviously different. In early historic times the Ainu occupied a large area of northern Japan; now there are only a few thousand left, living in scattered settlements in Hokkaido and Sakhalin. Quite possibly they were the original inhabitants of all Japan and extended to the adjacent areas of Siberia. An Upper Paleolithic skull from North

China has been characterized as like that of an Ainu (Hooton, 1946).

Unlike any of the other populations for thousands of miles, the Ainu are apt to have quite wavy hair. Most adult males grow heavy beards and mustaches and body hair as well. A majority of the Ainu have long heads, and short faces are equally common. They are apt to have heavy browridges, wide noses, and depressed nasal roots. The eyes of the males lack epicanthic folds, but many females have them. Most Ainu have dark brown eyes and hair. Their skins lack the ivory tint which is typical of the Chinese. The average Ainu is short in stature but as burly as his neighbors. The incidence of the blood type allele I^B is much lower among Ainu than among the Chinese, while that of allele I^A is higher. The frequency of the blood type allele L^N is also higher than it is among any of the neighboring peoples. At the Rh locus the frequency of r″ is higher than among any other population yet tested, but otherwise the various alleles are in proportions similar to those of the Japanese.

Further genetic studies are urgently needed, inasmuch as this rather unique people is vanishing rapidly. In some respects the Ainu certainly resemble Europeans; in some, Australians; and it has been suggested that they are a "branch" of the hypothetical Caucasoid major racial stock. A less improbable speculation is that they are the only remaining remnant of a Paleolithic population which occupied the Pacific coast of Asia before the appearance of the Monogloid peoples. Birdsell (1951) has suggested that people like the Ainu were among the earliest arrivals in the New World. If this is so, it might help explain the existence of dolichocephalic skulls and wavy hair in remote parts of America.

JAPANESE

Phenotypic distinctions between the Japanese population and that of southern China are not great, but they do exist. For instance, a larger proportion of Japanese have narrow foreheads, low-bridged but aquiline noses, deep jaws with slightly retreating chins, rather hairy legs, greater facial dimensions, or dolichocephalic skulls. A Japanese family is shown in Figure 12–7.

Except for the Ainu, facial hair is more common among Japanese than among the other peoples of eastern Asia, and many females have temporal hair reaching to the eyebrows. The incidence of wavy hair is higher, too, but their hair is always dark and so are their eyes. They often have pale skin color, females being lighter than males, and the upper classes lighter than the lower (Hulse, 1967). Many young people get rosy cheeks when they are exposed to cool, rainy weather. The frequency of the blood-type allele I^B

is lower and that of I^A distinctly higher than among the Chinese. At the Rh locus, the allele R^0 seems to be absent, but r and R^2 are slightly more frequent than among southern Chinese. The peroneus tertius muscle is absent less often, and there is a higher percentage of those who can taste PTC. Carabelli's cusp is very much more frequently found than among the Chinese and red-green color blindness rather less frequently.

Some people think that the Japanese are of Malay origin, except for a ruling class from the part of Asia north of China. Neither genetics nor morphology substantiate this notion. Studies of the offspring of immigrants (Shapiro, 1939; Lasker, 1946; Froelich, 1970) show that, in general, class difference in body build depends upon nutrition and the type of labor performed. Insofar as the Japanese population differs from the Chinese, indications of kinship to Ainu, to Northwest Coast Indians, to Alaskan Eskimos, or even to South Europeans are suggested as strongly as they are to the Malays. Japan is some distance from the coast of Asia, and gene flow into the country has certainly been small for at least a hundred generations. Furthermore, Japan has not been exposed to the steady pressure of Chinese expansion as Southeast Asia has. This fact may be enough to explain the minor difference in allele frequencies between Japan and China.

Improved standards of health and nutrition during childhood have resulted in a considerable increase in adult stature among populations of Chinese and Japanese descent during recent dec-

FIGURE 12-7. Japanese— Professor Watanabe and His Family

ades. Among Europeans, such growth is commonly accompanied by increased linearity of bodily form and decreased cephalic index. The opposite is true of both Chinese and Japanese; when they have enough to eat, they are likely to become burlier and more brachycephalic than ever.

PEOPLES OF THE PACIFIC

INDONESIANS

There are many islands southeast of Asia, some of them very large. During the glacial periods of prehistory many of them formed part of the continent. Human beings of one variety or another have inhabited this area since the time of *Homo erectus*. The present population is sometimes called Malayan, sometimes Indonesian. Its kinship to the Mongoloid populations of Asia is obvious, but so are its differences. As in the peninsula of Southeast Asia, there are a large number of small, distinctive gene pools, especially in refuge areas such as jungles and mountaintops, as well as a smaller number of groups each having millions of members.

Most of these Indonesians are not only short but slight in build, rather more so in fact than Indians in the hotter areas of the American tropics. Their skin color also tends to be darker, although, excepting in a few Pygmy isolates, it is not nearly so dark as it is among other Old World equatorial populations. The Indonesians are more likely to have wavy hair than the more northern Mongoloids. In most cases nasal roots are deeper and narrower, and the nasal wings are usually broader among the islanders than among Chinese or Thai. Such signs of sexual dimorphism as browridges among males and well-developed breasts among females are not uncommon. Figure 12–8 shows an Indonesian scientist.

Like their northern relatives, however, the Indonesians have a higher frequency of I^B than of I^{A1} at the ABO blood-type locus, a higher frequency of L^M than of L^N, and they lack the Kell positive and the I^{A2} allele. At the Rh locus, there is a very high frequency of R^1 and apparent absence of r. The alleles leading to primaquine sensitivity and to the thalassemia are both known to be present in the Philippine Islands and may exist in some of the other islands.

NEGRITOS

There are Negrito groups scattered among the Indonesians, especially in the Philippines and near the tip of the Malay peninsula.

A third population of this sort lives in the Andaman Islands, just west of the Malay peninsula. The very scanty information available indicates that there are no differences of blood-type frequencies between these groups and their Indonesian neighbors. In bodily and facial appearance, however, differences are obvious. As their name would suggest, the Negritos are both shorter and darker than the Indonesians. Their hair is woolly rather than straight or wavy and sometimes abundant on the body among adult males. Negritos frequently have bulbous foreheads and exceptionally flaring nasal wings.

Many Indonesians look as though they might have had a few Negritos among their ancestors, but few Negritos show traces of Mongoloid ancestry. Since all the evidence indicates that there has been a continuous movement of peoples from Asia into the islands, this sort of mixture probably has taken place and perhaps it has helped the Indonesians adapt to life in equatorial regions. The expansion of Mongoloid populations toward the east is continuing, and differences from continental Mongoloids are most marked in the smaller islands which are furthest from Asia.

NEW GUINEANS AND MELANESIANS

The populations of New Guinea, just east of Indonesia, are of a separate race entirely. Here the effects of long continued selection for life in the tropics are clearly apparent. At the same time, both the distribution of blood types and many anatomical details differ so greatly from what is found among Africans that it seems unreasonable to lump the peoples of these islands together with those of the western tropics. The natives of New Guinea and of the

FIGURE 12-8. Professor Teuku Jacob, an Indonesian Scholar (Photo: Ramli A. Rahman)

Melanesian islands which extend beyond it as far east as Fiji are, in almost all instances, as dark as the Negroes of Africa. They both develop keloid scar tissue when the skin is cut; they both have woolly or frizzly hair; they are both considerably elongated in body build, especially in the limbs. Figures 11–20 and 11–23 show Melanesians.

However, among Melanesians, lip eversion and prognathism are less frequent and usually less marked, though browridges and depressed nasal roots are more frequent and more marked than they are among African Negroes. In New Guinea, especially, many people have high-bridged aquiline noses with depressed tips, and many adult males have ample facial and body hair. Inhabitants of the islands further east commonly have long and frizzly hair on their heads. And whereas few Melanesians are very tall, the average Melanesian is taller than the average Indonesian. There are, however, some highland groups of typical Negrito stature, and they resemble their taller neighbors in appearance and in known gene frequencies (Graydon *et al.*, 1958).

The frequency of blood group B is about half as great among Melanesians as among Indonesians, but blood group O is more frequent. A^1 is variable, and A^2 is absent. Blood type N is very much more frequent than M, and some tribes may lack the allele L^M entirely. The incidence of the allele R^1 approaches or passes 90 percent. R^2 and R^0 are present in about equal proportions, and r is absent. Apparently Kell positive and Duffy negative blood types are absent, too. Fewer Melanesians can taste PTC than Mongoloid or African groups which have been tested. The presence of a multitude of tiny gene pools is attested to by sharp differences between neighboring tribes in allele frequencies at one locus or another, yet all fall within the range described above.

NATIVE AUSTRALIANS

More meaningful differences separate the native peoples of Australia from the Melanesians, and the transitional zone between them is very small. In fact, the Australians are so distinctive that many scholars consider them among the major racial stocks, although others interpret the evidence to indicate an ancient mixture between very early, perhaps prototypic Negroids and Caucasoids. Like America, Australia is remote and was not easy to reach until recently, so that there has been little genetic continuity between its populations and any others.

Only among some tribes in Queensland where it approaches New Guinea is the allele I^B of the ABO blood-group system found, and even there its frequency is low. Elsewhere only alleles I^{A1} and I^0

exist. The parallel to the American situation is striking. But although the form is the same, the content differs. The allele I^{A_1} rarely has a frequency of less than 25 percent or more than 40 percent in any part of Australia, with the highest concentration in the south. As in Melanesia, the incidence of the allele L^N is exceedingly high, but the MNS system lacks the varient S, which makes the population of this continent unique. At the Rh locus, r is lacking, but R^z and r', rarely present in other populations, both exist. The allele R^1 has by far the highest frequency, but R^2 and R^0 are found as well. There is a great deal of variation between different tribes at this locus. All Australians tested have been Duffy positive and Diego negative. Less than half of those who have been tested are able to taste PTC.

The rare anomaly of fourth molars is present more frequently among Australians than among any other group. Their teeth are usually large and the jaws prognathous, while their lips are not often as everted as Africans' are, though they may be thick. The Australians' faces are typically short and broad and so are their noses. They are likely to have deep nasion depressions and heavy browridges, even the females, so that their eyes appear very deep set. Their foreheads as a rule are narrow and somewhat retreating, and frontal baldness is quite frequent. Almost all Australians have wavy or curly hair, as Figure 12–9 shows.

The frequency of linear build and dark skin color in the north, especially in Arnhem land, suggests Australians have adapted to climatic differences within the country. Moreover abundant facial and body hair is rare in the north, whereas both are common further south. Almost all Australian adults have brown hair and eyes, although the incidence of blond hair during childhood may reach 100 percent in some central Australian tribes and is high through-

FIGURE 12-9. Two Natives of Australia (Photos: Left, Ted Bumiller from Monkmeyer; Right, E. Lincoln)

out all the western part of the continent. Such hair has very little red pigment and never becomes completely dark. Gray hair is not uncommon among the elderly.

Almost all Australians are dolichocephalic, some of them having very narrow skulls indeed. The average cranial capacity is low. On the other hand, stature is quite variable. Some tribes in Queensland are almost as short as Negritos, and about half of these people have frizzly hair. The now extinct Tasmanians are thought to have resembled these tribes in many ways: they are said to have been very dark with very broad noses and heavy browridges.

Whatever their origin, the natives of Australia are certainly distinctive and indeed anatomically conservative in many ways. Their skeletal structure retains many features which were common throughout most of the world during the Upper Paleolithic. Since they continued to make their living by means of a simple technology in a somewhat difficult environment, their retention of such features can be interpreted as adaptive. The few skeletal remains dating from thousands of years ago in Australia and Indonesia bear a very close resemblance to the skeletons of the modern Australians.

POLYNESIANS AND MICRONESIANS

Among the very latest areas to be inhabited by man are the islands of Polynesia and Micronesia, which are scattered throughout much of the Pacific north and east of Melanesia and Australia. Probably none of them were inhabited much more than 3,000 years ago, while New Zealand may not have been occupied until after Iceland was. Adequate shipping and skillful navigational methods were needed to reach these tiny dots of land which are separated by hundreds or even thousands of miles of water. After being settled each island group developed, of necessity, into a sharply defined genetic isolate.

Micronesians are usually shorter and darker than Polynesians and more likely to have frizzly hair. Blood group B is found in higher proportion in Micronesia and Samoa than it is further east. In Polynesia the allele frequency of I^A is quite high, as it is in Australia. Micronesian populations are more apt to have high frequencies of the allele L^N, whereas those of Polynesia are apt to have a more even division between L^M and L^N. Almost all of the Micronesian groups have a very high incidence of R^1 at the Rh locus, while in Polynesia alleles R^1 and R^2 are equally frequent. The percentage of excretors of BAIB is several times higher among Micronesians than Polynesians. The allele Fy^b in the Duffy system has not been found in Micronesia but has a frequency of more than 20 percent in Polynesia.

There are more similarities between Micronesians and Melanesians than between Polynesians and Melanesians. The Polynesian's combination of characteristics is quite distinctive. Of all tropical peoples, they are the biggest, heaviest, and least deeply pigmented. Many Polynesians and Micronesians have broad noses, and their lips are at least medium in thickness. Females usually have large breasts. Adult males rarely have body hair, but many of them have facial hair, and wavy hair is common. They have dark hair and eyes, their eyes are often quite large, as may be seen in Figure 14–14, and epicanthic folds are rare. Brachycephaly is more frequent than dolichocephaly, and the occiput is ordinarily rather flat. Differences in allele frequencies between different island populations at one or another locus are common but so irregularly distributed that drift and historical accident are (Gajdusek, 1964) probably adequate to account for them.

PEOPLES OF INDIA

Like China, India has long been thickly inhabited. For historic and cultural reasons, however, the interconnections between separate gene pools in India have remained at a minimum. Caste distinctions have inhibited interbreeding to a great degree, so that any mapping of allele frequencies on a geographical basis alone is misleading. It has been shown that differences between castes are likely to be at least as great as differences between the populations of different areas (Sanghvi, 1953).

In many regions of India there are tribal groups not yet assimilated into the caste system but tending to be endogamous. The foothills and valleys of the Himalayas are occupied by peoples whose Mongoloid affinities are revealed equally well by examination of blood-type frequencies, fingerprint patterns, or facial appearance. Further south live tribes whose characteristics are reminiscent of Negritos, Australians, or even, in a few respects, Africans. Some of them are assimilating into the lower levels of the caste structure. The offspring of invading groups from Central Asia or the Middle East are more likely to be found in higher castes and less likely to live in the southern part of the peninsula.

More often than not, light skin color indicates high caste, but members of the highest castes in southern India are usually darker than members of the lowest castes in the northwest. The skin color of the peoples of southern India and Ceylon is as dark as that of Melanesians or African Negroes, whereas the people in Kashmir are likely to be no darker than Italians. Average body weight is less in the east than in the west, while stature is short to very short except in the extreme northwest. Nasal width is narrowest there. (See Figure 12–10, people from northwest India.)

FIGURE 12-10. These People Are All Natives of India (Photos: Michael Mahar)

Very few Indians have light hair or eyes, and their hair is more likely to be wavy or curly than straight. Beards and body hair among adult males and breast development among females are comparable to those of Europeans. A large majority are dolichocephalic with moderate browridges, large eyes, little prognathism, and narrow faces. The body build of a great many Indians gives the deceptive impression of a certain lack of muscularity.

In almost all Indian groups the blood type M is more frequent than N in the MNS system, but the incidence of S is greater than among any of the Mongoloid or Pacific Ocean peoples. At the ABO locus I^B is almost always more common than I^{A1}, but the allele I^{A2} is found, although it is less frequent than further west and is lacking in some jungle tribes. Frequencies at the Rh locus are sharply different from those of Mongoloids and Pacific Ocean peoples. The allele r has an incidence ranging from 7 percent in some tribal groups to 30 percent in the northwest and in some high castes. The allele R^1 has the highest incidence, but R^z, R^0, and the different rare alleles are all present in one group or another. The percentage of Duffy negatives resembles that of the Polynesians but is variable from gene pool to gene pool. Sicklemia has been found in a number of Indian castes and tribes, and both thalassemia and primaquine sensitivity are present in low frequency in most parts of India. Inability to taste PTC is very common:

in some groups its incidence reaches 45 percent. It seems clear that there has been little gene flow between India and China, although there has been some from both of these regions into the peninsula of Southeast Asia.

THE PEOPLES OF AFRICA

According to some authorities, there has been not only gene flow but large-scale migration in prehistoric times from India into East Africa. The presence of sicklemia in both areas as well as dark skin color is urged in favor of this view. The Negro populations in Africa, however, differ in allele frequencies from Indian populations at most loci about which we have ample data. For instance, only a very small percentage of Negroes are nontasters; the frequencies of blood group B and blood type M are less in Africa than in India; that of Duffy positive is very much less; and both the MNS and Duffy loci, among African populations, contain alleles rare or absent in the populations of India.

The few African groups tested have the highest known incidence of the Kidd positive allele. At the Rh locus, African populations have a high to very high frequency of the allele R^0 and include the variant D^u, which is extremely rare elsewhere in the world. The frequency of the allele R^1 is correspondingly reduced. The degree of hair curl reaches its extreme among African Negroes, none of whom have straight or wavy hair. Adult males rarely have much body hair but frequently have beards, and baldness in old age is not uncommon. Africans are likely to have gray hair when they are old. As a rule, females breasts are conical with enlarged nipples, and female hips are likely to be narrower than among most other peoples. The degree of lip eversion is typically greater among African Negroes than among other darkskinned peoples, such as those of India or Melanesia, and so is the frequency of alveolar prognathism.

The African Negro is likely to have a short face with small browridges and a rounded forehead. His nose is likely to be short and broad with a low bridge and flaring wings. As among some other tropical peoples, the forearms and lower legs of African Negroes are likely to be exceptionally long. Stature in most African populations is greater than among other tropical peoples except for the Polynesians, and so is weight. But there are very short populations in Africa, too, such as the Pygmies of the equatorial jungles and the Khoisans of South Africa.

KHOISANS

The Khoisans are a dual group, composed of the Bushmen hunters who still live at a Mesolithic level of technology and the Hottentots who were pastoral. In racial characteristics these peoples are at the opposite extreme from the Australians, a fact worth pondering as we attempt to understand the mode of adaptation in our species. Allele frequencies among the Khoisans, as among American Indians and Australians, are often at one extreme or the other of the human range. Their hair is commonly in tiny spirals, growing in peppercorns; their ears very frequently have a broad helix and no lobe. Adult females usually develop very protruding buttocks, a condition known as steatopygia.

The frequencies of Duffy negative, Henshaw positive, and R^o alleles are exceptionally to uniquely high; at these loci the Khoisans carry African trends to an extreme. In comparison with other Africans, however, the Bushmen have an exceedingly low frequency of I^B at the ABO locus and the Hottentots a very high frequency of L^M at the MNS locus. In the Rh system the incidence of r is very low among Hottentots and apparently zero among Bushmen. The Kell positive allele, rare among other African populations, is found among Khoisans as frequently as among northwest Europeans. Haptoglobin type 1 is more frequent among them than among other Africans.

This combination of genetic traits sets the Khoisan population apart from all others to a most unusual degree. Furthermore, not only are the Khoisans, especially Bushmen, very short, but their skin color is yellow-brown which is much lighter than that of the Negroid peoples. Details of facial appearance, such as projecting malars and epicanthic eyefolds, are reminiscent of Mongoloid characteristics and have led to speculations concerning ancient Mongoloid affinities. Khoisans often have bulbous and comparatively broad foreheads and small and narrow jaws, giving the faces a triangular appearance. Like the Negroes, Khoisans are usually dolichocephalic with broad noses and thick lips, and they have little or no body hair. Since they retain many juvenile characteristics, they are often described as pedomorphic. In the past some scholars considered Hottentots to be hybrids between Bushmen and Negroids, but their gene frequencies do not support this notion. There is much evidence to suggest, however, that the Khoisans at one time occupied a very much larger part of Africa than they have recently, perhaps extending as far as the equator.

NEGROES

For many centuries and probably for many millenia the inhabitants of equatorial Africa (see Figure 12–11) have been Negroes.

FIGURE 12-11. Congolese Mother and Baby (Photo: Fuji Hira from Monkmeyer)

Populations of this racial variety also extend throughout central and western Africa, as far north as the Sahara, and in a few places, well into the desert. Scattered among them live a number of Pygmy populations, especially in the Congo. The Bantu-speaking tribes of Negroes, who now occupy most of the area south of the equator, are often thought to differ from those of western Africa, but there seems to be no sharply marked break in genetic continuity.

The members of some Bantu groups are likely to have a stockier build and not quite so dark a skin color as other Negroes. But they do not differ consistently from other Negroes in allele frequencies for any character which has yet been tested, with the exception of the rare hemoglobin C. This allele is found only among peoples living in West Africa. As in the case with sicklemia, heterozygosity for this character seems to confer added survival value, reproductive potential, or both in regions heavily infested with malaria. Consequently, the incidence of either trait is associated with the degree to which malaria is endemic in a given area. Primaquine sensitivity is associated with malaria in the same manner, and its frequency varies greatly from one region to another. Some Pygmies, whose deep jungle habitat is relatively free of malaria, have a very low incidence of any of these traits. Both West Africans and Bantu have a high incidence of the P positive blood type and haptoglobin type 1 and a low incidence of the ability to secrete ABO substances in the saliva. Most of them have the palmaris longus muscle, but fewer have Carabelli's cusp and multiple foramina below the orbit, as contrasted with non-Negro populations.

PYGMIES

Like the Negritos of the Far East, African Pygmies do not differ much from their neighbors in characters of which we know the allele frequencies. They are said to be somewhat lighter in skin color than the Negroes and sometimes have peppercorn hair. Pygmies are more apt than Negroes to have infantile facial features, or abundant body hair, or both. Living as they do in scattered groups, they consistently differ from the surrounding Negro populations in size but less consistently in other ways.

THE MALAGASY

Madagascar, like Iceland and New Zealand, appears to have been among the land masses which remained uninhabited until relatively recently. The biological characteristics of its population have not been adequately investigated, but it seems that in origin the Malagasy are a mixture of Indonesian and Negro elements. The elements are so thoroughly mixed that it is said to be impossible to tell a Malagasy's place of origin from his appearance (Singer *et al.*, 1957). Tribal differences and even caste differences exist, but in each group there is a considerable range of variation. At the ABO locus the allele I^B has a higher frequency than I^A; this is especially true in the northeast. At the Rh locus R^1 has a higher and R^0 a lower frequency than among Negroes. In both respects the Malagasy vary from the African norm in the direction of Indonesian allele frequencies. The incidence of the sickle-cell trait is very low.

Malagasy frequently have light brown skin, and their lips are usually thinner than is common among Negroes. Many Malagasy have brachycephalic heads. Wavy or even straight hair is not uncommon, and slightly slanting eyes are very frequent, as Figure 13–3 shows. Most Malagasy have low nasal bridges with flaring alae. The malars are quite prominent and neither their foreheads nor jaws are very wide. As a population, the Malagasy are distinctive enough to be considered a perfectly valid race, even though they are not of remote antiquity in origin.

OTHER AFRICAN PEOPLES

In the eastern part of Africa, from the equator to as far north as Egypt, there are many tribes which differ from the Negroes to the south and west in numerous ways. It has usually been supposed that, like the Malagasy, they are of mixed ancestry, and this is probably true in some cases. In this part of Africa the gene flow between Caucasoid and Negroid populations has been facilitated by relative ease of communication, but most of the peoples in the valley of the upper Nile and some still further south show few signs of any such intermixture. These people constitute the racial variety known as Nilotics (see Figure 11–22). Many of them are very tall and most of them have very long arms and legs. Their body build is gracile, so that the ratio of mass to surface area is lower than among any other living population. Despite their stature, these people are not heavy.

Most of them are dolichocephalic and less prognathous than other African Negroids, but they usually have very broad noses and thick lips. Their skin is very dark, their hair frizzly or woolly, and they have little if any body and facial hair. At the ABO locus, there is considerable variation in the relative frequency of the alleles I^A and I^B, but among the few groups tested the ratio of I^{A2} to I^{A1} is quite high. At the Rh and Lutheran loci, allele frequencies differ from those of non-Africans even more markedly than among most of the African Negroids. The frequency of sicklemia is clearly related to the degree of malarial infestation. The Nilotics are not intermediate between other African Negroids and Caucasoids in any of these ways. Their racial characteristics are more plausibly explained as the result of adaptation to the local environment than as the result of intermixture. Some skeletal material of considerable antiquity suggests that this adaptation is by no means a recent phenomenon.

There are to be sure other populations like the Somalis which do appear to be of mixed origin. Arabs and others from the Middle East have been coming to Africa for thousands of years, while slaves have been taken from Negroid tribes into the Middle East and Europe for a long time, too. But we should not jump to the conclusion that such traits as dark skin and curly hair, which are found frequently throughout the Mediterranean basin and further east, must be of African derivation. A fair skin has little survival value in this part of the world, except for cultural reasons, and curly hair is not the result of a cross between woolly and wavy hair.

CAUCASOID PEOPLES

The lands between India and Spain are inhabited, as they have been since Paleolithic times, by populations more closely akin to those of Europe than of any other area. The use of Caucasoid as the name of a major racial stock recognizes this fact. As we have already

FIGURE 12-12. A Greek Anthropologist, Professor Aris Poulianos

made clear, it is impractical and unrealistic to attempt any sharply marked subdivisions of this race within the European continent. The genetic continuum appears to be unbroken. During prehistoric and early historic times population movements between Europe and nearby parts of Asia and Africa were frequent. The spread of the Moslem religion in the Near East and North Africa 1,200 years ago reduced genetic contacts between the European and non-European Caucasoid populations. Maps of gene frequencies show no sharp breaks within the area inhabited by Caucasoids, although populations living in northwestern Europe are certainly different from those living in Arabia, and those in Northwest Africa differ from those of Russia in many ways. Europeans appear in Figures 11–21, 11–23, 12–12, 13–2, and 13–4, whereas Figure 12–13 shows a Near Eastern father and child.

Reduced pigmentation, finer hair, baldness, graying with increased age, and absence of prognathism are characteristics found with high to very high frequency in all the Caucasoid populations. Facial hair among adult males, marked sexual dimorphism in the shoulder-hip index, high-bridged noses, and Carabelli's cusp are somewhat less frequent but very widespread. As in India, the inability to taste PTC has a high incidence. The female breast is usually hemispherical and well developed. At the MN locus the balance between the two alleles is very close in most groups; at the Duffy and Kidd loci the frequency of the positive allele is between 60 percent and 70 percent in most groups which have been tested.

FIGURE 12-13. Father and Child from the Near East (Photo: United Nations)

In very few Caucasoid populations is the incidence of the allele I^B as high as it is for I^A, but there are striking differences between relative frequencies at this locus among the various populations. In the Rh system the allele R^1 is usually some three times as frequent as R^2, and r is much more frequent than R^0. In fact, the allele r reaches its highest known frequencies in western Europe. A certain degree of genetic unity within the Caucasoid stock is shown by the similarities just noted. It is impossible, however, to draw any sharp line separating Caucasoid populations from those of northern Indian or central Asia. Gene flow in both directions has not only been continuous but large-scale.

There is genetic diversity within the Caucasoid stock despite the lack of clearly defined races within it. Not only does blood type r have a much higher incidence in western than in eastern Europe, but so do reddish shades in the head hair. Fair hair is most commonly found among northern Europeans. Northern Europeans are even more likely to have light eyes and skin which is fair until exposed to sunlight. Reduced pigmentation among children, nearly universal in the north, is found less frequently in the south. The alleles I^0 and I^{A2} have a much higher incidence in the south and west than elsewhere. Dolichocephalic skulls, narrow faces, and high-bridged noses are more common in the south and the north than in the area between. Tall stature is more common in the Balkans and in northwestern Europe than elsewhere.

But in every local population there is a variety of the types which used to be classified as races. In some areas like the Balkans, the Caucasus, and nearby regions of Asia the population is traditionally subdivided into a large number of ethnic groups which rarely interbreed. Often, like the castes of India, these differ from one another in allele frequencies at a number of loci. In other areas village endogamy used to be very common, leading to the occasional appearance of somewhat unusual gene frequencies. National, linguistic, religious, and class differences have also led to genetic distinctions between or within populations because of their influence upon the selection of mates. For example, in southern Spain members of the upper classes are more likely to be blond than their lower class compatriots, and Basques on the Atlantic coast in Spain and France have the highest known frequency of the allele r at the Rh locus. Gypsies have higher frequencies of B, R^1, and M blood types than their neighbors, as well as darker pigmentation. The Lapps of northern Scandinavia have a very high frequency of A^2 and N and a very low frequency of r, compared to other Europeans, as well as shorter stature, smaller teeth, and deeper pigmentation than their neighbors. The evidence of genetics demonstrates that the Lapps are not akin to the Mongoloids (Boyd, 1963), as was previously thought.

PEOPLES OF CENTRAL ASIA

Central Asia, however, is inhabited by peoples whose characteristics are intermediate between those of the Caucasoids and of the Mongoloids. They tend to be of robust build with broad faces and coarse dark hair. The incidence of narrow eyes, blood group B, and brachycephaly among them is as high as among the Mongols themselves. But the Central Asians often have wavy hair, the adult males usually have abundant facial hair, their nasal bridge is ordinarily high, and their pigmentation is unlike that of their eastern neighbors, though it may be swarthy. Since long before the dawn of history, this area has been the passageway for migrations from both east and west. The results are obvious.

RECENT ALTERATIONS IN RACIAL DISTRIBUTION *

During the last few centuries, enormous transoceanic migrations have taken place which have altered the racial distribution of the world's population to an extraordinary degree. Millions of Europeans departed to the Americas, and hundreds of thousands to South Africa, Australia, and New Zealand. Millions of Negroes, kidnapped into slavery, were brought to the Americas. As a result of these movements, opportunities for the creation of new races have emerged, and a number of them have come into existence. During the same period of time vast improvements in technology have led to very rapid increase among a few of the previously existing populations. Other groups, at one time numerous, have nearly been wiped out, although more by mixture with migrants than by intentional genocide. These three processes have resulted in drastic changes in the allele frequencies of the human species.

During the past four centuries, while the world population has increased some sixfold, that of British ancestry has grown at least fiftyfold. Those areas in Europe inhabited by populations which include a high percentage of blondes held perhaps 3 percent of the world's inhabitants in 1500 A.D., but now their descendants comprise at least 12 percent of the world's inhabitants. It is reasonable to assume that the alleles for blondness have increased proportionately. They have, furthermore, become much more widespread geographically. Almost all of the inhabitants of New Zealand and Australia and well over half of the inhabitants of North America are of Northwest European ancestry. Migrants from Spain and Portugal flocked to the tropical and southern parts of the New World and from

* Parts of this section are based on copyrighted material from my paper "Technological Advance and Major Stocks," *Human Biology*, Vol. 27 (1955), pp. 184–92 (Wayne State University Press).

France to Canada. Nearly half of the ancestry of the present populations of these areas come from those countries of western Europe. The blood type alleles I^A and r have increased in frequency as a result of the rapid multiplication of these migrant stocks, just as blondness has.

Probably about one-eighth of the ancestry of the populations of the Americas is of African derivation, but only in a few places, like some of the Caribbean islands, are there peoples of almost purely African origin. During the period of slavery there was constant intermixing between the slave-owning class and the Negro population. There was also an exceedingly high death rate among slaves, which could well have altered allele frequencies at some loci. Some admixture with American Indians is known to have taken place, especially in Latin America. As a result, a new race called American Colored, consisting of perhaps 60 million members, was formed. Genetic studies of the segment of this race which lives in the United States suggest that at least one-fifth of its ancestry is derived from Europe rather than Africa. Their skin color is rarely as dark as that of African Negroes, and they frequently have abundant body hair which often appears in spiral tufts (Garn, 1961). This tufting is a phenotypic trait lacking in either parent race. The frequency of the sickle-cell allele has been reduced more and that of the allele r raised less than might have been expected were the effects of selection on these traits unknown. There is great phenotypic variability in this race, of which two representatives are shown in Figures 11–21 and 13–2.

Just as numerous in continental Latin America is the Ladino race, which originated from the interbreeding of Spaniards and Portuguese with the local American Indian population. The Ladinos also have a much smaller amount of African ancestry. The opportunities for spreading the genetic characteristics of Iberians among the natives of Middle America, the Andes, and, to a lesser extent, Brazil, were ample after the conquest, and within a few generations a large class, accommodated to European culture but only partly European in ancestry, had come into existence in all these countries. The Indians were practically exterminated in the Antilles and in most of Argentina as they were throughout most of the United States and Canada, while in jungles and remote highlands comparatively little intermixture occurred. Variability in the phenotype is considerable, as among the American Colored. As a rule, Ladinos are short in stature and light brown in skin color, with scant body hair. Very scanty evidence of allele frequencies at the MN and Rh loci suggests that the proportions of Iberian and American Indian ancestry are about equal.

Throughout Polynesia there was a precipitous decline in population during the century after the arrival of Caucasoid whalers and missionaries. During the past two generations population has been increasing, but it is a different population. The Chinese and Japanese, as well as the British and French, have contributed to the present gene pool and are continuing to do so. The new Pacific Island race which is being formed differs from the Polynesian rather more in allele frequencies at the various blood type loci than in external body characteristics. It is impossible to predict the future characteristics of this race since it is still in the process of formation with a constant inflow of genes from other populations. As a laboratory for the study of human genetics, it deserves more attention.

More or less isolated breeding populations exist within the races mentioned and partly described in this chapter. They are so numerous that it would be impossible even to list them. In most cases, the changes in allele frequencies from one to the next are minor, though real. Studies of microevolution use such small-scale isolates as their raw material. Attempts to study human genetics in racially mixed isolates began more than fifty years ago, when the population of Rehoboth was examined by the best techniques available at the time (Fischer, 1913). This isolate is composed of Dutch-Hottentot hybrids who live in Southwest Africa. The people of Pitcairn's Island in the South Pacific, who are descended from the mutineers of the *Bounty* and their Tahitian consorts, are another group which has been examined (Shapiro, 1929, 1936). Recently, human geneticists have been studying such isolates as the Dunkers (Glass *et al.*, 1952), the American Colored in Charleston (Pollitzer, 1958), Hutterites (Steinberg *et al.*, 1967), and some of the many Jewish groups which are new in Israel. From studies such as these, we may expect to gain more understanding of the processes involved in race formation.

It should be clear that we cannot pigeonhole the races we find in the world today into two, three, or four original major stocks. Recently gained knowledge of human genetics demonstrates that the various Negrito or Pygmy peoples are by no means more closely related to each other than to their larger neighbors. It proves that the Khoisans cannot be explained as a mixture between Negritos and Mongoloids. It shows that the Ainu are not really similar to either Near Eastern or European Caucasoids. And the Nilotics, although they dwell between the Negroes and the Caucasoids, are not intermediate in gene frequencies between them. There are needless difficulties in the assumption that the major stocks are earlier and the living populations of the world just a later derivation.

Today at least 90 percent of the world's inhabitants can be squeezed somehow into one or another of the so-called major stocks or into known hybrids between them. This is, however, a result of the very recent expansion of a few of the earlier stocks at the expense of others. The development of agriculture, which led to a dependable source of food throughout the year, took place less than 500 generations ago and only in a few favored areas. The tribes which first benefited from this revolutionary change in the human way of life attained an immediate demographic advantage over others. With their subsistence assured their populations were able to increase rapidly. They had the incentive, the opportunity, and the technical means of expanding geographically as well. Regions which had previously supported only a few wandering families of hunters could now support hundreds or even thousands of farmers.

As it happened, agriculture was first practiced in the area between the Mediterranean and India. There is no evidence to suggest that this took place as a result of any biological peculiarities of the inhabitants of this area. The later and quite independent invention of plant cultivation by American Indians demonstrates that historical circumstances rather than genetic superiority was responsible for the growth and elaboration of this new way of making a living. Yet the biological consequences of agriculture have been profound. Farming and farmers too spread from the Near East into Europe, India, and beyond. They carried with them their genetic characteristics as well as their tools. We have ample archaeological and linguistic evidence of the spread of farming populations throughout most of Europe as peasants sought new lands to cultivate. The Sahara desert, however, was an effective barrier to expansion of populations from the Near East into Central Africa.

During the Paleolithic, when all the peoples of the world were hunters, fishers, or collectors of wild plant foods, the open parklands of eastern and southern Africa were as favorable a habitat for humans as the open parklands which stretch from the Atlantic through the Near East to India. Each of these regions has an area of about 2.5 million square miles. There is no reason to suppose that either region was more densely inhabited than the other. The skeletal evidence available leads us to infer that the tribes in the northern parklands were of the Caucasoid racial variety. The ancestors of the Khoisans and of the Nilotics, however, lived in southern and eastern Africa. Technological advances have led to an enormous increase in the numbers of Caucasoids. Lack of such technological advances has kept the numbers of Khoisans and Nilotics from increasing to the same extent. Ten thousand years ago populations with genetic systems similar to those of Europeans were probably no more numerous than populations with genetic systems similar to those of Khoisans. There is no reason to suppose that blondness was more common than steatopygia during the Paleolithic.

Just as the practice of agriculture led to rapid population growth among the Caucasoid populations in the Near East and in

Europe, it had the same effect among the Mongoloid populations of the Far East. Ever since food production began in China, the Chinese have been expanding to the south, spreading their genetic characteristics among their southern neighbors. Indeed, these processes are continuing today. As a result, more than a billion individuals with somewhat Mongoloid characteristics now live along the western shore of the Pacific, even as far south as the equator.

Before the development of farming the distribution of peoples was very different. Probably most of the peoples with Mongoloid characteristics lived in the open steppes to the north; so far as we know, none of them lived in the tropics, and there is no reason to suppose that they were numerous. A large number of darker-skinned peoples inhabited the tropical areas of the Old World, but there is no reason to postulate genetic similarities among them. Melanesians and Australians were probably as different from African Negroes and from each other during the Paleolithic as they are today. In the east as in the west it has been historical circumstance, not genetic virtue, which had led to population increase by a few stocks among the many which had been in existence during earlier times. It has also produced the illusion that the stocks most numerous now are fundamental and other stocks simply branches or mixtures of later origin.

Sources and Suggested Readings

BAKER, P. T. and J. S. WEINER, eds.
 1966   *The Biology of Human Adaptability.* Clarendon Press, Oxford.

BIRDSELL, J. B.
 1951   The Problem of the Early Peopling of the Americas as Viewed from Asia. *Physical Anthropology of the American Indian.* Viking Fund, New York.

BOYD, W. C.
 1963   Four Achievements of the Genetical Method in Physical Anthropology. *American Anthropologist,* **65,** 243–252.

COON, C. S.
 1962   *The Origin of Races.* Knopf, New York.

COON, C. S., S. M. GARN and J. B. BIRDSELL
 1950   *Races.* Thomas, Springfield, Ill.

DARWIN, C.
1858   *The Origin of Species.* Murray, London.

DOBZHANSKY, T.
1958   Species After Darwin. *A Century of Darwin.* Harvard University Press, Cambridge.

FISCHER, E.
1913   *Die Rehobother Bastards und das Bastardierungs Problem Beim Menschen.* Gustav Fischer Verlag, Jena.

FROELICH, J. W.
1970   Migration and the Plasticity of Physique in the Japanese Americans of Hawaii. *American Journal of Physical Anthropology*, new series, **32**, 429–442.

GAJDUSEK, D. C.
1964   Factors Governing the Genetics of Primitive Human Populations. *Cold Spring Harbor Symposia in Quantitative Biology*, **29**, 121–136.

GARN, S. M.
1961   *Human Races.* Thomas, Springfield, Ill.

GLASS, B., M. S. SACKS, E. F. JOHN, and C. HESS
1952   Genetic Drift in a Religious Isolate. *American Naturalist*, **86**, 145–159.

GRAYDON, G. G., M. M. SEMPLE, R. T. SIMMONS, and S. FRANKLIN
1958   Blood Groups in Pygmies of the Wissellakes in Netherlands New Guinea. *American Journal of Physical Anthropology*, new series, **16**, 172–185.

HOOTON, E. A.
1946   *Up from the Ape*, revised edition. Macmillan, New York.

HULSE, F. S.
1967   Selection for Skin Color Among the Japanese. *American Journal of Physical Anthropology*, new series, **27**, 143–155.

HUXLEY, J. S. and A. C. HADDON
1936   *We Europeans.* Harper, New York.

LASKER, G. W.
  1946 Migration and Physical Differentiation. *American Journal of Physical Anthropology*, new series, **4**, 273–300.

LAUGHLIN, W. S., ed.
  1951 *Physical Anthropology of the American Indian.* Viking Fund, New York.

LEWIS, J. H.
  1942 *The Biology of the Negro.* University of Chicago Press, Chicago.

NEWMAN, M. T.
  1953 The Application of Ecological Rules to Racial Anthropology of the Aboriginal New World. *American Anthropologist*, **55**, 311–327.
  1960 Adaptation in the Physique of American Aborigines to Nutritional Factors. *Human Biology*, **32**, 288–313.
  1962 Evolutionary Changes in Body Size and Head Form in American Indians. *American Anthropologist*, **64**, 237–257.

OLIVIER, G.
  1956 *Les Populations du Cambodge.* Masson et Cie, Paris.

OSCHINSKY, L.
  1954 *The Racial Affinities of the Baganda.* Heffer, Cambridge.
  1957 Personal Communication.

POLLITZER, W. S.
  1958 The Negroes of Charleston (S.C.), A Study of Hemoglobin Types, Serology and Morphology. *American Journal of Physical Anthropology*, new series, **16**, 244–263.

SANGHVI, L. D.
  1953 Comparison of Genetical and Morphological Methods for a Study of Biological Differences. *American Journal of Physical Anthropology*, new series, **11**, 385–404.

SAUTER, M. R.
  1952 *Les Race de l'Europe.* Payot, Paris.

SIMPSON, G. G.
1961 *Principles of Animal Taxonomy.* Columbia University Press, New York.

SINGER, R., O. E. BUDTZ-OLSEN, P. BRAIN, and J. SAUGRAIN
1957 Physical Features, Sickling and Serology of the Malagasy of Madagascar. *American Journal of Physical Anthropology,* new series, **15,** 91–124.

SHAPIRO, H. L.
1929 *Descendants of the Mutineers of the Bounty.* Memoirs of the B. P. Bishop Museum, **9.**
1936 *Heritage of the Bounty.* Simon and Schuster, New York.
1939 *Migration and Environment.* Oxford University Press, New York.

STEINBERG, A. G., H. K. BLEIBTREU, T. W. KURCZYNSKI, A. O. MARTIN, and E. M. KURCZYNSKI
1967 Genetic Studies in an Inbred Human Isolate. *Proceedings of the Third International Congress of Human Genetics.* John Hopkins University Press, Baltimore.

WEIDENREICH, F.
1947 Facts and Speculations Concerning the Origin of Homo sapiens. *American Anthropologist,* **49,** 187–203.

CHAPTER 13

The Problem of Race, Language, and Culture

SOME THEORIES OF RACIAL SUPERIORITY

When anyone first visits a country other than his own, he will notice that the people who live there differ from him in many ways. He cannot see their blood type frequencies, but he is very likely to see their complexions. He will not be aware of the incidence of the ability to taste PTC among them, but he will be aware that their food does not taste like what his mother used to cook. He will not, as a rule, understand what these strange people are trying to say, for their language differs from his. Their manners as well as their appearance are likely to strike him as odd; they may even drive on the "wrong" side of the road or eat with chopsticks. Since he cannot help but feel that his own way of doing things is the sensible and correct way, it may upset him to see how foolish these foreigners are. It will be very easy for him to jump to the conclusion that their strange jargon, their exotic customs, and their unusual body appearance are all aspects of just one thing: their ancestors were different from his. They must have inherited these differences. Since their ways are clearly wrong, these foreigners are clearly inferior by nature. They belong to a lower race.

Such naïve xenophobia is nothing new. The ancient Greeks divided the population of the world into themselves and the "Barbarians"; the ancient Hebrews into themselves and the Gentiles; the

391

Zuñi, secure on the top of their mesa in New Mexico, knew that they were cooked, whereas all other people were raw. The name by which the people of a preliterate tribe call themselves, as distinct from everyone else, can very often be translated as *men*, or *real men*. Social responsibilities extend to members of one's own group: outsiders are fair game. Since pride in one's ancestral traditions and exploits does help to raise the esprit de corps or morale in any conflict situation, this is not surprising. In cases such as these the principles of genetics, being unknown, were not invoked to support notions of racial superiority. Indeed, the youngsters of a defeated tribe might often be adopted into the conquering one, and thus acquire new and better ancestors.

Even before recorded history, one consequence of improved technology was the development of different social classes within a community, or tribe, or nation. By one means or another some families acquired more property, power, or prestige than others. In such circumstances upper class families take pride in their distinguished ancestry, too; it sets them apart from the common herd. Sometimes one tribe will conquer another and become an aristocracy ruling over it. Sometimes thousands or even millions of people from other lands are captured and forced into slavery. Sometimes more or less endogamous castes will develop within a country, each with its own peculiar rules of conduct and ways of speech. In all of these situations, differences in physical appearance, in customary behavior, and in dialect or accent are likely to be associated. What is more natural than to suppose that all are due equally to ancestry? And what could be more convenient for those who happen to be on top?

During the nineteenth century at the time that anthropology was beginning to become an independent field of study, the peoples of Europe and especially of northwestern Europe were on top. European and American scholars noted the strong correlation between economic prosperity and the physical features, such as blondness, dolichocephaly, and tall stature, so common among their own friends and kinfolk. Ammon (1899) noted that in the part of Germany where he lived, the cities, centers of business enterprise, were full of such folk, while the peasantry in the countryside were more frequently dark and round-headed. He bewailed the fact that the countryfolk had more children. De Lapouge (Klineberg, 1935) found a greater proportion of long, narrow skulls in the cemetery of a rich, fashionable parish and of short, broad skulls in the cemetery of a working-class district in Paris. To him this proved the basic inferiority of brachycephals. The myth of the three races of Europe—Nordic, Alpine, and Mediterranean—was elaborated during this period. Each was supposed to have its own inborn psychological traits as well as a distinctive exterior appearance. Nordics were alleged to be brave, intelligent, and honest; Alpines dull, thrifty, and stubborn; Mediterraneans frivolous, treacherous, and passionate.

More than 2,000 years before, Aristotle (355 B.C.) had said that the northern Europeans were brave but too stupid to amount to anything, the Asiatics were intelligent but too cowardly to amount to anything, whereas his own people, the Greeks, were both brave and intelligent and therefore fitted by nature to rule the earth. Now it was the authority of Darwin or, if one did not like Darwin, the Old Testament that was called upon to support notions of racial superiority. Natural selection was pictured as the survival of those fittest to subdue all potential competitors. Ham, who had been cursed by Noah, was pictured as the ancestor of all Negroes.

In any long settled community the opportunities for social mobility are likely to be slim, and Europe in the last century was full of communities which had been settled since time immemorial. Peasants were the sons of peasants and the fathers of peasants. Fishermen were the sons of fishermen and the fathers of fishermen. Dukes were the sons of dukes and the fathers of dukes. The hereditary principle was well established. Dukes inherited blue eyes and landed property. Peasants inherited brown eyes and debts. It is very easy to confuse biological inheritance and social inheritance. It has been a long, slow process involving a great deal of skilled laboratory work and precise observation to attain even our present incomplete understanding of human genetics. It is not surprising that some of the best scholars of recent generations understood even less than we do and came to faulty conclusions. The continuously varying traits, such as stature and head shape, attracted their attention more often than not. They had no information which would have enabled them to differentiate between the effect of genes and of external circumstances upon the phenotypes which they studied.

The human body is quite plastic in many respects, and a great deal of diversity which we see when we look at each other is due to this fact. Purely cultural factors are responsible for some of the most obvious ways in which we differ from one another. Fashions may change but we must follow them while they exist. Females, for instance, are not only anatomically different from males, but they dress differently and decorate the exposed parts of their bodies in different ways. A girl may borrow her brother's shirt and pants, but she does not wear them as he will.

In all cultures the mannerisms of the sexes differ to some extent as well. Members of different social classes and ethnic groups have been distinguishable by means of bodily ornamentation. This is less obvious in modern America than it has been elsewhere during most of history. Romans wore togas, Eskimos fur parkas, American Indians feathers, South Sea Islanders a piece of tapa about their hips. Sailors were tattooed, cannibals filed their teeth, bankers had top hats, Moslem women veiled their faces, and Chinese ladies bound their feet. British army officers were required to grow mustaches but not beards, Japanese women blackened their front teeth when they married, musicians and artists let their hair grow long, but monks shaved off most of theirs, as did Iroquois on the warpath. An excellent mural in the National Museum at Washington, D.C., shown in Figure 13–1, portrays a variety of bodily decorations.

It is not difficult to penetrate the varied disguises, such as those listed above, with which different societies mask their members. They involve the body, but they are not of the body. Yet they have entered into the stereotypes which we carry in our minds and which enable us to recognize the status of a stranger. The fact that these disguises are cultural in origin leads to a greater degree of apparent similarity between members of any cultural group than their genes would do. Thus, it supports the stereotype of an inherent affinity between race and culture.

Some other aspects of learned behavior are even more deceptive. The way in which the body is handled is dependent upon learning, too, and different societies teach different standards, often unconscious. Chinese and Japanese raised in their own countries stand and walk in quite different style. The gestures which people of different ethnic backgrounds in Europe employ are far more diagnostic of origin than any anatomical items. Italians have elabororated upon the symbolism of gestures, raising their hands high and sweeping their arms freely in all directions. Jewish gestures de-

FIGURE 13-1. How We Make Ourselves More Beautiful (Photo: Courtesy of Smithsonian Institution)

pend much more upon the forearm and fingers, with jerky movements and less precise symbolism (Boas, 1938). Differences in facial expression appropriate to a given occasion may be used to identify members of different groups, for like gestures, they are standardized by culture. It has been alleged that the tempo and pitch of snoring is culturally determined, but no serious research has been undertaken in this field. In any case, the musculature and other anatomical details involved in these activities do not differ in different breeding populations in such a way as to account for the behavior.

BIOLOGICAL ADAPTATIONS TO CULTURE

Culturally determined activities often have a less superficial effect upon human biology. Instead of one's ancestral race determining one's cultural characteristics, it is often the other way around. The cultural behavior of one's ancestors may determine many of one's own biological characteristics. Sometimes their behavior will affect the phenotype only, but in many cases it will have brought about genetic changes as well. Since culture is the ecological plateau to which the human species has had to adapt, this is not strange. It is, however, a reversal of the opinion maintained by the greater number of scholars during the nineteenth century. It also contradicts the deeply felt emotions of a vast number of people today.

We have already mentioned some of the ways in which the fossil record of human evolution reveals adaptation to the exacting requirements of culture. The difference between an ape's hand and a person's is the result of selection working over thousands of generations: the ape's hand has become adapted to grasping branches, the man's to manipulating tools. Selection against small brains continued to operate among our ancestors until a few thousand generations ago or less. Brains of at least a certain minimum size are needed to cope with the demands of culture and of life with other people. It is perfectly possible that complexity of organization of the brain and consequent improvements of its operating efficiency have continued to be selected for during the past few tens of thousands of years. The fossil record cannot tell us. But human societies make such complex demands, even when technology is poorly developed, that we can be sure that our ancestors needed just as good brains to cope with their problems 10,000 years ago as we need to cope with the problems of the modern world.

Growing plasticity of response characterizes the evolution of vertebrates, of mammals from reptiles, of primates among the mammals, and of man from his primate ancestors. The development of social organization among primates put a premium upon such mental traits as emotional adjustability and educability to one's social role. The further development of society among our early ancestors increased the premium, adding further complexities. Ability to communicate meaning through language has had survival value for any group which practices such a technique in contrast to competitive groups. This ability demands a far more powerful intellect than any other creatures possess, yet it is an absolute necessity for human culture. And this ability is equally characteristic of all known peoples. No language can be called a better instrument for communication than any other language, nor is any language more difficult to learn than another. Each has its own complexities and subtleties, yet very young children in every society learn to speak with ease. Long ago, selection eliminated those whose genes did not grant this potentiality.

Language is but a single example of the intricacy of cultural behavior. In all fields of human activity, those who display fixity of response suffer in contrast to those who are supple and aware, who can learn rapidly to do what a new situation requires. A genetic constitution which enables educability is appropriate to a species which, like our own, must adapt to constantly changing conditions. The activities of human beings continually alter the natural environment. These alterations take place too rapidly for useful fixed responses to evolve. Selection favors plasticity or educability.

In all societies with which ethnographers are acquainted such characteristics as wisdom, poise, and ability to get along with others are favored. These seem to be pretty basic. The manner of their expression may differ with time and place, and additional characteristics may have survival value, too, but the Pygmies' culture calls for such personalities as strongly as the Englishmen's. It is for such reasons that we must be dubious about the notion that selection could have led to different psychic traits in different breeding populations. In not one of them is it profitable to be stupid.

You will recall from the example of balanced polymorphism at the sickle-cell locus that alleles are selected with reference to the advantage of the breeding population rather than of any individual within it. Some individuals are bound to suffer from anemia, and some individuals suffer from stupidity, too. Intelligence tests have been given to millions of people in many countries and to members of many different ethnic groups and genetic isolates. It has been debated whether intelligence is a single entity which can be measured with any degree of validity. The tests which have been given attempt to ascertain the effectiveness of a person's mental response to a variety of problems. They do show a very considerable range in ability within any large group. Some people are certainly much brighter than others, and the variability within all groups as shown by the standard deviation is rather high. The conditions of life in any form of human society involve so much communication that not all of us have to be geniuses.

Differences have been noted in the average scores of different ethnic groups, social classes, and breeding populations. The meaning of such findings depends upon a number of factors. We can safely draw one conclusion immediately: we cannot properly stereotype anyone as stupid or brilliant on grounds of group membership. The three brilliant scientists who appear in Figure 13–2 exemplify this fact. There is a high incidence of red hair in Scotland, but not all Scots are red-haired. Likewise there is a high incidence of blood group A in Australia, but not all Australians are of this blood group. The same principle applies to responses given to intelligence tests.

Other conclusions are less certain. It would appear that the culture of the group as such greatly affects average scores. Tests which are suitable in one culture may be ridiculous in another. Motivation to do well depends upon social circumstances. Members of one group may seek personal distinction, whereas members of another group may evade it. A pretense of stupidity often has survival value for members of a lower caste. Malnourished subjects do more poorly than well-nourished ones. On the whole, any attempt to relate the results of intelligence tests to human genetics seems premature. There are too many intervening variables, and culture obviously is one of the major factors affecting the mental phenotype.

During the past few years, attempts have been made by a few

FIGURE 13-2. Three Eminent Anthropologists. Professor L. K. Hsu from China, Professor W. Montague Cobb from the United States, and Professor Koski from Finland. (Photos: Left to Right, Herb Comess, Northwestern University; Scurlock; and University of Turku)

scientists who lack any degree of anthropological sophistication to show that the American Colored are unable to learn as readily or as rapidly as are members of other racial groups and that their alleged lack of ability must be attributed to an inferior genetic endowment. It should be noted that two quite separate and distinct propositions are advanced: proof of inability to learn is by no means proof that the genetic endowment is involved, as the first part of this chapter should have made clear. But in fact the most recent data submitted to support the opinion that American Colored children cannot learn is no more convincing than earlier data: it still takes no account of the motivation, the vocabulary, the family and social backgrounds, the state of health or the tensions suffered by the children who were tested. Conclusions which depend upon evidence which is so tainted are of no scientific importance at all.

CASTE DIVISIONS AND SOCIAL SELECTION

The fact that outsiders—however an outsider may be defined—have been so commonly thought of as inferior in some sense is an aspect of culture which has affected the distribution of genes in the human species. In the same way, the fact that inferiors are considered unworthy of equal treatment has had effects upon both genotype and phenotype. Slavery is an example.

This peculiar social institution dates from antiquity but attained real economic significance only twice: during the classical period in the Mediterranean area and again much more recently in the warmer parts of the Americas. Slavery far from their homeland was the best fate which war prisoners might expect in classical times. Sometimes whole populations were enslaved and transported far from home. The use of slaves for all sorts of unskilled or even highly skilled labor was well established by the time that the Romans began to extend their dominion throughout the Mediterranean basin. As their empire expanded, the slave markets were constantly replenished by fresh supplies of captives from all directions.

Slaves were given the most perilous tasks as well as the most arduous, so their life expectancy was low. Even those lucky enough to escape such a fate almost never succeeded in rejoining their own societies; and they must have been unable to breed rapidly enough to supply the next generation's demands for slave labor, since new captives were constantly being sought. Whatever genes they contributed to later generations were left among populations foreign to their own, since Syrians were transported to Britain and Berbers to Romania to suit the convenience of their owners.

Improvements in shipping led to the transportation of slaves, and their genes, to far greater distances during recent centuries.

The tropical African origin of approximately one gene out of eight. in the present population of the Americas—as we noted in Chapter Twelve—is entirely due to slavery. Whether or not this shifted allele frequencies in Africa we can never know, but it has certainly done so in the whole area from the United States to Brazil. Here, too, the death rate has been exceptionally high, and the reproductive potential consequently low. Census figures from Cuba and from the United States presented in Tables 8 and 9 demonstrate this. Al-

TABLE 8. POPULATION GROWTH AND THE IMPORTATION OF SLAVES INTO
CUBA DURING THE COLONIAL PERIOD.

	Population			
	White	Free Colored	Slave	Slaves Imported Since Previous Count
1792	107,000	75,000	90,000	85,000
1817	257,000	116,000	199,000	200,000
1827	311,000	107,000	287,000	80,000
1841	418,000	153,000	432,000	112,000
1861	793,000	226,000	377,000	94,000

Total importation of slaves: 571,000
Total Colored population by 1861: 603,000

TABLE 9. POPULATION GROWTH IN THE UNITED STATES DURING THE
PERIOD PRECEDING HEAVY EUROPEAN IMMIGRATION, BY THOUSANDS.

	1790	1800	1810	1820	1830	1840
White	3,172	4,304	5,862	7,867	10,532	14,190
Percent	80.7	81.1	81.2	81.5	81.9	83.2
Free Colored	59	108	186	234	320	386
Percent	1.5	2.0	2.4	2.5	2.5	2.2
Slave	698	893	1,191	1,538	2,000	2,487
Percent	17.8	16.9	16.4	16.0	15.6	14.6
Total	3,930	5,306	7,240	9,638	12,866	17,069
White Increase Since Previous Count		1,132	1,558	2,005	2,665	3,658
Percent		36	36	34	34	35
Slave Increase Since Previous Count		195	298	347	471	478
Percent		28	33	25	31	24

though freed or escaped Negro slaves competed successfully with Indians in many parts of tropical America, any natural advantages due to climatic adaptation which they may have possessed were more than counterbalanced by their unfavorable economic and social status in competition with populations of European ancestry. Since the abolition of slavery, improvements in public sanitation and nutrition have begun to change this situation—again demonstrating the importance of culture in determining allele frequencies.

Slavery is perhaps the most extreme example of the caste divisions which human culture has created and which have served as barriers to gene flow, for caste endogamy is standard practice. In places such as India, where many castes exist, the barriers must be strong, for Sanghvi and Khanolkar (1949) have found that marked differences at several loci separate such endogamous groups, all sharing the same territory. Despite the fact that selection by means of disease should be equivalent for all the castes concerned, blood groups A and B varied from 20 to 30 percent and the sickle-cell trait from 0 to 17 percent among these castes. In observable morphological traits, caste differences are just as great. Females especially are restrained from mating with males of a lower caste; sometimes the sanctions employed are quite violent. Males, on the other hand, are less easily restrained; in some cultures society pretends not to notice their breaches of etiquette. The genetic barrier is far from absolute, and as a result of this there is often a tendency for lower caste allele frequencies to approximate those of the upper caste.

Members of a dominant caste set aesthetic ideals, so that individuals showing physical features thought to be typical of that caste are likely to be regarded as desirable matches. Henriques (1953) illustrates this situation with an example from Jamaica. Only 3 percent of that island's population are of purely European ancestry, yet more than 25 percent display enough European characteristics to be classified as Colored rather than Negro. Children with such features have a higher survival rate than children who lack them, as well as opportunities for better jobs, so that they in turn can raise more children of their own than their darker cousins. Social selection supplements, if it does not replace, natural selection, for the social environment has become at least as important as the natural environment.

Sometimes the results of social selection are quite irrelevant to its stated purpose. For instance, shortly after the discovery of America by Columbus the Spanish government forbade the migration of anyone having Moslem or Jewish ancestry to their new overseas colonies. Most of the migrants to America came from southern Spain, which was that part of the country most recently recovered from the Moors. A great proportion of the population was descended, at least in part, from Moors and Jews, but the upper classes were mostly of Castilian origin. The migrants were drawn in the main from the upper classes, in which alleles for dark pigmentation were less frequent than among the lower classes. Even today, 400 years later, Cubans of Spanish rather than mixed ancestry resemble the upper rather than the lower classes of southern

Spain in appearance. There was no prejudice against brunettes on the part of the Spanish lawgivers; they just wanted to keep heretics out of their colonies. But the biological result, though unintended, was effective.

A woman is rarely able to give birth to more than twenty children, but a man is quite capable of fathering several hundred. In societies where polygyny is practiced, men who can afford to accumulate a large number of wives may have a very great many children. Their contribution to the gene pool of the next generation is likely to be high. In many societies where polygyny is not legally established, upper class males are left rather free to do the same thing. The Ladino race mentioned in the previous chapter owes its creation to the efforts of a relatively small number of European males who came as conquerors and exploited their advantageous situation. Small ruling aristocracies have undoubtedly altered the allele frequencies of the countries which they dominated on many occasions. If selection has not altered allele frequencies, it is possible to calculate the proportions of gametes contributed to a hybrid population by each of the parent stocks, but this need not reflect the proportion of individuals from each stock who were involved in the process.

RELIGIOUS BARRIERS

More or less endogamous castes, like those of India and those which are the leftover relics of past slavery in North and South America, are not the only breeding populations which owe their boundaries to social rules. Differences in religion have often served as barriers to gene flow in areas where several religious organizations coexist. Here in the United States there are some religious isolates, such as the Dunkers (Glass *et al.*, 1952), which have allele frequencies at some loci which are quite distinctive not only from their neighbors but from the populations from which they originated. Blood group B, for instance, has been almost lost from the Dunker gene pool although their ancestors came from central Europe. This is very probably the result of chance or genetic drift, for the Dunkers are a small group and do not intermarry with people of other faiths.

Members of many denominations are often encouraged to marry only within their group, but the extent to which this fact may be correlated with varied allele frequencies has rarely been examined in the United States. The Jewish isolate of Rome, however, is the subject of a classic study by Dunn (1959). This community has been in existence for a very long time, possibly as much as 2,000 years. It has been largely endogamous for at least several hundred years. And like the Dunkers, it has some distinctive allele frequencies, notably a very high incidence of the allele r′ of the Rh system.

Religion, occupation, and ethnic origin have been quite likely to be associated in many Balkan and Near Eastern countries. Each city contained several communities, each organized about a certain denomination and tending to follow specified trades (Coon, 1951). Craft skills as well as religious membership are handed down from one generation to the next, and endogamy is strictly adhered to, since marriages are arranged by the elders of the families. As might be expected, allele frequencies at various loci differ from one community to another. In Cairo, for instance, the percentage of tasters of PTC is greater among Moslems than among native Christians, whereas the Christians are much more likely to have hair on the central segment of their fingers (Boyd, 1950). Since communities of the same faith in different cities differ from one another too, it seems probable that genetic drift, rather than the retention of some ancient racial trait, is responsible for the allele frequencies which have been noted.

Even within a single community, different inbred lineages may vary in allele frequencies. Among the Jews from Habban in southern Arabia, Bonné (1969) found that the Sameach family has a distinctly higher frequency of the V, Sutter, and Duffy-amorph alleles than the other three families studied. In the same group I found (Hulse, 1970) that the Matoof family are distinctly light in skin color. Marriage to someone of the same surname is widely practiced in this isolate; presumably the founder effect is responsible for the genetic differences found at the loci responsible for these traits.

OCCUPATIONAL BARRIERS

In a few cases occupation alone sets people apart from their neighbors, leading to reproductive isolation. The Gypsies in Europe have remained wandering traders and repairmen of household utensils since they first entered the continent six centuries or more ago. The idea that their original homeland was India is supported by analysis of blood-group frequencies as well as by observation of their external physical features. In both they resemble certain lower caste groups of northwestern India rather than the Europeans among whom they dwell. The professional Sumo wrestlers of Japan are quite a bit taller and very much fatter than almost all other Japanese. Wrestlers almost always marry the daughters of other wrestlers. It is possible to become a wrestler, but one must be very big to succeed in this trade. Alleles for large size continue to enter this occupational group, but occupational endogamy serves as a selective force to maintain the appropriate physical type.

LINGUISTIC BARRIERS

Linguistic barriers to gene flow have been noted in a number of cases. Such barriers tend to preserve ethnic identity in circumstances where it would otherwise be lost. The Basques, who live both in France and Spain at the western end of the Pyrenees, are a case in point. This ethnic group shares the religion and the occupations of their neighbors and have no political status of their own. Their bond of unity is their language, which is quite unrelated to any other so far as anyone has been able to discover. Yet it has long been noted that the frequency of certain distinctive features, such as the combination of broad foreheads and narrow jaws, is most unusually high among them. They are equally unique in the incidence of various blood type alleles, as examination of the maps in Chapter Eleven shows. Their exclusiveness, expressed in their retention of their mother tongue, has led to a retention of genetic distinctiveness.

There are similar examples on the other side of the world and in another cultural context. Tribes of the Athapaskan linguistic stock, whether in Arizona or Canada, differ from their neighbors in a standard fashion. They have a higher frequency of blood group A, a lower frequency of blood type N, and a greater variety of Rh types. Apparently they have mated very little with the members of other tribes. In South America allele frequencies at the Diego locus differ very considerably between tribes of Arawak and Carib linguistic affiliation for the same reason (Layrisse and Wilbert, 1960).

Since there is no causal correlation between the cultural phenomenon of language on the one hand and the genetic phenomenon of blood types on the other, these findings must be regarded as signifying the importance of mating preferences in the flow of genes. A person's racial characteristics are incapable of determining the language which he speaks. The language which he learned as a child, however, is a most vital part of the culture in which he lives, and it influences his behavior profoundly. In most cases, he learned how to speak from his biological parents from whom he derived whatever genes he has. In most cases, too, it is convenient to be able to talk with one's husband or wife. Casual mating, to be sure, does not require speech, but most children are born of married couples. Cultural differences are the cause rather than the result of genetic differences. This is just as true of language as it is of economic circumstance.

MISCEGENATION

Despite all the barriers to gene flow which exist, mating between members of different groups has been constant for as long as

we have any evidence concerning human sexual behavior. There is
no reason to suppose that once upon a time all races were "pure,"
just as there is no evidence that human diversity is a recent phenomenon. Certainly, throughout recorded history all sorts of
groups have been forming, mingling, and vanishing. Miscegenation
is the term applied to the genetic mixing of groups which had been
distinct, but like the word inheritance, this word has been used in
several different ways and applied to at least three totally distinct
processes (Hulse, 1969). Sometimes it is used in reference to matings between members of different castes; sometimes with reference to mating between members of ethnic groups; and sometimes
with reference to mating between members of genetically distinct
breeding populations. This is very natural, although it is unfortunate, because these three sorts of human groupings are very likely
to overlap in their composition. It is very unfortunate, although it
is natural, because this overlapping makes it possible to claim that
the results of one sort of mixture are really due to another sort of
mixture. Since explanations of this sort are often emotionally comforting, they have been readily accepted and form part of the common folklore.

A caste is a socioeconomic group which is set apart rather rigidly from other groups living in the same geographic area. Ritual
sanctions are applied to enforce the separation. Often the members
of a caste are engaged in specified occupations, or their ancestors
were. As a rule, different castes within a society are hierarchically
arranged; at least some are regarded as better than others. As a
rule, matings between members of different castes are forbidden by
custom or even by law; although in some cases females may marry
males of a higher caste, and in some cases males may take lower
caste females for their pleasure. Sanctions against a male who attempts to mate upward are frequently ferocious. Consequently,
gene flow between different castes tends to be minimized. Yet different castes need not be genetically distinguishable. The Eta of
Japan have been called "Japan's Invisible Race" (DeVos and Wagatsuma, 1966) since, despite segregation, there is no way to spot a
member of this group by physical appearance. The keymarks of
caste are rank and rigidity.

An ethnic group is a recognizable sociocultural unit based upon
some form of national or tribal distinction, which lives among other
people rather than in its own country. The unity is one of senti-
ment and tradition and need not involve economic factors or hierarchical status. Both its own members and their neighbors recognize the existence of an ethnic group. Yet it is not rigid, nor even
necessarily stable. In a New England town (Warner, 1963) only
the members of old families of eighteenth-century vintage are
thought of as Yankees. In New York and further west all New

Englanders are thought of as Yankees. In the ex-Confederate States all northerners are thought of as Yankees. In Europe all people from the United States are thought of as Yankees. Nor need an ethnic group be in any sense a genetic group. In Hawaii the Portuguese comprise an ethnic group of whom some members are from the Cape Verde Islands and are obviously dark, while others are from the Azores and are obviously light. Neither physical appearance nor allele frequencies are useful criteria for distinguishing the Yankees from the Irish at Newburyport. But all the neighbors know who belongs to which group.

A genetically distinct breeding population is an entity of a thoroughly different sort, since it may be characterized in biological terms. Castes and ethnic groups are found only in the human species, but breeding populations exist in most if not all bisexual animal species. The barriers between castes and ethnic groups are the result of human culture and human imagination. The barriers between breeding populations may be oceans, mountains, deserts, and climatic zones as well. Society often determines the composition of a breeding population, but it is less able to determine its genetic characteristics. In many cases, at least within the human species, social regulations may be effective in causing genetic distinctions to be retained, but it is far more doubtful that social regulations caused them to originate.

As previous chapters have made clear, human breeding populations whose ancestors lived for thousands of generations in different parts of the globe have evolved varied peculiarities. Depigmentation is most frequent among Northwest Europeans, blood type B among East Asians, steatopygia among Bushmen and Hottentots, blood type R^2 among American Indians, and so on. Breeding populations which are genetically distinct from each other have come, in almost all cases, from different parts of the world. It is reasonable to suppose that they would have evolved no matter what form of social organization might have existed among them.

In the course of human history, however, migrations have become extensive, and during the last few hundred years millions of people have traveled thousands of miles to a new home. Consequently, we find individuals, families, and entire genetic isolates now living at a great distance from their ancestral areas and among others who came from an entirely different place. In many instances they have brought with them not only their genes but many or most aspects of their parental culture. Thus we find a great many genetic isolates or at least somewhat distinctive breeding populations, which are also ethnic groups. The Italian Swiss in California are an example of this; so are the group in Hawaii known as Haoles, that is, those of European ancestry; and so are the Indians of South Africa, Trinidad, and Guyana. As time goes on, ethnic distinctions may break down and genetic distinctions vanish. They tend to be mutually dependent, but it must never be forgotten that their origins are different.

Also, in the course of history, conquests have been made, ruling aristocracies of foreigners have been imposed upon local populations, and captives transported into slavery in distant lands. More or less rigidly stratified castes have originated from these activities, as well as from other historic causes, such as the degradation of certain occupations. Thus castes may be, but need not be, genetically distinct breeding populations just as they may be, but need not be, ethnic groups as well. The Eta of Japan appear to be a caste with neither ethnic nor genetic distinctions. Many castes in India differ in allele frequencies but do not differ ethnically. Many of the Ashkenazic Jews of Europe resembled their Gentile neighbors in allele frequencies much more closely than in ethnic characteristics. The Colored population of the United States resemble their Caucasian neighbors much more closely in ethnic characteristics than in allele frequencies. The French colonists in Algeria differed from their Berber neighbors ethnically and genetically as well as in being the dominant caste.

All possible combinations of caste, ethnic group, and race can be found. It is really not surprising that the term miscegenation has been used in such a loose way, not that its results have been so frequently misinterpreted. There can be no question but that, when forbidden matings occur, the offspring can be made to suffer and may be so badly mistreated that they learn undesirable forms of behavior. Furthermore, scholars and scientists are no more free of prejudice than are other people. Davenport and Steggerda (1929) wrote of anatomical disharmonies among mulattoes in Jamaica: long legs inherited from the African and short arms from the European ancestors. Interestingly enough, they were quite unable to find instances of these disharmonies; arms and legs can be measured precisely. They also claimed mental disharmonies: although the mulattoes to whom they gave intelligence tests did not do badly, they allege that many of them "were muddled and wuzzleheaded." What this means, if anything, is obscure. It is not something which can be measured precisely. Mjøen (1921) found Lapp-Norwegian hybrids to suffer from "want of balance" and "unwillingness to work"—characteristics which are certainly not subject to measurement of any sort.

It has also been alleged that the offspring of miscegenation are less fertile than members of "pure" races. But there is no shred of evidence to support this notion. Fischer (1913), in his classic study of the Rehobother Bastards, found 7.7 children per family among them more than a century after the group originated. Shapiro (1929, 1936) found that the descendants of mutineers of the *Bounty* multiplied at an equally rapid rate. Other investigators report similar findings in similar circumstances. To be sure, if they dwell in places where they are despised outcasts, hybrids may lack the opportunity and the incentive to rear large families. If they are striving to better their position in life or that of their children, the same thing is true. Family size among human beings is not a measure of fertility and has little to do with biological abilities; since our ancestors attained cortical control of their sexual impulses, it has been determined by sociocultural factors.

It has also been alleged that miscegenation brings out the worst characteristics of the two ancestral stocks which are hybridizing. What, if anything, does this statement mean? It certainly is not a statement concerning genetics or any other aspect of biology. In a cultural context, it is understandable, whether it be true or false. When two societies are in close contact, individuals who have some understanding of the culture of both have an advantage which they may exploit. This often proves disconcerting to their neighbors who are less empathetic or less alert. At the same time, an individual of mixed ancestry is commonly at a social disadvantage to start with and needs to take every advantage to get along. Thus those who are prejudiced against him from the beginning can easily condemn him for playing the game according to two sets of rules. If, on the other hand, the hybrid becomes discouraged with his lot, it is just as easy to condemn him for not playing the game at all, but in both cases behavior which is condemned is culturally, not genetically determined. Furthermore, such evidence as has been advanced in support of this statement is purely anecdotal and totally lacking in scientific value.

In summary, we can say with complete confidence that all statements alleging disadvantageous effects from miscegenation refer either to caste or to ethnic miscegenation. Most of them concern caste miscegenation and simply reflect the speakers' prejudices in regard to status. There is no indication that genetics is concerned in any way. The essential mistake made by those who assert disadvantageous effects has been a total disregard of cultural factors and an assumption that all human behavior is genetically determined.

There are, of course, scientists, scholars, and publicists who assert that miscegenation is beneficial rather than unfortunate. The high birth rates noted earlier have been taken to indicate hybrid vigor, or heterosis, for instance, and Shapiro (1929) goes on to proclaim that the Pitcairn Islanders created a social structure superior to that of either Tahiti or England. Rodenwaldt (1927) praised the vigor of the "Mestizen auf Kisar" whom he studied, and Williams (1931) wrote of the vitality of the Maya-Spanish crosses in Yucatan. Many historically minded scholars have noted cultural efflorescence after two groups of people have merged, and they have attributed this to the beneficial effects of introducing "new blood" into the population. Certainly cultural interchange can have a stimulating effect, but this is true whether genes are exchanged or not. The Japanese, whose island country has taken in a smaller proportion of immigrants during the last 1,500 years than any other nation I know of, have been as stimulated by culture contact as any people in the world.

Hybrid vigor has been claimed as one of the chief virtues resulting from miscegenation, but this is almost certainly due to a misunderstanding. Mendel (1866) noted that, in the F_1 generation of some of his hybrid peas, the plants grew extra large. As a phenomenon of the first filial generation after crossing of two genetically distinct strains, many later investigators have noted such hybrid vigor as well. Biologically, however, this is evanescent. Later generations, if inbred, do not continue to manifest this characteristic. If indeed extra vigor is noted among such groups as those studied by Shapiro and Fischer, it can scarcely be termed hybrid vigor, and in any case Trevor (1953), in reviewing a number of studies of miscegenation, was unable to confirm its existence in any of them. As Penrose (1955) has pointed out, the classic studies of race mixture have described cases of hybridization between groups neither of which were in fact genetically pure strains like Mendel's peas.

Another, but possibly related, advantage attributed to miscegenation is the lessened frequency of appearance in the phenotype of harmful recessives. This is a reasonable expectation in accordance with genetic knowledge and theory. One has to remember, however, that not all genetic recessives can be described as harmful, nor are all deleterious alleles recessive. Let us consider the case of blue eyes, which are found among about half of northwestern Europeans—so that the allele frequency may be calculated at about 70 percent—but not at all among aboriginal North American Indians. A good deal of miscegenation has taken place between these two groups during the last few hundred years, and it has been genetic as well as ethnic miscegenation. The allele frequencies in a population of hybrids would then be about 35 percent, and, if they mated only with one another, the phenotype frequency of blue eyes would be one in eight. Is this advantageous, disadvantageous, or simply irrelevant except aesthetically? We would expect the allele frequency for Rh negatives to be halved in such a mixed group, too, so that the phenotypic incidence would drop to one-fourth of that found in West European populations. This might be considered advantageous from the European point of view, but an American Indian might become indignant at the introduction of a new hazard into his population.

In the malarial regions of Africa a mulatto population would, at first, have a lower frequency of sickle-cell alleles and, consequently, a lower incidence of heterozygotes useful as a buffer against malaria than a Negro population long resident in the area. But natural selection might remedy this misfortune within a few generations. In the United States or England, on the other hand, since malaria is a minor hazard in these countries at the present time, the allele Hb^s is properly considered deleterious. Whether a certain genetic factor is harmful or not depends upon the environmental stresses to which a population is subject. It is rash and prejudicial to consider it a matter of absolute good or bad. We may conclude, however, that extensive outbreeding, whether or not it involves caste or ethnic miscegenation, does serve to retain recessives in the gene pool, and this is good insurance against possible environmental changes in the future. What we deplore now may serve a useful function for later generations.

Heterozygote advantage, which seems to have been pretty well demonstrated in the case of the sickle-cell locus, has been another of the arguments advanced in favor of miscegenation. There may well be many cases in which heterozygotes do enjoy an advantage of some sort. At any rate it is difficult to explain the numerous cases of balanced polymorphism in any other way; and the excess of the phenotype MN over expectation in so many family studies supports this opinion too. But, in fact, genetic polymorphism is so common at so many loci within each caste or ethnic group which has been studied that intermarriage between members of different social groups is not required to ensure its continuance.

Studies of miscegenation, as distinct from polemics, date at least as far back as Boas's (1894) publication, "The Half Blood Indian." As our understanding of the mechanisms of biological inheritance and of the relationships between genetics and environment have improved, investigators have turned more and more to the analysis of special problems rather than all-embracing population surveys. This has permitted more precise analysis of the particular problem chosen but has sometimes resulted in a neglect of factors which are relevant to the dynamics of miscegenation. Stuckert (1958) published a provocative paper on "African Ancestry of the White American Population" which neglected to take into account the fact that most of the American Colored were concentrated in a relatively small area within the United States, the fact that about 40 percent of American Whites are of quite recent European extraction, the fact that sanctions against Colored males mating with White females have been of the utmost ferocity, and the fact that "passing" as White has been exceedingly difficult. In any study of genetic miscegenation both cultural and geographical circumstances have to be considered.

FIGURE 13-3. A Man from Madagascar
(Photo: United Nations)

Mating is never at random in the human species, and among those who mate across the barriers of caste or ethnic group it is clearly less random than among those who mate within their own social group. Slave owners have been more likely to mate with slaves than have members of the slave owners' stocks who do not own slaves. Wandering fur traders were more likely to mate with American Indians than were their kinsmen who remained at home. Sailors whose ships took them to the South Seas were almost the only Europeans to mate with Polynesians. There is no reason to suppose that the Indonesians and Africans who became the ancestors of the Malagasy (see Figure 13–3) were a random sample of the populations from which they were derived. We have very little information on the physical, let alone the genetic, characteristics of those particular European males who were the ancestors of the hybrid groups which have been analyzed in the classic studies of race mixture. Nor do we know much about their consorts. We can imagine that slave owners picked the girls who pleased them most, but we do not know what standards they used.

Furthermore, since, in cases of ethnic miscegenation, at least one of the participating groups must have come from another region, they may be subject and their offspring may be subject to unfamiliar selective stresses which would result in shifts in allele frequencies whether or not race mixture took place. This was found to be the case by Workman, Blumberg, and Cooper (1963): the incidence of Hb^s among the Colored in Georgia had declined much more than it would have if hybridization with North Europeans alone had been responsible. When we are dealing with populations which have resulted from miscegenation several centuries ago, it becomes very difficult to estimate the relative proportions of alleles contributed by each of the ancestral stocks concerned. Pollitzer (1958) in a beautifully designed study of "The Negroes of Charleston, South Carolina" compared this population with West Africans, American Whites, and the larger group of American Colored for serological and morphological traits. He found that in blood-type frequencies both the Charleston Negroes and the United States Colored as a whole resemble West Africans more closely than they do in morphology. Manuila (1956) noted a higher incidence of blood type B in those parts of eastern Europe overrun by the Mongols than in neighboring areas, yet the inhabitants do not look in the least Mongoloid. It is quite possible that social selection has been operative in both these cases, inasmuch as humans have not yet developed such prejudices about blood types as they have about external anatomical features. Further studies are needed, of course, to confirm or deny this guess of mine.

Harrison and Owen (1964) in Liverpool studied the skin color of a group of mixed European-West African ancestry and many of their European and West African parents. Since there is no overlapping at all in the degree of pigmentation of the unexposed skin in West Africans and North Europeans, a study of this sort is most suitable to determine the number of loci involved in the inheritance of skin color. Much more precise genetic analyses can be made in a situation such as this: here we see the essential difference between cultural and genetic inheritance. Cultural characteristics are transmitted from one generation to the next at large; genetic characteristics are transmitted only from biological parents to their own personal offspring. Thus it was possible in the Liverpool study to compare children with their own parents and reach conclusions concerning the number of loci involved in the determination of pigmentation. Only by a study of genetic miscegenation conducted in this manner can this sort of information be uncovered. Caste and ethnic factors are eliminated, and selection can scarcely have had time to operate in the course of two generations.

During the present and the coming generation it seems to me that the best place in the world to study genetic miscegenation will be Israel. Populations of Jews from many different parts of the world have just been gathered together into this state. Many of these populations have been highly inbred for centuries, and they differ from one another in a great number of sets of allele frequencies. They are just beginning to interbreed with one another. Parental as well as first and second filial generations will all be available for study during the next two or three decades. Ethnic and even castelike differences exist but are minimized and can readily be factored out by careful analysis. The cultural atmosphere of the nation favors scientific research, and its compact size makes field work easy. It can therefore be hoped that many important discoveries concerning the consequences of miscegenation will be made by physical anthropologists and human geneticists working in unison in the natural laboratory of Israel.

We have already mentioned that diet, which is determined by culture, has observable effects upon the biological characteristics of human beings and that agriculture sometimes benefits mosquitoes as well as men. Food preferences and changes in food preferences have effects as well. Too great dependence upon one staple crop may lead to vitamin deficiencies, and these in turn may act as selective forces within a population. Maize appears to be associated with pellagra, which is due to niacin deficiency, and rice with beri-beri, caused by thiamine deficiency. Any diet very low in protein, as diets of grains and roots are likely to be, may result in kwashiorkor (Newman, 1962). All of these deficiency diseases eliminate large numbers of children from the population, and in almost all places where they have been endemic the average body size of adults is small. It is apparent that nonlethal cases delay growth and strongly suspected that permanent stunting is a common result. It would be logical to expect that certain genotypes may be favored at the expense of others in environments which include vitamin or protein deficiency as standard hazards to life; but we cannot be at all sure that alleles leading to short stature or light weight would be those selected.

Changes in diet have had a variety of interesting results. The potato was introduced into Europe only a few hundred years ago, for it had previously been cultivated only in the Andes. It does well in damp, cool climates, and therefore proved a most suitable crop for northern Europe. Agricultural improvements, including the provision of much winter fodder for farm animals, were being made at the time that the cultivation of the potato was spreading. With more and better food available human health improved and population increased. This increase was especially marked in the areas where the incidence of alleles for blondness and for blood group B were high. The result, of course, has been an increase in the frequency of both of these characteristics among Europeans. This increased frequency has nothing whatever to do with any possible adaptive value of the alleles concerned. It is the fortuitous consequence of cultural change. It should serve as another reminder to caution in attributing cultural achievements to the possession of one set of alleles rather than another.

PLASTICITY IN BODY FORM: AN EXAMPLE

We have noted repeatedly that the conditions of life, including diet, affect the phenotype in various ways. Greater growth, it will be remembered, is commonly the result of better circumstances.

The environment is rarely perfect enough to permit the full expression of genetic potential. At times, a change in size is accompanied by and very likely the cause of certain changes in shape or proportion. Differences in proportion have been thought of as characteristic of different races. Brachycephaly, for instance, has been used as a diagnostic trait to differentiate Alpines from Nordics within the European population. Yet comparisons between migrants from Europe to the United States and their American-born offspring have noted changes in the cephalic index. In some cases, these changes are great enough to justify including parents in one race and their children in another. This, of course, is rather fantastic. It reduces the use of the word race to an absurdity. Differences in the phenotype which are not the result of differences in allele frequencies must not be considered as racial, no matter what their magnitude may be. They serve rather to measure the degree of plasticity in body form.

A study of the people of the Canton Ticino in Switzerland (see Figure 13–4) and their close relatives in California (Hulse, 1968) may be used as an example of such phenotypic plasticity. No differences in allele frequencies exist, as we noted in Chapter Ten. All the subjects were members of the same breeding population. About half of the group were the offspring of marriages between natives of the same small villages; the other half were sons of marriages between men of one village and women from another. All the villages were within a few miles of each other, yet it had been customary for many generations to marry within one's own village. Such village endogamy served to protect local property rights from the claims of outsiders and to strengthen the emotional bonds uniting the community. Only during the present century is the rule of local endogamy breaking down, as industrialization attracts young people away and leads to more outside contacts. Migrants to California preferred spouses from Ticino which, as the only Italian-speaking canton in Switzerland, had a vigorous sense of ethnic identity. It was not easy for a migrant to marry someone from his own hometown, however, even though that might have been best. Village exogamy has been much more common in California than in Switzerland.

The standard diet of the villager until quite recently contained much cornmeal, cheese, vegetable soups, and bread, but very little meat and fresh fruit only during brief seasons. His cousin or nephew in California, in contrast, had much less cornmeal, a greater variety of vegetables, fresh fruit almost throughout the year, and several times as much meat. Both milk and wine were in good supply in both countries, and in neither were children permitted to indulge in sweets to the extent that most Americans do. Changes in both quantity and quality of nutrition are obvious.

FIGURE 13-4. Europeans in America (Photo: Frederick S. Hulse)

They were taking place at the same time as the change in the type of marriage. Tables 10 and 11, which follow, indicate the extent

TABLE 10. STATURE OF MEN OF EXOGAMOUS AND ENDOGAMOUS PARENTAGE BORN IN SWITZERLAND AND IN CALIFORNIA.

	Number N	Range R	Mean $\overline{X}$	Standard Deviation σ
Swiss Born				
Exogamous	249	148–184	168.75 ± .39	6.16
Endogamous	310	147–184	166.98 ± .32	5.66
California Born				
Exogamous	85	159–189	172.33 ± .71	6.56
Endogamous	64	150–188	170.41 ± .80	6.43

to which changes in bodily form followed the alterations in cultural practice. We can see that the California born are taller and less brachycephalic than the Swiss born, and that those of exogamous parentage are taller and less brachycephalic than those of endogamous parentage, no matter where they were born.

Of course, we should explain the meaning of these tables, as well as the methods of calculation involved. You will recall that, in dealing with measurable characteristics which show continuous variation within a population, it is possible to describe what that population is like by calculating the mean and the standard deviation, as well as by showing the total range of variation. Since the size of the sample affects the reliability of the results, this should be given as well. Other things being equal, a large sample is more reliable than a small one. As the tables show, the symbol N represents the total number of items in the sample, R the total range, $\overline{X}$ the arithmetic mean, and the Greek letter σ the standard deviation. The first two need no calculation: simple inspection of the data which has been collected shows what they are. The arithmetic mean is very simple to calculate. Add the values of all the items together and divide by the total number N. The total of all the statures of endogamous born Swiss is 51,764 centimeters; divide this by the number of individuals, which is 310, and the result is 166.98 centimeters, as the table shows.

The standard deviation shows the degree of variability on both sides of the mean. Most individuals will be somewhat taller or shorter than the mean, for instance, and the standard deviation shows how much taller or shorter one can expect them to be. In a group consisting of adult males, the amount of deviation from the average stature will be much less than in a group consisting of men, women, and children of the same population.

To compute the standard deviation, first measure the deviation of each individual item from the mean. The shortest of the endogamous Swiss born, for instance, is 147 centimeters tall; he deviates from the mean by 19.98 centimeters. Measure this devia-

TABLE 11. CEPHALIC INDEX OF MEN OF EXOGAMOUS AND ENDOGAMOUS PARENTAGE BORN IN SWITZERLAND AND IN CALIFORNIA

	Number N	Range R	Mean $\overline{X}$	Standard Deviation σ
Swiss Born				
Exogamous	249	74–93	83.24 ± .22	3.51
Endogamous	310	74–92	84.10 ± .20	3.60
California Born				
Exogamous	85	72–92	80.76 ± .44	4.09
Endogamous	64	73–90	81.23 ± .51	4.05

tion for each of the 310 persons in the sample. Next, square each of these individual deviations: $19.98 \times 19.98 = 399.2004$. Then add together all of these squared deviations. In this case, the sum will be 9,931. Then divide this figure by N and take its square root. The result is 5.66 centimeters, which is the standard deviation of this particular sample. The formula to remember is:

$\sigma = \sqrt{\dfrac{\Sigma x^2 f}{N}}$. The symbol Σ means the sum of; the symbol x stands

for the deviation, or distance of an individual measurement from the mean; and the symbol f stands for the frequency with which one finds an individual whose measurement is that far from the mean. Thus only one person is the shortest of all and only one the very tallest, but perhaps three or four will be ten centimeters shorter or taller and fifteen or twenty will be five centimeters shorter or taller than the mean. If many individuals have measurements close to the mean, the standard deviation will be small. If many of them have measurements which are a great deal more or less than the mean, it will be large.

Sometimes it is worthwhile to know whether a population is more variable in one trait than in another. Do the endogamous Swiss born vary more in stature or in cephalic index, for instance? Since the units of measurements for these separate traits are different and the means are different too, a direct comparison is impossible, but the solution is easy. The coefficient of variability, which permits such a comparison, is found by computing the

formula $V = \dfrac{\sigma}{x}(100)$. In other words, divide the standard devia-

tion by the mean in each case: $5.66 \div 166.98 = .0339 \times 100 = 3.39$, whereas $3.60 \div 84.10 = .0426 \times 100 = 4.26$. The percentage of variation is greater in cephalic index than it is in stature, so far as this particular population is concerned.

It is always worthwhile to know how reliable the mean which has been calculated for any measurement or index may be. Unless we know this, it is impossible to find out the degree of probability that differences between the means of two groups are greater than might be expected by chance alone. Samples which we obtain from any population are no more than samples: they are not complete populations. We attempt to pick the members of the sample at random, so that they will represent the populations accurately, but absolute precision is out of the question. A certain amount of error is inevitable, but the extent of this, called the

standard error, can be calculated. The formula is $E = \dfrac{\sigma}{\sqrt{N}}$, be-

cause it depends upon the relationship between the size of the sample and the amount of variability within the sample. A small sample is less likely to give an accurate picture than a large one; and a sample which is highly variable is less likely to be precise than one which is less variable. In the case of the endogamous Swiss born we find that $\frac{5.66}{\sqrt{310}} = .32$, but it will be noted that, since there are fewer endogamous California born, $E = \frac{6.43}{\sqrt{85}}$, or .80, which is more than twice as much.

There are several formulas in use for computing the probability that the difference between the means of two groups is due to something other than chance alone. A simple method precise enough for our purposes depends upon the expression E of the difference $= \sqrt{E_1^2 + E_2^2}$. Let us use this formula to find out whether the difference in cephalic index between the endogamous Swiss born and the endogamous California born is great enough to be worth trying to explain. The standard error of the Swiss group for this index is .32, of which the square is .1024; that of the California group is .80, of which the square is .64. The sum of the decimals is .7424, and $\sqrt{.7424} = .86$, which is the standard error of the difference between the means of the two groups. The Swiss group has a mean cephalic index of 84.10, the Californian of 81.23, as Table 10 shows. The difference between these two numbers is $2.87 \pm .86$. This difference is more than three times its own standard error. By chance alone, a difference of twice the standard error can be expected in less than one case out of twenty, in samples of sixty or more items; a difference of more than three times, less than once in a hundred cases. Such a difference calls for explanation, since it is so highly improbable that it is due to chance.

Indeed, all the differences between Swiss born and California born and most of those between those of endogamous and exogamous origin are great enough so that we can feel confident that they are real. We know that we cannot seek the cause of these differences in genes: all the members of the samples are drawn from a single extended gene pool. The fact that the diet of the California born provided superior nutrition may perhaps be enough to explain their greater stature. The negative correlation between stature and cephalic index is more than enough to explain the shift from brachycephaly of the taller Californians. Both of these changes have been noted in other migrant groups. They are purely phenotypic. It is quite likely that poor food or adverse conditions might reduce the stature and increase the cephalic index of the descendants of these men in later years.

The differences which separate those of exogamous and endogamous parentage cannot be explained in this way. A comparison of fathers and sons who were members of the sample leads to the conclusion that heterosis is responsible for the observed difference in stature. Some men, of endogamous parentage themselves, married women from another village. Their sons are on average five centimeters taller than they are. Other men average only a little more than two centimeters taller than their fathers. From breeding experiments with other sorts of creatures, it is known that heterosis is a phenomenon of the first filial generation, and so it is here. The drop in cephalic index is a secondary and incidental result of the greater stature. It is not a sign of racial change or evolution. It is not an adaptation. It is not even, of itself, a useful adjustment of the phenotype. Yet it is the sort of change which could have misled even the most careful scholars had skulls alone been available for study. The factors causing a change in bodily type are purely cultural in origin although they have had a biological effect. Improved living conditions are an aspect of culture, and so is the shift in marriage patterns.

This example of bodily plasticity has been given in order to show both the utility of anthropometry and the pitfalls which lie in the path of one who depends upon such measurements alone in attempting racial analyses. Until the development of techniques for determining blood types and other discrete biochemical and physiological traits, the data available to the physical anthropologist consisted largely of measurable anatomical features. Measurements and indices derived from measurements enabled scholars to describe more precisely what anyone who cared to look could see. But all of these measurements by their very nature lump together genetic potentialities and environmental effects. The idea that, for this reason, measurements should be discarded is rather silly. People have bones as well as blood. Adaptations may be anatomical as well as physiological. What should be discarded are the false conclusions drawn from imperfect knowledge.

The idea that the cephalic index alone, or the type of hair alone, or the incidence of any given allele alone will enable you to classify a population is dangerously misleading. The idea that hereditary differences, whether phrased in terms of phenotypic averages or of allele frequencies, cause cultural differences gains no support from comparisons of different groups, whether we call such groups ethnic or racial. The idea that we can safely stereotype all members of any group as identical turns out to be false. On the contrary, the idea that genetically based plasticity in form and behavior have been favored by selection is supported. The idea that culture, as it grew in content and evolved in form, has become a more and more important part of our environment is supported, too. Our ancestors, of course, had to evolve the capacity for culture as they were creating it, but once created, it molded the bodies and the minds of its participants. Our species continues to evolve subject to its direction.

Sources and Suggested Readings

AMMON, O.
 1895   *Zur Anthropologie der Badener.* Gustav Fischer Verlag, Jena.

BOAS, F.
 1894   The Half Blood Indian. *Popular Science Monthly,* **14,** 761.

BONNÉ, B.
 1969   Polymorphic Systems in the Habbanite Isolate. *Abstracts of the XII International Congress of Genetics,* **1,** Tokyo.

BOYD, W. C.
 1950   *Genetics and the Races of Man.* D. C. Heath, Boston.

COON, C. S.
 1951   *Caravan, the Story of the Middle East.* Knopf, New York.

DAVENPORT, C. B. and M. STEGGERDA
 1929   *Race Crossing in Jamaica.* Carnegie Institution, Washington.

DE VOS, G. and H. WAGATSUMA
 1966   *Japan's Invisible Race.* University of California Press, Berkeley.

DUNN, L. C.
 1959   *Heredity and Evolution in Human Populations.* Harvard University Press, Cambridge.

FISCHER, E.
 1913   *Die Rehobother Bastards und das Bastardierungsproblem beim Menschen.* Gustav Fischer, Jena.

GLASS, B., M. S. SACKS, E. F. JAHN, and C. HESS
 1952   Genetic Drift in a Religious Isolate. *The American Naturalist,* **86,** 145–159.

HARRISON, G. A. and J. J. T. OWEN
 1964   Studies on the Inheritance of Human Skin Colour. *Annals of Human Genetics,* **28,** 27.

HENRIQUES, F. N.
    1953   *Family and Color in Jamaica.* George Allen & Unwin, London.

HULSE, F. S.
    1957   Some Factors Influencing the Relative Proportions of Human Racial Stocks. *Cold Spring Harbor Symposia on Quantitative Biology,* **22,** 33–46.
    1968   Migration and Cultural Selection in Human Genetics. *The Anthropologist,* Special Volume, 1968, 1–21, Delhi.
    1969   Ethnic, Caste and Genetic Miscegenation. *Journal of Biosocial Science,* Supplement 1, 31–41.
    1970   Skin Color Among the Habbanite Jews of the Isolate from Habban. *Proceedings of the VIII International Congress of Anthropological and Ethnological Sciences,* **1,** 226–228, Tokyo.

KLINEBERG, OTTO
    1935   *Race Differences.* Harper and Bros., New York.

LAYRISSE, M. and J. WILBERT
    1960   *El Antigeno del Sistema Sanguineo Diego.* Fundacion Creole and Fundacion Eugenio Mendoza, Caracas.

MANUILA, A.
    1956   Distribution of ABO Genes in Eastern Europe. *American Journal of Physical Anthropology,* new series, **14,** 577–588.

MASON, PHILIP
    1961   *Common Sense About Race.* Macmillan, New York.

MENDEL, G.
    1866   Experiments in Plant Hybridization. *Proceedings of the Natural History Society of Brünn.* English Translation, Harvard University Press, Cambridge, 1948.

MJØEN, J. A.
    1921   Harmonic and Disharmonic Race Crossings. *Eugenics in Race and State,* **2,** 41.

NEWMAN, M. T.
    1962   Ecology and Nutritional Stress in Man. *American Anthropologist,* **64,** 22–34.

PENROSE, L. S.
   1955   Evidence of Heterosis in Man. *Proceedings of the Royal Society B,* **140,** 203.

POLLITZER, W. S.
   1958   The Negroes of Charleston (S.C.): A Study of Hemoglobin Types, Serology and Morphology. *American Journal of Physical Anthropology,* new series, **16,** 241–263.

RODENWALDT, E.
   1927   *Die Mestizen auf Kisar.* Gustav Fischer, Jena.

SANGHVI, L. D. and V. R. KHANOLKAR
   1949   Data Relating to Seven Genetical Characters in Six Endogamous Groups in Bombay. *Annals of Eugenics,* **15,** 52–64.

SHAPIRO, H. L.
   1929   *Descendants of Mutineers of the Bounty.* Memoirs of the Bernice P. Bishop Museum, **9.**
   1936   *Heritage of the Bounty.* Simon and Schuster, New York.

STUCKERT, R. P.
   1958   African Ancestry of the White American Population. *Ohio Journal of Science,* **58,** 155.

TREVOR, J. C.
   1953   Race Crossing in Man: The Analysis of Metrical Characters. *Eugenics Laboratory Memoirs,* **36.**

WARNER, W. L.
   1963   *Yankee City,* abridged edition. Yale University Press, New Haven.

WILLIAMS, G. D.
   1931   Maya-Spanish Crosses in Yucatan. *Papers of the Peabody Museum,* **13.** Harvard University Press, Cambridge.

WORKMAN, P. L., B. S. BLUMBERG, and A. J. COOPER
   1963   Selection, Gene Migration and Polymorphic Stability in a U.S. White and Negro Population. *American Journal of Human Genetics,* **15,** 429–437.

CHAPTER 14

Continuing Human Evolution

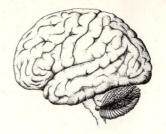

Evolution is accomplished by a change in allele frequencies. Phenotypic changes, when observed, may or may not have been the result of evolution. In the case of the migrants from Switzerland to California we can be quite sure that no evolution has taken place; human plasticity only can be demonstrated. In some other instances we can quite reasonably suspect that allele frequencies have shifted. Whether it is justifiable in all such cases to speak of evolution is much less certain. A shift in the frequency of one or two alleles between one generation and the next may portend evolution but does not guarantee that selection is really in process. Continued changes, or trends which persist, rather than fluctuating back and forth, may be called evolutionary. Evidence exists for such changes within relatively recent times even though we may be unable to measure their extent in terms of allele frequencies. Some such changes appear to be in process right now. A few may even be predicted for the future—with reservations.

The plasticity which is characteristic of so many of the details of human biology minimizes the necessity for selection. It is, after all, the phenotype which is subjected to environmental stress, even though it is the genotype which is transmitted from generation to generation. The previous chapter should have made it clear that plasticity of bodily form, just as much as flexibility of mental function, has had adaptive value of a high order for our species. The ecological zone which we exploit has been characterized by diversity in space and rapid changeability in time. Technological improvements and ideological shifts are typical of culture. Those humans who have responded most effectively to changing circumstances become the ancestors of later generations. Any mutations which tend to promote plasticity are likely to have been selected in the past, and we have no reason to suppose that this sort of selection has ceased, for adaptation to culture requires this quality.

At the same time, although culture mediates the impact upon us of a great number of environmental stresses, it has not abolished nature. To some, our mastery of nature has appeared so complete that they find it difficult to think in terms of adaptation so far as the human species is concerned. Human evolution has sometimes been pictured as the goal of all past events, but this is naïve megalomania. We are people, not gods. There are also some highly competent biologists who hold the opinion that the possibilities of anatomical and physiological adaptation have, by now, been exhausted. They believe that biological evolution, having reached its peak with the development of culture, is grinding to a halt. In their view any future changes in man's biology are bound to be trivial, irrelevant, and uninteresting. Only the evolution of culture itself, they write, has been significant during the last few thousand years (Huxley, 1955).

We should receive the conclusions of such authorities with respect, but there is room for difference of opinion. Judgments about what is or is not trivial depend upon the point of view. Who can tell how significant it might have seemed long ago that a lungfish was able to survive a dry period during which other fish perished? or that a baby obtained nourishment from its mother's breast? or that an ape was born with a pelvis so distorted in shape that he found it comfortable to stand up straight? The future of man as a biological organism may, perhaps, be brought under control. Our technological achievements appear to be capable of abolishing the future entirely. But in our present state of knowledge, it seems rash to predict that we will continue as we are for an indefinite period. We can demonstrate alterations in allele frequencies even within the past few hundred generations, both on a world-wide and on a local scale. There is plenty of evidence that selection, whether we call it natural or social, has continued to operate on modern mankind.

THE INCREASING BRACHYCEPHALIZATION OF THE SPECIES

The best documented but least well understood case of recent evolution has been the increasing brachycephalization of the species. This phenomenon has been neither constant nor universal, but it has been noted in many different parts of the world. The fact that most skulls from the Paleolithic in all areas are long and rather narrow has been mentioned. Archaeological sites from more recent periods are rather more likely to contain a certain proportion of brachycranial skulls. Much more often than not, there is a clear trend in the direction of round-headedness. Recent sites contain the greatest percentage of comparatively broad skulls. The percentage frequency of brachycephaly among the native populations of the world at the present time is shown in Figure 14–1. It has remained low, even up to now, throughout most of Africa and in Australia and Melanesia as well. Peoples living in such remote areas as Greenland, Lower California, and Tierra del Fuego tend to be even more dolichocephalic. In Europe the average is lower in Scandinavia, the British Isles, the Iberian peninsula, and southern Italy than elsewhere. It is lower in southern than in northern India and lower in Japan than in China. The highest averages are found in a belt of land stretching from Siberia through central Asia into the Near East and central Europe. But the greater number of native peoples of Southeast Asia, the Pacific islands, and America are brachycephalic also. The variation within each population is greater than the difference between the averages of any two known populations, so there is a great deal of overlapping.

It should be noted that a skull is classified as being brachycranial if its greatest width is four-fifths, or 80 percent, of its greatest length. The skin, and sometimes hair, which cover the skull of a living person, add a few millimeters to the length and breadth of a head, and this alters the shape slightly. Consequently, we classify a head as brachycephalic if its greatest width is 82 percent of its greatest length. Twin studies by Osborne and De George (1959) demonstrate a high degree of heritability in head breadth and cephalic index, at least among persons of European origin. But we really do not know how many genes are involved in these traits nor, indeed, whether shape or size is the factor most involved. More recently, Sekla and Soukup (1969) have provided evidence that a child is very likely indeed to resemble one parent in head shape rather than being equally similar in both, which suggests that not many loci are involved. However, environmental modification of the cephalic index is so likely that anthropologists remain in ignorance concerning the details of its mode of inheritance.

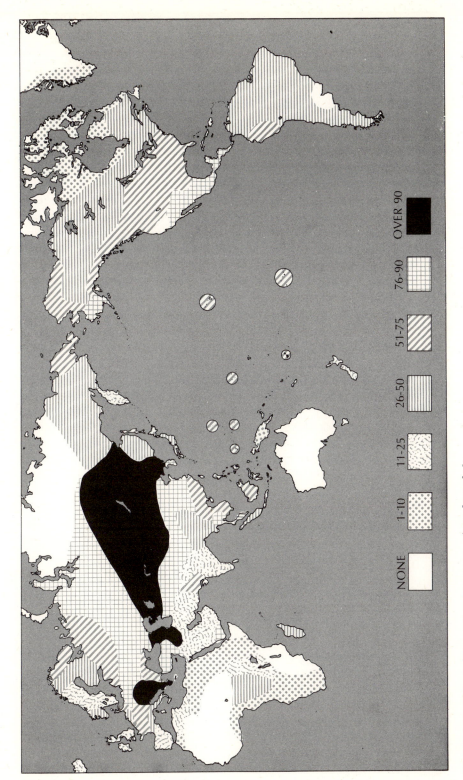

FIGURE 14-1. Estimated Percentage Frequency of Brachycephaly

Until Boas (1911) published his work on the physical differences between immigrants to the United States and their offspring, it had been assumed that environment did not affect head shape. However, a series of later studies in many parts of the world have demonstrated very clearly that the cephalic index is among the more plastic traits of the human species. The length of the head is positively correlated to stature, but its breadth is not. An increase in stature in a population of European origin is usually accompanied by a decrease in cephalic index, for the head becomes longer without becoming broader. Interestingly enough, this phenomenon has not yet been found in studies among populations of East Asian origin. Women commonly have slightly rounder heads than do men of the same population. Minor changes in the cephalic index are sometimes found as children grow up too. It has been fashionable among some tribes to beautify their offspring by molding their skulls during infancy, just as other tribes seek to improve on nature by tattooing, circumcision, foot-binding, or the wearing of uplift brassieres. The bones of the cranial vault are still malleable during the first few years of life, and the sutures are open as well. Thus by fastening boards or pads to an infant's head or by wrapping thongs about it, a parent can make sure that the child's head will grow into the shape that local fashion demands.

Somewhat similar results are produced inadvertently by cradling practices in at least a few parts of the world. Both in Lebanon (Ewing, 1950) and the Balkans (Ehrich and Coon, 1947) it has been shown that the custom of fastening babies into cradles with wooden head boards has had this effect. The occiput is pressed constantly upon this hard surface, so that growth has to take place in other directions, and the back of the head is flattened. Neither intentional or unintentional skull deformation has any effect whatever upon the mentality of the growing child. But, of course, either form of deformation makes the task of determining the hereditary component in head shape even more difficult.

Newman (1962) has shown, however, that neither a depression of stature nor deformation can explain the growing frequency of brachycephaly which undoubtedly took place as time went on among American Indians. Almost all of the skulls from very early periods found in America are long and narrow. A great majority of the skulls from later but still early periods have the same shape. But in more recent times this has become less and less true.

In the southeastern part of the United States the mean cranial index of adult males rose from less than seventy-six to more than eighty during a period of some 200 generations. During a somewhat briefer period the average index among the Indians of the southwestern desert rose from seventy-three to seventy-eight or more, and a similar change is noted among those of California. In the Andean region of South America, from Ecuador to Tierra del Fuego, the trend toward broad-headedness may have started at a later time, but there can be no doubt of its existence. In no area is there any evidence of a reverse trend. During the period of brachycephalization the Indians of the eastern United States were becoming taller, which makes it clear that head shape was changing quite independently of body size.

Comparable trends have been noted among the Japanese by Suzuki (1960), accompanied by a narrowing of the nasal root. The growth in size of Japanese born in Hawaii (Shapiro, 1939) and of Chinese born in the United States (Lasker, 1946) is also associated with broadening of the skull and narrowing of the nose. Polynesians, whose ancestry certainly includes a large component of southeastern Asians, are bigger and in general more brachycephalic than any known inhabitants of that area, past or present. You will recall that the Polynesians are among the more recently formed races. Without much doubt, brachycephalization has been taking place among all the peoples of east Asia or Mongoloid ancestry during the past few thousand years, no matter what the reason may be.

The same process can be documented in Europe and the Mediterranean area. A few Neanderthaloid and Upper Paleolithic crania were brachycranial. In Mesolithic times the proportion of such skulls becomes greater, and during the Bronze Age it increases still more. The custom of cremation, so widely practiced during late prehistoric and classical times, destroys the evidence and thus leaves us in ignorance about any widespread trends in the evolution of head shape during those periods. Brachycephaly increased greatly during the centuries after the fall of the Roman Empire, however. In most of the countries of central and eastern Europe graves dating from the fifth to the eighth century have not more than 25 percent to 30 percent of the skulls with indices of eighty or above. By the nineteenth century the proportions are reversed, and the mean index has risen by five or six points in most places. (See Figure 14–2.) Such a pronounced change over so wide an

FIGURE 14-2. The Increase of Brachycephaly in Europe. This Chart Indicates the Change in Head Shape which Took Place in Central Europe during the Middle Ages. The Solid Line Shows the Percentage Distribution of Cranial Indices of Skulls from Graves of the Fifth to Eighth Centuries; the Broken Line Shows the Percentage Distribution of Cranial Indices of Skulls from Graves of the Nineteenth Century.

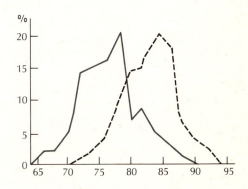

area demands explanation. Yet it has not been a universal phenomenon. Australia, Melanesia, and most of Africa as well as many of the peninsula areas of Europe are inhabited by peoples who have not become round-headed.

A globular-shaped container has a smaller surface per unit volume than any other shape, and the temporal areas on the sides of the head have many sweat glands. Coon (1955) has suggested that for creatures living in warm areas, especially open plains which are not too humid, dolichocephaly might serve to promote heat loss. Our tropical ancestors were long-headed, and those populations which have never left the tropics have retained this characteristic. Is this an example of Allen's rule? Plenty of heat is generated by the metabolism of the brain, whether one is asleep or awake. The quantity of blood supplied to the brain, as shown by the number and size of arteries and veins, is very great among mammals in general and anthropoids in particular. The brain, of course, cannot tolerate such variations in temperature as the arms or legs: its continued functioning at a high level of efficiency is required for life. Climatic stress could be among the factors which affect head shape, according to Coon (1962). This line of reasoning may explain the retention of dolichocephaly in Africa and India but does not account for the long heads of the Greenland Eskimo and Neanderthal Man, inhabitants of frigid lands. Spherical heads would have seemed more appropriate for them. Nor does it explain the increase in cephalic index among desert dwellers in Arizona and New Mexico. Nor do the inhabitants of northwestern Europe, who are dolichocephalic and who inhabit a cool wet area, fit the model.

Weidenreich (1945) suggested that a round head balances more readily at the top of the spine than an oval one. This is plausible but not necessarily true. Expansion to the rear can counterbalance projection in front. Should the jaws be large and heavy, as in the case of so many early hominids, adequate expansion might be difficult to attain. Neanderthal men had very strong neck muscles as well as expanded occiputs. But the reduction in facial projection found among all races of modern mankind has been very considerable. And the comparative recency of brachycephaly, which did not become widespread until we had been on our hind legs for two million years or more, causes one to doubt the validity of this suggestion. So does the speed with which the cephalic index increased after the trend set in. It has been suggested that the continued incursions of nomads from Central Asia increased the incidence of brachycephaly in eastern Europe, as they may well have increased the incidence of blood type B. The distribution of round heads does not support this notion, nor does the period during which the increase was taking place. It is also possible that the difficulties of childbirth are reduced as brachycephaly increases. Babies' heads are quite flexible but not infinitely so.

During recent decades the trend toward increased round-headedness among European populations has apparently been reversed: this may be a secondary result of increase in stature, as it certainly is among the offspring of Swiss and Jewish migrants to the United States. Nevertheless, brachycephalization has been a true evolutionary trend. So have a number of other changes in the bones of the head.

OTHER CHANGES IN THE SKULL

Early hominids had very thick skulls. Those of the men of the Upper Paleolithic were thinner. In still later times some but not all of the populations of the world came to have still thinner skulls. With the invention and spread of intensive agriculture, which took place in several regions and was practiced by peoples of quite different skeletal features, thin skulls become common. The farmers of Mexico and Peru, like those of Egypt and Meso-potamia, had thinner skulls than their hunting predecessors. Very few peoples of today are characterized by skulls as thick as those which were typical during the Upper Paleolithic. In many places, during these same few tens of thousands of years, the evidence indicates a decrease in average cranial capacity. In no place has cranial capacity increased during this length of time.

The evolution of the jaws and teeth has followed the same line in most but not all parts of the world. They have become smaller; chins have become more prominent; the frequency of congenitally missing teeth has increased. This process has not been confined to agricultural peoples, nor is it universal among them. The reindeer-herding Lapps of the European Arctic and the hunting Bushmen of South Africa are among the peoples with small jaws and teeth, while agricultural Polynesians are among those with a large chewing apparatus. It may be worth noting that the body size of Lapps and Bushmen tends to be well below the world average, whereas that of Polynesians is above it. It is quite possible that among the factors leading to the changes in size and proportion of the head and face a reduction in body size in general may be important.

DIET AND HABITAT

A reduction in body size has often followed the development of intensive grain agriculture and may be a reflection of nutritional stress. Newman (1960) has analyzed the relationship between average weight, ambient temperature, and caloric intake among many tribes of American Indians. In the temperate and arctic areas he found a regression of average weight on the temperature of the coldest month. These have been areas where dependence upon agriculture was far from complete; in many cases no food crops at all were raised. The peoples of Mexico, Central America, and Peru have cultivated maize for several thousand years, and it became their staple food source long ago. Studies by nutritionists show that the caloric intake has been very low indeed for most people in this region. Protein and vitamin deficiencies exist. The average weight falls well below what would be expected as a response to climate alone. Growth and maturation are delayed among these tribes and adult body size reduced. As an adaptation to the conditions of life, this makes good sense. Selection has probably removed children who could not get along on what would be, for us, a most inadequate diet.

THE RURAL PEASANT

It is not unlikely that both phenotype and genotype have been affected in the adjustment of one population after another to dependence upon cultivated grains as a major source of nourishment. The peoples of the plains in the whole vast region stretching from the Mediterranean eastward as far as the Pacific Ocean are, in general, dependent upon grain for their livelihood, as their ancestors have been for thousands of years. Meat is a rare item in the diet of the peasant, whether he is a Spaniard, a Persian or a Japanese. He earns his bread by the sweat of his brow and is likely to have to work hard from early childhood to old age. He probably remembers at least one famine during his lifetime, but he does not remember many feasts. The soil in which he raises his crops is likely to be deficient in calcium. He lives in a completely unsanitary village where epidemics will spread with lightning speed. He is infested with parasites and bitten by malarial-transmitting mosquitoes. In need of extra hands for farm work, he propagates as many children as possible, expecting quite correctly that many of them will die.

The type of constitution which evolves in response to all of these stresses will have to be one which can resist both bronchial and intestinal infections, for all the peasant's children will have been exposed to both. Immunological defenses against malaria, plague, and smallpox were discussed in a previous chapter. It has been alleged that slow growth may give some protection against tuberculosis. An efficient or, as it is sometimes called, a low rate of basal metabolism may help solve his nutritional problems. Small body size is likely to do the same thing. Devices for calcium economy, such as small bones, will be useful, too. If by some stroke of luck the peasant becomes prosperous and is able to feed and care for his children well, they will almost certainly grow up faster and, as adults, be larger than he is. This phenotypic phenomenon is known to have accompanied improvements in diet and sanitation in Japan. But selection has been at work for so long, disposing of individuals who might have been very tall, that the average stature and weight continue to be less than those of many other peoples. Evolution for adaptation to the conditions of peasant life has been in process for several thousand years and it continues today.

Agricultural conditions are not the same everywhere, to be sure. Soil varies, and crops vary. Growing rice is quite a different matter from growing bananas or yams: the rice involves producing artificial swamps, and using human manure as fertilizer. These, in turn, lead to their own particular health hazards. Thiamine deficiency is a consequence of too great a dependence upon polished rice in the diet. Yet unhusked rice cannot be stored for so long a period as polished rice, and people must eat between one harvest and the next. Furthermore, in China and Japan where rice is the preferred food, there has been a tabu against using milk and milk products, which would have made up some of the dietary deficiencies. The human imagination has imposed new burdens upon mankind while it has alleviated old ones. Food tabus have often had unfortunate results, since vitamins and trace minerals lacking in one food may be present in another which is shunned.

Diets which are rich in protein, such as meat, milk, and to a lesser extent fish, seem to be associated with populations of larger body size or greater weight, but the correlation is far from perfect. An ample amount of animal protein is just one of the necessary causes of growth. Climatic factors also enter into the equation. Perhaps the degree of exposure to contagious diseases does, too. Hunters, herdsmen, and farmers who can include meat in their diet and who live in a temperate climate are likely to be tall and heavy. Polynesians, who had plenty of fish, an ample amount of calcium from taro, whose islands were cooled by the trade winds, and who were so isolated as to escape the spread of contagions, attained a large size. So did many farmers of northwestern Europe who kept dairy cattle, sheep, and pigs, raised a variety of grains and root crops, and who poached the game on their lord's manor as much as they dared. So did the Indian tribes of the eastern United States who continued to hunt extensively even after they put their wives to work cultivating maize and a few other crops. Such peoples were able to escape the full force of the varied stresses imposed upon the peasantry of warmer regions.

LACTASE AND DAIRYING

Rather recently, it has been suggested that the practice of dairying has led to still further evolutionary changes in some human populations. All infant mammals, of course, produce the enzyme lactase which enables them to metabolize milk sugar. After being weaned, however, they no longer need this enzyme and cease to synthesize it. It has been found that some adult humans, as well, are lactase deficient and may even suffer from gastric distress when they drink milk. Cheese and butter, although extracted from milk, contain little or no lactase and can be safely consumed. As we have gained more knowledge of the physiology of non-Europeans, it has been noted that in many populations lactase deficiency is common or almost universal among adults in many parts of the world, although it is rare in the United States. In many populations, too, milk is never consumed except by unweaned babies. It would be most interesting to find out the degree to which the cultural practice is related to the biological characteristics.

McCracken (1971) has reviewed the available data bearing upon this problem. Studies have been made in many countries, but the procedures used have been far from uniform, and the samples are often very small. However, such data as exist are, for the most part, in agreement with the hypothesis that selection has operated, in milk-drinking populations, to increase the precentage of adults who retain the ability to synthesize the enzyme lactase. Such diverse peoples as native Australians, American Indians, East Asians, and non-milk-drinking African Negroes become, in most cases, lactase deficient as they grow up. So do a majority of the American Colored, whose African ancestors came from tribes where milk was not consumed by adults. Some of the Nilotic and other dairying tribes of East Africa, however, include only a minority of lactase-deficient adults. In this they resemble most Europeans, whose ancestors have been drinking milk for thousands of years. Contrary evidence comes from India, however, where a few studies of very small samples indicate a high frequency of lactase deficiency despite the widespread use of milk in that country.

The practice of dairying cannot have started before the Neolithic and has never been established among many peoples even today. Milk drinking is far from universal even among nations where cheese and butter are commonly used. Evolution has not yet had more than a few hundred generations at most in which to operate, selecting for survival and parentage those who retained the infantile or predomorphic trait of synthesizing lactase—if, indeed, the selection hypothesis proves, after more extensive studies, to be accurate. Should it turn out to be the correct explanation of population differences in this ability, we can be more sure than ever of the vital importance of cultural practices in guiding the direction of human evolution.

SELECTION FOR URBAN LIFE

Life in a peasant village subjects the individual to forms of selection which had not affected his ancestors, but life in any city, until about a century ago, accentuated such selection still more. Cities grew up as centers of trade and government by the beginning of the Bronze Age some 5,000 years ago in the Near East. Contagions which might affect the countryside were certain to decimate the cities. Typically more than half of any children born would die within a year. The number of interpersonal contacts in a city is bound to be much greater than in a village, and such contacts help to spread disease. Urban sanitation, until very recently, was totally unthought of. People might try to be clean, but the water they used simply spread disease. Until antiseptic sanitary procedures were adequately developed, no city could maintain its population except by constant immigration from the countryside.

Yet the ambitious, the adventurous, and the clever continued to stream in, for the opportunities and amusements of urban as distinct from farming life have long been known. Plague after plague would take its toll, but still people continued to come. Selection for resistance to one disease after another began to evolve, whereas muscular strength, useful both in farming and hunting, was far less necessary for making a living as a craftsman, a trader, or a clerk. Measles, chicken pox, and many other diseases which were highly lethal in earlier days became, as time went on, nuisances rather than selective factors among populations which had been exposed to them for many generations.

Stoudt (1961), analyzing data collected by Marett, characterizes the slum dweller of Colombo, Ceylon, as differing markedly from the rural inhabitants of that island in a number of ways which illustrate how selection has operated in a typical Oriental city. These people have long legs and are not depressed in stature; they are lean, with narrow chests and shoulders; and they have short arms. They are more brachycephalic than other Ceylonese but have long narrow faces and large noses. The effects of nutritional deficiencies and the heterosis resulting from mixed ancestry seem to be in conflict here. We must remember that people who live in cities must buy their food, whereas their country cousins grow their own. It must be remembered, too, that until the most recent times affluence has been almost as rare as sanitation in cities.

Constant exposure to hunger and disease have been the fate of most city dwellers for hundreds of years. Populations which had not been so exposed lacked the opportunity to evolve adequate resistance to many diseases. After the introduction of such contagions Polynesians and American Indians died in great numbers.

ADAPTING TO HIGH ALTITUDE

The selection of alleles which enhance resistance to disease may but need not alter one's exterior appearance. It is, nevertheless, an example of continuing human evolution, and as new types of microorganisms evolve, we may anticipate that further evolution of the same sort will take place in the future. Evolution of adaptation to life at high altitudes involves both anatomical and physiological change. Populations which have been native to plateaus or mountain valleys two miles or more above sea level are subjected to a number of special stresses. Although there are plenty of mountain ranges and even more isolated peaks which exceed such altitudes, there are only two regions of large extent which do so. These are the areas centering on Tibet, between India and China, and the Andean massif stretching from Ecuador into Bolivia. Both have been inhabited for some thousands of years, but certainly not for tens of thousands. Adaptation to extreme altitudes must be a recent acquisition, separately attained in Asia and in South America. An Andean is shown in Figure 14–3.

FIGURE 14-3. An Andean Anthropologist, Dr. Roberto Frisancho (Photo: Palmer Studio)

As we know, atmospheric air pressure decreases as the height above sea level increases. There are fewer molecules of oxygen per cubic centimeter, and they do not transfuse so readily from the lungs into the bloodstream. Yet any reduction in the supply of oxygen to the tissues is disastrous to all physiological functions, the nervous system suffering first. The primary reaction is an increase in the heartbeat and the speed of breathing, but this soon becomes self-defeating. The heart tires, and excessive breathing results in expelling carbon dioxide from the blood. Yet carbon dioxide serves as a stimulus for breathing, which consequently becomes difficult. Bodily activity becomes exhausting, and one feels dizzy and nauseated. It is difficult to eat. At night, the temperature falls rapidly, and it is difficult to sleep, too. If, however, one survives, the body is stimulated to produce greater and greater quantities of hemoglobin. This process takes a few days, or at most a few weeks. The addition of hemoglobin permits more efficient transport of all available oxygen to the various tissues of the body, thus overcoming the problems of living at a high altitude to some extent. The physiological plasticity of most human beings is great enough to permit this adjustment. We can accommodate to the problem of living at altitudes of between two and three miles above sea level.

The problem of reproducing is more difficult to solve. The discovery of silver mines at Potosi in Bolivia attracted both Spaniards and Indians to the place, and a large city grew up at an altitude of three miles. Yet fifty-three years passed before the first Spanish baby was born, although the Indians continued to reproduce as regularly as ever (Monge, 1948). There is evidence that sexual desire and sexual ability are reduced by any considerable decrease in air pressure. There is even more evidence that mothers experience varied difficulties in completing their pregnancies with success. Oxygen does not transfuse so readily through the placental walls at high altitudes as it does at sea level. McClung (1969) has found that placentas are more extensive, proportionately heavier, and display more signs of damage in Cuzco, 11,000 feet above sea level, than at Lima, which is close to sea level. She also reports that birth weight is reduced and neonatal mortality increased among humans and other mammals born in the Andes. Populations cannot become established in such regions until they have acquired the ability to reproduce as well as to work.

Nor is attaining adulthood an easy task in the Andean highlands. Hanna (1968) finds that young boys, who shepherd the flocks, are exposed to more severe stress than are adults. Physical growth is slow; the adolescent spurt in stature and the attainment of full sexual dimorphism are both delayed by several years beyond sea-level norms; but there is an accelerated development in chest dimensions (Frisancho and Baker 1970).

A broad deep chest and a lowered diaphragm, permitting lungs of larger volume, is very useful for continued life at a height of 12,000 feet or more. An expansion of lung surface by increased size of the alveoli, where gaseous exchange takes place, and dilation of the capillaries are helpful, too. The lungs of animals and men native to such altitudes have these features (Hurtado, 1932). Some of the adaptations found among the Indians of the Andes are presented in Table 12. These men, though short in stature and not

TABLE 12. SOME PHYSIOLOGICAL ADAPTATIONS OF MEN LIVING AT
HIGH ALTITUDES IN PERU.

	Sea Level	5,000 Meters (3 miles)
Oxygen Pressure	100 %	60 %
Total Blood Volume	5,000 ccs.	7,000 ccs.
Total Hemoglobin	750 grms	1,500 grms
Thoracic Volume	10,100 ccs.	12,150 ccs.
Lung Blood Volume	750 ccs.	1,400 ccs.
Lung Hemoglobin	110 grms	300 grms

heavy in build, have chest dimensions which are well above average in proportion to their size. This has been noted especially for children. Survival during the period of growth is what really matters for the continuance of the stock. It should be noted, too, that abnormal hemoglobins are, so far as we know, quite lacking among any mountain-dwelling populations. Any degree of anemia would be lethal at high altitudes, and with mosquitoes absent malaria is not a problem. Stature appears to be irrelevant. Many Himalayan peoples are tall, in contrast to the Andeans, but large chests and enhanced vital capacity are characteristic of both.

It is worth noting, too, that the native populations of both areas are of Mongoloid affinity. Rather sturdy body build and broad chests are commonly found in the various races which are subsumed under this name. These characteristics are adaptive for cold climates as well as rarefied air. It is quite possible that they may be regarded as preadaptations for living at high altitudes. For, although tribes of Mongoloid and of Caucasoid ancestry are both found in the Himalayas, Coon (1958) states that Mongoloids alone inhabit the higher valleys and plateaus. This could be a historic accident. It would seem just as probable, however, that this geographical distribution reflects a greater degree of inherited ability to overcome the stresses imposed by life at great heights on the part of the Mongoloids. In any case, the final and most vital steps in reaching such an adaptation are another example of recent and continuing human evolution.

THE POLYNESIANS

The technological achievements of human culture have made it possible to exploit such forbidding habitats as high mountain ranges and elevated plateaus and have provided the incentive to invade such areas. Such achievements also led to the populating of other and more pleasant parts of the world, such as Polynesia. We have mentioned that these islands, so far-flung throughout the South Pacific, were not inhabited until a few thousand years ago and that their populations differ in many respects from those of other tropical regions. Adequate shipping and navigational skills, as well as the will and stamina to undertake most hazardous voyages, were required before they could be reached and settled. Suggs (1960) provides evidence to support the thesis that the southward expansion of the Chinese during the Bronze Age provided the stimulus for such voyages. Southern China and the large islands near Southeast Asia supplied the migrants themselves, and large outrigger canoes with sails supplied the transportation. Settlers frequently sailed in fleets of such canoes, taking with them such animals as dogs, pigs, and chickens, and the various food plants which they hoped to grow in their new homes. The Maori tradition asserts that seven canoes brought their ancestors to New Zealand, and similar stories are told in other islands. These tales need not be taken at their face value but do suggest the small number of original migrants needed to populate the different island groups.

The technical skills of this population were of a high order, so that at the time of first contact with Europeans, most of the islands were densely populated. The natives were uniformly described as large, healthy, and vigorous to the point of exuberance. Their beauty was often extolled: a glance at Figure 14–4 shows why. Polynesians are distinctive in allele frequencies, although in some characteristics, such as size, they may differ only phenotypically from a number of the tribes of Southeast Asia. They escaped the prevalence of infection, the constant humid heat, and the inadequacy of diet which are characteristic of that area. We do not know how numerous the actual migrants into Polynesia were, but the degree of similarity in physical type which extends from Hawaii to New Zealand suggests that there were not many. Uniform selection throughout the area is an alternate or supplementary hypothesis. Certainly, selection must have operated during the period of exploration and settlement, which called for physical strength, athletic skill, and daring. These characteristics were still highly prized among Polynesians in recent times. Perhaps the evolution of the Polynesian race is the consequence of selection for such factors. Whether or not this speculation is accurate, the evolution took place.

Until recently, it was orthodox to consider the Polynesians a

FIGURE 14-4. Two Polynesians (Photos: Edwin Ferdon)

trihybrid population originating from a mixture of Caucasoids, Mongoloids, and Negroids. Such genetic data as are available lend no support to this notion, nor do phenotypic data require it. One might conjecture a contribution to Polynesian ancestry from some pre-Mongoloid and partly Mongoloid populations of Southeast Asia, or Japan, or both. Certain aspects of Polynesian culture suggest contacts with India, but there is little or no evidence of gene flow from that country. The Polynesian languages are affiliated with those of the New Hebrides in Melanesia—islands inhabited by groups having some resemblances to the natives of Australia. Contributions to the Polynesian gene pool from all of these sources are perfectly possible.

Migration, the intermixing of previously distinct populations, and the expansion of some breeding groups at the expense of others have taken place on a growing scale during the past few thousand, and especially the past few hundred, years. Insofar as these phenomena involve a change in allele frequencies, either for the species as a whole or for any of its constituent parts, they may properly be included as aspects of continuing human evolution. All of them have involved changes in allele frequencies on numerous occasions. The expansion of agricultural populations, such as those of the Near East, later of China, and during the past dozen generations of Europe, has been mentioned in previous chapters. During the present century, with the spread of sanitation and industrialization, populations of northwest European origin have not increased in numbers as rapidly as those of Latin America and Asia. Alleles for reduced pigmentation have become so well established in so many parts of the world, however, that we may predict with some confidence that their frequency will remain higher than it was before the great overseas migrations from Europe.

RELAXATION OR REDIRECTION OF SELECTION?

It has often been maintained that natural selection has been relaxed as the protective screen of culture has been spread between the human species and the natural environment. Certainly, it is true that each technological revolution has been followed by a very considerable population increase. Exploiting new resources and new sources of energy makes it possible for more people to live in any given region. Obviously, many individuals who would have died, or who would never have been born, can and do live and reproduce if more food becomes available and if diseases are mastered. Does this not imply a lessening in the pressure of natural selection? The question may seem reasonable, but in fact it is based upon false premises and is therefore misleading. As any species shifts its ecological position, selective stresses are redirected. Millions of years ago, in our ancestral line, selective pressure favoring the ability to grasp branches with our toes was relaxed—but, at the same time, selective pressure favoring the ability to manufacture tools was increased. In more recent millennia selective pressure favoring abilities useful for the Paleolithic life style may well have been relaxed—but, as the examples given in the last few pages indicate, it has increased in other directions. Were we, today, as well adapted to the circumstances of the Paleolithic as our ancestors used to be, we would be even less well adapted to the circumstances of today. It is perfectly possible that, as Post (1962) maintains, myopia is more frequent in agricultural than in hunting populations; but if this is true, redirection rather than overall relaxation in selection is illustrated.

Gene pools semi-isolated from one another exist in all large populations, and these are more than likely to have birth rates and death rates which vary to some degree from one another. The inability of slave populations to reproduce their numbers has already been mentioned in another context. In nonindustrialized societies which lack slavery but in which some families are very much better off than others, the well-to-do are often found to increase disproportionately in numbers, since they can take better care of their children. This was true until recently in China, for instance (Ta Chen, 1947). In some other countries, however, property-owning and other prosperous families have fewer children than do poor people. This is standard practice among the middle classes of industrialized societies. A large number of children may cost money which the parents would prefer to save or invest in order to better their position. In order to preserve the status of a family in later generations, they have often preferred to have as few heirs as possible so that property need not be divided. Many parents feel that their children need higher education but that they cannot afford to send more than one or two to college.

ARE WE BECOMING MORE STUPID?

As public health and general prosperity have improved, the death rate of children born to poor parents has declined. The genetic contribution of the wealthier classes to the next generation becomes proportionately smaller than that of the poorer classes. In the United States, for instance, the wives of professional men and business proprietors have given birth to an average of two children by the time they have ceased reproducing, while the wives of farm laborers have given birth to an average of four children. Insofar as genetic differences between social classes exist, it can be expected that allele frequencies will shift under such circumstances. Sometimes, of course, genetic differences do exist. In the United States, for instance, the descendants of early settlers have had better opportunities to accummulate wealth than later arrivals and their offspring. Most of the early settlers came from the British Isles and other parts of northwestern Europe. Many of the later migrants came from other parts of Europe. People of African, American Indian, and Asian ancestry have had the fewest opportunities. At the present time it seems certain that genetic characteristics typical of northwestern Europe are decreasing in frequency in the United States, just as during the preceding few centuries they were increasing in the world at large. In both cases social circumstance rather than biological virtue is the responsible agent.

There exists a rather widespread fear that one current trend in human evolution is a decrease in the frequency of whatever alleles are involved in a high order of intelligence. Are we becoming more and more stupid as the generations pass? Since adaptation to our ecological circumstances involves using our minds to such a great extent, such a trend would be unfortunate. There are great difficulties in attempting to answer this question, but many scholars have tried, nevertheless. Proper definition of terms is one difficulty. As the previous chapter showed, we do not really know what intelligence is, and we have found out that intelligence tests are most imperfect. The assumption most commonly made by those who fear that we are becoming less intelligent is that the upper or well-to-do classes owe their favored position to better genetic endowment and that the lower or poorer classes are genetically less well equipped. Since the latter are at present increasing in numbers more rapidly than the former, average intelligence is bound to fall. The propositions involved in this hypothesis need to be examined.

Since the British population is ethnically more homogeneous than that of the United States, tests made in Great Britain give results which can be interpreted more clearly. Distortions which might be caused by contrasting rich, Protestant, Yankee professionals with poor, Catholic, Indian farm hands are possible in this country but impossible there. Several sets of intelligence tests given to school children in Scotland provide data from which it is possible to draw interesting conclusions. In all the tests, as a glance at Table 13 demonstrates, the children of professional people and large employers made the highest scores, those of salaried employees the next highest, while the children of unskilled wage earners

TABLE 13. INTELLIGENCE TEST SCORES OF CHILDREN IN SCOTLAND. (Scottish Council for Research in Education, 1949 and 1953.)

Father's Occupation	Sibship Size	Persons per Room	Mean Score of Children
Professional and large employer			52
Salaried employee			48
		<1	47
Non-manual wage earner			44
Small employer			43
	1,2		41
		1–2	39
Skilled manual wage earner	3,4		37
Farmer			36
		2–3	34
Semi-skilled manual wage earner			33
Agricultural worker			32
Unskilled manual wage earner	5,6	3+	31
	7,8		29
	9+		26

and agricultural workers made the lowest scores. The greatest percentage of really feeble-minded children were found in families of the poorer classes, too. But there were some other correlations. Single children scored higher than those with brothers and sisters: in fact, the greater the number of siblings, the worse the score. Those who lived in homes which had fewer occupants than rooms did well, while those who came from homes which had three occupants for each room did very poorly. Farmers' children did rather poorly in contrast with those of city dwellers. If, in fact, the results of these tests give a true picture of the distribution in the population of genetic systems controlling intelligence, one would have to expect a decline in intelligence as time went by.

But in fact, just the opposite trend has been demonstrated in Scotland. More than 90 percent of eleven-year-old Scottish school children were given a verbal intelligence test in 1932, and the same proportion were given the same test fifteen years later. The average score attained in the earlier year was 34.5, but in the later year it had risen to 36.7. We should mention that the later generation of girls had an average score three points higher than the earlier generation, whereas boys improved their score only half as much.

Those who claim that intelligence tests measure innate, genetically determined intellectual ability would have to conclude that the Scottish population, at least, is evolving in the direction of increased intelligence. The sudden appearance of a difference between the braininess of boys and girls, the lower scores of rural children in general, and the correlations between high scores and small families, as well as low scores and overcrowded households, all indicate that environmental factors must influence the ability to score well on intelligence tests. In any case, there is no evidence that the human species is becoming more stupid as a consequence of differential birth rates.

As a matter of fact, there is no real reason to expect evolution to proceed in that direction. While it is true that, in a society with a structure such as ours, those who are intellectually most gifted do not have as many children as do people of average mentality, it is also true that those who are least intelligent have few or no offspring. The feeble-minded are rarely in a position to reproduce at all. Any combination of alleles which may be responsible for their unfortunate condition are eliminated from the gene pool almost as rapidly as they appear. Very commonly, severe mental disability is accompanied by, and doubtless in part is an aspect of, severe body disability. The reproductive performance of those who suffer from such combined misfortune is far below average, while the death rate is high. Just as in the case of the sickle-cell trait, a condition of balanced polymorphism exists; elimination of alleles at both ends of the scale is constant. But, as long as external circumstances are constant, the population average remains the same. Evolution will occur only as these circumstances change.

RECENT MIGRATIONS

The very extensive migrations of the past few centuries have brought millions of people into environments quite unlike those in which their ancestors grew up. The results have varied. The selective forces at work upon the descendants of farmers who came to live in cities have already been discussed. Overseas migration is quite a different matter, since, even today, it is more difficult to move from California to Switzerland than to walk from a Swiss city back to one's home village. Both trips may take an equal length of time, but the longer one is much more expensive. The incentives must be great to persuade people to cut themselves off forever from their kinfolk and friends, their accustomed ways and familiar surroundings. We might expect that certain personality types would be attracted to settle in distant lands, whereas others would prefer to get along as best they might at home. Indeed, it used to be common folklore in rural New England that only the ne'er-do-wells and the shiftless failures went out West, whereas in the West the orthodox dogma was that only the bold and the strong had come, leaving the timid and the weaklings at home.

We might expect, too, that certain physical characteristics would be more favored among migrants. A survey by Martin (1949) showed that young men who migrated from one county to another within England have a greater average stature than those who remained at home. Japanese who migrated to Hawaii tend to be slightly taller than their relatives who remained at home (Shapiro, 1939). Since migrants had usually left home before the completion of their growth period, it is possible that better conditions in the places to which they moved led to extra growth. We do not know.

But we dare not assume in an offhand manner that migrants are genetically a perfectly random and therefore representative sample of the population from which they were derived. They are known to be nonrepresentative demographically and sociologically. Young men are those most likely to migrate. Those least likely to inherit property have an added incentive to migrate, as have members of large families. In Ticino Canton of Switzerland sibships which contained no migrants averaged 4.6 members; those which included one migrant averaged 5.5 members; and those having two or more averaged 7.2 members. People who already have kinfolk in their place of destination are more apt to go than those who can expect no one to turn to in case of emergency. Sometimes entire families move.

From the data collected so far differences in allele frequencies between migrants and their cousins at home appear to be minimal. My own studies have shown that the distribution of ABO and Rh blood types among the American-born Japanese of Seattle is the same as that found in the parts of Japan from which their parents came. Persons with Irish surnames in Seattle have the same frequencies at these loci as the Irish of Dublin, and those with Scottish surnames have the same as those of Scots in Edinburgh. Migration provides an opportunity for new selective forces to operate on a population and may involve some selection at the beginning. But from the point of view of continuing human evolution, its greatest role seems to be that of draining old gene pools and creating new ones.

Migrants to another land have a hard job finding mates from their own hometown. It is common practice for them to seek out, if they can, spouses of similar background. But even this may be difficult. As generations pass, there is a strong tendency for old barriers to gene flow to break down. The awareness of ethnic identity with the land of origin decays, and the girl next door seems more attractive than the girl who would have been next door had grandpa stayed home.

Most of the migrants from Ticino to California married girls from the same canton or girls whose parents had come from there. Many of their children married Italians, and some married Irish or German Catholics. But the third generation rarely marries into its ancestral group: the Italian Swiss colony in California is dissolving into the melting pot. The bonds of religion and preferences for spouses of one's own social class replace the bonds of ethnic origin. This process goes on at varying rates among different groups, but it always goes on. A majority of students in most classes which I have taught know of ancestors from more than one country. In Hawaii, as census records show, the most rapidly expanding group of the population is that of mixed Asian, Hawaiian, and European ancestry.

Modern migrations have taken millions of people very far from home, and they have met and begun to breed with others whose ancestry had been separated from their own for many hundreds of generations. Several of the races listed in Chapter Twelve are among the products of such intermixture. The Ladino, the American Colored, and the South Pacific are still receiving genetic contributions from outsiders. They are still in the process of evolving characteristic allele frequencies, and it is impossible to predict what these may be. Indeed, it is impossible to predict whether genetic equilibrium will ever be established among any of these groups at any time in the future. Any one of them may merge into still other groups before such a balance is attained. The Ladino and American Colored groups are merging at the moment. Meanwhile, adaptation to new environments continues to be as necessary in groups of recently mixed as in groups of anciently mixed origin. There is evidence, as previously mentioned, that the incidence of the sickle-cell allele in the American Colored population of the United States is less than might be expected from their estimated degree of European ancestry.

Not all cases of race mixture produce recognizable new breeding populations which require taxonomic recognition. In a great many instances gene flow between one population and another is known to take place without causing a new isolate. In colonial days or even somewhat later in the United States, people of European origin joined Indian tribes and left descendants among them. An individual of 100 percent pure aboriginal ancestry would now be hard to find and harder to identify. People of Indian and African ancestry have passed into the group commonly labeled White, despite the caste barriers. The frequency of alleles for epicanthic eyefolds should be noticeably greater among the members of the next generation in the United States than it was before, because of Japanese wives brought home by servicemen. The number of blue-eyed babies in Tokyo will rise, a generation from now, when the recessive alleles introduced after 1945 recombine in the matings which give rise to the second filial generation. But such trickles between one gene pool and another are not creating new races.

In fact, as travel becomes easier, we may expect the present racial divisions within the world's population to be submerged by an increasing flow of genes between what have been separate groups. Perhaps a whole set of new races will evolve in response to new environmental pressures. Perhaps if the current drive for technological identity throughout the world creates the same sort of environment in all places, there will be an even mixture of existing allele frequencies everywhere. Should this be so, there would be some interesting alterations in the phenotypic frequencies of recessive traits. At present there is a concentration of alleles for blue eyes in populations of European origin, which comprise about one-fourth of the world's inhabitants. Among them the allele frequency may be estimated at 60 percent and the phenotypic frequency at 36 percent, or 270 million people. The same number of alleles evenly distributed throughout the world would give a frequency of 15 percent and a phenotypic frequency of 2.25 percent, or 67.5 million people. The reader for his own amusement may care to make similar calculations concerning color blindness, the Rh negative factor, or other genetic traits. The breakdown of genetic isolates always provides new phenotypic frequencies upon which selection can operate in the continuing process of evolution.

Sources and Suggested Readings

BAKER, P. T.
1966   Ecological and Physiological Adaptation in Indigenous South Americans, in *The Biology of Human Adaptability*, edited by P. T. Baker and J. S. Weiner. Clarendon Press, Oxford.

BOAS, F.
1911   *Changes in Bodily Form of Descendants of Immigrants.* Government Printing Office, Washington, D.C.

COON, C. S.
1955   Some Problems of Human Variability and Natural Selection in Climate and Culture. *American Naturalist*, **89**, 257–280.
1958   An Anthropo-geographic Excursion Around the World. Natural Selection in Man. *Memoir 86*, American Anthropological Association.
1962   *The Origin of Races.* Knopf, New York.

EHRICH, R. W. and C. S. COON
1947   Occipital Flattening Among the Dinarics. *American Journal of Physical Anthropology*, new series, **6**, 181–186.

EWING, J. F.
1950   *Hyperbrachycephaly as Influenced by Cultural Conditioning.* Papers of the Peabody Museum, **23**, no. 2.

FRISANCHO, A. R. and P. T. BAKER
1970   Altitude and Growth: A Study of the Patterns of Physical Growth of a High Altitude Peruvian Quechua Population. *American Journal of Physical Anthropology*, new series, **32**, 279–292.

HANNA, J. M.
1968   *Cold Stress and Microclimate in the Quechua Indians of Southern Peru.* Appendix H, in Occasional Papers in Anthropology, no. 1. Pennsylvania State University, University Park.

HULSE, F. S.
   1968   Migration and Cultural Selection in Human Genetics.
          The Anthropologist, Special Volume, 1–21, Delhi.

HURTADO, A.
   1932   Respiratory Adaptation in the Indians Native to the
          Peruvian Andes. *American Journal of Physical Anthro-
          pology*, **17**, 137–165.

HUXLEY, J. S.
   1955   Evolution, Cultural and Biological. *Yearbook of An-
          thropology*. Wenner-Gren Foundation, New York.

KATZ, S. H., ed.
   1970   Symposium on Human Adaptation. *American Journal
          of Physical Anthropology*, new series, **32**, 221–319.

LASKER, G. W.
   1946   Migration and Physical Differentiation. *American
          Journal of Physical Anthropology*, new series, **4**, 273–
          300.

MARTIN, W. J.
   1949   *The Physique of Young Adult Males*. Medical Research
          Council Memorandum, no. 20. Her Majesty's Station-
          ery Office, London.

McCLUNG, J.
   1969   *Effects of High Altitude on Human Birth*. Harvard
          University Press, Cambridge.

McCRACKEN, R. D.
   1971   Lactase Deficiency: An Example of Dietary Evolution.
          Current Anthropology.

MONGE, C.
   1948   *Acclimatization in the Andes*. Johns Hopkins Univer-
          sity Press, Baltimore.

NEWMAN, M. T.
   1960   Adaptations in the Physique of American Aborigines to
          Nutritional Factors. *Human Biology*, **32**, 288–313.
   1962   Evolutionary Changes in Body Size and Head Form in
          American Indians. *American Anthropologist*, **64**, 237–
          257.

OSBORNE, R. H. and F. V. DE GEORGE
>1959 *Genetic Basis of Morphological Variation: An Evaluation and Application of the Twin Study Method.* Harvard University Press, Cambridge.

POST, R.
>1962 Population Differences in Vision Acuity. *Eugenics Quarterly,* **9,** 189–212.

SCOTTISH COUNCIL FOR RESEARCH IN EDUCATION
>1949 *The Trend of Scottish Intelligence.* University of London Press, London.
>1953 *Social Implications of the 1947 Scottish Mental Survey.* University of London Press, London.

SEKLA, B. and F. SOUKUP
>1969 Inheritance of the Cephalic Index. *American Journal of Physical Anthropology,* new series, **30,** 137–140.

SHAPIRO, H. L.
>1939 *Migration and Environment.* Oxford University Press, New York.

STOUDT, H.
>1961 *The Physical Anthropology of Ceylon.* Ceylon Museum Ethnographic Series, no. 2, Colombo.

SUGGS, R. C.
>1960 *The Island Civilizations of Polynesia.* New American Library, New York.

SUZUKI, H.
>1960 Changes in the Skull Features of the Japanese People from Ancient to Modern Times. *Selected Papers of the Fifth International Congress of Anthropological and Ethnological Sciences,* Philadelphia, 717–724.

TA CHEN
>1947 *Population in Modern China.* University of Chicago Press, Chicago.

WEIDENREICH, F.
>1945 The Brachycephalization of Recent Mankind. *Southwestern Journal of Anthropology,* **1,** 1–54.

CHAPTER 15

Natural History and Laboratory Analysis

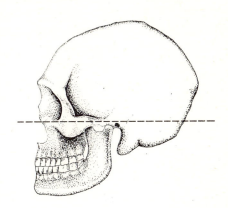

EXPERIMENTS IN HUMAN PHYSIOLOGY

Removing his clothes, the Australian rolled them up in a ball for a pillow and cheerfully lay down, naked, to go to sleep. With some reluctance, for the temperature after sunset was already falling, the young physiologist from the United States followed his example. He knew that the temperature might be expected to reach forty degrees Fahrenheit or lower before the night was over. Gauges for recording skin temperature and metabolic rate were attached to both human guinea pigs, and they tried to make themselves comfortable. The Australian had no difficulty and was soon sleeping peacefully, but the American began to shiver. He tried to control himself, but soon his teeth were chattering. He found it almost impossible to lie still. In fact, his movements awakened his companion, who observed his plight with amusement and then rolled over and went back to sleep.

These two were among a number of volunteers in an experiment designed to discover the mechanism of adjustment to cold among the native Australians. In the desert the temperature may rise and fall by fifty degrees or more every day. Aboriginally, the people who lived there wore no clothing whatsoever: extra material possessions were a bother rather than a benefit, and finding enough to eat took up most of everyone's time. They needed and had bodies adapted

449

to exercise during the heat of the day. How did they keep warm at night?

The answer provided by the experiment is that they did not waste body heat by radiating it to the outside world. The skin temperature on the physiologist's feet after he took off his shoes rose and fell more than once during the night but was never less than eighty-six degrees Fahrenheit. The Australian had no shoes to take off, and his foot's skin temperature fell steadily from seventy-three to forty-five degrees. The capillaries which bring blood close to the surface of the body contracted, blood almost ceased to run through them, and the vital organs within his body remained warm. When he awoke in the morning and began to exercise, the capillaries expanded again. In contrast, the American continued to lose the body heat which his circulatory system brought to the surface in the futile attempt to keep his skin warm. Furthermore, after falling, the American's metabolism rose to a higher rate than ever, whereas that of the native of the desert remained not only lower but much more regular. His physiology is either phenotypically adjusted or genetically adapted for the sort of life which his ancestors have lived for a thousand generations.

This experiment (Hammel *et al.*, 1959) and others like it have shown how the human body can operate under conditions of climatic stress. Baker (1958) tested forty pairs of American White and American Colored soldiers matched for size, weight, body build, and thickness of the layer of subcutaneous fat by having them exercise nude in a very hot desert. He found that body temperature rose more rapidly among the Colored soldiers: in other words, their bodies suffered a greater strain under these conditions. He also found that the average White absorbed 13 percent more solar radiation after his body was tanned than it had before. The amount of absorption of solar radiation by the skin of the American Colored soldiers increased by only 6 percent, since it was so much darker to begin with. As these experiments show, very dark skins reflect too little heat from the body. Heat stroke and death may be the result of overheating. Schickele (1947) has reported from examining army medical records that the greater a man's relative body weight, the more susceptible he was to fatal heat stroke.

The combination of a very dark skin and a thick-set body or one with much subcutaneous fat is not very functional for active work in a hot desert. Newman (1956) found that American Colored soldiers have, on average, substantially less subcutaneous fat than American White soldiers. Dupertuis (1948) noted that men of spare, lean body build have a greater volume of blood per pound of weight than burlier men and especially than men who tend to become fat. Extra liquid content in the body can act as a reserve to enable more sweating and less rapid dehydration under hot dry conditions. Information derived from experiment, from measurements, and from the study of records combines to indicate something of the nature of climatic adaptation in the human species. In attacking any problem the physical anthropologist must seek for knowledge in the laboratory and the field, by giving tests and taking measurements, by examining, abstracting, and analyzing all sorts of records.

Each new fragment of knowledge, each increase in the depth of our understanding of the processes which shape the human body and determine its reactions leads to further questions. Discovering the way in which the Australian natives protect themselves against the chill of night does not, as yet, tell us whether the mechanisms involved are inborn or individually acquired. The environment, we know, molds the phenotype as well as selecting genotypes for death or survival. These are two very distinct processes which we must not confuse. We will have to test many individuals of mixed ancestry and all the members of a number of families in order to find out whether there is a genetic basis for the ability to contract the skin capillaries. Nor do we know yet what mechanisms are involved in the greater tolerance to humid heat which Negroes appear to have in comparison to Europeans. The prevalence of very dark skin color in so many parts of the torrid zone of the Old World still needs to be explained. To say that it exemplifies Gloger's rule may be true but does not answer the question. We need more experiments.

In 1950 Coon, Garn, and Birdsell suggested, in their stimulating book *Races*, that climatic adaptation had played a major role in the evolution of human diversity. Since that time more and more studies have been made, both in the field and in the laboratory, in order to determine the extent to which this hypothesis should be accepted. As this work continues, it is becoming clear that not all of their provocative hypotheses can be accepted. Steegman (1965, 1970) tested the idea that the broad smooth face, with few sharp projections, which is found so commonly among Mongoloids, is adapted to life in the Arctic, and he has not been able to confirm it at all. Both in Michigan and in Hawaii he subjected volunteers of European and Japanese ancestry to frigid temperatures with their faces exposed. He measured, with great care, the degree to which any parts of the face projected; and he measured, with great care, the temperature of the skin before and at the end of exposure to cold. He found, as a result, that temperature is related to subcutaneous fat thickness rather than to any aspects of facial shape. The suggestion that climate engineered the shape of the Mongoloid face was plausible: it was also testable, and the tests indicate that we will have to look for some other explanation. Careful measurements under controlled conditions were the method of choice for this test.

ANTHROPOMETRY

Interest in the extent of human biological diversity is hardly new, but using measurements to record its type and extent dates from the late eighteenth century. Petrus Camper, a Dutch anthropologist, measured the degree of the facial angle in order to show the amount of prognathism of a skull. His technique was to place a skull in such a position that a horizontal line passed through the ear hole and the nasal spine. Another line was drawn from the most forwardly projecting point of the upper jaw to the forehead and the angle between these two lines was measured. An angle of ninety degrees represented a face in which the jaw was directly below the forehead; the greater the projection of the jaw the smaller the angle. By using this angle it was possible to measure the amount of variability within any group and the difference between the averages of different groups. Thus anthropometry as a method of study began. In time Camper's technique was found rather clumsy to use and lacking in precision. In 1884, an agreement was made at a congress of the International Anthropological Association held in Frankfort to adopt another way of placing the skull in position for measurement as a standard (Garson, 1884). The Frankfort horizontal is a plane running from the top of each auditory meatus, or ear hole, through the upper margin of the lower border of each orbit. This is a very close approximation to the position in which a person will hold his head when looking directly forward, and an instrument known as a craniophore will hold the skull in this position easily. Figure 15–1 shows the difference between these horizontals.

It was not until 1838 that measurements of limb bones were taken and their relative lengths compared. In that year Humphrey

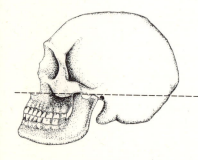
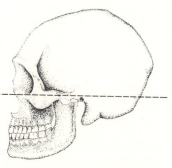

FIGURE 15-1. Two Methods of Placing Skulls in Position for Study. Note How Different the Same Skull Appears When Viewed in Different Positions. It Is Seen to the Left in the Horizontal Used by Camper; to the Right as Placed in the Frankfort Plane.

measured the humeri, radii, femora, and tibiae of twenty-five European and an equal number of Negro skeletons in order to test the widespread assertion that Negroes have long forearms and long shins. He found that the average humerus and the average femur in the two racial samples had the same proportions to total stature; but in his Negro sample, the average radius was more than 15 percent of stature, whereas among the Europeans, the average was only 14 percent. Negro tibiae averaged more than 23 percent of stature, but those of Europeans only 22 percent. Since the museums of western Europe and of the United States had quantities of skeletal remains—especially skulls—of humans from many regions of the world, other scholars during the nineteenth century devised all sorts of measurements, indices, and angles with which to describe them. A great deal of potentially useful information was collected in this way, but some men became so devoted to technique that they seem to have forgotten that their work might have any purpose except description. Von Torok (1890) enumerates 5,371 measurements, in addition to indices which may be calculated between them, and hundreds of angles just for the skull. It is said that he considered the complete measurement of one skull an adequate subject for a doctoral dissertation.

Although it reached fantastic extremes, this devotion to bones is understandable. They were available; they were hard. Their hardness facilitated precise measurements. They were easy to transport from the field: they do not decay as the soft parts of the body are likely to do. They keep their shape even when dehydrated, which is a great convenience. Furthermore, the use of bones makes it possible to compare the characteristics of modern men with those of earlier varieties. The growing interest in human evolution stimulated digging for fossils, which could not be directly compared to living people but only to bones. This led to the unfounded hope that the skeleton might be more stable and resistant to change than other parts of the body and, consequently, more useful in studying the relationships and ancestry of different racial groups. In fact, bones grow just as muscles, skin, and hair do and are subject to all sorts of external influences while they are doing so.

Washburn has been among the scholars whose experiments have demonstrated the effects of muscular activity upon the pattern of bone growth. Since the necessary experiments required the surgical removal of some muscles, he was unable to use human infants as his subjects. Rats, however, are mammals just as we are, with a growth pattern and a relation of bone to muscle which is subject to the same mechanical factors. The temporal muscle in the rat, as in man, originates from a considerable area on the side of the head, its upper margin being marked by a line or crest. It inserts on the coronoid process of the ascending ramus of the mandible, and it functions to move that bone in biting or chewing. The reader can locate this muscle by placing his fingertips to the side of his head and moving his lower jaw.

In order to find out the manner in which the temporal muscle is related to the shape of the skull, Washburn (1947) removed this muscle from one side of the head of twenty-two one-day-old rats. All survived, but they were killed and dissected several months later after they had matured. In all cases the coronoid process, already present at birth, had vanished. The temporal line on the skull had not developed. It is clear that the mechanical stress of muscular activity is essential for bones to attain their normal shapes. In ten cases neck muscles were also removed, and the nuchal crest at the rear of the skull, to which they attach, failed to grow as a result. Where loss of muscle caused less growth, the sutures between the bones of the skull lacked their ordinary complexity. On the other hand, the internal shape of the brain case was altered very little as a result of the lack of muscle. Rapid growth of the brain typically takes place at a very early age both in rats and people. The growth of the jaw muscles and the stresses which they impose upon the exterior surface of the skull do not occur until later.

The study of bones alone is clearly inadequate to an understand-ing of human evolution, racial differences, or age changes. They are, however, all that remains from archaeological excavations, and skeletons and skeletal fragments have been delivered from such sites to the laboratories of physical anthropologists by the thou-sands. Standardized techniques for taking measurements, calculat-ing indices, and recording as precisely as possible the appearance of discrete but not measureable features have been developed. Thus it becomes possible to compare the characteristics of popula-tions from different archaeological sites. The deductions which can be drawn from such studies are less revealing than studies of living peoples. They are, nevertheless, valuable, and as we learn more of the ways in which bone grows and bones grow to reach adult sizes and shapes, the raw data which formed the basis of past studies may provide us with even more valuable information, allowing us to make better deductions. It would be a pity to throw all the old bones away, just because we have learned to study man's biological characteristics in other ways.

The primary tools used in studying skeletal material are few and simple. The most important of all are a keen eye and a steady hand. Accurate observation is always vital, for we strongly suspect there are numerous characters of which the presence or absence is genetically determined. Carabelli's cusp, an extra cusp on a molar tooth, is an instance; foramina for the passage of nerves and blood vessels on the maxilla and mandible are others. At the lower end of the humerus there may or may not be a supra-condyloid process projecting from the inner surface of the bone. A foramen for the passage of a nerve and artery is located at this point among many mammals; some fossil human humeri have a groove or a hook here. This bony spike is found in less than one modern man per thousand, although it has been alleged that its frequency is ten times higher among the criminal insane. When I was a graduate student—one of twenty on the campus—our teacher was somewhat mordantly amused to find this odd excresence on my left humerus, and on that of one other graduate student in anthropology: a ratio of one in ten! The mode of inheritance of this trait or of any potentiality to develop it remains unknown.

Sliding or spreading calipers are used for measuring any relatively small linear dimension. The latter is provided with curved arms, so that it may be used to measure distances between two points separated by some protruding shape: cranial dimensions, for instance. The former is preferable in other cases. Both tools should be graduated to millimeters, since the metric scale is universally employed in anthropometry because of its greater ease in calculations. For larger dimensions an osteometric board or an anthropometer should be used.

It is simple to construct an osteometric board. A steel tape may be stretched and secured firmly upon a piece of hard wood, at one end of which a crosspiece is immovably fastened. A second cross-piece slides back and forth along the tape. The anthropometer is, in essence, a very large sliding caliper, made in four lengths of steel which can be separated or joined by firm sockets. Its stand-

---

TABLE 14. LIST OF TRADITIONAL LANDMARKS ON THE SKULL.

Bregma: the meeting point of the coronal and sagittal sutures, where the parietal and frontal bones all meet.

Basion: the median point on the anterior margin of the foramen magnum.

Frontotemporale: the medial point on the incurve of the temporal ridge.

Glabella: the most prominent point in the median line between the two browridges above the root of the nose.

Gnathion: the lowest median point on the lower border of the mandible.

Gonion: the lowest exterior point of the angle between the tooth-bearing section of the mandible and the ascending ramus.

Lambda: the meeting point of the lambdoidal and sagittal sutures, where the parietal and occipital bones all meet.

Nasion: the upper end of the internasal suture, where the nasal and frontal bones all meet.

Porion: the uppermost point of the upper margin of the ear hole.

Prosthion: the lowest point of the intermaxillary suture, between the two central incisors.

Vertex: the highest median point of a skull which is placed in the Frankfort horizontal.

Zygion: the most laterally projecting point of the cheekbones.

---

ard length is two meters or just over six feet six inches. A flexible steel tape is needed for measuring arcs and circumferences, such as that of the skull. A glass graduated cylinder of 2,000 cubic centimeters capacity is used to measure cranial capacity. Mustard seed is poured by means of a funnel through the foramen magnum into the skull until it is full. It is then emptied into the cylinder, and the volume read. Many other instruments have been devised for one special purpose or another, but those which have been mentioned previously have been in most widespread use.

Anthropologists have made international agreements with respect to the points on various bones between which measurements are taken, and they have given many such points names. As our understanding of the processes of growth has increased, many measurements which suit the purpose of some particular investigation have been devised. However the names of the points or landmarks retain their importance, and a list of those on the skull which are most commonly found in the literature is given in Table 14, in alphabetical order. It should be stressed that these are the traditional landmarks. For new purposes new points may be defined.

A few of the measurements which have been most widely used in studies of the human skull are described in Table 15, and Figure 15–2 pictures the location of landmarks on the skull.

TABLE 15. MEASUREMENTS TRADITIONALLY TAKEN ON THE SKULL.

Maximum cranial length: from glabella to the point on the median line which is furthest to the rear.

Maximum cranial breadth: the widest diameter, perpendicular to the length, which can be ascertained.

Basion-bregmatic height: from basion to bregma. This is always less than the auricular height.

Auricular height: the difference in level between porion and vertex. The skull should be placed in a craniophore to obtain this measurement. Its virtue is that it may also be obtained on living people, which basio-bregmatic height obviously cannot.

Minimum frontal breadth: the distance between the two fronto-temporalia.

Bizygomatic breadth: the distance between the two zygia.

Bigonial breadth: the distance between the two gonia.

Total face height: the distance between nasion and gnathion with the mandible in place.

Upper face height: the distance between nasion and prosthion.

Nasal height: the distance between nasion and the lower margin of the nasal opening, at the intermaxillary suture.

Nasal breadth: the greatest diameter of the nasal opening, perpendicular to the nasal height.

Nasion-basion line: the distance between these two points.

Prosthion-basion line: the distance between these two points.

Cranial capacity: one method of measurement has been given above.

Except for nasal breadth and the measurements using basion as one of the points, these measurements can be taken on living subjects. Nasal breadth on the living is measured between the alae, or fleshy wings of the nostril, which gives a far greater dimension than the diameter of the nasal opening. Locating nasion and gonion involves extra careful palpation, to be sure, but this can be learned. The thickness of the soft tissues is minimal at all the points mentioned, but it does add a few millimeters to the measurements. The use of measurements which are equally applicable to a living subject and to a bone, such as the skull, enables rather direct comparisons to be made between the sizes and shapes most prevalent in past and present generations.

Shapes and proportions are represented by various indices which state in numerical terms the relationship between one measurement and another. The cranial index is obtained by dividing the maximum breadth of the skull by its maximum length, as was stated in the previous chapter. A few of the other indices which show a considerable amount of variation between different human beings are listed in Table 16.

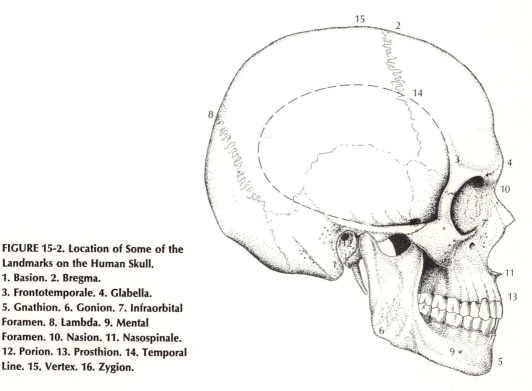

FIGURE 15-2. Location of Some of the Landmarks on the Human Skull.
1. Basion. 2. Bregma.
3. Frontotemporale. 4. Glabella.
5. Gnathion. 6. Gonion. 7. Infraorbital Foramen. 8. Lambda. 9. Mental Foramen. 10. Nasion. 11. Nasospinale.
12. Porion. 13. Prosthion. 14. Temporal Line. 15. Vertex. 16. Zygion.

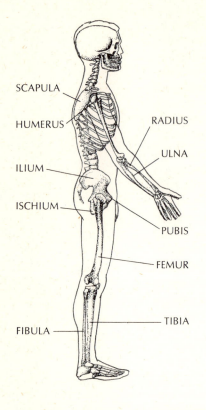

SCAPULA

HUMERUS

RADIUS

ULNA

ILIUM

ISCHIUM

PUBIS

FEMUR

TIBIA

FIBULA

FIGURE 15-3. The Position of the Bones of the Skeleton

TABLE 16. A FEW SKULL INDICES.

Length-height index: basion-bregma, or auricular height divided by maximum length.

Breadth-height index: either height, as above, divided by maximum breadth.

Cranio-facial index (called cephalo-facial on living subjects): bizygomatic breadth divided by maximum cranial (or head) breadth.

Frontal-parietal index: minimum frontal divided by maximum cranial (or head) breadth.

Gnathic index: basion-prosthion line divided by basion-nasion line.

Total facial index: total face height divided by bizygomatic breadth.

Upper facial index: upper face height divided by bizygomatic breadth.

Zygo-frontal index: minimal frontal divided by bizygomatic breadth.

Zygo-gonial index: bigonial divided by bizygomatic breadth.

Nasal index: nasal breadth divided by nasal height. This index is always very much higher on living subjects than on skulls. An index of fifty on a skull is equivalent to one of seventy-five on a living person.

In measuring the bones of the limbs, of which the positions are displayed in Figure 15–3, the maximum length is usually taken as well as diameters at various places, so that the caliber or relative stoutness of the bone may be calculated. Some populations are characterized by a certain amount of flattening of the femur, known as platymeria; or of the tibia, known as platycnemia. Measuring the antero-posterior and lateral diameters of the shafts enables one to calculate indices which show the degree of such flattening. The maximum diameter of the head of the femur, which articulates into the acetabulum of the pelvis, may be of assistance in determining sex, for it is almost always larger among adult males in any population. The characteristics of the pelvis are naturally much more influenced by sex, females usually having pelves which are broader relative to the anterior-posterior diameter as shown in Figure 15–4. The pelvic brim index represents the shape by comparing these diameters. Other sex differences include greater proportionate breadth of the sacrum, a wider pubic angle, and shallower ischiatic notches among females. All of these differences relate to the female function of childbearing.

Measurements of living individuals is in many ways a more challenging and as a rule a more fruitful activity than work with old dead bones. Only by dealing with live specimens can we observe processes at work as, for instance, in growth studies. A skull cannot talk back and does not have to be persuaded to cooperate with the investigator. Dimensions can be measured with great precision on a skull. It can be opened up so that its inner surface may be studied. A person, on the other hand, can place all sorts of obstacles in the anthropologist's way. It is only decent to explain the object of one's research to anyone kind enough to submit to rather intimate bodily investigation. For some studies captive samples may prove adequate. Soldiers under orders provided the raw material for a number of studies of climatic adaptation, for instance. Even in such cases, however, active cooperation rather than reluctant obedience is needed to complete a project successfully.

In many cases, a captive sample may be quite unrepresentative and therefore cannot be used. Soldiers are likely to be in better physical trim than other young males, since they are selected as well as trained. Hospital patients are likely to be in worse shape than the population from which they are drawn. For many studies more time and effort must be put into insuring a group's continued interest and persuading each separate individual to assist the investigator than is devoted to actual observation and measurement. But such time is well spent.

Measurements and observations should be tailored to the purposes of the research and to the necessities of the situation. This last item very definitely includes the convenience and the tabus of the subjects. It is almost always a waste of time to argue with someone who does not care to cooperate. It arouses nothing but hostility to insist that a woman undo an elaborate coiffure which

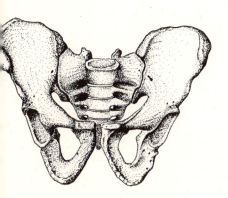
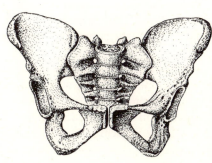

FIGURE 15-4. Male Pelvis (Left) Contrasted to Female Pelvis (Right). The Figure Indicates Sexual Dimorphism for the Sake of Child-Bearing.

has taken hours to arrange. The rules of the group concerning bodily modesty must be observed, whatever they happen to be. Moslem girls may be more reluctant to unveil their faces than American girls are to remove their bikini tops. The interruption of work hours may please some people but annoy others. These rules apply to any anthropological research done with living people, whether measuring, taking blood samples, studying nutrition, or anything else. For work in the field or for work in the laboratory people must be shown the respect due to them as human beings.

SAMPLES: RANDOM AND OTHERWISE

The problem of sample selection is a recurrent one. A sample must reflect, as accurately as possible, a defined universe. Should I wish to make a meaningful comparison between the Bushmen of South Africa and any other group, it would be more than desirable to have in my series individuals from both groups, in equivalent proportions, who differed only in one respect: that of group membership. In fact, it is quite out of the question that such samples would be obtainable. We are able to make statements concerning the Bushmen only insofar as we have sound assurance that other variables than group membership are irrelevant to the problem which is being investigated. Since we have every reason to believe that age and sex have nothing to do with the distribution of ABO blood groups, it is not necessary to take account of these two variables in comparing Bushmen and Polynesians. If, however, we find that the Polynesians are taller or heavier than Bushmen, we cannot know without further investigation whether this difference is due to diet, disease, genes, or a combination.

Shapiro (1939), in comparing Japanese in Hawaii to those in Japan, was interested in whether or not the migrants were a random sample of the population from which they were derived, or whether they had been selected with reference to any particular characteristics. The population from which they were derived was not the entire population of Japan. It was the population of the villages from which the migrants came and, most especially, the kindreds from which they originated. Japanese migrants, in his study, were quite properly compared to their own brothers and cousins back home. A further question might well be whether these families were in any sense a random sample of the Japanese population as a whole, but one of the soundest rules in research is to ask one question at a time. Too many cooks spoil the broth, and too many variables spoil research design.

In comparing the thermal insulative properties of body fat among American White and Colored populations, Baker (1959) was faced with a similar problem. American Colored soldiers have less subcutaneous fat than American White soldiers. In this they may or may not correctly represent the populations from which they are drawn. It does not matter so far as this piece of research is concerned. He selected an equal number of subjects from each population matched within one kilogram for weight, one centimeter for stature, and as closely as possible for body fat as measured by skin fold thickness. Body temperatures were measured continuously during the experiment by thermocouples at eleven points on the skin and within the rectum.

The subjects were first kept in a room with a temperature of eighty degrees Fahrenheit for an hour, then exposed to a temperature of fifty degrees for 105 minutes, then returned for fifteen minutes of warming up. The humidity was constantly maintained at 50 percent. Mean skin temperature among the Colored fell faster and further than among the White sample and recovered more slowly. In rectal temperature, a difference of the same sort was less pronounced. The Colored had a much lower variance than the White sample, despite the fact that the amount of subcutaneous fat was equally variable in the two groups. In both groups the skin temperature of the leaner individuals fell less but the rectal temperature more than the same temperature of the fatter men. The differences attributable to body fat were significantly greater among the White than among the Colored soldiers, however. This experiment was well enough designed to take account of known variables. As a result, we are in a position to make valid inferences. Had Baker attempted to compare "average" Colored soldiers with "average" White soldiers, several alternate speculations of equal plausibility would have been possible.

In 1965 I wished to test the hypothesis that sexual selection had been among the forces guiding the course of human evolution. In order to do this it was necessary to find a population which had not been much disturbed by the influx of genes from other populations, in which the cultural definition of sexual attractiveness had not altered for many generations, in which the different social classes were sharply separated, and in which marriages were arranged in accordance with well-established rules. Japan was the obvious country to pick, and it had the added convenience of being a nation where education has long been universal and where anthropology is a well-established science. The characteristic which I chose to study was skin color, because the Japanese have, for many centuries, agreed that a fair skin is sexually attractive and because the reflectance spectrophotometer is capable of recording skin color at several wavelengths in an objective numerical fashion. However, skin color alters during growth and quite possibly during adulthood too; so it was necessary to restrict the sample to individuals of more or less the same age. Skin color also deepens upon exposure to sunlight; thus it was necessary to measure it upon a part of the body which is not often exposed to sunlight. Students in high school were the obvious subjects to select, since the age-range was minimal, they were sexually mature, they were intellectually interested, and they came from all classes of society. Furthermore, schools in Japan have electric current—which is needed to operate the reflectance spectrophotometer; the students could be easily assembled; and the school officials could assist in innumerable ways. The inner surface of the upper arms was the obvious region to measure, for it is difficult to expose it to sunlight, and yet few people are embarrassed about uncovering it.

As a result of designing the project in a manner which reduced inconveniences to a minimum and took account of the known or suspected variables, I was able to record the percentage of reflectance at eight wavelengths, from red to blue, or over 500 late teenagers, both male and female, in the course of a few months. It was also possible to classify the members of the sample into subgroups by social class and geographical origin within the country, so that they might be compared. As it turned out, those whose ancestors came from northern Japan proved to have slightly fairer skin than those from southwestern Japan, which agrees with Japanese popular opinion. Those of the upper socioeconomic class were the lightest and those of the lower class the darkest, while middle-class students were intermediate in degree of pigmentation at all wavelengths in the visible spectrum; this finding supports the hypothesis that sexual selection can indeed, under the proper circumstances, lead to a concentration of the most favored genes in the most favored class. Had the problem attacked been a different one, a different project design and method of procedure would have been required. It should be noted, for instance, that the study outlined here tells us absolutely nothing about the mode of inheritance of skin color. If we seek information on this question, the work done by Harrison and Owen (1964) in Liverpool, which was briefly described in Chapter Thirteen, gives us one of the proper approaches.

NATURAL LABORATORIES

From time to time geography, the sequence of historical events, or some other factor extraneous to human biology has been found to have created a natural laboratory. We are in no position to subject human beings to laboratory control, but sometimes this is done for us and we can exploit the circumstances to the advantage of science.

A few of the populations which originated from matings between members of different races have lived in almost total isolation ever since their formation. These isolates provide us with natural laboratories. The people of Rehoboth in Southwest Africa are descended from early European settlers—mostly Dutch—and Hottentots. They were studied early in the present century by Fischer (1913). He was quite aware of the principles of Mendelian inheritance, and his work with the Rehoboth population was a pioneer attempt to apply these principles to the study of human genetics. Unfortunately knowledge of genetics was meager at that time, so that the data which he collected is scarcely amenable to analysis by the methods later developed. For instance, proper equipment for recording skin color had not been invented at the time. The existence of such simply inherited characters as blood types was unsuspected, save for the ABO system. The tools which are now available for studying process did not exist when Fischer did his work. He was therefore unable to find out the sorts of things about the biological results of race mixture which could now be discovered. This population is, however, still available for study.

The descendants of the mutineers of the *Bounty* and their Tahitian consorts have, for the most part, preferred to live in isolation, too, some on Pitcairn and others on Norfolk island in the South Pacific. Shapiro (1929, 1936) has made anthropometric studies of both these related populations and has been careful to record the circumstances under which they live. Data concerning the individual Tahitians and British who were involved is almost completely lacking, however. The assumption had to be made that they were a representative sample of the populations from which they were drawn, since this is the least improbable guess. Further study of known genetic characteristics of the living members of these isolates would probably be most enlightening, since geneologies are very well known.

The two settlements involved separated from one another several generations ago and have had little or no genetic contact since that time. The earlier ancestry of both is practically identical. A study of differences in allele frequencies which may exist between them at various loci—if any such differences should be found— would reveal the speed at which genetic drift had taken place and serve as a valuable check upon theoretical calculations concerning the speed and importance of this phenomenon.

In dealing with large populations the problem of sampling can be and has been dealt with in various ways. The first requisite is to realize that some bias is inevitable: captive samples are by definition selected, and samples of volunteers are almost certain to be nonrepresentative in some way. The proper way to deal with this situation is to recognize it and attempt to adjust one's research in such a way as to take account of it. Baker's experiment concerning body heat, cited previously, is a good illustration of this.

Some research on the distribution of blood types may have depended too much upon samples of hospital or clinic patients. The accumulating evidence of significant associations between blood types and diseases makes such data suspect. Volunteer samples, on the other hand, may well be skewed in ways which are quite obscure but may easily be important. In my own experience it has been difficult to persuade people who felt themselves to be aberrant in any way to submit either to anthropometry or blood typing. Some felt themselves too superior because of wealth or official position; others too inferior for any one of a number of reasons. On the other hand, kinfolk of individuals already examined needed less persuasion than anyone else. It is necessary in field work to be aware of such things and to consider the ways in which they may skew the data which is being collected.

Very small populations present different problems. It is best, if possible, to examine all members of such groups; in this way, the problem of representativeness does not arise. Many of the populations which are subject to unusual environmental conditions, which have unusual allele frequencies, or which attract the interest of physical anthropologists for any other reason have only a few hundred members. The greater number of tribes of American Indians in the United States are far from numerous. Almost everyone in such a group is related to almost everyone else, so that exclusion of known relatives from the group to be studied, which is orthodox in dealing with samples drawn from a large population, is self-defeating under the circumstances.

Inasmuch as all human communities contain members of at least two or three generations and since some parents are bound to have more children than others, the statistics devised for analyzing populations of maize or fruit flies are not quite appropriate in such cases. Nevertheless, a more precise picture of existing evolutionary circumstances can be obtained if no one is excluded from the series to be studied. Sometimes it is possible to observe, by comparing the allele frequencies of the old and the young, the manner in which genetic change is taking place. Chagnon *et al.* (1970) collected cultural, historical, and geneological data from a community of Yanomama Indians in the Amazonian rain forest of South America whose genetic characteristics they were studying. Thus they were able to document the exact circumstances which led to the rather unusual allele frequencies of this population. It appears that in this tribe, women who are captured in warfare give birth to a greater than average number of children. A single captured woman, in this case, had enough children to explain the allele frequencies which were found. Thus we see how very important it is for the anthropologist to be aware of all the circumstances affecting the behavior of any group which he is studying.

Similarly small groups are found scattered in many parts of the world. Many have already been mentioned. In many cases, they are the last remnants of previously more numerous peoples. From research among such groups we may obtain valuable clues concerning the adaptive value in the past of characteristics which may be less functional in the technological environment of the present. They must not be neglected.

After several hundred years of contact with people from distant lands, we must expect that some admixture of nonlocal alleles will be found in every tribe. It is prudent to be skeptical about claims to racial purity. Official documents, purporting to record proportions of tribal ancestry, deal, as they should, with social rather than biological reality. Attempts at reconstruction of aboriginal allele frequencies or phenotypical characteristics are likely, in many cases, to be speculative, but they are perfectly legitimate. If data exist concerning the identity of foreign visitors, it will be possible to make reasonable estimates of the genetic contribution which they could have made to the local gene pool. Historic knowledge of the personnel engaged in the fur trade with American Indians, for instance, should be used in attempting to reconstruct the earlier genetic systems of the Plains tribes.

There is little doubt that work in a laboratory can be kept to a higher standard of precision. All necessary instruments are available and in order. Persons willing to come to a laboratory will, as a rule, be willing to adjust themselves to the requirements of the research. Having taken the time and made the effort to do so, they are likely to cooperate further. A well-designed and equipped laboratory will provide for the comfort and ease of the subjects as well as the investigator. Procedures may be kept at a high degree of efficiency and the subjects favorably impressed by the scientific atmosphere which, in our country and others, arouses a certain degree of respect. A long-term project, such as a growth study, can only be conducted under such conditions as these.

GROWTH STUDIES

The study of human growth and development is, of course, one of the most significant and essential aspects of physical anthropology. There are many approaches to analyzing the processes involved in growth. Baer and Gavan (1968) have listed quite a variety of methods and techniques which are very helpful in discovering exactly where bone growth is taking place. Children of various ages may be measured, and the degree of maturation recorded by noting whether one or another adult characteristic has developed yet. The myth of early sexual maturity in the tropics has been disposed of by such studies. It is clear that constant heat is among the factors which delay rather than promote maturity. Malnutrition and illness are other factors which have the same effect, and they are especially prevelant in tropical regions.

Healthy, well-nourished boys and girls in temperate lands mature more rapidly than any others. As prosperity and public sanitation have improved, biological maturity is reached at an earlier age. But some aspects of maturity are more subject to such environmental influences than are others. Chagula (1960) finds that native boys of East Africa, whose nutrition is not up to par, almost always have some and usually all of their wisdom teeth by the age of twenty. A majority have at least one erupted wisdom tooth before the age of fifteen. In the United States such an early age for the completion of dentition is rare.

In sharp contrast is the age at which girls first menstruate. The poorly nourished Bantu of South Africa, like their tropical cousins in Nigeria and many natives of India, are unlikely to menstruate before the age of fourteen. The average age is closer to fifteen. A considerable majority of Europeans exhibit this sign of approaching sexual maturation more than a year earlier. Kralj-Cercek (1956) finds correlations between menarche and body build, social class, nutrition, and climate. In Slovenia girls who had eaten meat twice a day during childhood reached menarche, or first menstruation, at an average age of eleven years and eight months; whereas those who had eaten meat once a week or less did not have this experience until an average age of fourteen years and one month. Girls having the most feminine body build first menstruated on average almost two years earlier than those having the least feminine build. Nutritional status does not correspond to social status at all but rather to family food habits. Nevertheless, the average age of menarche among girls whose parents are of higher status is almost a year earlier than it is among girls whose parents are of the lower class. Girls from the island of Susak in the Adriatic usually reached menarche four months later than those in Ljubljana, which is in the mountains and has much colder winters.

In the highlands of Peru, however, the stress of constant cold and reduced oxygen pressure appear to delay maturity for both sexes to a marked degree (Frisancho and Baker, 1970). No doubt the rather poor nutrition and the amount of strenuous exercise required of growing children contributes to slow growth in this and quite a few other areas of the world. Even the way in which children are treated, which is dictated by custom as much as by economic circumstance, probably has an effect upon the growth rate. A youngster who stays up late every night requires more calories to keep going than one whose bedtime is early. If little boys are given the best food, and their sisters eat only what is left afterward, boys may well grow more rapidly—unless they also have to work a lot harder. We need far more information on growth among peoples who have not yet benefited from modern technology.

Most studies of growth in which one ethnic, social, geographical, or racial group is contrasted to another have necessarily been cross-sectional. Longitudinal studies, in which the growth pattern of each single child is studied through the years from infancy to maturity, provide us with even more revealing and significant data. Growth is much more than simply a swelling out in size. The rate at which it proceeds varies from one period to another. Certain organs or whole sections of the body may increase in size and change in shape without relation to other parts. The early growth of the brain, in contrast to the musculature, is an example of this which has been noted earlier. By examining Figure 15–5 you can see that the anatomical features which distinguish the sexes undergo their most rapid growth even later. Girls experience a growth spurt a year or two earlier than their brothers, as is shown in Figure 15–6. And the periods of accelerated growth in different individuals, even belonging to the same gene pool, are far from identical. For these reasons it is wise to follow the pattern of growth of each child separately for as many years as possible.

Many children must be studied for purposes of statistical validity, and they must all be members of a single group if the results are to be meaningful. There must be a well-founded expectation, not just a pious hope, that the families of which the children are members will neither move away nor drop out of the program. A town from which people are always moving is a poor place in which

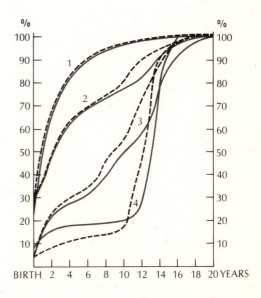

FIGURE 15-5. Aspects of Human Growth. The Curves Represent the Percentage of Adult Size Attained at Various Ages by: 1. Central Nervous System. 2. Stature. 3. Weight. 4. Sexual Characteristics. The Solid Lines Show the Growth Curves of Boys; the Broken Lines Show the Growth Curves of Girls

to start a growth study. It is best to set up shop at a locality where jobs are reasonably secure and to work with families who will maintain an intelligent interest in the program over the years. Only in this way can attrition be kept at a minimum.

Rhythms of growth and rates of aging, too, have as much biological significance as the characteristics of young maturity. Individual rhythms vary just as adult features do, although the sequence of events in growth is relatively constant. Chronological age in years is not necessarily an accurate measure of physiological age. The relative effect of genetic constitution and environmental conditions upon the rate and rhythm of growth can be determined only as a result of longitudinal studies in which the hereditary background and living circumstances of the subjects are known. Not very many anthropologists have been in a position to spend twenty years or more, as is necessary, on such a project, but fortunately a few are doing so. Such work involves applying practically all the techniques and instrumental apparatus used in any form of research in physical anthropology, for the subjects of a

FIGURE 15-6. How Boys and Girls Grow. This Girl and Boy Are the Same Age. Note that She Grows and Develops Earlier than He Does, But that He Eventually Catches Up and Surpasses Her in Stature. Such a Difference between Males and Females in the Rhythm of Growth Is an Aspect of Sexual Dimorphism.

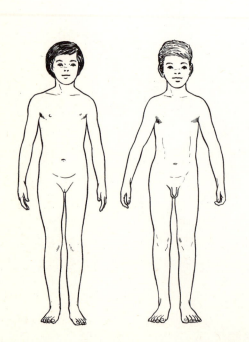
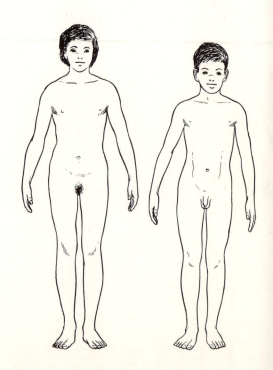

growth study should be thoroughly, not superficially, examined at
regular stated intervals. Anthropometric measurements are involved, but even more can be learned by the use of X-rays. They
have been invaluable for precise measurements of bone growth and
for ascertaining the sequence in which the epiphyses ossify. As we
have become more aware of the potential hazards involved in exposure to powerful radiation, this technique has, naturally, become
less popular. Careful dietary and health records need to be kept
in order to ascertain the existence and degree of any correlations
between nutrition or disease and the rate of development of one
part or another of the body.

As children approach maturity, the alterations in hair and eye
color and of the parts of the body from which hair grows have long
been obvious. As part of a long-term growth study, Garn, Selby,
and Crawford (1956) have measured the age changes in skin pigmentation on various areas of the body. Although the forehead and
inner arm remain light, the areolae and genitals become much
darker in response to the increased production of sex hormones during and after puberty, as measured by the degree of reflectance.
Now that the reflectance spectrophotometer is available, we can
expect to learn much more about the effects of growth, and of aging,
and of exposure to sunlight than was possible before. Tools for
precise measurements are required for fuller understanding of all
the changes which take place during life.

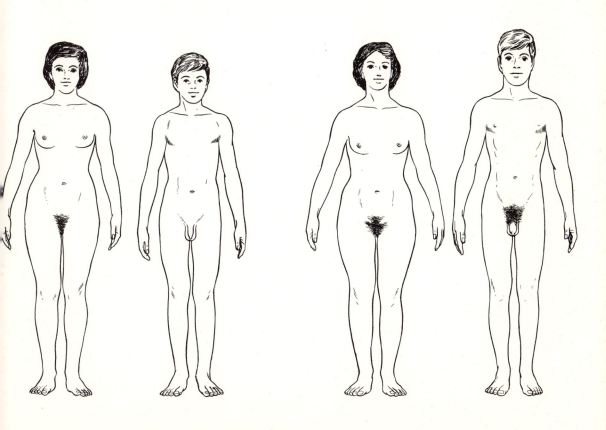

Of course, tools which are adequate for measuring bones may well be useless in studies of the living, for we are composed of fat, muscle, and other tissues as well. Research by physical anthropologists in the field of body composition is not yet well advanced. Very few of the needed techniques are possible outside of a laboratory, since they require equipment which cannot readily be transported to remote areas or from house to house at which the investigator calls. One useful tool which can readily be carried, however, is a skin-fold caliper for measuring the amount of subcutaneous fat. Such a caliper is provided with a spring so that it is in constant tension and therefore able to measure soft tissues with a high degree of consistency. At certain areas of the body: just below the shoulder blade, the back of the arm over the triceps muscle, the forearm, and the side of the chest at the level of the lowest rib, for instance, the skin is loose enough to be plucked or pinched up without giving pain to the subject. The double layer of skin plus fat which is raised may be measured with a skin-fold caliper. Differences related to age, sex, and race as well as nutritional state are quite consistently found in such measurements.

TWIN STUDIES

Research into the details of human growth has obvious applications in the field of health as well as in anthropology. Among other things longitudinal growth studies have shown rather clearly the extent of human individuality, the normal range within which we can expect children of any particular group to vary. It is an old idea that no two children are alike, but growth studies demonstrate the ways in which they are not alike. By means of such research we are beginning to understand the reasons for different sorts of similarities and dissimilarities. The problems involved in disentangling the various circumstances which influence growth and in learning to distinguish the effect upon the growth pattern of one circumstance from another are enormously complex. A problem of continuing interest to physical anthropologists is that of assessing the relative weight to assign to hereditary and environmental influences upon the development of dimensional characteristics. It is clear enough that the genetic constitution and the conditions of life both affect stature, for instance. But such a statement, despite its truth, is most unsatisfying. We want to know: How much?

One quite promising approach to this problem is the study of twins. Some twin pairs are derived from a single egg which was fertilized by a single sperm. These are properly termed monozygotic, although the name "identical" is quite commonly used. Other twin pairs are derived from two eggs which happened to be available for fertilization at the same time. These are properly termed dizygotic, but such names as "unlike" or "fraternal" are often given to them. Dizygotic twins are simply siblings who by chance shared their mother's uterus. There is no more reason to expect them to be genetically similar than other brothers or sisters who were born several years apart. They are, of course, very likely to share many environmental conditions in common, both before and after their birth. In contrast, monozygotic twins necessarily and by definition share an identical genetic constitution. Should twins who appear very similar to one another be found to have different blood types or to possess contrasting alleles at any locus, we must conclude that they are in fact dizygotic. The first task of anyone engaged in twin research is to make certain that he knows which twin pairs are monozygotic.

The frequency of monozygotic twin births is rather close to one in 250 among all of the world's populations, so far as we know, but the frequency of dizygotic twin births is far more variable. Among the American Colored population in the United States, for instance, it is almost four times as high as among the Japanese, nor are these the extreme limits of variation. Other evidence also suggests heritability in dizygotic twinning. The frequency of dizygotic twin confinements, at least in the United States, rises sharply with increase in the age of the mother, up to the age of forty. The frequency of monozygotic twin confinements rises less. Prenatal deaths are much more frequent among twins than in the population at large. This is most especially true of monozygotic twins and, among them, of males. Stillbirths and deaths at a very early age are more common among twins than among children born singly. Two embryos which share a single uterus are subject to extra strain, and the small size so typical of twins at birth enhances the difficulties of survival. It is clear that selection operates quite strongly against the phenomenon of twinning in the human species by eliminating so many twins.

Pairs of adult twins available for study are not easy to find, but a number of studies have been made. Each has benefited from the criticisms received by previous work. Methodology and project design have become more sophisticated. The findings of the most recent studies are therefore more meaningful and more easily interpreted.

The work of Osborne and De George (1959) exemplifies this. Basically, their method has been that of simple variance analysis. All work was done under carefully controlled laboratory conditions. Both members of each twin pair were measured and observed at the same time. All possible tests were given to determine whether a pair were monozygotic or dizygotic. Since the differences between siblings of the same sex for any given dimension are likely to be less than between people picked at random from a population, extra special care had to be given to precision in measurement. The set of measurements and observations used was designed to show body composition and constitution as well as size and shape. The difference between the two members of each twin pair was calculated for each measurement. Monozygotic twins were included in one series, dizygotic twins in another series. The mean variance was determined separately for each series by the formula $\frac{\Sigma x^2}{2n}$; n stands for the number of twin pairs and x for the difference between the two members of each pair. Thus it became possible to find out in what ways monozygotic twins resemble one another more closely than dizygotic twins do and to give tests of significance to such differences as were found.

This technique can measure the degree to which various characteristics depend for their expression more upon genetic constitution than environmental circumstances. But even within a single household no two individuals can possibly have identical experiences, even though they may have identical genes. Some interesting findings were made. Monozygotic twins were much closer in stature than were dizygotic twins: the difference is significant at the .001 level of probability. In weight, on the other hand, the effect of environment is much more strongly shown. Members of twin pairs of both types differed from one another considerably, showing that the genetic component in weight is much less important than in stature. Environmental influence seems to be especially marked in such measurements as upper arm and thigh circumstance, chest depth, and foot breadth. Genetic influence appears to be strongest in some of the facial dimensions: minimum frontal and bigonial diameters and the height of the upper face and nose. The mode of inheritance of these characteristics remains unknown, and twin studies are not designed to reveal this. Like other dimensions, they reflect the influence of several or many genes rather than one or two.

TESTING PROCEDURES

Twin studies like growth studies involve the collection of much data from each subject. It would be impractical to the highest degree to attempt either sort of study in the field rather than in the laboratory. Much research in physical anthropology, however, involves the combination of field work with laboratory analysis. This is often true, for instance, of blood typing. The actual determination of the blood type involves laboratory equipment and procedures, but the samples of blood to be tested may be collected in the place or places where people live and sent to a laboratory. If refrigeration is available, samples of blood or any other body fluid may be transported for great distances. At times it is possible to transport testing equipment and technicians to the field, and sometimes this is much more convenient. Or a field laboratory may be established on a more permanent basis if continued studies prove to be worthwhile. For quite a few years such a laboratory has been maintained at Nuñoa, a Peruvian town slightly over 13,000 feet above sea level (Baker, 1969). At this place all sorts of hypotheses concerning human adaptability to high altitudes can be tested; the local inhabitants are almost all of local ancestry, field situations can be compared easily to those in the laboratory, and the cultural practices of the people can be studied concurrently with their biological characteristics. At the same time, communications with institutions which have more elaborate equipment is far from difficult. Blood samples, for instance, can be refrigerated and sent by air, within a few hours, to whatever laboratory is most appropriate.

The list of equipment required for research into blood characteristics is rather extensive. Much of it is far too bulky for transportation to remote spots and can be used only in an established laboratory. Blood for testing may be collected into a capillary tube from the finger tip or earlobe, which is first cleaned and disinfected with alcohol and then punctured with a disposable lancet. If a larger quantity of blood is needed, it may be obtained from a vein and collected into a test tube. It has frequently been found that subjects are more willing to have a few drops taken from the ear—an operation which is invisible to the donor—than to have a greater amount drained from the vein in the arm. The container of blood is then sealed to prevent contamination, carefully labeled, and put in a cold place until it may be tested. Sometimes it is advisable to add a special preservative if the blood cannot be tested for several days. The most rigid sanitary precautions must be observed to protect each donor, but the equipment needed for collection as distinct from the testing of blood is simple and easy to carry into and back from the field.

There are a number of testing methods in current use. Such methods are improved as more experience is gained, and a complete description of any one of them would be out of place in this book. A very simple technique, suitable for field conditions, for determining the presence of the antigens of the ABO system is to place two drops of blood from the same person, diluted by a saline solution, on a sterile glass slide. A small drop of anti-A serum is added to one of the bloods and a small drop of anti-B serum to the other. Anti-A serum will agglutinate the red cells of group A blood, so that visible clumps are formed. Anti-B serum will do the same to cells of group B blood. Consequently, if neither drop of blood agglutinates, it is of group O; if both agglutinate, it is of group AB. This technique is illustrated by Figure 15–7. For most determinations more complex procedures are required. Blood may need to be centrifuged, incubated, or both before it is suitable for testing. Centrifuges, incubators, sterilizing materials, test tube racks, constant temperature water baths, and microscopes are among the items of equipment which must be on hand in a blood typing laboratory. For the examination of other properties of the blood still further instruments are required.

Haptoglobins, for instance, which are among the glycoproteins of blood plasma, are found in more than one form in human blood. The precise form depends upon the presence of one allele or another of a gene, and allele frequencies differ from population to population. The techniques for determining the type of haptoglobin which is present involve the use of electrophoresis, since the electrical charge present on molecules of one type differs from that found on another. Consequently, these molecules migrate at varying speeds through suitably porous material in a magnetic field. A variety of electrophoretic instruments have been invented and are in use. Those depending upon the use of starch gel seem to give the most sensitive readings, but improvements in this type of equipment are constantly being made.

Hemoglobin types, such as those involved in the sickle-cell trait, may be determined by the use of the same equipment. Blood which is to be analyzed for the type of haptoglobin or hemoglobin which it possesses must be sent to a laboratory possessing electrophoretic equipment. The β-globulins or transferrins of human blood plasma may also be distinguished by electrophoresis, because some move more rapidly than others. The γ-globulins, such as Gm and Inv, are among other characteristics of serum protein which are found in more than one form. These can be distinguished from one another by still further, rather complex laboratory procedures (Steinberg, 1962). As time goes on, more and more genetic polymorphisms in the composition of the body fluids continue to be discovered by laboratory tests; and in the greater number of these, differences in allele frequencies distinguish the various human populations.

There is also hope, rather uncertain hope at the present time, that laboratory analysis may yield reliable data concerning the dis-

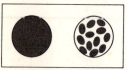

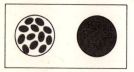

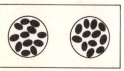

FIGURE 15-7. Reactions Shown by the Slide Test for Blood Grouping

tribution of the ABO blood group frequencies among ancient as well as among living populations. The A and B antigens are not restricted to the red cells of the bloodstream but exist in many if not most tissues, including bone. Tests of mummified tissue from Egypt and Peru were made as long ago as 1937 by Boyd and appeared to show the presence of A and B antigens which had remained chemically intact for many hundreds or even several thousand years. Candela (1940) extended the technique to cancellous bone tissue. However, Salazar (1951) reported that the soil surrounding bones as well as the bones themselves at Monte Alban, an archaeological site in Mexico, gave A type reactions. It has already been mentioned that the smallpox virus appears to be almost identical with A antigen, and a number of other bacterial components resemble blood group antigens. Such a situation gives cause for concern. Experiments to test the reliability of the results obtained from typing aged bone were in order.

Thieme and Otten (1957) report upon such an experiment. More than forty bones from autopsy specimens of previously determined blood group were buried in stone jars in sandy soil. After several years they were dug up, and nineteen of them were typed, the others being still too full of fat to be usable. The bones were ground and tested for the presence of A and B antigens by the standard inhibition technique. Each specimen was subjected to twelve individual testings. The results of the testing are presented in Table 17. A high proportion (47 percent) of tests yielded false results. The experimenters attributed this to bacterial action in the soil. It will be noticed that in most cases the blood group substance had been destroyed, although one known group O was converted into A. Some antigenic elements in the soil may be picked up by aging bone. The standard techniques used in the past do not appear to be specific enough to be reliable.

At least two major factors have hindered progress in perfecting reliable techniques in paleoserology. The inhibition tests which

TABLE 17. RESULTS OF BLOOD GROUP TESTS ON BONE AGED TWO YEARS IN SANDY SOIL.

Known Blood Group	Typing Results			
	O	*A*	*B*	*AB*
7 O	6	1	–	–
8 A	5	3	–	–
3 B	2	–	1	–
1 AB	1	–	–	–

have been standard tell us only that certain substances are absent from the material which is being studied. We reach positive conclusions only by a process of elimination, no matter how successful we have been in removing contaminating substances. Furthermore, we do not yet know as much as we need to about the precise chemical nature of the organic residues found in ancient bone. Only when these have been more fully identified can we have confidence in the accuracy of test results. At the same time, it is fair to say that serum for testing, conditions for testing, and the techniques used in preparation for testing are constantly being improved. Problems which appeared to defy solution, like that of the Piltdown bones, were solved by proper work in the laboratory. Problems which now appear most confusing will continue to be solved by proper work in the laboratory as time goes on.

Sources and Suggested Readings

BAER, M. J., and J. A. GAVAN, eds.
   1968   Symposium on Bone Growth as Revealed by in Vivo Markers. *American Journal of Physical Anthropology*, new series, **29**, 155–310.

BAKER, P. T.
   1958   The Biological Adaptation of Man to Hot Deserts. *American Naturalist*, **92**, 337–357.
   1959   American Negro-White Differences in the Thermal Insulative Aspects of Body Fat. *Human Biology*, **31**, 316–324.
   1969   Human Adaptation to High Altitude. *Science*, **163**, 1149–1156.

BOYD, W. C. and L. G. BOYD
   1937   Blood Grouping Tests on 300 Mummies. *Journal of Immunology*, **32**, 307–319.

CANDELA, P. B.
   1940   Reliability of Blood-Group Tests on Human Bones. *American Journal of Physical Anthropology*, **27**, 365–381.

CHAGNON, N. A., J. V. NEEL, L. WEINKAMP, M. LAYRISSE, H. GERSHO-
WITZ, and M. AYERS
1970   The Influence of Cultural Factors on the Demography
and Pattern of Gene-Flow from the Makiritare to the
Yanomama Indians. *American Journal of Physical
Anthropology*, new series, **32**, 339–349.

CHAGULA, A. K.
1960   The Age of Eruption of Third Permanent Molars in
Male East Africans. *American Journal of Physical Anthropology*, new series, **18**, 77–82.

DUPERTUIS, C. W.
1948   Somatotypes and Blood Volume. *American Journal of
Physical Anthropology*, new series, **6**, 232–243.

FISCHER, E.
1913   *Die Rehobother Bastards und das Bastardierungs
Problem beim Menschen.*   Gastav Fischer Verlag, Jena.

FRISANCHO, A. R. and P. T. BAKER
1970   Altitude and Growth: A Study of the Patterns of Physical Growth of a High Altitude Peruvian Quechua Population. *American Journal of Physical Anthropology*,
new series, **32**, 279–292.

GARN, S. M., S. SELBY, and M. R. CRAWFORD
1956   Skin Reflectance Studies in Children and Adults.
American Journal of Physical Anthropology, new series, **14**, 101–117.

GARN, S. M. and Z. SHAMIR
1958   *Methods for Research in Human Growth.*   Thomas,
Springfield, Ill.

GARSON, J. G.
1884   The Frankfort Craniometric Agreement. *Journal of
the Anthropological Institute*, **14**, 64.

HAMMEL, H. T., R. W. ELSNER, D. H. LEMESSURIER, K. L. ANDERSON,
and F. A. MILAN
1959   Thermal and Metabolic Response of the Australian
Aborigine Exposed to Moderate Cold in Summer.
Journal of Applied Physiology, **14**, 605–615.

HARRISON, G. A. and J. J. T. OWEN
   1964   Studies in the Inheritance of Human Skin Color. An-
          nals of Human Genetics, **28**, 27.

KATZ, S. H., ed.
   1970   Symposium on Human Adaptation. *American Journal
          of Physical Anthropology*, new series, **32**, 221–319.

KRALJ-CERCEK, L.
   1956   The Influence of Food, Body-Build and Social Origin
          on the Age at Menarche. *Human Biology*, **28**, 293–406.

NEWMAN, R. W.
   1956   Skinfold Measurements in Young American Males.
          Human Biology, **28**, 154–164.

OSBORNE, R. H. and F. V. DE GEORGE
   1959   *Genetic Basis of Morphological Variation: An Evalua-
          tion and Application of the Twin Study Method.* Har-
          vard University Press, Cambridge.

SALAZAR, M. M.
   1951   Estudio Immunilogico de Restos Oseos Antiquos. *Ga-
          ceta Medica de Mexico*, **81**, 122–127.

SCHICKELE, E.
   1947   Environment and Fatal Heat Stroke; an Analysis of
          157 Cases Occurring in the Army of the U.S. During
          World War II. *The Military Surgeon*, **100**, 235–256.

SHAPIRO, H. L.
   1929   Descendants of the Mutineers of the Bounty, *Memoirs
          of the B. P. Bishop Museum*, **9**, Honolulu.
   1936   *Heritage of the Bounty.* Simon and Schuster, New
          York.
   1939   *Migration and Environment.* Oxford University Press,
          New York.

STEINBERG, A. G.
   1962   Progress in the Study of Genetically Determined Hu-
          man Gamma Globulin Types (the Gm and Inv groups).
          Progress in Medical Genetics **2**, 1–33.

STEEGMAN, A. J.
   1965   A Study of Relationships Between Facial Cold Re-
          sponse and Some Variables of Facial Morphology.

American Journal of Physical Anthropology, new series, **23**, 355–362.

1970   Cold Adaptation and the Human Face. *American Journal of Physical Anthropology*, new series, **32**, 243–250.

TANNER, J. M.

1966   *Growth at Adolescence*, 2nd edition. Blackwell Scientific Publications, Oxford.

THIEME, F. P. and C. M. OTTEN

1957   The Unreliability of Blood-Typing Aged Bone. *American Journal of Physical Anthropology*, new series, **15**, 387–398.

VON TOROK, A.

1890   *Grundzuge einer Systematischen Kraniometric.* Stuttgart.

CHAPTER **16**

Where We Stand

The problems involved in studying human beings are as unique as the species itself. Laboratory analysis of data and laboratory experiment, too, are becoming more and more vital as means of increasing our understanding of human biology. But we must continue to exploit the natural laboratories which we find in the world at large. Results obtained from each sort of study stimulate further work in the others. The era in which description of traits and schemes of classification dependent upon description were the major objectives of physical anthropology has come to an end. An attempt to understand the processes involved in the development and expression of human traits has always been the aim of most of those engaged in research in this field, but a long period of pure description was required first. Emotionally based reluctance to study man as a biological organism has always been an obstacle to research in physical anthropology. Description has seemed less revolting than analysis, and taxonomy less dangerous than the study of process. Most of us are very sensitive about our uniqueness, and many of us very fearful that the results of biological research may deflate our pretensions.

A lady of the Victorian period is said to have been told during a dinner conversation of Darwin's conclusion regarding the evolution of mankind. She remarked in some distress that she must hope he had been mistaken and that she was not related to a monkey. If Darwin were right, however, she trusted that such embarrassing news could be kept quiet.

The news, of course, was not kept quiet. The good lady, like all the rest of us, was indeed related to a monkey and to all other forms of life as well. It is most unprofitable to view this as embarrassing news, or as good news, either. The fact of evolution is neither a scandal nor an excuse for unseemly behavior. It is, however, very important, very interesting, and very significant. We are in a position to comprehend far more about ourselves and one another when we are emotionally capable of accepting our place in nature. Our uniqueness, which is unquestionable, does not mean that we have no place in nature or that we are exempt from the regularities which are so often called laws of nature. On the contrary, it means that we are subject to all these laws and to others as well. In adding culture to the world of life, we have not subtracted biology. We have abolished neither the environment nor our ancestry.

During the past decade there has been a growing awareness, among nature lovers at first but among the general public more recently, of the vital importance of realizing, and accepting, our place in nature. Traditionally, in the Western world at least, man's uniqueness was taken to imply that he was the master of the universe, that he was above nature, that he had no responsibility to the world. The lethal naïveté of such assumptions is now becoming apparent. As a species, we have indeed been very clever and have learned how to manipulate not only knives and forks but microorganisms and atoms. By 1940 we had learned how to reduce the death rate drastically by the use of antibiotics. By 1950 we had learned how to increase the death rate drastically by the use of the energy of atomic fusion. By 1960 we had learned how to increase food production enormously by the use of insecticides. By 1970 we had learned that we didn't know how to use these powerful inventions of ours, which may well be in the process of destroying us. Is the human species in the position of the sorcerer's apprentice, who learned the magic word that made the water flow but not the counter-charm to turn it off?

Having reduced the death rate but not the birth rate, we find the human population of the world doubling with each generation. Yet the surface area of the world remains the same. Having developed enormously powerful weapons, we find ourselves using greater and greater proportions of our resources to defend ourselves against them. Yet the resources of the world remain the same. Having devised effective insecticides, we find that they kill creatures we call useful as well as their intended victims. Yet they are long lasting and now poison the air, the water, and the soil all over the world. Without half trying, we have succeeded in polluting our

total environment, upsetting the balance of nature in many catas-
trophic ways, wasting irreplaceable resources, and at the same time
doubling the effective demand upon those resources with each decade. It is legitimate to wonder how much longer this can go on.

It is easy to say, as many people have, that this state of affairs
is due to unfortunate, unfair, and inefficient economic, social, or
political arrangements. In this case, the obvious cure would be to
transform such arrangements, after which pollution would cease,
the environment would be restored, and population increase
wouldn't matter. It is easy to say, but is it relevent?

It is easy to say, as other people have, that our present hazardous condition is due to the innate wickedness of man. If only virtue can be restored, either by religious conversion or the improvement of our genes, everyone would be nice to everyone else. Therefore pollution would cease, the environment would be restored, and
population increase wouldn't matter. It is easy to say this, but
does it have anything to do with the problem?

It is much less easy to view any human problem from a scientific view, which requires dispassionate analysis, than it is to pro-
pose solutions such as these. Yet, in fact, the proper diagnosis of
any problem improves the chance of finding a solution. The assumption that man is wicked and the assumption that the system
is wicked are both agreeable to certain aspects of our traditional
culture. Excellent drama is provided by the conflict between virtue
and wickedness, so that emotional satisfaction comes from phrasing problems in such terms. It is not, however, likely to cure a patient who suffers from elephantiasis. Different ailments call for
different treatments, and the casting out of devils seems unlikely to
be an effective remedy for the pollution, destruction, and overcrowding which threaten the human species at the present time.

No matter how virtuous we may become, the surface of the
globe provides standing room for only a finite number of persons.
No matter how just the economic system may become, the resources of the globe provide sustenance for only a finite number of
organisms. No matter how perfect our social relations and political
arrangements may become, we will remain living, physical organisms which occupy space and require air, food, and water. We will
continue to produce wastes which must be taken care of. We will
continue to die even if we cease to breed. The more of us there
are, the greater will become the problems of pollution and the overexploitation of finite resources. This is simple elementary arithmetic which cannot be avoided.

Overcrowding appears to be a basic factor, therefore, in all of
the problems which face us during the last third of the twentieth
century. Like any other species, ours has responded to favorable
circumstances by an increase in numbers. Unlike any other species,

however, ours is composed of individuals who are capable of long-range forethought. We are not required to let natural selection be the sole agent of population adjustment. But we are required to act in accordance with our biological as well as our cultural capacities. Consequently, a fuller understanding of the nature of man and of man's place in nature is required if we are to begin to deal effectively with the problems which face our species today. We must accept the fact that we do have a place in nature, not above it. To discover what that place is, how we came to occupy it, and how our nature has evolved in response to it are the tasks of the physical anthropologist. To accomplish these tasks, a great deal of research is needed.

OUR GROWING UNDERSTANDING OF MAN'S PLACE IN NATURE

Whether research is conducted in a laboratory or in the field will depend upon the problem at hand. In either case, the design of the project and the selection of the sample are matters of the utmost importance. Appreciation of these points is one of the real advances which have been made in physical anthropology during the present century. The earliest information to reach scholars concerning the diversity of human characteristics was somewhat casually collected and therefore most inadequate. There could be no assurance that it was in any way representative. Nor could the early anthropologists know what clues to seek nor which characteristics might be relevant to the study of any particular problem.

It is not necessarily self-evident that the features which were observed are in any significant sense real entities. It is not really likely that a functional entity will be identical with a genetic entity. Finding that there is a strong hereditary component in the height of the nose (Osborne and De George, 1959) does not imply that there is a single gene controlling this dimension. On the contrary, it is known that as teeth grow, the size of surrounding bone tissue grows also. This must be considered when we think about the meaning of nasal breadth and, consequently, of the nasal index. The nose, as Washburn (1952) reminds us, is an integral part of the face: it does not stand alone. It has its own function, and its shape may reflect climate stress among other things. But if large incisors have enough selective value, the nostrils may have to be wide, the climate notwithstanding, for these openings are directly above the roots of the teeth. We must adapt to all aspects of our environment, not just to one; and each part of a man's body must fit the other parts. The example of nasal shape is simply one of many which might be given to illustrate this point.

The extent of our knowledge concerning the biological characteristics of the human species is constantly increasing, but it remains most inadequate. Descriptive studies have been extensive enough to permit their practical application in many situations. Physical anthropologists are often able to help the authorities identify skeletal remains. In cases of disputed paternity they are frequently able by means of genetic analysis to determine whether a suspected individual could have fathered a certain child; they cannot state that he alone could have done so. Knowledge of the frequency with which persons with certain dimensions are found in a population assists the government in supplying clothing which will fit members of the armed forces. Such knowledge has proved useful in the design of equipment as well. But such applications are only the incidental products of anthropological research. They do not help us in our continued search for the causes of variation within the human species and for the circumstances which have led to human evolution. The search for such causes must involve studies of process and must take into account the importance of culture.

THE NATURE OF PHYSICAL ANTHROPOLOGY

Physical anthropology is not, of course, the only scientific discipline which centers its attention upon the structure and operation of the human body. In the historic development of the sciences during the past few centuries, both medicine on the one hand and zoology on the other have been deeply involved in studying human biology. The medical tradition, of course, has risen from the desire to alleviate suffering, and, if possible to cure the sick. The interest of the physician, the surgeon, and the psychiatrist has been to promote the return to health of those who are ailing or in pain. Extensive knowledge of anatomy, of physiology, and of psychology are required for these endeavors. But variations from the norm have commonly been treated as pathologies, or at best as oddities, while the norm most usually accepted has been the condition supposed to be typical in the population to which the practitioner belongs. The interest of the zoologist, on the other hand, has been in man as an animal rather than in the human animal. In zoological studies man is often treated as though he had two natures, a biological and a spiritual, and many zoologists are explicit in stating that their only interest is in the biological nature. Both disciplines have had a tradition, not easily overcome, of thinking in terms of dichotomies: the sick versus the well, or the beast versus the angel.

The distinction of physical anthropology is that it can serve and, as time goes on, is coming more to serve to unite the purely physical studies and the purely social studies of mankind. Its claim to a separate place in the field of science is based upon its ability to interpret the biological variability of the human species within a cultural setting. Modern physical anthropologists are interested in the relationship, rather than the difference, between health and disease and between culture and biology. Culture is seen as the unifying theme of our studies, whether we are observing the behavior of baboons, subjecting laboratory animals to environmental stress, operating an electrophoresis apparatus, or engaged in statistical calculations. The cultural nature of man is an aspect and a product of his biological nature, and his biological nature is an aspect and a product of his cultural nature. Man in nature is not distinguishable from man in culture, for our nature is cultural. The point has been made in several earlier chapters that we can view culture as the ecological plateau upon which our species makes its living, and to which, consequently, it must adapt and adjust. It is impossible to emphasize this point too strongly, for it is a most significant aspect of the essential unity of anthropology.

This is what makes the varied tasks of the physical anthropologist just a little different in method but vastly different in aim and attitude from those of his colleagues in the fields of medicine and zoology. The attempt to understand all the varied implications of the fact that culture is truly our ecological zone is a vast, absorbing, and important job. A human is not only a being who has the sort of pelvis which enables him to stand upright, but one whose upright posture has facilitated the elaboration of culture. He is not only a creature with an elaborate brain, but one whose braininess had freed him from some of the hazards of life only to devise new ones. The physical aspects and the cultural aspects of being human are so intimately related to one another that attempts to separate them are not only fatuous but dangerously misleading. We have come to realize that there is no real conflict between nature and nurture but that genetic systems and their environments react upon each other in most subtle ways. In just the same sense human biology and human culture are in a state of dynamic interdependence upon one another. Attempts to explain either one without taking the other into account are doomed to failure.

Physical anthropology does not serve to bridge a gap between the purely biological and the purely social studies of man. Its function is rather to demonstrate that no such gap exists. The entire discipline of anthropology applies, as best it may, the techniques and viewpoints of the natural sciences to the study of man. Other fields of study within anthropology find it methodologically convenient or even necessary to take the human animal for granted and center their attention upon social, linguistic, or psychological phenomena as such. Physical anthropology treats man himself as the phenomenon worth intensive study. Man, at least as we know him today, is the product and creature of past social, linguistic, and psychological events which have guided and modified his ancestors' activities. Man is a phenomenon of culture. But this statement does not contradict the fact that man is equally a phenomenon of nature. It merely elaborates upon it.

The strategy of physical anthropology, as Washburn (1952) calls it, is being directed to research designed to pin down the processes involved in human development to a greater degree now than it used to be. As we come to understand the growth of the individual more thoroughly, we become better able to appreciate the manner in which the stock has evolved. As we discover a greater number of details concerning the circumstances of evolution, we are able to make better sense out of the patterns and rhythms of individual growth. Individual development and species development fit together and are dependent upon each other, since they both reflect our adaptation to life in culture. This is what has made our evolution and our characteristics so unique in the world of life.

MAN'S LIFE

We share a great deal with all other living creatures. Like them, we are composed of complex chemical compounds organized into protoplasm. The reactions of these compounds with one another constitute the process of living. They are facilitated by some environmental circumstances and inhibited by others. Only a very narrow range of conditions permits life to operate at all. The temperature must be appropriate. The strength of the gravitational field and other cohesive forces must be appropriate. The quantities and types of radiation must be appropriate. The raw material in the form of elements and simpler chemical compounds must be appropriate. In other words, the environment must be fit for life, just as life must be fit for the environment. Without water we would dry out and die. Without oxygen we would suffocate and die. Without the sun's radiations plants would cease to manufacture food, and we would starve and die. Like other living things we are subject to these conditions.

Our living activities are subject to the control of exceedingly complex molecules of Deoxyribonucleic acid, or DNA. It is this substance which determines the potentialities for development of each individual, and it is this substance which is transmitted from each generation to the next. The continued life of any individual is dependent upon the adequacy of his response to environmental stress, and this in turn is dependent upon the precise nature of his DNA. The continued life of any species, including our own, is dependent upon the existence of properly functioning mechanisms for its transmission. Bisexual reproduction, by which a high degree of genetic recombination and potential diversity within a species is promoted, is widespread among plants and animals alike, including the human species. The added complications to life imposed by this method of reproduction would seem to have been a low price to pay for the advantages which it conveys. Indeed, among many creatures, including human beings, these added complications have served as one of the stimuli promoting social life, which has a high degree of survival value in itself.

There is no evidence which would suggest that the discoveries of Mendel concerning the way in which inherited potentialities are transmitted and distributed are not fully applicable to our species. It is possible, with a large class whose members know their parents' eye colors, to demonstrate the working of the Hardy-Weinberg law in human populations. I do this every semester. Despite the impossibility of conducting controlled breeding experiments with human beings and despite the plastic response of the human organism to environment, it is quite clear that we are not exempt from the ordinary rules of genetics. Our mating habits have added new rules, such as the incest tabu, and a complete set of unique prejudices, which appear to have had some effect upon the distribution of contrasting alleles. Our lack of a well-defined rutting season has certainly had an effect upon the structure of human society. Our use of atomic energy may alter the mutation rate of all organisms, not just mankind alone. But the principles of genetics remain the same.

In basic structure, physiology, and behavior we are clearly animals rather than plants and obviously many-celled animals with a variety of differentiated tissues and specialized organs. There can be no question about the fact that we are vertebrates, tetrapods, amniotes, and mammals. The recognition of this long antedates the development of anthropology. The whole pattern of our anatomy permits no other conclusion. Our bones, our brains, and our blood are as typically mammalian as are those of a dog or a horse. We enjoy the successes and feel the pains which other mammals do. We share their sensations. As embryos we are protected, as infants we are nourished by the resources of our mothers' bodies, just as other mammals are. Long before the idea of organic evolution became popular, Linnaeus had no hesitation in classifying us among the mammals.

Nor could he question our place among the primates. Man's anatomy is so remarkably similar to the monkey's that early surgeons such as Galen eighteen centuries ago were able to learn about people by dissecting monkeys. The more data we collect, the more basic the similarity turns out to be, in body chemistry as well as body form. In tracing out the evolutionary pathway which led eventually to man, the final step from nonhuman primate to human primate is the shortest and easiest of all. Dependence upon the sense of vision and facility in manipulation, socially learned behavior, and slow growth are characteristics equally of monkeys, apes, and men. Stereoscopic color vision, large brains, and grasping hands are typical of all three. These similarities have embarrassed or even annoyed many people, but they exist and must be accounted for.

MAN'S EVOLUTION

Darwin, a century ago, accounted for them and for the other similarities found among all living things by suggesting the idea of evolution by means of natural selection. Various objections were raised, then and later, to Darwin's explanation and to the concept of evolution in general. But no other hypothesis fits the data, and none of the data deny the hypothesis. The geographical distribution of the forms of life can be explained in no other way. The sequence of the forms of life as revealed by paleontology can be explained in no other way. The embryological development of individual creatures can be explained in no other way. The diversity in function of homologous parts of various animals can be explained in no other way. The retention of vestigial organs and habits can be explained in no other way. The concept of evolution is the unifying principle which guides biological research, as it has done since Darwin realized that natural selection was the means whereby evolution continued to operate. Mendel's discovery of the particulate nature of inheritance overcame the technical difficulties in explaining how diversity might continue or even be increased to provide the raw material for selection. Due to the patient labors and keen insights of these two men, it became possible to explain the phenomenon of man in nature.

During the century which has elapsed since Darwin demonstrated that evolution is an inescapable inference rather than a plausible speculation, the accumulation of fossil evidence has revealed the actual steps of human evolution. We do not as yet fully understand all of these steps. More fossil evidence will be most welcome. But the application of ecological theory, and experiments designed to find out how the body grows and what responses it makes to different environmental stresses, have illuminated our understanding.

The sequence of events which led to the origin of man as a really new sort of creature is beginning to be clarified. The evolution of the capacity for culture had to take place as a preparatory step. It seems clear that a predisposition for life in culture exists among many mammalian species. The behavior of the domestic dog as contrasted to that of the wolf illustrates this. But it is significant that this predisposition has remained dormant or at best very poorly developed except among primates. Capacity for domestication mimics capacity for culture, but something more is needed. Primates are notoriously not amenable to domestication, yet many species reveal by their behavior some of the attributes required by culture. The utility of arboreal life and of social organization as preparatory steps have been documented by many studies. Such preadaptations as grasping hands and primary dependence upon vision are required for existence upon the human ecological plateau.

The habitat exploited by our ancestors must have been one in which cultural conditioning had survival value. They seem to have begun to develop the necessary capabilities several million years ago. We can only suppose that this was because of the particular manner in which they exploited their environment. The fossil evidence shows us that both erect posture and tool use came into existence before the great increase in brain size upon which we pride ourselves. Washburn (1959) speculates on the importance of tool use in setting the direction of human evolution, which created new selective pressures favoring the survival of those whose brains were capable of memory, foresight, and originality. Etkin (1962), on the other hand, stresses the importance of the division of labor between the sexes. He believes that this encouraged a psychological as well as an economic revolution in the way in which the protohominids lived. We may take these two ideas as being supplementary rather than contradictory. In any case, culture evolved because of the preexisting biological capacities of certain primates, and the biological evolution of their offspring has been guided by culture ever since.

CULTURE AND BIOLOGY

Thus, it is worth repeating that the concept of culture is as necessary as the concept of evolution to an understanding of the distinctively human aspects of human biology. The activities of living creatures, not just the anatomical structures which facilitate their activities, are the vital factors in the struggle for existence. Since the time when culture first began to develop, it has influenced the activities of our ancestors. Culture is not only our creation but our creator. Selection for the possession of the capacity for culture has been one of the most, if not the very most, important factor in determining the line of human evolution. The cultural aspects of our environment are those which have continued to promote the unity of the human species and of the ancestral species which preceded *Homo sapiens*. Indeed as our ancestors' efforts improved the utility and thereby the quality of culture, its importance in selection increased more and more. Even many of the ways in which human populations have become diversified would have been impossible without culture. Research in physical anthropology continues to point up the intimacy of the relationship between culture and biology.

The full extent of polymorphism in man is slowly being revealed by studies of human physiology and biochemistry. Differences in external appearance have been perfectly apparent from the earliest times, but it used to be said that these were only skin deep. Nothing could be more misleading. It used to be said that the diversity of man was restricted to nonadaptive characteristics. Nothing could be more inaccurate. These two misunderstandings combined to create the impression that biological diversity within the species, being superficial and due to chance, has no significance. Nothing could serve better to discourage research and experimentation than such a sterile dogma. Descriptions of minutiae could be refined, new classifications of mankind into types could be devised, and new conjectural reconstructions of prehistoric migrations could be dreamed up, but that was about all. The supposed fact that natural selection had ceased to operate upon mankind was lamented by some scholars who were thereby enabled to make morbid forecasts about the future of the species.

THE NEED FOR EXPERIMENT

But the realization that living processes as well as structural forms may be studied breathes new vitality into research in physical anthropology. As yet we know very little about the manner in which we grow as individuals and even less about the way in which selection has operated to adapt different populations to the conditions under which they live. Ideas derived from experiments upon other animals or from studies of other animals in the field suggest hypotheses to us. But the actual testing of such hypotheses is just beginning. Rats appear to be capable of far greater expansion in bulk, if properly fed and protected from infections, than do human beings. Why should this be so? Or are appearances deceptive? As yet, we do not know, but by further research we should be able to find out. To what extent are the differences in weight which correlate so well with climate phenotypic adjustments, and to what extent are they the results of selection of proper genotypes? We don't know the answer to this question either, but it is the sort of question which research can answer. Precisely how does heterozygosity at the sickle-cell locus operate to confer added chances for survival in malarial regions? Several answers have been given, but only by well-designed experimental studies will we be able to decide among them.

The general outline of human evolution from a prehuman stock has become much clearer within the past generation than it had been previously. The discovery of large numbers of Australopithecine fossils has been very helpful. Functional analyses of the significance of their pelvic shape continue, but there is general agreement that these creatures were not pronograde. The discovery of tools with some of the specimens can mean that both erect posture and tool use preceded the expansion of the brain. The discrediting of the Piltdown fraud by means of chemical analysis reinforced this point. The use of radioactive materials as clocks has begun, but only begun, to clarify the chronology of human evolution. We have every reason to expect that the outline of this historic process will be filled in as more discoveries are made and as, by experiment, we learn to understand the significance of various anatomical characteristics found in fossil types of man. We do not yet know why they had thick skulls or broad noses. We do not yet know why Neanderthaloid browridges were so different from those of "Sinanthropus" or modern Australians. Finding more fossils can scarcely give us an answer, but laboratory research may do so.

The fact of racial diversity is plain, but its causes are not. About the only things we can be at all sure of are that many causes for such diversity exist, that adaptations are frequently involved, and that racial groups are episodic rather than permanent. If we study the process of raciation within an evolutionary framework, we may expect to gain useful insights. If we blithely dismiss the operation of genetic principles, neglect the lessons to be drawn from field studies and laboratory experiments on other animals, and assume that racial characteristics must be nonadaptive, we are unlikely to find out much worth knowing. But if we are open-minded about the merits of contrasting hypotheses until further research has confirmed one or the other, we will save ourselves needless disappointments should our dearest speculation prove false. If we set out to prove the total and eternal accuracy of any preconceived dogma, we are certain to lead ourselves astray, no matter how great the technical virtuosity of our work. Carefully designed experiments and the patient collection of data in the field are beginning to give us a few answers concerning the processes involved in the evolution of racial differences. Further questions are being constantly suggested by these answers. By asking the right questions one at a time we can expect to continue to increase our understanding.

Physical anthropologists are often asked to predict the biological future of mankind. Such essays into science fiction, if adequately gruesome, can certainly give the reader a thrill. But scientific prediction is not prophecy: it assumes the continuance of existing circumstances. Since evolution is the consequence of changing circumstances, statements concerning future evolution can be nothing but guesses. Trends which are quite obvious now will not necessarily continue into the future. It is probably safer to prophesy that certain events will not take place than that other events will occur. Any further expansion in brain size, for instance, would be likely to involve such added hazards to childbirth as to be rather unlikely. Since human evolution is still going on, and since our technology is still modifying the physical world about us, it would be surprising if no shifts in allele frequencies took place in the future. But we do not know what they will be. As we learn more about the processes involved in human growth and evolution, we may be able to command their future course. Programs for the genetic improvement of the species might become possible should general agreement be reached as to the meaning of improvement. As matters stand, it is more interesting, more profitable, and more enlightening to continue research designed to assist us in understanding the biological processes which have led us to our present state.

Sources and Suggested Readings

BATES, M.
   1961   *Man in Nature.*   Prentice-Hall.   Englewood Cliffs.

BERRILL, N. J.
   1955   *Man's Emerging Mind.*   Dodd, Mead and Co., New York.

CARSON, R.
   1962   *Silent Spring.*   Houghton Mifflin, Boston.

COLD SPRING HARBOR SYMPOSIA, Vol. 15
   1951   *The Origin and Evolution of Man.*   Long Island Biological Association, Cold Spring Harbor.

EHRLICH, P. R.
  1968   *The Population Bomb.*   Ballantine, New York.

ETKIN, W.
  1962   Social Behavior and the Evolution of Man's Mental
         Faculties.   *Culture and the Evolution of Man.*   Oxford
         University Press, New York.

HARDIN, G., ed.
  1969   *Population, Evolution and Birth Control.*   Freeman,
         San Francisco.

HUXLEY, T. H.
  1890   *Evidence as to Man's Place in Nature.*   Appleton, New
         York.

OSBORNE, R. H. and F. V. DE GEORGE
  1959   *Genetic Basis of Morphological Variation.   An Evalua-
         tion and Application of the Twin Study Method.*   Har-
         vard University Press, Cambridge.

WASHBURN, S. L.
  1953   The Strategy of Physical Anthropology.   *Anthropology
         Today.*   University of Chicago Press, Chicago.
  1959   Speculations on the Interrelations of the History of
         Tools and Biological Evolution.   *The Evolution of
         Man's Capacity for Culture.*   Wayne State University
         Press, Detroit.

Glossary

ACETABULUM The socket in the pelvis to which the head of the femur is articulated.

ACHEULIAN A toolmaking tradition of the Lower Paleolithic period. The typical tools are finely made bifacial cutting implements of stone.

ADAPT To come to possess a genetic system suitable for existing ecological conditions. Populations adapt.

ALBINISM Inability to synthesize tyrosinase, a precursor of melanin. This condition is due to a recessive allele.

ALLELE One of two or more forms of a gene.

ALLEN'S RULE The tendency for homothermal animals living in cold places to have shorter appendages than their close relatives in warmer areas.

ALLOMETRY Differential growth, in a standard proportion, of a certain part of the body.

ALVEOLAR Pertaining to the tooth-bearing part of the jaw.

AMINO ACIDS The building blocks of proteins. They are organic acids containing nitrogen among other elements.

AMNION An embryonic sac, containing liquid, which serves to protect the unborn creature which floats within it. *See* Figure 5–1.

AMNIOTE The grade of vertebrates with an amnion—reptiles, mammals, and birds.

ANNELID A phylum of segmented wormlike animals.

ANTHROPOIDEA The infraorder of primates containing apes, monkeys, and men.

ANTHROPOMORPHIC Attributing human characteristics to nonhumans.

ANTIBODY A chemical in a body fluid which serves to destroy a specific foreign protein.

ANTIGEN Any substance capable, when introduced into an organism, of producing an antibody.

APE Common name of the family Pongidae.

494

ARTHROPOD The phylum comprising crustaceans, insects, and similar segmented animals with an external skeleton.

AUSTRALOPITHECINE A Villafranchian to Middle Pleistocene hominid taxon.

BALANCE OF NATURE The equilibrium which is supported to characterize a natural community of animals and plants, all of which are mutually dependent in many complex ways. This equilibrium can be readily disturbed, and has been violently upset by the overexploitation resulting from human ingenuity.

BALANCED POLYMORPHISM The continued equilibrium between contrasting alleles in cases where heterozygote advantage exists, or when each of the alleles has an equal selective value.

BERGMAN'S RULE The tendency for homothermal animals living in cold areas to have greater body bulk than their close relatives in warmer areas.

BETA-AMINOISOBUTYRIC ACID (BAIB) An amino acid of which small quantities are normally excreted. Some people excrete much greater amounts, often from genetic causes.

BILOPHODONT MOLAR A molar tooth having two pairs of cusps joined by sharp ridges, longer than it is wide, and typical of Old World monkeys.

BRACHIATION Moving about in the trees by swinging by the arms underneath branches.

BRACHYCEPHALIC Having a head 82 percent or more as wide as it is long.

BRACHYCRANIAL Having a skull 80 percent or more as wide as it is long.

BREEDING POPULATION The group within which most mating takes place, and within which one is as likely to mate with any one person as with any other person of the opposite sex.

BRONZE AGE The period, usually at or before the dawn of history, during which bronze rather than iron was used for weapons, ornaments, and some implements.

CALCANEUS Bone on the lateral aspect of the foot, which in humans forms the heel and the rear section of the arch, and which in tarsiers is very much elongated, giving them added leverage for jumping.

CARBONIFEROUS The fifth period of the Paleozoic era, from more than 200 million back to about 300 million years ago.

CARBON-14 DATING A technique for dating the time at which an organism died by measuring the degree to which its carbon 14, which is radioactive, has vanished.

CAROTID ARTERIES The chief suppliers of blood to the brain, head, and neck.

CASTE A social group in which membership is ascribed in accordance with ancestry, and which practices endogamy.

CATALYST A substance which causes or speeds up chemical reactions without undergoing permanent changes itself.

CATARRHINE The taxon of primates which includes men, apes, and Old World monkeys.

CENOZOIC The geological era which began about 70 million years ago, and in which we are living.

CENTRIOLE A small body lying just outside the nucleus of a cell, which duplicates itself, as chromosomes do, just before cell division.

CEREBELLUM A section of the brain between the medulla and the cerebrum. Its functions include the maintenance of equilibrium.

CEREBRAL CORTEX The outer layer of nerve cells of the cerebrum, much expanded among some mammals, and especially cetaceans and primates, by the presence of convolutions.

CEREBRUM, or CEREBRAL HEMISPHERES The foremost section of the vertebrate brain. Its functions include the highest level of the integration of behavior.

CHELLEAN The toolmaking tradition which preceded and evolved into the Acheulian (*q.v.*). The typical tools are coarsely made bifacial cutting implements of stone.

CHI-SQUARE A method of estimating degrees of probability.

CHORDATE The phylum of creatures containing, at sometime during life, a notochord. It includes vertebrates and a few other, rather obscure, sea-dwelling animals. *See* Figure 4–5.

CHROMOSOME A threadlike structure within the nucleus composed of or containing the genes. Except in gametes, chromosomes occur in pairs.

CLASS A taxon more inclusive than an order and less than a phylum. Members of a class share basic structural similarities although they may have undergone great adaptive radiation.

CLINE A gradient in the frequency of a biological characteristic which is common in one area but uncommon in another.

CLOACA The duct, among all vertebrates except Eutheria, formed by the joining of the intestine and the ureters, so that all wastes are discharged in common.

CODOMINANCE The situation in which some alleles in a system of multiple alleles are not dominant over each other, but are dominant over still others.

COLLAGEN A somewhat gelatinous protein present in bone and cartilege.

COLOR BLINDNESS Common term for several different defects in the ability to distinguish colors, including total absence of color vision. All of them are inherited and transmitted on the X chromosome.

CONGENITAL Existing at birth. Often thought of as due to inheritance, but this is not necessarily so.

CONVOLUTIONS Foldings or wrinklings on the surface of the cerebrum which increase the area of the cerebral cortex.

CRANIAL CAPACITY The volume of the skull: this approximates the volume of the brain. Consequently, measuring it is the best means available for estimating how large the brains of extinct creatures, including our ancestors, may have been.

CRANIUM, pl. CRANIA All of the skull except for the mandible.

CRETACEOUS The last period of the Mesozoic era, almost as long as all succeeding time. *See* Figures 4–3 and 6–1.

CULTURE Behavior which is learned, shared in society, and transmitted from one generation to the next.

CYTOPLASM The protoplasm which is not within the nucleus of a cell.

DEOXYRIBONUCLEIC ACID (DNA) The very stuff of life. It is composed of sugar-phosphate chains to which are attached organic bases in patterned alternation. It has the property of synthesizing precise replicas of itself from materials in its environment, and it directs life's activities.

DEVONIAN The fourth period of the Paleozoic era, ending more than 300 million years ago.

DIABETES MELLITUS An inborn error of metabolism which inhibits storage of sugar in the liver and causes excessive urination. Although genetically caused, the condition may not become apparent until later life.

DIAPHRAGM The strong sheet of muscle separating the abdominal and thoracic cavities of mammals.

DIASTEMA A gap between two teeth: especially the gap which accommodates a projecting canine from the other jaw.

DECIDUOUS TEETH The first, temporary set of teeth found among mammals.

DISTAL Away from the center of the body.

DIZYGOTIC Derived from two separate ova, fertilized by different spermatozoa.

DOLICHOCEPHALIC Having a head 77 percent or less as wide as it is long.

DOLICHOCRANIAL Having a skull 75 percent or less as wide as it is long.

DOMINANCE In genetics having an allele which is expressed in the phenotype even if heterozygous. In ethology having a social position which gives one unquestioned priority in access to whatever is desired.

DONAU An early Pleistocene glaciate which took place before the better known Alpine glaciations. *See* Figure 8–1.

DORSAL Pertaining to the back side of the body.

DOWN'S SYNDROME A genetic defect due to faulty meiosis which produces an extra chromosome. Sometimes known as Mongolism.

DRIFT In genetics a shift in allele frequencies which is due to chance alone—like a run of good or bad luck in gambling. Consequently, it is most likely to be effective in quite small populations.

DRYOPITHECINE A Miocene and Pliocene taxon of apes which may be ancestral to the hominids as well as pongids.

ECHINODERM The phylum comprising sea urchins, starfish and the like, which are probably the closest kin of the chordates.

ECOLOGY The study of the mutual relations of organisms with one another and with the nonliving environment.

ECOLOGICAL NICHE The position which a creature occupies in relation to its environment: its way of life as that fits into the living community of which it is a part.

ECTOMORPHY In somatotyping one of the three components recognized by constitutional typologists: it records the degree of linearity in body build.

ELECTROPHORESIS The separating of various protein molecules which have different electric charges. An electric current is passed through filter paper, starch gel, or the like, which has been impregnated with a liquid containing such proteins. This process will cause the protein molecules to move through the porous material, and their rate of speed will depend upon their electric charge.

EMBRYOLOGY The scientific study of the formation and development of an organism from the time when it is a fertilized egg until it is born.

ENDOCRANIAL CAST A cast of the inner side of the skull, which simulates the shape and to some degree the surface conformation of the brain which that skull once held.

ENDOCRINE GLAND A gland which discharges a hormone directly into the blood stream.

ENDOGAMOUS Marrying or mating within a social group of any nature—kin, class, religious, ethnic, or otherwise.

ENDOMORPHY In somatotyping one of the three components recognized by constitutional typologists: it records the degree of visceral and fat development in body build.

ENVIRONMENT In biology the sum total of conditions in which an organism, a population, or a community is living, and to which it must adjust or adapt.

ENZYME A biological compound which causes changes in other substances by catalytic action.

EOCENE The second epoch of the Cenozoic. *See* Figure 6–1.

EPICANTHIC EYEFOLD A fold of skin on the eyelid which covers its inner corner, next to the nose. Such an eyefold is very common among Mongoloids, especially in China, Japan, and Siberia.

EPIPHYSIS Articular section of a long bone which in mammals has a separate center of ossification from the shaft, to which it becomes united only at the end of growth.

ERYTHROCYTE A "red cell" in the blood stream, which carries oxygen to, and carbon dioxide from, the tissues of the body.

ESTIVATION A slowing down almost to the point of suspension of biologic activity for a prolonged period when it is hot or dry.

ESTRUS The period of maximum female sexual receptiveness, coinciding with maximum fertility. Although apparently lacking in *Homo sapiens*, it is a cyclic phenomenon among most mammals, at least. Estrus may recur many times a year in some species, but only every few years in others.

ETHNIC GROUP A social group which is distinguished from others by cultural characteristics which are assumed, truly or falsely, to be of national origin.

ETHOLOGY In zoology the study of the naturalistic behavior of animals in groups.

EUTHERIA Infraclass of mammals which nourish the unborn young by means of a well developed placenta. *See* Figure 5–4.

EVOLUTION Descent with modification. A shift in the allele frequencies of a population as time goes on.

EXOGAMOUS The opposite of *endogamous*.

FAMILY A taxon more inclusive than a genus and less than an order. Members of a family share many structural peculiarities, as for example the Canidae, which includes dogs, wolves, and foxes.

FAVISM An enzyme deficiency resulting from a sex-linked gene. It causes severe reactions to primaquine and to fava beans, but seems to provide some protection against certain forms of malaria.

FEMUR, pl. FEMORA The long bone of the thigh. *See* Figure 15–3.

FIBULA The smaller of the two bones of the lower leg.

FORAMEN, pl. FORAMINA A hole, specifically an opening in a bone.

FORAMEN MAGNUM The opening in the skull through which the spinal cord emerges.

FOSSIL A remaining part of any ancient form of life. Commonly it is a hard part which has become mineralized, but prints or casts, when preserved, are also called fossils.

FRANKFORT PLANE A way of placing a skull for observation, so that a horizontal plane intersects the upper margin of the ear holes and the lower margin of the eye sockets.

FRONTAL BONE The bone of the forehead, extending back to form the foremost part of the skull vault. *See* Figure 15–2.

FRONTAL LOBE The foremost part of the cerebrum. There is evidence that the functions of this part of the brain involve such characteristics as foresight, inhibition, and worry.

FOUNDER EFFECT An aspect of genetic drift. It is the consequence of the fact that the alleles of the founders of a population, no matter how few they were, are the only ones available to their descendants, no matter how numerous they become.

GAMETE A sex cell, either sperm or ovum.

GASTROCNEMIUS The muscle, very well developed in *Homo*, which runs dorsally from the lower part of the femur to merge into the Achilles tendon: this in turn reaches the heel. Thus it flexes the ankle joint, and secondarily the knee joint.

GENE The unit of inheritance. At present it is commonly supposed that each gene is concerned with the synthesis of a particular enzyme.

GENE FLOW Spreading of genes from one population to the next and the next which does not require permanent migration of individuals, but depends simply upon mating along the boundaries of the populations concerned.

GENE POOL *See* breeding population.

GENETIC DRIFT A shift in allele frequencies due to chance rather than selection, such as may take place in a population too small to constitute a true statistical sample.

GENETIC ISOLATE *See* breeding population.

GENIOGLOSSAL MUSCLES Among the more important muscles which control tongue movements. They arise from within the foremost part of the lower border of the mandible.

GENOTYPE The genetic constitution which reacts with the environment to produce the phenotype.

GENUS, pl. GENERA A taxon more inclusive than a species and less than a family. The species of a genus share so many characteristics that they are likely to be in sharp competition.

GLUCOSE 6 PHOSPHATE DEHYDROGENASE (G6PD) DEFICIENCY *See* Favism.

GLOGER'S RULE The tendency for homothermal animals living in hot damp places to have very dark skins, and in hot dry places yellow-tan skins.

GLUTEUS MAXIMUS In the Hominidae, the largest muscle of the hip and thigh: its strength permits erect posture without conscious strain. In other primates, it is smaller and weaker, and its course somewhat different.

GRACILIS The muscle meagerly developed in *Homo*, but much larger in other anthropoids, which runs on the inner side of the thigh from the pubis to the upper part of the tibia. Thus it helps to pull the thighs together and turn the knees toward each other.

GRADE In taxonomy a level of organizational efficiency. *See* Figures 5–4 and 6–3.

GÜNZ The first of the four Alpine glaciations. *See* Figure 8–1.

HAPTOGLOBIN A blood serum protein, of which several genetically determined varieties exist.

HEMOGLOBIN A red blood cell protein containing iron, which serves to transport oxygen to, and carbon dioxide from, all the cells of the body.

HEMOPHILIA Hereditary defect in ability to coagulate blood, so that no scab forms and death from bleeding may result. Any one of several loci, some at least sex-linked, are concerned with this misfortune.

HETEROGONY Differential or allometric growth of separate parts of the body, so that a larger creature will have a different shape from a smaller relative.

HETEROSIS Hybrid vigor. Extra strength, growth, or resistance due to heterozygosity at one or more loci.

HETEROZYGOUS Having two different alleles of a given gene.

HIBERNATION The slowing down, almost to the point of suspension, of biologic activity for a prolonged period when it is very cold.

HOMEOSTASIS Maintaining a steady state by self-regulation: the ability to adjust to change and continue normal life.

HOMINIDAE The family including all species of *Homo* as well as the Australopithecines.

HOMINOIDEA The superfamily including the Hominidae and the Pongidae: that is, men and apes.

HOMO The genus to which we belong.

HOMO ERECTUS The extinct species directly ancestral to *Homo sapiens*.

HOMO HABILIS An alleged species based by fossils from Olduvai Gorge which may represent forms transitional between Australopithecus and *Homo*. Not a valid taxonomic title.

HOMO SAPIENS The only living species of the genus *Homo*.

HOMOTHERM The grade of vertebrates capable of maintaining a more or less constant internal temperature. These are birds and mammals.

HOMOZYGOUS Having identical alleles of a given gene.

HORMONE A chemical substance, transmitted through the blood stream, which stimulates or inhibits some functional activity.

HUMERUS The bone of the upper arm. *See* Figure 15–3.

ILIUM, pl. ILIA The uppermost flaring bone of the pelvis which, during growth, fuses with the other pelvic bones.

INCA BONE An extra bone, most frequently found among Mongoloids, at the uppermost part of the occipital bone.

INCEST TABU A cultural prohibition, found in all societies, against sexual intercourse between kinfolk defined as too closely related. The result of this strong sanctioned practice include the promotion of gene flow.

INSULIN A hormone which affects carbohydrate metabolism to regulate the amount of glucose in the blood stream.

ISCHIAL CALLOSITY A hairless, toughened area of skin covering the ischium. It is found in all Old World monkeys and some apes.

ISCHIUM, pl. ISCHIA The lowermost bone of the pelvis which, during growth fuses with the other pelvic bones. *See* Figure 15–3.

JURASSIC The second period of the Mesozoic era. *See* Figure 4–3.

LACTASE The enzyme which enables unweaned mammals to digest milk sugar. Among many human populations, most adults continue to synthesize this enzyme: this may well be an ability under genetic control.

LATIMERIA The only surviving genus of a Mesozoic order of fish, found recently to be still living in the Indian Ocean.

LINEA ASPERA A roughened ridge on the back of the femur which provides added area for muscular attachment.

LOCUS The area on a chromosome presumably occupied by a single gene.

MAMMAL The class of vertebrates possessing hair at some time during life, a lower jaw composed of a single bone, and, among females, means of suckling the young.

MANDIBLE The lower jaw: in mammals a single bone. The mandible fossilizes much more readily than do many other bones.

MARSUPIAL The order of mammals whose young are sheltered in a pouch after birth. *See* Figure 5–4.

MASTOID PROCESS A rounded protuberance on the under side of the temporal bone, in men and some apes, which provides added area for muscular attachment.

MAXILLA, pl. MAXILLAE In *Homo* the bones which form the upper jaw and surround most of the bony nasal aperture. In other anthropoids the most forward part of the upper jaw is formed by separate bones, the premaxillae: this fact was strongly urged as an argument against evolution by Darwin's opponents.

MEDULLA The rearmost part of the vertebrate brain.

MEIOSIS The process whereby the number of chromosomes is reduced by half, in the preparation of gametes. *See* Figure 3–4.

MELANIN A pigmented substance formed in the body and deposited in varying amounts in such structures as the skin, hair, and brain surface.

MENARCHE The time of first menstruation.

MESOMORPHY In somatotyping one of the three components recognized by constitutional typologists: it records the degree of skeletal and muscular development in body build.

MESOZOIC A geological era lasting from 200 million to 70 million years ago. *See* Figure 4–3.

METABOLISM The processes of physical and chemical change, continuously constructing protoplasm and breaking it down with release of energy, which takes place in living organisms.

METACARPALS The bones of the hand, between the wrist and the fingers.

METATARSALS The bones of the foot, between the tarsus and the toes.

METATHERIA The infraclass of mammals containing the Marsupials. *See* Figure 5–4.

METAZOAN An animal with many cells.

MINDEL The second of the four Alpine glaciations. *See* Figure 8–4.

MIOCENE The fourth epoch of the Cenozoic. *See* Figure 6–1.

MITOSIS Ordinary cell division, in which the chromosomes duplicate before separating, so that their number is maintained. *See* Figure 3–1.

MOLLUSCA The phylum comprising clams, snails, squid, and similar creatures.

MONGOLISM *See* Down's Syndrome.

MONKEY A grade of the Anthropoidea having tails. Two distinct taxa, the Ceboidea of the New World, and the Ceropithecoidea of the Old World, are of this grade.

MONOTREME The order of mammals which lay eggs. *See* Figure 5–4.

MONOZYGOTIC Derived from a single ovum fertilized by one spermatozoan.

MOUSTERIAN The major toolmaking tradition of the Middle Paleolithic, closely associated with Neanderthal Man. A great variety of tools were made, including knives, scrapers, points, and augers.

MUTATION A physical or chemical change in the structure of a gene which leads to a change in the gene's activity.

MYOPIA A defect in the shape of the lens of the eye, resulting in shortsightedness.

NATURAL SELECTION Selection (*q.v.*) which takes place without intention or control by anyone, as contrasted to artificial selection by a breeder who wishes to produce a certain sort of creature.

NEANDERTHAL A valley in Germany where remains of a Pleistocene variety of man were found and after which this variety is named.

NEANDERTHALOID Basically similar to the Neanderthal man in anatomy. A vague but useful term.

NEOLITHIC The period when men cultivated plants and made many of their tools of ground stone. Self-contained farming villages were typical.

NEOPALLIUM The area of the cerebral cortex not devoted to the sense of smell. It has expanded greatly among mammals.

NEOTENY Retention during adulthood of childish or even fetal characteristics.

NOTOCHORD A dorsally located stiffening rod, unsegmented, which precedes the backbone in embryonic development among vertebrates, but is more lasting in some other chordates.

NUCLEIC ACID A chemical compound containing carbon, hydrogen, nitrogen, oxygen, and phosphorus which is necessary for continued life.

NUCLEUS That part of a cell containing the chromosomes. Usually surrounded by its own membrane and thought to function as the executive center of the cell.

OCCIPITAL BONE The rearmost bone of the skull, penetrated by the foramen magnum (q.v.), so that in many animals including man it forms most of the skull base as well. *See* Figure 15–2.

OCCIPUT The rear part of the head or skull.

OLDUWAN A toolmaking tradition in Africa during Villafranchian times. The standard tool was a crudely made cleaver or chopper.

OLFACTORY LOBES Section of the forebrain devoted to appreciating and integrating stimuli from the smelling organs.

OLIGOCENE The third epoch of the Cenozoic. *See* Figure 6–1.

ORDER A taxon more inclusive than a family but less than a class. Members of an order share adaptations to some broad ecological zone, but may differ as much as seals from cats, or people from lemurs.

OREOPITHECUS An anthropoid genus of the Pliocene.

ORTHOSELECTION Selection for improved performance of whatever a taxon is doing, so that existing traits become more strongly developed.

OSMOTIC PRESSURE The pressure which causes a fluid to seep through a semipermeable membrane into a more concentrated solution.

OSSIFICATION The process whereby bone replaces cartilage.

OSTEODONTOKERATIC The alleged culture of the Australopithecines, who, Dart claims, made tools out of bones, teeth, and horn.

OVUM, pl. OVA The female reproductive cell, or unfertilized egg.

PALEOCENE The first epoch of the Cenozoic. *See* Figure 6–1.

PALEOLITHIC The time during which men cultivated no plants and made stone tools by chipping or flaking rather than grinding: the first 99 percent of human history.

PALEOZOIC A geological era lasting from 500 million to 200 million years ago. *See* Figure 4–3.

PALMARIS LONGUS This muscle runs from near the distal end of the humerus down the front of the forearm, becoming a tendon which flexes the palm of the hand. It is often absent, and its frequency varies between different populations.

PARALLEL EVOLUTION Evolution in the same direction by two related taxa, so that they do not become less similar despite lack of interbreeding, but instead both acquire similar new characteristics.

PARIETAL BONES One on either side of the skull, these form the top and uppermost part of the sides of the skull vault. *See* Figure 15–2.

PECTORAL Situated on the foremost or upper part of the chest.

PEDOMORPHISM *See* Neoteny.

PERMIAN The final period of the Paleozoic era, about 200 million years ago.

PESTICIDE Poison intended for creatures which annoy us, but which, all too often, are effective against other creatures, and tend to upset the balance of nature.

PHENOTYPE A biological characteristic which may be observed or tested.

PHENYLPYRUSIC ACID A metabolic derivative of phenylahanine, which is normally decarbolized, but may be excreted because of lack of the proper enzymes.

PHENYLTHIOCARBOMIDE (PTC) A synthetic chemical which to some people tastes bitter, but to others is quite tasteless.

PHYLOGENY The evolutionary history of a taxon.

PHYLUM, pl. PHYLA A taxon including all creatures which have a similar basic structural pattern, and which, therefore, are quite surely related to one another.

PITHECANTHROPUS A fossil hominid of the lower middle Pleistocene. No longer acceptable as a taxonomic title.

PLACENTA The tissue, closely attached to the lining of the uterus, and joined by the umbilical cord to the fetus, by means of which a mother provides nourishment to and absorbs waste material from her unborn baby.

PLANTARIS A muscle lying next to gastrocnemius (*q.v.*). It is almost vestigial in *Homo*, but larger than gastocnemius in most mammals. Among them it extends under the foot and serves to flex the toes: but among us it merges into the tendon of Achilles.

PLANTIGRADE Standing and walking on the soles of the feet rather than the toes.

PLASMODIUM The generic name of the microorganism which causes malaria.

PLASTICITY The ability to respond to environmental pressure by phenotypic modifications during growth. Said of an individual, not of a group.

PLATYRRHINE Having a broad nose. An older term used to distinguish the monkeys of the New World.

PLEIOTROPY The causation of several quite different effects upon the phenotype by the action of a single gene.

PLEISTOCENE The sixth epoch of the Cenozoic, during which extensive glaciations took place in various regions. *See* Figures 8–1 and 9–1. Not synonymous with Paleolithic.

PLIOCENE The fifth epoch of the Cenozoic. *See* Figures 6–1 and 8–1.

PLUVIAL A rainy period. Pluvial periods in tropical lands may have been contemporaneous with glacial periods in colder areas.

POLYANDRY Marriage of one woman to several men: a very rare custom.

POLYGENIC Characteristics which are under the control of several genes rather than one: these include nearly but not quite all traits apparent to the naked eye.

POLYGYNY Marriage of one man to several women, a very widespread custom.

POLYMORPHIC Having two or more alleles at one or more loci, so that variability exists within the population. Said of a species or lesser taxon.

POLYTYPIC Occurring in several readily distinguishable breeds. Said of a species.

PONGIDAE The family including all the genera of apes.

POTASSIUM-ARGON DATING A technique for dating the time at which a rock was formed by measuring the extent to which potassium has been transformed into argon.

PREADAPTATION A characteristic useful for ecological conditions in which a creature does not yet live.

PRECIPITIN TEST A test of the degree of similarity between the plasma proteins of blood from different species, from which we can infer how closely or distantly related they are. It depends upon the fact that blood produces antibodies which react against foreign proteins and form a precipitate.

PREFERENTIAL MATING The choice of one sex partner rather than another. This is standard practice in our species.

PRIMATE The order or mammals to which we belong.

PROCONSUL Miocene hominoids of which numerous fossils have been found in East Africa. No longer acceptable as a taxonomic title.

PROGNATHISM Forward protrusion of the jaws. In alveolar prognathism only the tooth-bearing parts project, whereas in facial prognathism the entire area below the eyes is thrust forward.

PROPLIOPITHECUS An anthropoid genus of the Oligocene, which may be ancestral to all hominoids and is probably ancestral to gibbons.

PRONOGRADE Walking on four legs, with the body more or less horizontal.

PROTEIN A constituent of protoplasm formed by combinations of amino acids. There are innumerable proteins each slightly different from all others, but all are exceedingly complex in structure.

PROTOPLASM A clear, viscid colloid composed of carbon, hydrogen, oxygen, nitrogen, and at least eight other elements in complex and unstable combinations. It is the stuff of life.

PROTOTHERIA The subclass of mammals containing the monotremes. *See* Figure 5–4.

PUBIS, pl. PUBES The foremost bone of the pelvis which, during growth, fuses with the other two pelvic bones.

RACE A population within a species which can be readily distinguished from other such populations on genetic grounds alone.

RADIUS One of the two bones of the forearm.

RAMAPITHECUS A late Miocene and early Pliocene hominoid taxon having teeth which strongly suggest close hominoid affinities.

RECESSIVE In genetics, an allele which is not expressed in the phenotype except when homozygous.

RHESUS Common name for an Indian species of the genus Macaca, a monkey much used in medical and psychological experiments. A blood type system is named after this variety.

RIBONUCLEIC ACID (RNA) Enzymes synthesized by the genes which serve as messengers to the cytoplasm, within which their catalytic action organizes the proper forms of biochemical reactions.

RISS The third of the four Alpine glaciations. *See* Figure 8–1.

SACROSPINALIS The muscle group which runs behind the backbone from the sacrum to the thorax and neck. Thus it is useful in holding the torso in balance above the pelvis.

SACRUM The fused vertebrae (five in number in *Homo*) which articulate with the two ilia, and complete the pelvic girdle.

SECTORIAL PREMOLAR A first lower premolar of which the outer cusp projects much more than the inner. This projection, found among apes but not men, sheers against the projecting upper canine.

SELECTION The survival of some genotypes at the expense of contrasting ones, because the latter are less well adapted.

SEXLINKED A gene is termed sex-linked if it is located on either the X or the Y chromosomes, which determine sex. Its mode of inheritance is determined by the fact of its location.

SEXUAL DIMORPHISM Marked difference in the characteristics of males and females of a species.

SHOVEL-SHAPED INCISORS Upper incisors which are buttressed on either side, lingually, by ridges of enamel. Such incisors are very common among Mongoloid, especially American Indians.

SIBLING Brother or sister.

SICKLE CELL A red blood cell which assumes a collapsed and distorted shape and is unable to carry the normal amount of oxygen. Such cells are due to an incompletely recessive allele: in heterozygous individuals relatively few sickle cells are found.

SICKLEMIA The condition of having some sickle cells in the blood stream.

SILURIAN The third period of the Paleozoic era, nearly 400 million years ago.

SIMIAN SHELF A bony bar between the two sides of the foremost part of an ape's mandible, which is quite wide and would be structurally weak without such buttressing.

SINANTHROPUS A fossil hominid of the middle Pleistocene. No longer acceptable as a taxonomic title.

SOLEUS The large muscle, deeper than gastrocnemius and plantaris (*q.v.*) which runs from the upper part of the tibia and fibula to the tendon of Achilles. Thus it helps to flex the ankle and also to steady the leg above the foot when we stand up.

SOMATOTYPING A system for classifing body build which recognizes three components, endomorphy, mesomorphy, and ectomorphy, each developed to a greater or lesser degree in each individual.

SPECIES, pl. SPECIES The basic taxon among bisexual creatures. The lines of genetic communication are open within a species, but at best ajar between species. The name of a species is always given in small letters after the name of the genus to which it belongs.

SPERM, SPERMATOZOON The male reproductive cell.

STANDARD DEVIATION A measure of the extent of variation within a group. Two-thirds of all individuals are within one standard deviation, and 95 percent within two standard deviations of the mean measurement.

STANDARD ERROR A measurement of the degree of error in a statistical calculation: this depends upon the size of the sample used as well as its amount of variability.

STEATOPYGIA Having a protrusive deposit of fat on the buttocks, commonly associated with a strong lumbar curve.

STEREOSCOPIC VISION Depth perception due to fusion in the brain of images seen by two eyes so close together that their field of vision is almost but not quite the same. *See* Figure 6–9.

SYMBIOSIS Mutually advantageous living together of very different species: for example, cats and farmers, since the cats kill rodents which eat stored grain.

SYNAPSE Approximation between two nerves so close that impulses are sent from one nerve to the other.

SYNAPSIDA The subclass of reptiles from which mammals evolved. *See* Figure 4–5.

SUTURE Where the edges of the different bones of the skull come in contact with each other. Growth takes place along these edges, and eventually two adjacent bones may fuse and the suture become obliterated.

TARSUS The bones of the heel and part of the arch of the foot.

TAXON, pl. TAXA A group of creatures related by descent from a common ancestor, and distinctive enough to deserve a name.

TAXONOMY The science of systematic classification of living things in such a manner as to indicate their relationship to one another.

TEMPORAL BONES One on either side of the skull, these form the lower part of the sides of the skull, include the ear cavities, and extend below to form part of the skull base. *See* Figure 15–2.

TERRITORIALISM In ethology, a concept often used to "explain" the behavior of animals in the wild. It depends upon the idea that defence of a creature's home territory is vital, because it serves to space out individuals and thus conserve resources. Among primates, some species are much more territorial than are others.

TETRAPOD The grade of vertebrates having four limbs, or, like snakes and whales, descended from four-limbed ancestors.

THALASSEMIA An inherited anemia. Its existence in malarial areas strongly suggests that the heterozygous condition must confer some advantage to counteract the peril of the homozygous state.

THERIODONTS Synapsid reptiles having teeth somewhat like mammals, and from which mammals evolved.

THERIA The subclass of mammals which do not lay eggs. *See* Figure 5–4.

THUMB A digit that is set apart from the others, which facilitates grasping. In most primates, thumbs are found on hands and feet alike: a few lack thumbs on their hands, and we lack thumbs on our feet.

TIBIA The larger of the two bones of the lower leg. *See* Figure 15–3.

TORUS A thickened ridge of bone, such as the browridge.

TRANSFERRIN A plasma protein of the blood which binds iron and may be involved in protection against infections.

TRIASSIC The first period of the Mesozoic era.

ULNA One of the two bones of the forearm.

VENTRAL The belly side of a creature.

VERTEBRATE The subphylum of chordates having a segmented backbone.

VILLAFRANCHIAN The first part of the Pleistocene, before the

Günz glaciation. Modern genera of animals begin to appear during this time.

WALLACE'S LINE The set of deep troughs in the ocean, in existence since the Eocene at least, which separate the Asian from the Australasian faunal regions.

WÜRM The fourth and latest of the Alpine glaciations. *See* Figures 8–1 and 9–1.

XENOPHOBIA Unreasoned suspicion of and contempt for strangers and foreigners.

ZINJANTHROPUS Name given to an Australopithecine of East Africa. Not a valid taxonomic label.

ZYGOTE Cell formed by the union of a sperm with an ovum.

Index

About the Author

Frederick S. Hulse is Professor of Anthropology at the University of Arizona. Extensive field work has taken him to Cuba, England, Hawaii, Israel, Japan, Mexico, Spain, and Switzerland. In all his research, he has attempted to uncover the effects of social and cultural aspects of environment upon human physique and gene frequencies.

He has been President of the American Association of Physical Anthropologists, Associate Editor of the *American Anthropologist*, and Editor of the *American Journal of Physical Anthropology*. In addition, he represented the United States as a Vice President of the VIII International Congress of Anthropological and Ethnological Sciences at Tokyo in 1968.

He has frequently contributed articles to the *American Journal of Physical Anthropology*, the *Southwestern Journal of Anthropology*, *American Anthropologist*, and *Eugenics Quarterly*.

A Note on the Type

The text of this book was set on the Linotype in Aster, a typeface designed by Francesco Simoncini (born 1912 in Bologna, Italy) for Ludwig and Mayer, the German type foundry. Starting out with the basic old-face letterforms that can be traced back to Francesco Griffo in 1495, Simoncini emphasized the diagonal stress by the simple device of extending diagonals to the full height of the letterforms and squaring off. By modifying the weights of the individual letters to combat this stress, he has produced a type of rare balance and vigor. Introduced in 1958, Aster has steadily grown in popularity wherever type is used.

This book was composed, printed, and bound by Kingsport Press Inc., Kingsport, Tennessee.